CompTIA®
Network+®
Study Guide
Second Edition

D0572459

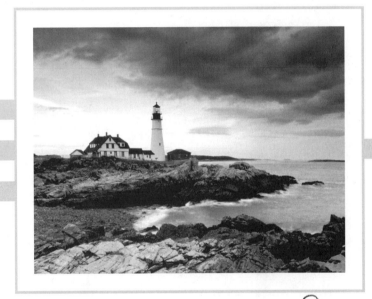

TEAM VIEWER SOFTWARE

CompTIA®
Network+®
Study Guide
Second Edition

Todd Lammle

WILEY

John Wiley & Sons, Inc.

Senior Acquisitions Editor: Jeff Kellum
Development Editor: Kim Wimpsett
Technical Editors: Troy McMillan and Tom Carpenter
Production Editor: Christine O'Connor
Copy Editor: Judy Flynn
Editorial Manager: Pete Gaughan
Production Manager: Tim Tate
Vice President and Executive Group Publisher: Richard Swadley
Vice President and Publisher: Neil Edde
Project Manager 1: Laura Moss-Hollister
Associate Producer: Marilyn Hummel
Quality Assurance: Josh Frank
Book Designers: Judy Fung and Bill Gibson
Compositor: Craig Woods, Happenstance Type-O-Rama
Proofreader: Rebecca Rider
Indexer: Robert Swanson
Project Coordinator, Cover: Katherine Crocker
Cover Designer: Ryan Sneed

Copyright © 2012 by John Wiley & Sons, Inc., Indianapolis, Indiana

Published simultaneously in Canada

ISBN: 978-1-118-13755-0

ISBN: 978-1-118-22533-2 (ebk.)

ISBN: 978-1-118-23886-8 (ebk.)

ISBN: 978-1-118-26346-4 (ebk.)

No part of this publication may be reproduced, stored in a retrieval system or transmitted in any form or by any means, electronic, mechanical, photocopying, recording, scanning or otherwise, except as permitted under Sections 107 or 108 of the 1976 United States Copyright Act, without either the prior written permission of the Publisher, or authorization through payment of the appropriate per-copy fee to the Copyright Clearance Center, 222 Rosewood Drive, Danvers, MA 01923, (978) 750-8400, fax (978) 646-8600. Requests to the Publisher for permission should be addressed to the Permissions Department, John Wiley & Sons, Inc., 111 River Street, Hoboken, NJ 07030, (201) 748-6011, fax (201) 748-6008, or online at http://www.wiley.com/go/permissions.

Limit of Liability/Disclaimer of Warranty: The publisher and the author make no representations or warranties with respect to the accuracy or completeness of the contents of this work and specifically disclaim all warranties, including without limitation warranties of fitness for a particular purpose. No warranty may be created or extended by sales or promotional materials. The advice and strategies contained herein may not be suitable for every situation. This work is sold with the understanding that the publisher is not engaged in rendering legal, accounting, or other professional services. If professional assistance is required, the services of a competent professional person should be sought. Neither the publisher nor the author shall be liable for damages arising herefrom. The fact that an organization or Web site is referred to in this work as a citation and/or a potential source of further information does not mean that the author or the publisher endorses the information the organization or Web site may provide or recommendations it may make. Further, readers should be aware that Internet Web sites listed in this work may have changed or disappeared between when this work was written and when it is read.

For general information on our other products and services or to obtain technical support, please contact our Customer Care Department within the U.S. at (877) 762-2974, outside the U.S. at (317) 572-3993 or fax (317) 572-4002.

Wiley publishes in a variety of print and electronic formats and by print-on-demand. Some material included with standard print versions of this book may not be included in e-books or in print-on-demand. If this book refers to media such as a CD or DVD that is not included in the version you purchased, you may download this material at http://booksupport.wiley.com. For more information about Wiley products, visit www.wiley.com.

Library of Congress Control Number: 2011944531

TRADEMARKS: Wiley, the Wiley logo, and the Sybex logo are trademarks or registered trademarks of John Wiley & Sons, Inc. and/or its affiliates, in the United States and other countries, and may not be used without written permission. CompTIA and Network+ are registered trademarks of Computing Technology Industry Association. All other trademarks are the property of their respective owners. John Wiley & Sons, Inc. is not associated with any product or vendor mentioned in this book.

10 9 8 7 6 5 4

Dear Reader,

Thank you for choosing *CompTIA Network+ Study Guide, Second Edition*. This book is part of a family of premium-quality Sybex books, all of which are written by outstanding authors who combine practical experience with a gift for teaching.

Sybex was founded in 1976. More than 30 years later, we're still committed to producing consistently exceptional books. With each of our titles, we're working hard to set a new standard for the industry. From the paper we print on, to the authors we work with, our goal is to bring you the best books available.

I hope you see all that reflected in these pages. I'd be very interested to hear your comments and get your feedback on how we're doing. Feel free to let me know what you think about this or any other Sybex book by sending me an email at nedde@wiley.com. If you think you've found a technical error in this book, please visit http://sybex.custhelp.com. Customer feedback is critical to our efforts at Sybex.

Best regards,

Neil Edde
Vice President and Publisher
Sybex, an Imprint of Wiley

Acknowledgments

Kim Wimpsett was the development editor of this, the newest book in the Sybex CompTIA series. Thank you, Kim, for working so hard on this book with me.

Jeff Kellum is instrumental to my success in the Cisco world and is my acquisitions editor for this new CompTIA Network+ book. Jeff, thanks for your guidance and continued patience with all the books we've published together!

In addition, Christine O'Connor was an excellent production editor, and she worked really hard to get the book done as quickly as possible, without missing the small mistakes that are so easy to overlook. I am always very pleased when I hear that she will be working with me on a new project. Judy Flynn was my copy editor, and she was patient, helpful, and detailed but yet worked extremely hard to get this book on the shelf as quickly as possible, and for that I thank her tremendously.

Troy McMillian literally hashed and rehashed each topic in this guide with me at all hours of the day and night, scrutinizing the material until we both agreed it was verifiably solid. Thank you, Troy, yet once again!

About the Author

Todd Lammle, CompTIA Network+, CCSI, CCNA/CCNP, CCSP/CCVP, MCSE, CEH/CHFI, FCC RF Licensed,   is the authority on network certification and internetworking. He is a world-renowned author, speaker, trainer, and consultant. Todd has over 25 years of experience working with LANs, WANs, and large licensed and unlicensed wireless networks. He's president and CEO of GlobalNet Training and Consulting, Inc., a network-integration and training firm based in Boulder, Colorado; Dallas, Texas; and San Francisco, California. You can reach Todd through his forum at www.lammle.com/forum.

Contents at a Glance

Foreword		*xxv*
Introduction		*xxix*
Assessment Test		*li*
Chapter 1	Introduction to Networks	1
Chapter 2	The Open Systems Interconnection Specifications	27
Chapter 3	Networking Topologies, Connectors, and Wiring Standards	53
Chapter 4	The Current Ethernet Specifications	87
Chapter 5	Networking Devices	115
Chapter 6	Introduction to the Internet Protocol	155
Chapter 7	IP Addressing	189
Chapter 8	IP Subnetting, Troubleshooting IP, and Introduction to NAT	211
Chapter 9	Introduction to IP Routing	253
Chapter 10	Routing Protocols	273
Chapter 11	Switching and Virtual LANs	297
Chapter 12	Wireless Networking	335
Chapter 13	Authentication and Access Control	375
Chapter 14	Network Threats and Mitigation	413
Chapter 15	Physical and Hardware Security	449
Chapter 16	Wide Area Networks	485
Chapter 17	Troubleshooting Tools	515
Chapter 18	Software and Hardware Tools	569
Chapter 19	Network Troubleshooting	595
Chapter 20	Management, Monitoring, and Optimization	635
Appendix A	Answers to Review Questions	669
Appendix B	Answers to Written Labs	703
Appendix C	Subnetting Class A	717
Appendix D	About the Additional Study Tools	725
Index		*729*

Contents

Foreword xxv

Introduction xxix

Assessment Test li

Chapter 1   Introduction to Networks 1

First Things First: What's a Network? 2
The Local Area Network (LAN) 3
Common Network Components 5
Wide Area Network (WAN) 7
Network Architecture: Peer-to-Peer or Client-Server? 9
Physical Network Topologies 12
Bus Topology 12
Star Topology 13
Ring Topology 14
Mesh Topology 15
Point-to-Point Topology 16
Point-to-Multipoint Topology 17
Hybrid Topology 18
Topology Selection, Backbones, and Segments 18
Selecting the Right Topology 19
The Network Backbone 20
Network Segments 21
Summary 21
Exam Essentials 21
Written Labs 22
Review Questions 23

Chapter 2   The Open Systems Interconnection Specifications 27

Internetworking Models 28
The Layered Approach 28
Advantages of Reference Models 29
The OSI Reference Model 30
The Application Layer 31
The Presentation Layer 33
The Session Layer 33
The Transport Layer 33
The Network Layer 39
The Data Link Layer 42
The Physical Layer 44
Introduction to Encapsulation 45

	Summary	46
	Exam Essentials	46
	Written Lab	47
	Review Questions	48

Chapter 3 **Networking Topologies, Connectors, and Wiring Standards** **53**

Physical Media		55
	Coaxial Cable	55
	Twisted-Pair Cable	58
	Fiber-Optic Cable	61
	Media Converters	66
	Broadband over Power Line	67
	Serial Cables	68
Cable Properties		71
	Transmission Speeds	71
	Distance	71
	Duplex	71
	Noise Immunity (Security, EMI)	71
	Frequency	72
Wiring Standards		72
	568A vs. 568B	73
	Straight-Through Cable	75
	Crossover Cable	75
	T1 Crossover Cable	76
Installing Wiring Distributions		79
Summary		80
Exam Essentials		81
Written Lab		81
Review Questions		83

Chapter 4 **The Current Ethernet Specifications** **87**

Network Basics		88
Ethernet Basics		90
	Collision Domain	90
	Broadcast Domain	90
	CSMA/CD	91
	Half- and Full-Duplex Ethernet	92
Ethernet at the Data Link Layer		94
	Binary to Decimal and Hexadecimal Conversion	94
	Ethernet Addressing	98
	Ethernet Frames	98
	Channel Bonding	101
Ethernet at the Physical Layer		101
Summary		106

	Exam Essentials	107
	Written Lab	107
	Review Questions	111
Chapter 5	**Networking Devices**	**115**
	Common Network Connectivity Devices	117
	Hub	118
	Network Interface Card	118
	Bridge	120
	Switch	120
	Router	121
	Firewall	125
	Dynamic Host Configuration Protocol Server	126
	Other Specialized Devices	129
	Multilayer Switch	130
	Load Balancer	130
	Domain Name Service Server	130
	Proxy Server	135
	Encryption Devices	136
	VPN Concentrator	137
	Planning and Implementing a Basic SOHO Network Using	
	Network Segmentation	137
	Determining Requirements	138
	Switches and Bridges at the Data Link Layer	144
	Hubs at the Physical Layer	146
	Environmental Considerations	147
	Summary	147
	Exam Essentials	148
	Written Lab	149
	Review Questions	150
Chapter 6	**Introduction to the Internet Protocol**	**155**
	Introducing TCP/IP	157
	A Brief History of TCP/IP	157
	TCP/IP and the DoD Model	158
	The Process/Application Layer Protocols	159
	The Host-to-Host Layer Protocols	168
	The Internet Layer Protocols	173
	Data Encapsulation	178
	Summary	182
	Exam Essentials	182
	Written Lab	183
	Review Questions	184

Chapter 7	**IP Addressing**	**189**
	IP Terminology	190
	The Hierarchical IP Addressing Scheme	191
	Network Addressing	192
	Private IP Addresses	196
	IPv4 Address Types	198
	Layer 2 Broadcasts	198
	Layer 3 Broadcasts	198
	Unicast Address	199
	Multicast Address	199
	Internet Protocol Version 6 (IPv6)	200
	Why Do We Need IPv6?	200
	The Benefits of and Uses for IPv6	201
	IPv6 Addressing and Expressions	202
	Shortened Expression	203
	Address Types	203
	Special Addresses	204
	Summary	205
	Exam Essentials	205
	Written Lab	206
	Review Questions	207
Chapter 8	**IP Subnetting, Troubleshooting IP, and Introduction to NAT**	**211**
	Subnetting Basics	212
	How to Create Subnets	213
	Subnet Masks	214
	Classless Inter-Domain Routing (CIDR)	215
	Subnetting Class C Addresses	217
	Subnetting Class B Addresses	226
	Troubleshooting IP Addressing	234
	Determining IP Address Problems	237
	Introduction to Network Address Translation (NAT)	241
	Types of Network Address Translation	243
	NAT Names	243
	How NAT Works	244
	Summary	245
	Exam Essentials	246
	Written Labs	246
	Review Questions	247

Chapter 9	**Introduction to IP Routing**	**253**
	Routing Basics	254
	The IP Routing Process	257
	Testing Your IP Routing Understanding	263
	Static and Dynamic Routing	264
	Summary	267
	Exam Essentials	267
	Written Lab	267
	Review Questions	269
Chapter 10	**Routing Protocols**	**273**
	Routing Protocol Basics	274
	Administrative Distances	275
	Classes of Routing Protocols	277
	Distance Vector Routing Protocols	278
	Routing Information Protocol (RIP)	279
	RIP Version 2 (RIPv2)	280
	VLSM and Discontiguous Networks	280
	EIGRP	282
	Border Gateway Protocol (BGP)	285
	Link State Routing Protocols	286
	Open Shortest Path First (OSPF)	287
	Intermediate System-to-Intermediate System (IS-IS)	289
	IPv6 Routing Protocols	290
	RIPng	290
	EIGRPv6	291
	OSPFv3	291
	Summary	291
	Exam Essentials	292
	Written Lab	292
	Review Questions	293
Chapter 11	**Switching and Virtual LANs**	**297**
	Networking Before Layer 2 Switching	298
	Switching Services	302
	Limitations of Layer 2 Switching	303
	Bridging vs. LAN Switching	303
	Three Switch Functions at Layer 2	304
	Spanning Tree Protocol	309
	Spanning-Tree Port States	310
	STP Convergence	311
	Rapid Spanning Tree Protocol 802.1w	311

Virtual LANs	313
VLAN Basics	313
Quality of Service	316
VLAN Memberships	317
Static VLANs	317
Dynamic VLANs	318
Identifying VLANs	318
VLAN Identification Methods	320
VLAN Trunking Protocol	321
VTP Modes of Operation	322
Configuring VTP	323
Two Additional Advanced Features of Switches	324
Power over Ethernet	324
Port Mirroring/Spanning	326
Summary	328
Exam Essentials	328
Written Lab	329
Review Questions	330

Chapter 12	**Wireless Networking**	**335**
	Introduction to Wireless Technology	337
	The 802.11 Standards	340
	2.4GHz (802.11b)	341
	2.4GHz (802.11g)	342
	5GHz (802.11a)	343
	5GHz (802.11h)	344
	2.4GHz/5GHz (802.11n)	345
	Comparing 802.11 Standards	346
	Range Comparisons	346
	Wireless Network Components	347
	Wireless Access Points	347
	Wireless Network Interface Card	348
	Wireless Antennas	349
	Installing a Wireless Network	351
	Ad Hoc Mode: Independent Basic Service Set	351
	Infrastructure Mode: Basic Service Set	352
	Signal Degradation	354
	Installing and Configuring Hardware	355
	Wireless Security	362
	Open Access	363
	Service Set Identifiers, Wired Equivalent Privacy, and Media Access Control Address Authentication	364
	Remote Authentication Dial In User Service	365

Temporal Key Integrity Protocol	366
Wi-Fi Protected Access or WPA 2 Pre-Shared Key	367
Summary	368
Exam Essentials	369
Written Lab	369
Review Questions	370

Chapter 13   Authentication and Access Control   375

Security Filtering	377
Access Control Lists	378
Tunneling	379
Encryption	386
Remote Access	390
Managing User Account and Password Security	393
Managing User Accounts	393
Managing Passwords	396
Single Sign-On	400
Multifactor Authentication	400
User-Authentication Methods	400
Public Key Infrastructure (PKI)	401
Kerberos	402
Authentication, Authorization, and Accounting (AAA)	402
Network Access Control (NAC)	405
Challenge Handshake Authentication Protocol (CHAP)	405
MS-CHAP	405
Extensible Authentication Protocol (EAP)	406
Summary	406
Exam Essentials	407
Written Lab	407
Review Questions	409

Chapter 14   Network Threats and Mitigation   413

Recognizing Security Threats	414
Denial of Service	415
Viruses	417
Worms	421
Buffer Overflow	421
Wireless Threats	421
Attackers and Their Tools	424
Social Engineering (Phishing)	427
Understanding Mitigation Techniques	428
Active Detection	429
Passive Detection	429
Proactive Defense	429

Policies and Procedures	430
Security Policies	431
Security Training	436
Patches and Upgrades	437
Updating Antivirus Components	439
Fixing an Infected Computer	441
Summary	441
Exam Essentials	442
Written Lab	442
Review Questions	444

Chapter 15   Physical and Hardware Security   449

Using Hardware and Software Security Devices	450
Defining Firewalls	452
Network-Based Firewalls	453
Host-Based Firewalls	453
Firewall Technologies	453
Access Control Lists	453
Port Security	456
Demilitarized Zone	456
Protocol Switching	457
Dynamic Packet Filtering	459
Proxy Services	460
Firewalls at the Application Layer vs. the Network Layer	461
Stateful vs. Stateless Network Layer Firewalls	462
Application Layer Firewalls	463
Scanning Services and Other Firewall Features	464
Content Filtering	465
Signature Identification	466
Zones	466
Intrusion Detection and Prevention Systems	468
Network-Based IDS	469
Host-Based IDS	471
Vulnerability Scanners	472
VPN Concentrators	473
Understanding Problems Affecting Device Security	474
Physical Security	474
Logical Security Configurations	476
Summary	478
Exam Essentials	479
Written Lab	480
Review Questions	481

Chapter 16   Wide Area Networks   485

What's a WAN?   488
    Defining WAN Terms   488
    The Public Switched Telephone Network   489
    WAN Connection Types   490
    Bandwidth or Speed   492
T-Series Connections   492
    The T1 Connection   494
    The T3 Connection   494
Transmission Media   495
    Wired Connections   495
    Dense Wavelength Division Multiplexing   496
    Passive Optical Network   496
    Wireless Technologies   497
Broadband Services   498
    DSL Technology and xDSL   500
    Cable Modem   501
Wireless WAN Technologies   503
    Cellular WAN   503
WAN Protocols   504
    Integrated Services Digital Network   504
    Frame Relay Technology   506
    Asynchronous Transfer Mode   508
Summary   509
Exam Essentials   509
Written Lab   510
Review Questions   511

Chapter 17   Troubleshooting Tools   515

Protocol Analyzers   517
Throughput Testers   518
Connectivity Software   519
Using *Traceroute*   520
Using *ipconfig* and *ifconfig*   521
    Using the *ipconfig* Utility   521
    Using the *ifconfig* Utility   525
Using the *ping* Utility   526
Using the Address Resolution Protocol   529
    The Windows ARP Table   529
    Using the *arp* Utility   530
Using the *nslookup* Utility   533
Resolving Names with the Hosts Table   535
Using the *Mtr* Command   536

Using the *route* Command   537
  Using the *route* Command Options   538
  Some Examples of the *route* Command   540
Using the *nbtstat* Utility   540
  The *−a* Switch   541
  The *−A* Switch   543
  The *−c* Switch   543
  The *−n* Switch   544
  The *−r* Switch   544
  The *−R* Switch   545
  The *−S* Switch   545
  The *−s* Switch   546
Using the *netstat* Utility   546
  The *−a* Switch   549
  The *−e* Switch   550
  The *−r* Switch   551
  The *−s* Switch   551
  The *−p* Switch   551
  The *−n* Switch   553
Using the File Transfer Protocol   554
  Starting FTP and Logging In to an FTP Server   555
  Downloading Files   557
  Uploading Files   559
Using the *Telnet* Utility   560
  How to Enable Telnet in Vista   560
  Don't Use Telnet, Use Secure Shell   561
Summary   562
Exam Essentials   562
Written Lab   563
Review Questions   564

Chapter 18   **Software and Hardware Tools**   **569**

Understanding Network Scanners   570
  Packet Sniffers   570
  Intrusion Detection and Prevention Software   572
  Port Scanners   574
Identifying Hardware Tools   576
  Cable Testers   577
  Protocol Analyzer   579
  Certifiers   580
  Time-Domain Reflectometer   581
  Optical Time-Domain Reflectometer   581

Multimeter 582
Toner Probe 582
Butt Set 584
Punch-Down Tool 585
Cable Stripper/Snips 586
Voltage Event Recorder 587
Environmental Monitors 588
Summary 589
Exam Essentials 589
Written Lab 590
Review Questions 591

Chapter 19   Network Troubleshooting   595

Narrowing Down the Problem 598
Are There Any Cabling Issues? Did You Check
the Super Simple Stuff? 599
Is Hardware or Software Causing the Problem? 603
Is It a Workstation or a Server Problem? 604
Which Segments of the Network Are Affected? 604
Is It Bad Cabling? 604
Troubleshooting Steps 609
Step 1: Identify the Problem 610
Step 2: Establish a Theory of Probable Cause 613
Step 3: Test the Theory to Determine Cause 616
Step 4: Establish a Plan of Action to Resolve the
Problem and Identify Potential Effects 618
Step 5: Implement the Solution or Escalate as Necessary 620
Step 6: Verify Full System Functionality and
If Applicable Implement Preventative Measures 622
Step 7: Document Findings, Actions, and Outcomes 623
Troubleshooting Tips 623
Don't Overlook the Small Stuff 624
Prioritize Your Problems 624
Check the Software Configuration 625
Don't Overlook Physical Conditions 625
Don't Overlook Cable Problems 626
Check for Viruses 626
Summary 626
Exam Essentials 627
Written Lab 628
Review Questions 629

Chapter 20   **Management, Monitoring, and Optimization**   **635**

Managing Network Documentation   638
  Using SNMP   638
  Schematics and Diagrams   639
  Baselines   645
  Policies, Procedures, and Regulations   647
Monitoring the Network and Optimizing Its Performance   649
  Network Monitoring and Logging   650
  Reasons to Optimize Your Network's Performance   652
  How to Optimize Performance   654
  Virtual Networking   658
Summary   661
Exam Essentials   662
Written Lab   663
Review Questions   664

Appendix A   **Answers to Review Questions**   **669**

Chapter 1: Introduction to Networks   670
Chapter 2: The Open Systems Interconnection Specifications   672
Chapter 3: Networking Topologies, Connectors, and
  Wiring Standards   673
Chapter 4: The Current Ethernet Specifications   675
Chapter 5: Networking Devices   676
Chapter 6: Introduction to the Internet Protocol   677
Chapter 7: IP Addressing   679
Chapter 8: IP Subnetting, Troubleshooting IP, and
  Introduction to NAT   681
Chapter 9: Introduction to IP Routing   683
Chapter 10: Routing Protocols   684
Chapter 11: Switching and Virtual LANs   686
Chapter 12: Wireless Networking   688
Chapter 13: Authentication and Access Control   689
Chapter 14: Network Threats and Mitigation   691
Chapter 15: Physical and Hardware Security   692
Chapter 16: Wide Area Networks   694
Chapter 17: Troubleshooting Tools   695
Chapter 18: Software and Hardware Tools   697
Chapter 19: Network Troubleshooting   699
Chapter 20: Management, Monitoring, and Optimization   700

Appendix B   **Answers to Written Labs**   **703**

Chapter 1: Introduction to Networks   704
Chapter 2: The Open Systems Interconnection Specifications   704
Chapter 3: Networking Topologies, Connectors, and
  Wiring Standards   705

Chapter 4: The Current Ethernet Specifications   705

Chapter 5: Networking Devices   708

Chapter 6: Introduction to the Internet Protocol   708

Chapter 7: IP Addressing   709

Chapter 8: IP Subnetting, Troubleshooting IP, and Introduction to NAT   710

Chapter 9: Introduction to IP Routing   710

Chapter 10: Routing Protocols   711

Chapter 11: Switching and Virtual LANs   711

Chapter 12: Wireless Networking   712

Chapter 13: Authentication and Access Control   712

Chapter 14: Network Threats and Mitigation   712

Chapter 15: Physical and Hardware Security   713

Chapter 16: Wide Area Networks   713

Chapter 17: Troubleshooting Tools   714

Chapter 18: Software and Hardware Tools   714

Chapter 19: Network Troubleshooting   715

Chapter 20: Management, Monitoring, and Optimization   715

Appendix C   Subnetting Class A   717

Subnetting Practice Examples: Class A Addresses   718

    Practice Example #1A: 255.255.0.0 (/16)   719

    Practice Example #2A: 255.255.240.0 (/20)   719

    Practice Example #3A: 255.255.255.192 (/26)   720

Subnetting in Your Head: Class A Addresses   720

Written Lab 1   721

Written Lab 2   722

Answers to Written Lab 1   722

Answers to Written Lab 2   723

Appendix D   About the Additional Study Tools   725

Additional Study Tools   726

    Sybex Test Engine   726

    Electronic Flashcards   726

    PDF of Glossary of Terms   726

    Adobe Reader   726

System Requirements   727

Using the Study Tools   727

Troubleshooting   727

    Customer Care   728

Index   729

Foreword

CompTIA Network+:

The CompTIA Network+ (2011 Edition) certification ensures that the successful candidate has the important knowledge and skills necessary to manage, maintain, troubleshoot, install, operate, and configure basic network infrastructure; describe networking technologies and basic design principles; adhere to wiring standards; and use testing tools.

It Pays to Get Certified

In a digital world, digital literacy is an essential survival skill. Certification proves you have the knowledge and skill to solve business problems in virtually any business environment.

CompTIA Network+ certification is held by many IT Staff in organizations. 21% of IT staff within a random sampling of U.S. organizations within a cross section of industry verticals hold Network+ certification.

The CompTIA Network+ credential Proves knowledge of networking features and functions and is the leading vendor-neutral certification for networking professionals.

Starting Salary The average starting salary of network engineers can be up to $70,000.

Career Pathway CompTIA Network+ is the first step in starting a networking career and is recognized by Microsoft as part of their MS program. Other corporations, such as Novell, Cisco, and HP also recognize CompTIA Network+ as part of their certification tracks.

More than 260,000 Individuals worldwide are CompTIA Network+ certified.

Mandated/Recommended by organizations worldwide Such as Cisco, HP, Ricoh, the U.S. State Department, and U.S. government contractors such as EDS, General Dynamics, and Northrop Grumman.

How Certification Helps Your Career

It Is Everywhere	IT Knowledge and Skills Get Jobs	Retain Your Job and Salary	Want to Change Jobs?	Stick Out from the Resume Pile
IT is ubiquitous and needed by most organizations. Globally, there are over 600,000 IT job openings.	Certifications are essential credentials that qualify you for jobs, increased compensation, and promotion.	Make your expertise stand above the rest. Competence is usually retained during times of change.	Certifications qualify you for new opportunities, whether you are locked into a current job, see limited advancement, or need to change careers.	Hiring managers can demand the strongest skill set.

CompTIA Career Pathway

CompTIA offers a number of credentials that form a foundation for your career in technology and allow you to pursue specific areas of concentration. Depending on the path you choose to take, CompTIA certifications help you build upon your skills and knowledge, supporting learning throughout your entire career.

Steps to Getting Certified

Review exam objectives.   Review the certification objectives to make sure you know what is covered in the exam.

> www.comptia.org/certifications/testprep/practicetests.aspx

Practice for the exam.   After you have studied for the certification, take a free assessment and sample test to get an idea of what type of questions might be on the exam.

> certification.comptia.org/Training/testingcenters/examobjectives.aspx

Purchase an exam voucher.   Purchase your exam voucher on the CompTIA Marketplace, which is located at www.comptiastore.com.

Take the test!   Select a certification exam provider and schedule a time to take your exam. You can find exam providers at the following link:

`certification.comptia.org/Training/testingcenters/`

Stay certified through continuing Education!   Effective January 1, 2011, new CompTIA Security+ certifications are valid for three years from the date of your certification. There are a number of ways the certification can be renewed. For more information go to

`http://certification.comptia.org/getCertified/steps_to_certification/`
`stayCertified.aspx`

Join the IT Professional Community

The free IT Pro online community at `http://itpro.comptia.org` provides valuable content to students and professionals.

- Career IT job resources
    - Where to start in IT
    - Career assessments
    - Salary trends
    - US job board
- Forums on networking, security, computing, and cutting-edge technologies
- Access to blogs written by industry experts
- Current information on cutting-edge technologies
- Access to various industry resource links and articles related to IT and IT careers

Content Seal of Quality

This text bears the seal of CompTIA Approved Quality Content. This seal signifies that this content covers 100% of the exam objectives and implements important instructional design principles. CompTIA recommends multiple learning tools to help increase coverage of the learning objectives. Look for this seal on other materials you use to prepare for your certification exam.

Why CompTIA?

Global recognition   CompTIA is recognized globally as the leading IT nonprofit trade association and has enormous credibility. Plus, CompTIA's certifications are vendor neutral and offer proof of foundational knowledge that translates across technologies.

Valued by hiring managers   Hiring managers value CompTIA certification because it is vendor- and technology-independent validation of your technical skills.

Recommended or required by government and businesses   Many government organizations and corporations either recommend or require technical staff to be CompTIA certified (Dell, Sharp, Ricoh, the US Department of Defense, and many more).

Top ranking   Three CompTIA certifications ranked in the top 10. In a study by DICE of 17,000 technology professionals, certifications helped command higher salaries at all experience levels.

How to Obtain More Information

- Visit us online at www.comptia.org to learn more about getting a CompTIA certification. And while you're at it, take a moment to learn a little more about CompTIA. We're the voice of the world's IT industry. Our membership includes companies on the cutting edge of innovation.
- To contact CompTIA with any questions or comments, please call 866-835-8020, ext. 5, or email questions@comptia.org.
- Find us on the following social media sites:
    - Facebook
    - LinkedIn
    - Twitter
    - YouTube

Terry Erdle
Executive Vice President, Skills Certification,
CompTIA

Introduction

If you're like most of us in the networking community, you probably have one or more network certifications. If that's you, you're very wise in choosing a CompTIA Network+ (N10-005) certification to proudly add to your repertoire because that achievement will make you all the more valuable as an employee. In these challenging economic times, keeping ahead of the competition—even standing out among your present colleagues—could make a big difference in whether you gain a promotion or possibly keep your job instead of being the one who gets laid off! Or maybe this is your first attempt at certification because you've decided to venture into a new career in information technology (IT). You've realized that getting into the IT sector is a good way to go because as the information age marches on, the demand for knowledgeable professionals in this dynamic field will only intensify dramatically.

Either way, obtaining certification is one of the best things you can do for your career if you are working in, or want to break into, the networking profession because it proves that you know what you're talking about regarding the subjects in which you're certified. It also powerfully endorses you as a professional in a way that's very similar to a physician being board certified in a certain area of expertise.

In this book, you'll find out what the Network+ exam is all about because each chapter covers a part of the exam. I've included some great review questions at the end of each chapter to help crystallize the information you learned and solidly prepare you to ace the exam.

A really cool thing about working in IT is that it's constantly evolving, so there are always new things to learn and fresh challenges to master. Once you obtain your Network+ certification and discover that you're interested in taking it further by getting into more complex networking (and making more money), the Cisco CCNA certification is definitely your next step; you can get the skinny on that and even more in-depth certifications on my blog at www.lammle.com/forum.

What Is the Network+ Certification?

Network+ is a certification developed by the Computing Technology Industry Association (CompTIA) that exists to provide resources and education for the computer and technology community. This is the same body that developed the A+ exam for PC technicians.

Way back in 1995, members of the organization got together to develop a new certification that tests skills for IT. To ensure industry-wide support, it was sponsored by many past and present IT industry leaders like these:

- Compaq Computers
- Digital Equipment Corporation (a part of Compaq)
- IBM
- Lotus
- Microsoft

- Novell
- TSS
- U.S. Robotics
- US West
- Wave Technologies

The Network+ exam was designed to test the skills of network technicians with 18 to 24 months of experience in the field. It tests areas of networking technologies such as the definition of a protocol, the Open Systems Interconnection (OSI) model and its layers, and the concepts of network design and implementation—the minimum knowledge required for working on a network and some integral prerequisites for network design and implementation.

Why Become Network+ Certified?

Because CompTIA is a well-respected developer of vendor-neutral industry certifications, becoming Network+ certified proves you're competent in the specific areas tested by the Network+ exam.

The following are the major benefits are associated with becoming Network+ certified:

Proof of professional achievement   Networking professionals are pretty competitive when it comes to collecting more certifications than their peers. And because the Network+ certification broadly covers the entire field of networking, technicians want this certification a lot more than having just Microsoft certifications—Network+ is a lot more prestigious and valuable. Because it's rare to gain something that's worth a lot with little effort, I'll be honest—preparing for the Network+ exam isn't exactly a lazy day at the beach. (However, beaches do happen to be really high on my personal list of great places to study!) And people in IT know that it isn't all that easy to pass the Network+ exam, so they'll definitely respect you more and know that you've achieved a certain level of expertise about vendor-independent networking-related subjects.

Opportunity for advancement   We all like to get ahead in our careers—advancement results in more responsibility and prestige, and it usually means a fatter paycheck, greater opportunities, and added options. In the IT sector, a great way to make sure all that good stuff happens is by earning a lot of technology certifications, including Network+.

Fulfillment of training requirements   Network+, because of its wide-reaching industry support, is recognized as a baseline of networking information. Some companies actually specify the possession of a Network+ certification as a job requirement before they'll even consider hiring you, or as a goal to be met before your next review. And often, gaining a Network+ certification will get you a pay raise at review time.

Customer confidence   As companies discover the CompTIA advantage, they will undoubtedly require qualified staff to achieve these certifications. Many companies outsource their work to consulting firms with experience working with security. Firms that have certified staff have a definite advantage over firms that don't.

How to Become Network+ Certified

As this book goes to press, there are two Network+ exam providers: Prometric and Pearson VUE. The following table contains all the necessary contact information and exam-specific details for registering. Exam pricing might vary by country or by CompTIA membership.

Vendor	Website phone	Phone number
Prometric	`http://securereg3.prometric.com`	US and Canada: 800-977-3926
Pearson VUE	`www.vue.com/comptia`	US and Canada: 877-551-PLUS (7587)

When you schedule the exam, you'll receive instructions regarding appointment and cancellation procedures, ID requirements, and information about the testing center location. In addition, you'll receive a registration and payment confirmation letter. Exams can be scheduled up to six weeks out or as late as the next day (or, in some cases, even the same day).

Exam prices and codes may vary based on the country in which the exam is administered. For detailed pricing and exam registration procedures, refer to CompTIA's website at www.comptia.com.

After you've successfully passed your Network+ exam, CompTIA will award you a certification. Within four to six weeks of passing the exam, you'll receive your official CompTIA Network+ certificate and ID card. (If you don't receive these within eight weeks of taking the test, contact CompTIA directly using the information found in your registration packet.)

Tips for Taking the Network+ Exam

Here are some general tips for taking your exam successfully:

- Bring two forms of ID with you. One must be a photo ID, such as a driver's license. The other can be a major credit card or a passport. Both forms must include a signature.

- Arrive early at the exam center so you can relax and review your study materials, particularly tables and lists of exam-related information. After you are ready to enter the testing room, you will need to leave everything outside; you won't be able to bring any materials into the testing area.

- Read the questions carefully. Don't be tempted to jump to an early conclusion. Make sure you know exactly what each question is asking.

- Don't leave any unanswered questions. Unanswered questions are scored against you. There will be questions with multiple correct responses. When there is more than one correct answer, a message at the bottom of the screen will prompt you to either "choose two" or "choose all that apply." Be sure to read the messages displayed to know how many correct answers you must choose.

- When answering multiple-choice questions you're not sure about, use a process of elimination to get rid of the obviously incorrect answers first. Doing so will improve your odds if you need to make an educated guess.

- On form-based tests (nonadaptive), because the hard questions will take the most time, save them for last. You can move forward and backward through the exam.

- For the latest pricing on the exams and updates to the registration procedures, visit CompTIA's website at www.comptia.org.

Who Should Read This Book?

You—if want to pass the Network+ exam, and pass it confidently! This book is chock full of the exact information you need and directly maps to Network+ exam objectives (listed later in this introduction), so if you use it to study for the exam, your odds of passing shoot way up.

And in addition to including every bit of knowledge you need to learn to pass the exam, I've included some really great tips and solid wisdom to equip you even further to successfully work in the real IT world.

What Does This Book Cover?

This book covers everything you need to know to pass the Network+ exam. But in addition to studying the book, it's a good idea to practice on an actual network if you can.

Here's a list of the 20 chapters in this book.

Chapter 1, "Introduction to Networks"   An introduction to what a network is, and an overview of the most common physical network topologies you'll find in today's networks.

Chapter 2, "The Open Systems Interconnection Specifications"   This chapter covers the OSI model, what it is, what happens at each of its layers, and how each layer works.

Chapter 3, "Networking Topologies, Connectors, and Wiring Standards"   This chapter covers the various networking media and topologies, plus the cable types and properties used in today's networks.

Chapter 4, "The Current Ethernet Specifications"   This chapter covers how a basic Ethernet LAN works and describes and categorizes the different Ethernet specifications.

Chapter 5, "Networking Devices"   It's important for you to understand all the various devices used in today's networks, and this chapter will describe how hubs, routers, and switches, and some other devices work within a network.

Chapter 6, "Introduction to the Internet Protocol"   This is your introduction to the all-important IP protocol stack.

Chapter 7, "IP Addressing"   This chapter will take up from where Chapter 6 left off and move into IP addressing. It also contains information about public versus private addressing and DHCP.

Chapter 8, "IP Subnetting, Troubleshooting IP, and Introduction to NAT"   Beginning where Chapter 7 ends, we'll be tackling IP subnetting in this one. But no worries here—I've worked hard to make this not-so-popular-yet-vital topic as painless as possible.

Chapter 9, "Introduction to IP Routing"   This is an introduction to routing that basically covers what routers do and how they do it. This chapter, along with Chapter 10 and Chapter 11, cover routing and switching in much more detail than what is necessary to meet the CompTIA Network+ objectives because this knowledge is so critical to grasp when working with today's networks.

Chapter 10, "Routing Protocols"   This chapter goes into detail describing the protocols that run on routers and that update routing tables to create a working map of the network.

Chapter 11, "Switching and Virtual LANs"   This chapter covers Layer 2 switching, the Spanning Tree Protocol (STP), and virtual LANs. Just as I went in deeper than needed for the exam with the routing chapters, I'll cover switching and virtual LANs (which are also vital in today's corporate networks) more thoroughly.

Chapter 12, "Wireless Networking"   Because wireless is so important for both home and business networks today, this chapter is loaded with all the information you need to be successful at wireless networking at home and work.

Chapter 13, "Authentication and Access Control"   This is the first of three security chapters. There are tons of exam objectives about network security that are so important that I took three chapters to cover all of them. In this chapter, I'll introduce security, security filtering, tunneling, and user authentication.

Chapter 14, "Network Threats and Mitigation"   This is probably the most fun of the three security chapters because I'll tell you all about security threats and how to stop them. The only way to get good at network security is to implement it, and this chapter shows you how.

Chapter 15, "Physical and Hardware Security"   This chapter's focus is on explaining basic firewalls, security devices, and device security.

Chapter 16, "Wide Area Networks"   In this chapter, you get to learn all about things like Frame Relay, E1/T1, DSL, cable modems, and more. All of the CompTIA Network+ WAN objectives are covered in this chapter.

Chapter 17, "Troubleshooting Tools"   This is also a fun chapter because again, you can follow along and run all the troubleshooting commands yourself. And I repeat, it's a really good idea to run through all the commands, again and again!

Chapter 18, "Software and Hardware Tools"   This chapter introduces you to the network tools you will use to help you run your networks. Both software and hardware tools will be discussed.

Chapter 19, "Network Troubleshooting"   In almost every chapter, I discuss how to verify and fix problems, but this chapter will really get into the nuts and bolts of detailed network troubleshooting and documentation.

Chapter 20, "Management, Monitoring, and Optimization"   This last chapter will provide configuration-management documentation and covers wiring, logical diagrams, baselines, policies, and regulations.

What's Included in the Book

I've included several learning tools throughout the book:

Assessment test   At the end of this introduction is an assessment test that you can use to check your readiness for the exam. Take this test before you start reading the book; it will help you determine the areas you might need to brush up on. The answers to the assessment test questions appear on a separate page after the last question of the test. Each answer includes an explanation and a note telling you the chapter in which the material appears.

Objective map and opening list of objectives   On the inside front cover of this book is a detailed exam objective map showing you where each of the exam objectives is covered in this book. In addition, each chapter opens with a list of the exam objectives it covers. Use these to see exactly where each of the exam topics is covered.

Exam essentials   Each chapter, just before the summary, includes a number of exam essentials. These are the key topics you should take from the chapter in terms of areas to focus on when preparing for the exam.

Written lab   Each chapter includes a written lab. These are short exercises that map to the exam objectives. Answers to these can be found in Appendix B.

Chapter review questions   To test your knowledge as you progress through the book, there are review questions at the end of each chapter. As you finish each chapter, answer the review questions and then check your answers—the correct answers and explanations are in Appendix A. You can go back to reread the section that deals with each question you got wrong to ensure that you answer correctly the next time you're tested on the material.

We've included a number of additional study tools that can be found on the book's companion site at www.sybex.com/go/netplus2e:

Sybex test engine   Using this custom software, you can identify up front the areas in which you are weak and then develop a solid studying strategy using the test engine for each of the robust testing features included with this book. In addition to taking the assessment test and the chapter review questions with the test engine, you'll find two practice exams. Take these practice exams just as if you were taking the actual exam (without any reference material). When you've finished the first exam, move on to the next one to solidify your test-taking skills. If you get more than 90 percent of the answers correct, you're ready to take the certification exam.

Electronic flashcards   Use these handy flashcards for quick and convenient review.

PDF of glossary of terms   The glossary of terms is on the companion site in PDF format.

Readers can get the additional study tools by visiting www.lammle.com/forum and www.sybex.com/go/netplus2e. The Additional Study Tools appendix includes instructions on how to download the files to your hard drive.

How to Use This Book

If you want a solid foundation for the serious effort of preparing for the Network+ exam, then look no further because I've spent countless hours putting together this book with the sole intention of helping you to pass it!

This book is loaded with valuable information, and you will get the most out of your study time if you understand how I put the book together. Here's a list that describes how to approach studying:

1. Take the assessment test immediately following this introduction. (The answers are at the end of the test, but no peeking!) It's okay if you don't know any of the answers—that's what this book is for. Carefully read over the explanations for any question you get wrong, and make note of the chapters where that material is covered.

2. Study each chapter carefully, making sure that you fully understand the information and the exam objectives listed at the beginning of each one. Again, pay extra-close attention to any chapter that includes material covered in questions you missed on the assessment test.

3. Complete the written lab at the end of each chapter. Do *not* skip these written exercises because they directly map to the CompTIA objectives and what you've got to have nailed down to meet them.

4. Answer all the review questions related to each chapter. Specifically note any questions that confuse you, and study those sections of the book again. And don't just skim these questions—make sure you understand each answer completely.

5. Try your hand at the practice exams. In addition, check out www.lammle.com for more CompTIA Network+ exam prep questions. The questions found on my site will be updated at least monthly, maybe weekly or even daily. Before you take your test, be sure to visit my website for questions, videos, audios, and other useful information.

6. Test yourself using all the electronic flashcards. These are brand-new and updated flashcard programs to help you prepare for the latest CompTIA Network+ exam, and they're really great study tools.

I tell you no lies—learning every bit of the material in this book is going to require applying yourself with a good measure of discipline. So try to set aside the same time period every day to study, and select a comfortable and quiet place to do so. If you work hard, you will be surprised at how quickly you learn this material.

If you follow the steps listed here and study with the review questions, practice exams, electronic flashcards, and all the written labs, you would almost have to try to fail the CompTIA Network+ exam. However, studying for the Network+ exam is like training for a marathon—if you don't go for a good run every day, you're not likely to finish very well.

This book covers everything about CompTIA Network+. For up-to-date information about Todd Lammle CompTIA boot camps, audio training, and training videos, please see www.lammle.com and/or www.lammle.com/forum.

Exam Objectives

Speaking of objectives, you're probably pretty curious about those, right? CompTIA asked groups of IT professionals to fill out a survey rating the skills they felt were important in their jobs, and the results were grouped into objectives for the exam and divided into six domains.

This table gives you the extent by percentage that each domain is represented on the actual examination.

Domain	% of Examination
1.0 Network Technologies	21%
2.0 Network Installation and Configuration	23%
3.0 Network Media and Topologies	17%
4.0 Network Management	20%
5.0 Network Security	19%
Total	100%

Next, I'm going to give you the outline of the Network+ exam objectives.

 The specific objectives and weighting percentages can change at any time, so check CompTIA's website at www.comptia.org for a list of the most current ones.

1.0 Network Concepts

1.1 Compare the layers of the OSI and TCP/IP models.

- OSI model:
    - Layer 1 – Physical
    - Layer 2 – Data link
    - Layer 3 – Network
    - Layer 4 – Transport
    - Layer 5 – Session

- Layer 6 – Presentation
- Layer 7 – Application
- TCP/IP model:
  - Network Interface Layer
  - Internet Layer
  - Transport Layer
  - Application Layer
    - (Also described as: Link Layer, Internet Layer, Transport Layer, Application Layer)

1.2 Classify how applications, devices, and protocols relate to the OSI model layers.

- MAC address
- IP address
- EUI-64
- Frames
- Packets
- Switch
- Router
- Multilayer switch
- Hub
- Encryption devices
- Cable
- NIC
- Bridge

1.3 Explain the purpose and properties of IP addressing.

- Classes of addresses
  - A, B, C and D
  - Public vs. Private
- Classless (CIDR)
- IPv4 vs. IPv6 (formatting)
- MAC address format
- Subnetting
- Multicast vs. unicast vs. broadcast
- APIPA

1.4 Explain the purpose and properties of routing and switching.

- EIGRP
- OSPF
- RIP
- Link state vs. distance vector vs. hybrid
- Static vs. dynamic
- Routing metrics
  - Hop counts
  - MTU, bandwidth
  - Costs
  - Latency
- Next hop
- Spanning-Tree Protocol
- VLAN (802.1q)
- Port mirroring
- Broadcast domain vs. collision domain
- IGP vs. EGP
- Routing tables
- Convergence (steady state)

1.5 Identify common TCP and UDP default ports.

- SMTP – 25
- HTTP – 80
- HTTPS – 443
- FTP – 20, 21
- TELNET – 23
- IMAP – 143
- RDP – 3389
- SSH – 22
- DNS – 53
- DHCP – 67, 68

1.6 Explain the function of common networking protocols.

- TCP
- FTP
- UDP

- TCP/IP suite
- DHCP
- TFTP
- DNS
- HTTPS
- HTTP
- ARP
- SIP (VoIP)
- RTP (VoIP)
- SSH
- POP3
- NTP
- IMAP4
- Telnet
- SMTP
- SNMP2/3
- ICMP
- IGMP
- TLS

1.7 Summarize DNS concepts and its components.

- DNS servers
- DNS records (A, MX, AAAA, CNAME, PTR)
- Dynamic DNS

1.8 Given a scenario, implement the following network troubleshooting methodology:

- Identify the problem:
    - Information gathering
    - Identify symptoms
    - Question users
    - Determine if anything has changed
- Establish a theory of probable cause
    - Question the obvious
- Test the theory to determine cause:
    - Once theory is confirmed determine next steps to resolve problem.
    - If theory is not confirmed, re-establish new theory or escalate.

- Establish a plan of action to resolve the problem and identify potential effects
- Implement the solution or escalate as necessary
- Verify full system functionality and if applicable implement preventative measures
- Document findings, actions and outcomes

1.9 Identify virtual network components.

- Virtual switches
- Virtual desktops
- Virtual servers
- Virtual PBX
- Onsite vs. offsite
- Network as a Service (NaaS)

2.0 Network Installation and Configuration

2.1 Given a scenario, install and configure routers and switches.

- Routing tables
- NAT
- PAT
- VLAN (trunking)
- Managed vs. unmanaged
- Interface configurations
    - Full duplex
    - Half duplex
    - Port speeds
    - IP addressing
    - MAC filtering
- PoE
- Traffic filtering
- Diagnostics
- VTP configuration
- QoS
- Port mirroring

2.2 Given a scenario, install and configure a wireless network.

- WAP placement
- Antenna types
- Interference

- Frequencies
- Channels
- Wireless standards
- SSID (enable/disable)
- Compatibility (802.11 a/b/g/n)

2.3 Explain the purpose and properties of DHCP.

- Static vs. dynamic IP addressing
- Reservations
- Scopes
- Leases
- Options (DNS servers, suffixes)

2.4 Given a scenario, troubleshoot common wireless problems.

- Interference
- Signal strength
- Configurations
- Incompatibilities
- Incorrect channel
- Latency
- Encryption type
- Bounce
- SSID mismatch
- Incorrect switch placement

2.5 Given a scenario, troubleshoot common router and switch problems.

- Switching loop
- Bad cables/improper cable types
- Port configuration
- VLAN assignment
- Mismatched MTU/MUT black hole
- Power failure
- Bad/missing routes
- Bad modules (SFPs, GBICs)
- Wrong subnet mask
- Wrong gateway
- Duplicate IP address
- Wrong DNS

2.6 Given a set of requirements, plan and implement a basic SOHO network.

- List of requirements
- Cable length
- Device types/requirements
- Environment limitations
- Equipment limitations
- Compatibility requirements

3.0 Network Media and Topologies

3.1 Categorize standard media types and associated properties.

- Fiber:
  - Multimode
  - Singlemode
- Copper:
  - UTP
  - STP
  - CAT3
  - CAT5
  - CAT5e
  - CAT6
  - CAT6a
  - Coaxial
  - Crossover
  - T1 Crossover
  - Straight-through
- Plenum vs. non-plenum
- Media converters:
  - Singlemode fiber to Ethernet
  - Multimode fiber to Ethernet
  - Fiber to Coaxial
  - Singlemode to multimode fiber
- Distance limitations and speed limitations
- Broadband over powerline

3.2 Categorize standard connector types based on network media.

- Fiber:
    - ST
    - SC
    - LC
    - MTRJ
- Copper:
    - RJ-45
    - RJ-11
    - BNC
    - F-connector
    - DB-9 (RS-232)
    - Patch panel
    - 110 block (T568A, T568B)

3.3 Compare and contrast different wireless standards.

- 802.11 a/b/g/n standards
    - Distance
    - Speed
    - Latency
    - Frequency
    - Channels
    - MIMO
    - Channel bonding

3.4 Categorize WAN technology types and properties.

- Types:
    - T1/E1
    - T3/E3
    - DS3
    - OCx
    - SONET
    - SDH
    - DWDM
    - Satellite
    - ISDN

- Cable
- DSL
- Cellular
- WiMAX
- LTE
- HSPA+
- Fiber
- Dialup
- PON
- Frame relay
- ATMs
- Properties:
  - Circuit switch
  - Packet switch
  - Speed
  - Transmission media
  - Distance

3.5 Describe different network topologies.

- MPLS
- Point to point
- Point to multipoint
- Ring
- Star
- Mesh
- Bus
- Peer-to-peer
- Client-server
- Hybrid

3.6 Given a scenario, troubleshoot common physical connectivity problems.

- Cable problems:
  - Bad connectors
  - Bad wiring
  - Open, short
  - Split cables

- DB loss
- TXRX reversed
- Cable placement
- EMI/Interference
- Distance
- Cross-talk

3.7 Compare and contrast different LAN technologies.

- Types:
    - Ethernet
    - 10BaseT
    - 100BaseT
    - 1000BaseT
    - 100BaseTX
    - 100BaseFX
    - 1000BaseX
    - 10GBaseSR
    - 10GBaseLR
    - 10GBaseER
    - 10GBaseSW
    - 10GBaseLW
    - 10GBaseEW
    - 10GBaseT
- Properties:
    - CSMA/CD
    - CSMA/CA
    - Broadcast
    - Collision
    - Bonding
    - Speed
    - Distance

3.8 Identify components of wiring distribution.

- IDF
- MDF
- Demarc

- Demarc extension
- Smart jack
- CSU/DSU

4.0 Network Management

4.1 Explain the purpose and features of various network appliances.

- Load balancer
- Proxy server
- Content filter
- VPN concentrator

4.2 Given a scenario, use appropriate hardware tools to troubleshoot connectivity issues.

- Cable tester
- Cable certifier
- Crimper
- Butt set
- Toner probe
- Punch down tool
- Protocol analyzer
- Loop back plug
- TDR
- OTDR
- Multimeter
- Environmental monitor

4.3 Given a scenario, use appropriate software tools to troubleshoot connectivity issues.

- Protocol analyzer
- Throughput testers
- Connectivity software
- Ping
- Tracert/traceroute
- Dig
- Ipconfig/ifconfig
- Nslookup
- Arp
- Nbtstat

- Netstat
- Route

4.4 Given a scenario, use the appropriate network monitoring resource to analyze traffic.

- SNMP
- SNMPv2
- SNMPv3
- Syslog
- System logs
- History logs
- General logs
- Traffic analysis
- Network sniffer

4.5 Describe the purpose of configuration management documentation.

- Wire schemes
- Network maps
- Documentation
- Cable management
- Asset management
- Baselines
- Change management

4.6 Explain different methods and rationales for network performance optimization.

- Methods:
  - QoS
  - Traffic shaping
  - Load balancing
  - High availability
  - Caching engines
  - Fault tolerance
  - CARP
- Reasons:
  - Latency sensitivity
  - High bandwidth applications (VoIP, video applications, unified communications)
  - Uptime

5.0 Network Security

5.1 Given a scenario, implement appropriate wireless security measures.

- Encryption protocols:
  - WEP
  - WPA
  - WPA2
  - WPA Enterprise
- MAC address filtering
- Device placement
- Signal strength

5.2 Explain the methods of network access security.

- ACL:
  - MAC filtering
  - IP filtering
  - Port filtering
- Tunneling and encryption:
  - SSL VPN
  - VPN
  - L2TP
  - PPTP
  - IPSec
  - ISAKMP
  - TLS
  - TLS1.2
  - Site-to-site and client-to-site
- Remote access:
  - RAS
  - RDP
  - PPPoE
  - PPP
  - ICA
  - SSH

5.3 Explain methods of user authentication.

- PKI
- Kerberos
- AAA (RADIUS, TACACS+)
- Network access control (802.1x, posture assessment)
- CHAP
- MS-CHAP
- EAP
- Two-factor authentication
- Multifactor authentication
- Single sign-on

5.4 Explain common threats, vulnerabilities, and mitigation techniques.

- Wireless:
  - War driving
  - War chalking
  - WEP cracking
  - WPA cracking
  - Evil twin
  - Rogue access point
- Attacks:
  - DoS
  - DDoS
  - Man in the middle
  - Social engineering
  - Virus
  - Worms
  - Buffer overflow
  - Packet sniffing
  - FTP bounce
  - Smurf
- Mitigation techniques:
  - Training and awareness
  - Patch management
  - Policies and procedures
  - Incident response

5.5 Given a scenario, install and configure a basic firewall.

- Types:
  - Software and hardware firewalls
- Port security
- Stateful inspection vs. packet filtering
- Firewall rules:
  - Block/allow
  - Implicit deny
  - ACL
- NAT/PAT
- DMZ

5.6 Categorize different types of network security appliances and methods.

- IDS and IPS:
  - Behavior based
  - Signature based
  - Network based
  - Host based
- Vulnerability scanners:
  - NESSUS
  - NMAP
- Methods:
  - Honeypots
  - Honeynets

 Exam objectives are subject to change at any time without prior notice and at CompTIA's sole discretion. Please visit CompTIA's website (www.comptia.org) for the most current listing of exam objectives.

Assessment Test

1. What is the basic purpose of a local area network (LAN)?
   A. To interconnect networks in several different buildings
   B. To connect one or more computers together so they can share resources
   C. To interconnect 2 to 10 routers
   D. To make routers unnecessary

2. You need a topology that is easy to troubleshoot and scalable. Which would you use?
   A. Bus
   B. Star
   C. Mesh
   D. Ring

3. IP resides at which layer of the OSI model?
   A. Application
   B. Data Link
   C. Network
   D. Physical

4. Layer 2 of the OSI model is named _____.
   A. Application layer
   B. Network layer
   C. Transport layer
   D. Data Link layer

5. Which RG rating of coax is used for cable modems?
   A. RG-59
   B. RG-58
   C. RG-6
   D. RG-8

6. Which UTP wiring uses four twisted wire pairs (eight wires) and is rated for 250MHz?
   A. Category 3 UTP
   B. Category 5 STP
   C. Category 5 UTP
   D. Category 6 UTP

7. If you are running half-duplex Internet, which of the following is true?

   A. Your digital signal cannot transmit and receive data at the same time.

   B. Hosts use the CSMA/CD protocol to prevent collisions.

   C. The physical connection consists of one wire pair.

   D. All of the above.

8. You need to connect a hub to a switch. You don't like this idea because you know that it will create congestion. What type of cable do you need to use to connect the hub to the switch?

   A. EtherIP

   B. Crossover

   C. Straight-through

   D. Cable Sense, Multiple Access

9. Your boss asks you why you just put in a requisition to buy a bunch of switches. He said he just bought you a bunch of hubs five years ago! Why did you buy the switches?

   A. Because each switch port is its own collision domain.

   B. The cable connecting devices to the hub wore out, and switches were cheaper than new cable.

   C. There were too many broadcast domains, and a switch breaks up broadcast domains by default.

   D. The hubs kept repeating signals but quit recognizing frames and data structures.

10. Which device would connect network segments together, creating separate collision domains for each segment but only a single broadcast domain?

    A. Hub

    B. Router

    C. Switch

    D. Modem

11. Most Application layer protocols use only UDP or TCP at the Transport layer. Which of the following could use both?

    A. TCP

    B. Microsoft Word

    C. Telnet

    D. DNS

12. HTTP, FTP, and Telnet work at which layer of the OSI model?

   A. Application

   B. Presentation

   C. Session

   D. Transport

13. IPv6 uses multiple types of addresses. Which of the following would describe an any-cast address used by an IPv6 host?

   A. Communications are routed to the most distant host that shares the same address.

   B. Packets are delivered to all interfaces identified by the address. This is also called one-to-many addressing.

   C. This address identifies multiple interfaces, and the anycast packet is only delivered to one address. This address can also be called one-to-one-of-many.

   D. Anycast is a type of broadcast.

14. Which of the following IP addresses are not allowed on the Internet? (Choose all that apply.)

   A. 11.255.255.1

   B. 10.1.1.1

   C. 172.33.255.0

   D. 192.168.0.1

15. What is the subnetwork address for a host with the IP address 200.10.5.168/28?

   A. 200.10.5.156

   B. 200.10.5.132

   C. 200.10.5.160

   D. 200.10.5.0

   E. 200.10.5.255

16. If you wanted to verify the local IP stack on your computer, what would you do?

   A. Ping 127.0.0.0

   B. Ping 127.0.0.1

   C. Telnet 1.0.0.127

   D. Ping 169.5.3.10

   E. Telnet 255.255.255.255

17. The OSI model uses an encapsulation method to describe the data as it is encapsulated at each layer. What is the encapsulation named at the Data Link layer?

   A. Bits

   B. Packets

   C. Frames

   D. Data

   E. Segments

18. Where does a Data Link layer frame have to carry a Network layer packet if the packet is destined for a remote network?

   A. Router

   B. Physical medium

   C. Switch

   D. Another host

19. Which of the following are not distance vector routing protocols? (Choose all that apply.)

   A. OSPF

   B. RIP

   C. RIPv2

   D. IS-IS

20. Which of the following uses both distance vector and link state properties?

   A. IGRP

   B. OSPF

   C. RIPv1

   D. EIGRP

   E. IS-IS

21. You need to break up broadcast domains in a Layer 2 switched network. What strategy will you use?

   A. Implement a loop-avoidance scheme.

   B. Create a flatter network structure using switches.

   C. Create a VLAN.

   D. Disable spanning tree on individual ports.

22. Why do most switches run the Spanning Tree Protocol by default?

    A. It monitors how the network is functioning.

    B. It stops data from forwarding until all devices are updated.

    C. It prevents switching loops.

    D. It manages the VLAN database.

23. Which of the following describes MIMO correctly?

    A. A protocol that requires acknowledgment of each and every frame

    B. A data-transmission technique in which several frames are sent by several antennae over several paths and are then recombined by another set of antennae

    C. A modulation technique that allows more than one data rate

    D. A technique that packs smaller packets into a single unit, which improves throughput

24. Which two practices help secure your wireless access points from unauthorized access? (Choose all that apply.)

    A. Assigning a private IP address to the AP

    B. Changing the default SSID value

    C. Configuring a new administrator password

    D. Changing the mixed-mode setting to single mode

    E. Configuring traffic filtering

25. IPSec is defined at what layer of the OSI model?

    A. Network

    B. Physical

    C. Layer 4

    D. Layer 7

26. You want your users to log in and authenticate before they can get onto your network. Which of the following services would you use?

    A. RADIUS

    B. DNS

    C. Virtual Network Computing

    D. Remote Desktop Protocol

27. Someone calls you and asks for your bank account number because the bank is having problems with your account. You give them this information and later find out that you were scammed. What type of attack is this?

   A. Phishing

   B. Calling scam

   C. Analog scam

   D. Trust-exploration attack

   E. Man-in-the-middle attack

   F. Rogue access point

28. Which three of the following are types of denial of service attacks?

   A. Ping of Death

   B. Stacheldraht

   C. SYN flood

   D. Virus FloodSyn

29. You want to stop a hacker in their tracks. Which of the following devices are proactive in providing this service?

   A. Access control list (ACL)

   B. Content filtering

   C. Security zones

   D. Intrusion prevention system (IPS)

   E. Network Address Translation

   F. Virtual LANs

30. You connected your company to the Internet, and security is a concern. What should you install?

   A. Higher-quality cables

   B. Firewall

   C. DNS

   D. Switches

31. Which of the following are WAN protocols or technologies? (Choose all that apply.)

   A. ATM

   B. ISDN

   C. MPLS

   D. RIP

32. The rate at which the Frame Relay switch agrees to transfer data is referred to as _____.

   A. BE

   B. FECN

   C. CIR

   D. BECN

33. Which two arp utility switches perform the same function?

   A. –g

   B. –Z

   C. –d

   D. –a

   E. –h

   F. –b

34. You need to purge and reload the remote NetBIOS name table cache. Which nbtstat utility switch will you use?

   A. –r

   B. –R

   C. /r

   D. /R

   E. –a

   F. –A

35. Which tool is used to attach ends to network cables?

   A. Punch-down tool

   B. Crimper

   C. VLAN tool

   D. Strippers

   E. ARP tool

36. You are using a TDR. Which three of the following actions can you do with this device?

   A. Estimate cable lengths

   B. Find splice and connector locations and their associated loss amounts

   C. Display unused services

   D. Define cable-impedance characteristics

37. Which of the following are considered cabling issues? (Choose all that apply.)

   A. Crosstalk

   B. Shorts

   C. Open impedance mismatch

   D. DNS configurations

38. You have just tested your theory of a problem to determine the cause. Based on the standard troubleshooting model, what is your next step?

   A. Question the obvious.

   B. Establish a theory of probable cause.

   C. Establish a plan of action to resolve the problem and identify potential effects.

   D. Verify full system functionality and if applicable implement preventative measures.

39. Which network performance optimization technique can delay packets that meet certain criteria to guarantee usable bandwidth for other applications?

   A. Traffic shaping

   B. Jitter control

   C. Logical network mapping

   D. Load balancing

   E. Access lists

40. You need to optimize network traffic by spreading it across multiple connections. Which strategy should be used?

   A. Load balancing

   B. Traffic shaping

   C. Add VLANs

   D. A 1Gbps connection

   E. Following the regulations

Answers to Assessment Test

1. B. LANs generally have a geographic scope of a single building or smaller. They can be simple (two hosts) to complex (with thousands of hosts). See Chapter 1 for more information.

2. B. Star topologies are the easiest to troubleshoot and can easily scale to large sizes. See Chapter 1 for more information.

3. C. IP is a Network layer protocol. Internet Explorer is an example of an Application layer protocol. Ethernet is an example of a Data Link layer protocol, and T1 can be considered a Physical layer protocol. See Chapter 2 for more information.

4. D. Layer 2 of the OSI model is the Data Link layer, which provides the physical transmission of the data and handles error notification, network topology, and flow control. See Chapter 2 for more information.

5. C. Cable modems use RG-6 coax cables. See Chapter 3 for more information.

6. D. To get the high data-transfer speed, like 1Gbps, you need to use a wire standard that is highly rated, such as Category 5e or Category 6. See Chapter 3 for more information.

7. D. A, B, and C are true. With half duplex, you are using one wire pair with a digital signal either transmitting or receiving (but not both at once). Carrier Sense Multiple Access with Collision Detection (CSMA/CD) helps packets that are transmitted simultaneously from different hosts share bandwidth evenly. See Chapter 4 for more information.

8. B. To connect two switches together or a hub to a switch, you need a crossover cable. See Chapter 4 for more information.

9. A. For the most part, switches are not cheap; however, one of the biggest benefits of using switches instead of hubs in your internetwork is that each switch port is actually its own collision domain. A hub creates one large collision domain. Switches still can't break up broadcast domains (do you remember which devices do?). Hubs do not recognize frames and data structures but switches do. See Chapter 5 for more information.

10. C. A switch creates separate collision domains for each port but does not break up broadcast domains by default. See Chapter 5 for more information.

11. D. DNS uses TCP for zone exchanges between servers and UDP when a client is trying to resolve a hostname to an IP address. See Chapter 6 for more information.

12. A. HTTP, FTP and Telnet use TCP at the Transport layer; however, they are all Application layer protocols, so the Application layer is the best answer for this question. See Chapter 6 for more information.

13. C. Anycast is a new type of communication that replaces broadcasts in IPv4. Anycast addresses identify multiple interfaces, which is the same as multicast; however, the big difference is that the anycast packet is delivered to only one address: the first one it finds defined in the terms of routing distance. This address can also be called one-to-one-of-many. See Chapter 7 for more information.

14. B, D. The addresses in the range 10.0.0.0 through 10.255.255.255 and 172.16.0.0 through 172.31.255.255 as well as 192.168.0.0 through 192.168.255.255 are all considered private, based on RFC 1918. Use of these addresses on the Internet is prohibited so that they can be used simultaneously in different administrative domains without concern for conflict. See Chapter 7 for more detail on IP addressing and information on private IP addresses.

15. C. This is a pretty simple question. A /28 is 255.255.255.240, which means that our block size is 16 in the fourth octet. 0, 16, 32, 48, 64, 80, 96, 112, 128, 144, 160, 176, and so on. The host is in subnet 160. See Chapter 8 for more information.

16. B. To test the local stack on your host, ping the loopback interface of 127.0.0.1. As a matter of fact, the entire range from 127.0.0.1-127.255.255.254 will test the IP stack. See Chapter 8 for more information.

17. C. The Data Link layer is responsible for encapsulating IP packets into frames and for providing logical network addresses. See Chapter 9 for more information.

18. A. Packets specifically have to be carried to a router in order to be routed through a network. See Chapter 9 for more information.

19. A, D. RIP and RIPv2 are distance vector routing protocols. OSPF and IS-IS are link state. See Chapter 10 for more information.

20. D. EIGRP is called a hybrid routing protocol because it uses the characteristics of both distance vector and link state routing protocols. However, EIGRP can only be run on Cisco routers and is not vendor neutral. See Chapter 10 for more information.

21. C. Virtual LANs break up broadcast domains in Layer 2 switched internetworks. See Chapter 11 for more information.

22. C. The Spanning Tree Protocol (STP) was designed to stop Layer 2 loops. All enterprise model switches have STP by default. See Chapter 11 for more information.

23. B. Part of the 802.11n wireless standard, MIMO sends multiple frames by several antennae over several paths; they are then recombined by another set of antennae to optimize throughput and multipath resistance. This is called spatial multiplexing. See Chapter 12 for more information.

24. B, C. At a minimum, you need to change the default SSID value on each AP and configure new usernames and passwords on the AP. See Chapter 12 for more information.

25. A. IPSec works at the Network layer of the OSI model (Layer 3) and secures all applications that operate above it (Layer 4 and above). Additionally, because it was designed by the IETF and designed to work with IPv4 and IPv6, it has broad industry support and is quickly becoming the standard for VPNs on the Internet. See Chapter 13 for more information.

26. A. RADIUS combines user authentication and authorization into one profile. See Chapter 13 for more information.

27. A. Social engineering, or phishing, refers to the act of attempting to illegally obtain sensitive information by pretending to be a credible source. Phishing usually takes one of two forms: an email or a phone call. See Chapter 14 for more information.

28. A, B, C. A denial of service (DoS) attack prevents users from accessing the system. All of the options are all possible denial of service attacks except Virus FloodSyn. See Chapter 14 for more information.

29. D. Changing network configurations, terminating sessions, and deceiving the attacker are all actions that can be taken by an intrusion prevention system (IPS) device. These are all proactive approaches to security. See Chapter 15 for more information.

30. B. Firewalls help provide perimeter network security by allowing or denying connections and types of traffic in or out of the network. See Chapter 15 for more information.

31. A, B, C. Routing Information Protocol (RIP) is not a WAN protocol but a routing protocol used in local area connections. See Chapter 16 for more information.

32. C. The Committed Information Rate (CIR) is the rate, in bits per second, at which the Frame Relay switch agrees to transfer data. See Chapter 16 for more information.

33. A, D. The arp utility's –a and –g switches perform the same function. They both show the current ARP cache. See Chapter 17 for more information.

34. B. To purge and reload the remote NetBIOS name cache, you must use nbtstat –R. Remember that the R must be uppercase, and it will not work correctly without the hyphen before it. See Chapter 17 for more information.

35. B. A wire crimper or crimper is used to attach ends onto different types of network cables. See Chapter 18 for more information.

36. A, B, D. Due to sensitivity to any variation and impedance to cabling, options A, B, and D are all reasons you'd use a TDR. See Chapter 18 for more information.

37. A, B, C. Because most of today's networks still consist of large amounts of copper cable, they can continue to suffer from the physical issues (the options are not a complete list) that have plagued all networks since the very beginning of networking. See Chapter 19 for more information.

38. C. You have just tested your theory of a problem to determine the cause. Based on the standard troubleshooting model, the next step would be to Establish a plan of action to resolve the problem and identify potential effects. See Chapter 19 for more information.

39. A. Traffic shaping, also known as packet shaping, is another form of bandwidth optimization. See Chapter 20 for more information.

40. A. Load balancing refers to a technique used to spread work out to multiple computers, network links, or other devices. You can load-balance work on servers by clustering servers so that multiple machines all provide the same service. See Chapter 20 for more information.

Chapter

1

Introduction to Networks

THE FOLLOWING COMPTIA NETWORK+ EXAM OBJECTIVES ARE COVERED IN THIS CHAPTER:

✓ **3.5 Describe different network topologies.**

- MPLS
  - Point-to-point
  - Point-to-multipoint
- Ring
- Star
- Mesh
- Bus
- Peer-to-peer
- Client-server
- Hybrid

You'd have to work pretty hard these days to find someone who would argue when we say that our computers have become invaluable to us personally and professionally. Our society has become highly dependent on the resources they offer and on sharing them with each other. The ability to communicate with others—whether they're in the same building or in some faraway land—completely hinges on our capacity to create and maintain solid, dependable networks.

And those vitally important networks come in all shapes and sizes—ranging from small and simple to humongous and super complicated. But whatever their flavor, they all need to be maintained properly, and to do that well, you have to understand networking basics. The various types of devices and technologies that are used to create networks, as well as how they work together, is what this book is about, and I'll go through this critical information one step at a time with you. Understanding all of this will not only equip you with a rock-solid base to build on as you gain IT knowledge and grow in your career, it will also arm you with what you'll need to ace the Network+ certification exam!

To find up-to-the-minute updates for this chapter, please see www.lammle.com/forum or the book's web site at www.sybex.com/go/netplus2e.

First Things First: What's a Network?

The dictionary defines the word *network* as "a group or system of interconnected people or things." Similarly, in the computer world, the term *network* means two or more connected computers that can share resources such as data and applications, office machines, an Internet connection, or some combination of these, as shown in Figure 1.1.

FIGURE 1.1   A basic network

Okay—Figure 1.1 shows a really basic network made up of only two host computers connected; they share resources such as files and even a printer hooked up to one of the hosts. These two hosts "talk" to each other using a computer language called *binary code*, which consists of lots of 1s and 0s in a specific order that describes exactly what they want to "say."

Next, I'm going to tell you about local area networks (LANs), how they work, and even how we can connect LANs together. Then, later in this chapter, I'll describe how to connect remote LANs together through something known as a wide area network (WAN).

The Local Area Network (LAN)

Just as the name implies, a *local area network (LAN)* is usually restricted to spanning a particular geographic location such as an office building, a single department within a corporate office, or even a home office.

Back in the day, you couldn't put more than 30 workstations on a LAN, and you had to cope with strict limitations on how far those machines could actually be from each other. Because of technological advances, all that's changed now, and we're not nearly as restricted in regard to both a LAN's size and the distance a LAN can span. Even so, it's still best to split a big LAN into smaller logical zones known as *workgroups* to make administration easier.

> The meaning of the term workgroup in this context is slightly different than when the term is used in contrast to domains. In that context a workgroup is a set of devices with no security association with one another (whereas in a domain they do have that association). In this context, we simply mean they physically are in the same network segment.

In a typical business environment, it's a good idea to arrange your LAN's workgroups along department divisions; for instance, you would create a workgroup for Accounting, another one for Sales, and maybe another for Marketing—you get the idea. Figure 1.2 shows two separate LANS, each as its own workgroup.

FIGURE 1.2   Two separate LANs (workgroups)

First, don't stress about the devices labeled *hub* and *switch*—these are just connectivity devices that allow hosts to physically connect to resources on a LAN. Trust me; I'll describe them to you in much more detail in Chapter 5, "Networking Devices."

Anyway, back to the figure…. Notice that there's a Marketing workgroup and a Sales workgroup. These are LANs in their most basic form. Any device that connects to the Marketing LAN can access the resources of the Marketing LAN—in this case, the servers and printer. You must be physically connected (via cable or wireless) to a workgroup's LAN to get the resources from it.

There are two problems with this:

- You must be physically connected to a workgroup's LAN to get the resources from it.
- You can't get from one LAN to the other LAN and use its server data and printing resources remotely.

This is a typical network issue that's easily resolved by using a cool device called a *router* to connect the two LANs, as shown in Figure 1.3.

FIGURE 1.3   A router connects LANs.

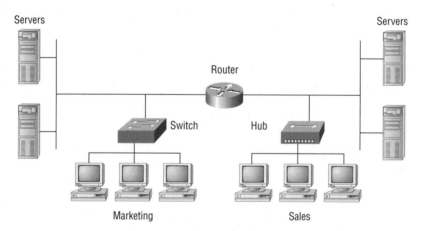

Nice—problem solved! Even though you can use routers for more than just connecting LANs, the router shown in Figure 1.3 is a great solution because the host computers from the Sales LAN can get to the resources (server data and printers) of the Marketing LAN, and vice versa.

Now, you might be thinking that we really don't need the router—that we could just physically connect the two workgroups with a type of cable that would allow the Marketing and Sales workgroups to hook up somehow. True, we could do that, but if we did, we would have only one big, cumbersome workgroup instead of separate workgroups for Marketing and Sales. And that kind of arrangement isn't practical for today's networks.

This is because with smaller, individual, yet connected groups, the users on each LAN enjoy much faster response times when accessing resources, and administrative tasks are a lot easier, too. Larger workgroups run more slowly because in them, a legion of hosts are all trying to get to the same resources simultaneously. So the router shown in Figure 1.3, which separates the workgroups while still allowing access between them, is a really great solution after all.

> As I said, don't worry about the network connectivity devices I've mentioned so far in this chapter, such as hubs, switches, and routers. I promise to cover them all in detail in Chapter 5. At this stage, I really want you to focus on understanding the concepts that I'm presenting. For now, all you need to know is that hubs and switches are devices that connect other devices together, and routers connect networks together.

So now, let me define those other terms I've used so far: *workstations*, *servers*, and *hosts*.

Common Network Components

There are a lot of different machines, devices, and media that make up our networks. Right now, I'm going to tell you about three of the most common:

- Workstations
- Servers
- Hosts

Workstations

Workstations are often seriously powerful computers that run more than one central processing unit (CPU) and whose resources are available to other users on the network to access when needed. Something this powerful is typically referred to only as a server today. Don't confuse workstations with client machines, which can be workstations but aren't always. A *client machine* is any device on the network that can ask for access to resources from a server or powerful workstation—that for instance, hosts a printer.

> The terms *workstation* and *host* can sometimes be used interchangeably. Computers have become more and more powerful and the terms have become somewhat fuzzy because hosts can be clients, workstations, servers, and more! The term *host* is used to describe pretty much anything that takes an IP address.

Servers

Servers are also powerful computers. They get their name because they truly are "at the service" of the network and run specialized software for the network's maintenance and control known as the *network operating system*.

In a good design that optimizes the network's performance, servers are highly specialized and are there to handle one important labor-intensive job. This is not to say that a single server can't do many jobs, but more often than not, you'll get better performance if you dedicate a server to a single task. Here's a list of common dedicated servers:

File server   Stores and dispenses files

Mail server   The network's post office; handles email functions

Print server   Manages printers on the network

Web server   Manages web-based activities by running Hypertext Transfer Protocol (HTTP) for storing web content and accessing web pages

Fax server   The "memo maker" that sends and receives paperless faxes over the network

Application server   Manages network applications

Telephony server   Handles the call center and call routing and can be thought of as a sophisticated network answering machine

Remote access server   Provides remote users with access to the network through modems and an IP connection

Proxy server   Handles tasks in the place of other machines on the network

See how the name of each kind of server indicates what it actually does—how it serves the network? This is an excellent way to remember them.

Okay, as I said, servers are usually dedicated to doing one specific important thing within the network. But not always—sometimes they have more than one job. But whether servers are designated for one job or are network multitaskers, they can maintain the network's data integrity by backing up the network's software and hardware. And no matter what, they all serve a number of client machines.

Back in Figure 1.2, I showed you an example of two really simple LAN networks. I want to make sure you know that servers must have considerably superior CPUs, hard-drive space, and memory—a lot more than a simple workstation's capacity—because they serve many client machines and provide any resources they require. Because they're so important, you should always put your servers in a very secure area. My company's servers are in a locked server room because not only are they really pricey workhorses, they also store huge amounts of important and sensitive company data, so, they need to be kept safe from any unauthorized access.

In Figure 1.4, you can see a network populated with both workstations and servers. You also see that the hosts can access the servers across the network—pretty much the general idea of having a network.

You probably noticed that there are more workstations here than servers, right? Think of why that is…. If you answered that it's because one server can provide resources to what can sometimes be a huge number of individual users at the same time, but workstations don't, you have it!

FIGURE 1.4   A network populated with servers and workstations

Hosts

It can be kind of confusing because when people refer to hosts, they really can be referring to almost any type of networking devices—including workstations and servers. But if you dig a bit deeper, you'll find that usually this term comes up when people are talking about resources and jobs that have to do with Transmission Control Protocol/Internet Protocol (TCP/IP). The scope of possible machines and devices is so broad because, in TCP/IP-speak, *host* means any network device with an IP address. Yes, you'll hear IT professionals throw this term around pretty loosely; for the Network+ exam, stick to the definition being network devices, including workstations and servers, with IP addresses.

Here's a bit of background: The name *host* harkens back to the Jurassic period of networking when those dinosaurs known as *mainframes* were the only intelligent devices to roam the network. These were called *hosts* whether they had TCP/IP functionality or not. In that bygone age, everything else in the network-scape was referred to as *dumb terminals* because only mainframes—hosts—were given IP addresses. Another fossilized term from way back then is *gateways* when it was used to talk about any Layer 3 machines like routers. We still use these terms today, but they've evolved a bit to refer to the many intelligent devices populating our present-day networks, each of which has an IP address. This is exactly the reason why you hear *host* used so broadly.

Wide Area Network (WAN)

There are legions of people who, if asked to define a *wide area network (WAN)*, couldn't do it. Yet most of them use the Big Dog of all WANs—the Internet—every day! With that in mind, you can imagine that WAN networks are what we use to span large geographic areas and truly go the distance. Like the Internet, WANs usually employ both routers and public links, so that's generally the criteria used to define them.

> WANs are so important that I have dedicated an entire chapter to them: Chapter 16, "Wide Area Networks."

Here's a list of some of the important ways that WANs are different from LANs:

- WANs usually need a router port or ports.
- WANs span larger geographic areas and/or can link disparate locations.
- WANs are usually slower.
- We can choose when and how long we connect to a WAN. A LAN is all or nothing— our workstation is either connected permanently to it or not at all, although most of us have dedicated WAN links now.
- WANs can utilize either private or public data transport media such as phone lines.

We get the word *Internet* from the term *internetwork*. An internetwork is a type of LAN and/or WAN that connects a bunch of networks, or *intranets*. In an internetwork, hosts still use hardware addresses to communicate with other hosts on the LAN. However, in an internetwork, hosts use logical addresses (IP addresses) to communicate with hosts on a different LAN (other side of the router).

And *routers* are the devices that make this possible. Each connection into a router is a different logical network. Figure 1.5 demonstrates how routers are employed to create an internetwork and how they enable our LANs to access WAN resources.

FIGURE 1.5   An internetwork

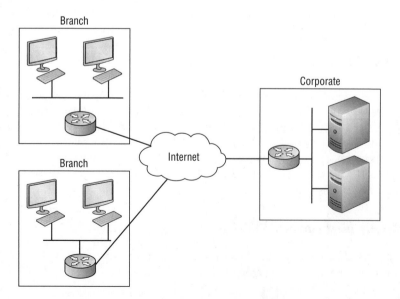

The Internet is a prime example of what's known as a *distributed WAN*—an internetwork that's made up of a lot of interconnected computers located in a lot of different places. There's another kind of WAN, referred to as *centralized*, that's composed of a main, centrally located computer or location that remote computers and devices can connect to. A good example is remote offices that connect to a main corporate office, as shown in Figure 1.5.

MPLS

MultiProtocol Label Switching (MPLS) will be defined clearly in Chapter 16, but for the objectives of the CompTIA Network+ exam, this chapter will define the actual layout of what is one of the most popular WAN protocols in use today. MPLS has become one of the most innovative and flexible networking technologies on the market and has several advantages compared to other WAN technologies:

- Physical layout flexibility
- Prioritizing of data
- Redundancy in case of link failure
- One-to-many connection

MPLS is a switching mechanism that imposes labels (numbers) to data and then uses those labels to forward data when the data arrives at the MPLS network, as shown in Figure 1.6.

FIGURE 1.6   MultiProtocol Label Switching layout

The labels are assigned on the edge of the MPLS network, and forwarding inside the MPLS network (cloud) is done solely based on labels through virtual links instead of physical links. Prioritizing data is a huge advantage, and voice data could have priority over basic data based on the labels, for example. And since there are multiple paths for the data to be forwarded through the MPLS cloud, there is some redundancy provided.

Network Architecture: Peer-to-Peer or Client-Server?

So, we've developed networking as a way to share resources and information, and how that's achieved directly maps to the particular architecture of the network operating system software. There are two main network types you need to know about: peer-to-peer and client-server. And by the way, it's really tough to tell the differences just by looking at a diagram or even by checking out live video of the network humming along, but the differences between peer-to-peer and client-server architectures are major. They're not just physical; they're logical differences. You'll see what I mean in a bit.

Peer-to-Peer Networks

Computers connected together in *peer-to-peer networks* do not have any central, or special, authority—they're all *peers*, meaning that when it comes to authority, they're all equals. This means it's up to the computer that has the resource being requested to perform a security check for access rights to its resources.

It also means that the computers existing in a peer-to-peer network can be client machines that access resources and server machines that provide them to other computers. This works really well if there's not a huge number of users on the network, if each user backs things up locally, and if your network doesn't require a lot of security.

If your network is running Windows, Mac, or Unix in a local LAN workgroup, you have a peer-to-peer network. Figure 1.7 gives you a snapshot of a typical peer-to-peer network. Peer-to-peer networks present some challenges. For example, backing up company data becomes an iffy proposition.

FIGURE 1.7   A peer-to-peer network

Users	Password	Access
Mickey	!Tails?	Full
Pluto	$NoKats	Read
Louie	^Wet#!	Read

Millie

Users	Password	Access
Millie	#Shorts?	Read
Mickey	My!Ears?	Read
Louie	^Wet#!	Full

Pluto

Hub

Users	Password	Access
Millie	#Shorts?	Read
Pluto	&LittleTail!	Full
Louie	^Wet#!	Full

Mickey

Users	Password	Access
Millie	#Shorts?	Read
Pluto	&LittleTail!	Full
Mickey	&&Boss!@	Full

Louie

Since it should be clear by now that peer-to-peer networks are all sunshine, backing up all that super-important data is not only vital, it can be really challenging. What if you forget where you put a badly needed file? (Haven't we all done that?) And then there's that security issue to tangle with. Because security is not centrally governed, each and every user has to remember and maintain a list of users and passwords on each and every machine. Worse, some of those all-important passwords for the same users change on different machines—even for accessing different resources. Yikes!

Client-Server Networks

Client-server networks are pretty much the polar opposite of peer-to-peer networks because in them, a single server uses a network operating system for managing the whole network. So a client machine's request for a resource goes to the main server, which responds by handling security and directing the client to the resource it wants, instead of the request going directly to the machine with the desired resource. This arrangement definitely has its benefits. First, because the network is much better organized and doesn't depend on users remembering where needed resources are, it's a whole lot easier to find the files you need because everything is stored in one spot—on that special server. Your security also gets a lot tighter because all usernames and passwords are on that server (which, by the way, isn't ever used as a workstation). You even gain scalability—client-server networks can have legions of workstations on them. And even with all those demands, their performance is actually optimized.

Check out Figure 1.8, which shows a client-server network with a server that has a database of access rights, user accounts, and passwords.

FIGURE 1.8   A client-server network

Users	Password	Access
Millie	#Shorts?	Read
Pluto	&LittleTail!	Full
Louie	^Wet#!	Full
Mickey	—Ear!s?	Write

Many of today's networks are a healthy (we hope) combination of the peer-to-peer and client-server architectures with carefully specified servers that permit the simultaneous sharing of resources from devices running workstation operating systems. Even though the supporting machines can't handle as many inbound connections at a time, they still run the server service reasonably well. If this type of mixed environment is designed well, most networks benefit greatly by having the capacity to take advantage of the positive aspects of both worlds.

Physical Network Topologies

Just as a topographical map is a type of map that shows the shape of the terrain, the *physical topology* of a network is also a type of map. It defines the specific characteristics of a network, such as where all the workstations and other devices are located and the precise arrangement of all the physical media such as cables. On the other hand, *logical topologies*, which were covered earlier, delineate exactly how data moves through the network. And though these two topologies are usually a lot alike, a particular network can have physical and logical topologies that are very different. But basically, what you want to remember is that a network's physical topology gives you the lay of the land and the logical topology shows how digital signal or data navigates through that layout.

The following are the topologies you're most likely to run in to these days:

- Bus
- Star
- Ring
- Mesh
- Point-to-point
- Point-to-multipoint
- Hybrid

Bus Topology

This type of topology is the most basic one of the bunch, and it really does sort of resemble a bus. (Well, okay—actually, it looks more like a bus that's been in a pretty nasty wreck!) Anyway, the *bus topology* consists of two distinct and terminated ends, with each of its computers connecting to one unbroken cable running its entire length. Back in the day, we used to attach computers to that main cable with wire taps, but this didn't work all that well so we began using drop cables in their place (unless you're dealing with 10Base2 Ethernet, in which case you would slip a "T" into the main cable anywhere you wanted to connect a device to it instead of using drop cables).

Figure 1.9 depicts what a typical bus network's physical topology looks like.

Even though all the computers on this kind of network see all the data flowing through the cable, only the one computer that the data is specifically addressed to actually *gets* the data. Some of the benefits in favor of using a bus topology are that it's easy to install and it's not very expensive, in part because it doesn't require as much cable as the other types of physical topologies. But it also has some drawbacks: For instance, it's hard to troubleshoot, change, or move, and it really doesn't offer much in the way of fault tolerance because everything is connected to that single cable.

FIGURE 1.9   A typical bus network's physical topology

Laser Printer

Server S1

By the way, *fault tolerance* is the capability of a computer or a network system to respond to a condition automatically, often resolving it, which reduces the impact on the system. If fault-tolerance measures have been implemented correctly on a network, it's highly unlikely that any of that network's users will know that a problem even existed.

Star Topology

A star topology's computers are connected to a central point with their own individual cables or wireless connections. You'll often find that central spot inhabited by a device like a hub, a switch, or an access point.

Star topology offers a lot of advantages over bus topology, making it more widely used even though it obviously requires more physical media. One of its best features is that because each computer or network segment is connected to the central device individually, if the cable fails, it brings down only that particular machine or network segment. That's truly a great benefit because it makes the network much more fault tolerant as well as a lot easier to troubleshoot. Another great thing about a star topology is that it's a lot more scalable—all you have to do if you want to add to it is run a new cable and connect to the machine at the core of the star. In Figure 1.10, you'll find a great example of a typical star topology.

Okay, although it is called a *star* topology, it really looks a lot more like the imaginary pictures people draw of the sun. (Yes, the sun is a star—but it definitely doesn't look like how we usually depict it, does it?) You could also get away with saying it looks like a bike wheel with spokes connecting to the hub in the middle of the wheel and extending outward to connect to the rim. And just like that bike wheel, it's the hub device at the center of a star topology network that can give you the most grief if something goes wrong with it. If that hub in the middle of it all happens to fail, down comes the whole network, so it's a very good thing hubs don't fail often!

FIGURE 1.10   Typical star topology with a hub

Just as it is with pretty much everything, a star topology has its pros and cons. But the good news far outweighs the bad, which is why people are choosing to go with a star topology more and more. Here's a list of benefits gained by opting for a star topology:

- New stations can be added easily and quickly.
- A single cable failure won't bring down the entire network.
- It is relatively easy to troubleshoot.

Here are the disadvantages of a star topology:

- The total installation cost can be higher because of the larger number of cables (but prices are constantly becoming more competitive).
- It has a single point of failure (the hub or other central device).

There are two more sophisticated implementations of a star topology. The first is called *point-to-point link*, where you have not only the device in the center of the spoke acting as a hub, but also the one on the other end. This is still a star-wired topology, but as I'm sure you can imagine, it gives you a huge amount of scalability!

Another refined version is the wireless flavor, but to understand this version well, you've really got to have a solid grasp of the capabilities and features of all the devices populating the wireless star topology. No worries, though—I'll be covering wireless access points later on in Chapter 12, "Wireless Networking." For now, it's good enough for you to know that access points are pretty much just wireless hubs or switches that behave like their wired counterparts. Basically, they create a point-by-point connection to endpoints and other wireless access points.

Ring Topology

In this type of topology, you'll find that each computer is directly connected to other computers within the same network. Looking at Figure 1.11, you can see that the network's data flows from computer to computer back to the source, with the network's primary cable forming a ring. The problem is, the *ring topology* has a lot in common with the bus topology because if you want to add to the network, you have no choice but to break the cable ring—something that is probably going to bring down the entire network.

FIGURE 1.11   A typical ring topology

   This is one big reason this topology isn't all that popular—you just won't run into it a lot as I did in the 1980s and early 1990s. It's also pricey because you need several cables to connect each computer, it's really hard to reconfigure, and as you've probably guessed, it's not fault tolerant.

   However, with all that being said, if you work at an ISP, you may find a physical ring topology in use for a technology called SONET or possibly some other WAN technology. You just won't find any LANs in physical rings anymore.

Mesh Topology

In this type of topology, you'll find that there's a path from every machine to every other one in the network. That's a lot of connections—in fact, the *mesh topology* wins the prize for "most physical connections per device"! You won't find it used in LANs very often, if ever, these days, but you will find a modified version of it known as a *hybrid mesh* used in a restrained manner on WANs, including the Internet.

   Often, hybrid mesh topology networks will have quite a few connections between certain places to create redundancy (backup). And other types of topologies can sometimes be found in the mix too, which is also why it's dubbed *hybrid*. At any rate, it isn't a full-on full mesh topology if there isn't a connection between all devices in the network. But it's still respectably complicated—Figure 1.12 shows just how much only four connections can complicate things.

FIGURE 1.12   A typical mesh topology

As shown in the figure, things just get more and more complex as both the wiring and the connections multiply. For each *n* locations or hosts, you end up with *n(n–1)/2* connections. This means that in a network consisting of only four computers, you have 4(4–1)/2, or 6 connections. And if that little network grows to, say, a population of 10 computers, you'll have a whopping 45 connections to cope with—yikes! That's a huge amount of overhead, so only small networks can really use this topology and manage it well. On the bright side, you get a very respectable level of fault tolerance. But it is nice that we don't use these in corporate LANs any longer because they were very complicated to manage.

A full mesh physical topology has the absolute least likelihood of having a collision.

This is the reason you will usually find the hybrid version in today's WANs. In fact, the mesh topology is actually pretty rare these days. It's mainly used because of the robust fault tolerance it offers—because you have a multitude of connections, if one goes on the blink, computers and other network devices can simply switch to one of the many redundant connections that are up and running. But as you can imagine, all that cabling in the mesh topology makes it really costly. Plus, you can make your network management much less insane by using what's known as a *partial mesh topology* solution instead, so why not go that way? You may lose a little fault tolerance, but if you go the partial mesh route, you still get to use the same technology between all the network's devices. Just remember that with partial mesh, not all devices will be interconnected, so it's very important to choose wisely the ones that are.

Point-to-Point Topology

As its name implies, in a *point-to-point* topology you have a direct connection between two routers, giving you one communication path. The routers in a point-to-point topology can either be linked by a serial cable, making it a physical network, or be far apart and connected only by a circuit within a Frame Relay or MPLS network, making it a logical network.

Figure 1.13 gives you a prime specimen of a T1, or WAN point-to-point connection.

What you see here is a lightning bolt and a couple of round things with a bunch of arrows projecting from them, right? Well, the two round things radiating arrows represent our network's two routers, and that lightning bolt represents a WAN link. (These symbols are industry standard, and I'll be using them throughout this book, so it would a good idea to get used to them.)

Part two of the diagram shows two computers connected by a cable—a point-to-point link. By the way, this should remind you of something we just went over…remember our talk about peer-to-peer networks? Good! I hope you also happen to remember that a big drawback related to peer-to-peer network sharing is that it is not very scalable. With this in mind, you probably won't be all that surprised that even if both machines have a wireless point-to-point connection, the network won't be very scalable.

You'll usually find point-to-point networks within many of today's WANs, and as you can see in part three of Figure 1.13, a link from a computer to a hub or switch is also a valid point-to-point connection. A common version of this setup consists of a direct wireless link between two wireless bridges that's used to connect computers in two different buildings together.

FIGURE 1.13   Three point-to-point connections

Serial Connection, Like a T1 between Routers

Direct Ethernet or Wireless

Cable Direct to Hub or Switch   Hub

Point-to-Multipoint Topology

Again as the name suggests, a *point-to-multipoint* topology consists of a succession of connections between an interface on one router and multiple destination routers—one point of connection to multiple points of connection. Each of the routers and every one of their interfaces involved in the point-to-multipoint connection are part of the same network.

Figure 1.14 shows a WAN to best demonstrate a point-to-multipoint network that depicts a single corporate router connecting to multiple branches.

Figure 1.15 shows another prime example of a point-to-multipoint network: a college or corporate campus.

FIGURE 1.14   A point-to-multipoint network, example 1

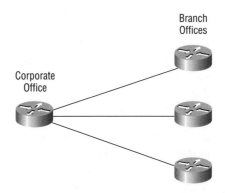

Branch
Offices

Corporate
Office

FIGURE 1.15 A point-to-multipoint network, example 2

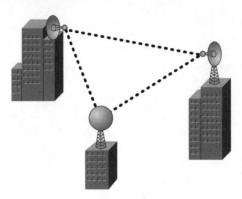

Hybrid Topology

I know I talked about hybrid network topology back in the section about mesh topology, but I didn't give you a picture of it in the form of a figure. I also want to point out that *hybrid topology* means just that—a combination of two or more types of physical or logical network topologies working together within the same network.

Figure 1.16 depicts a simple hybrid network topology; it shows a LAN switch or hub in a star topology configuration that connects to its hosts via bus topology.

FIGURE 1.16 A simple hybrid network

Hub

Physical Star, Logical Bus

Topology Selection, Backbones, and Segments

Now that you're familiar with many different types of network topologies, you're ready for some tips on selecting the right one for your particular network. You also need to know about backbones and segments—the very last part of this chapter.

⊕ **Real World Scenario**

They're Just Cables, Right?

Wrong! Regardless of the type of network you build, you need to start thinking about quality at the bottom and work up.

Think of it as if you were at an electronics store buying the cables for your sweet new home theater system. You've already spent a bunch of time and money getting the right components to meet your needs. In fact, you've probably parted with a respectable chunk of change, so why would you stop there and connect all these great devices together with the cable equivalent of twine? No, you're smarter than that. You know that picking out the exact cables that will maximize the sound and picture quality of your specific components can also protect them.

It's the same thing when you're faced with selecting the physical media for a certain network (such as your new client-server network). You just don't want to cut corners here. Because if it's the backbone of the network, you absolutely don't want to be faced with having to dig up everything that's already been installed after the fact. Doing this costs a lot more than taking the time to wisely choose the right cables and spending the money it takes to get them in the first place. The network downtime alone can cost a company a bundle (pun intended). Another reason for choosing the network's physical media correctly is that it's going to be there for a good 5 to 10 years. This means two things: It better be solid quality, and it better be scalable because that network is going to grow and change over the years.

Selecting the Right Topology

As you now know, not only do you have a buffet of network topologies to choose from, but each one also has pros and cons to implementing it. But it really comes down to that well-known adage "Ask the right questions." First, how much cash do you have? And how much fault tolerance do you really need? Also, is this network likely to grow like a weed—is it probably going to need to be quickly and easily reconfigured often? In other words, how scalable does your network need to be?

For instance, if your challenge is to design a nice, cost-effective solution that involves only a few computers in a room, getting a wireless access point and some wireless network cards is definitely your best way to go because you won't need to pony up for a bunch of cabling and it's super simple to set up. Alternatively, if you're faced with coming up with a solid design for a growing company's already-large network, you're probably good to go with using a wired star topology because it will nicely allow for future changes. Remember, a star topology really shines when it comes to making additions to the network, moving things around, and making any kind of changes happen quickly, efficiently, and cost effectively.

If, say, you're hired to design a network for an ISP that needs to be up and running 99.9 percent of the time with no more than 8 hours a year allowed downtime, well, you need Godzilla-strength fault tolerance. Do you remember which topology gives that up the best? (Hint: Internet.) Your primo solution is to go with either a hybrid or a partial mesh topology. Remember that partial mesh leaves you with a subset of $n(n-1)/2$ connections to maintain—a number that could very well blow a big hole in your maintenance budget!

Here's a list of things to keep in mind when you're faced with coming up with the right topology for the right network:

- Cost
- Ease of installation
- Ease of maintenance
- Fault-tolerance requirement

The Network Backbone

Today's networks can get pretty complicated, so we need to have a standard way of communicating with each other intelligibly about exactly which part of the network we're referencing. This is the reason we divide networks into different parts called *backbones* and *segments*.

Figure 1.17 illustrates a network and shows which part is the backbone and which parts are segments.

FIGURE 1.17   Backbone and segments on a network

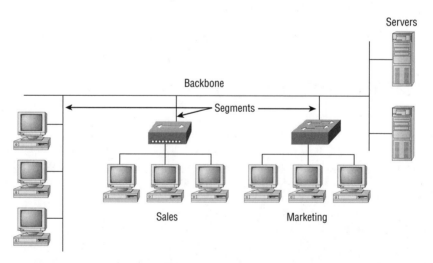

You can see that the network backbone is actually kind of like our own. It's what all the networks segments and servers connect to and what gives the network its structure. As you can imagine, being such an important nerve center, the backbone must use some kind of seriously fast, robust technology—often that's Gigabit Ethernet. And to optimize network performance (that is, speed and efficiency), it follows that you would want to connect all of the network's servers and segments directly to the network's backbone.

Network Segments

When we refer to a segment, we can mean any small section of the network that may be connected to, but isn't actually a piece of, the backbone. The network's workstations and servers organized into segments connect to the network backbone, which is the common connecting point for all segments; you can see this by taking another look at Figure 1.17, which displays three segments.

Summary

This chapter created a solid foundation for you to build your networking knowledge on as you go through this book.

In it, you learned what, exactly, a network is, and you got an introduction to some of the components involved in building one—routers, switches, and hubs—as well as the jobs they do in a network.

You also learned that having the components required to build a network isn't all you need. Understanding the various types of network connection methods like peer-to-peer and client-server is also vital.

Further, you learned about the various types of logical and physical network topologies and the features and drawbacks of each. I wrapped up the chapter with a short discussion about network backbones and segments and equipped you with the right questions to ask yourself to ensure that you come up with the right network topology for your networking needs.

Exam Essentials

Know your network topologies.   Know the names and descriptions of the topologies. Be aware of the difference between physical networks (what humans see) and logical networks (what the equipment "sees").

Know the advantages and disadvantages of the topologies.   It is important to know what each topology brings to the table. Knowing the various characteristics of each topology comes in handy during troubleshooting.

Understand the terms *LAN* and *WAN*.   You need to understand when you would use a LAN and when you would use a WAN. A LAN is used to connect a group of hosts together, and a WAN is used to connect various LANs together.

Written Labs

Provide the answers to the following questions:

1. What are the three primary LAN topologies?

2. What common WAN topology often results in multiple connections to a single site (leading to a high degree of fault tolerance) and has one-to-many connections?

3. What is the term for a device that shares its resources with other network devices?

4. What network model draws a clear distinction between devices that share their resources and devices that do not?

5. Which network topology or connection type can be implemented with only two endpoints?

6. What device is an example of an Ethernet technology implemented as a star topology?

7. What does MPLS stand for?

8. What does WAN stand for?

9. Will a computer that shares no resources most likely be connected to the backbone or to a segment?

10. Which LAN topology is characterized by all devices being daisy-chained together with the devices at each end being connected to only one other device?

    You can find the answers to the written labs in Appendix B.

Review Questions

You can find the answers in Appendix A.

1. You need a network that provides centralized authentication for your users. Which of the following logical topologies should you use?

   A. VLANs

   B. Peer-to-peer

   C. Client-server

   D. Mesh

2. You need a topology that is scalable to use in your network. Which of the following will you install?

   A. Bus

   B. Ring

   C. Star

   D. Mesh

3. Which of the following physical topologies has the most connections and is the least popular for LANs?

   A. Bus

   B. Start

   C. Ring

   D. Mesh

4. In a physical star topology, what happens when a workstation loses its physical connection to another device?

   A. The ring is broken, so no devices can communicate.

   B. Only that workstation loses its ability to communicate.

   C. That workstation and the device it's connected to lose communication with the rest of the network.

   D. No devices can communicate because there are now two unterminated network segments.

5. Which type of WAN technology uses labels, which enables priority of voice though the network?

   A. VPN

   B. T1

   C. MPLS

   D. LAN

   E. Bus

6. What is a logical grouping of network users and resources called?

   A. WAN

   B. LAN

   C. MPLS

   D. Host

7. Which of the following is a concern when using peer-to-peer networks?

   A. Where to place the server

   B. Whose computer is least busy and can act as the server

   C. The security associated with such a network

   D. Having enough peers to support creating such a network

8. Which of the following is an example of when a point-to-multipoint network is called for?

   A. When a centralized office needs to communicate with many branch offices

   B. When a full mesh of WAN links is in place

   C. When multiple offices are daisy-chained to one another in a line

   D. When there are only two nodes in the network to be connected

9. Which of the following is an example of a LAN?

   A. Ten buildings interconnected by Ethernet connections over fiber-optic cabling

   B. Ten routers interconnected by Frame Relay circuits

   C. Two routers interconnected with a T1 circuit

   D. A computer connected to another computer so they can share resources

10. Which of the following is a disadvantage of the star topology?

    A. When a port on the central concentrating device fails, the attached end device and entire network loses connectivity to the rest of the network.

    B. When the central concentrating device experiences a complete failure, all attached devices lose connectivity to the rest of the network.

    C. In a star topology, a more expensive type of host must be used compared to the host used when implementing a physical bus.

    D. It is more difficult to add stations and troubleshoot than with other topologies.

11. What is a difference between a LAN and a WAN?

    A. WANs need a special type of router port.

    B. WANs cover larger geographical areas.

    C. WANs can utilize either private or public data transport.

    D. All of the above.

12. Which of the following provides the most physical layout flexibility in a very large, geographically dispersed enterprise network?

    A. Bus topology

    B. LAN switch

    C. Star topology

    D. MPLS cloud network

13. In what type of network are all computers considered equals and they do not share any central authority?

    A. Peer-to-peer

    B. Client-server

    C. Physical topology

    D. None of the above

14. What advantage does the client-server architecture have over peer-to-peer?

    A. Easier maintenance

    B. Greater organization

    C. Tighter security

    D. All of the above

15. Which of the following is an example of a hybrid network?

    A. Ethernet switch

    B. Ring topology

    C. Bus topology

    D. Star topology

16. You have a network with multiple devices and need to have a smaller broadcast domain while working with a single device. Which of the following is the best solution?

    A. Use static IP addresses.

    B. Add more hubs.

    C. Implement more switches.

    D. Install a router.

17. Which type of topology has the greatest number of physical connections?

   A. Point-to-multipoint

   B. Star

   C. Point-to-point

   D. Mesh

18. What type of topology gives you a direct connection between two routers so that there is one communication path?

   A. Point-to-point

   B. Star

   C. Bus

   D. Straight

19. Which network topology is a combination of two or more types of physical or two or more types of logical topologies?

   A. Point-to-multipoint

   B. Hybrid

   C. Bus

   D. Star

20. When designing a network and deciding which type of network topology to use, which item(s) should be considered? (Select all that apply.)

   A. Cost

   B. Ease of installation

   C. Ease of maintenance

   D. Fault-tolerance requirements

Chapter

2

The Open Systems Interconnection Specifications

THE FOLLOWING COMPTIA NETWORK+ EXAM OBJECTIVES ARE COVERED IN THIS CHAPTER:

✓ **1.1 Compare the layers of the OSI and TCP/IP models.**

- OSI model:
    - Layer 1 – Physical
    - Layer 2 – Data Link
    - Layer 3 – Network
    - Layer 4 – Transport
    - Layer 5 – Session
    - Layer 6 – Presentation
    - Layer 7 – Application

In this chapter, I'll dissect the Open Systems Interconnection (OSI) model and describe each part to you in detail because you need a solid foundation on which to build your networking knowledge. The OSI model has seven hierarchical layers that were developed to enable different networks to communicate reliably between disparate systems.

Because this book is centering upon all things Network+, it's crucial for you to understand the OSI model as CompTIA sees it, so I'll present each of its seven layers in that light.

I'll finish this chapter with an introduction to encapsulation. *Encapsulation* is the process of encoding data as it goes down the OSI stack.

To find up-to-the-minute updates for this chapter, please see www.1ammle.com/forum or the book's web site at www.sybex.com/go/netplus2e.

Internetworking Models

When networks first came into being, computers could usually communicate only with computers from the same manufacturer. For example, companies ran either a complete DECnet solution or an IBM solution—not both together. In the late 1970s, the *Open Systems Interconnection (OSI) reference model* was created by the International Organization for Standardization (ISO) to break through this barrier.

The OSI model was meant to help vendors create interoperable network devices and software in the form of protocols so that different vendor networks could work with each other. Like world peace, it'll probably never happen completely, but it's still a great goal.

The OSI model is the primary architectural model for networks. It describes how data and network information are communicated from an application on one computer through the network media to an application on another computer. The OSI reference model breaks this approach into layers.

In the following section, I'll explain the layered approach and how you can use this approach to help troubleshoot internetworks.

The Layered Approach

Basically, a *reference model* is a conceptual blueprint of how communications should take place. It addresses all the processes required for effective communication and divides these processes into logical groupings called *layers*. When a communication system is designed in this manner, it's known as *layered architecture*.

Think of it like this: Say you and some friends want to start a company. One of the first things you'll do is sit down and think through what tasks must be done, who will do them, the order in which they will be done, and how they relate to each other. Ultimately, you might group these tasks into departments. Let's say you decide to have an order-taking department, an inventory department, and a shipping department. Each of your departments has its own unique tasks, keeping its staff members busy and requiring them to focus only on their own duties.

In this scenario, I'm using departments as a metaphor for the layers in a communication system. For things to run smoothly, the staff of each department has to trust and rely heavily on the others to do their jobs and competently handle their unique responsibilities. In your planning sessions, you'll probably take notes, recording the entire process to facilitate later discussions about standards of operation that will serve as your business blueprint or reference model.

Once your business is launched, your department heads, each armed with the part of the blueprint relating to their own department, will need to develop practical methods to implement their assigned tasks. These practical methods, or protocols, must be compiled into a standard operating procedures manual and followed closely. The procedures in your manual will have been included for different reasons and have varying degrees of importance and implementation. If you form a partnership or acquire another company, it will be imperative that its business protocols—its business blueprint—match yours (or at least are compatible with it).

Similarly, software developers can use a reference model to understand computer communication processes and see what types of functions need to be accomplished on any one layer. If they're developing a protocol for a certain layer, all they need to concern themselves with is that specific layer's functions, not those of any other layer. Another layer and protocol will handle the other functions. The technical term for this idea is *binding*. The communication processes that are related to each other are bound, or grouped together, at a particular layer.

Advantages of Reference Models

The OSI model is hierarchical, and the same benefits and advantages can apply to any layered model. The primary purpose of all such models, especially the OSI model, is to allow different vendors' networks to interoperate.

Advantages of using the OSI layered model include, but are not limited to, the following:

- The OSI model divides the network communication process into smaller and simpler components, thus aiding component development, design, and troubleshooting.
- It allows multiple-vendor development through standardization of network components.
- It encourages industry standardization by defining what functions occur at each layer of the model.
- It allows various types of network hardware and software to communicate.
- It prevents changes in one layer from affecting other layers, so it doesn't hamper development and makes application programming easier.

The OSI Reference Model

One of the greatest functions of the OSI specifications is to assist in data transfer between disparate hosts—meaning, for example, that they enable you to transfer data between a Unix host and a PC or a Mac.

The OSI model isn't a physical model, though. Rather, it's a set of guidelines that application developers can use to create and implement applications that run on a network. It also provides a framework for creating and implementing networking standards, devices, and internetworking schemes. The OSI model has seven layers:

- Application (Layer 7)
- Presentation (Layer 6)
- Session (Layer 5)
- Transport (Layer 4)
- Network (Layer 3)
- Data Link (Layer 2)
- Physical (Layer 1)

Figure 2.1 summarizes the functions defined at each layer of the OSI model. With this in hand, you're now ready to explore each layer's functions in detail.

FIGURE 2.1   Layer functions

Some people like to use the mnemonic Please Do Not Throw Sausage Pizza Away to remember the seven layers (starting at Layer 1 and moving up to Layer 7).

The seven layers are divided into two groups. The top three layers define how the applications within the end stations will communicate with each other and with users. The bottom four layers define how data is transmitted end to end. Figure 2.2 shows the three upper layers and their functions, and Figure 2.3 shows the four lower layers and their functions.

FIGURE 2.2   The upper layers

When you study Figure 2.2, understand that the user interfaces with the computer at the Application layer and also that the upper layers are responsible for applications communicating between hosts. Remember that none of the upper layers knows anything about networking or network addresses. That's the responsibility of the four bottom layers.

Figure 2.3 illustrates that the four bottom layers define how data is transferred through physical media, switches, and routers. These bottom layers also determine how to rebuild a data stream from a transmitting host to a destination host's application.

Let's start at the Application layer and work our way down the stack.

The Application Layer

The *Application layer* of the OSI model marks the spot where users actually communicate with the computer (technically users communicate with the network stack through application processes interfaces or APIs that connect the application in use to the operating system of the computer). The Application layer chooses and determines the availability of communicating partners along with the resources necessary to make the connection, coordinates partnering applications, and forms a consensus on procedures for controlling data integrity and error recovery. The Application layer comes into play only when it's apparent that access to the network will be needed soon. Take the case of Internet Explorer (IE). You could uninstall every trace of networking components from a system, such as TCP/IP, the network card, and so on, and you could still use IE to view a local HTML document—no problem. But things would definitely get messy if you tried to do something like view an HTML document that had to be retrieved using HTTP or nab a file with FTP or TFTP. That's because IE responds to requests such as those by attempting to access the Application layer. And what's happening is that the Application layer acts as an interface between the application program—which isn't part of the layered structure—and the next layer down by providing ways for the application to send information down through the protocol stack. In other words, IE doesn't reside within the Application layer—it interfaces with Application layer protocols when it needs to deal with remote resources.

FIGURE 2.3 The lower layers

Transport	• Provides reliable or unreliable delivery • Performs error correction before retransmit
Network	• Provides logical addressing, which routers use for path determination
Data Link	• Combines packets into bytes and bytes into frames • Provides access to media using MAC addresses • Performs error detection, not correction
Physical	• Moves bits between devices • Specifies voltage, wire speed, and pin-out of cables

The Application layer is also responsible for identifying and establishing the availability of the intended communication partner and determining whether sufficient resources for the intended communication exist.

These tasks are important because computer applications sometimes require more than just desktop resources. Often, they unite communicating components from more than one network application. Prime examples are file transfers and email as well as enabling remote access, network-management activities, and client-server processes like printing and information location. Many network applications provide services for communication over enterprise networks, but for present and future internetworking, the need is fast developing to reach beyond the limits of current physical networking.

It's important to remember that the Application layer acts as an interface between application programs. This means that Microsoft Word, for example, doesn't reside at the Application layer but instead interfaces with the Application layer protocols. Chapter 6, "Introduction to the Internet Protocol," will present some programs or processes that actually reside at the Application layer—for example, FTP and TFTP.

The Presentation Layer

The *Presentation layer* gets its name from its purpose: It presents data to the Application layer and is responsible for data translation and code formatting.

This layer is essentially a translator and provides coding and conversion functions. A successful data-transfer technique is to adapt the data into a standard format before transmission. Computers are configured to receive this generically formatted data and then convert it back into its native format for reading (for example, EBCDIC to ASCII). By providing translation services, the Presentation layer ensures that data transferred from one system's Application layer can be read by the Application layer of another system.

The OSI has protocol standards that define how standard data should be formatted. Tasks like data compression, decompression, encryption, and decryption are associated with this layer. In addition, some Presentation layer standards are involved in multimedia operations.

The Session Layer

The *Session layer* is responsible for setting up, managing, and then tearing down sessions between Presentation layer entities. This layer also provides dialog control between devices, or nodes. It coordinates communication between systems and serves to organize their communication by offering three different modes: *simplex*, *half duplex*, and *full duplex*. To sum up, the Session layer basically keeps applications' data separate from other applications' data.

The Transport Layer

The *Transport layer* segments and reassembles data into a data stream. Services located in the Transport layer segment and reassemble data from upper-layer applications and unite it onto the same data stream. They provide end-to-end data transport services and can establish a logical connection between the sending host and destination host on an internetwork.

The Transport layer is responsible for providing mechanisms for multiplexing upper-layer applications, establishing virtual connections, and then tearing down virtual circuits. It also hides details of any network-dependent information from the higher layers by providing transparent data transfer.

You may be familiar with Transmission Control Protocol (TCP) and User Datagram Protocol (UDP) already. (If you're not, no worries—I'll tell you all about them in Chapter 6, "Introduction to the Internet Protocol.") If so, you know that both work at the Transport layer and that TCP is a reliable service and UDP is not. This means application developers have more options because they have a choice between the two protocols when working with TCP/IP protocols.

The term *reliable networking* can be used at the Transport layer. It means that acknowledgments, sequencing, and flow control will be used.

The Transport layer can be connectionless or connection-oriented. However, it's important that you understand the connection-oriented portion of the Transport layer. The following sections will provide the skinny on the connection-oriented (reliable) protocol of the Transport layer.

Connection-Oriented Communication

Before a transmitting host starts to send segments down the model, the sender's TCP process contacts the destination's TCP process to establish a connection. What is created is known as a *virtual circuit*. This type of communication is called *connection-oriented*. During this initial *handshake*, the two TCP processes also agree on the amount of information that will be sent in either direction before the respective recipient's TCP sends back an acknowledgment. With everything agreed on in advance, the path is paved for reliable communication to take place.

Figure 2.4 depicts a typical reliable session taking place between sending and receiving systems. Looking at it, you can see that both hosts' application programs begin by notifying their individual operating systems that a connection is about to be initiated. The two operating systems communicate by sending messages over the network confirming that the transfer is approved and that both sides are ready for it to take place. After all of this required synchronization takes place, a connection is fully established and the data transfer begins. This virtual circuit setup is called *overhead*.

While the information is being transferred between hosts, the two machines periodically check in with each other, communicating through their protocol software to ensure that all is going well and that the data is being received properly.

Let me sum up the steps in the connection-oriented session—the three-way handshake—pictured in Figure 2.4:

- The first "connection agreement" segment is a request for synchronization.

- The next segments acknowledge the request and establish connection parameters—the rules—between hosts. These segments request that the receiver's sequencing is synchronized here as well so that a bidirectional connection is formed.

- The final segment is also an acknowledgment. It notifies the destination host that the connection agreement has been accepted and that the connection has been established. Data transfer can now begin.

Although I broke this connection setup into much detail, it really is just called the three-way handshake as I already mentioned and is known as SYN, SYN/ACK, ACK, or synchronize, synchronize-acknowledgment, acknowledgement.

That sounds pretty simple, but things don't always flow so smoothly. Sometimes congestion can occur during a transfer because a high-speed computer is generating data traffic a lot faster than the network can handle transferring it. A bunch of computers simultaneously sending datagrams through a single gateway or to a destination can also botch things up.

In the latter case, a gateway or destination can become congested even though no single source caused the problem. In either case, the problem is basically akin to a freeway bottleneck—too much traffic for too small a capacity. It's not usually one car that's the problem; it's that there are simply too many cars on that particular freeway.

FIGURE 2.4   Establishing a connection-oriented session

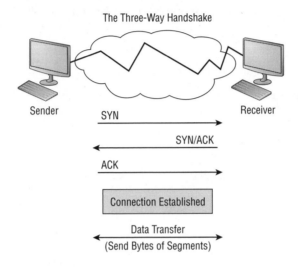

Flow Control
============

Flow Control

Data integrity is ensured at the Transport layer by maintaining *flow control* and by allowing users to request reliable data transport between systems. Flow control provides a means for the receiver to govern the amount of data sent by the sender. It prevents a sending host on one side of the connection from overflowing the buffers in the receiving host—an event that can result in lost data. Reliable data transport employs a connection-oriented communications session between systems, and the protocols involved ensure that the following will be achieved:

- The segments delivered are acknowledged back to the sender upon their reception.
- Any segments not acknowledged are retransmitted.
- Segments are sequenced back into their proper order upon arrival at their destination.
- A manageable data flow is maintained in order to avoid congestion, overloading, and data loss.

Okay, so what happens when a machine receives a flood of datagrams too quickly for it to process? It stores them in a memory section called a *buffer*. But this buffering action can solve the problem only if the datagrams are part of a small burst. If not, and the datagram deluge continues, a device's memory will eventually be exhausted, its flood capacity will be exceeded, and it will react by discarding any additional datagrams that arrive.

This sounds pretty bad, but there aren't really any huge worries here thanks to the transport function—network flood-control systems actually work quite well. How do they work? Well, instead of just dumping resources and allowing data to be lost, the transport can issue a "not ready" indicator to the sender, or source, of the flood (as shown in Figure 2.5). This mechanism works kind of like a stoplight, signaling the sending device to stop transmitting segment traffic to its overwhelmed peer. After the peer machine's receiver processes the segments abounding in its memory reservoir (its buffer), it sends out a "ready" transport indicator. When the machine waiting to transmit the rest of its datagrams receives this "go" indictor, it resumes its transmission.

FIGURE 2.5   Transmitting segments with flow control

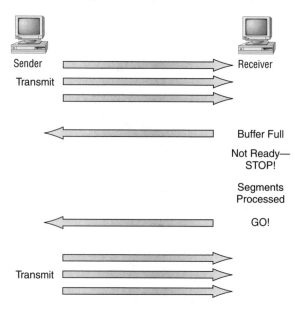

During fundamental, reliable, connection-oriented data transfer, datagrams are delivered to the receiving host in exactly the same sequence they're transmitted—and the transmission fails if this order is breached! So if any data segments are lost, duplicated, or damaged along the way, a failure notice is transmitted. This problem is solved by making sure the receiving host acknowledges that it has received each and every data segment in the correct order.

To summarize, a service is considered connection-oriented if it has the following characteristics:

- A virtual circuit is set up (such as a three-way handshake).
- It uses sequencing.
- It uses acknowledgments.
- It uses flow control.

Windowing

Ideally, data throughput happens quickly and efficiently. And as you can imagine, it would be slow if the transmitting machine had to wait for an acknowledgment after sending each segment. But because time is available *after* the sender transmits the data segment and *before* it finishes processing acknowledgments from the receiving machine, the sender uses the break as an opportunity to transmit more data. The quantity of data segments (measured in bytes) that the transmitting machine is allowed to send without receiving an acknowledgment is represented by what is called a *window*.

 Windows are used to control the amount of outstanding, unacknowledged data segments.

It's important to understand that the size of the window controls how much information is transferred from one end to the other. Although some protocols quantify information by observing the number of packets, TCP/IP measures it by counting the number of bytes.

Figure 2.6 illustrates two window sizes—one set to 1 and one set to 3. In our simplified example, both the sending and receiving machines are workstations.

FIGURE 2.6 Windowing

When you've configured a window size of 1, the sending machine waits for an acknowledgment for each data segment it transmits before transmitting another. If you've configured a window size of 3, the sending machine is allowed to transmit three data segments before an acknowledgment is received. In reality, this isn't done in simple numbers but in the amount of bytes that can be sent.

If a receiving host fails to receive all the segments that it should acknowledge, the host can improve the communication session by decreasing the window size.

Acknowledgments

Reliable data delivery ensures the integrity of a stream of data sent from one machine to the other through a fully functional data link. It guarantees that the data won't be duplicated or lost. This is achieved through something called *positive acknowledgment with retransmission*—a technique that requires a receiving machine to communicate with the transmitting source by sending an acknowledgment message back to the sender when it receives data. The sender documents each segment it sends and waits for this acknowledgment before sending the next segment. When it sends a segment, the transmitting machine starts a timer and retransmits if it expires before an acknowledgment is returned from the receiving end.

In Figure 2.7, the sending machine transmits segments 1, 2, and 3. The receiving node acknowledges it has received them by requesting segment 4. When it receives the acknowledgment, the sender then transmits segments 4, 5, and 6. If segment 5 doesn't make it to the destination, the receiving node acknowledges that event with a request for the segment to be resent. The sending machine will then resend the lost segment and wait for an acknowledgment, which it must receive in order to move on to the transmission of segment 7.

FIGURE 2.7 Transport layer reliable delivery

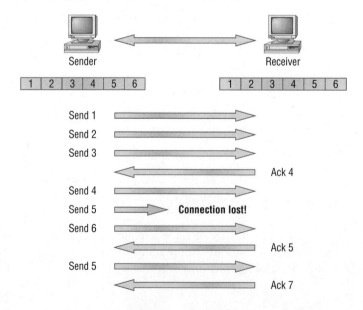

The Transport layer doesn't need to use a connection-oriented service (this is up to the application developer). It's safe to say that if you're connection-oriented, meaning that you've created a virtual circuit, you're using TCP. If you aren't setting up a virtual circuit, then you're using UDP and are considered connectionless.

 Transport Control Protocol (TCP) and User Datagram Protocol (UDP) are protocols that work at the Transport layer and are covered in detail in Chapter 6.

Devices Used in an Internetwork

The following network devices operate at all seven layers of the OSI model:

- Network management stations (NMSs)
- Web and application servers
- Gateways (not default gateways)
- Network hosts

Several devices operate primarily at the Physical layer of the OSI model. These devices manipulate mainly the physical aspects of a network data stream (such as the voltages, signal direction, and signal strength). The following devices are the most popular:

- Network Interface Cards (NICs)
- Transceivers
- Repeaters
- Hubs

These devices are discussed in detail in Chapter 5.

The Network Layer

The *Network layer* manages device addressing, tracks the location of devices on the network, and determines the best way to move data, which means that the Network layer must transport traffic between devices that aren't locally attached. Routers (Layer 3 devices) are specified at the Network layer and provide the routing services within an internetwork.

It happens like this: First, when a packet is received on a router interface, the destination IP address is checked. If the packet isn't destined for that particular router, the router looks up the destination network address in the routing table. Once the router chooses an exit inter-face, the packet is sent to that interface to be framed and sent out on the local network. If the router can't find an entry for the packet's destination network in the routing table, the router drops the packet.

Two types of packets are used at the Network layer:

Data packets   These are used to transport user data through the internetwork. Protocols used to support data traffic are called *routed protocols*. Two examples of routed protocols are Internet Protocol (IP) and Internet Protocol version 6 (IPv6), which you'll learn about in Chapter 7, "IP Addressing."

Route-update packets   These are used to update neighboring routers about the networks connected to all routers within the internetwork. Protocols that send route-update packets are called routing protocols; some common ones are Routing Information Protocol (RIP), RIPv2, Enhanced Interior Gateway Routing Protocol (EIGRP), and Open Shortest Path First (OSPF). Route-update packets are used to help build and maintain routing tables on each router.

Figure 2.8 shows an example of a routing table. The routing table used by a router includes the following information:

Network addresses   These are protocol-specific network addresses. A router must main-tain a routing table for individual routing protocols because each routing protocol keeps track of a network with a different addressing scheme (IP and IPv6, for example). Think of it as a street sign in each of the different languages spoken by the residents who live on a particular street. If there were American, Spanish, and French folks on a street named Cat, the sign would read Cat/Gato/Chat.

Interface   This is the exit interface a packet will take when destined for a specific network.

Metric   This value equals the distance to the remote network. Different routing protocols use different ways of computing this distance. I'll cover routing protocols in Chapter 9, "Introduction to IP Routing." For now, just know that some routing protocols (namely RIP) use something called a *hop count*—the number of routers a packet passes through en route to a remote network—whereas others use bandwidth, delay of the line, or something known as a tick count (1/18 of a second).

Routers break up broadcast domains, which means that by default, broadcasts aren't forwarded through a router. Why is this a good thing? Routers also break up collision domains, but this can be accomplished using Layer 2 (Data Link layer) switches as well.

> Broadcast and collision domains are covered in detail in Chapter 5. For now, remember that routers break up broadcast domains and switches break up collision domains.

Because each interface in a router represents a separate network, it must be assigned unique network identification numbers, and each host on the network connected to that router must use the same network number. Figure 2.9 demonstrates how a router works within an internetwork.

FIGURE 2.8 Routing table used in a router

FIGURE 2.9 A router in an internetwork

Each router interface is a broadcast domain.
Routers break up broadcast domains by
default and provide WAN services.

Here are some points about routers that you should definitely commit to memory:

- Routers, by default, won't forward any broadcast or multicast packets.

- Routers use the logical address in a Network layer header to determine the next-hop router to forward the packet to.

- Routers can use access lists, created by an administrator, to control security on the types of packets that are allowed to enter or exit an interface.

- Routers can provide Layer 2 bridging functions if needed and can simultaneously route through the same interface.

- Layer 3 devices (routers, in this case) provide connections between virtual LANs (VLANs).

- Routers can provide quality of service (QoS) for specific types of network traffic.

Routers can also be referred to as a Layer 3 switch. These terms are interchangeable.

The Data Link Layer

The *Data Link layer* provides the physical transmission of the data and handles error notification, network topology, and flow control. This means the Data Link layer ensures that messages are delivered to the proper device on a LAN using hardware addresses and translates messages from the Network layer into bits for the Physical layer to transmit.

The Data Link layer formats the message into pieces, each called a *data frame*, and adds a customized header containing the destination and source hardware address. This added information forms a sort of capsule that surrounds the original message in much the same way that engines, navigational devices, and other tools attached to the lunar modules of the Apollo project. These various pieces of equipment were useful only during certain stages of flight and were stripped off the module and discarded when their designated stage was complete. This is a great analogy for data traveling through networks because it works very similarly.

It's important for you to understand that routers, which work at the Network layer, don't care about where a particular host is located. They're only concerned about where networks are located and the best way to reach them—including remote ones. Routers are totally obsessive when it comes to networks. And for once, this obsession is a good thing! The Data Link layer is responsible for the unique identification of each device that resides on a local network.

For a host to send packets to individual hosts on a local network as well as transmit packets between routers, the Data Link layer uses hardware addressing. Each time a packet is sent between routers, it's framed with control information at the Data Link layer. However, that information is stripped off at the receiving router, and only the original packet is left completely intact. This framing of the packet continues for each hop until the packet is finally delivered to the correct receiving host. It's important to understand that the packet itself is never altered along the route; it's only encapsulated with the type of control information required for it to be properly passed on to the different media types.

Figure 2.10 shows the Data Link layer with the Ethernet and Institute of Electrical and Electronics Engineers (IEEE) specifications. When you check it out, notice that the IEEE 802.2 standard is not only used in conjunction with the other IEEE standards, it also adds functionality to those standards.

FIGURE 2.10   Data Link layer

| 802.5 | 802.3 | 802.2 | Logical Link Control (LLC) |
| | | | Media Access Control (MAC) |

The IEEE Ethernet Data Link layer has two sublayers:

Media Access Control (MAC)   Defines how packets are placed on the media. Contention media access is "first come/first served" access where everyone shares the same bandwidth—hence the name. Physical addressing is defined here as are logical topologies. What's a logical topology? It's the signal path through a physical topology. Line discipline, error notification (not correction), ordered delivery of frames, and optional flow control can also be used at this sublayer.

Logical Link Control (LLC)   Responsible for identifying Network layer protocols and then encapsulating them. An LLC header tells the Data Link layer what to do with a packet once a frame is received. It works like this: A host receives a frame and looks in the LLC header to find out where the packet is destined—say, the IP protocol at the Network layer. The LLC can also provide flow control and sequencing of control bits.

Project 802

One of the major components of the Data Link layer is the result of the IEEE's 802 sub-committees and their work on standards for local area and metropolitan area networks (LANs/MANs). The committee met in February 1980, so they used the 80 from 1980 and the 2 from the second month to create the name Project 802. The designation for an 802 standard always includes a dot (.) followed by either a single or a double digit. These numeric digits specify particular categories within the 802 standard. These standards are listed in the following table.

Standard	Topic
802.1	LAN/MAN Management (and Media Access Control Bridges)
802.2	Logical Link Control
802.3	CSMA/CD
802.4	Token Passing Bus
802.5	Token Passing Ring
802.6	Distributed Queue Dual Bus (DQDB) Metropolitan Area Network (MAN)
802.7	Broadband Local Area Networks
802.8	Fiber-Optic LANs and MANs
802.9	Isochronous LANs
802.10	LAN/MAN Security

Standard	Topic
802.11	Wireless LAN
802.12	Demand Priority Access Method
802.15	Wireless Personal Area Network
802.16	Wireless Metropolitan Area Network (also called WiMAX)
802.17	Resilient Packet Ring
802.18	LAN/MAN Standards Committee

The Physical Layer

Finally, we're hitting bottom. Well, not in a bad way—we've now arrived at the *Physical layer*, which does two important things: It sends bits and receives bits. Bits come only in values of 1 or 0—a Morse code with numerical values. The Physical layer communicates directly with the various types of actual communication media. Different kinds of media represent these bit values in different ways. Some use audio tones, and others employ *state transitions*—changes in voltage from high to low and low to high. Specific protocols are needed for each type of media to describe the proper bit patterns to be used, how data is encoded into media signals, and the various qualities of the physical media's attachment interface.

The Physical layer specifies the electrical, mechanical, procedural, and functional requirements for activating, maintaining, and deactivating a physical link between end systems. This layer is also where you identify the interface between the *data terminal equipment (DTE)* and the *data communication equipment (DCE)*. (Some older phone company employees still call DCE data circuit-terminating equipment.) The DCE is usually located at the customer, whereas the DTE is the attached device. The services available to the DTE are most often accessed via the DCE device, which is a modem or *channel service unit/data service unit (CSU/DSU)*.

The Physical layer's connectors and different physical topologies are defined by the standards, allowing disparate systems to communicate.

Finally, the Physical layer specifies the layout of the transmission media (its topology, in other words). A physical topology describes the way the cabling is physically laid out (as opposed to a logical topology, discussed earlier in the section "The Data Link Layer"). The physical topologies include bus, star, ring, and mesh and were described in Chapter 1, "Introduction to Networks."

Introduction to Encapsulation

When a host transmits data across a network to another device, the data goes through *encapsulation*: It's wrapped with protocol information at each layer of the OSI model. Each layer communicates only with its peer layer on the receiving device.

To communicate and exchange information, each layer uses *Protocol Data Units (PDUs)*. These hold the control information attached to the data at each layer of the model. They're usually attached to the header in front of the data field but can also be in the trailer, or end, of it.

At a transmitting device, the data-encapsulation method works like this:

1. User information is converted to data for transmission on the network.

2. Data is converted to segments, and a reliable connection is set up between the transmitting and receiving hosts.

3. Segments are converted to packets or datagrams, and a logical address is placed in the header so each packet can be routed through an internetwork.

4. Packets or datagrams are converted to frames for transmission on the local network. Hardware (Ethernet) addresses are used to uniquely identify hosts on a local network segment.

5. Frames are converted to bits, and a digital encoding and clocking scheme is used.

Figure 2.11 shows how user data is encapsulated at a transmitting host.

FIGURE 2.11   Data encapsulation

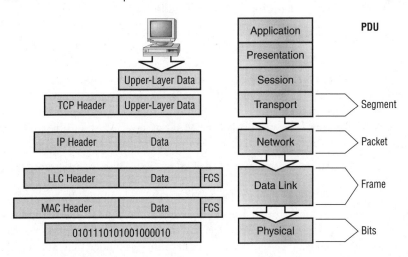

After you learn more foundational material about networking in the next few chapters, I'll come back to the encapsulation method and discuss it in more detail in Chapter 6.

Summary

You're now armed with a ton of fundamental information. You're set to build on it and are well on your way to certification.

Let's take a minute to go over what you've learned in this chapter. We started by discussing internetworking models and the advantages of having them. I then discussed the OSI model—the seven-layer model used to help application developers design applications that can run on any type of system or network. Each layer has its special jobs and select responsibilities within the model to ensure that solid, effective communications do, in fact, occur. I provided you with complete details of each layer and discussed how you need to view the specifications of the OSI model.

This chapter finished with a brief introduction to the encapsulation method used in networking. Encapsulation is a highly important concept to understand, and I'll continue to discuss it throughout this book.

Exam Essentials

Remember the OSI layers.   You absolutely must remember and understand the seven layers of the OSI model as well as what function each layer provides. The Application, Presentation, and Session layers are upper layers and are responsible for communicating from a user interface to an application. The Transport layer provides segmentation, sequencing, and virtual circuits. The Network layer provides logical network addressing and routing through an internetwork. The Data Link layer provides framing and placing of data on the network medium. The Physical layer is responsible for taking 1s and 0s and encoding them into a digital signal for transmission on the network segment.

Know the sublayers of the Data Link layer.   In addition to the OSI layers, knowing the only layer that has sublayers and the functions of those sublayers is extremely important. The Data Link layer has two sublayers: LLC and MAC. The LLC sublayer is responsible primarily for the multiplexing of Network layer protocols. The MAC sublayer is responsible for physical addressing and determining the appropriate time to place data on the network.

Know the devices that operate at each layer of the OSI model.   Hubs and repeaters see only bits, making them Layer 1 devices. Because all networking devices have physical connectivity to the network, they all operate at Layer 1, but hubs and repeaters operate only at this layer. Nevertheless, we generally consider that a device operates at the highest layer it supports; that layer's functionality is the main reason we implement the device on the network. For example, switches and bridges are considered Layer 2 devices because they understand and make decisions based on Layer 2 addresses. Routers are Layer 3 devices for a similar reason; they deal with Layer 3 addresses. Networking devices, such as workstations, that run applications, are said to operate at the Application layer (or you may hear that they operate at all layers) because they must include Application layer protocols that offer services to networked applications.

Written Lab

1. Which layer chooses and determines the availability of communicating partners along with the resources necessary to make the connection, coordinates partnering applications, and forms a consensus on procedures for controlling data integrity and error recovery?

2. Which layer is responsible for converting frames from the Data Link layer into electrical signals?

3. At which layer is routing implemented, enabling connections and path selection between two end systems?

4. Which layer defines how data is formatted, presented, encoded, and converted?

5. Which layer is responsible for creating, managing, and terminating sessions between applications?

6. Which layer manages the transmission of data across a physical link and is primarily concerned with physical addressing and the ordered delivery of frames?

7. Which layer is used for reliable communication between end nodes over the network and provides mechanisms for establishing, maintaining, and terminating virtual circuits as well as controlling the flow of information?

8. Which layer provides logical addressing that routers use for path determination?

9. Which layer specifies voltage, wire speed, and connector pin-outs and moves bits between devices?

10. Which layer combines bits into bytes and bytes into frames and uses MAC addressing?

    You can find the answers in Appendix B.

Review Questions

You can find the answers in Appendix A.

1. Host 1 sent a SYN packet to Host 2. What will Host 2 send in response?

   A. ACK

   B. NAK

   C. SYN-ACK

   D. SYN-NAK

   E. SYN

2. TCP and UDP reside at which layer of the OSI model?

   A. 1

   B. 2

   C. 3

   D. 4

3. Which layer of the OSI model provides a user interface in the form of an entry point for programs to access the network infrastructure?

   A. Application

   B. Transport

   C. Network

   D. Physical

4. You are connected to a server on the Internet and you click a link on the server and receive a time-out message. What layer could be the source of this message?

   A. Application

   B. Transport

   C. Network

   D. Physical

5. Which layer of the OSI model is responsible for code and character-set conversion as well as recognizing data formats?

   A. Application

   B. Presentation

   C. Session

   D. Network

6. At which layers of the OSI model do bridges, hubs, and routers primarily operate, respectively?

   A. Physical, Physical, Data Link

   B. Data Link, Data Link, Network

   C. Data Link, Physical, Network

   D. Physical, Data Link, Network

7. Which layer of the OSI model is responsible for converting data into signals appropriate for the transmission medium?

   A. Application

   B. Network

   C. Data Link

   D. Physical

8. A receiving host has failed to receive all the segments that it should acknowledge. What can the host do to improve the reliability of this communication session?

   A. Send a different source port number.

   B. Restart the virtual circuit.

   C. Decrease the sequence number.

   D. Decrease the window size.

9. Which Layer 1 devices can be used to enlarge the area covered by a single LAN segment? (Choose two.)

   A. Firewall

   B. NIC

   C. Hub

   D. Repeater

   E. RJ-45 transceiver

10. Segmentation of a data stream happens at which layer of the OSI model?

   A. Physical

   B. Data Link

   C. Network

   D. Transport

11. When data is encapsulated, which is the correct order?

    A. Data, frame, packet, segment, bits

    B. Segment, data, packet, frame, bits

    C. Data, segment, packet, frame, bits

    D. Data, segment, frame, packet, bits

12. What are two purposes for segmentation with a bridge?

    A. To add more broadcast domains

    B. To create more collision domains

    C. To add more bandwidth for users

    D. To allow more broadcasts for users

13. Acknowledgments, sequencing, and flow control are characteristic of which OSI layer?

    A. Layer 2

    B. Layer 3

    C. Layer 4

    D. Layer 7

14. Which if the following is true regarding sequencing and acknowledgments?

    A. The segments delivered are acknowledged back to the sender upon their reception.

    B. If a segment is not received, the virtual circuit must be restarted from the beginning at a slower transmit interval.

    C. Any segments not acknowledged are retransmitted.

    D. Segments are sequenced back into their proper order upon arrival at their destination.

    E. All segments are retransmitted on time slot intervals.

15. What is the purpose of flow control?

    A. To ensure that data is retransmitted if an acknowledgment is not received

    B. To reassemble segments in the correct order at the destination device

    C. To provide a means for the receiver to govern the amount of data sent by the sender

    D. To regulate the size of each segment

16. At which layer of the OSI model would you find IP?

    A. Transport

    B. Network

    C. Data Link

    D. Physical

17. Of the following, which is the highest layer in the OSI model?

   A. Transport

   B. Session

   C. Network

   D. Presentation

18. Routers perform routing at which OSI layer?

   A. Physical

   B. Data Link

   C. Network

   D. Transport

   E. Application

19. Which of the following mnemonic devices can you use to remember the first letter of the name of each layer of the OSI model in the proper order?

   A. All People Seem To Need Processed Data

   B. Always Should People Never Threaten Dog Police

   C. Please Do Not Throw Sausage Pizza Away

   D. All Day People Should Try New Professions

20. Which IEEE standard specifies the protocol for CSMA/CD?

   A. 802.2

   B. 802.3

   C. 802.5

   D. 802.11

Chapter

3

Networking Topologies, Connectors, and Wiring Standards

THE FOLLOWING COMPTIA NETWORK+ EXAM OBJECTIVES ARE COVERED IN THIS CHAPTER:

✓ **3.1 Categorize standard media types and associated properties.**

- Fiber:
  - Multimode
  - Singlemode
- Copper:
  - UTP
  - STP
  - CAT3
  - CAT5
  - CAT5e
  - CAT6
  - CAT6a
  - Coaxial
  - Crossover
  - T1 Crossover
  - Straight-through
- Plenum vs. non-plenum

- Media converters:
  - Singlemode fiber to Ethernet
  - Multimode fiber to Ethernet
  - Fiber to Coaxial
  - Singlemode to multimode fiber
- Distance limitations and speed limitations
- Broadband over powerline

✓ **3.2 Categorize standard connector types based on network media.**

- Fiber:
  - ST
  - SC
  - LC
  - MTRJ
- Copper:
  - RJ-45
  - RJ-11
  - BNC
  - F-connector
  - DB-9 (RS-232)
  - Patch panel
  - 110 block (T568A, T568B)

✓ **3.8 Identify components of wiring distribution.**

- IDF
- MDF
- Demarc
- Demarc extension
- Smart jack
- CSU/DSU

The idea of connecting a bunch of computers together hasn't changed a whole lot since the mid-1980s, but how we go about doing that certainly has. Like everything else, the technologies and devices we create our networks with have evolved dramatically and will continue to do so in order to keep up with the ever-quickening pace of life and the way we do business.

When you connect computers together to form a network, you want error-free, blazingly fast communication, right? Although "error-free" and reality don't exactly walk hand in hand, keeping lapses in communication to a minimum and making that communication happen really fast is definitely possible. But it isn't easy, and understanding the types of media and network topologies used in networking today will go far in equipping you to reach these goals. So will being really knowledgeable about and familiar with the array of components and devices used to control network traffic.

All of these networking ingredients are going to be the focus of this chapter. In it, I'll cover different types of networking media, discuss common topologies and devices, and compare the features that they all bring into designing a solid network that's as problem free and turbo charged as possible.

To find up-to-the-minute updates for this chapter, please see www.lammle .com/forum or www.sybex.com/netplus2e.

Physical Media

A lot of us rely on wireless networking methods that work using technologies like radio frequency and infrared, but even wireless depends on a physical media backbone in place somewhere. And the majority of installed LANs today communicate via some kind of cabling, so let's take a look at the three types of popular cables used in modern networking designs:

- Coaxial
- Twisted-pair
- Fiber optic

Coaxial Cable

Coaxial cable, referred to as *coax*, contains a center conductor made of copper that's surrounded by a plastic jacket with a braided shield over it. A plastic such as polyvinyl chloride (PVC) or fluoroethylenepropylene (FEP, commonly known as Teflon) covers this metal shield. The Teflon-type covering is frequently referred to as a *plenum-rated coating*, and it's definitely expensive but often mandated by local or municipal fire code when cable is hidden in walls and ceilings. Plenum rating applies to all types of cabling and is an approved replacement for all other compositions of cable sheathing and insulation like PVC-based assemblies.

The difference between plenum and non-plenum cable comes down to how each is constructed and where you can use it. Many large multistory buildings are designed to circulate air through the spaces between the ceiling of one story and the floor of the next; this space between floors is referred to as the *plenum*. And it just happens to be a perfect spot to run all the cables that connect the legions of computers that live in the building. Unless there's a fire—if that happens, the plenum cable becomes a serious hazard because its insulation gives off poisonous smoke that gets circulated throughout the whole building. Plus, plenum cables can actually become "wicks" for the fire, helping it quickly spread from room to room and floor to floor—yikes!

Because it's a great goal to prevent towering infernos, the National Fire Protection Association (NFPA) demands that cables run within the plenum have been tested and guaranteed as safe. They must be fire retardant and create little or no smoke and poisonous gas when burned. This means you absolutely can't use a non-plenum-type cable in the plenum, but it doesn't mean you can't use it in other places where it's safe. And because it's a lot cheaper, you definitely want to use it where you can.

Thin Ethernet, also referred to as *thinnet* or *10Base2*, is a thin coaxial cable. It is basically the same as thick coaxial cable except it's only about ¼ inch in diameter. Thin Ethernet coaxial cable is Radio Grade 58, or just RG-58. Figure 3.1 shows an example of thinnet. This connector resembles the coaxial connector used for cable TV which is called an *F connector*.

FIGURE 3.1   A stripped-back thinnet cable

Oh, by the way, if you use thinnet cable, you've got to use *BNC* connectors to attach stations to the network, as shown in Figure 3.2.

FIGURE 3.2   Male and female BNC connectors

Male

Female

You don't have to know much about most coax cable types in networks anymore, especially the thinnet and thicknet types of coaxial cable. Thicknet was known as RG-58 A/U. Nowadays, we use 75 ohm coax for cable TV; using coax in the Ethernet world is pretty much a thing of the past. RG-6, or CATV coax, is used in our brave new broadband world.

You can attach a BNC connector with a crimper that looks like a weird pair of pliers and has a die to crimp the connector. A simple squeeze crimps the connector to the cable. You can also use a screw-on connector, but I avoid doing that because it's not very reliable.

Table 3.1 lists some specifications for the different types of coaxial cable, but understand that we use only RG-59 and RG-6 in today's world.

TABLE 3.1   Coaxial cable specifications

RG rating	Popular name	Ethernet implementation	Type of cable
RG-58 U	N/A	None	Solid copper
RG-58 A/U	Thinnet	10Base2 *185m*	Stranded copper
RG-8	Thicknet	10Base5 *500m*	Solid copper
RG-59	Cable television		
Low cost, short distance	N/A	Solid copper	

TABLE 3.1   Coaxial cable specifications *(continued)*

RG rating	Popular name	Ethernet implementation	Type of cable
RG-6	Cable television, cable modems		
Longer distances than RG-59; some power implementations	N/A	Solid copper	
RG-62	ARCnet (obsolete)	N/A	Solid/stranded

> An advantage of using coax cable is the braided shielding that provides resistance to electronic pollution like *electromagnetic interference (EMI)*, *radio frequency interference (RFI)*, and other types of stray electronic signals that can make their way onto a network cable and cause communications problems.

Twisted-Pair Cable

Twisted-pair cable consists of multiple individually insulated wires that are twisted together in pairs. Sometimes a metallic shield is placed around them, hence the name *shielded twisted-pair (STP)*. Cable without outer shielding is called *unshielded twisted-pair (UTP)*, and it's used in twisted-pair Ethernet (10BaseT, 100BaseTX, 1000BaseTX) networks.

Ethernet Cable Descriptions

Ethernet cable types are described using a code that follows this format: *N<Signaling>X*. The *N* refers to the signaling rate in megabits per second, *<Signaling>* stands for the signaling type—either baseband or broadband—and the *X* is a unique identifier for a specific Ethernet cabling scheme.

Here's a common example: 100Base*X*. The 100 tells us that the transmission speed is 100Mb, or 100 megabits. The *X* value can mean several different things, and the *T* is short for *twisted-pair*. This is the standard for running 100-Megabit Ethernet over two pairs (four wires) of Category 5, 5e, or 6 UTP.

So why are the wires in this cable type twisted? Because when electromagnetic signals are conducted on copper wires in close proximity—like inside a cable—it causes interference called *crosstalk*. Twisting two wires together as a pair minimizes interference and even protects against interference from outside sources. This cable type is the most common today for the following reasons:

- It's cheaper than other types of cabling.
- It's easy to work with.
- It allows transmission rates that were impossible 10 years ago.

UTP cable is rated in these categories:

Category 1   Two twisted wire pairs (four wires). It's the oldest type and is only voice grade—it isn't rated for data communication. People refer to it as plain old telephone service (POTS). Before 1983, this was the standard cable used throughout the North American telephone system. POTS cable still exists in parts of the Public Switched Telephone Network (PSTN) and supports signals limited to the 1MHz frequency range.

> *Category* is often shortened to *Cat.* Today, any cable installed should be a minimum of Cat 5e because some cable is now certified to carry bandwidth signals of 350MHz or beyond. This allows unshielded twisted-pair cables to exceed speeds of 1Gbps—fast enough to carry broadcast-quality video over a network.

Category 2   Four twisted wire pairs (eight wires). It handles up to 4Mbps, with a frequency limitation of 10MHz, and is now obsolete.

Category 3   Four twisted wire pairs (eight wires) with three twists per foot. This type can handle transmissions up to 16MHz. It was popular in the mid-1980s for up to 10Mbps Ethernet, but it's now limited to telecommunication equipment and, again, is obsolete for networks.

Category 4   Four twisted wire pairs (eight wires), rated for 20MHz. Also obsolete.

Category 5   Four twisted wire pairs (eight wires), rated for 100MHz. But why use Cat 5 when you can use Cat 5e for the same price? I am not sure you can even buy plain Cat 5 anymore!

Category 5e (enhanced)   Four twisted wire pairs (eight wires), rated for 100MHz, but capable of handling the disturbance on each pair that's caused by transmitting on all four pairs at the same time—a feature that's needed for Gigabit Ethernet. Any category below 5e shouldn't be used in today's network environments.

Figure 3.3 shows a basic Cat 5e cable with the four wire pairs twisted to reduce crosstalk.

Category 6   Four twisted wire pairs (eight wires), rated for 250MHz. Cat 6 became a standard back in June 2002. You would usually use it as riser cable to connect floors together. If you're installing a new network in a new building, there's no reason to use anything but Category 6 UTP cabling as well as running fiber runs between floors.

Category 6a (Augmented)   Basic category 6 cable has a reduced maximum length when used for 10GBaseT; however, Category 6a cable, or Augmented Category 6, is characterized to

500MHz and has improved crosstalk characteristics, which allows10GBaseT to be run for up to 100 meters. The most important point is a performance difference between ISO/IEC and EIA/TIA component specifications for the NEXT (near-end crosstalk) transmission parameter. Running at a frequency of 500MHz, an ISO/IEC Cat 6a connector provides double the power (3db) of a Cat 6A connector that conforms with the EIA/TIA specification. Note that 3 dB equals a 100 percent increase of a near-end crosstalk noise reduction. This is our future cable indeed!

FIGURE 3.3   Cat 5e UTP cable

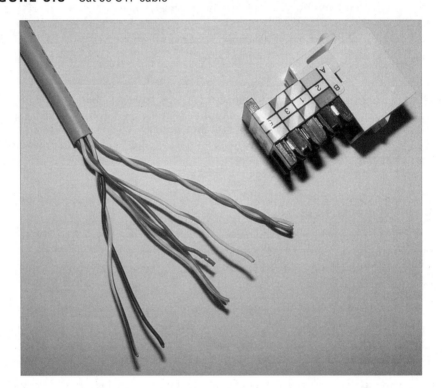

Connecting UTP

BNC connectors won't fit very well on UTP cable, so you need to use a *registered jack (RJ)* connector, which you're familiar with because most telephones connect with them. The connector used with UTP cable is called RJ-11 for phones that use four wires; RJ-45 has four pairs (eight wires), as shown in Figure 3.4.

Figure 3.5 shows the pin-outs used in a typical RJ-45 connector. Looking from the bottom of the connector, pin 1 would be on the left.

FIGURE 3.4 RJ-11 and RJ-45 connectors

FIGURE 3.5 The pin-outs in an RJ-45 connector

Most of the time, UTP uses RJ connectors; you use a crimper to attach them to a cable, just as you would with BNC connectors. The only difference is that the die that holds the connector is a different shape. Higher-quality crimping tools have interchangeable dies for both types of cables. We do not use RJ-11 for local area networks (LANs), but we do use them for our home Digital Subscriber Line (DSL) connections.

 RJ-11 uses two wire pairs, and RJ-45 uses four wire pairs.

Fiber-Optic Cable

Because fiber-optic cable transmits digital signals using light impulses rather than electricity, it's immune to EMI and RFI.

🌐 Real World Scenario

Category 5e Cabling Tips

If you want data rates faster than 10Mbps over UTP, ensure that all components are rated to deliver this and be really careful when handling all components. If you yank on Cat 5e cable, it will stretch the number of twists inside the jacket, rendering the Cat 5e label on the outside of the cable invalid. Also, be certain to connect and test all four pairs of wire. Although today's wiring usually uses only two pairs (four wires), the standard for Gigabit Ethernet over UTP requires that all four pairs (eight wires) be in good condition.

Also be aware that a true Cat 5e cabling system uses rated components from end to end, patch cables from workstation to wall panel, cable from wall panel to patch panel, and patch cables from patch panel to hub. So if any components are missing, or if the lengths don't match the Category 5e specification, you just don't have a Category 5e cabling installation. And certify that the entire installation is Category 5e compliant. Be warned that doing this requires some pretty pricey test equipment to make the appropriate measurements.

Anyone who's seen a network's UTP cable run down an elevator shaft would definitely appreciate this fiber feature. Fiber cable allows light impulses to be carried on either a glass or a plastic core. Glass can carry the signal a greater distance, but plastic costs less. Whichever the type of core, it's surrounded by a glass or plastic cladding with a different refraction index that reflects the light back into the core. Around this is a layer of flexible plastic buffer that can be wrapped in an armor coating that's usually Kevlar, which is then sheathed in PVC or plenum.

The cable itself comes in either single-mode fiber (SMF) or multimode fiber (MMF); the difference between them is in the number of light rays (the number of signals) they can carry. Multimode fiber is most often used for shorter-distance applications and single-mode fiber for spanning longer distances.

Although fiber-optic cable may sound like the solution to many problems, it has pros and cons just like the other cable types.

Here are the pros:

- It's completely immune to EMI and RFI.
- It can transmit up to 40 kilometers (about 25 miles).

And here are the cons:

- It's difficult to install.
- It's more expensive than twisted-pair.

- Troubleshooting equipment is more expensive than twisted-pair test equipment.
- It's harder to troubleshoot.

Single-Mode Fiber

Single-mode fiber-optic cable (SMF) is a very high-speed, long-distance media that consists of a single strand—sometimes two strands—of glass fiber that carries the signals. Light-emitting diodes (LEDs) and laser are the light sources used with SMF. The light source is transmitted from end to end and pulsed to create communication. This is the type of fiber cable employed to span really long distances because it can transmit data 50 times further than multimode fiber at a faster rate.

Clearly, because the transmission media is glass, the installation of SMF can be a bit tricky. Yes, there are outer layers protecting the glass core, but the cable still shouldn't be crimped or pinched around any tight corners.

Multimode Fiber

Multimode fiber-optic cable (MMF) also uses light to communicate a signal, but with it, the light is dispersed on numerous paths as it travels through the core and is reflected back. A special material called *cladding* is used to line the core and focus the light back onto it. MMF provides high bandwidth at high speeds over medium distances (up to about 3,000 feet), but beyond that it can be really inconsistent. This is why MMF is most often used within a smaller area of one building; SMF can be used between buildings.

MMF is available in glass or in a plastic version that makes installation a lot easier and increases the installation's flexibility.

Fiber-Optic Connectors

A whole bunch of different types of connectors are available to use with fiber-optic cables, but the two most popular are the *straight tip (ST)* and *subscriber (or square) connector (SC)*. The ST fiber-optic connector (developed by AT&T) is one of the most widely used fiber-optic connectors; it uses a BNC attachment mechanism similar to thinnet's that makes connections and disconnections fairly frustration free. In fact, this is the feature that makes this connector so popular. Figure 3.6 shows an example of an ST connector. Notice the BNC attachment mechanism.

The SC connector is another type of fiber-optic connector. As you can see in Figure 3.7, SC connectors are *latched*—a mechanism holds the connector in securely and prevents it from falling out.

SC connectors work with either single-mode or multimode optical fibers and will last for around 1,000 matings. They're being used more now but still aren't nearly as popular as ST connectors for LAN connections.

Small Form Factor Fiber-Optic Connectors

Another cool fiber-optic connector is the *small form factor (SFF)* connector, which allows more fiber-optic terminations in the same amount of space than its standard-sized counterparts. The two most popular versions are the *mechanical transfer registered jack (MT-RJ or MTRJ)*, designed by AMP, and the *Local Connector (LC)*, designed by Lucent.

FIGURE 3.6   An example of an ST connector

FIGURE 3.7   A sample SC connector

🌐 Real World Scenario

Should I Use Copper or Fiber?

If your data runs are measured in miles, fiber optic is your cable of choice because copper just can't give you more than about 1,500 feet without electronics regenerating the signal. The standards limit UTP to a pathetic 328 feet.

Another good reason to opt for fiber is if you require high security because it doesn't create a readable magnetic field. Although fiber-optic technology was initially super expensive and nasty to work with, it's now commonly used for Gigabit or 10GB Internet backbones.

Ethernet running at 10Mbps over fiber-optic cable to the desktop is designated 10BaseFL; the 100Mbps version of this implementation is 100BaseFX. The *L* in the 10Mbps version stands for *link*. Other designations are *B* for *backbone* and *P* for *passive*.

The MT-RJ fiber-optic connector was the first small form factor fiber-optic connector to be widely used, and it's only one-third the size of the SC and ST connectors it most often replaces. It offers these benefits:

- Small size
- TX and RX strands in one connector
- Keyed for single polarity
- Pre-terminated ends that require no polishing or epoxy
- Easy to use

Figure 3.8 shows an example of an MT-RJ fiber-optic connector.

FIGURE 3.8　A sample MT-RJ fiber-optic connector

LC is a newer style of SFF fiber-optic connector that's pulling ahead of the MT-RJ. It is especially popular for use with Fibre-Channel adapters (FCs) and is a standard used for fast storage area networks and Gigabit Ethernet adapters. Figure 3.9 depicts an example of the LC connector.

It has similar advantages to MT-RJ and other SFF-type connectors but is easier to terminate. It uses a ceramic insert just as standard-sized fiber-optic connectors do.

FIGURE 3.9   A sample LC fiber-optic connector

Media Converters

There may be instances where you need to convert from one media type to another. It could be that you need to go from one mode of fiber to another mode, or it could be more extreme and you need to go from fiber to Ethernet. Here are some of the more common media converters:

Single-mode fiber to Ethernet   These devices accept a fiber connector and an Ethernet connector and convert the signal from Ethernet and single-mode fiber (see Figure 3.10).

FIGURE 3.10   Single-mode fiber to Ethernet

Multimode fiber to Ethernet   These devices accept a fiber connector and an Ethernet connector and convert the signal from Ethernet and multi-mode fiber (see Figure 3.11).

FIGURE 3.11   Multimode fiber to Ethernet

Fiber to coaxial   These devices accept a fiber connector and a coaxial connector and convert digital signals from optical to coax (see Figure 3.12).

FIGURE 3.12   Fiber to coaxial

Singlemode to multimode fiber   These devices accept a single-mode fiber connector and a multimode fiber connector and convert the signals between the two (see Figure 3.13).

FIGURE 3.13   Single-mode to multimode fiber

Broadband over Power Line

In February 2011, the IEEE finally published a standard for Broadband over Power Line (BPL) called IEEE 1901; this is also referred to as Power Line Communication (PLC) or even Power Line Digital Subscriber Line (PDSL). Although this technology has been available for decades in theory, without an IEEE standard it was just not adopted as an alternative to other high-speed media.

However, it is highly likely that this technology will really start to see some traction, especially from the power companies who will be able to gather data from every device in your house and specifically tell you how much power is being used by your refrigerator, washers and dryers, and especially your computer and televisions, among all the other devices plugged into a wall power outlet.

BPL will allow you to just plug a computer into a wall power socket and have more than 500Mbps (in the future) for up to 1,500 meters.

Near my home in Boulder, Colorado, Xcel Energy is using BPL in combination with radio links for its SmartGridCity pilot project, which will send data from power meters, hot water heaters, thermostats, and more.

An example of an adaptor is shown in Figure 3.14.

FIGURE 3.14   Powerline adapter sets

This technology can be used to deliver Internet access to the home as well. For a computer (or any other device), you would need only to plug a BPL modem into any outlet in an equipped building to have high-speed Internet access. The basic BPL installation is shown in Figure 3.15.

After the gateway is connected through the coupler to the meter bank for the building, any electrical outlet can be used with the BPL modem to receive the ISP connection to the Internet. Challenges that still exist include (1) the fact that power lines are typically noisy and (2) the frequency at which the information is transmitted is used by shortwave and the unshielded power lines can act as antennas, thereby interfering with shortwave communications.

FIGURE 3.15   Basic BPL installation

Serial Cables

Except for multimode fiber, all the cable flavors I've talked about so far are considered serial cable types. In network communications, *serial* means that one bit after another is sent out onto the wire or fiber and interpreted by a network card or other type of interface on the other end.

Each 1 or 0 is read separately and then combined with others to form data. This is very different from parallel communication where bits are sent in groups and have to be read together to make sense of the message they represent. A good example of a parallel cable is an old printer cable—which has been replaced by USB, as I'll get to in a minute.

RS-232

Recommended Standard 232 (RS-232) was a cable standard commonly used for serial data signals connecting data-terminal equipment and data-communications equipment, such as computer's serial port to an external modem.

Figure 3.16 shows an example of one of the many types of RS-232 cables. These cables normally connect to a connector on the device called a *DB-9*.

Because most laptops don't even come with these types of connectors anymore, they've pretty much been replaced by things like USB and FireWire.

Universal Serial Bus

Universal Serial Bus (USB) is now the built-in serial bus du jour of most motherboards. You usually get a maximum of 4 external USB interfaces, but add-on adapters can take that up to as many as 16 serial interfaces. USB can actually connect a maximum of 127 external devices, and it's a much more flexible peripheral bus than either serial or parallel.

We use USB to connect printers, scanners, and a host of other input devices like keyboards, joysticks, and mice. When connecting USB peripherals, you've got to connect them either directly to one of the USB ports (as shown in Figure 3.17) on the PC or to a USB hub that is connected to one of those USB ports.

FIGURE 3.16   An RS-232 cable end

FIGURE 3.17   A USB port

Hubs can be chained together to provide multiple USB connections, but even though you can connect up to 127 devices, it's really not practical to go there. Each device has a USB plug, as shown in Figure 3.18.

FIGURE 3.18   A USB plug

Cable Properties

The reason we use so many different types of cables in a network is that each type has its own set of properties that specifically make it the best to use for a particular area or purpose. Different types vary in transmission speeds, distance, duplex, noise immunity, and frequency, and I'll cover each of these next.

Transmission Speeds

Based on the type of cable or fiber you choose and the network that it's installed in, network administrators can control the speed of a network to meet the network's traffic demands. Admins usually permit, or would like to have, transmission speeds of up to 10Gbps or higher on the core areas of their networks that connect various network segments. In the distribution and access areas, where users connect to switches, it's typically 100Mbps per connection, but transmission speeds are creeping up because the traffic demand is getting higher.

Distance

A deciding factor used in choosing what cable type to use is often the topology of a network and the distance between its components. Some network technologies can run much further than others without communication errors, but all network communications technologies are prone to *attenuation*—the degradation of signal due to the medium itself and the distance signals have to travel. Some cable types suffer from attenuation more than others. For instance, any network using twisted-pair cable should have a maximum segment length of only 328 feet (100 meters).

Duplex

All communications are either half duplex or full duplex. The difference is whether the communicating devices can "talk" and "listen" at the same time.

During half-duplex communication, a device can either send communication or receive communication, but not both at the same time. Think walkie-talkie—when you press the button on the walkie-talkie, you turn the speaker off and you can't hear anything the other side is saying.

In full-duplex communication, both devices can send and receive communication at the same time. This means that the effective throughput is doubled and communication is much more efficient. Full-duplex is typical in most of today's switched networks. I'll discuss both full and half duplex in more detail in Chapter 4, "The Current Ethernet Specifications."

Noise Immunity (Security, EMI)

Any time electrons are pushed through two wires next to each other, it creates a magnetic current. And we can create a current in the wires. This is good because without *magnetic flux*, we wouldn't be using computers—the power that surges through them is a result of it. The bad news is that it also creates two communications issues.

First, because the wire is creating a current based on the 1s and 0s coursing through it, with the right tools in hand, people can read the message in the wire without cutting it or even removing the insulation. You've heard of this—it's called *tapping* the wire, and it's clearly a valid security concern. In ancient history, high-security installations like the Pentagon actually encased communication wires in lead shielding to prevent them from being tapped. STP wires make tapping a little harder, but not hard enough.

The best way to solve the magnetic-flux problem caused by electricity is to not use these wires at all. As I said, fiber-optic cables carry the signal as light on a glass or a really pure plastic strand, and light is not susceptible to magnetic flux, making fiber optics a whole lot harder to tap. It's still not impossible—you can do it at the equipment level, but you have to actually cut and then repair the cable to do that, which isn't likely to go unnoticed.

The second magnetic-flux issue comes from the outside in instead of from the inside out. Because wires can take on additional current if they're near any source of magnetism, you've got to be really careful where you run your cables. You can avoid EMI by keeping copper cables away from all powerful magnetic sources like electric motors, speakers, amplifiers, fluorescent light ballasts, and so on. Just keep them away from anything that can generate a magnetic field!

Frequency

Each cable type has a specified maximum frequency that gives you the transmission bandwidth it can handle. Cat 5e cable is tested to 100MHz maximum frequency and can run 1Gbps signals for relatively short distances. That's maxing it out, but it's still good for connecting desktop hosts at high speeds. On the other hand, Cat 6 is a 250MHz cable that can handle 1Gbps data flow all day long with ease. Cat 6 has a lot more twists and thicker cables, so it is best used when connecting floors of a building.

 Although signal is measured as bandwidth, the capacity to carry the signal in a cable is measured as frequency.

Wiring Standards

Ethernet cabling is an important thing to understand, especially if you're planning to work on any type of LAN. There are different types of wiring standards available:

- 568A
- 568B
- Straight-through
- Crossover

We will look into each one of these, and then I'll end this discussion with some examples for you.

568A vs. 568B

If you look inside a network cable, you will find four pairs of wires twisted together to prevent crosstalk; they're also twisted like this to help prevent EMI and tapping. The same pins have to be used on the same colors throughout a network to receive and transmit, but how do you decide which color wire goes with which pin? The good news is that you don't have to decide—at least not completely.

Two wiring standards have surfaced that have been agreed on by over 60 vendors, including AT&T, 3Com, and Cisco (although there isn't 100 percent agreement). In other words, over the years, some network jacks have been pinned with the 568A standard and some have used the 568B standard, which can cause a bit of confusion if you don't know what you're looking at in your network.

568A   By looking at Figure 3.19, you can see that the green pair is used for pins 1 and 2 but the orange pair is split to pins 3 and 6, separated by the blue pair.

568B   Now take a look at Figure 3.20. The orange pair is pins 1 and 2 and the green pair is pins 3 and 6, again separated by the blue pair.

FIGURE 3.19   568A wireless standard   *568A*

Pin	Pair	Wire	Color
1	3	1	white/green
2	3	2	green
3	2	1	white/orange
4	1	2	blue
5	1	1	white/blue
6	2	2	orange
7	4	1	white/brown
8	4	2	brown

Note that the only difference between T568A and T568B is that pairs 2 and 3 (orange and green) are swapped.

If you're thinking, "What's the difference, and why does it matter?" the answer is the position of four wires on one side of the cable—that's it! There are eight wires in each UTP cable; pins 4, 5, 7, and 8 aren't used in either standard.

 If you're installing new cabling to each cubicle and/or office, you need to make sure to connect all eight pins—and use Cat 5e or Cat 6. Voice over IP (VoIP) uses all eight pins, and it's really common to have voice and data on the same wire at the same time in today's networks.

This only leaves the wire pairs to connect to pins 1, 2, 3, and 6. Remember, if we connect the green-white, green, orange-white, and orange wires to pins 1, 2, 3, and 6, respectively, on both sides of the cable, we're using the 568A standard and creating the kind of straight-through cable that's regularly implemented as a regular *patch cable* for most networks. On the other hand, if we switch from pin 1 to pin 3 and from pin 2 to pin 6 on one side only, we've created a *crossover cable* for most networks. Let's take a look.

FIGURE 3.20   568A wireless standard

Pin	Pair	Wire	Color
1	2	1	white/orange
2	2	2	orange
3	3	1	white/green
4	1	2	blue
5	1	1	white/blue
6	3	2	green
7	4	1	white/brown
8	4	2	brown

Straight-Through Cable

The straight-through cable is used to connect a host to a switch or hub or a router to a switch or hub.

 No worries—I'll tell you all about devices like switches, hubs, and routers in detail in Chapter 5, "Networking Devices."

Four wires are used in straight-through cable to connect Ethernet devices. It's really pretty simple to do this; Figure 3.21 depicts the four wires used in a straight-through Ethernet cable.

FIGURE 3.21   Straight-through Ethernet cable

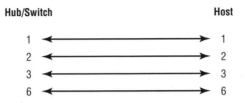

Notice that only pins 1, 2, 3, and 6 are used. Connect 1 to 1, 2 to 2, 3 to 3, and 6 to 6, and you'll be up and networking in no time. Just remember that this would be a 10/100 Ethernet-only cable, and it wouldn't work with 1000Mbps Ethernet, voice, Token Ring, ISDN, and so on.

Crossover Cable

The same four wires are used in this cable, and just as with the straight-through cable, you just connect the different pins together. Crossover cables can be used to connect these devices:

- Switch to switch
- Hub to hub
- Host to host
- Hub to switch
- Router direct to host

Check out Figure 3.22, which demonstrates how each of the four wires are used in a crossover Ethernet cable.

Okay—did you notice that instead of connecting 1 to 1, 2 to 2, and so on, we connected pins 1 to 3 and 2 to 6 on each side of the cable? A crossover cable is typically used to connect two switches together, but it can also be used to test communications between two workstations directly, bypassing the switch.

A crossover cable is used only in Ethernet UTP installations. You can connect two workstation NICs or a workstation and a server NIC directly with it.

FIGURE 3.22   Crossover Ethernet cable

If you are trying to match the straight-through and crossover cables with the 568A and 568B standard, here is how it would look:

568A+568A = straight through

568B+568B = straight through

568A+568B = crossover

You're going to find out a lot more about how important it is to label basically everything. But for now, make sure to label a crossover cable as what it is so that no one tries to use it as a workstation patch cable. If they do that, the workstation won't be able to communicate with the hub and the rest of the network!

It's really cool that you can carry a crossover cable with you in your tool bag along with your laptop—then, if you want to ensure that a server's NIC is functioning correctly, you can just connect your laptop directly to the server's NIC using your handy crossover cable. You should be able to log in to the server if both NICs are configured correctly.

Use a cable tester to make sure that what you're dealing with is in fact a crossover cable. The tester can also tell you if there's a problem with the cable. Figure 3.23 shows an inexpensive cable tester for UTP.

This cost-effective little tool will tell you beyond a shadow of a doubt if you have a straight-through or crossover cable—or even if there's a problem with the cable.

T1 Crossover Cable

In Chapter 5 you will be introduced to a device called the CSU/DSU. This device may be your connection to the Internet for the enterprise. The type of cable you use to connect to this device from your router depends on the interface types that are available on the router.

The router may connect with several types of serial cables if a T1 connection is not built into the router. If a T1 connection is built into the router, you will use an Ethernet cable. Figure 3.24 shows a T1 crossover cable connected to a T568B connection.

In rare instances you may have the need to run a cable between two CSU/DSUs. In that case you will need a T1 crossover cable. A T1 cable uses T568B pairs 1 and 2, so to connect two T1 CSU/DSU devices back-to-back requires a crossover cable that swaps these pairs. Specifically, pins 1, 2, 4, and 5 are connected to 4, 5, 1, and 2, respectively.

FIGURE 3.23   An inexpensive cable tester

FIGURE 3.24   A T1 crossover cable

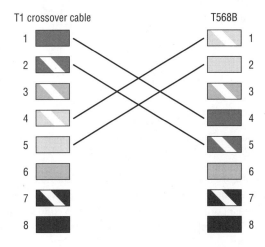

Test Your Cable Understanding

You've taken a look at the various RJ-45 UTP cables. With that in mind, what cable is used between the switches in the following?

For host A to ping host B, you need a crossover cable to connect the two switches together. But what types of cables are used in the network shown in the following?

In the second example, there are a variety of cables in use. For the connection between the switches, we'd clearly use a crossover cable like the one you saw in the earlier example. The trouble is, here we have a console connection that uses a rolled cable. Plus, the connection from the router to the switch is a straight-through cable, which is also what's running between the hosts to the switches.

Installing Wiring Distributions

By now, you're probably getting the idea that there are a lot more components in the average computer networks than meets the eye, right? If this isn't exactly a news bulletin to you, then you either already are, or have been, involved in the initial installation of the network. If the latter describes you, you probably will be, or already are, involved in the purchase and installation of the components that will connect the computers throughout your organization's building. And it may also be up to you to verify that all of the network components have been installed properly and tested. So, let's go over each of these components and the process of verifying their proper installation.

MDF/IDF

The main distribution frame (MDF) is a wiring point that's generally used as a reference point for telephone lines. It's also considered the WAN termination point. It's installed in the building as part of the prewiring, and the internal lines are connected to it. After that, all that's left is to connect the external (telephone company) lines to the other side to complete the circuit. Often, another wire frame called an intermediate distribution frame (IDF) is located in an equipment or telecommunications room. It is connected to the MDF and is used to provide greater flexibility for the distribution of all the communications lines to the building. It is typically (and better be) a sturdy metal rack designed to hold the bulk of cables coming from all over the building!

25 Pair

A *25-pair cable* consists of 25 individual pairs of wires all inside one common insulating jacket. It's not generally used for data cabling, just for telephone cabling, and especially for backbone and cross-connect cables because it reduces the cable clutter significantly. This type of cable is often referred to as a *feeder cable* because it supplies signal to many connected pairs.

110 Block

A newer type of wiring distribution point called a *110 block* has replaced most telephone wire installations and is also used for computer networking. On one side, wires are punched down; the other side has RJ-11 (for phone) or RJ-45 (for network) connections.

You'll find 110 blocks in sizes from 25 to more than 500 wire pairs, and some are capable of carrying 1Gpbs connections when used with Category 6 cables. The hitch is that using Cat 6 with the 110 block is really difficult because of the size of the Cat 6 wiring.

Demarc/Demarc Extension

The *demarc* (short for demarcation) is the last point of responsibility of the service provider. It's often at the MDF in your building connection (if your building is large), but it's usually just an RJ-45 jack that your channel service unit/data service unit (CSU/DSU) connects into from your router to wide area network (WAN) connections (CSU/DSUs are explained in detail in Chapter 16 "Wide Area Networks").

When troubleshooting, network admins often test for connectivity on both sides of the demarc to determine if the problem is internal or external. The length of copper or fiber that begins after the demarc but still doesn't reach all the way up to your office is referred to as a *demarc extension*.

Smart Jack

A *smart jack*, also called a network interface device (NID) or network interface unit, is owned by the PSTN and is a special network interface that's often used between the service provider's network and the internal network. You can't physically test to an actual demarc because it is just an RJ-45 jack, but the service provider may install a NID that has power and can be looped for testing purposes.

The smart-jack device may also provide for code and protocol conversion, making the signal from the service provider usable by the devices on the internal network like the CSU/DSU.

 Real World Scenario

Above and Beyond the Network+!

If you have a Cisco router that is having a problem—such as a serial WAN connection issue—and you're using a serial port on your router to connect to a port on a CSU/DSU, type this at the enabled Cisco router console or Telnet port:

```
config t
int s0/0
loopback
```

At this point, your interface will come up and look like it is working. That is, of course, if your connection from the router to the CSU/DSU is working properly. If not, you have a local problem.

Summary

I know getting through this chapter probably wasn't the most fun you've had recently. But understanding all those types of wires and cabling, along with their unique capacities, their associated standards, and the right connectors to use with them plus where to place them is integral to having a solid, foundational understanding of the things that make a great network run quickly and reliably.

It's critical for you to grasp the basics of networking. Having the facts about how a good network is designed and implemented and what goes into that process will make you an effective and efficient technician—and maybe, some day, a highly paid system administrator.

Exam Essentials

Understand the various types of cables used in today's networks.   Coaxial (other than for cable modems) is rarely used, but twisted-pair and fiber optic cable are very common in today's networks.

Understand the various types of ends that are used on each type of cable.   Coax uses BNC; twisted-pair uses RJ-11 for voice and RJ-45 for data; and fiber uses various ends, depending on its use.

Describe the various types of media converters that are available.   These include single mode fiber to Ethernet, multimode fiber to Ethernet, fiber to coaxial, and single mode to multimode fiber.

Understand what a 568A to 568A cable is.   A 568A to 568A cable is also known as an Ethernet straight-through cable and is used to connect hosts to switches, for example.

Understand what a 568A to 568B cable is.   A 568A to 568B cable is also known as an Ethernet crossover cable and is used to connect switches to switches, for example.

Define the function of a T1 crossover cable.   In rare instances, you may have the need to run a cable between two CSU/DSUs. In that case, you will need a T1 crossover cable. A T1 cable uses T568B pairs 1 and 2, so to connect two T1 CSU/DSU devices back-to-back requires a crossover cable that swaps these pairs. Specifically, pins 1, 2, 4, and 5 are connected to 4, 5, 1, and 2, respectively.

Describe the operation of Broadband over Power Line.   BPL allows for the transmission of data over existing power lines, both for networking home computers and for receiving Internet access to a building.

Written Lab

In this section, write the answers to the following questions:

1. Which UTP wiring uses four twisted wire pairs (eight wires) and is rated for 250MHz?

2. The point at which the operational control or ownership changes from your company to a service provider is referred to as _____.

3. Which type of cable will you use to connect switches?

4. Which RG rating of coax is used for cable modems?

5. Which UTP uses four twisted wire pairs (eight wires), is rated for 100MHz, and is capable of handling the disturbance on each pair caused by transmitting on all four pairs at the same time?

6. You want to connect a host to a switch port. What type of Ethernet cable will you use?

7. In what instance would you use T1 crossover cable?

8. 568A uses which pins to make a connection?

9. 568B uses which pins to make a connection?

10. What are two advantages of fiber-optic cabling?

    You can find the answers in Appendix B.

Review Questions

You can find the answers in Appendix A.

1. Why would a network administrator use plenum-rated cable during an installation? (Choose two.)

    A. Low combustion temperature

    B. High combustion temperature

    C. Reduces toxic gas released during a fire

    D. Is not susceptible to any interference

2. Which of the following Ethernet Unshielded twisted-pair cabling types are commonly used?

    A. 10BaseT

    B. 100BaseTX

    C. 1000BaseTX

    D. All of the above

3. In which of the following categories is UTP cable not rated?

    A. Category 2

    B. Category 3

    C. Category 5e

    D. Category 8

4. What type of connector does UTP cable typically use?

    A. BNC

    B. ST

    C. RJ-45

    D. SC

5. Which of the following provides the longest cable run distance?

    A. Single-mode fiber

    B. Multimode fiber

    C. Category 3 UTP

    D. Coax

6. You need to crimp on a connector using an RJ-45 connector. Which pin-out configuration would you use to connect a host into a switch?

    A. UTP

    B. Straight-through

    C. Crossover

    D. Rolled

7. Fiber-optic cable is immune to electromagnetic interference (EMI) and radio frequency interference (RFI) because it _____.

    A. Transmits analog signals using electricity

    B. Transmits analog signals using light impulses

    C. Transmits digital signals using light impulses

    D. Transmits digital signals using electricity

8. What type of cable transmits lights from end to end?

    A. Coax

    B. Fiber-optic

    C. UTP

    D. Category 2

9. What is the main difference between single-mode fiber (SMF) and multimode fiber (MMF)?

    A. Electrical signals.

    B. Number of light rays.

    C. Number of digital signals.

    D. Signal-mode can be run a shorter distance.

10. What type of cable should be used if you need to make a cable run longer than 100 meters?

    A. Category 5e

    B. Category 6

    C. Fiber-optic

    D. Coaxial

11. Which of the following are fiber-optic connectors? (Select three.)

    A. BNC

    B. ST

    C. RJ-11

    D. SC

    E. LC

    F. RJ-45

12. You need to connect two devices on a vertical connect and they need to send voice traffic. Which of the following cable will you use?

    A. Cat 3

    B. Cat 5

    C. Cat 8

    D. Rolled

13. How many hosts on a half-duplex segment can talk at one time?

    A. 0

    B. 1

    C. 2

    D. Unlimited

14. Which type of cable does EMI have the least effect on?

    A. Coax

    B. Fiber-optic

    C. UTP

    D. STP

15. How many devices can be connected to a full-duplex segment?

    A. 0

    B. 1

    C. 2

    D. 4

16. How many wires are used in a 100 Mbps UTP transmission?

    A. 2

    B. 4

    C. 6

    D. 8

17. A crossover cable is used to connect all of the following except _____.

   A. Switch to switch

   B. Host to host

   C. Hub to switch

   D. Host to switch

18. How is a T1 crossover cable crosses wired?

   A. Pins 1, 2, 4, and 5 are connected to 4, 5, 1, and 2.

   B. Pins 2, 3, 4, and 5 are connected to 4, 5, 1, and 2.

   C. Pins 1, 2, 4, and 5 are connected to 3, 4, 5,and 6.

   D. Pins 4, 5, 6, and 7 are connected to 4, 5, 1, and 2.

19. The purpose of the demarcation point is to separate the customer from whom?

   A. The branch office

   B. Headquarters

   C. The data center

   D. The service provider

20. You need to make a 568B cable for a FastEthernet link. How many pairs will you use?

   A. 1

   B. 2

   C. 3

   D. 4

Chapter

4

The Current Ethernet Specifications

THE FOLLOWING COMPTIA NETWORK+ EXAM OBJECTIVES ARE COVERED IN THIS CHAPTER:

✓ **3.7 Compare and contrast different LAN technologies.**

- Types:
  - Ethernet
  - 10BaseT
  - 100BaseT
  - 1000BaseT
  - 100BaseTX
  - 100BaseFX
  - 1000BaseX
  - 10GBaseSR
  - 10GBaseLR
  - 10GBaseER
  - 10GBaseSW
  - 10GBaseLW
  - 10GBaseEW
  - 10GBaseT
- Properties
  - CSMA/CD
  - Broadcast
  - Collision
  - Bonding
  - Speed
  - Distance

Before we move on and explore networking devices, the TCP/IP and DoD models, IP addressing, subnetting, and routing in the upcoming chapters, you have to understand the big picture of LANs and learn the answer to these key questions: How is Ethernet used in today's networks? What are Media Access Control (MAC) addresses, and how are they used?

This chapter will answer those questions and more. I'll not only discuss the basics of Ethernet and the way MAC addresses are used on an Ethernet LAN, I'll also cover the protocols used with Ethernet at the Data Link layer. You'll also learn about the various Ethernet specifications.

So now, let's get started with the fundamentals of connecting two hosts together.

 To find up-to-the-minute updates for this chapter, please see www.lammle.com/forum or the book's web site at www.sybex.com/go/netplus2e.

Network Basics

Networks and networking have grown exponentially over the last 20 years—understandably so. They've had to evolve at light speed just to keep up with huge increases in basic mission-critical user needs ranging from sharing data and printers to more advanced demands like videoconferencing. Unless everyone who needs to share network resources is located in the same office area (an increasingly uncommon situation), the challenge is to connect the sometimes large number of relevant networks together so all users can share the networks' wealth.

Let's take a look at how communication happens on a basic local area network (LAN), which I started to discuss in Chapter 1, "Introduction to Networks." Starting with Figure 4.1, you get a picture of a basic LAN network that's connected together using an Ethernet connection to a hub. This network is actually one collision domain and one broadcast domain, but don't stress if you have no idea what this means—I'm going to talk about both collision and broadcast domains in depth in Chapter 5, "Networking Devices."

Okay, about Figure 4.1...How would you say the PC named Bob communicates with the PC named Sally? Well, they're both on the same LAN connected with a multiport repeater (a hub). So does Bob just send out a data message, "Hey Sally, you there?" or does Bob use Sally's IP address and put things more like, "Hey 192.168.0.3, are you there?" I hope you picked the IP address option, but even if you did, the news is still bad—both answers are wrong! Why? Because Bob is actually going to use Sally's MAC address (known as a *hardware address*), which is burned right into the network card of Sally's PC, to get ahold of her.

FIGURE 4.1   The basic network

This is all good, but how does Bob get Sally's MAC address when Bob knows only Sally's name and doesn't even have her IP address? Bob is going to start by using name resolution (hostname-to-IP-address resolution), something that's usually accomplished using Domain Name Service (DNS). And note that if these two hosts are on the same LAN, Bob can just broadcast to Sally asking her for the information (no DNS needed)—welcome to Microsoft Windows, Vista included!

Here's the output from a network analyzer depicting a simple name-resolution process from Bob to Sally:

```
Time         Source         Destination    Protocol    Info
53.892794    192.168.0.2    192.168.0.255  NBNS        Name query NB SALLY<00>
```

As I already mentioned, because the two hosts are on a local LAN, Windows (Bob) will broadcast to resolve the name Sally (the destination 192.168.0.255 is a broadcast address). Let's take a look at the rest of the information:

```
EthernetII,Src:192.168.0.2(00:14:22:be:18:3b),Dst:Broadcast(ff:ff:ff:ff:ff:ff)
```

This output shows that Bob knows his own MAC address and source IP address but not Sally's IP address or MAC address; so, Bob sends a broadcast address of all *f*s for the MAC address (a Data Link layer broadcast) and an IP LAN broadcast of 192.168.0.255. Again, no worries—you're going to learn all about broadcasts in Chapter 6, "Introduction to the Internet Protocol."

Before the name is resolved, the first thing Bob has to do is broadcast on the LAN to get Sally's MAC address so he can communicate to her PC and resolve her name to an IP address:

```
Time        Source         Destination Protocol Info
5.153054    192.168.0.2    Broadcast    ARP Who has 192.168.0.3? Tell 192.168.0.2
```

Next, check out Sally's response:

```
Time         Source       Destination  Protocol  Info
5.153403     192.168.0.3  192.168.0.2  ARP  192.168.0.3 is at 00:0b:db:99:d3:5e
5.53.89317   192.168.0.3  192.168.0.2  NBNS Name query response NB 192.168.0.3
```

Okay, sweet—Bob now has both Sally's IP address and her MAC address. These are both listed as the source address at this point because this information was sent from Sally back to Bob. So, *finally*, Bob has all the goods he needs to communicate with Sally. And just so you know, I'm going to tell you all about Address Resolution Protocol (ARP) and show you exactly how Sally's IP address was resolved to a MAC address a little later in Chapter 6.

By the way, I want you to understand that Sally still had to go through the same resolution processes to communicate back to Bob—sounds crazy, huh? Consider this a welcome to IPv4 and basic networking with Windows—and we haven't even added a router yet.

Ethernet Basics

Ethernet is a contention media-access method that allows all hosts on a network to share the same bandwidth of a link. Ethernet is popular because it's readily scalable, meaning that it's comparatively easy to integrate new technologies, such as Fast Ethernet and Gigabit Ethernet, into an existing network infrastructure. It's also relatively simple to implement in the first place, and with it, troubleshooting is reasonably straightforward. Ethernet uses both Data Link and Physical layer specifications, and this section of the chapter will give you both the Data Link layer and Physical layer information you need to effectively implement, troubleshoot, and maintain an Ethernet network.

Collision Domain

The term *collision domain* is an Ethernet term that refers to a particular network scenario wherein one device sends a packet out on a network segment and thereby forces every other device on that same physical network segment to pay attention to it. This is bad because if two devices on one physical segment transmit at the same time, a *collision event*—a situation where each device's digital signals interfere with another on the wire—occurs and forces the devices to retransmit later. Collisions have a dramatically negative effect on network performance, so they're definitely something we want to avoid!

The situation I just described is typically found in a hub environment where each host segment connects to a hub that represents only one collision domain and one broadcast domain. This begs the question, "What's a broadcast domain?"

Broadcast Domain

Here's that answer…A *broadcast domain* refers to the set of all devices on a network segment that hear all the broadcasts sent on that segment.

Even though a broadcast domain is typically a boundary delimited by physical media like switches and repeaters, it can also reference a logical division of a network segment where all hosts can reach each other via a Data Link layer (hardware address) broadcast.

That's the basic story, but rest assured that I'll be delving deeper into the skinny on collision and broadcast domains a bit later in Chapter 5.

CSMA/CD

Ethernet networking uses *Carrier Sense Multiple Access with Collision Detection (CSMA/CD)*, a protocol that helps devices share the bandwidth evenly without having two devices transmit at the same time on the network medium. CSMA/CD was created to overcome the problem of those collisions that occur when packets are transmitted simultaneously from different hosts. And trust me—good collision management is crucial because when a host transmits in a CSMA/CD network, all the other hosts on the network receive and examine that transmission. Only bridges and routers can effectively prevent a transmission from propagating throughout the entire network.

So, how does the CSMA/CD protocol work? Let's start by taking a look at Figure 4.2, where a collision has occurred in the network.

FIGURE 4.2   CSMA/CD

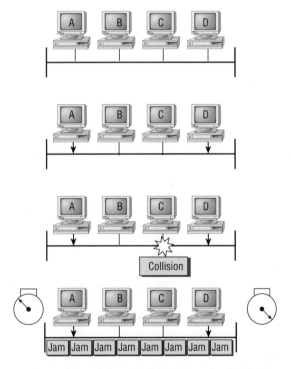

Carrier Sense Multiple Access with Collision Detection (CSMA/CD)

When a host wants to transmit over the network, it first checks for the presence of a digital signal on the wire. If all is clear, meaning that no other host is transmitting, the host will then proceed with its transmission. But it doesn't stop there. The transmitting host constantly monitors the wire to make sure no other hosts begin transmitting. If the host detects another signal on the wire, it sends out an extended jam signal that causes all hosts on the segment to stop sending data (think busy signal). The hosts respond to that jam signal by waiting a while before attempting to transmit again. Backoff algorithms (represented by the clocks counting down on either side of the jammed devices) determine when the colliding stations can retransmit. If collisions keep occurring after 15 tries, the hosts attempting to transmit will then time out. Pretty clean!

When a collision occurs on an Ethernet LAN, the following happens:

▪ A jam signal informs all devices that a collision occurred.

▪ The collision invokes a random backoff algorithm.

▪ Each device on the Ethernet segment stops transmitting for a short time until the timers expire.

▪ All hosts have equal priority to transmit after the timers have expired.

And following are the effects of having a CSMA/CD network that has sustained heavy collisions:

▪ Delay

▪ Low throughput

▪ Congestion

> Backoff on an 802.3 network is the retransmission delay that's enforced when a collision occurs. When a collision occurs, a host will resume transmission after the forced time delay has expired. After this backoff delay period has expired, all stations have equal priority to transmit data.

In the following sections, I'm going to cover Ethernet in detail at both the Data Link layer (Layer 2) and the Physical layer (Layer 1).

Half- and Full-Duplex Ethernet

Just so you know, half-duplex Ethernet is defined in the original 802.3 Ethernet specification. Basically, when you run half duplex, you're using only one wire pair with a digital signal either transmitting or receiving. This really isn't all that different from full duplex because you can both transmit and receive—you just don't get to do that at the same time running half duplex as you can if you're running full duplex.

Here's how it works: If a host hears a digital signal, it uses the CSMA/CD protocol to help prevent collisions and to permit retransmitting if a collision does occur. Half-duplex Ethernet—typically 10BaseT—is only about 30 to 40 percent efficient because a large 10BaseT network will usually provide only 3Mbps to 4Mbps at most. Although it's true that 100Mbps Ethernet can and sometimes does run half duplex, it's just not very common to find that happening these days.

In contrast, full-duplex Ethernet uses two pairs of wires at the same time instead of one measly wire pair like half duplex employs. Plus, full duplex uses a point-to-point connection between the transmitter of the sending device and the receiver of the receiving device (in most cases the switch). This means that with full-duplex data transfer, you not only get faster data-transfer speeds, but you also get collision prevention too—sweet!

You don't need to worry about collisions because now it's like a freeway with multiple lanes instead of the single-lane road provided by half duplex. Full-duplex Ethernet is supposed to offer 100 percent efficiency in both directions—for example, you can get 20Mbps with a 10Mbps Ethernet running full duplex or 200Mbps for Fast Ethernet. But this rate is something known as an *aggregate rate*, which translates as "you're supposed to get" 100 percent efficiency. No guarantees, in networking as in life.

Full-duplex Ethernet can be used in many situations; here are some examples:

- With a connection from a switch to a host
- With a connection from a switch to a switch
- With a connection from a host to a host using a crossover cable

NOTE   You can run full duplex with just about any device except a hub.

You may be wondering: If it's capable of all that speed, why wouldn't it deliver? Well, when a full-duplex Ethernet port is powered on, it first connects to the remote end and then negotiates with the other end of the Fast Ethernet link. This is called an *auto-detect mechanism*. This mechanism first decides on the exchange capability, which means it checks to see if it can run at 10, 100, or even 1000Mbps. It then checks to see if it can run full duplex, and if it can't, it will run half duplex instead.

Hosts usually auto-detect both the Mbps and the duplex type available (the default setting), but you can manually set both the speed and duplex type on the Network Interface Card (NIC) card, as shown in the following graphic.

It is pretty rare these days to go into a NIC configuration on a host and change these settings, but this example shows that you can do that if you want.

 Remember that half-duplex Ethernet shares a collision domain and provides a lower effective throughput than full-duplex Ethernet, which typically has a private collision domain and a higher effective throughput.

Last, remember these important points:

- There are no collisions in full-duplex mode.
- A dedicated switch port is required for each full-duplex host.
- The host network card and the switch port must be capable of operating in full-duplex mode.

Now let's take a look at how Ethernet works at the Data Link layer.

Ethernet at the Data Link Layer

Ethernet at the Data Link layer is responsible for Ethernet addressing, commonly referred to as *hardware addressing* or *MAC addressing*. Ethernet is also responsible for framing packets received from the Network layer and preparing them for transmission on the local network through the Ethernet contention media-access method.

Ethernet MAC addresses are made up of hexadecimal addresses. So before I discuss MAC addresses, let's start by talking about binary, decimal, and hexadecimal addresses and how to convert one to another.

Binary to Decimal and Hexadecimal Conversion

Understanding the differences between binary, decimal, and hexadecimal numbers and how to convert one format into the other is very important before we move on to discussing the TCP/IP protocol stack and IP addressing in Chapter 6 and Chapter 7, "IP Addressing."

So let's get started with binary numbering. It's pretty simple, really. Each digit used is limited to being either a 1 (one) or a 0 (zero), and each digit is called 1 bit (short for *bi*nary digi*t*). Typically, you count either 4 or 8 bits together, with these being referred to as a *nibble* and a *byte*, respectively.

What's interesting about binary numbering is the value represented in a decimal format—the typical decimal format being the base-10 number scheme that we've all used since kindergarten. The binary numbers are placed in a value spot, starting at the right and moving left, with each spot having double the value of the previous spot.

Table 4.1 shows the decimal values of each bit location in a nibble and a byte. Remember, a nibble is 4 bits and a byte is 8 bits.

TABLE 4.1 Binary values

Nibble values	Byte values
8 4 2 1	128 64 32 16 8 4 2 1

What all this means is that if a one digit (1) is placed in a value spot, then the nibble or byte takes on that decimal value and adds it to any other value spots that have a 1. And if a zero (0) is placed in a bit spot, you don't count that value.

 Hex is short for *hexadecimal*, which is a numbering system that uses the first six letters of the alphabet (*A* through *F*) to extend beyond the available 10 digits in the decimal system. Hexadecimal has a total of 16 digits.

Let me clarify things for you—if we have a 1 placed in each spot of our nibble, we then add up 8 + 4 + 2 + 1 to give us a maximum value of 15. Another example for our nibble values is 1010, which means that the 8 bit and the 2 bit are turned on and equal a decimal value of 10. If we have a nibble binary value of 0110, then our decimal value is 6 because the 4 and 2 bits are turned on.

But the byte values can add up to a value that's significantly higher than 15. This is how— if we count every bit as a one (1), then the byte binary value looks like this (remember, 8 bits equal a byte):

11111111

We then count up every bit spot because each is turned on. It looks like this, which demonstrates the maximum value of a byte:

128 + 64 + 32 + 16 + 8 + 4 + 2 + 1 = 255

A binary number can equal plenty of other decimal values. Let's work through a few examples:

10010110

Which bits are on? The 128, 16, 4, and 2 bits are on, so we'll just add them up: 128 + 16 + 4 + 2 = 150.

01101100

Which bits are on? The 64, 32, 8, and 4 bits are on, so we add them up: 64 + 32 + 8 + 4 = 108.

11101000

Which bits are on? The 128, 64, 32, and 8 bits are on, so we add the values: 128 + 64 + 32 + 8 = 232.

You should memorize Table 4.2 before braving the IP sections in Chapter 6 and Chapter 7 since this lists all available subnet masks.

TABLE 4.2   Binary-to-decimal memorization chart

Binary value	Decimal value
10000000	128
11000000	192
11100000	224
11110000	240
11111000	248
11111100	252
11111110	254
11111111	255

Hexadecimal addressing is completely different than binary or decimal—it's converted by reading nibbles, not bytes. By using a nibble, we can convert these bits to hex pretty simply. First, understand that the hexadecimal addressing scheme uses only the numbers 0 through 9. And because the numbers 10, 11, 12, and so on can't be used (because they are two-digit numbers), the letters *A*, *B*, *C*, *D*, *E*, and *F* are used to represent 10, 11, 12, 13, 14, and 15, respectively.

Table 4.3 shows both the binary value and the decimal value for each hexadecimal digit.

TABLE 4.3   Hex-to-binary-to-decimal chart

Hexadecimal value	Binary value	Decimal value
0	0000	0
1	0001	1
2	0010	2
3	0011	3
4	0100	4
5	0101	5
6	0110	6

Hexadecimal value	Binary value	Decimal value
7	0111	7
8	1000	8
9	1001	9
A	1010	10
B	1011	11
C	1100	12
D	1101	13
E	1110	14
F	1111	15

Did you notice that the first 10 hexadecimal digits (0–9) are the same values as the decimal values? If not, look again. This handy fact makes those values super easy to convert.

So suppose you have something like this: 0x6A. (Some manufacturers put *0x* in front of characters so you know that they're a hex value, while others just give you an *h*. It doesn't have any other special meaning.) What are the binary and decimal values? To correctly answer that question, all you have to remember is that each hex character is one nibble and two hex characters together make a byte. To figure out the binary value, first put the hex characters into two nibbles and then put them together into a byte. 6 = 0110 and A (which is 10 in hex) = 1010, so the complete byte is 01101010.

To convert from binary to hex, just take the byte and break it into nibbles.

Here's how you do that: Say you have the binary number 01010101. First, break it into nibbles—0101 and 0101—with the value of each nibble being 5 because the 1 and 4 bits are on. This makes the hex answer 0x55. And in decimal format, the binary number is 01010101, which converts to 64 + 16 + 4 + 1 = 85.

Okay, now try another binary number:

11001100

Our answer is 1100 = 12 and 1100 = 12 (therefore, it's converted to CC in hex). The decimal conversion answer is 128 + 64 + 8 + 4 = 204.

One more example, and then we need to get working on the Physical layer. Suppose we're given the following binary number:

10110101

The hex answer is 0xB5 because 1011 converts to B and 0101 converts to 5 in hex value. The decimal equivalent is 128 + 32 + 16 + 4 + 1 = 181.

See the written lab at the end of this chapter for more practice with binary/hex/decimal conversion.

Ethernet Addressing

Now that you've got binary to decimal and hexadecimal address conversion down, we can get into how Ethernet addressing works. It uses the *Media Access Control (MAC) address* burned into each and every Ethernet NIC. The MAC, or hardware, address is a 48-bit (6-byte) address written in a hexadecimal format.

Figure 4.3 shows the 48-bit MAC addresses and how the bits are divided.

FIGURE 4.3   Ethernet addressing using MAC addresses

The *organizationally unique identifier (OUI)* is assigned by the Institute of Electrical and Electronics Engineers (IEEE) to an organization. It's composed of 24 bits, or 3 bytes. The organization, in turn, assigns a globally administered address (24 bits, or 3 bytes) that is unique (supposedly—no guarantees) to each and every adapter it manufactures. Look closely at the figure. The high-order bit is the Individual/Group (I/G) bit. When it has a value of 0, we can assume that the address is the MAC address of a device and may well appear in the source portion of the MAC header. When it is a 1, we can assume that the address represents either a broadcast or multicast address in Ethernet or a broadcast.

The next bit is the Global/Local bit (G/L, also known as U/L, where *U* means *Universal*). When set to 0, this bit represents a globally administered address (as standardized by the IEEE). When the bit is a 1, it represents a locally governed and administered address. The low-order 24 bits of an Ethernet address represent a locally administered or manufacturer-assigned code. This portion commonly starts with 24 0s for the first card made and continues in order until there are 24 1s for the last (16,777,216th) card made. You'll find that many manufacturers use these same six hex digits as the last six characters of their serial number on the same card.

Ethernet Frames

The Data Link layer is responsible for combining bits into bytes and bytes into frames. Frames are used at the Data Link layer to encapsulate packets handed down from the Network layer for transmission on a type of physical media access.

The function of Ethernet stations is to pass data frames between each other using a group of bits known as a MAC frame format. This provides error detection from a cyclic redundancy check (CRC). But remember—this is error detection, not error correction. The 802.3 frames and Ethernet frame are shown in Figure 4.4.

FIGURE 4.4   802.3 and Ethernet frame formats

Ethernet_II

Preamble 8 Bytes	DA 6 Bytes	SA 6 Bytes	Type 2 Bytes	Data	FCS 4 Bytes

802.3_Ethernet

Preamble 8 Bytes	DA 6 Bytes	SA 6 Bytes	Length 2 Bytes	Data	FCS

Encapsulating a frame within a different type of frame is called *tunneling*.

The following information regarding frame headings and the various types of Ethernet frames are beyond the CompTIA Network+ objectives. Throughout the rest of this book, I will show you screen shots from a network analyzer. It's always good to understand what you are looking at, so I put this information in to help you understand a frame structure.

Following are the details of the different fields in the 802.3 and Ethernet frame types:

Preamble   An alternating 1,0 pattern provides a 5MHz clock at the start of each packet, which allows the receiving devices to lock the incoming bit stream.

Start frame delimiter (SFD)/synch   The preamble is seven octets, and the SFD is one octet (synch). The SFD is 10101011, where the last pair of 1s allows the receiver to come into the alternating 1,0 pattern somewhere in the middle and still synch up and detect the beginning of the data (this field is not shown in the figure).

Destination Address (DA)   This transmits a 48-bit value using the least significant bit (LSB) first. The DA is used by receiving stations to determine whether an incoming packet is addressed to a particular host. The DA can be an individual address or a broadcast or multicast MAC address. Remember that a broadcast is all 1s (or *F*s in hex) and is sent to all devices but a multicast is sent only to a similar subset of hosts on a network.

Source Address (SA)   The SA is a 48-bit MAC address used to identify the transmitting device, and it uses the LSB first. Broadcast and multicast address formats are illegal within the SA field.

Length or Type   802.3 uses a Length field, but the Ethernet frame uses a Type field to identify the Network layer protocol. 802.3 by itself cannot identify the upper-layer routed protocol and must be used with a proprietary LAN protocol—Internetwork Packet Exchange (IPX), for example.

Data   This is a packet sent down to the Data Link layer from the Network layer. The size can vary from 64 to 1500 bytes.

Frame Check Sequence (FCS)   FCS is a field that is at the end of the frame and is used to store the CRC.

Okay—let's take a minute to look at some frames caught on our trusty network analyzer. You can see that the following frame has only three fields: Destination, Source, and Type (shown as Protocol Type on this analyzer):

```
Destination:   00:60:f5:00:1f:27
Source:        00:60:f5:00:1f:2c
Protocol Type: 08-00 IP
```

This is an Ethernet_II frame. Notice that the Type field is IP, or 08-00 (mostly just referred to as 0x800) in hexadecimal.

The next frame has the same fields, so it must be an Ethernet_II frame too:

```
Destination:   ff:ff:ff:ff:ff:ff Ethernet Broadcast
Source:        02:07:01:22:de:a4
Protocol Type: 08-00 IP
```

Did you notice that this frame was a broadcast? You can tell because the destination hardware address is all 1s in binary, or all *F*s in hexadecimal.

Let's take a look at one more Ethernet_II frame. You can see that the Ethernet frame is the same Ethernet_II frame we use with the IPv4 routed protocol. The difference is that the Type field has 0x86dd when we are carrying IPv6 data, and when we have IPv4 data, we use 0x0800 in the Protocol field:

```
Destination: IPv6-Neighbor-Discovery_00:01:00:03 (33:33:00:01:00:03)
Source: Aopen_3e:7f:dd (00:01:80:3e:7f:dd)
Type: IPv6 (0x86dd)
```

This is the beauty of the Ethernet_II frame. Because of the Protocol field, we can run any Network layer routed protocol and it will carry the data because it can identify that particular Network layer protocol.

Channel Bonding

Channel bonding (also known as *Ethernet bonding*) is a computer-networking arrange-ment where two or more network interfaces on a host are combined for redundancy and/or increased throughput. There are various names for this technology, but Link Aggregation is the most common. Cisco calls this EtherChannel. Figure 4.5 shows some examples of Ethernet channel bonding.

FIGURE 4.5   Ethernet channel bonding example

In Figure 4.5, you can see that bonding can be used to attach multiple connections to a server, between switches, and even for connections to the Internet, providing fault tolerance as well as improved throughput.

Ethernet at the Physical Layer

Ethernet was first implemented by a group called DIX (Digital, Intel, and Xerox). They created and implemented the first Ethernet LAN specification, which the IEEE used to cre-ate the IEEE 802.3 Committee. This was a 10Mbps network that ran on coax, then on twisted-pair, and finally on fiber physical media.

The IEEE extended the 802.3 Committee to two new committees known as 802.3u (Fast Ethernet) and 802.3ab (Gigabit Ethernet on Category 5+) and then finally to 802.3ae (10Gbps over fiber and coax).

Figure 4.6 shows the IEEE 802.3 and original Ethernet Physical layer specifications.

When designing your LAN, it's really important to understand the different types of Ethernet media available to you. Sure, it would be great to run Gigabit Ethernet to each desk-top and 10Gbps between switches (and to servers), and although this is just starting to hap-pen, justifying the cost of that network today for most companies would be a pretty hard sell. But if instead you mix and match the different types of Ethernet media methods currently available, you can come up with a cost-effective network solution that works great.

FIGURE 4.6   Ethernet Physical layer specifications

Data Link (MAC Layer)	Ethernet	802.3						
Physical		10Base2	10Base5	10BaseT	10BaseF	100BaseTX	100BaseFX	100BaseT4

The Electronic Industries Association and the newer Telecommunications Industry Alliance (EIA/TIA) together form the standards body that creates the Physical layer specifications for Ethernet. The EIA/TIA specifies that Ethernet use a *registered jack (RJ) connector* with a 4 5 wiring sequence on *unshielded twisted-pair (UTP)* cabling (RJ-45). However, the industry is calling this just an 8-pin modular connector.

Each Ethernet cable type that is specified by the EIA/TIA has something known as *inherent attenuation*, which is defined as the loss of signal strength as it travels the length of a cable and is measured in decibels (dB). The cabling used in corporate and home markets is measured in categories. A higher-quality cable will have a higher-rated category and lower attenuation. For example, Category 5 is better than Category 3 because Category 5 cables have more wire twists per foot and therefore less crosstalk. *Crosstalk* is the unwanted signal interference from adjacent pairs in the cable.

Here are the original IEEE 802.3 standards:

10Base2   10Mbps baseband technology, using coax up to 185 meters in length. Known as *thinnet* and can support up to 30 workstations on a single segment. Uses a physical and logical bus with Attachment Unit Interface (AUI) connectors. The 10 means 10Mbps, *Base* means baseband technology—a signaling method for communication on the network— and the 2 means almost 200 meters. 10Base2 Ethernet cards use BNC (British Naval Connector, Bayonet Neill-Concelman, or Bayonet Nut Connector) and T-connectors to connect to a network.

10Base5   10Mbps baseband technology, using coax up to 500 meters in length. Known as *thicknet*. Uses a physical and logical bus with AUI connectors. Up to 2,500 meters with repeaters and 1,024 users for all segments.

10BaseT   10Mbps using Category 3 UTP wiring. Unlike on 10Base2 and 10Base5 networks, each device must connect into a hub or switch, and you can have only one host per segment or wire. Uses an RJ-45 connector (8-pin modular connector) with a physical star topology and a logical bus.

Each of the 802.3 standards defines an AUI, which allows a one-bit-at-a-time transfer to the Physical layer from the Data Link media-access method. This allows the MAC address to remain constant but means the Physical layer can support both existing and new technologies. The original AUI interface was a 15-pin connector, which allowed a transceiver (transmitter/receiver) that provided a 15-pin-to-twisted-pair conversion.

There's an issue, though—the AUI interface can't support 100Mbps Ethernet because of the high frequencies involved. So basically, 100BaseT needed a new interface, and the 802.3u specifications created one called the Media Independent Interface (MII) that provides 100Mbps throughput. The MII uses a nibble, which you of course remember is defined as 4 bits. Gigabit Ethernet uses a Gigabit Media Independent Interface (GMII) and transmits 8 bits at a time.

802.3u (Fast Ethernet) is compatible with 802.3 Ethernet because they share the same physical characteristics. Fast Ethernet and Ethernet use the same maximum transmission unit (MTU) and the same MAC mechanisms, and they both preserve the frame format that is used by 10BaseT Ethernet. Basically, Fast Ethernet is just based on an extension to the IEEE 802.3 specification, and because of that, it offers us a speed increase of 10 times 10BaseT.

Here are the expanded IEEE Ethernet 802.3 standards, starting with Fast Ethernet:

100BaseTX (IEEE 802.3u)   100BaseTX, most commonly known as Fast Ethernet, uses EIA/TIA Category 5 or 5E or 6, UTP two-pair wiring. One user per segment; up to 100 meters long (328 feet). It uses an RJ-45 connector with a physical star topology and a logical bus.

> 100BaseT and 100BaseTX: What's the difference? 100BaseT is the name of a group of standards for Fast Ethernet that include 100BaseTX. Also included are 100BaseT4 and 100BaseT2.The same can be said about 1000BaseT and 1000BaseX.

100BaseFX (IEEE 802.3u)   Uses 62.5/125-micron multimode fiber cabling. Point-to-point topology; up to 412 meters long. It uses ST and SC connectors, which are media-interface connectors.

> Ethernet's implementation over fiber can sometimes be referred to as 100BaseTF, although this isn't an actual standard. It just means that Ethernet technologies are being run over fiber cable.

1000BaseCX (IEEE 802.3z)   Copper twisted-pair called twinax (a balanced coaxial pair) that can run only up to 25 meters and uses a special 9-pin connector known as the High Speed Serial Data Connector (HSSDC).

1000BaseT (IEEE 802.3ab)   Category 5, four-pair UTP wiring up to 100 meters long (328 feet).

1000BaseSX (IEEE 802.3z)   The implementation of Gigabit Ethernet running over multimode fiber-optic cable (instead of copper twisted-pair cable) and using short wavelength laser. Multimode fiber (MMF) using 62.5- and 50-micron core; uses an 850 nanometer (nm) laser and can go up to 220 meters with 62.5-micron, 550 meters with 50-micron.

1000BaseLX (IEEE 802.3z)   Single-mode fiber that uses a 9-micron core and 1300 nm laser and can go from 3 km up to 10 km.

10GBaseT   10GBaseT is a standard created by the IEEE 802.3an committee to provide 10Gbps connections over conventional UTP cables (Category 5e, 6, or 7 cables). 10GBaseT allows the conventional RJ-45 used for Ethernet LANs. It can support signal transmission at the full 100-meter distance specified for LAN wiring. If you need to implement a 10 Gbps link, this is the most economical way to go!

10GBaseSR   An implementation of 10 Gigabit Ethernet that uses short-wavelength lasers at 850 nm over multimode fiber. It has a maximum transmission distance of between 2 and 300 meters (990 feet), depending on the size and quality of the fiber.

10GBaseLR   An implementation of 10 Gigabit Ethernet that uses long-wavelength lasers at 1,310 nm over single-mode fiber. It also has a maximum transmission distance between 2 meters and 10 km (which is 6 miles!), depending on the size and quality of the fiber.

10GBaseER   An implementation of 10 Gigabit Ethernet running over single-mode fiber. It uses extra-long-wavelength lasers at 1,550 nm. It has the longest transmission distances possible of the 10 Gigabit technologies: anywhere from 2 meters up to 40 km, depending on the size and quality of the fiber used.

10GBaseSW   10GBaseSW, as defined by IEEE 802.3ae, is a mode of 10GBaseS for MMF with a 850 nm laser transceiver with a bandwidth of 10Gbps. It can support up to 300 meters of cable length. This media type is designed to connect to SONET equipment.

10GBase-LW   10GBaseLW is a mode of 10GBaseL supporting a link length of 10 km on standard single-mode fiber (SMF) (G.652). This media type is designed to connect to SONET equipment.

10GBaseEW   10GBaseEW is a mode of 10GBaseE supporting a link length of up to 40 km on SMF based on G.652 using optical-wavelength 1550 nm. This media type is designed to connect to SONET equipment.

> If you want to implement a network medium that is not susceptible to electromagnetic interference (EMI), fiber-optic cable provides a more secure, long-distance cable that is not susceptible to EMI at high speeds as UTP is.

Table 4.4 summarizes the cable types.

TABLE 4.4   Common Ethernet cable types

Ethernet name	Cable type	Maximum speed	Maximum transmission distance	Notes
10Base5	Coax	10Mbps	500 meters per segment	Also called thicknet, this cable type uses vampire taps to connect devices to cable.

Ethernet name	Cable type	Maximum speed	Maximum transmission distance	Notes
10Base2	Coax	10Mbps	185 meters per segment	Also called thinnet, a very popular implementation of Ethernet over coax.
10BaseT	UTP	10Mbps	100 meters per segment	One of the most popular network cabling schemes.
100BaseTX	UTP, STP	100Mbps	100 meters per segment	Two pairs of Category 5 UTP.
10BaseFL	Fiber	10Mbps	Varies (ranges from 500 meters to 2,000 meters)	Ethernet over fiber optics to the desktop.
100BaseFX	MMF	100Mbps	2,000 meters	100Mbps Ethernet over fiber optics.
1000BaseT	UTP	1000Mbps	100 meters	Four pairs of Category 5e or higher.
1000BaseSX	MMF	1000Mbps	550 meters	Uses SC fiber connectors. Max length depends on fiber size.
1000BaseCX	Balanced, shielded copper	1000Mbps	25 meters	Uses a special connector, the HSSDC.
1000BaseLX	MMF and SMF	1000Mbps	550 meters multimode/2,000 meters single mode	Uses longer wavelength laser than 1000BaseSX. Uses SC and LC connectors.
10GBaseT	UTP	10Gbps	100 meters	Connects to the network like a Fast Ethernet link using UTP.
10GBaseSR	MMF	10Gbps	300 meters	850 nm laser. Max length depends on fiber size and quality.

TABLE 4.4 Common Ethernet cable types *(continued)*

Ethernet name	Cable type	Maximum speed	Maximum transmission distance	Notes
10GBaseLR	SMF	10Gbps	10 kilometers	1310 nm laser. Max length depends on fiber size and quality.
10GBaseER	SMF	10Gbps	40 kilometers	1550 nm laser. Max length depends on fiber size and quality.
10GBaseSW	MMF	10Gbps	300 meters	850 nm laser transceiver.
10GBaseLW	SMF	10Gbps	10 kilometers	Typically used with SONET.
10GBaseEW	SMF	10Gbps	40 kilometers	1550 nm optical wavelength.

 An advantage of 100BaseFX over 100BaseTX is longer cable runs; however, 100BaseTX is easier to install.

I know there's a lot of information to remember about the various Ethernet and fiber types used in today's networks, but for the CompTIA Network+ exam, you really need to know them. Trust me, I haven't inundated you with unnecessary information!

Armed with the basics covered in the chapter, you're equipped to go to the next level and put Ethernet to work using various network devices. But to ensure that you're really ready, read the summary, go over the exam essentials and do the written lab and review questions for this chapter.

Summary

In this chapter, you learned the fundamentals of Ethernet networking, how hosts communicate on a network, and how CSMA/CD works in an Ethernet half-duplex network.

I also showed you the differences between half- and full-duplex modes and discussed how Ethernet channel bonding can be used to attach multiple connections between Ethernet devices.

I finished the chapter with a description of the common Ethernet cable types used in today's networks. And by the way, you'd be wise to study that section really well!

Exam Essentials

Understand basic Ethernet communication.   Know how hosts use hardware addresses to communicate on an Ethernet LAN.

Understand Ethernet addressing.   Know the hexadecimal addressing scheme used to create an Ethernet address.

Understand binary, decimal, and hexadecimal addressing.   Know the different addressing types, and also use the written lab to practice your conversions.

Understand the basic definition of channel bonding.   Know the various ways you can use channel bonding to make your network more resilient and add bandwidth between devices.

Written Lab

In this section, you will write in the answer to the following conversion tables.

1. Convert from decimal IP address to binary format.

    Complete the following table to express 192.168.10.15 in binary format.

128	64	32	16	8	4	2	1	Binary

Complete the following table to express 172.16.20.55 in binary format.

128	64	32	16	8	4	2	1	Binary

Complete the following table to express 10.11.12.99 in binary format.

128	64	32	16	8	4	2	1	Binary

2. Convert the following from binary format to decimal IP address.

Complete the following table to express 11001100.00110011.10101010.01010101 in decimal IP address format.

128	64	32	16	8	4	2	1	Decimal

Complete the following table to express 11000110.11010011.00111001.11010001 in decimal IP address format.

128	64	32	16	8	4	2	1	Decimal

Complete the following table to express 10000100.11010010.10111000.10100110 in decimal IP address format.

128	64	32	16	8	4	2	1	Decimal

3. Convert the following from binary format to hexadecimal.

Complete the following table to express 11011000.00011011.00111101.01110110 in hexadecimal.

128	64	32	16	8	4	2	1	Hexadecimal

Complete the following table to express 11001010.11110101.10000011.11101011 in hexadecimal.

128	64	32	16	8	4	2	1	Hexadecimal

Complete the following table to express 10000100.11010010.01000011.10110011 in hexadecimal.

128	64	32	16	8	4	2	1	Hexadecimal

You can find the answers in Appendix B.

Review Questions

You can find the answers in Appendix A.

1. On an Ethernet switched network, what address does one host computer use to communicate with another?

   A. IP address

   B. MAC address

   C. Street address

   D. HUB address

2. Which of the following can run full duplex and achieve 200Mbps with CAT5e cable?

   A. 100BaseF

   B. 100BaseTX

   C. 1000BaseF

   D. 1000BaseT

3. How many devices in a collision domain have to listen when a single host talks?

   A. 2

   B. 3

   C. 1

   D. All

4. If you are using a cable medium called 100BaseTF, what does this mean?

   A. That you are running Ethernet over cable

   B. That you are running Ethernet over fiber

   C. That you are running Ethernet over ThickNet

   D. That you are bundling multiple connections

5. What protocol helps devices share the bandwidth evenly without having two devices transmit at the same time on the network medium?

   A. TCP/IP

   B. CSMA/CD

   C. HTTPS

   D. TFTP

6. What is the maximum distance of 10GBaseSR?

   A. 100 meters (328 feet)

   B. 302 meters (990 feet)

   C. 305 meters (1000 feet)

   D. 1593 km (6 miles)

7. How many wire pairs are used with half duplex?

   A. 2

   B. 1

   C. 4

   D. None of the above

8. How many wire pairs are used with 100BaseT full duplex?

   A. 2

   B. 1

   C. 4

   D. A or C

9. What is the maximum distance of 10GBaseLR?

   A. 1 mile

   B. 3 miles

   C. 6 miles

   D. 25 miles

10. What is the effective total throughput increase with a full-duplex connection?

    A. None

    B. Twice as much

    C. Four times as much

    D. Ten times as much

11. What device can you not use full-duplex communication with?

    A. Host

    B. Hub

    C. Switch

    D. Router

12. What is the decimal equivalent of this binary number:
    11000000.10101000.00110000.11110000?

    A. 192.168.48.192

    B. 192.168.48.240

    C. 192.168.64.224

    D. 192.168.32.248

13. Which technology increases the bandwidth for network transmission by joining
    together multiple connections in one logical connection?

    A. Bonding

    B. VLANs

    C. STP

    D. Traffic shaping

14. How is the decimal value 10 represented in binary?

    A. 1000

    B. 1001

    C. 1010

    D. 1011

15. What is the decimal value for the binary number 11101000?

    A. 128

    B. 194

    C. 224

    D. 232

16. What is the decimal number 10 in hexadecimal?

    A. 9

    B. A

    C. C

    D. B

17. How many bits is a MAC address?

    A. 16

    B. 32

    C. 48

    D. 64

18. What is the maximum distance of 1000BaseT?

  A. 100 meters (328 feet)

  B. 128 meters (420 feet)

  C. 1000 meters (3280 feet)

  D. 1024 meters (3360 feet)

19. What is the purpose of the Frame Check Sequence (FCS) in an Ethernet frame?

  A. Error correction

  B. Error detection

  C. Error recovery

  D. Creating errors

20. What does the *Base* mean in 100BaseTX?

  A. Broadband

  B. 100Mbps

  C. Baseband

  D. Twisted-pair at 100Mbps

Chapter

5

Networking Devices

✓ **1.2 Classify how applications, devices, and protocols relate to the OSI model layers.**

- Frames
- Packets
- Switch
- Router
- Multilayer switch
- Hub
- Encryption devices
- Cable
- NIC
- Bridge

✓ **1.4 Explain the purpose and properties of routing and switching.**

- Broadcast domain vs. collision domain

✓ **1.7 Summarize DNS concepts and its components.**

- DNS servers
- DNS records (A, MX, AAAA, CNAME, PTR)
- Dynamic DNS

✓ **2.1 Given a scenario, install and configure routers and switches.**

- Managed vs. unmanaged
- Interface configurations
  - Full duplex
  - Half duplex
  - Port speeds
  - IP addressing
- Traffic filtering
- Diagnostics

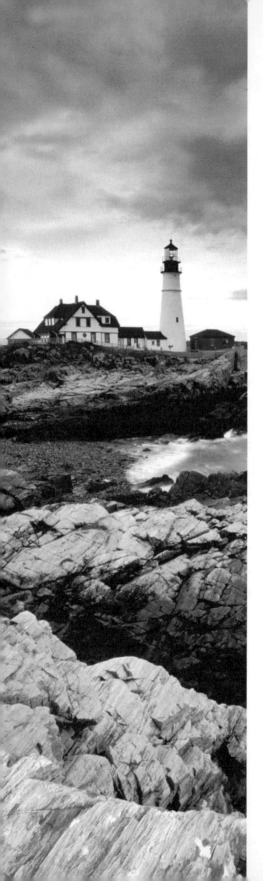

✓ **2.3 Explain the purpose and properties of DHCP.**

- Static vs. dynamic IP addressing
- Reservations
- Scopes
- Leases
- Options (DNS servers, suffixes)

✓ **2.6 Given a set of requirements, plan and implement a basic SOHO network.**

- List of requirements
- Cable length
- Device types/requirements
- Environment limitations
- Equipment limitations
- Compatibility requirements

✓ **4.1 Explain the purpose and features of various network appliances.**

- Load balancer
- Proxy server
- Content filter
- VPN concentrator

In this chapter, I'll tell you all about the networking devices I've introduced so far. I'll go into much greater detail about each device, and yes—I'm going to present even more of them to you! Because all the components that you'll learn about shortly are typically found in today's networks and internetworks, it's very important that you be familiar with them.

We'll start by covering the more common network devices that you would be most likely to come across, and then move on to discuss some of the more specialized devices that you may or may not always find running in a network.

I'll finish the chapter by using examples to discuss how routers, hubs, and switches work within internetworks today.

For up-to-the-minute updates for this chapter, please see www.lammle.com/forum or www.sybex.com/go/netplus2e.

Common Network Connectivity Devices

By now, you should be fairly savvy regarding the various types of network media and connections, so it's time to learn about some of the devices they hook up to that are commonly found on today's networks.

First, I'll define the basic terms; then, later in this chapter, I'll show you how these devices actually work within a network. At that time, I'll give you more detailed descriptions of these devices and terms used along with them.

Because these devices connect network entities, they're known as *connectivity devices*. Here's a list of the devices I'll be covering in this chapter:

- Hub
- Network Interface Card (NIC)
- Bridge
- Basic switch
- Basic router
- Basic firewall
- Dynamic Host Configuration Protocol (DHCP) server
- Other specialized devices

Hub

As you learned earlier, a *hub* is the device that connects all the segments of the network together in a star topology Ethernet network. Each device in the network connects directly to the hub through a single cable and is used to connect multiple devices without segmenting a network. Any transmission received on one port will be sent out all the other ports in the hub, including the receiving pair for the transmitting device, so that Carrier Sense Multiple Access with Collision Detection (CSMA/CD) on the transmitter can monitor for collisions.

So, basically, this means that if one station sends a broadcast, all the others will receive it; yet based on the addressing found in the frame, only the intended recipient will actually listen to it. This arrangement simulates the physical bus that the CSMA/CD standard was based on, and it's why we call the use of a hub in an Ethernet environment a physical star/logical bus topology.

Figure 5.1 depicts a typical hub as you might find it employed within a home network. Most of the time, hubs really aren't recommended for corporate networks because of their limitations.

FIGURE 5.1   A typical hub

It's important to note that hubs are nothing more than glorified repeaters that are incapable of recognizing frames and data structures—the reason why they act with such a lack of intelligence. A broadcast sent out by any device on the hub will be propagated to all devices connected to it. And just as in a physical bus topology configuration, any two or more of those connected devices have the potential of causing a collision with each other, which means that this hardware device will create a LAN with the most network traffic collisions. Hubs are not suggested in today's corporate network for this reason.

Network Interface Card

Those of you who aren't familiar with NICs probably want to be, at this point, so here goes: a *Network Interface Card* (NIC) is installed in your computer to connect, or interface, your computer to the network. It provides the physical, electrical, and electronic connections to the network media.

A NIC either is an expansion card or is built right into the computer's motherboard. The NIC usually connects to the computer through *expansion slots* located on the motherboard that allow peripherals to be plugged in directly. In some notebook computers, NIC adapters can be connected to the printer port or through a PC card slot.

Figure 5.2 shows a typical 100Mbps Ethernet NIC.

FIGURE 5.2   Network Interface Card

Nowadays, most PCs and laptops of all types come with an Ethernet connector built into the motherboard, so you usually don't need a separate card. It's also rare to find a laptop today without a built-in wireless network card, but you can buy external wireless cards for desktops and laptops if you've got legacy equipment that needs them.

NIC cards generally have one or two light-emitting diodes (LEDs) that help in diagnosing any functional problems. If there are two separate LEDs on the NIC, one of them is most likely the Link LED, which illuminates when proper connectivity to an active network has been detected. But it's not always that cut and dried—that blinking LED can mean the NIC is receiving a proper signal from the hub or switch, but it can also indicate connectivity to and detection of a carrier on a segment. Another possibility is that it's found connectivity with a router or other end device using a crossover cable.

The other LED is the aptly named Activity LED, which tends to flicker constantly. That activity indicates the intermittent transmission and reception of frames arriving at the network or leaving it.

The first LED you should verify is the Link LED because if it's not illuminated, the Activity LED simply cannot illuminate.

Bridge

A *bridge*—specifically, a transparent bridge—is a network device that connects two similar network segments together. Its primary function is to keep traffic separated on either side of the bridge, breaking up collision domains, as pictured in Figure 5.3.

FIGURE 5.3 Bridges break up collision domains.

What we can see here is that traffic is allowed to pass through the bridge only if the transmission is intended for a station on the opposite side. The main reasons you would place a bridge in your network would be to connect two segments together or to divide a busy network into two segments.

Bridges are software based; so, interestingly, you can think of a switch as a hardware-based, multiport bridge. In fact, the terms, *bridge* and *switch* are often used interchangeably because the two devices used basically the same bridging technologies. The past tense is there for a reason—you'd be hard-pressed to buy a bridge today.

Switch

Switches connect multiple segments of a network together much like hubs do, but with three significant differences—a switch recognizes frames and pays attention to the source and destination MAC address of the incoming frame as well as the port on which it was received. Hubs don't do those things. They simply send anything they receive on one port out to all the others.

So, if a switch determines that a frame's final destination happens to be on a segment that's connected via a different port than the one on which the frame was received, the switch will only forward the frame out from the specific port on which its destination is located. If the switch can't figure out the location of the frame's destination, it will flood the frame out every port except the one on which the frame port was received.

Figure 5.4 shows a typical low-cost Ethernet switch. It looks a lot like a hub. However, switches can come in very large, expensive sizes. Switches that can perform the basic switching process and do not allow you to configure more advanced features—like adding an IP address for telnetting to the device or adding VLANs—are called unmanaged switches. Others, like Cisco switches that do allow an IP address to be configured for management with such applications as SNMP and do allow special ports to be configured (as in VoIP) are called managed switches.

FIGURE 5.4   Typical Ethernet switch

That's as far as we're going with switches right now. I'll bring them up later on in this chapter and cover them in much greater detail in Chapter 11, "Switching and Virtual LANs." For now, you can think of a switch as a faster, smarter bridge that has more ports.

 Switches are a Layer 2 device, which means they segment the network with MAC addresses. If you see the term "Layer 3 switch," that means you are talking about a router, not a Layer 2 switch. The terms router and Layer 3 switch are interchangeable.

Router

A *router* is a network device used to connect many, sometimes disparate, network segments together, combining them into what we call an *internetwork*. A well-configured router can make intelligent decisions about the best way to get network data to its destination. It gathers the information it needs to make these decisions based on a network's particular performance data.

Figure 5.5 shows a Small Office, Home Office (SOHO) router that provides wired and wireless access for hosts and connects them to the Internet without any necessary configuration. But know that I certainly don't recommend leaving a router with the default configuration! No worries, though—I'll go over the configuration process with you in Chapter 10, "Routing Protocols."

Routers can be multifaceted devices that behave like computers unto themselves with their own complex operating systems—for example, Cisco's IOS. You can even think of them as CPUs that are totally dedicated to the process of routing packets. And due to their complexity and flexibility, you can configure them to actually perform the functions of other types of network devices (like firewalls, for example) by simply implementing a specific feature within the router's software.

FIGURE 5.5   Router connected to the Internet, providing access for hosts

 Routers can have many different names: Layer 3 switch and multilayer switch are the most common, besides the name router, of course. Remember, if you just hear the word "switch," that means a Layer 2 device. Routers, Layer 3 switches, and multilayer switches are all Layer 3 devices.

Interface Configurations

When configuring interfaces on a router or switch, unless you're doing complex configurations such as connecting up a Voice over IP (VoIP) network, the interface configurations are pretty straightforward.

There is a major difference between a router interface and a switch interface configuration, however. On a switch, you do not add an IP address since they only read to Layer 2, and most of the time, you never even need to configure a switch interface. First, they are enabled by default, and second, they are very good at auto-detecting the speed, duplex, and in newer switches, even the Ethernet cable type (crossover or straight through). A router is much different and an IP address is expected on each interface; they are not enabled by default, and a good Layer 3 network design must be considered before installing a router.

Let's start by taking a look at a basic Cisco switch configuration. First, notice by the output shown that there is no configuration on the interfaces, but yet you can plug this switch into your network and it would work. This is because all ports are enabled and there are some very basic configurations that allow the switch to run without any configuration—they can be considered plug-and-play in a small or home network.

```
Switch#sh running-config
[output cut]
!
interface FastEthernet0/1
!
interface FastEthernet0/2
!
interface FastEthernet0/3
!
interface FastEthernet0/4
!
interface FastEthernet0/5
!
interface FastEthernet0/6
!
interface FastEthernet0/7
!
interface FastEthernet0/8
!
```

Let's take a look at a configuration of a simple switch interface. First we'll notice the duplex options:

```
Switch(config-if)#duplex ?
   auto  Enable AUTO duplex configuration
   full  Force full duplex operation
   half  Force half-duplex operation
```

All switch ports are set to duplex auto by default, and usually you can just leave this configuration alone. However, be aware that if your Network Interface Card is set to half-duplex and the switch port is configured for full-duplex, the port will receive errors and you'll eventually get a call from the user. This is why it is advised to just leave the defaults on your hosts and switch ports, but it is a troubleshooting spot to check when a problem is reported from a single user.

The next configuration and/or troubleshooting spot you may need to consider is the speed of the port.

```
Switch(config-if)#speed ?
  10    Force 10 Mbps operation
  100   Force 100 Mbps operation
  auto  Enable AUTO speed configuration
```

Again, this is set to auto, but you may want to force the port to be 100 and full-duplex. Typically, the NIC will run this without a problem and you'll be sure you're getting the most bang for your buck on your switch port.

Let's take a look at a router interface. We're pretty much going to configure (or not configure) the same parameters. However, you should be very aware that a router interface and a switch interface perform different functions. A router interface will break up collisions domains just as a switch interface does, but the purpose of a router interface is to create and maintain broadcast domains and connectivity of WAN services. Basic Layer 2 switches cannot do these services. As I mentioned, you must have a Layer 3 design before you can implement a router, meaning you must have your subnet design laid out on your network diagram and your IP addressing scheme must be completely understood. You cannot start configuring router interfaces randomly, there must be a design and it needs to be correct.

Unlike switches, router interfaces do not just work when you plug them into the network—they must be configured and enabled. All ports are shut down by default and why shouldn't they be? Unless you have a network design and understand IP addressing, what good is a router to your network?

Let's take a look:

```
Router(config-if)#duplex ?
  auto  Enable AUTO duplex configuration
  full  Force full duplex operation
  half  Force half-duplex operation
```

```
Router(config-if)#speed ?
  10    Force 10 Mbps operation
  100   Force 100 Mbps operation
  auto  Enable AUTO speed configuration
```

```
Router(config-if)#ip address ?
  A.B.C.D  IP address
  dhcp     IP Address negotiated via DHCP
  pool     IP Address autoconfigured from a local DHCP pool
```

First we can see that the basics are there, duplex and speed, but also to make a router interface useful at all we must add an IP address. Notice the options allow you to configure a specific IP address or allow the interface to receive the address for the interface from a

DHCP server. You would only use this option if you had an IP address reservation for the router interface on your DHCP server since having your router get a random IP address from a DHCP server would be hard to manage. Let's finish the basics:

```
Router(config-if)#ip address 1.1.1.1 255.0.0.0
Router(config-if)#no shutdown
Router(config-if)#
*Oct  5 17:26:46.522: %LINK-3-UPDOWN: Interface FastEthernet0/0, changed state
to up
*Oct  5 17:26:47.522: %LINEPROTO-5-UPDOWN: Line protocol on Interface
FastEthernet0/0, changed state to up
```

The interface can now be connected to a Layer 2 switch and the hosts connected to the same broadcast domain must set their default gateway address to 1.1.1.1, and viola, they can now send packets to the router.

Firewall

So what, exactly, is a *firewall*? Basically, firewalls are your network's security guards; and to be real, they're probably the most important thing to implement on your network. That's because today's networks are almost always connected to the Internet—a situation that makes security crucial! A firewall protects your LAN resources from invaders that prowl the Internet for unprotected networks, while simultaneously preventing all or some of your LAN's computers from accessing certain services on the Internet. You can employ them to filter packets based on rules that you or the network administrator create and configure to strictly delimit the type of information allowed to flow in and out of the network's Internet connection.

A firewall can be either a stand-alone "black box" or a software implementation placed on a server or router. Either way, the firewall will have at least two network connections: one to the Internet (known as the *public* side) and one to the network (known as the *private* side). Sometimes, there is a second firewall, as shown in Figure 5.6. This firewall is used to connect servers and equipment that can be considered both public and private (like web and email servers). This intermediary network is known as a *demilitarized zone (DMZ)*.

FIGURE 5.6   Example of firewalls with a DMZ

Firewalls are the first line of defense for an Internet-connected network. Without them in place, any network that's connected to the Internet is essentially wide open to anyone with a little technical savvy who seeks to exploit LAN resources and/or access your network's sensitive information.

Dynamic Host Configuration Protocol Server

Even though I'm going to get into the finer points of DHCP soon, in Chapter 6, "Introduction to the Internet Protocol," I want to give you some basic insight into this server service here.

In essence, DHCP servers assign IP addresses to hosts. This protocol gives us a much easier way to administrate—by automatically providing IP information—than the alternative and tedious method known as static IP addressing, where we have to address each host manually. It works well in any network environment, from tiny to huge, and allows all types of hardware to be employed as a DHCP server, including routers.

It works like this: A DHCP server receives a request for IP information from a DHCP client using a broadcast (as Chapter 6 will show you in detail). The only hitch is that if the DHCP server isn't on the same segment as the DHCP client, the broadcast won't be received by the server because by default, routers won't forward broadcasts, as shown in Figure 5.7.

FIGURE 5.7   DHCP client sends broadcasts looking for a DHCP server

In Figure 5.7, Router A is configured with the IP helper address command on interface E0 of the router. Whenever interface E0 receives a broadcast request, Router A will forward those requests as a unicast (meaning instead of a broadcast, the packet now has the destination IP address of the DHCP server).

So, as shown in the figure, you can configure Router A to forward these requests and even use multiple DHCP servers for redundancy, if needed. This works because the router has been configured to forward the request to a single server using a unicast or by sending the request to multiple servers via a directed broadcast.

Personally, most of the time I use a Windows server to act as the DHCP server for my entire internetwork and have my routers forward client requests. It is possible to have a DHCP server on every network segment, but that is not necessary because of the routers' forwarding ability.

Figure 5.8 shows a picture of a Windows server with something called Scope Options.

FIGURE 5.8 A Windows DHCP server's Scope Options

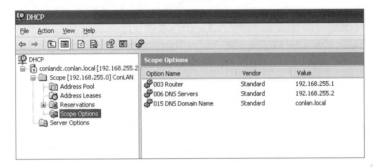

Scope Options provide IP configuration for hosts on a specific subnet. Below the Scope Options, you'll find Server Options, which provide IP information for all scopes configured on the server. If I had just one Domain Name Service (DNS) server for the entire network, I'd configure the Server Options with my DNS server information; that DNS server information would then show up automatically in all scopes configured on my server.

So, what exactly does a DHCP client ask for, and what does a DHCP server provide? Is it just an IP address, a mask, and a default gateway? No, it is much more than that. Let's take a look at a DHCP client request on an analyzer. Figure 5.9 shows the options that the client is requesting from the DHCP server.

First, you can see that the DHCP service runs on top of the BootP protocol (port 68) and that the DHCP client is looking for a BootP server (port 67). The client IP address is 0.0.0.0, and the client doesn't know the DHCP server address either because this is a broadcast to 255.255.255.255 (the Data Link layer broadcast shows ff:ff:ff:ff:ff:ff). Basically, all the DHCP client knows for sure is its own MAC address.

The DHCP client Parameter Request List option shown at the end of Figure 5.9 has been expanded and is shown in Figure 5.10. The client is "requesting" a certain IP address because this is the IP address it received from the server the last time it requested an IP address.

FIGURE 5.9   DHCP client request to a DHCP server

```
⊞ Frame 33 (344 bytes on wire, 344 bytes captured)
⊞ Ethernet II, Src: Usi_d0:e9:35 (00:1e:37:d0:e9:35), Dst: Broadcast (ff:ff:ff:ff:ff:ff)
⊞ Internet Protocol, Src: 0.0.0.0 (0.0.0.0), Dst: 255.255.255.255 (255.255.255.255)
⊞ User Datagram Protocol, Src Port: bootpc (68), Dst Port: bootps (67)
⊟ Bootstrap Protocol
     Message type: Boot Request (1)
     Hardware type: Ethernet
     Hardware address length: 6
     Hops: 0
     Transaction ID: 0xb16f1532
     Seconds elapsed: 0
  ⊞ Bootp flags: 0x8000 (Broadcast)
     Client IP address: 0.0.0.0 (0.0.0.0)
     Your (client) IP address: 0.0.0.0 (0.0.0.0)
     Next server IP address: 0.0.0.0 (0.0.0.0)
     Relay agent IP address: 0.0.0.0 (0.0.0.0)
     Client MAC address: Usi_d0:e9:35 (00:1e:37:d0:e9:35)
     Server host name not given
     Boot file name not given
     Magic cookie: (OK)
  ⊞ Option: (t=53,l=1) DHCP Message Type = DHCP Discover
  ⊞ Option: (t=116,l=1) DHCP Auto-Configuration
  ⊞ Option: (t=61,l=7) Client identifier
  ⊞ Option: (t=50,l=4) Requested IP Address = 10.100.36.38
  ⊞ Option: (t=12,l=14) Host Name = "globalnet-todd"
  ⊞ Option: (t=60,l=8) Vendor class identifier = "MSFT 5.0"
  ⊞ Option: (t=55,l=12) Parameter Request List
     End Option
```

FIGURE 5.10   DHCP client parameter request list

```
⊟ Option: (t=55,l=12) Parameter Request List
     Option: (55) Parameter Request List
     Length: 12
     Value: 010F03062C2E2F1F2179F92B
     1 = Subnet Mask
     15 = Domain Name
     3 = Router
     6 = Domain Name Server
     44 = NetBIOS over TCP/IP Name Server
     46 = NetBIOS over TCP/IP Node Type
     47 = NetBIOS over TCP/IP Scope
     31 = Perform Router Discover
     33 = Static Route
     121 = Classless Static Route
     249 = Classless Static Route (Microsoft)
     43 = Vendor-Specific Information
  End Option
```

That is quite a request list! The DHCP server will respond with the options that it has configured and available to provide to a DHCP client. Let's take a look and see what the server responds with. Figure 5.11 shows the DHCP server response.

The client is going to get the IP address that it asked for (10.100.36.38), a subnet mask of 255.255.255.224, a lease time of 23 hours (the amount of time before the IP address and other DHCP information expires on the client), the IP address of the DHCP server, the default gateway (router), the DNS server IP address (it gets two), the domain name used by DNS, and some NetBIOS information (used by Windows for name resolution).

The lease time is important and can even be used to tell you if you have a DHCP problem, or more specifically, that the DHCP server is no longer handing out IP addresses to hosts. If hosts start failing to get onto the network one at a time as they try to get a new IP address as their lease time expires, you need to check your server settings.

FIGURE 5.11   DHCP server response

```
⊞ Frame 34 (359 bytes on wire, 359 bytes captured)
⊞ Ethernet II, Src: Cisco_90:ed:80 (00:0b:5f:90:ed:80), Dst: Broadcast (ff:ff:ff:ff:ff:ff)
⊞ Internet Protocol, Src: 10.100.36.33 (10.100.36.33), Dst: 255.255.255.255 (255.255.255.255)
⊞ User Datagram Protocol, Src Port: bootps (67), Dst Port: bootpc (68)
⊟ Bootstrap Protocol
    Message type: Boot Reply (2)
    Hardware type: Ethernet
    Hardware address length: 6
    Hops: 0
    Transaction ID: 0xb16f1532
    Seconds elapsed: 0
  ⊞ Bootp flags: 0x8000 (Broadcast)
    Client IP address: 0.0.0.0 (0.0.0.0)
    Your (client) IP address: 10.100.36.38 (10.100.36.38)
    Next server IP address: 10.100.36.12 (10.100.36.12)
    Relay agent IP address: 10.100.36.33 (10.100.36.33)
    Client MAC address: Usi_d0:e9:35 (00:1e:37:d0:e9:35)
    Server host name not given
    Boot file name not given
    Magic cookie: (OK)
  ⊞ Option: (t=53,l=1) DHCP Message Type = DHCP Offer
  ⊞ Option: (t=1,l=4) Subnet Mask = 255.255.255.224
  ⊞ Option: (t=58,l=4) Renewal Time Value = 11 hours, 30 minutes
  ⊞ Option: (t=59,l=4) Rebinding Time Value = 20 hours, 7 minutes, 30 seconds
  ⊞ Option: (t=51,l=4) IP Address Lease Time = 23 hours
  ⊞ Option: (t=54,l=4) Server Identifier = 10.100.36.12
  ⊞ Option: (t=15,l=16) Domain Name = "globalnet.local"
  ⊞ Option: (t=3,l=4) Router = 10.100.36.33
  ⊞ Option: (t=6,l=8) Domain Name Server
  ⊞ Option: (t=44,l=4) NetBIOS over TCP/IP Name Server = 10.100.36.13
  ⊞ Option: (t=46,l=1) NetBIOS over TCP/IP Node Type = H-node
    End Option
```

Here is another example of a possible DHCP problem: you arrive at work after a weekend where some hosts were left on and some were shut down. The hosts that were left running and not shut down are still working, but the hosts that were shut down and were restarted on Monday morning do not get a new IP address. This is a good indication that you need to head over to your DHCP server and take a look at what is going on.

A DHCP server can also be configured with a reservation list so that a host always receives the same IP address. You would use this reservation list for routers or servers if they were not statically assigned. However, you can use reservation lists for any host on your network as well.

Other Specialized Devices

In addition to the network connectivity devices I've discussed with you, there are several devices that, while they may not be directly connected to a network, do actively participate in moving network data. Here's a list of them:

- Multilayer switch
- Load balancer
- DNS server
- Proxy server

- Encryption devices
- Content filter
- VPN concentrator

Multilayer Switch

A *multilayer switch* (MLS) is a computer networking device that switches on Open Systems Interconnection (OSI) Layer 2 like an ordinary network switch but provides routing. A 24 port MLS gives you the best of both worlds. It operates at Layer 3 (routing) while still providing 24 collision domains which a router could not do.

The major difference between the packet-switching operation of a router and that of a Layer 3 or multilayer switch lies in the physical implementation. In routers, packet switching takes place using a microprocessor, whereas a Layer 3 switch handles this by using application-specific integrated circuit (ASIC) hardware. I'd show you a picture of a Layer 3 switch, but they look just like regular Layer 2 switches and you already know what those look like. The differences are the hardware inside and the operating system.

Load Balancer

Your average router just sends incoming packets to their specified, correlative IP address on the network; but a *load balancer* can actually send incoming packets to multiple machines hidden behind one IP address—cool, right?

Today's load-balancing routers follow various rules to determine specifically how they will route network traffic. Depending on your needs, you can set rules based on the least load, fault tolerance, the fastest response times, or just dividing up (balancing) outbound requests for smooth network operations.

In fact, the fault tolerance, or redundancy, as well as the scalability so vital to large networking environments and e-commerce include some of the great benefits we gain using load balancers.

Think about this scenario: Say you have a website where people are placing orders for the stuff you've got for sale. Obviously, the orders placed vary in size and the rate at which they come in varies; and you definitely wouldn't want your servers becoming so overloaded that they hose up and crash your site, causing you to lose lots of money, now would you? That's where balancing the load of traffic between a group of servers comes to the rescue, because even if one of them freezes, your customers will still be able to access your site and place orders.

Domain Name Service Server

A *Domain Name Service (DNS) server* is one of the most important servers in your network and on the Internet as well. Why? Because without a DNS server, you would have to type `http://206.123.114.186` instead of simply entering `www.lammle.com`. So it follows that you can pretty much think of the DNS system as the phone book of the Internet.

A host name is typically the name of a device that has a specific IP address; on the Internet, it is part of what is known as a fully qualified domain name (FQDN). An FQDN consists of a host name and a domain name.

The process of finding the IP address for any given host name is known as *name resolution*, and it can be performed in several ways: a HOSTS file (meaning you statically type in all names and IP addresses on each and every host), a request broadcast on the local network (Microsoft's favorite—why ask a server when you can just broadcast, right?), DNS, and Microsoft's Windows Internet Naming Service (WINS). DNS is the most popular today and is the resolution method you really need to know.

On the Internet, domains are arranged in a hierarchical tree structure. The following list includes some of the top-level domains currently in use:

`.com` A commercial organization. Most companies end up as part of this domain.

`.edu` An educational establishment, such as a university.

`.gov` A branch of the U.S. government.

`.int` An international organization, such as NATO or the United Nations.

`.mil` A branch of the U.S. military.

`.net` A network organization.

`.org` A nonprofit organization.

Your local ISP is probably a member of the `.net` domain, and your company is probably part of the `.com` domain. The `.gov` and `.mil` domains are reserved strictly for use by the government and the military within the United States. In other parts of the world, the final part of a domain name represents the country in which the server is located (`.ca` for Canada, `.jp` for Japan, `.uk` for Great Britain, and `.ru` for Russia, for example). Well over 130 countries are represented on the Internet.

The `.com` domain is by far the largest, followed by the `.edu` domain. Some new domain names are becoming popular, however, because of the increasing number of domain-name requests. These include `.firm` for businesses and companies, `.store` for businesses selling goods rather than services, `.arts` for cultural and entertainment organizations, and `.info` for informational services. The domains `.cc`, `.biz`, `.travel`, and `.post` are also in use on the Internet.

Let's see how a basic DNS server works in your network. Figure 5.12 shows how, when you type in a human name, the DNS server resolves it, allowing the host to send the HTTP packets to the server.

This DOS screen shows how the DNS server can resolve the human name to the IP address of the `Lammle.com` server when I ping the server by the name instead of the IP address.

It should be easy to imagine how hard life would be without DNS translating human names to IP addresses, routing your packet through the Internet, or internetwork to get to your servers. Figure 5.13 gives you an example of a Windows server configured as a DNS server.

Now the hosts can receive the IP address of this DNS server, and then this server will resolve host names to correct IP address. This is a mission-critical service in today's networks, don't you think? As shown in Figure 5.13, if I ping from a host to conlanpc1, the host will send the name-resolution request to the DNS server and translate this name to IP address 192.168.255.8.

FIGURE 5.12   DNS resolution example

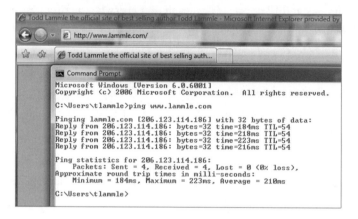

FIGURE 5.13   A Windows DNS server

Host (A) is called an A record and is what gives you the IP address of a domain or host. In IPv6, it's called a quad-A or AAAA record. As shown in Figure 5.13, you can see that each name has an A record, which is associated to an IP address. So, "A" records resolve hostnames to IP addresses, but what happens if you know the IP address and want to know the hostname? There is a record for this too! It's called the pointer record (PTR).

Other typical records found on DNS servers are *mail exchanger (MX) records*, which are used to translate mail records. The MX record points to the mail exchanger for a particular host. DNS is structured so that you can actually specify several mail exchangers for one host. This feature provides a higher probability that email will arrive at its intended destination. The mail exchangers are listed in order in the record, with a priority code that indicates the order in which they should be accessed by other mail-delivery systems.

If the first-priority mail exchanger doesn't respond in a given amount of time, the mail-delivery system tries the second one, and so on. Here are some sample mail-exchange records:

```
hostname.company.com.    IN    MX    10 mail.company.com.
hostname.company.com.    IN    MX    20 mail2.company.com.
hostname.company.com.    IN    MX    30 mail3.company.com.
```

In this example, if the first mail exchanger, `mail.company.com`, does not respond, the second one, `mail2.company.com`, is tried, and so on.

Another important record type on a DNS is the canonical name *(CNAME) record*. This is also commonly known as the *alias record* and allows hosts to have more than one name. For example, suppose your web server has the host name www, and you want that machine to also have the name ftp so that users can use FTP to access a different portion of the file system as an FTP root. You can accomplish this with a CNAME record. Given that you already have an address record established for the host name www, a CNAME record that adds ftp as a host name would look something like this:

```
www.company.com.    IN    A        204.176.47.2
ftp.company.com.    IN    CNAME    www.company.com.
```

When you put all these record types together in a zone file, or DNS table, it might look like this:

```
mail.company.com.        IN    A        204.176.47.9
mail2.company.com.       IN    A        204.176.47.21
mail3.company.com.       IN    A        204.176.47.89
yourhost.company.com.    IN    MX       10 mail.company.com.
yourhost.company.com.    IN    MX       20 mail2.company.com.
yourhost.company.com.    IN    MX       30 mail3.company.com.
www.company.com.         IN    A        204.176.47.2
ftp.company.com.         IN    CNAME    www.company.com.
```

Finally two other record types you should know about include AAAA (for authentication servers such as RADIUS or TACACS+) and PTR or pointer records. PTR records are an IP address to name mapping rather than a name to IP address mapping. They reside in what is called a *reverse lookup zone* (or table) in the server and are used when an IP address is known but not a name.

Let's take a look a tad deeper for a minute into how resolution takes place between a host and a DNS server. Figure 5.14 shows a DNS query from my host to www.lammle.com from a browser.

FIGURE 5.14 A DNS query to www.lammle.com

```
⊞ Frame 119 (74 bytes on wire, 74 bytes captured)
⊞ Ethernet II, Src: Cisco_3c:78:00 (00:05:9a:3c:78:00), Dst: 00:00:00_00:00:00 (00:00:00:00:00:00)
⊞ Internet Protocol, Src: 10.100.10.55 (10.100.10.55), Dst: 10.100.36.12 (10.100.36.12)
⊞ User Datagram Protocol, Src Port: 62595 (62595), Dst Port: domain (53)
⊟ Domain Name System (query)
     Transaction ID: 0x6e64
   ⊞ Flags: 0x0100 (Standard query)
     Questions: 1
     Answer RRs: 0
     Authority RRs: 0
     Additional RRs: 0
   ⊟ Queries
      ⊟ www.lammle.com: type A, class IN
          Name: www.lammle.com
          Type: A (Host address)
          Class: IN (0x0001)
```

This figure shows that DNS uses User Datagram Protocol (UDP) at the Transport layer (it uses Transport Control Protocol [TCP] if it is updating its phone book pages—we call these *zone updates*), and this query is asking destination port 53 (the DNS service) on host 10.100.36.13 who the heck www.lammle.com is.

Let's take a look at the server's response. Figure 5.15 shows the DNS answer to our query for www.lammle.com.

FIGURE 5.15 The DNS answer to our query

```
⊞ Frame 36 (104 bytes on wire, 104 bytes captured)
⊞ Ethernet II, Src: Cisco_90:ed:80 (00:0b:5f:90:ed:80), Dst: Usi_d0:e9:35 (00:1e:37:d0:e9:35)
⊞ Internet Protocol, Src: 10.100.36.13 (10.100.36.13), Dst: 10.100.36.38 (10.100.36.38)
⊞ User Datagram Protocol, Src Port: domain (53), Dst Port: 59259 (59259)
⊟ Domain Name System (response)
     [Request In: 35]
     [Time: 0.000302000 seconds]
     Transaction ID: 0x070e
   ⊞ Flags: 0x8180 (Standard query response, No error)
     Questions: 1
     Answer RRs: 2
     Authority RRs: 0
     Additional RRs: 0
   ⊟ Queries
      ⊟ www.lammle.com: type A, class IN
          Name: www.lammle.com
          Type: A (Host address)
          Class: IN (0x0001)
   ⊟ Answers
      ⊠ www.lammle.com: type CNAME, class IN, cname lammle.com
      ⊟ lammle.com: type A, class IN, addr 206.123.114.186
          Name: lammle.com
          Type: A (Host address)
          Class: IN (0x0001)
          Time to live: 3 hours, 6 minutes, 27 seconds
          Data length: 4
          Addr: 206.123.114.186
```

Port 53 answered from server 10.100.36.13 with the IP address of 206.123.114.186. My host can now go to that server requesting HTTP pages using the IP address.

Dynamic DNS

At one time all DNS records had to be manually entered into the DNS server and edited manually when changes occurred. Today DNS is dynamic and works in concert with the DHCP function. Hosts register their names with the DNS sever as they receive their IP address configuration from the DHCP server. Some older operating systems are nor capable of self-registration (such as Windows NT) but the DHCP server can even be configured to perform registration on behalf of these clients with the DNS server.

This doesn't mean that manual records cannot be created if desired. In fact some of the record types we have discussed can only be created manually. These include MX and CNAME records.

Proxy Server

A *proxy server* is basically a type of server that handles its client-machine requests by forwarding them on to other servers while allowing granular control over the traffic between the local LAN and the Internet. When it receives a request, the proxy will then connect to the specific server that can fulfill the request for the client that wants it.

Sometimes the proxy modifies the client's request or a server's response to it—or even handles the client's request itself. It will actually cache or "remember" the specific server that would have normally been contacted for the request in case it's needed another time. This behavior really speeds up the network's function, thereby optimizing its performance. However, proxy servers can also limit the availability of the types of sites that users on a LAN have access to, which is a benefit for an administrator of the network if users are constantly connected to nonwork sites and using all the WAN bandwidth.

Figure 5.16 shows where a proxy server would be typically found in a small to medium-size network.

There are two main types of proxy servers you'll typically find working in present-day networks:

Caching proxy server   A caching proxy server speeds up the network's service requests by recovering information from a client's or clients' earlier request. Caching proxies keep local copies of the resources requested often, which really helps minimize the upstream use of bandwidth. These servers can greatly enhance network performance.

Web proxy server   A web proxy server is usually used to create a web cache. You experience this when you Google a site you've visited before. The web proxy "remembers" you, and the site not only loads faster, but sometimes even recalls your personal information by automatically filling in your username—or even your billing/shipping information when you place another order.

FIGURE 5.16   A proxy server

Encryption Devices

Although a number of the devices we have discussed earlier can perform encryption services, there are appliances that can perform encryption. The advantage of using these devices is that they normally provide more choice of encryption methods and stronger encryption options. They also offload the process from other devices like routers and servers, which is a good thing since the encryption /decryption process is very processer intensive and interferes with other functions that those routers and servers might be performing.

Sometimes these devices are called encryption gateways. They can either sit in line with a server or a local network, encrypting and decrypting all traffic, or they can function as an application server, encrypting any file sent to them within a network. Examples of encryption appliances are shown in Figure 5.17.

FIGURE 5.17   Encryption appliance

While an encryption appliance is dedicated to encryption, a content filtering appliance scans the content of what goes through it and filters out specific content or content types. Dedicating a device to this process offloads the work from servers or routers that could do this but at a cost of greatly slowing the devices. Also there is usually more functionality and granular control available with a dedicated appliance.

Email is a good example of what you might run through one of these devices before the email is delivered to filter out spam and objectionable content. Another example of the use of a content filter might be to block websites based on the content of the web pages rather than on the basis of the URL or IP address. An example of a content filtering appliance is shown in Figure 5.18.

FIGURE 5.18   Content filtering appliance

VPN Concentrator

A VPN concentrator is a device that accepts multiple VPN connections from remote locations. Although this function can be performed by a router or server, as with the encryption gateways and content filtering devices discussed earlier, the same performance benefits can be derived from dedicating a device to this. Moreover, additional functionality usually comes with these devices, one of which is shown in Figure 5.19.

FIGURE 5.19   VPN concentrator

Planning and Implementing a Basic SOHO Network Using Network Segmentation

It's very likely that at some point you'll have to break up one large network into a bunch of smaller ones because user response will have dwindled to a slow crawl as the network grew and grew. With all that growth, your LAN's traffic congestion will have reached epic proportions.

Determining Requirements

When implementing a SOHO network, the first thing to be done is to identify the requirements of the network and the constraints around which you must operate. This should drive your design and device choices. An example set of requirements and constraints might be as follows:

1. Small number of computers

2. No need for Internet access

3. Need to share resources

With these constraints in mind, you might find that you need only a switch and some CAT 5E cabling for this project. There is no need for a router or firewall in this case.

Let's look at how to use the segmentation devices I have defined so far in this chapter. Here's a list of some of the nasty things that commonly cause LAN traffic congestion:

- Too many hosts in a broadcast domain

- Broadcast storms

- Multicasting

- Low bandwidth

- Adding hubs for connectivity to the network

The answer to fixing a huge but slow network is to break it up into a number of smaller networks—something called *network segmentation*. You do this by using devices like routers and switches, which are sometimes still referred to as bridges because switches still use bridging technologies. Figure 5.20 displays a network that's been segmented with a switch so each network segment connected to the switch is now a separate collision domain. But make note of the fact that this network is actually still one *broadcast domain*—the set of all devices on a network segment that hear all the broadcasts sent on that segment.

FIGURE 5.20 A switch can replace the hub, breaking up collision domains.

And keep in mind that the hub used in Figure 5.20 just extended the one collision domain from the switch port.

Routers are used to connect networks together and route packets of data from one network to another. (Cisco has become the de facto standard for routers because of its high-quality router products, great selection, and fantastic service.) Routers, by default, break up a broadcast domain. Figure 5.21 shows a router in our little network that creates an internetwork and breaks up broadcast domains.

The network in Figure 5.21 is pretty cool. Each host is connected to its own collision domain, and the router has created two broadcast domains. And don't forget that the router provides connections to WAN services as well. The router uses something called a serial interface for WAN connections: specifically, a V.35 physical interface.

FIGURE 5.21   Routers create an internetwork.

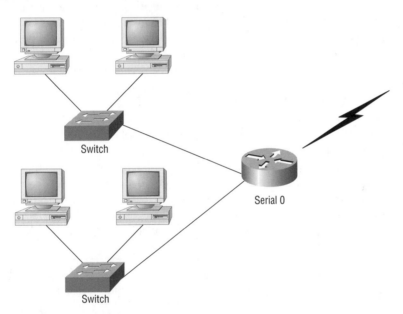

Breaking up a broadcast domain is important because when a host or server sends a network broadcast, every device on the network must read and process that broadcast—unless you've got a router. When the router's interface receives this broadcast, it can respond by basically saying, "Thanks, but no thanks," and discard the broadcast without forwarding it on to other networks. Even though routers are known for breaking up broadcast domains by default, it's important to remember that they break up collision domains as well.

There are two advantages of using routers in your network:

- They don't forward broadcasts by default.

- They can filter the network based on Layer 3 (Network layer) information (such as IP address).

Four router functions in your network can be listed as follows:

- Packet switching
- Packet filtering
- Internetwork communication
- Path selection

Remember that routers are really switches; they're actually what we call Layer 3 switches. Unlike Layer 2 switches, which forward or filter frames, routers (Layer 3 switches) use logical addressing and provide what is called *packet switching*. Routers can also provide packet filtering by using access lists; and when routers connect two or more networks together and use logical addressing (IP or IPv6), this is called an *internetwork*. Last, routers use a *routing table* (map of the internetwork) to make path selections and to forward packets to remote networks.

Conversely, switches aren't used to create internetworks (they do not break up broadcast domains by default); they're employed to add functionality to a network LAN. The main purpose of a switch is to make a LAN work better—to optimize its performance—providing more bandwidth for the LAN's users. And switches don't forward packets to other networks as routers do. Instead, they only "switch" frames from one port to another within the switched network. Okay, you may be thinking, "Wait a minute, what are frames and packets?" I'll tell you all about them later in this chapter, I promise.

By default, switches break up collision domains, as mentioned in Chapter 4, "The Current Ethernet Specifications." This is an Ethernet term used to describe a network scenario wherein one particular device sends a packet on a network segment, forcing every other device on that same segment to pay attention to it. At the same time, a different device tries to transmit, leading to a collision, after which both devices must retransmit, one at a time. Not very efficient! This situation is typically found in a hub environment where each host segment connects to a hub that represents only one collision domain and only one broadcast domain. By contrast, each and every port on a switch represents its own collision domain.

 Switches create separate collision domains but a single broadcast domain. Routers provide a separate broadcast domain for each interface.

The term *bridging* was introduced before routers and hubs were implemented, so it's pretty common to hear people referring to bridges as switches. That's because bridges and switches basically do the same thing—break up collision domains on a LAN (in reality, you cannot buy a physical bridge these days, only LAN switches; but these switches use bridging technologies, so Cisco still calls them multiport bridges).

So this means a switch is basically just a multiple-port bridge with more brainpower, right? Well, pretty much, but there are differences. Switches do provide this function, but they do so with greatly enhanced management ability and features. Plus, most of the time, bridges only had two or four ports. Yes, you could get your hands on a bridge with up to 16 ports, but that's nothing compared to the hundreds available on some switches.

You would use a bridge in a network to reduce collisions within broadcast domains and to increase the number of collision domains in your network. Doing this provides more bandwidth for users. And keep in mind that using hubs in your network can contribute to congestion on your Ethernet network. As always, plan your network design carefully!

Figure 5.22 shows how a network would look with all these internetwork devices in place. Remember that the router will not only break up broadcast domains for every LAN interface but also break up collision domains.

When you look at Figure 5.22, do you see the router at center stage and see how it connects each physical network together? We have to use this layout because of the older technologies involved—bridges and hubs.

FIGURE 5.22   Internetworking devices

On the top internetwork in Figure 5.22, you'll notice that a bridge is used to connect the hubs to a router. The bridge breaks up collision domains, but all the hosts connected to both hubs are still crammed into the same broadcast domain. Also, the bridge creates only two collision domains, so each device connected to a hub is in the same collision domain as every other device connected to that same hub. This is actually pretty lame, but it's still better than having one collision domain for all hosts.

Notice something else: The three hubs at the bottom that are connected also connect to the router, creating one collision domain and one broadcast domain. This makes the bridged network look much better indeed.

 Although bridges/switches are used to segment networks, they will not isolate broadcast or multicast packets.

The best network connected to the router is the LAN switch network on the left. Why? Because each port on that switch breaks up collision domains. But it's not all good—all devices are still in the same broadcast domain. Do you remember why this can be a really bad thing? Because all devices must listen to all broadcasts transmitted, that's why. And if your broadcast domains are too large, the users have less bandwidth and are required to process more broadcasts, and network response time will slow to a level that could cause office riots.

Once we have only switches in our network, things change a lot. Figure 5.23 shows the network that is typically found today.

FIGURE 5.23   Switched networks creating an internetwork

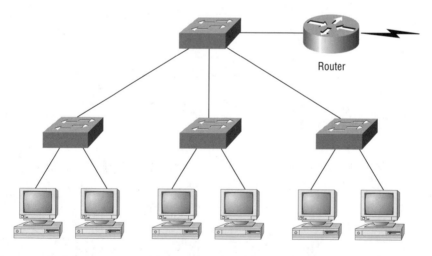

Router

Here I've placed the LAN switches at the center of the network world so the router is connecting only logical networks together. If I implement this kind of setup, I've created virtual LANs (VLANs), something I'm going to tell you about in Chapter 11. So don't stress. But it is really important to understand that even though you have a switched network, you still need a router to provide your inter-VLAN communication, or internetworking. Don't forget that.

Obviously, the best network is one that's correctly configured to meet the business require-ments of the company it serves. LAN switches with routers, correctly placed in the network, are the best network design. This book will help you understand the basics of routers and switches so you can make tight, informed decisions on a case-by-case basis.

Let's go back to Figure 5.22 again. Looking at the figure, how many collision domains and broadcast domains are in this internetwork? I hope you answered nine collision domains and three broadcast domains.

The broadcast domains are definitely the easiest to see because only routers break up broadcast domains by default. And because there are three connections, that gives you three broadcast domains. But do you see the nine collision domains? Just in case that's a no, I'll explain. The all-hub network is one collision domain; the bridge network equals three col-lision domains. Add in the switch network of five collision domains—one for each switch port—and you've got a total of nine.

Now, in Figure 5.23, each port on the switch is a separate collision domain and each VLAN is a separate broadcast domain. But you still need a router for routing between VLANs. How many collision domains do you see here? I'm counting 10— remember that connections between the switches are considered a collision domain.

Real World Scenario

Should I Replace All My Hubs with Switches?

You're a network administrator at a large company in San Jose. The boss comes to you and says that he got your requisition to buy a switch and is not sure about approving the expense; do you really need it?

Well, if you can, sure—why not? Switches really add a lot of functionality to a network that hubs just don't have. But most of us don't have an unlimited budget. Hubs still can create a nice network—that is, of course, if you design and implement the network correctly.

Let's say that you have 40 users plugged into four hubs, 10 users each. At this point, the hubs are all connected together so that you have one large collision domain and one large broadcast domain. If you can afford to buy just one switch and plug each hub into a switch port, as well as plug the servers into the switch, then you now have four collision domains and one broadcast domain. Not great; but for the price of one switch, your network is a much better thing. So, go ahead! Put that requisition in to buy all new switches. What do you have to lose?

So now that you've gotten an introduction to internetworking and the various devices that live in an internetwork, it's time to head into internetworking models.

As I mentioned earlier, routers break up broadcast domains, which means that by default, broadcasts aren't forwarded through a router. Do you remember why this is a good thing? Routers break up collision domains, but you can also do that using Layer 2

(Data Link layer) switches. Because each interface in a router represents a separate network, it must be assigned unique network identification numbers, and each host on the network connected to that router must use the same network number. Figure 5.24 shows how a router works in an internetwork.

FIGURE 5.24   A router in an internetwork

Here are some points about routers that you should commit to memory:

- Routers, by default, will not forward any broadcast or multicast packets.
- Routers use the logical address in a Network-layer header to determine the next hop router to forward the packet to.
- Routers can use access lists, created by an administrator, to control security on the types of packets that are allowed to enter or exit an interface.
- Routers can provide Layer 2 bridging functions if needed and can simultaneously route through the same interface.
- Layer 3 devices (routers, in this case) provide connections between virtual LANs (VLANs).
- Routers can provide quality of service (QoS) for specific types of network traffic.

Switching and VLANs are covered in Chapter 11.

Switches and Bridges at the Data Link Layer

Layer 2 switching is considered hardware-based bridging because it uses specialized hardware called an *application-specific integrated circuit (ASIC)*. ASICs can run up to gigabit speeds with very low latency rates.

Latency is the time measured from when a frame enters a port to the time it exits a port.

Bridges and switches read each frame as it passes through the network. The Layer 2 device then puts the source hardware address in a filter table and keeps track of which port the frame was received on. This information (logged in the bridge's or switch's filter table) is what helps the machine determine the location of the specific sending device. Figure 5.25 shows a switch in an internetwork.

The real-estate business is all about location, location, location, and it's the same way for both Layer 2 and Layer 3 devices. Although both need to be able to negotiate the network, it's crucial to remember that they're concerned with very different parts of it. Primarily, Layer 3 machines (such as routers) need to locate specific networks, whereas Layer 2 machines (switches and bridges) need to eventually locate specific devices. So, networks are to routers as individual devices are to switches and bridges. And routing tables that "map" the internetwork are for routers as filter tables that "map" individual devices are for switches and bridges.

After a filter table is built on the Layer 2 device, it will forward frames only to the segment where the destination hardware address is located. If the destination device is on the same segment as the frame, the Layer 2 device will block the frame from going to any other segments. If the destination is on a different segment, the frame can be transmitted only to that segment. This is called *transparent bridging*.

FIGURE 5.25   A switch in an internetwork

Each segment has its own collision domain.
All segments are in the same broadcast domain.

When a switch interface receives a frame with a destination hardware address that isn't found in the device's filter table, it will forward the frame to all connected segments. If the unknown device that was sent the "mystery frame" replies to this forwarding action, the switch updates its filter table regarding that device's location. But in the event that the destination address of the transmitting frame is a broadcast address, the switch will forward all broadcasts to every connected segment by default.

All devices that the broadcast is forwarded to are considered to be in the same broadcast domain. This can be a problem; Layer 2 devices propagate Layer 2 broadcast storms that choke performance, and the only way to stop a broadcast storm from propagating through an internetwork is with a Layer 3 device—a router.

The biggest benefit of using switches instead of hubs in your internetwork is that each switch port is actually its own collision domain. (Conversely, a hub creates one large collision domain.) But even armed with a switch, you still can't break up broadcast domains. Neither switches nor bridges will do that. They'll typically simply forward all broadcasts instead.

Another benefit of LAN switching over hub-centered implementations is that each device on every segment plugged into a switch can transmit simultaneously—at least, they can as long as there is only one host on each port and a hub isn't plugged into a switch port. As you might have guessed, hubs allow only one device per network segment to communicate at a time.

Hubs at the Physical Layer

As you know, a hub is really a multiple-port repeater. A repeater receives a digital signal and reamplifies or regenerates that signal and then forwards the digital signal out all active ports without looking at any data. An active hub does the same thing. Any digital signal received from a segment on a hub port is regenerated or reamplified and transmitted out all ports on the hub. This means all devices plugged into a hub are in the same collision domain as well as in the same broadcast domain. Figure 5.26 shows a hub in a network.

FIGURE 5.26   A hub in a network

All devices in the same collision domain
All devices in the same broadcast domain
Devices share the same bandwidth.

Hubs, like repeaters, don't examine any of the traffic as it enters and is then transmitted out to the other parts of the physical media. Every device connected to the hub, or hubs, must listen if a device transmits. A physical star network—where the hub is a central device and cables extend in all directions out from it—is the type of topology a hub creates. Visually, the design really does resemble a star, whereas Ethernet networks run a logical bus topology, meaning that the signal has to run through the network from end to end.

Hubs and repeaters can be used to enlarge the area covered by a single LAN segment, although I do not recommend this. LAN switches and/or wireless APs are affordable for almost every situation.

Environmental Considerations

All of the equipment discussed in this chapter, switches, routers, hubs, and so on, require proper environmental conditions to operate correctly. These devices have the same needs as any computing device. These environmental concerns can be categorized thusly:

Temperature   Like any device with a CPU, infrastructure devices such as routers, switches, and specialty appliances must have a cool area to operate. When temperatures rise, servers start rebooting and appliance CPUs start overworking as well. The room(s) where these devices are located should be provided with heavy duty HVAC systems and ample ventilation. It may even be advisable to dedicate a suite for this purpose and put the entire system on a UPS with a backup generator in the case of a loss of power.

Humidity   The air around these systems can be neither too damp, nor too dry; it must be "just right." If it is too dry static electricity will build up in the air making the situation ripe for damaging a system. Its take very little static electricity to fry some electrical components. If it is too damp, connections start corroding and shorts being to occur. A humidifying system should be used to maintain the level above 50 percent. The air conditioning should keep it within acceptable levels on the upper end.

Summary

Whew, this chapter covered quite a bit of information. In this chapter, you learned the difference between a router, a switch (bridge), and a hub and when to use each one. I also covered some devices that you might find in a network today, but not as often, such as VPN Concentrators and Content Filters.

The information I discussed about DNS and DHCP is critical to your success on the Network+ objectives, and I highly suggest that you reread those sections. I covered how both the DNS and DHCP services work on a network.

In addition to the most common devices, I discussed the specialized network devices mentioned in the Network+ objectives. I finished the chapter by discussing collision and broadcast domains in detail as well as how you would use a router, switch, and hub in your networks today.

All of the information in this chapter is fundamental, and you must understand it before moving on to the other chapters in this book.

Exam Essentials

Understand how DHCP works and its purpose. Dynamic Host Configuration Protocol (DHCP) provides IP configuration information to hosts. It is important to know how a DHCP client requests information from a server, how a server receives this information, and also how the server responds to the client and with what type of information.

Understand how DNS works and its purpose. Domain Name Service (DNS) is used to resolve human names to binary format. Understanding how DNS resolves these names is critical, as is understanding how a DNS query is sent and how a DNS server responds.

Understand the difference between a hub, a switch (bridge), and a router. A hub just connects network segments together. A switch/bridge segments the network using MAC addresses, and a router segments the network using logical addressing (IP and IPv6).

Remember the different names for a router. A router is a Layer 3 hardware device, but can also be called a Layer 3 switch, or a multilayer switch.

Remember the various devices used on networks today and when you would use each one and how. Understand the differences and how each device works: routers, switches, hubs, DNS servers and DHCP servers.

Identify the purpose, benefits, and characteristics of using a proxy service. A proxy server keeps a LAN somewhat separated from the Internet. Doing so increases security and filtering control and has the tendency to speed up Internet access through caching of recently used web pages.

Describe the proper use of network segmentation when planning and implementing a basic SOHO network. Understand and apply the concepts of proper network segmentation when planning the use of various devices in the design of a SOHO network.

Describe the benefits of using dedicated appliances for certain services. Using appliances to offload functions such as encryption, content filtering, and VPN concentration can decrease the workload of other systems and add functionality that may be present in these dedicated devices.

Identify the environmental requirements of infrastructure devices. A cool temperature, ample ventilation, and the proper humidity level are all key to maintaining the operation of devices like routers, switches, and appliances.

Written Lab

Complete the table by filling in the appropriate layer of the OSI or hub, switch, or router device.

Description	Device or OSI Layer
This device sends and receives information about the Network layer.	
This layer creates a virtual circuit before transmitting between two end stations.	
A Layer 3 switch or multilayer switch	
This device uses hardware addresses to filter a network.	
Ethernet is defined at these layers.	
This layer supports flow control and sequencing.	
This device can measure the distance to a remote network.	
Logical addressing is used at this layer.	
Hardware addresses are defined at this layer.	
This device creates one big collision domain and one large broadcast domain.	
This device creates many smaller collision domains, but the network is still one large broadcast domain.	
This device can never run full duplex.	
This device breaks up collision domains and broadcast domains.	

You can find the answers in Appendix B.

Review Questions

You can find the answers in Appendix A.

1. Which of the following is not a term used when making SOHO Internet connections?

    A. Hub

    B. Repeater

    C. NIC

    D. Switch

2. What advantage does a switch have over a hub?

    A. It discards frames.

    B. Transmissions received on one port will be sent out all the other ports.

    C. It recognizes frame boundaries and destination MAC addresses of incoming frames.

    D. Any two or more devices the switch connects have are capable of causing a collision with each other.

3. Which device is used to segment a network?

    A. Hub

    B. Switch

    C. Repeater

    D. All of the above

4. What is the primary function of a bridge?

    A. Breaks up collision domains

    B. Allows a NIC or other networking device to connect to a different type of media than it was designed for

    C. Allows mobile users to connect to a wired network wirelessly

    D. None of the above

5. A network device that is used to connect multiple devices together without segmenting a network is a

    A. Hub

    B. Wireless access point

    C. Switch

    D. Router

6. Which of the following is among the benefits of a switch?

   A. Protects LAN resources from attackers on the Internet

   B. Provides extra bandwidth

   C. Reduces throughput

   D. Allows access to all computers on a LAN

7. Which of the following devices can work at both Layers 2 and 3 of the OSI model?

   A. Hub

   B. Switch

   C. Multi-layer switch

   D. Bridge

8. What is an advantage of using DHCP in a network environment?

   A. More difficult administration of the network

   B. Static IP addressing

   C. Can send an operating system for the PC to boot from

   D. Assigns IP address to hosts

9. What is a benefit of a multilayer switch (MLS) over a Layer 2 switch?

   A. Less bandwidth

   B. Routing functions

   C. Fewer features

   D. Fewer ports

10. Which device should be used if you need to send incoming packets to one or more machines that are hidden behind a single IP address?

   A. Switch

   B. Load balancer

   C. Hub

   D. Repeater

11. What role does the "A" record in a Domain Name Service (DNS) server have in your network?

   A. Translates human name to IP address

   B. Translates IP address to human name

   C. Enables printing, copying, and faxing from one device

   D. Controls network packets to optimize performance

12. Which device does not aid in network segmentation?

    A. Router

    B. Switch

    C. Hub

    D. Bridge

13. What is the most common use for a web proxy?

    A. Web cache

    B. Increases throughput

    C. DHCP services

    D. Supports user authentication

14. Which is not an advantage of network segmentation?

    A. Reduced congestion

    B. Improved security

    C. Containing network problems

    D. Preventing broadcast storms

15. Users arrive at the office after a weekend and the hosts that were shut down over the weekend are restarted but cannot access the LAN or Internet. Hosts that were not shut down are working fine. Where can the problem be?

    A. The DNS server

    B. The DHCP server

    C. The proxy server

    D. The firewall

16. You need a device that can prevent your users from accessing certain web sites . Which device should you install?

    A. Firewall

    B. IDS

    C. IPS

    D. Proxy server

17. Which device creates separate collision domains and a single broadcast domain?

    A. Hub

    B. Router

    C. Switch

    D. Modem

18. Which of the following is NOT an advantage of using appliances to offload services like encryption and content filtering?

  A. Less expensive

  B. Takes load off other devices

  C. Additional functionality

  D. Better performance

19. Which type of server in your network uses pointer and A records?

  A. NAT Translation server

  B. IPS/IDS Server

  C. DNS Server

  D. Proxy Server

20. Users on your network are saturating your bandwidth because they are using too many non-work-related sites. What device would limit the availability of the types of sites that users on a LAN have access to while providing granular control over the traffic between the local LAN and the Internet?

  A. Switch

  B. DHCP server

  C. DNS server

  D. Proxy server

Chapter

6

Introduction to the Internet Protocol

THE FOLLOWING COMPTIA NETWORK+ EXAM OBJECTIVES ARE COVERED IN THIS CHAPTER:

✓ **1.1 Compare the layers of the OSI and TCP/IP models.**

- TCP/IP model:
    - Network Interface Layer
    - Internet Layer
    - Transport Layer
    - Application Layer
    - (Also described as: Link Layer, Internet Layer, Transport Layer, Application Layer)

✓ **1.5 Identify common TCP and UDP default ports.**

- SMTP – 25
- HTTP – 80
- HTTPS – 443
- FTP – 20, 21
- TELNET – 23
- IMAP – 143
- RDP – 3389
- SSH – 22
- DNS – 53
- DHCP – 67, 68

✓ **1.6 Explain the function of common networking protocols.**

- TCP
- FTP
- UDP
- TCP/IP suite
- DHCP
- TFTP
- DNS
- HTTPS
- HTTP
- ARP
- SIP (VoIP)
- RTP (VoIP)
- SSH
- POP3
- NTP
- IMAP4
- Telnet
- SMTP
- SNMP2/3
- ICMP
- IGMP
- TLS

The *Transmission Control Protocol/Internet Protocol (TCP/IP)* suite was created by the Department of Defense (DoD) to ensure and preserve data integrity, as well as to maintain communications in the event of catastrophic war. So it follows that if designed and implemented correctly, a TCP/IP network can truly be a solid, dependable, and resilient network solution. In this chapter, I'll cover the protocols of TCP/IP.

I'll begin by covering the DoD's version of TCP/IP and then compare this version and its protocols with the OSI reference model discussed in Chapter 2, "The Open Systems Interconnection Specifications."

After going over the various protocols found at each layer of the DoD model, I'll finish the chapter by adding more detail to the explanation of data encapsulation that I started in Chapter 2.

To find up-to-the-minute updates for this chapter, please see www.lammle.com/forum or the book's web site at www.sybex.com/go/netplus2e.

Introducing TCP/IP

Because TCP/IP is so central to working with the Internet and intranets, it's essential for you to understand it in detail. I'll begin by giving you some background on TCP/IP and how it came about and then move on to describe the important technical goals defined by the original designers. After that, you'll find out how TCP/IP compares to a theoretical model—the Open Systems Interconnection (OSI) model.

A Brief History of TCP/IP

The very first Request for Comments (RFC) was published in April 1974, which paved the way for today's Internet and its protocols. Each of these protocols is specified in the multitude of RFCs, which are observed, maintained, sanctioned, filed, and stored by the Internet Engineering Task Force (IETF).

TCP first came on the scene in 1974. In 1978, it was divided into two distinct protocols: TCP and IP. Then, in 1983, TCP/IP replaced the Network Control Protocol (NCP) and was authorized as the official means of data transport for anything connecting to ARPAnet.

ARPAnet was the Internet's ancestor, created by ARPA, the DoD's Advanced Research Projects Agency, way back in 1957 in reaction to the Soviet's launching of Sputnik. ARPA was soon redubbed DARPA, and it was divided into ARPAnet and MILNET (also in 1983); both were finally dissolved in 1990.

But contrary to what you might think, most of the development work on TCP/IP happened at UC Berkeley in Northern California, where a group of scientists were simultaneously working on the Berkeley version of Unix, which soon became known as the BSD, or Berkeley Software Distribution series of Unix versions. Of course, because TCP/IP worked so well, it was packaged into subsequent releases of BSD Unix and offered to other universities and institutions if they bought the distribution tape. Basically, BSD Unix bundled with TCP/IP began as shareware in the world of academia and, as a result, became the basis of the huge success and exponential growth of today's Internet as well as smaller, private, and corporate intranets.

As usual, what may have started as a small group of TCP/IP aficionados evolved, and as it did, the US government created a program to test any new published standards and make sure they passed certain criteria. This was to protect TCP/IP's integrity and to ensure that no developer changed anything too dramatically or added any proprietary features. It's this very quality—this open-systems approach to the TCP/IP family of protocols—that pretty much sealed its popularity because it guarantees a solid connection between myriad hardware and software platforms with no strings attached.

TCP/IP and the DoD Model

The DoD model is basically a condensed version of the OSI model; it's composed of four, instead of seven, layers:

- Process/Application layer
- Host-to-Host layer
- Internet layer
- Network Access layer

Figure 6.1 shows a comparison of the DoD model and the OSI reference model. As you can see, the two are similar in concept, but each has a different number of layers with different names.

When the different protocols in the IP stack are discussed, two layers of the OSI and DoD models are interchangeable. In other words, the Internet layer and the Network layer describe the same thing, as do the Host-to-Host layer and the Transport layer. The other two layers of the DoD model, Process/Application and Network Access, are composed of multiple layers of the OSI model.

A vast array of protocols operate at the DoD model's *Process/Application layer* to integrate the various activities and duties spanning the focus of the OSI's corresponding top three layers (Application, Presentation, and Session). We'll be looking closely at those protocols in the next part of this chapter. The Process/Application layer defines protocols for node-to-node application communication and also controls user-interface specifications.

FIGURE 6.1   The DoD and OSI models

The *Host-to-Host layer* parallels the functions of the OSI's Transport layer, defining protocols for setting up the level of transmission service for applications. It tackles issues such as creating reliable end-to-end communication and ensuring the error-free delivery of data. It handles packet sequencing and maintains data integrity.

The *Internet layer* corresponds to the OSI's Network layer, designating the protocols relating to the logical transmission of packets over the entire network. It takes care of the logical addressing of hosts by giving them an IP address, and it handles the routing of packets among multiple networks.

At the bottom of the DoD model, the *Network Access layer* monitors the data exchange between the host and the network. The equivalent of the Data Link and Physical layers of the OSI model, the Network Access layer oversees hardware addressing and defines protocols for the physical transmission of data.

The DoD and OSI models are alike in design and concept and have similar functions in similar layers. Figure 6.2 shows the TCP/IP protocol suite and how its protocols relate to the DoD model layers.

We'll now look at the different protocols in more detail, starting with the Process/Application layer protocols.

The Process/Application Layer Protocols

In the following sections, I'll describe the different applications and services typically used in IP networks.

FIGURE 6.2 The TCP/IP protocol suite

DoD Model

Process/Application	Telnet	FTP	LPD	SNMP
	TFTP	SMTP	NFS	X Window

Host-to-Host	TCP	UDP

Internet	ICMP	ARP	RARP
	IP		

Network Access	Ethernet	Fast Ethernet	Token Ring	FDDI

Telnet

Telnet is the chameleon of protocols—its specialty is terminal emulation. It allows a user on a remote client machine, called the Telnet client, to access the resources of another machine, the Telnet server. Telnet achieves this by pulling a fast one on the Telnet server and making the client machine appear as though it were a terminal directly attached to the local network. This projection is actually a software shell—a virtual terminal that can interact with the chosen remote host.

These emulated terminals are of the text-mode type and can execute refined procedures such as displaying menus that give users the opportunity to choose options and access the applications on the duped server. Users begin a Telnet session by running the Telnet client software and then logging into the Telnet server.

Telnet offers no security or encryption and is being replaced by Secure Shell (SSH) when security across the remote-configuration session is needed or desired.

File Transfer Protocol

File Transfer Protocol (FTP) is the protocol that actually lets you transfer files across an IP network, and it can accomplish this between any two machines that are using it. But FTP isn't just a protocol; it's also a program. Operating as a protocol, FTP is used by applications. As a program, it's employed by users to perform file tasks by hand. FTP also allows for access to both directories and files and can accomplish certain types of directory operations, such as relocating files into different directories.

Accessing a host through FTP is only the first step, though. Users must then be subjected to an authentication login that's probably secured with passwords and usernames implemented by system administrators to restrict access. You can get around this somewhat by adopting the username *anonymous*—although what you'll gain access to will be limited.

Even when employed by users manually as a program, FTP's functions are limited to listing and manipulating directories, typing file contents, and copying files between hosts. It can't execute remote files as programs.

Secure File Transfer Protocol

Secure File Transfer Protocol (SFTP) is used when you need to transfer files over an encrypted connection. It uses an SSH session (more on this later), which encrypts the connection. Apart from the secure part, it's used just as FTP is—for transferring files between computers on an IP network, such as the Internet.

Trivial File Transfer Protocol

Trivial File Transfer Protocol (TFTP) is the stripped-down, stock version of FTP, but it's the protocol of choice if you know exactly what you want and where to find it—plus it's easy to use, and it's fast too! It doesn't give you the abundance of functions that FTP does though. TFTP has no directory-browsing abilities; it can do nothing but send and receive files. This compact little protocol also skimps in the data department, sending much smaller blocks of data than FTP, and there's no authentication as with FTP, so it's insecure. Few sites support it because of the inherent security risks.

 Real World Scenario

When Should You Use FTP?

The folks at your San Francisco office need a 50 MB file emailed to them right away. What do you do? Most email servers would reject the email because they have size limits. Even if there's no size limit on the server, it would still take a while to send this big file. FTP to the rescue!

If you need to give someone a large file or you need to get a large file from someone, FTP is a nice choice. Smaller files (less than 10 MB) can be sent via email if you have the bandwidth of DSL or a cable modem. However, most ISPs don't allow files larger then 10 MB to be emailed, so FTP is an option you should consider if you need to send and receive large files (who doesn't these days?), even if they're compressed. To use FTP, you'll need to set up an FTP server on the Internet so that the files can be shared.

Besides, FTP is faster than email, which is another reason to use FTP for sending or receiving large files. In addition, because it uses TCP and is connection-oriented, if the session dies, FTP can sometimes start up where it left off. Try that with your email client!

Simple Mail Transfer Protocol

Simple Mail Transfer Protocol (SMTP), answering our ubiquitous call to email, uses a spooled, or queued, method of mail delivery. Once a message has been sent to a destination, the message is spooled to a device—usually a disk. The server software at the destination posts a vigil, regularly checking the queue for messages. When it detects them, it proceeds to deliver them to their destination. SMTP is used to send mail; POP3 is used to receive mail.

Post Office Protocol

Post Office Protocol (POP) gives us a storage facility for incoming mail, and the latest version is called POP3 (sound familiar?). Basically, how this protocol works is when a client device connects to a POP3 server, messages addressed to that client are released for downloading. It doesn't allow messages to be downloaded selectively, but once they are, the client-server interaction ends and you can delete and tweak your messages locally at will. Lately we're seeing a newer standard, IMAP, being used more and more in place of POP3. Why?

Internet Message Access Protocol, Version 4

Because *Internet Message Access Protocol (IMAP)* makes it so you get control over how you download your mail, with it, you also gain some much-needed security. It lets you peek at the message header or download just a part of a message—you can now just nibble at the bait instead of swallowing it whole and then choking on the hook hidden inside!

With it, you can choose to store messages on the email server hierarchically and link to documents and user groups too. IMAP even gives you search commands to use to hunt for messages based on their subject, header, or content. As you can imagine, it has some serious authentication features—it actually supports the Kerberos authentication scheme that MIT developed. And yes, IMAP4 is the current version.

Remote Desktop Protocol

Remote Desktop Protocol (RDP) is a proprietary protocol developed by Microsoft. It allows you to connect to another computer and run programs. RDP operates somewhat like Telnet, except instead of getting a command-line prompt as you do with Telnet, you get the actual graphical user interface (GUI) of the remote computer. Clients exist for most versions of Windows, and Macs now come with a preinstalled RDP client.

Microsoft currently calls its official RDP server software Remote Desktop Services, which used to be called Terminal Services for a while. Microsoft's official client software is currently referred to as Remote Desktop Connection, which was called Terminal Services Client in the past.

RDP is an excellent tool for remote clients, allowing them to connect to their work computer from home, for example, and get their email or perform work on other applications without running or installing any of the software on their home computer.

Transport Layer Security

Both *Transport Layer Security (TLS)* and its forerunner, Secure Sockets Layer (SSL), are cryptographic protocols that come in really handy for enabling secure online data-transfer activities like browsing the Web, instant messaging, Internet faxing, and so on. They're so similar it's not within the scope of this book to detail the differences between them.

SIP (VoIP)

Session Initiation Protocol (SIP) is a hugely popular signaling protocol used to construct and deconstruct multimedia communication sessions for many things like voice and video calls, videoconferencing, streaming multimedia distribution, instant messaging, presence information, and online games over the Internet.

RTP (VoIP)

Real-time Transport Protocol (RTP) describes a packet-formatting standard for delivering audio and video over the Internet. Although initially designed as a multicast protocol, it's now used for unicast applications too. It's commonly employed for streaming media, video-conferencing, and push-to-talk systems—all things that make it a de facto standard in Voice over IP (VoIP) industries.

Simple Network Management Protocol

Simple Network Management Protocol (SNMP) collects and manipulates valuable network information. It gathers data by polling the devices on the network from a management station at fixed or random intervals, requiring them to disclose certain information. When all is well, SNMP receives something called a *baseline*—a report delimiting the operational traits of a healthy network. This protocol can also stand as a watchdog over the network, quickly notifying managers of any sudden turn of events. The network watchdogs are called *agents*, and when aberrations occur, agents send an alert called a *trap* to the management station. In addition, SNMP can help simplify the process of setting up a network as well as the administration of your entire internetwork.

SNMP Versions 1, 2, and 3

SNMP versions 1 and 2 are pretty much obsolete. This doesn't mean you won't see them in a network at some time, but v1 is super old and, well, outdated. SNMPv2 provided improvements, especially in security and performance. But one of the best additions was what was called GETBULK, which allowed a host to retrieve a large amount of data at once. However, v2 never really caught on in the networking world. SNMPv3 is now the standard and uses both TCP and UDP, unlike v1, which used only UDP. Version 3 added even more security and message integrity, authentication, and encryption. So, be careful when running SNMPv1 and v2 because they are susceptible to a packet sniffer reading the data.

Secure Shell

Secure Shell (SSH) protocol sets up a secure Telnet session over a standard TCP/IP connection and is employed for doing things like logging into other systems, running programs on remote systems, and moving files from one system to another. And it does all of this while maintaining a nice, strong, encrypted connection. You can think of it as the new-generation protocol that's now used in place of `rsh` and `rlogin`—even Telnet.

Hypertext Transfer Protocol

All those snappy websites comprising a mélange of graphics, text, links, and so on—the *Hypertext Transfer Protocol (HTTP)* is making it all possible. It's used to manage communications between web browsers and web servers and opens the right resource when you click a link, wherever that resource may actually reside.

Hypertext Transfer Protocol Secure

Hypertext Transfer Protocol Secure (HTTPS) is a secure version of HTTP that arms you with a whole bunch of security tools for keeping transactions between a web browser and a server secure. It's what your browser needs to fill out forms, sign in, authenticate, and encrypt an HTTP message when you make a reservation or buy something online.

Both SSH (port 22) and HTTPS (port 443) are used to encrypt packets over your intranet and the Internet.

Network Time Protocol

Kudos to Professor David Mills of the University of Delaware for coming up with this handy protocol that's used to synchronize the clocks on our computers to one standard time source (typically, an atomic clock). *Network Time Protocol (NTP)* works in conjunction with other synchronization utilities to ensure that all computers on a given network agree on the time. This may sound pretty simple, but it's very important because so many of the transactions done today are time- and date-stamped. Think about your precious databases, for one. It can mess up a server pretty badly if it's out of sync with the machines connected to it, even by mere seconds (think crash!). You can't have a transaction entered by a machine at, say, 1:50 a.m. when the server records that transaction as having occurred at 1:45 a.m. So basically, NTP works to prevent "back to the future sans DeLorean" from bringing down the network—very important indeed!

The Requests for Comments (RFCs) form a series of notes, started in 1969, about the Internet (originally the ARPAnet). The notes discuss many aspects of computer communication; they focus on networking protocols, procedures, programs, and concepts but also include meeting notes, opinion, and sometimes humor. You can find the RFCs by visiting www.iana.org.

Secure Copy Protocol

FTP is great. It's a super easy, user-friendly way to transfer files—if you don't need to transfer those files securely. That's because when you use FTP for transferring data, usernames and passwords get sent right along with the file request in the clear for all to see with no encryption whatsoever! Kind of like Hail Mary passes, you basically just throw them out there and hope your information doesn't fall into the wrong hands and get intercepted.

That's where *Secure Copy Protocol (SCP)* comes to your rescue—its whole purpose is to protect your precious files. Through SSH, it first establishes and then sustains a secure, encrypted connection between the sending and receiving hosts until file transfer is complete. When armed with SCP, your Hail Mary pass can be caught only by your intended receiver—snap! In today's networks, however, the more robust SFTP is used more commonly than SCP.

Lightweight Directory Access Protocol

If you're the system administrator of any decent-sized network, odds are you have a type of directory in place that keeps track of all your network resources, such as devices and users. But how do you access those directories? Through the *Lightweight Directory Access Protocol (LDAP),* that's how. This protocol standardizes how you access directories, and its first and second inceptions are described in RFCs 1487 and 1777, respectively. There were a few glitches in those two earlier versions, so a third version—the one most commonly used today—was created to address those issues and is described in RFC 3377.

Internet Group Management Protocol

Internet Group Management Protocol (IGMP) is the TCP/IP protocol used for managing IP multicast sessions. It accomplishes this by sending out unique IGMP messages over the network to reveal the multicast-group landscape and to find out which hosts belong to which multicast group. The host machines in an IP network also use IGMP messages to become members of a group and to quit the group too. IGMP messages come in seriously handy for tracking group memberships as well as active multicast streams.

Domain Name Service

Domain Name Service (DNS) resolves hostnames—specifically, Internet names, such as www.lammle.com, to their corresponding IP addresses.

You don't have to use DNS; you can just type in the IP address of any device you want to communicate with. An IP address identifies hosts on a network and the Internet as well. However, DNS was designed to make our lives easier. Think about this: What would happen if you wanted to move your web page to a different service provider? The IP address would change, and no one would know what the new one was. DNS allows you to use a domain name to specify an IP address. You can change the IP address as often as you want, and no one will know the difference.

DNS is used to resolve a *fully qualified domain name (FQDN)*—for example, www.lammle .com or todd.lammle.com—to an IP address. An FQDN, or DNS namespace, is a hierarchy that can logically locate a system based on its domain identifier.

If you want to resolve the name *todd*, you must either type in the FQDN of todd.lammle .com or have a device, such as a PC or router, add the suffix for you. For example, on a Cisco router, you can use the command ip domain-name lammle.com to append each request with the lammle.com domain. If you don't do that, you'll have to type in the FQDN to get DNS to resolve the name.

> An important thing to remember about DNS is that if you can ping a device with an IP address but can't use its FQDN, you might have some type of DNS configuration failure.

Dynamic Host Configuration Protocol/Bootstrap Protocol

Dynamic Host Configuration Protocol (DHCP) assigns IP addresses to hosts with information provided by a server. It allows easier administration and works well in small to even very large network environments. Many types of hardware can be used as a DHCP server, including routers.

DHCP differs from Bootstrap Protocol (BootP) in that BootP assigns an IP address to a host but the host's hardware address must be entered manually in a BootP table. You can think of DHCP as a dynamic BootP. But remember that BootP is also used to send an operating system that a host can boot from. DHCP can't do that.

> Please also read the section on DHCP and DNS in Chapter 5, "Networking Devices," if you have not done so; both figure largely in the exam objectives.

But there is a lot of information a DHCP server can provide to a host when the host is requesting an IP address from the DHCP server. Here's a partial list of the information a DHCP server can provide:

- IP address
- Subnet mask
- Domain name
- Default gateway (routers)
- DNS
- Windows Internet Naming Service (WINS) information

A DHCP server can give even more information than this, but the items in the list are the most common.

A client that sends out a DHCP DISCOVER message in order to receive an IP address sends out a broadcast at both Layer 2 and Layer 3. The Layer 2 broadcast is all *F*s in hex, which looks like this: FF:FF:FF:FF:FF:FF. The Layer 3 broadcast is 255.255.255.255, which means all networks and all hosts. DHCP is connectionless, which means it uses User Datagram

Protocol (UDP) at the Transport layer, also known as the Host-to-Host layer, which we'll talk about next.

In case you don't believe me, here's an example of output from my trusty analyzer:

```
Ethernet II,Src:192.168.0.3(00:0b:db:99:d3:5e),Dst:Broadcast(ff:ff:ff:ff:ff:ff)
Internet Protocol,Src:0.0.0.0(0.0.0.0),Dst:255.255.255.255(255.255.255.255)
```

The Data Link and Network layers are both sending out "all hands" broadcasts saying, "Help—I don't know my IP address!"

Figure 6.3 shows the process of a client-server relationship using a DHCP connection.

FIGURE 6.3   DHCP client four-step process

The following is the four-step process a client takes to receive an IP address from a DHCP server:

1. The DHCP client broadcasts a DHCP Discover message looking for a DHCP server (Port 67).

2. The DHCP server that received the DHCP Discover message sends a unicast DHCP Offer message back to the host.

3. The client then broadcasts to the server a DHCP Request message asking for the offered IP address and possibly other information.

4. The server finalizes the exchange with a unicast DHCP Acknowledgment message.

What happens if you have a few hosts connected together with a switch or hub and you don't have a DHCP server? You can add IP information by hand (this is called *static IP addressing*), or Windows provides what is called Automatic Private IP Addressing (APIPA), a feature of later Windows operating systems. With APIPA, clients can automatically self-configure an IP address and subnet mask (basic IP information that hosts use to communicate, which is covered in detail in Chapter 7, "IP Addressing," and Chapter 8, "IP Subnetting, Troubleshooting IP, and Introduction to NAT") when a DHCP server isn't available. The IP address range for APIPA is 169.254.0.1 through 169.254.255.254. The client also configures itself with a default class B subnet mask of 255.255.0.0. If you have a DHCP server and your host is using this IP address, this means your DHCP client on your host is not working or the server is down or can't be reached because of a network issue.

Now, let's take a look at the Transport layer, or what the DoD calls the Host-to-Host layer.

The Host-to-Host Layer Protocols

The main purpose of the Host-to-Host layer is to shield the upper-layer applications from the complexities of the network. This layer says to the upper layer, "Just give me your data stream, with any instructions, and I'll begin the process of getting your information ready to send."

The following sections describe the two protocols at this layer:

▪   Transmission Control Protocol (TCP)

▪   User Datagram Protocol (UDP)

In addition, we'll look at some of the key host-to-host protocol concepts, as well as the port numbers.

Transmission Control Protocol

Transmission Control Protocol (TCP) takes large blocks of information from an application and breaks them into segments. It numbers and sequences each segment so that the destination's TCP process can put the segments back into the order the application intended. After these segments are sent, TCP (on the transmitting host) waits for an acknowledgment from the receiving end's TCP process, retransmitting those segments that aren't acknowledged.

Remember that in reliable transport operation, a device that wants to transmit sets up a connection-oriented communication with a remote device by creating a session. The transmitting device first establishes a connection-oriented session with its peer system; that session is called a *call setup* or a *three-way handshake*. Data is then transferred, and when the transfer is complete, a call termination takes place to tear down the virtual circuit.

TCP is a full-duplex, connection-oriented, reliable, and accurate protocol, but establishing all these terms and conditions, in addition to error checking, is no small task.

TCP is very complicated and, not surprisingly, costly in terms of network overhead. And because today's networks are much more reliable than those of yore, this added reliability is often unnecessary.

Because the upper layers just send a data stream to the protocols in the Transport layers, I'll demonstrate how TCP segments a data stream and prepares it for the Internet layer. When the Internet layer receives the data stream, it routes the segments as packets through an internetwork. The segments are handed to the receiving host's Host-to-Host layer protocol, which rebuilds the data stream to hand to the upper-layer protocols.

Figure 6.4 shows the TCP segment format. The figure shows the different fields within the TCP header.

FIGURE 6.4   TCP segment format

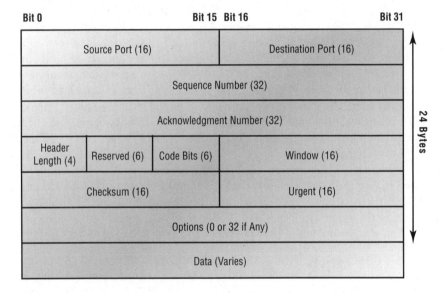

The TCP header is 20 bytes long, or up to 24 bytes with options.

For more detailed information regarding the TCP header, which is beyond the scope of the CompTIA Network+ exam objectives, please see my book *CCNA: Cisco Certified Network Associate Study Guide, 7th Edition* (Sybex, 2011).

User Datagram Protocol

If you were to compare *User Datagram Protocol (UDP)* with TCP, the former is basically the scaled-down economy model that's sometimes referred to as a *thin protocol*. Like a thin person on a park bench, a thin protocol doesn't take up a lot of room—or in this case, much bandwidth on a network.

UDP doesn't offer all the bells and whistles of TCP either, but it does do a fabulous job of transporting information that doesn't require reliable delivery—and it does so using far fewer network resources.

There are some situations in which it would definitely be wise for developers to opt for UDP rather than TCP. Remember the watchdog SNMP up there at the Process/Application layer? SNMP monitors the network, sending intermittent messages and a fairly steady flow of status updates and alerts, especially when running on a large network. The cost in overhead to establish, maintain, and close a TCP connection for each one of those little messages would reduce what would be an otherwise healthy, efficient network to a dammed-up bog in no time!

Another circumstance calling for UDP over TCP is when reliability is already handled at the Process/Application layer. DNS handles its own reliability issues, making the use of TCP both impractical and redundant. But ultimately, it's up to the application developer to decide whether to use UDP or TCP, not the user who wants to transfer data faster.

UDP does *not* sequence the segments and doesn't care in which order the segments arrive at the destination. But after that, UDP sends the segments off and forgets about them. It doesn't follow through, check up on them, or even allow for an acknowledgment of safe arrival—complete abandonment. Because of this, it's referred to as an *unreliable* protocol. This doesn't mean that UDP is ineffective, only that it doesn't handle issues of reliability. Because UDP assumes that the application will use its own reliability method, it doesn't use any. This gives an application developer a choice when running the IP stack: TCP for reliability or UDP for faster transfers.

Further, UDP doesn't create a virtual circuit, nor does it contact the destination before delivering information to it. Because of this, it's also considered a *connectionless* protocol.

Figure 6.5 clearly illustrates UDP's markedly low overhead as compared to TCP's hungry usage. Look at the figure carefully—can you see that UDP doesn't use windowing or provide for acknowledgments in the UDP header?

FIGURE 6.5 UDP segment

 For more detailed information regarding the UDP header, which is beyond the scope of the CompTIA Network+ exam objectives, please see my book *CCNA: Cisco Certified Network Associate Study Guide, 7th Edition* (Sybex, 2011).

Key Concepts of Host-to-Host Protocols

Now that you've seen both a connection-oriented (TCP) and connectionless (UDP) protocol in action, it would be good to summarize the two here. Table 6.1 highlights some of the key concepts that you should keep in mind regarding these two protocols. You should memorize this table.

TABLE 6.1   Key features of TCP and UDP

TCP	UDP
Sequenced	Unsequenced
Reliable	Unreliable
Connection-oriented	Connectionless
Virtual circuit	No virtual circuit
High overhead	Low overhead
Acknowledgments	No acknowledgment
Windowing flow control	No windowing or flow control

A telephone analogy could really help you understand how TCP works. Most of us know that before you speak to someone on a phone, you must first establish a connection with that other person—wherever they are. This is like a virtual circuit with TCP. If you were giving someone important information during your conversation, you might say, "You know?" or ask, "Did you get that?" Saying something like this is a lot like a TCP acknowledgment—it's designed to get your verification. From time to time (especially on cell phones), people also ask, "Are you still there?" They end their conversations with a "Goodbye" of some kind, putting closure on the phone call. TCP also performs these types of functions.

Alternatively, using UDP is like sending a postcard. To do that, you don't need to contact the other party first. You simply write your message, address the postcard, and mail it. This is analogous to UDP's connectionless orientation. Because the message on the postcard is probably not a matter of life or death, you don't need an acknowledgment of its receipt. Similarly, UDP doesn't involve acknowledgments.

Port Numbers

TCP and UDP must use *port numbers* to communicate with the upper layers because they're what keep track of different simultaneous conversations originated by or accepted by the local host. Originating-source port numbers are dynamically assigned by the source host and will usually have a value of 1024 or higher. Ports 1023 and below are defined in RFC 3232, which discusses what are called *well-known port numbers*.

Virtual circuits that don't use an application with a well-known port number are assigned port numbers randomly from a specific range instead. These port numbers identify the source and destination application or process in the TCP segment.

Figure 6.6 illustrates how both TCP and UDP use port numbers.

FIGURE 6.6   Port numbers for TCP and UDP

You just need to remember that numbers below 1024 are considered well-known port numbers and are defined in RFC 3232. Numbers 1024 and above are used by the upper layers to set up sessions with other hosts and by TCP as source and destination identifiers in the TCP segment.

Table 6.2 gives you a list of the typical applications used in the TCP/IP suite, their well-known port numbers, and the Transport layer protocols used by each application or process. It's important that you study and memorize this table for the CompTIA Network+ exam.

TABLE 6.2   Key protocols that use TCP and UDP

TCP	UDP
Telnet 23	SNMP 161
SMTP 25	TFTP 69
HTTP 80	DNS 53
FTP 20, 21	BOOTPS/DHCP 67,68
DNS 53	
HTTPS 443	
SSH 22	
POP3 110	

TCP	UDP
NTP 123	
IMAP4 143	
RDP 3389	

Notice that DNS uses both TCP and UDP. Whether it opts for one or the other depends on what it's trying to do. Even though it's not the only application that can use both protocols, it's certainly one that you should remember in your studies.

The Internet Layer Protocols

In the DoD model, there are two main reasons for the Internet layer's existence: routing and providing a single network interface to the upper layers.

None of the other upper- or lower-layer protocols have any functions relating to routing—that complex and important task belongs entirely to the Internet layer. The Internet layer's second duty is to provide a single network interface to the upper-layer protocols. Without this layer, application programmers would need to write what are called *hooks* into every one of their applications for each different Network Access protocol. This would not only be a pain in the neck, it would also lead to different versions of each application—one for Ethernet, another one for Token Ring, and so on. To prevent this, IP provides one single network interface for the upper-layer protocols. That accomplished, it's then the job of IP and the various Network Access protocols to get along and work together.

All network roads don't lead to Rome—they lead to IP. And all the other protocols at this layer, as well as all those at the upper layers, use it. Never forget that. All paths through the DoD model go through IP. The following sections describe the protocols at the Internet layer:

- Internet Protocol (IP)
- Internet Control Message Protocol (ICMP)
- Address Resolution Protocol (ARP)
- Reverse Address Resolution Protocol (RARP)

Internet Protocol

Internet Protocol (IP) essentially is the Internet layer. The other protocols found here merely exist to support it. IP holds the big picture and could be said to "see all" in that it's aware of all the interconnected networks. It can do this because all the machines on the network have a software, or logical, address called an IP address, which I'll cover more thoroughly in the next chapter.

IP looks at each packet's destination address. Then, using a routing table, it decides where a packet is to be sent next, choosing the best path. The protocols of the Network Access layer at the bottom of the DoD model don't possess IP's enlightened scope of the entire network; they deal only with physical links (local networks).

Identifying devices on networks requires answering these two questions: Which network is it on? And what is its ID on that network? The answer to the first question is the *software address*, or *logical address* (the correct street). The answer to the second question is the *hardware address* (the correct mailbox). All hosts on a network have a logical ID called an IP address. This is the software, or logical, address and contains valuable encoded information, greatly simplifying the complex task of routing. (IP is discussed in RFC 791.)

IP receives segments from the Host-to-Host layer and fragments them into packets if necessary. IP then reassembles packets back into segments on the receiving side. Each packet is assigned the IP address of the sender and of the recipient. Each router (Layer 3 device) that receives a packet makes routing decisions based on the packet's destination IP address.

Figure 6.7 shows an IP header. This will give you an idea of what IP has to go through every time user data is sent from the upper layers to a remote network.

FIGURE 6.7 IP header

For more detailed information regarding the IP header, which is beyond the scope of the CompTIA Network+ exam objectives, please see my book *CCNA: Cisco Certified Network Associate Study Guide, 7th Edition* (Sybex, 2011).

Internet Control Message Protocol

Internet Control Message Protocol (ICMP) works at the Network layer and is used by IP for many different services. ICMP is a management protocol and messaging service provider for IP. Its messages are carried as IP packets.

ICMP packets have the following characteristics:

- They can provide hosts with information about network problems.

- They are encapsulated within IP datagrams.

The following are some common events and messages that ICMP relates to and the two most popular programs that use ICMP:

Destination Unreachable   If a router can't send an IP datagram any further, it uses ICMP to send a message back to the sender, advising it of the situation. For example, take a look at Figure 6.8, which shows that the Ethernet interface of the Lab B router is down.

FIGURE 6.8   ICMP error message is sent to the sending host from the remote router.

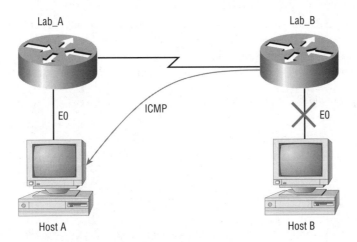

EO on Lab B is down. Host A is trying to communicate to Host B. What happens?

When Host A sends a packet destined for Host B, the Lab B router will send an ICMP Destination Unreachable message back to the sending device (directly to Host A, in this example).

Buffer Full   If a router's memory buffer for receiving incoming datagrams is full, it will use ICMP to send out this message until the congestion abates.

Hops   Each IP datagram is allotted a certain number of routers, called *hops*, to pass through. If a datagram reaches its limit of hops before arriving at its destination, the last router to receive it deletes it. The executioner router then uses ICMP to send an obituary message, informing the sending machine of the demise of its datagram.

Ping   Ping uses ICMP echo request and reply messages to check the physical and logical connectivity of machines on an internetwork.

Traceroute   Traceroute uses IP packet Time-to-Live time-outs to discover the path a packet takes as it traverses an internetwork.

Both Ping and Traceroute (also just called Trace, and Microsoft Windows uses tracert) allow you to verify address configurations in your internetwork.

Address Resolution Protocol

Address Resolution Protocol (ARP) finds the hardware address of a host from a known IP address. Here's how it works: When IP has a datagram to send, it must inform a Network Access protocol, such as Ethernet or Token Ring, of the destination's hardware address on the local network. (It has already been informed by upper-layer protocols of the destination's IP address.) If IP doesn't find the destination host's hardware address in the ARP cache, it uses ARP to find this information.

As IP's detective, ARP interrogates the local network by sending out a broadcast asking the machine with the specified IP address to reply with its hardware address. So basically, ARP translates the software (IP) address into a hardware address—for example, the destination machine's Ethernet address. Figure 6.9 shows how an ARP broadcast looks to a local network.

FIGURE 6.9   Local ARP broadcast

ARP resolves IP addresses to Ethernet (MAC) addresses.

The following trace shows an ARP broadcast—notice that the destination hardware address is unknown and is all 0s in the ARP header. In the Ethernet header, a destination of all *F*s in hex (all 1s in binary), a hardware-address broadcast, is used to make sure all devices on the local link receive the ARP request.

```
Flags:          0x00
Status:         0x00
Packet Length:  64
Timestamp:      09:17:29.574000 12/06/03
Ethernet Header
Destination:    FF:FF:FF:FF:FF:FF Ethernet Broadcast
Source:         00:A0:24:48:60:A5
Protocol Type:  0x0806 IP ARP
ARP - Address Resolution Protocol
Hardware:                   1 Ethernet (10Mb)
Protocol:                   0x0800 IP
Hardware Address Length: 6
Protocol Address Length: 4
Operation:                  1 ARP Request
Sender Hardware Address: 00:A0:24:48:60:A5
Sender Internet Address: 172.16.10.3
Target Hardware Address: 00:00:00:00:00:00 (ignored)
Target Internet Address: 172.16.10.10
Extra bytes (Padding):
.............. 0A 0A 0A 0A 0A 0A 0A 0A 0A 0A 0A 0A 0A
 0A 0A 0A 0A 0A
Frame Check Sequence: 0x00000000
```

Reverse Address Resolution Protocol

When an IP machine happens to be a diskless machine, it has no way of initially knowing its IP address. But it does know its MAC address. *Reverse Address Resolution Protocol (RARP)* discovers the identity of the IP address for diskless machines by sending out a packet that includes its MAC address and a request for the IP address assigned to that MAC address. A designated machine, called a *RARP server*, responds with the answer, and the identity crisis is over. RARP uses the information it does know about the machine's MAC address to learn its IP address and complete the machine's ID portrait.

Figure 6.10 shows a diskless workstation asking for its IP address with a RARP broadcast.

FIGURE 6.10   RARP broadcast example

Data Encapsulation

I started to discuss data encapsulation in Chapter 2, but I could only provide an overview at that point in the book because you needed to have a firm understanding of how ports work in a virtual circuit. With the last five chapters of foundational material under your belt, you're ready to get more into the details of encapsulations.

When a host transmits data across a network to another device, the data goes through *encapsulation*: It's wrapped with protocol information at each layer of the OSI model. Each layer communicates only with its peer layer on the receiving device.

To communicate and exchange information, each layer uses *Protocol Data Units (PDUs)*. These hold the control information attached to the data at each layer of the model. They're usually attached to the header in front of the data field but can also be in the trailer, or end, of it.

Each PDU attaches to the data by encapsulating it at each layer of the OSI model, and each has a specific name depending on the information provided in each header. This PDU information is read only by the peer layer on the receiving device. After it's read, it's stripped off, and the data is then handed to the next layer up.

Figure 6.11 shows the PDUs and how they attach control information to each layer. This figure demonstrates how the upper-layer user data is converted for transmission on the network. The data stream is then handed down to the Transport layer, which sets up a virtual circuit to the receiving device by sending over a synch packet. Next, the data stream is broken up into smaller pieces, and a Transport layer header (a PDU) is created and attached to the header of the data field; now the piece of data is called a *segment*. Each segment is sequenced so the data stream can be put back together on the receiving side exactly as it was transmitted.

FIGURE 6.11   Data encapsulation

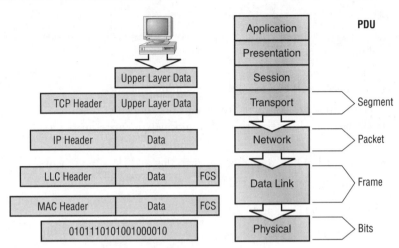

Each segment is then handed to the Network layer for network addressing and routing through the internetwork. Logical addressing (for example, IP) is used to get each segment to the correct network. The Network layer protocol adds a control header to the segment handed down from the Transport layer, and what we have now is called a *packet* or *datagram*. Remember that the Transport and Network layers work together to rebuild a data stream on a receiving host, but it's not part of their work to place their PDUs on a local network segment—which is the only way to get the information to a router or host.

It's the Data Link layer that's responsible for taking packets from the Network layer and placing them on the network medium (cable or wireless). The Data Link layer encapsulates each packet in a *frame*, and the frame's header carries the hardware address of the source and destination hosts. If the destination device is on a remote network, then the frame is sent to a router to be routed through an internetwork. Once it gets to the destination network, a new frame is used to get the packet to the destination host.

To put this frame on the network, it must first be put into a digital signal. Because a frame is really a logical group of 1s and 0s, the Physical layer is responsible for encoding these digits into a digital signal, which is read by devices on the same local network. The receiving devices will synchronize on the digital signal and extract (decode) the 1s and 0s from the digital signal. At this point, the devices build the frames, run a cyclic redundancy check (CRC), and then check their answer against the answer in the frame's Frame Check Sequence (FCS) field. If it matches, the packet is pulled from the frame and what's left of the frame is discarded. This process is called *de-encapsulation*. The packet is handed to the Network layer, where the address is checked. If the address matches, the segment is pulled from the packet and what's left of the packet is discarded. The segment is processed at the Transport layer, which rebuilds the data stream and acknowledges to the transmitting station that it received each piece. It then happily hands the data stream to the upper-layer application.

In summary, at a transmitting device, the data-encapsulation method works like this:

1. User information is converted to data for transmission on the network.

2. Data is converted to segments, and a reliable connection is set up between the transmitting and receiving hosts.

3. Segments are converted to packets or datagrams, and a logical address is placed in the header so each packet can be routed through an internetwork.

4. Packets or datagrams are converted to frames for transmission on the local network. Hardware (Ethernet) addresses are used to uniquely identify hosts on a local network segment.

5. Frames are converted to bits, and a digital encoding and clocking scheme is used.

To explain this in more detail using the layer addressing, I'll use Figure 6.12.

FIGURE 6.12 PDU and layer addressing

Remember that a data stream is handed down from the upper layer to the Transport layer. As technicians, we really don't care who the data stream comes from because that's a programmer's problem. Our job is to rebuild the data stream reliably and hand it to the upper layers on the receiving device.

Before we go further in our discussion of Figure 6.12, let's review port numbers and make sure you understand them. The Transport layer uses port numbers to define both the virtual circuit and the upper-layer process, as you can see from Figure 6.13.

The Transport layer takes the data stream, makes segments out of it, and establishes a reliable session by creating a virtual circuit. It then sequences (numbers) each segment and uses acknowledgments and flow control. If you're using TCP, the virtual circuit is defined by the source port number. Remember, the host just makes this up starting at port number 1024 (0 through 1023 are reserved for well-known port numbers). The destination port number defines the upper-layer process (application) that the data stream is handed to when the data stream is reliably rebuilt on the receiving host.

FIGURE 6.13   Port numbers at the Transport layer

Now that you understand port numbers and how they're used at the Transport layer, let's go back to Figure 6.12. Once the Transport layer header information is added to the piece of data, it becomes a segment and is handed down to the Network layer along with the destination IP address. (The destination IP address was handed down from the upper layers to the Transport layer with the data stream, and it was discovered through a name resolution method at the upper layers—probably DNS.)

The Network layer adds a header, and adds the logical addressing (IP addresses), to the front of each segment. Once the header is added to the segment, the PDU is called a *packet*. The packet has a protocol field that describes where the segment came from (either UDP or TCP) so it can hand the segment to the correct protocol at the Transport layer when it reaches the receiving host.

The Network layer is responsible for finding the destination hardware address that dictates where the packet should be sent on the local network. It does this by using ARP. IP at the Network layer looks at the destination IP address and compares that address to its own source IP address and subnet mask. If it turns out to be a local network request, the hardware address of the local host is requested via an ARP request. If the packet is destined for a remote host, IP will look for the IP address of the default gateway (router) instead.

The packet, along with the destination hardware address of either the local host or default gateway, is then handed down to the Data Link layer. The Data Link layer will add a header to the front of the packet, and the piece of data then becomes a *frame*. (We call it a frame because both a header and a trailer are added to the packet, which makes the data resemble bookends or a frame, if you will.) This is shown in Figure 6.12. The frame uses an Ether-Type field to describe which protocol the packet came from at the Network layer. Now a CRC is run on the frame, and the answer to the CRC is placed in the FCS field found in the trailer of the frame.

The frame is now ready to be handed down, one bit at a time, to the Physical layer, which will use bit-timing rules to encode the data in a digital signal. Every device on the network segment will synchronize with the clock, extract the 1s and 0s from the digital signal, and build a frame. After the frame is rebuilt, a CRC is run to make sure the frame is okay. If everything turns out to be good, the hosts will check the destination address to see if the frame is for them.

If all this is making your eyes cross and your brain freeze, don't freak—things will become much clearer as we go through the book—really! Soon, I'll be going over exactly how data is encapsulated and routed through an internetwork in even more detail, in an easy to understand, step-by-step manner, in Chapter 9, "Introduction to IP Routing."

Summary

Protocols, protocols everywhere—so many different reasons for them, and so many jobs they do for us! And sometimes they even work in conjunction with each other. This can seem like way too much information, but no worries—as you become familiar with the various layers and their functions, I promise it will soon become clear that this hierarchical structure is a seriously tight, robust networking foundation.

Similarly, as you understand the TCP/IP big picture, the reason why all those protocols exist and are necessary will also become much easier to understand. They're really like a team that works jointly, from layer to layer, to make our TCP/IP networks the wonderful, great tools they are.

Exam Essentials

Remember the Process/Application layer protocols.   Telnet is a terminal-emulation program that allows you to log into a remote host and run programs. File Transfer Protocol (FTP) is a connection-oriented service that allows you to transfer files. Trivial FTP (TFTP) is a connectionless file transfer program. Simple Mail Transfer Protocol (SMTP) is a send-mail program.

Remember the Host-to-Host layer protocols.   Transmission Control Protocol (TCP) is a connection-oriented protocol that provides reliable network service by using acknowledgments and flow control. User Datagram Protocol (UDP) is a connectionless protocol that provides low overhead and is considered unreliable.

Remember the Internet layer protocols.   Internet Protocol (IP) is a connectionless protocol that provides network address and routing through an internetwork. Address Resolution

Protocol (ARP) finds a hardware address from a known IP address. Internet Control Message Protocol (ICMP) provides diagnostics and Destination Unreachable messages.

Remember the difference between connection-oriented and connectionless network services.   Connection-oriented services use acknowledgments and flow control to create a reliable session. More overhead is used than in a connectionless network service. Connectionless services are used to send data with no acknowledgments or flow control. This is considered unreliable.

Written Lab

Provide the answers to the following questions:

You can find the answers in Appendix B.

1. What might be the problem if a DHCP client suddenly finds itself in a different IP subnet from the one it should be in?

2. Name the protocol that uses both TCP ports 20 and 21.

3. What two Transport layer protocols does a DNS server use?

4. Which protocol dynamically reports errors to source hosts by using IP directly to build packets?

5. What could cause a server that you can ping not to provide the particular TCP/IP service, such as FTP, HTTP, and so on, that you expect it to offer?

6. What might cause your email to stop functioning properly when you change Internet service providers?

7. Which Unix command is used for terminal emulation in the same way Telnet is used?

8. What protocol is at the heart of the `ping` and `tracert` commands in a Windows operating system?

9. Which destination Transport layer protocol and port number does a TFTP client use to transfer files over the network?

10. What well-known port numbers do SMTP, POP3, RDP, and IMAP4 servers use?

    You can find the answers to the written labs in Appendix B.

Review Questions

You can find the answers in Appendix A.

1. The OSI model has seven layers and the DoD has four. At which layer does SMTP work in both models?

   A. Network

   B. Transport

   C. Session

   D. Application

   E. Internet

2. You need to have secure communications using HTTPS. What port number is used by default?

   A. 69

   B. 23

   C. 21

   D. 443

3. You want to implement a mechanism that automates the IP configuration, including IP address, subnet mask, default gateway, and DNS information. Which protocol will you use to accomplish this?

   A. SMTP

   B. SNMP

   C. DHCP

   D. ARP

4. What protocol is used to find the hardware address of a local device?

   A. RARP

   B. ARP

   C. IP

   D. ICMP

   E. BootP

5. You need to log in to a Unix server across a network that is not secure. Which of the following protocols will allow you to remotely administrator this server securely?

   A. Telnet

   B. SSH

   C. SFTP

   D. HTTP

6. If you can ping by IP address but not by hostname, or FQDN, which of the following port numbers is related to the server process that is involved?

    A. 21

    B. 23

    C. 53

    D. 69

    E. 80

7. Which of the following describe the DHCP Discover message? (Choose two.)

    A. It uses FF:FF:FF:FF:FF:FF as a Layer 2 broadcast.

    B. It uses UDP as the Transport layer protocol.

    C. It uses TCP as the Transport layer protocol.

    D. It does not use a Layer 2 destination address.

8. What Layer 4 protocol is used for a Telnet connection, and what is the default port number?

    A. IP, 6

    B. TCP, 21

    C. UDP, 23

    D. ICMP, 21

    E. TCP, 23

9. Which statements are true regarding ICMP packets? (Choose two.)

    A. They acknowledge receipt of a TCP segment.

    B. They guarantee datagram delivery.

    C. They can provide hosts with information about network problems.

    D. They are encapsulated within IP datagrams.

    E. They are encapsulated within UDP datagrams.

10. Which of the following services use TCP? (Choose three.)

    A. DHCP

    B. SMTP

    C. SNMP

    D. FTP

    E. HTTP

    F. TFTP

11. Which of the following services use UDP? (Choose three.)

    A. DHCP

    B. SMTP

    C. SNMP

    D. FTP

    E. HTTP

    F. TFTP

12. Which of the following TCP/IP protocols are used at the Application layer of the OSI model? (Choose three.)

    A. IP

    B. TCP

    C. Telnet

    D. FTP

    E. TFTP

13. Which of the following protocols is used by email servers to exchange messages with one another? Choose all that appply.

    A. POP3

    B. IMAP

    C. SMTP

    D. HTTP

14. You need to have a connection to run applications that are installed on only your desktop computer at your office. Which protocol will provide a GUI interface to your work computer?

    A. Telnet

    B. FTP

    C. RDP

    D. IMAP

    E. SMTP

15. Which of the following protocols can use TCP and UDP, permits authentication and secure polling of network devices, and allows for automated alerts and reports on network devices? Choose all that appply.

    A. DNS

    B. SNMP

    C. SMTP

    D. TCP

16. You need to transfer files between two hosts. Which two protocols can you use?

   A. SNMP

   B. SCP

   C. RIP

   D. NTP

   E. FTP

17. What layer in the IP stack is equivalent to the Transport layer of the OSI model?

   A. Application

   B. Host-to-Host

   C. Internet

   D. Network Access

18. You need to make sure that the time is consistent across all your network devices. What protocol do you need to run on your network?

   A. FTP

   B. SCP

   C. NTP

   E. RTP

19. Which of the following allows a server to distinguish among different simultaneous requests from the same host? Choose all that appply.

   A. They have different port numbers.

   B. A NAT server changes the IP address for subsequent requests.

   C. A server is unable to accept multiple simultaneous sessions from the same host. One session must end before another can begin.

   D. The MAC address for each one is unique.

20. Which of the following uses both TCP and UDP? Choose all that appply.

   A. FTP

   B. SMTP

   C. Telnet

   D. DNS

Chapter

7

IP Addressing

THE FOLLOWING COMPTIA NETWORK+ EXAM OBJECTIVES ARE COVERED IN THIS CHAPTER:

✓ **1.3 Explain the purpose and properties of IP addressing.**

- Classes of addresses
  - A, B, C, and D
  - Public vs. Private
- Classless (CIDR)
- IPv4 vs. IPv6 (formatting)
- MAC address format
- Multicast vs. unicast vs. broadcast
- APIPA

One of the most important topics in any discussion of TCP/IP is IP addressing. An *IP address* is a numeric identifier assigned to each machine on an IP network. It designates the specific location of a device on the network.

An IP address is a software address, not a hardware address—the latter is hard-coded on a network interface card (NIC) and used for finding hosts on a local network. IP addressing was designed to allow hosts on one network to communicate with a host on a different network regardless of the type of LANs the hosts are participating in.

Before we get into the more complicated aspects of IP addressing, you need to understand some of the basics. First I'm going to explain some of the fundamentals of IP addressing and its terminology. Then you'll learn about the hierarchical IP addressing scheme and private IP addresses.

I'll define unicast, multicast, and broadcast addresses and then finish the chapter with a discussion on IPv6. And I promise to make it all as painless as possible.

The reason that we would even discuss IPv6 (besides to cover the objectives, of course) is because of the lack of IPv4 addresses available for use in future networks, which we need to keep our corporate and private networks and even the Internet running. Basically, we're running out of addresses for all our new hosts! IPv6 will fix this for us.

To find up-to-the-minute updates for this chapter, please see www.lammle.com/forum or the book's web site at www.sybex.com/go/netplus2e.

IP Terminology

Throughout this chapter, you'll learn several important terms vital to your understanding of the Internet Protocol. Here are a few to get you started:

Bit   A *bit* is one digit, either a 1 or a 0.

Byte   A *byte* is 7 or 8 bits, depending on whether parity is used. For the rest of this chapter, always assume a byte is 8 bits.

Octet   An octet, made up of 8 bits, is just an ordinary 8-bit binary number. In this chapter, the terms *byte* and *octet* are completely interchangeable.

Network address   This is the designation used in routing to send packets to a remote network—for example, 10.0.0.0, 172.16.0.0, and 192.168.10.0.

Broadcast address   The *broadcast address* is used by applications and hosts to send information to all hosts on a network. Examples include 255.255.255.255, which designates all networks and all hosts; 172.16.255.255, which specifies all subnets and hosts on network 172.16.0.0; and 10.255.255.255, which broadcasts to all subnets and hosts on network 10.0.0.0.

You will find the terms *subnet mask* and *slash notation* (for example, /24) used a few times in this chapter. These terms will be fully defined and used in Chapter 8, "IP Subnetting, Troubleshooting IP, and Introduction to NAT."

The Hierarchical IP Addressing Scheme

An IP address consists of 32 bits of information. These bits are divided into four sections, referred to as *octets* or bytes, and four octets sum up to 32 bits ($8 \times 4 = 32$). You can depict an IP address using one of three methods:

- Dotted-decimal, as in 172.16.30.56
- Binary, as in 10101100.00010000.00011110.00111000
- Hexadecimal, as in AC.10.1E.38

Each of these examples validly represents the same IP address. Hexadecimal isn't used as often as dotted-decimal or binary in IP addressing, but you still might find an IP address stored in hexadecimal in some programs. The Windows Registry is a good example of a program that stores a machine's IP address in hex.

The 32-bit IP address is known as a structured, or hierarchical, address as opposed to a flat, or nonhierarchical, address. Although either type of addressing scheme can be used, *hierarchical addressing* has been chosen for a very important reason. The major advantage of this scheme is that it can handle a large number of addresses, namely, 4.3 billion (a 32-bit address space with two possible values for each position—either 0 or 1—gives you 2^{32}, or 4,294,967,296). The disadvantage of the flat-addressing scheme, and the reason it's not used for IP addressing, relates to routing. If every address were unique, all routers on the Internet would need to store the address of each and every machine on the Internet. This would make efficient routing impossible, even if only a fraction of all possible addresses were used.

The solution to this problem is to use a two- or three-level hierarchical addressing scheme that is structured by network and host or by network, subnet, and host.

This two- or three-level scheme is comparable to a telephone number. The first section, the area code, designates a very large area. The second section, the prefix, narrows the scope to a local calling area. The final segment, the customer number, zooms in on the specific connection. IP addresses use the same type of layered structure. Rather than all 32 bits being treated as a unique identifier, as in flat addressing, a part of the address is designated as the network address and the other part is designated as either the subnet and host or just the host address.

Next, I'm going to cover IP network addressing and the different classes of addresses used for our networks.

Network Addressing

The *network address*—also called the network number—uniquely identifies each network. Every machine on the same network shares that network address as part of its IP address. In the IP address 172.16.30.56, for example, 172.16 is the network address.

The *host address* is assigned to, and uniquely identifies, each machine on a network. This part of the address must be unique because it identifies a particular machine—an individual—as opposed to a network, which is a group. This number can also be referred to as a *host address*. So in the sample IP address 172.16.30.56, the 30.56 is the host address.

The designers of the Internet decided to create classes of networks based on network size. For the small number of networks possessing a very large number of hosts, they created the rank *Class A network*. At the other extreme is the *Class C network*, which is reserved for the numerous networks with a small number of hosts. The class distinction for networks between very large and very small is predictably the *Class B network*.

Subdividing an IP address into a network and host address is determined by the class designation of your network. Figure 7.1 summarizes the classes of networks—a subject I'll explain in much greater detail throughout this chapter.

FIGURE 7.1 Summary of the three classes of networks

To ensure efficient routing, Internet designers defined a mandate for the leading-bits section of the address for each different network class. For example, since a router knows that a Class A network address always starts with a 0, the router might be able to speed a packet on its way after reading only the first bit of its address. This is where the address schemes define the difference between a Class A, a Class B, and a Class C address. Coming up, I'll discuss the differences between these three classes followed by a discussion of the Class D and Class E addresses. For now, know that Classes A, B, and C are the only ranges that are used to address hosts in our networks.

Class A Addresses

In a Class A network address, the first byte is assigned to the network address, and the three remaining bytes are used for the host addresses. The Class A format is as follows:

`network.host.host.host`

For example, in the IP address 49.22.102.70, the 49 is the network address and 22.102.70 is the host address. Every machine on this particular network would begin with the distinctive network address of 49.

Class A network addresses are 1 byte long, with the first bit of that byte reserved and the 7 remaining bits available for manipulation, or addressing. As a result, the maximum number of Class A networks that can be created is 128. Why? Well, each of the 7 bit positions can be either a 0 or a 1 and 2^7 gives you 128.

The designers of the IP address scheme said that the first bit of the first byte in a Class A network address must always be off, or 0. This means a Class A address must be between 0 and 127 in the first byte, inclusive.

Consider the following network address:

0xxxxxxx

If we turn the other 7 bits all off and then turn them all on, we'll find the Class A range of network addresses:

00000000 = 0
01111111 = 127

So, a Class A network is defined in the first octet between 0 and 127, and it can't be less or more.

To complicate matters further, the network address of all 0s (0000 0000) is reserved to designate the default route (see Table 7.1). Additionally, the address 127, which is reserved for diagnostics, can't be used either, which means that you can really only use the numbers 1 to 126 to designate Class A network addresses. This means the actual number of usable Class A network addresses is 128 minus 2, or 126.

TABLE 7.1   Reserved IP addresses

Address	Function
Network address of all 0s	Interpreted to mean "this network or segment."
Network address of all 1s	Interpreted to mean "all networks."
Network 127.0.0.1	Reserved for loopback tests. Designates the local host and allows that host to send a test packet to itself without generating network traffic.

TABLE 7.1   Reserved IP addresses *(continued)*

Address	Function
Host address of all 0s	Interpreted to mean "network address" or any host on specified network.
Host address of all 1s	Interpreted to mean "all hosts" on the specified network; for example, 128.2.255.255 means "all hosts" on network 128.2 (Class B address).
Entire IP address set to all 0s	Used by Cisco routers to designate the default route. Could also mean "any network."
Entire IP address set to all 1s (same as 255.255.255.255)	Broadcast to all hosts on the current network; sometimes called an "all 1s broadcast" or limited broadcast.

Each Class A address has 3 bytes (24 bit positions) for the host address of a machine. This means there are 2^{24}—or 16,777,216—unique combinations and, therefore, precisely that many potential unique host addresses for each Class A network. Because host addresses with the two patterns of all 0s and all 1s are reserved, the actual maximum usable number of hosts for a Class A network is 2^{24} minus 2, which equals 16,777,214. Either way, you can see that's a seriously huge number of hosts to have on a network segment!

Here's an example of how to figure out the valid host IDs in a Class A network address:

- All host bits off is the network address: 10.0.0.0.
- All host bits on is the broadcast address: 10.255.255.255.

The valid hosts are the numbers in between the network address and the broadcast address: 10.0.0.1 through 10.255.255.254. Notice that 0s and 255s can be valid host IDs. All you need to remember when trying to find valid host addresses is that the host bits can't ever be all be turned off or all turned on at the same time.

Class B Addresses

In a Class B network address, the first 2 bytes are assigned to the network address and the remaining 2 bytes are used for host addresses. The format is as follows:

network.network.host.host

For example, in the IP address 172.16.30.56, the network address is 172.16 and the host address is 30.56.

With a network address being 2 bytes (8 bits each), we're left with 2^{16} unique combinations. But the Internet designers decided that all Class B network addresses should start with the binary digit 1, then 0. This leaves 14 bit positions available to manipulate, so in reality, we get 16,384 (that is, 2^{14}) unique Class B network addresses.

In a Class B network, the RFCs state that the first bit of the first byte must always be turned on but the second bit must always be turned off. If we turn the other 6 bits all off and then all on, we will find the range for a Class B network:

10000000 = 128
10111111 = 191

As you can see, a Class B network is defined when the first byte is configured from 128 to 191.

A Class B address uses 2 bytes for host addresses. This is 2^{16} minus the two reserved patterns (all 0s and all 1s), for a total of 65,534 possible host addresses for each Class B network.

Here's an example of how to find the valid hosts in a Class B network:

- All host bits turned off is the network address: 172.16.0.0.
- All host bits turned on is the broadcast address: 172.16.255.255.

The valid hosts would be the numbers in between the network address and the broadcast address: 172.16.0.1 through 172.16.255.254.

Class C Addresses

The first 3 bytes of a Class C network address are dedicated to the network portion of the address, with only 1 measly byte remaining for the host address. Here's the format:

network.network.network.host

Using the example IP address 192.168.100.102, the network address is 192.168.100 and the host address is 102.

In a Class C network address, the first three bit positions are always the binary 110. The calculation is as follows: 3 bytes, or 24 bits, minus 3 reserved positions leaves 21 positions. Hence, there are 2^{21}, or 2,097,152, possible Class C networks.

For Class C networks, the RFCs define the first 2 bits of the first octet as always turned on, but the third bit can never be on. Following the same process as the previous classes, convert from binary to decimal to find the range. Here's the range for a Class C network:

11000000 = 192
11011111 = 223

So, if you see an IP address with a range from 192 up to 223, you'll know it's a Class C IP address.

Each unique Class C network has 1 byte to use for host addresses. This gets us to 2^8, or 256, minus the two reserved patterns of all 0s and all 1s for a total of 254 available host addresses for each Class C network.

Here's an example of how to find a valid host ID in a Class C network:

- All host bits turned off is the network ID: 192.168.100.0.
- All host bits turned on is the broadcast address: 192.168.100.255.

The valid hosts would be the numbers in between the network address and the broadcast address: 192.168.100.1 through 192.168.100.254.

Class D and E Addresses

The addresses 224 to 255 are reserved for Class D and E networks. Class D (224–239) is used for multicast addresses and Class E (240–255) for scientific purposes. But they're really beyond the scope of this book, so I'm not going to go into detail about them here. But you do need to know that the multicast range is from 224.0.0.0 through 239.255.255.255.

Special Purposes of Network Addresses

Some IP addresses are reserved for special purposes, so network administrators can't ever assign them to hosts. Table 7.1 listed the members of this exclusive little club and the reasons why they're included in it.

Private IP Addresses

The people who created the IP addressing scheme also created what we call *private IP addresses*. These addresses can be used on a private network, but they're not routable through the Internet. This is designed for the purpose of creating a measure of much-needed security, but it also conveniently saves valuable IP address space.

If every host on every network had to have real routable IP addresses, we would have run out of available IP addresses to hand out years ago. But by using private IP addresses, ISPs, corporations, and home users need only a relatively tiny group of bona fide IP addresses to connect their networks to the Internet. This is economical because they can use private IP addresses on their inside networks and get along just fine.

To accomplish this task, the ISP and the corporation—the end users, no matter who they are—need to use something called Network Address Translation (NAT), which basically takes a private IP address and converts it for use on the Internet. NAT provides security in that these IP addresses cannot be seen by external users. External users will only be able to see the public IP address to which the private IP address has been mapped. Moreover, multiple devices in the same private network can use the same, real IP address to transmit out onto the Internet. Doing things this way saves megatons of address space—a very good thing for us all!

Table 7.2 lists the reserved private addresses.

TABLE 7.2   Reserved IP address space

Address class	Reserved address space
Class A	10.0.0.0 through 10.255.255.255
Class B	172.16.0.0 through 172.31.255.255
Class C	192.168.0.0 through 192.168.255.255

> ### 🌐 Real World Scenario
>
> #### So, What Private IP Address Should I Use?
>
> That's a really great question: Should you use Class A, Class B, or even Class C private addressing when setting up your network? Let's take Acme Corporation in San Francisco as an example. This company is moving into a new building and needs a whole new network (what a treat this is!). It has 14 departments, with about 70 users in each. You could probably squeeze three or four Class C addresses to use, or maybe you could use a Class B, or even a Class A just for fun.
>
> The rule of thumb in the consulting world is, when you're setting up a corporate network—regardless of how small it is—you should use a Class A network address because it gives you the most flexibility and growth options. For example, if you used the 10.0.0.0 network address with a /24 mask, then you'd have 65,536 networks, each with 254 hosts. Lots of room for growth with that network! You would then subnet this network address space using Classless Internet Domain Routing (CIDR), which provides only the needed amount of hosts to each department or building without wasting IP addresses.
>
> (A /24 tells you that a subnet mask has 24 bits out of 32 bits turned on for subnetting a network. This will be covered, as well as CIDR, in more detail in Chapter 8.)
>
> But if you're setting up a home network, you'd opt for a Class C address because it is the easiest for people to understand and configure. Using the default Class C mask gives you one network with 254 hosts—plenty for a home network.
>
> With the Acme Corporation, a nice 10.1.*x*.0 with a /24 mask (the *x* is the subnet for each department) makes this easy to design, install, and troubleshoot.

APIPA

I discussed this in Chapter 6, "Introduction to the Internet Protocol," but it is worth repeating here. What happens if you have a few hosts connected together with a switch or hub and you don't have a DHCP server? You can add static IP information to a host or you can let Windows provides what is called Automatic Private IP Addressing (APIPA). I don't recommend this, but APIPA is a "feature," so you do need to remember it, hence mentioning it two chapters in a row!

With APIPA, clients can automatically self-configure an IP address and subnet mask, which is the minimum information needed for hosts to communicate when a DHCP server isn't available. In this way, it could be thought of as a DHCP failover scheme. If all of the hosts set themselves with an APIPA address, they could communicate with one another, but unfortunately not with any addresses that were statically configured such as default gateways!

The IP address range for APIPA is 169.254.0.1 through 169.254.255.254. The client also configures itself with a default class B subnet mask of 255.255.0.0.

However, when you're in your corporate network and you're running a DHCP server, and your host displays that it is using this IP address range, this means that either your DHCP client on the host is not working or the DHCP server is down or can't be reached because of a network issue. For example, if you plug a DHCP client into a port that is disabled, the host will receive an APIPA address. I don't know anyone who has seen a host in the APIPA address range and been happy about it!

IPv4 Address Types

Most people use *broadcast* as a generic term, and most of the time, we understand what they mean. But not always. For example, you might say, "The host broadcasted through a router to a DHCP server," but, well, it's pretty unlikely that this would ever really happen. What you probably mean—using the correct technical jargon—is, "The DHCP client broadcasted for an IP address; a router then forwarded this as a unicast packet to the DHCP server." Oh, and remember that with IPv4, broadcasts are pretty important, but with IPv6, there aren't any broadcasts sent at all—as you'll see in the next section!

Okay, I've referred to broadcast addresses throughout earlier chapters, and even showed you some examples of various IP addresses. But I really haven't gone into the different terms and uses associated with them yet, and it's about time I did. So here are the four IPv4 address types that I'd like to define for you:

Layer 2 broadcasts   These are sent to all nodes on a LAN.

Broadcasts (Layer 3)   These are sent to all nodes on the network.

Unicast   This is an address for a single interface, and these are used to send packets to a single destination host.

Multicast   These are packets sent from a single source and transmitted to many devices on different networks. Referred to as *one-to-many*.

Layer 2 Broadcasts

First, understand that Layer 2 broadcasts are also known as hardware broadcasts—they only go out on a LAN, and they don't go past the LAN boundary (router).

The typical hardware address is 6 bytes (48 bits) and looks something like 0c43.a4.f312.c2. The broadcast would be all 1s in binary, which would be all *F*s in hexadecimal, as in FF.FF .FF.FF.FF.FF.

Layer 3 Broadcasts

Then there are the plain old broadcast addresses at Layer 3. Broadcast messages are meant to reach all hosts on a broadcast domain. These are the network broadcasts that have all host bits on.

Here's an example that you're already familiar with: The network address of 172.16.0.0 255.255.0.0 would have a broadcast address of 172.16.255.255—all host bits on. Broadcasts can also be "any network and all hosts," as indicated by 255.255.255.255.

A good example of a broadcast message is an Address Resolution Protocol (ARP) request. When a host has a packet, it knows the logical address (IP) of the destination. To get the packet to the destination, the host needs to forward the packet to a default gateway if the destination resides on a different IP network. If the destination is on the local network, the source will forward the packet directly to the destination. Because the source doesn't have the MAC address to which it needs to forward the frame, it sends out a broadcast, something that every device in the local broadcast domain will listen to. This broadcast says, in essence, "If you are the owner of IP address 192.168.2.3, please forward your MAC address to me," with the source giving the appropriate information.

Unicast Address

A unicast address is assigned to a single interface, and this term is used both in IPv4 and IPv6 to describe your host interface IP address.

Multicast Address

Multicast is a different beast entirely. At first glance, it appears to be a hybrid of unicast and broadcast communication, but that isn't quite the case. Multicast does allow point-to-multipoint communication, which is similar to broadcasts, but it happens in a different manner. The crux of *multicast* is that it enables multiple recipients to receive messages without flooding the messages to all hosts on a broadcast domain. However, this is not the default behavior—it's what we can do with multicasting if it's configured correctly!

Multicast works by sending messages or data to IP multicast group addresses. Routers then forward copies (unlike broadcasts, which are not forwarded) of the packet out every interface that has hosts subscribed to a particular group address. This is where multicast differs from broadcast messages—with multicast communication, copies of packets, in theory, are sent only to subscribed hosts. When I say in theory, this means that the hosts will receive, for example, a multicast packet destined for 224.0.0.10 (this is an EIGRP packet and only a router running the EIGRP protocol will read these). All hosts on the broadcast LAN (Ethernet is a broadcast multi-access LAN technology) will pick up the frame, read the destination address, and immediately discard the frame, unless they are in the multicast group. This saves PC processing, not LAN bandwidth. Multicasting can cause severe LAN congestion, in some instances, if not implemented carefully.

There are several different groups that users or applications can subscribe to. The range of multicast addresses starts with 224.0.0.0 and goes through 239.255.255.255. As you can see, this range of addresses falls within IP Class D address space based on classful IP assignment.

Internet Protocol Version 6 (IPv6)

People refer to IPv6 as "the next-generation Internet protocol," and it was originally created as the answer to IPv4's inevitable, looming address-exhaustion crisis. Though you've probably heard a thing or two about IPv6 already, it has been improved even further in the quest to bring us the flexibility, efficiency, capability, and optimized functionality that can truly meet our ever-increasing needs. The capacity of its predecessor, IPv4, pales in comparison—and that's the reason it will eventually fade into history completely.

The IPv6 header and address structure has been completely overhauled, and many of the features that were basically just afterthoughts and addendums in IPv4 are now included as full-blown standards in IPv6. It's well equipped, poised, and ready to manage the mind-blowing demands of the Internet to come.

Why Do We Need IPv6?

Well, the short answer is because we need to communicate and our current system isn't really cutting it anymore—kind of like how the Pony Express couldn't compete with airmail. Just look at how much time and effort we've invested in coming up with slick new ways to conserve bandwidth and IP addresses.

It's reality, the number of people and devices that connect to networks increases each and every day. That's not a bad thing at all—we're finding new and exciting ways to communicate with more people all the time, something that's become integral to our culture today. In fact, it's now pretty much a basic human need. But the forecast isn't exactly blue skies and sunshine because, as I alluded to in this chapter's introduction, IPv4, upon which our ability to communicate is presently dependent, is going to run out of addresses for us to use. IPv4 has only about 4.3 billion addresses available—in theory—and we know that we don't even get to use all of those. There really are only about 250 million addresses that can be assigned to devices. Sure, the use of Classless Inter-Domain Routing (CIDR) and NAT has helped to extend the inevitable dearth of addresses, but the truth is we will run out of them, and it's going to happen within a few years. China is barely online, and we know a huge population of people and corporations there surely want to be. There are a lot of reports that give us all kinds of numbers, but all you really need to think about to convince yourself that I'm not just being an alarmist is the fact that there are about 6.5 billion people in the world today, and it's estimated that just over 10 percent of that population is connected to the Internet—wow! IPv6 to the rescue!

That statistic is basically screaming at us the ugly truth that, based on IPv4's capacity, every person can't have a single computer with an IP address—let alone all the other devices we use with them. I have more than one computer, and it's pretty likely you do too. And I'm not even including in the mix phones, laptops, game consoles, fax machines, routers, switches, and a mother lode of other devices we use every day! So I think I've made it pretty clear that we've got to do something before we run out of addresses and lose the ability to connect with each other as we know it. And that "something" just happens to be implementing IPv6.

The Benefits of and Uses for IPv6

What's so fabulous about IPv6? Is it really the answer to our coming dilemma? Is it really worth it to upgrade from IPv4? All good questions—you may even think of a few more. Of course, there's going to be that group of people with the time-tested and well-known "resistance-to-change syndrome," but don't listen to them. If we had done that years ago, we'd still be waiting weeks, even months for our mail to arrive via horseback. Instead, just know that the answer is a resounding YES! Not only does IPv6 give us lots of addresses (3.4×10^{38} = definitely enough), but there are many other features built into this version that make it well worth the cost, time, and effort required to migrate to it.

Today's networks, as well as the Internet, have a ton of unforeseen requirements that simply were not considerations when IPv4 was created. We've tried to compensate with a collection of add-ons that can actually make implementing them more difficult than mandating them by a standard. By default, IPv6 has improved upon and included many of those features as standard and mandatory. One of these sweet new standards is IPSec—a feature that provides end-to-end security and that I'll cover in Chapter 13, "Authentication and Access Control." Another little beauty is known as *mobility*, and as its name suggests, it allows a device to roam from one network to another without dropping connections.

But it's the efficiency features that are really going to rock the house! For starters, the header in an IPv6 packet has half the fields, and they are aligned to 64 bits, which gives us some seriously souped-up processing speed—compared to IPv4, lookups happen at light speed. Most of the information that used to be bound into the IPv4 header was taken out, and now you can choose to put it, or parts of it, back into the header in the form of optional extension headers that follow the basic header fields.

And of course there's that whole new universe of addresses (3.4×10^{38}) we talked about already. But where did we get them? Did that *Criss Angel Mindfreak* dude just show up and, blammo, they all materialized? The obvious answer is no, but that huge proliferation of addresses, had to come from somewhere, right? Well, it just so happens that IPv6 gives us a substantially larger address space, meaning the address is a whole lot bigger—four times bigger, as a matter of fact! An IPv6 address is actually 128 bits in length, and no worries—I'm going to break down the address piece by piece and show you exactly what it looks like coming up in the next section, "IPv6 Addressing and Expressions." For now, let me just say that all that additional room permits more levels of hierarchy inside the address space and a more flexible address architecture. It also makes routing much more efficient and scalable because the addresses can be aggregated a lot more effectively. And IPv6 also allows multiple addresses for hosts and networks. Plus, the new version of IP now includes an expanded use of multicast communication (one device sending to many hosts or to a select group), which will also join in to boost efficiency on networks because communications will be more specific.

IPv4 uses broadcasts very prolifically, causing a bunch of problems, the worst of which is of course the dreaded broadcast storm—an uncontrolled deluge of forwarded broadcast traffic that can bring an entire network to its knees and devour every last bit of bandwidth. Another nasty thing about broadcast traffic is that it interrupts each and every device on the network. When a broadcast is sent out, every machine has to stop what it's doing and analyze the traffic, whether the broadcast is meant for it or not.

But smile, everyone: There is no such thing as a broadcast in IPv6 because it uses multicast traffic instead. And there are two other types of communication as well: unicast, which is the same as it is in IPv4, and a new type called *anycast*. Anycast communication allows the same address to be placed on more than one device so that when traffic is sent to one device addressed in this way, it is routed to the nearest host that shares the same address. This is just the beginning—we'll get more into the various types of communication later in this chapter in the section "Address Types."

IPv6 Addressing and Expressions

Just as understanding how IP addresses are structured and used is critical with IPv4 addressing, it's also vital when it comes to IPv6. You've already read about the fact that at 128 bits, an IPv6 address is much larger than an IPv4 address. Because of this, as well as because of the new ways the addresses can be used, you've probably guessed that IPv6 will be more complicated to manage. But no worries! As I said, I'll break it down into the basics and show you what the address looks like, how you can write it, and what many of its common uses are. It's going to be a little weird at first, but before you know it, you'll have it nailed.

So let's take a look at Figure 7.2, which has a sample IPv6 address broken down into sections.

FIGURE 7.2 IPv6 address example

```
2001:0db8:3c4d:0012:0000:0000:1234:56ab
_____I____I_____
Global Prefix    Subnet      Interface ID
```

As you can now see, the address is truly much larger—but what else is different? Well, first, notice that it has eight groups of numbers instead of four and also that those groups are separated by colons instead of periods. And hey, wait a second…there are letters in that address! Yep, the address is expressed in hexadecimal just like a MAC address is, so you could say this address has eight 16-bit hexadecimal colon-delimited blocks. That's already quite a mouthful, and you probably haven't even tried to say the address out loud yet.

One other thing I want to point out is for when you set up your test network to play with IPv6, because I know you're going to want to do that. When you use a web browser to make an HTTP connection to an IPv6 device, you have to type the address into the browser with brackets around the literal address. Why? Well, a colon is already being used by the browser for specifying a port number. So basically, if you don't enclose the address in brackets, the browser will have no way to identify the information.

Here's an example of how this looks:

`http://[2001:0db8:3c4d:0012:0000:0000:1234:56ab]/default.html`

Now obviously, if you could, you would rather use names to specify a destination (like `www.lammle.com`); but even though it's definitely going to be a pain in the rear, you just have to accept the fact that sometimes you have to bite the bullet and type in the address number. It should be pretty clear that DNS is going to become extremely important when implementing IPv6.

Shortened Expression

The good news is, there are a few tricks to help rescue you when you're writing these monster addresses. For one thing, you can actually leave out parts of the address to abbreviate it, but to get away with doing that you have to follow a couple of rules. First, you can drop any leading zeros in each of the individual blocks. After you do that, the sample address from earlier would then look like this:

`2001:db8:3c4d:12:0:0:1234:56ab`

Okay, that's a definite improvement—at least you don't have to write all of those extra zeros! But what about whole blocks that don't have anything in them except zeros? Well, you can kind of lose those too—at least some of them. Again referring to our sample address, you can remove the two blocks of zeros by replacing them with double colons, like this:

`2001:db8:3c4d:12::1234:56ab`

Cool—you replaced the blocks of all zeros with double colons. The rule you have to follow to get away with this is that you can only replace one contiguous block of zeros in an address. So if my address has four blocks of zeros and each of them is separated, I don't get to replace them all. Check out this example:

`2001:0000:0000:0012:0000:0000:1234:56ab`

And just know that you *can't* do this:

`2001::12::1234:56ab`

Instead, this is the best that you can do:

`2001::12:0:0:1234:56ab`

The reason why this example is your best shot is that if you remove two sets of zeros, the device looking at the address will have no way of knowing where the zeros go back in. Basically, the router would look at the incorrect address and say, "Well, do I place two blocks into the first set of double colons and two into the second set, or do I place three blocks into the first set and one block into the second set?" And on and on it would go because the information the router needs just isn't there.

Address Types

We're all familiar with IPv4's unicast, broadcast, and multicast addresses, which basically define who or at least how many other devices we're talking to. But as I mentioned, IPv6 adds to that trio and introduces the anycast address type. Broadcasts, as we know them, have been eliminated in IPv6 because of their cumbersome inefficiency.

Since a single interface can have multiple types of IPv6 addresses assigned for various purposes, let's find out what each of these types of IPv6 addresses are and the communication methods of each:

Unicast   Packets addressed to a unicast address are delivered to a single interface, same as in IPv4. For load balancing, multiple interfaces can use the same address.

Global unicast addresses   These are your typical publicly routable addresses, and they're used the same way globally unique addresses are in IPv4.

Link-local addresses   These are like the private addresses in IPv4 in that they're not meant to be routed and are unique for each link (LAN). Think of them as a handy tool that gives you the ability to throw a temporary LAN together for meetings or for creating a small LAN that's not going to be routed but still needs to share and access files and services locally. However, link-local is used on every LAN that connects to a router interface(s) as well.

Unique local addresses   These addresses are also intended for nonrouting purposes, but they are nearly globally unique, so it's unlikely you'll ever have one of them overlap with any other address. Unique local addresses were designed to replace site-local addresses, so they basically do almost exactly what IPv4 private addresses do—allow communication throughout a site while being routable to multiple local networks. The difference between link-local and unique local is that unique local can be routed within your organization or company.

Multicast   Again, as in IPv4, packets addressed to a multicast address are delivered to all interfaces identified by the multicast address. Sometimes people call them *one-to-many addresses*. It's really easy to spot multicast addresses in IPv6 because they always start with *FF*.

Anycast   Like multicast addresses, an anycast address identifies multiple interfaces, but there's a big difference: The anycast packet is delivered to only one address—actually, to the first IPv6 address it finds defined in terms of routing distance. And again, this address is special because you can apply a single address to more than one interface. You could call them one-to-one-of-many addresses, but just saying anycast is a lot easier.

You're probably wondering if there are any special, reserved addresses in IPv6 because you know they're there in IPv4. Well, there are—plenty of them! Let's go over them now.

Special Addresses

I'm going to list some of the addresses and address ranges that you should definitely make a point to remember because you'll eventually use them. They're all special or reserved for specific use; but unlike IPv4, IPv6 gives us a galaxy of addresses, so reserving a few here and there doesn't hurt a thing.

0:0:0:0:0:0:0:0   Equals ::. This is the equivalent of IPv4's 0.0.0.0 and is typically the source address of a host when you're using stateful configuration (DHCP).

0:0:0:0:0:0:0:1   Equals ::1. The equivalent of 127.0.0.1 in IPv4.

0:0:0:0:0:0:192.168.100.1   This is how an IPv4 address would be written in a mixed IPv6/IPv4 network environment.

2000::/3   The global unicast address range.

FC00::/7   The unique local unicast range.

FE80::/10   The link-local unicast range.

FF00::/8   The multicast range.

3FFF:FFFF::/32   Reserved for examples and documentation.

2001:0DB8::/32   Also reserved for examples and documentation.

2002::/16   Used with *6to4*, which is the transition system—the structure that allows IPv6 packets to be transmitted over an IPv4 network without the need to configure explicit tunnels.

Summary

In this chapter, I covered the very basics of both IPv4 and IPv6 and how they work in an internetwork (remember that if the word *IP* is used alone, it is referring to just IPv4). As you now know by reading this chapter, even when discussing and configuring the basics, there is a lot to understand—and we just scratched the surface. But trust me when I say this—you now know more than you'll need to meet the Network+ objectives.

I discussed in detail the difference between each class of address and how to find a network address, broadcast address, and valid host range.

I explained why we need IPv6 and the benefits associated with it. I followed that up by covering addressing with IPv6 as well as how to use the shortened expressions. And during the discussion on addressing with IPv6, I showed you the different address types, plus the special addresses reserved in IPv6.

The next chapter is very important, but it's one that some people find rather challenging, so take a break and get ready for a really fun but long chapter on IP subnetting. I promise not to torture you too much!

Exam Essentials

Remember the Class A range.   The IP range for a Class A network is 1 through 126. This provides 8 bits of network addressing and 24 bits of host addressing by default.

Remember the Class B range.   The IP range for a Class B network is 128 through 191. Class B addressing provides 16 bits of network addressing and 16 bits of host addressing by default.

Remember the Class C range.   The IP range for a Class C network is 192 through 223. Class C addressing provides 24 bits of network addressing and 8 bits of host addressing by default.

Remember the Private IP ranges.   The Class A private address range is 10.0.0.0 through 10.255.255.255.

The Class B private address range is 172.16.0.0 through 172.31.255.255.

The Class C private address range is 192.168.0.0 through 192.168.255.255.

Remember the APIPA range.   The IP address range for APIPA is 169.254.0.1 through 169.254.255.254. The client also configures itself with a default class B subnet mask of 255.255.0.0.

Understand why we need IPv6.   Without IPv6, the world would soon be depleted of IP addresses.

Understand link-local.   Link-local is like an IPv4 private IP address, but it can't be routed at all, not even in your organization.

Understand unique local.   This, like link-local, is like a private IP address in IPv4 and cannot be routed to the Internet. However, the difference between link-local and unique local is that unique local can be routed within your organization or company.

Remember IPv6 addressing.   IPv6 addressing is not like IPv4 addressing. IPv6 addressing has much more address space and is 128 bits long, represented in hexadecimal, unlike IPv4, which is only 32 bits long and represented in decimals.

Written Lab

Provide the answers to the following questions:

1. What is the valid range used for a class C private IP address?

2. Name some of the benefits of IPv6 over IPv4.

3. What is the term for the auto-configuration technology responsible for addresses that start with 169.254?

4. What defines a unicast address?

5. What defines a multicast address?

6. What is the name for a 48-bit (6-byte) numerical address physically assigned to a network interface, such as a NIC?

7. What gives IPv6 the ability to reference more addresses than IPv4?

8. What is the private address range for class B networks?

9. What is the Class C range of values for the first octet in decimal and in binary?

10. What is the 127.0.0.1 address used for?

   You can find the answers in Appendix B.

Review Questions

You can find the answers in Appendix A.

1. Which of the following addresses is not allowed on the Internet?

   A. 191.192.168.1

   B. 191.168.169.254

   C. 172.32.255.0

   D. 172.31.12.251

2. A host automatically configured with an address from which of the following ranges indicates an inability to contact a DHCP server?

   A. 169.254.0.x with a mask of 255.255.255.0

   B. 169.254.x.x with a mask of 255.255.0.0

   C. 169.254.x.x with a mask of 255.255.255.0

   D. 169.255.x.x with a mask of 255.255.0.0

3. Which statement regarding private IP addresses is most accurate?

   A. Private addresses cannot be used in intranets that require routing.

   B. Private addresses must be assigned by a registrar or ISP.

   C. A remote host across the Internet cannot ping your host if it has a private address.

   D. Private addresses can only be used by a single administrative domain.

4. Which of the following is a valid Class A address?

   A. 191.10.0.1 255.0.0.0

   B. 127.10.0.1 255.0.0.0

   C. 128.10.0.1 255.0.0.0

   D. 126.10.0.1 255.0.0.0

5. Which of the following is a valid Class B address?

   A. 10.1.1.1 255.255.0.0

   B. 126.1.1.1 255.255.0.0

   C. 129.1.1.1 255.255.0.0

   D. 192.168.1.1 255.255.0.0

6. Which of the following describes a broadcast address?

   A. All network bits are on (1s).

   B. All host bits are on (1s).

   C. All network bits are off (0s).

   D. All host bits are off (0s).

7. Which of the following is a Layer 2 broadcast?

   A. FF.FF.FF.EE.EE.EE

   B. FF.FF.FF.FF.FF.FF

   C. 255.255.255.255

   D. 255.0.0.0

8. In a Class C IP address, how long is the network address?

   A. 8 bits

   B. 16 bits

   C. 24 bits

   D. 32 bits

9. Which of the following is true when describing a unicast address?

   A. Packets addressed to a unicast address are delivered to a single interface.

   B. These are your typical publicly routable addresses, just like regular publicly routable addresses in IPv4.

   C. These are like private addresses in IPv4 in that they are not meant to be routed.

   D. These addresses are meant for nonrouting purposes, but they are almost globally unique so it is unlikely they will have an address overlap.

10. A host is rebooted and you view the IP address that it was assigned. The address is 169.123.13.34. Which of the following happened?

    A. The host received an APIPA address.

    B. The host received a multicast address.

    C. The host received a public address.

    D. The host received a private address.

11. An IPv4 addresses uses 32 bits. How many bits is an IPv6 address?

    A. 64

    B. 128

    C. 192

    D. 255

12. Which of the following is true when describing a multicast address?

    A. Packets addressed to a unicast address from a multicast address are delivered to a single interface.

    B. Packets are delivered to all interfaces identified by the address. This is also called a one-to-many address.

    C. It identifies multiple interfaces and is delivered to only one address. This address can also be called one-to-one-of-many.

    D. These addresses are meant for nonrouting purposes, but they are almost globally unique so it is unlikely they will have an address overlap.

13. Which of the following is true when describing an anycast address?

    A. Packets addressed to a unicast address from an anycast address are delivered to a single interface.

    B. Packets are delivered to all interfaces identified by the address. This is also called a one-to-many address.

    C. This address identifies multiple interfaces, and the anycast packet is delivered to only one address. This address can also be called one-to-one-of-many.

    D. These addresses are meant for nonrouting purposes, but they are almost globally unique so it is unlikely they will have an address overlap.

14. You want to ping the loopback address of your local host. Which two addresses could you type?

    A. `ping 127.0.0.1`

    B. `ping 0.0.0.0`

    C. `ping ::1`

    D. `trace 0.0.::1`

15. What two statements about IPv6 addresses are true?

    A. Leading zeros are required.

    B. Two colons (::) are used to represent successive hexadecimal fields of zeros.

    C. Two colons (::) are used to separate fields.

    D. A single interface will have multiple IPv6 addresses of different types.

16. What two statements about IPv4 and IPv6 addresses are true?

    A. An IPv6 address is 32 bits long, represented in hexadecimal.

    B. An IPv6 address is 128 bits long, represented in decimal.

    C. An IPv4 address is 32 bits long, represented in decimal.

    D. An IPv6 address is 128 bits long, represented in hexadecimal.

17. Which of the following is a Class C network address?

    A. 10.10.10.0 255.255.255.0

    B. 127.0.0.1 255.255.255.0

    C. 128.0.0.0 255.255.0.0

    D. 192.255.254.0 255.255.255.0

18. Which of the following are private IP addresses? (Choose two.)

    A. 12.0.0.1

    B. 168.172.19.39

    C. 172.20.14.36

    D. 172.33.194.30

    E. 192.168.24.43

19. Which of the following is a valid IP address that can be used on the Internet (meaning the public addressing scheme)?

    A. 10.10.1.1

    B. 168.16.1.1

    C. 234.1.1.1

    D. 172.30.1.1

20. Which of the following is an invalid IP address for a host?

    A. 10.0.0.1

    B. 128.0.0.1

    C. 224.0.0.1

    D. 172.0.0.1

Chapter

8

IP Subnetting, Troubleshooting IP, and Introduction to NAT

THE FOLLOWING COMPTIA NETWORK+ EXAM OBJECTIVES ARE COVERED IN THIS CHAPTER:

✓ **1.3 Explain the purpose and properties of IP addressing**

- Classless (CIDR)

- Subnetting

✓ **2.1 Given a scenario, install and configure routers and switches.**

- NAT

- PAT

This chapter's focus will really zoom in on IP addressing to ensure that you have it nailed down tight. This is an integral aspect of networking, and it's important to your success on the exams and as a professional too!

We'll start with subnetting an IP network. You're going to have to really apply yourself because it takes time and practice in order to do subnetting correctly and quickly. So be patient and do whatever it takes to get this stuff dialed in. This chapter truly is important—possibly the most important chapter in this book for you to understand. Make it part of you!

I'll thoroughly cover IP subnetting from the very beginning. I know this might sound weird to you, but I think you'll be much better off if you can try to forget everything you've learned about subnetting before reading this chapter—especially if you've been to a Microsoft class!

I'll also take you through IP address troubleshooting and walk you through each of the steps recommended when you're faced with troubleshooting an IP network. Finally, I'll finish up with an introduction to Network Address Translation (NAT)—there are various types of NAT, and you need to know when you would use each one.

So get psyched—you're about to go for quite a ride! This chapter will truly help you understand IP addressing and networking, so don't get discouraged or give up. If you stick with it, I promise that one day you'll look back on this and be really glad you decided to stay the course. It's one of those things that after you understand it, you'll laugh at that time, way back when, when you thought this was hard. So, are you ready now? Let's go!

To find up-to-the-minute updates for this chapter, please see www.lammle.com/forum or the book's web site at www.sybex.com/go/netplus2e.

Subnetting Basics

In Chapter 7, "IP Addressing," you learned how to define and find the valid host ranges used in a Class A, Class B, or Class C network address by turning the host bits all off and then all on. This is very good, but here's the catch: You were defining only one network. What would happen if you wanted to take one network address and create six networks from it? You would have to do something called *subnetting*, because that's what allows you to take one larger network and break it into a bunch of smaller networks.

There are loads of reasons in favor of subnetting, including the following benefits:

Reduced network traffic   We all appreciate less traffic of any kind. With networks, it's no different. Without trusty routers, packet traffic could grind the entire network down to a near standstill. With routers, most traffic will stay on the local network; only packets destined for other networks will pass through the router. Routers create broadcast domains. The more broadcast domains you create, the smaller the broadcast domains are and the less network traffic is on each network segment.

Optimized network performance   This is the very cool reward you get when you reduce network traffic!

Simplified management   It's easier to identify and isolate network problems in a group of smaller connected networks than within one gigantic network.

Facilitated spanning of large geographical distances   Because WAN links are considerably slower and more expensive than LAN links, a single large network that spans long distances can create problems in every area previously listed. Connecting multiple smaller networks makes the system more efficient.

Next, we're going to move on to subnetting a network address. This is the good part—ready?

How to Create Subnets

To create subnetworks, you take bits from the host portion of the IP address and reserve them to define the subnet address. This means fewer bits for hosts, so the more subnets, the fewer bits are left available for defining hosts.

Soon, I'll show you how to create subnets, starting with Class C addresses. But before you actually implement subnetting, you really need to determine your current requirements as well as plan for future conditions.

Follow these steps—they're your recipe for solid design:

1. Determine the number of required network IDs:
   - One for each subnet
   - One for each wide area network (WAN) connection

2. Determine the number of required host IDs per subnet:
   - One for each TCP/IP host
   - One for each router interface

3. Based on the previous requirements, create the following:
   - One subnet mask for your entire network
   - A unique subnet ID for each physical segment
   - A range of host IDs for each subnet

Understanding the Powers of 2

By the way, powers of 2 are really important to memorize for use with IP subnetting. To review powers of 2, remember that when you see a number with another number to its upper right (an exponent), this means you should multiply the number by itself as many times as the upper number specifies. For example, 2^3 is $2 \times 2 \times 2$, which equals 8. Here's a list of powers of 2 that you should commit to memory:

$2^1 = 2$

$2^2 = 4$

$2^3 = 8$

$2^4 = 16$

$2^5 = 32$

$2^6 = 64$

$2^7 = 128$

$2^8 = 256$

$2^9 = 512$

$2^{10} = 1,024$

$2^{11} = 2,048$

$2^{12} = 4,096$

$2^{13} = 8,192$

$2^{14} = 16,384$

If you hate math, don't get stressed out about knowing all these exponents—it's helpful to know them, but it's not absolutely necessary. Here's a little trick, because you're working with 2s: Each successive power of 2 is double the previous one.

For example, all you have to do to remember the value of 2^9 is to first know that $2^8 = 256$. Why? Because when you double 2 to the eighth power (256), you get 2^9 (or 512). To determine the value of 2^{10}, simply start at $2^8 = 256$, and then double it twice.

You can go the other way as well. If you needed to know what 2^6 is, for example, you just cut 256 in half two times: once to reach 2^7 and then one more time to reach 2^6. Not bad, right?

Subnet Masks

For the subnet address scheme to work, every machine on the network must know which part of the host address will be used as the subnet address. This is accomplished by assigning a *subnet mask* to each machine. A subnet mask is a 32-bit value that allows the recipient of IP packets to distinguish the network ID portion of the IP address from the host ID portion of the IP address.

The network administrator creates a 32-bit subnet mask composed of 1s and 0s. The 1s in the subnet mask represent the positions that refer to the network, or subnet, addresses.

Not all networks need subnets, meaning they use the default subnet mask. This is basically the same as saying that a network doesn't have a subnet address. Table 8.1 shows the default subnet masks for Classes A, B, and C. These default masks cannot and do not change. In other words, you can't make a Class B subnet mask read 255.0.0.0. If you try, the host will read that address as invalid and usually won't even let you type it in. For a Class A network, you can't change the first byte in a subnet mask; it must read 255.0.0.0 at a minimum. Similarly, you cannot assign 255.255.255.255, because this is all 1s—a broadcast address. A Class B address must start with 255.255.0.0, and a Class C has to start with 255.255.255.0. Check out Table 8.1.

TABLE 8.1 Default subnet mask

Class	Format	Default subnet mask
A	*network.host.host.host*	255.0.0.0
B	*network.network.host.host*	255.255.0.0
C	*network.network.network.host*	255.255.255.0

Classless Inter-Domain Routing (CIDR)

Another term you need to know is *Classless Inter-Domain Routing (CIDR)*. It's basically the method that Internet service providers (ISPs) use to allocate a number of addresses to a company or a home connection. They provide addresses in a certain block size; I'll be going into that in greater detail later in this chapter.

When you receive a block of addresses from an ISP, what you get will look something like this: 192.168.10.32/28. This is telling you what your subnet mask is. The slash notation (/) means how many bits are turned on (1s). Obviously, the maximum could only be /32 because a byte is 8 bits and there are 4 bytes in an IP address: $4 \times 8 = 32$. But keep in mind that the largest subnet mask available (regardless of the class of address) can only be a /30 because you have to keep at least 2 bits for host bits.

Take, for example, a Class A default subnet mask, which is 255.0.0.0. This means that the first byte of the subnet mask is all ones (1s), or 11111111. When referring to a slash notation, you need to count all the 1s bits to figure out your mask. The 255.0.0.0 is considered a /8 because it has 8 bits that are 1s—that is, 8 bits that are turned on.

A Class B default mask would be 255.255.0.0, which is a /16 because 16 bits are (1s): 11111111.11111111.00000000.00000000.

Table 8.2 offers a listing of every available subnet mask and its equivalent CIDR slash notation.

TABLE 8.2 CIDR values

Subnet Mask	CIDR Value
255.0.0.0	/8
255.128.0.0	/9
255.192.0.0	/10
255.224.0.0	/11
255.240.0.0	/12
255.248.0.0	/13
255.252.0.0	/14
255.254.0.0	/15
255.255.0.0	/16
255.255.128.0	/17
255.255.192.0	/18
255.255.224.0	/19
255.255.240.0	/20
255.255.248.0	/21
255.255.252.0	/22
255.255.254.0	/23
255.255.255.0	/24
255.255.255.128	/25

Subnet Mask	CIDR Value
255.255.255.192	/26
255.255.255.224	/27
255.255.255.240	/28
255.255.255.248	/29
255.255.255.252	/30

Make a note to self that the /8 through /15 can be used only with Class A network addresses; /16 through /23 can be used by Class A and B network addresses; /24 through /30 can be used by Class A, B, and C network addresses. This is a big reason why most companies use Class A network addresses. By being allowed the use of all subnet masks, they gain the valuable benefit of maximum flexibility for their network design.

Subnetting Class C Addresses

There are many different ways to subnet a network. The right way is the way that works best for you. In a Class C address, only 8 bits are available for defining the hosts. Remember that subnet bits start at the left and go to the right, without skipping bits. This means that the only Class C subnet masks can be those listed here:

Binary	Decimal	CIDR
00000000	0	/24
10000000	128	/25
11000000	192	/26
11100000	224	/27
11110000	240	/28
11111000	248	/29
11111100	252	/30

We can't use a /31 or /32 because, remember, we have to leave at least 2 host bits for assigning IP addresses to hosts.

Okay—get ready for something special…I'm going to teach you an alternate method of subnetting that makes it a whole lot easier to subnet larger numbers in no time. And trust me, you really do need to be able to subnet fast!

Subnetting a Class C Address: The Fast Way!

When you've chosen a possible subnet mask for your network and need to determine the number of subnets, valid hosts, and broadcast addresses of a subnet that the mask provides, all you need to do is answer five simple questions:

- How many subnets does the chosen subnet mask produce?
- How many valid hosts per subnet are available?
- What are the valid subnets?
- What's the broadcast address of each subnet?
- What are the valid hosts in each subnet?

At this point, it's important that you both understand and have memorized your powers of 2. Please refer to the sidebar "Understanding the Powers of 2" earlier in this chapter if you need some help. Here's how you get the answers to those five big questions:

- *How many subnets?* 2^x = number of subnets. x is the number of masked bits, or the 1s. For example, in 11000000, the number of 1s gives us 2^2 subnets. In this example, there are 4 subnets.

- *How many hosts per subnet?* $2^y - 2$ = number of hosts per subnet. y is the number of unmasked bits, or the 0s. For example, in 11000000, the number of 0s gives us $2^6 - 2$ hosts. In this example, there are 62 hosts per subnet. You need to subtract 2 for the subnet address and the broadcast address, which are not valid hosts.

- *What are the valid subnets?* 256 – subnet mask = block size, or increment number. An example would be 256 – 192 = 64. The block size of a 192 mask is always 64. Start counting at zero in blocks of 64 until you reach the subnet mask value, and these are your subnets. 0, 64, 128, 192. Easy, huh?

- *What's the broadcast address for each subnet?* Now here's the really easy part. Because we counted our subnets in the last section as 0, 64, 128, and 192, the broadcast address is always the number right before the next subnet. For example, the 0 subnet has a broadcast address of 63 because the next subnet is 64. The 64 subnet has a broadcast address of 127 because the next subnet is 128. And so on. And remember, the broadcast of the last subnet is always 255.

- *What are the valid hosts?* Valid hosts are the numbers between the subnets, omitting all the 0s and all 1s. For example, if 64 is the subnet number and 127 is the broadcast address, then 65–126 is the valid host range—it's *always* the numbers between the subnet address and the broadcast address.

I know this can truly seem confusing. But it really isn't as hard as it seems to be at first—just hang in there! Why not try a few and see for yourself?

Subnetting Practice Examples: Class C Addresses

Here's your opportunity to practice subnetting Class C addresses using the method I just described. Exciting, isn't it? We're going to start with the first Class C subnet mask and work through every subnet that we can using a Class C address. When we're done, I'll show you how easy this is with Class A and B networks too!

Practice Example #1C: 255.255.255.128 (/25)

Because 128 is 10000000 in binary, there is only 1 bit for subnetting, and there are 7 bits for hosts. We're going to subnet the Class C network address 192.168.10.0.

192.168.10.0 = Network address

255.255.255.128 = Subnet mask

Now, let's answer the big five:

- *How many subnets?* Because 128 is 1 bit on (**1**0000000), the answer is $2^1 = 2$.

- *How many hosts per subnet?* We have 7 host bits off (1**0000000**), so the equation is $2^7 - 2 = 126$ hosts.

- *What are the valid subnets?* $256 - 128 = 128$. Remember, we'll start at zero and count in our block size, so our subnets are 0, 128.

- *What's the broadcast address for each subnet?* The number right before the value of the next subnet is all host bits turned on and equals the broadcast address. For the 0 subnet, the next subnet is 128, so the broadcast of the 0 subnet is 127.

- *What are the valid hosts?* These are the numbers between the subnet and broadcast address. The easiest way to find the hosts is to write out the subnet address and the broadcast address. This way, the valid hosts are obvious. The following table shows the 0 and 128 subnets, the valid host ranges of each, and the broadcast address of both subnets:

Subnet	0	128
First host	1	129
Last host	126	254
Broadcast	127	255

Before moving on to the next example, take a look at Figure 8.1. Okay, looking at a Class C /25, it's pretty clear there are two subnets. But so what—why is this significant? Well actually, it's not, but that's not the right question. What you really want to know is what you would do with this information!

FIGURE 8.1   Implementing a Class C /25 logical network

```
Router#show ip route
[output cut]
C 192.168.10.0 is directly connected to Ethernet 0.
C 192.168.10.128 is directly connected to Ethernet 1.
```

The key to understanding subnetting is to understand the very reason you need to do it. And I'm going to demonstrate this by going through the process of building a physical network—and let's add a router. (We now have an internetwork, as I truly hope you already know!) Because we added that router, in order for the hosts on our internetwork to communicate, they must now have a logical network addressing scheme. We could use IPv6, but IPv4 is still the most popular, and it also just happens to be what we're studying at the moment, so that's what we're going with.

Now take a look back at Figure 8.1. (By the way, the output you see below the diagram is the routing table of the router which was displayed by executing the show ip route command on the router. The same output is shown in Figure 8.2 as well.) There are two physical networks, so we're going to implement a logical addressing scheme that allows for two logical networks. As always, it's a really good idea to look ahead and consider any likely growth scenarios—both short and long term, but for this example, a /25 will do the trick.

Practice Example #2C: 255.255.255.192 (/26)

In this second example, we're going to subnet the network address 192.168.10.0 using the subnet mask 255.255.255.192.

192.168.10.0 = Network address

255.255.255.192 = Subnet mask

It's time to answer the big five:

- *How many subnets?* Because 192 is 2 bits on (**11**000000), the answer is $2^2 = 4$ subnets.

- *How many hosts per subnet?* We have 6 host bits off (11**000000**), so the equation is $2^6 - 2 = 62$ hosts.

- *What are the valid subnets?* 256 − 192 = 64. Remember, we start at zero and count in our block size, so our subnets are 0, 64, 128, and 192.

- *What's the broadcast address for each subnet?* The number right before the value of the next subnet is all host bits turned on and equals the broadcast address. For the 0 subnet, the next subnet is 64, so the broadcast address for the 0 subnet is 63.

- *What are the valid hosts?* These are the numbers between the subnet and broadcast address. The easiest way to find the hosts is to write out the subnet address and the broadcast address. This way, the valid hosts are obvious. The following table shows the 0, 64, 128, and 192 subnets, the valid host ranges of each, and the broadcast address of each subnet:

The subnets (do this first)	0	64	128	192
Our first host (perform host addressing last)	1	65	129	193
Our last host	62	126	190	254
The broadcast address (do this second)	63	127	191	255

Again, before getting into the next example, you can see that we can now subnet a /26. And what are you going to do with this fascinating information? Implement it! We'll use Figure 8.2 to practice a /26 network implementation.

FIGURE 8.2   Implementing a Class C /26 logical network

```
Router#show ip route
[output cut]
C 192.168.10.0 is directly connected to Ethernet 0.
C 192.168.10.64 is directly connected to Ethernet 1.
C 192.168.10.128 is directly connected to Ethernet 2.
```

The /26 mask provides four subnetworks, and we need a subnet for each router interface. With this mask, in this example, we actually have room to add another router interface.

Practice Example #3C: 255.255.255.224 (/27)

This time, we'll subnet the network address 192.168.10.0 and subnet mask 255.255.255.224.

192.168.10.0 = Network address

255.255.255.224 = Subnet mask

- *How many subnets?* 224 is 11100000, so our equation is $2^3 = 8$.

- *How many hosts?* $2^5 - 2 = 30$.

- *What are the valid subnets?* 256 − 224 = 32. We just start at zero and count to the subnet mask value in blocks (increments) of 32: 0, 32, 64, 96, 128, 160, 192, and 224.

- *What's the broadcast address for each subnet (always the number right before the next subnet)?*

- *What are the valid hosts (the numbers between the subnet number and the broadcast address)?*

To answer the last two questions, first just write out the subnets, and then write out the broadcast addresses—the number right before the next subnet. Last, fill in the host addresses. The following table gives you all the subnets for the 255.255.255.224 Class C subnet mask:

The subnet address	0	32	64	96	128	160	192	224
The first valid host	1	33	65	97	129	161	193	225
The last valid host	30	62	94	126	158	190	222	254
The broadcast address	31	63	95	127	159	191	223	255

Practice Example #4C: 255.255.255.240 (/28)

Let's practice on another one:

> 192.168.10.0 = Network address
>
> 255.255.255.240 = Subnet mask

- *Subnets?* 240 is 11110000 in binary. 2^4 = 16.
- *Hosts?* 4 host bits, or $2^4 - 2$ = 14.
- *Valid subnets?* 256 − 240 = 16. 0, 16, 32, 48, 64, 80, 96, 112, 128, 144, 160, 176, 192, 208, 224, 240.
- *Broadcast address for each subnet?*
- *Valid hosts?*

To answer the last two questions, check out the following table. It gives you the subnets, valid hosts, and broadcast addresses for each subnet. First, find the address of each subnet using the block size (increment). Second, find the broadcast address of each subnet increment (it's always the number right before the next valid subnet); then, just fill in the host addresses. The following table shows the available subnets, hosts, and broadcast addresses provided by a Class C network 255.255.255.240 mask:

Subnet	0	16	32	48	64	80	96	112	128	144	160	176	192	208	224	240
First host	1	17	33	49	65	81	97	113	129	145	161	177	193	209	225	241
Last host	14	30	46	62	78	94	110	126	142	158	174	190	206	222	238	254
Broadcast	15	31	47	63	79	95	111	127	143	159	175	191	207	223	239	255

Practice Example #5C: 255.255.255.248 (/29)

Let's keep practicing:

> 192.168.10.0 = Network address
>
> 255.255.255.248 = Subnet mask

- *Subnets?* 248 in binary = 11111000. 2^5 = 32.
- *Hosts?* $2^3 - 2$ = 6.

- *Valid subnets?* 256 – 248 = 8, start at zero: 0, 8, 16, 24, 32, 40, 48, 56, 64, 72, 80, 88, 96, 104, 112, 120, 128, 136, 144, 152, 160, 168, 176, 184, 192, 200, 208, 216, 224, 232, 240, and 248.
- *Broadcast address for each subnet?*
- *Valid hosts?*

Take a look at the following table. It shows some of the subnets (first four and last four only), valid hosts, and broadcast addresses for the Class C 255.255.255.248 mask:

Subnet	0	8	16	24	...	224	232	240	248
First host	1	9	17	25	...	225	233	241	249
Last host	6	14	22	30	...	230	238	246	254
Broadcast	7	15	23	31	...	231	239	247	255

Practice Example #6C: 255.255.255.252 (/30)

I know, I know—but just one more:

192.168.10.0 = Network address

255.255.255.252 = Subnet mask

- *Subnets?* 64.
- *Hosts?* 2.
- *Valid subnets?* 0, 4, 8, 12, and so on, all the way to 252.
- *Broadcast address for each subnet (always the number right before the next subnet)?*
- *Valid hosts (the numbers between the subnet number and the broadcast address)?*

The following table shows you the subnet, valid host, and broadcast address of the first four and last four subnets in the 255.255.255.252 Class C subnet:

Subnet	0	4	8	12	...	240	244	248	252
First host	1	5	9	13	...	241	245	249	253
Last host	2	6	10	14	...	242	246	250	254
Broadcast	3	7	11	15	...	243	247	251	255

Subnetting in Your Head: Class C Addresses

It really is possible to subnet in your head by looking at a valid IP address and subnet mask. This is extremely important for IP addressing and troubleshooting. Even if you don't believe me that you can subnet in your head, I'll show you how. And it's not all that hard, either—take the following example: What is the subnet, broadcast address, and valid host range that this host IP address is a part of?

192.168.10.33 = Host address

255.255.255.224 = Subnet mask

Real World Scenario

Should We Really Use This Mask That Provides Only Two Hosts?

Imagine you are the network administrator for Acme Corporation in San Francisco, with dozens of WAN links connecting to your corporate office. Right now your network is a classful network, which means that the same subnet mask is on each host and router interface. You've read about classless routing where you can have different size masks, but you don't know what to use on your point-to-point WAN links. Is 255.255.255.252 (/30) a helpful mask in this situation?

Yes, this is a very helpful mask in wide area networks.

If you use the 255.255.255.0 mask, then each network will have 254 hosts, but you only use two addresses with a WAN link! That is a waste of 252 hosts per subnet. If you use the 255.255.255.252 mask, then each subnet has only 2 hosts, and you don't waste precious addresses.

First, determine the subnet and broadcast address of this IP address. You can do this by answering question 3 of the big five questions: 256 − 224 = 32. Start at zero: 0, 32, 64. The address of 33 falls between the two subnets of 32 and 64 and must be part of the 192.168.10.32 subnet. The next subnet is 64, so the broadcast address of the 32 subnet is 63. (Remember that the broadcast address of a subnet is always the number right before the next subnet.) The valid host range is 33–62 (the numbers between the subnet and broadcast address). I told you this is easy!

Okay, let's try another one. What is the subnet, broadcast address, and valid host range that this host IP address is a part of?

192.168.10.33 = Host address

255.255.255.240 = Subnet mask

256 − 240 = 16. Start at zero and count till you pass the valid host in the problem: 0, 16, 32, 48. Bingo—the host address is between the 32 and 48 subnets. The subnet is 192.168.10.32, and the broadcast address is 47 (the next subnet is 48). The valid host range is 33–46 (the numbers between the subnet number and the broadcast address).

Okay, we need to do more, just to make sure you have this down.

You have a host address of 192.168.10.174 with a mask of 255.255.255.240. What is the subnet, broadcast address, and valid host range that this host IP address is a part of?

The mask is 240, so we need our block size: 256 − 240 = 16. Just keep adding 16 until we pass the host address of 174, starting at zero, of course: 0, 16, 32, 48, 64, 80, 96, 112, 128, 144, 160, 176. The host address of 174 is between 160 and 176, so the subnet is 160. The broadcast address is 175; the valid host range is 161–174. That was a tough one.

Let's do one more just for fun. This is the easiest one of all Class C subnetting:

192.168.10.17 = Host address

255.255.255.252 = Subnet mask

What subnet and broadcast address is this IP address a part of? 256 – 252 = 4. Start at zero (always start at zero unless told otherwise), 0, 4, 8, 12, 16, 20, and so on. You've got it! The host address is between the 16 and 20 subnets. The subnet is 192.168.10.16, and the broadcast address is 19. The valid host range is 17–18.

Now that you're all over Class C subnetting, let's move on to Class B subnetting. But before we do, let's do a quick review.

So What Do You Know Now?

Here's where you can really apply what you've learned so far and begin committing it all to memory. This is a very cool section that I've been using in my classes for years. It will really help you nail down subnetting!

When you see a subnet mask or slash notation (CIDR), you should know the following when working with class C networks:

/25

What do you know about a /25?

- 128 mask
- 1 bits on and 7 bits off (10000000)
- Block size of 128
- 2 subnets, each with 126 hosts

/26

And what do you know about a /26?

- 192 mask
- 2 bits on and 6 bits off (11000000)
- Block size of 64
- 4 subnets, each with 62 hosts

/27

What about a /27?

- 224 mask
- 3 bits on and 5 bits off (11100000)
- Block size of 32
- 8 subnets, each with 30 hosts

/28

And what about a /28?

- 240 mask
- 4 bits on and 4 bits off
- Block size of 16
- 16 subnets, each with 14 hosts

/29

What do you know about a /29?

- 248 mask
- 5 bits on and 3 bits off
- Block size of 8
- 32 subnets, each with 6 hosts

/30

And last, what about a /30?

- 252 mask
- 6 bits on and 2 bits off
- Block size of 4
- 64 subnets, each with 2 hosts

Regardless of whether you have a Class A, Class B, or Class C address, the /30 mask will provide you with only two hosts, ever. This mask is suited almost exclusively for use on point-to-point links.

If you can memorize this "So What Do You Know Now?" section, you'll be much better off in your day-to-day job and in your studies. Try saying it out loud, which helps you memorize things—yes, your significant other and/or coworkers will think you've lost it, but they probably already do if you're in the networking field. And if you're not yet in the networking field but are studying all this to break into it, you might as well have people start thinking you're a little "different" now because they will eventually anyway.

It's also helpful to write these on some type of flashcards and have people test your skill. You'd be amazed at how fast you can get subnetting down if you memorize block sizes as well as this "So What Do You Know Now?" section.

Subnetting Class B Addresses

Before we dive into this, let's look at all the possible Class B subnet masks. Notice that we have a lot more possible subnet masks than we do with a Class C network address:

255.255.0.0   (/16)

255.255.128.0   (/17)

255.255.192.0	(/18)
255.255.224.0	(/19)
255.255.240.0	(/20)
255.255.248.0	(/21)
255.255.252.0	(/22)
255.255.254.0	(/23)
255.255.255.0	(/24)
255.255.255.128	(/25)
255.255.255.192	(/26)
255.255.255.224	(/27)
255.255.255.240	(/28)
255.255.255.248	(/29)
255.255.255.252	(/30)

We know the Class B network address has 16 bits available for host addressing. This means we can use up to 14 bits for subnetting (because we have to leave at least 2 bits for host addressing). Using a /16 means you are not subnetting with class B, but it is a mask you can use.

 By the way, do you notice anything interesting about that list of subnet values—a pattern, maybe? Ah-ha! That's exactly why I had you memorize the binary-to-decimal numbers at the beginning of this section. Because subnet mask bits start on the left and move to the right and bits can't be skipped, the numbers are always the same regardless of the class of address. Memorize this pattern.

The process of subnetting a Class B network is pretty much the same as it is for a Class C, except that you have more host bits and you start in the third octet.

Use the same subnet numbers for the third octet with Class B that you used for the fourth octet with Class C, but add a 0 to the network portion and a 255 to the broadcast section in the fourth octet. The following table shows you an example host range of two subnets used in a Class B 240 (/20) subnet mask:

First subnet	Second Subnet
16.0	32.0
31.255	47.255

Notice that these are the same numbers we used in the fourth octet with a /28 mask, but we moved them to the third octet and added a .0 and .255 at the end. Just add the valid hosts between the numbers, and you're set!

Subnetting Practice Examples: Class B Addresses

This section will give you an opportunity to practice subnetting Class B addresses. Again, I have to mention that this is the same as subnetting with Class C, except we start in the third octet—with the exact same numbers!

Practice Example #1B: 255.255.128.0 (/17)

Let's take a look at our first example:

173.16.0.0 = Network address

172.16.0.0 = Network address

255.255.128.0 = Subnet mask

- *Subnets?* $2^1 = 2$ (same as Class C).
- *Hosts?* $2^{15} - 2 = 32,766$ (7 bits in the third octet, and 8 in the fourth).
- *Valid subnets?* 256 − 128 = 128. 0, 128. Remember that subnetting in class B starts in the third octet, so the subnet numbers are really 0.0 and 128.0, as shown in the next table. These are the exact numbers we used with Class C; we use them in the third octet and add a 0 in the fourth octet for the network address.
- *Broadcast address for each subnet?*

The following table shows the two subnets available, the valid host range, and the broadcast address of each:

Subnet	0.0	128.0
First host	0.1	128.1
Last host	127.254	255.254
Broadcast	127.255	255.255

Okay, notice that we just added the fourth octet's lowest and highest values and came up with the answers. And again, it's done exactly the same way as for a Class C subnet. We just use the same numbers in the third octet and added 0 and 255 in the fourth octet—pretty simple, huh? I really can't say this enough: It's not hard. The numbers never change. We just use them in different octets!

Practice Example #2B: 255.255.192.0 (/18)

Let's take a look at a second example with class B.

172.16.0.0 = Network address

255.255.192.0 = Subnet mask

- *Subnets?* $2^2 = 4$.

- *Hosts?* $2^{14} - 2 = 16,382$ (6 bits in the third octet, and 8 in the fourth).
- *Valid subnets?* $256 - 192 = 64$. 0, 64, 128, 192. Remember that we're in the third octet, so the subnet numbers are really 0.0, 64.0, 128.0, and 192.0, as shown in the next table.
- *Broadcast address for each subnet?*
- *Valid hosts?*

The following table shows the four subnets available, the valid host range, and the broadcast address of each:

Subnet	0.0	64.0	128.0	192.0
First host	0.1	64.1	128.1	192.1
Last host	63.254	127.254	191.254	255.254
Broadcast	63.255	127.255	191.255	255.255

Again, it's pretty much the same as it is for a Class C subnet—we just added 0 and 255 in the fourth octet for each subnet in the third octet.

Practice Example #3B: 255.255.240.0 (/20)

172.16.0.0 = Network address

255.255.240.0 = Subnet mask

- *Subnets?* $2^4 = 16$.
- *Hosts?* $2^{12} - 2 = 4094$.
- *Valid subnets?* $256 - 240 = 0, 16, 32, 48$, and so on, up to 240. Notice that these are the same numbers as a Class C 240 mask—we just put them in the third octet and add a 0 and 255 in the fourth octet.
- *Broadcast address for each subnet?*
- *Valid hosts?*

The following table shows the first four subnets, valid hosts, and broadcast addresses in a Class B 255.255.240.0 mask:

Subnet	0.0	16.0	32.0	48.0
First host	0.1	16.1	32.1	48.1
Last host	15.254	31.254	47.254	63.254
Broadcast	15.255	31.255	47.255	63.255

Practice Example #4B: 255.255.254.0 (/23)

172.16.0.0 = Network address

255.255.254.0 = Subnet mask

- *Subnets?* $2^7 = 128$.
- *Hosts?* $2^9 - 2 = 510$.
- *Valid subnets?* $256 - 254 = 0, 2, 4, 6, 8$, and so on, up to 254.
- *Broadcast address for each subnet?*
- *Valid hosts?*

The following table shows the first five subnets, valid hosts, and broadcast addresses in a Class B 255.255.254.0 mask:

Subnet	0.0	2.0	4.0	6.0	8.0
First host	0.1	2.1	4.1	6.1	8.1
Last host	1.254	3.254	5.254	7.254	9.254
Broadcast	1.255	3.255	5.255	7.255	9.255

Practice Example #5B: 255.255.255.0 (/24)

Contrary to popular belief, 255.255.255.0 used with a Class B network address is not called a Class B network with a Class C subnet mask. It's amazing how many people see this mask used in a Class B network and think it's a Class C subnet mask. This is a Class B subnet mask with 8 bits of subnetting—it's considerably different from a Class C mask. Subnetting this address is fairly simple:

172.16.0.0 = Network address

255.255.255.0 = Subnet mask

- *Subnets?* $2^8 = 256$.
- *Hosts?* $2^8 - 2 = 254$.
- *Valid subnets?* $256 - 255 = 1. 0, 1, 2, 3$, and so on, all the way to 255.
- *Broadcast address for each subnet?*
- *Valid hosts?*

The following table shows the first four and last two subnets, the valid hosts, and the broadcast addresses in a Class B 255.255.255.0 mask:

Subnet	0.0	1.0	2.0	3.0	...	254.0	255.0
First host	0.1	1.1	2.1	3.1	...	254.1	255.1
Last host	0.254	1.254	2.254	3.254	...	254.254	255.254
Broadcast	0.255	1.255	2.255	3.255	...	254.255	255.255

Practice Example #6B: 255.255.255.128 (/25)

This is one of the hardest subnet masks you can play with. And worse, it actually is a really good subnet to use in production because it creates over 500 subnets with a whopping 126 hosts for each subnet—a nice mixture. So, don't skip over it!

> 172.16.0.0 = Network address
>
> 255.255.255.128 = Subnet mask

- *Subnets?* $2^9 = 512$.
- *Hosts?* $2^7 - 2 = 126$.
- *Valid subnets?* Now for the tricky part. $256 - 255 = 1$. 0, 1, 2, 3, and so on for the third octet. But you can't forget the one subnet bit used in the fourth octet. Remember when I showed you how to figure one subnet bit with a Class C mask? You figure this out the same way. (Now you know why I showed you the 1-bit subnet mask in the Class C section—to make this part easier.) You actually get two subnets for each third octet value, hence the 512 subnets. For example, if the third octet is showing subnet 3, the two subnets would actually be 3.0 and 3.128.
- *Broadcast address for each subnet?*
- *Valid hosts?*

The following table shows how you can create subnets, valid hosts, and broadcast addresses using the Class B 255.255.255.128 subnet mask (the first eight subnets are shown, and then the last two subnets):

Subnet	0.0	0.128	1.0	1.128	2.0	2.128	3.0	3.128	...	255.0	255.128
First host	0.1	0.129	1.1	1.129	2.1	2.129	3.1	3.129	...	255.1	255.129
Last host	0.126	0.254	1.126	1.254	2.126	2.254	3.126	3.254	...	255.126	255.254
Broadcast	0.127	0.255	1.127	1.255	2.127	2.255	3.127	3.255	...	255.127	255.255

Practice Example #7B: 255.255.255.192 (/26)

Now, this is where Class B subnetting gets easy. Because the third octet has a 255 in the mask section, whatever number is listed in the third octet is a subnet number. However, now that we have a subnet number in the fourth octet, we can subnet this octet just as we did with Class C subnetting. Let's try it:

> 172.16.0.0 = Network address
>
> 255.255.255.192 = Subnet mask

- *Subnets?* $2^{10} = 1024$.
- *Hosts?* $2^6 - 2 = 62$.
- *Valid subnets?* $256 - 192 = 64$. The subnets are shown in the following table. Do these numbers look familiar?

- *Broadcast address for each subnet?*
- *Valid hosts?*

The following table shows the first eight subnet ranges, valid hosts, and broadcast addresses:

Subnet	0.0	0.64	0.128	0.192	1.0	1.64	1.128	1.192
First host	0.1	0.65	0.129	0.193	1.1	1.65	1.129	1.193
Last host	0.62	0.126	0.190	0.254	1.62	1.126	1.190	1.254
Broadcast	0.63	0.127	0.191	0.255	1.63	1.127	1.191	1.255

Notice that for each subnet value in the third octet, you get subnets 0, 64, 128, and 192 in the fourth octet.

Practice Example #8B: 255.255.255.224 (/27)

This is done the same way as the preceding subnet mask, except that we have more subnets and fewer hosts per subnet available.

172.16.0.0 = Network address

255.255.255.224 = Subnet mask

- *Subnets?* $2^{11} = 2048$.
- *Hosts?* $2^5 - 2 = 30$.
- *Valid subnets?* $256 - 224 = 32$. 0, 32, 64, 96, 128, 160, 192, 224.
- *Broadcast address for each subnet?*
- *Valid hosts?*

The following table shows the first eight subnets:

Subnet	0.0	0.32	0.64	0.96	0.128	0.160	0.192	0.224
First host	0.1	0.33	0.65	0.97	0.129	0.161	0.193	0.225
Last host	0.30	0.62	0.94	0.126	0.158	0.190	0.222	0.254
Broadcast	0.31	0.63	0.95	0.127	0.159	0.191	0.223	0.255

This next table shows the last eight subnets:

Subnet	255.0	255.32	255.64	255.96	255.128	255.160	255.192	255.224
First host	255.1	255.33	255.65	255.97	255.129	255.161	255.193	255.225
Last host	255.30	255.62	255.94	255.126	255.158	255.190	255.222	255.254
Broadcast	255.31	255.63	255.95	255.127	255.159	255.191	255.223	255.255

Subnetting in Your Head: Class B Addresses

Are you nuts? Subnet Class B addresses in our heads? It's actually easier than writing it out—I'm not kidding! Let me show you the steps:

1. What subnet and broadcast address is the IP address 172.16.10.33 255.255.255.224 (/27) a member of?

    The interesting octet is the fourth octet. 256 – 224 = 32. 32 + 32 = 64. Bingo: 33 is between 32 and 64. However, remember that the third octet is considered part of the subnet, so the answer is the 10.32 subnet. The broadcast is 10.63 because 10.64 is the next subnet. That was a pretty easy one.

2. What subnet and broadcast address is the IP address 172.16.66.10 255.255.192.0 (/18) a member of?

    The interesting octet is the third octet instead of the fourth octet. 256 – 192 = 64. 0, 64, 128. The subnet is 172.16.64.0. The broadcast must be 172.16.127.255 because 128.0 is the next subnet.

 Notice in the last example I started counting at zero. This is called *ip subnet-zero*. It is a command that if executed on a router, allows us to use the zero subnet as our first subnet. This may or may not be enabled on your router. If it is not enabled, then you cannot start counting subnets at zero. Most routers, if not all routers these days, support ip subnet-zero.

3. What subnet and broadcast address is the IP address 172.16.50.10 255.255.224.0 (/19) a member of?

    256 – 224 = 0, 32, 64 (remember, we always start counting at zero). The subnet is 172.16.32.0, and the broadcast must be 172.16.63.255 because 64.0 is the next subnet.

4. What subnet and broadcast address is the IP address 172.16.46.255 255.255.240.0 (/20) a member of?

    256 – 240 = 16. The third octet is interesting to us. 0, 16, 32, 48. This subnet address must be in the 172.16.32.0 subnet, and the broadcast must be 172.16.47.255 because 48.0 is the next subnet. So, yes, 172.16.46.255 is a valid host.

5. What subnet and broadcast address is the IP address 172.16.45.14 255.255.255.252 (/30) a member of?

    Where is the interesting octet? 256 – 252 = 0, 4, 8, 12, 16 (in the fourth octet). The subnet is 172.16.45.12, with a broadcast of 172.16.45.15 because the next subnet is 172.16.45.16.

6. What is the subnet and broadcast address of the host 172.16.88.255/20?

    What is a /20? If you can't answer this, you can't answer this question, can you? A /20 is 255.255.240.0, which gives us a block size of 16 in the third octet, and because no subnet bits are on in the fourth octet, the answer is always 0 and 255 in the fourth octet. 0, 16, 32, 48, 64, 80, 96...bingo. 88 is between 80 and 96, so the subnet is 80.0 and the broadcast address is 95.255.

7. A router receives a packet on an interface with a destination address of 172.16.46.191/26. What will the router do with this packet?

Discard it. Do you know why? 172.16.46.196/26 is a 255.255.255.192 mask, which gives us a block size of 64. Our subnets are then 0, 64, 128, 192. 191 is the broadcast address of the 128 subnet, so a router, by default, will discard any broadcast packets.

Troubleshooting IP Addressing

Troubleshooting IP addressing is obviously an important skill because running into trouble somewhere along the way is pretty much a sure thing, and it's going to happen to you. No—I'm not a pessimist; I'm just keeping it real. Because of this nasty fact, it will be great when you can save the day because you can both figure out (diagnose) the problem and fix it on an IP network whether you're at work or at home!

Let's use Figure 8.3 as an example of your basic IP trouble—poor Sally can't log in to the Windows server. Do you deal with this by calling the Microsoft team to tell them their server is a pile of junk and causing all your problems? Probably not such a great idea—let's first double-check our network instead. Check out Figure 8.3.

FIGURE 8.3 Basic IP troubleshooting

Let's get started by going over the basic troubleshooting steps. They're pretty simple, but important nonetheless. Pretend you're at Sally's host and she's complaining that she can't communicate to a server that just happens to be on a remote network:

1. Open a command prompt window on Sally's host, and ping 127.0.0.1.

```
C:\>ping 127.0.0.1
Pinging 127.0.0.1 with 32 bytes of data:
Reply from 127.0.0.1: bytes=32 time<1ms TTL=128
```

```
Reply from 127.0.0.1: bytes=32 time<1ms TTL=128
Reply from 127.0.0.1: bytes=32 time<1ms TTL=128
Reply from 127.0.0.1: bytes=32 time<1ms TTL=128
Ping statistics for 127.0.0.1:
    Packets: Sent = 4, Received = 4, Lost = 0 (0% loss),
Approximate round trip times in milli-seconds:
    Minimum = 0ms, Maximum = 0ms, Average = 0ms
```

This is the diagnostic, or loopback, address, and if you get a successful ping, your IP stack is considered to be initialized. If it fails, then you have an IP stack failure and need to reinstall TCP/IP on the host.

> **NOTE** If you ping the loopback address and receive an "unable to contact IP driver, error code 2" message, you need to reinstall the TCP/IP protocol suite on the host.

2. Now, from the same command prompt window, ping the IP address of the local host.

```
C:\>ping 172.16.10.2
Pinging 172.16.10.2 with 32 bytes of data:
Reply from 172.16.10.2: bytes=32 time<1ms TTL=128
Reply from 172.16.10.2: bytes=32 time<1ms TTL=128
Reply from 172.16.10.2: bytes=32 time<1ms TTL=128
Reply from 172.16.10.2: bytes=32 time<1ms TTL=128
Ping statistics for 172.16.10.2:
    Packets: Sent = 4, Received = 4, Lost = 0 (0% loss),
Approximate round trip times in milli-seconds:
    Minimum = 0ms, Maximum = 0ms, Average = 0ms
```

If that's successful, your Network Interface Card (NIC) is functioning. If it fails, there is a problem with the NIC. Success here doesn't mean that a cable is plugged into the NIC, only that the IP protocol stack on the host can communicate to the NIC (via the LAN driver).

3. From the command prompt window, ping the default gateway (router).

```
C:\>ping 172.16.10.1
Pinging 172.16.10.1 with 32 bytes of data:
Reply from 172.16.10.1: bytes=32 time<1ms TTL=128
Reply from 172.16.10.1: bytes=32 time<1ms TTL=128
Reply from 172.16.10.1: bytes=32 time<1ms TTL=128
Reply from 172.16.10.1: bytes=32 time<1ms TTL=128
```

```
Ping statistics for 172.16.10.1:
    Packets: Sent = 4, Received = 4, Lost = 0 (0% loss),
Approximate round trip times in milli-seconds:
    Minimum = 0ms, Maximum = 0ms, Average = 0ms
```

If the ping works, it means that the NIC is plugged into the network and can communicate on the local network. If it fails, you have a local physical network problem that could be anywhere from the NIC to the router.

4. If steps 1 through 3 were successful, try to ping the remote server.

```
C:\>ping 172.16.20.2
Pinging 172.16.20.2 with 32 bytes of data:
Reply from 172.16.20.2: bytes=32 time<1ms TTL=128
Reply from 172.16.20.2: bytes=32 time<1ms TTL=128
Reply from 172.16.20.2: bytes=32 time<1ms TTL=128
Reply from 172.16.20.2: bytes=32 time<1ms TTL=128
Ping statistics for 172.16.20.2:
    Packets: Sent = 4, Received = 4, Lost = 0 (0% loss),
Approximate round trip times in milli-seconds:
    Minimum = 0ms, Maximum = 0ms, Average = 0ms
```

If that works, then you know that you have IP communication between the local host and the remote server. You also know that the remote physical network is working.

If the user still can't communicate with the server after steps 1 through 4 are successful, you probably have some type of name resolution problem and need to check your Domain Name System (DNS) settings. But if the ping to the remote server fails, then you know you have some type of remote physical network problem and need to go to the server and work through steps 1 through 3 until you find the snag.

Before we move on to determining IP address problems and how to fix them, I just want to mention some basic yet handy DOS commands that you can use to help troubleshoot your network from both a PC and a Cisco router (the commands might do the same thing, but they are implemented differently):

Packet InterNet Groper (ping)   Uses an Internet Control Message Protocol (ICMP) echo request and replies to test if a host IP stack is initialized and alive on the network.

traceroute   Displays the list of routers on a path to a network destination by using Time to Live (TTL) time-outs and ICMP error messages. This command will work on a router, MAC, or Linux box but not from a Windows command prompt.

tracert   Same command as traceroute, but it's a Microsoft Windows command and will not work on other devices, like a Cisco router or Unix box.

arp -a   Displays IP-to-MAC-address mappings on a Windows PC.

ipconfig /all   Used only from a DOS prompt. Shows you the PC network configuration.

Once you've gone through all these steps and used the appropriate DOS commands, if necessary, what do you do if you find a problem? How do you go about fixing an IP address configuration error? That's exactly what you're going to learn about next—how to determine specific IP address problems and what you can do to fix them.

Determining IP Address Problems

It's common for a host, router, or other network device to be configured with the wrong IP address, subnet mask, or default gateway. Because this happens way too often, I'm going to teach you how to both determine and fix IP address configuration errors.

Once you've worked through the four basic steps of troubleshooting and determined there's a problem, you obviously then need to find and fix it. It really helps to draw out the network and IP addressing scheme. If it's already done, consider yourself lucky and go buy a lottery ticket because although it should be done, it rarely is. And if it is, it's usually outdated or inaccurate anyway. Typically it is not done, and you'll probably just have to bite the bullet and start from scratch.

Once you have your network accurately drawn out, including the IP addressing scheme, you need to verify each host's IP address, mask, and default gateway address to determine the problem. (I'm assuming that you don't have a physical problem or that if you did, you've already fixed it.)

Let's check out the example illustrated in Figure 8.4. A user in the sales department calls and tells you that she can't get to Server A in the marketing department. You ask her if she can get to Server B in the marketing department, but she doesn't know because she doesn't have rights to log on to that server. What do you do?

FIGURE 8.4   IP address problem 1

You ask the client to go through the four troubleshooting steps that you learned about in the preceding section. Steps 1 through 3 work, but step 4 fails. By looking at the figure, can you determine the problem? Look for clues in the network drawing. First, the WAN link between the Lab_A router and the Lab_B router shows the mask as a /27. You should already know that this mask is 255.255.255.224 and then determine that all networks are using this mask. The network address is 192.168.1.0. What are our valid subnets and hosts? 256 – 224 = 32, so this makes our subnets 32, 64, 96, 128, and so on. So, by looking at the figure, you can see that subnet 32 is being used by the sales department, the WAN link is using subnet 96, and the marketing department is using subnet 64.

Now you have to determine what the valid host ranges are for each subnet. From what you learned at the beginning of this chapter, you should now be able to easily determine the subnet address, broadcast addresses, and valid host ranges. The valid hosts for the Sales LAN are 33 through 62—the broadcast address is 63 because the next subnet is 64, right? For the Marketing LAN, the valid hosts are 65 through 94 (broadcast 95), and for the WAN link, 97 through 126 (broadcast 127). By looking at the figure, you can determine that the default gateway on the Lab_B router is incorrect. That address is the broadcast address of the 64 subnet, so there's no way it could be a valid host.

Did you get all that? Maybe we should try another one, just to make sure. Figure 8.5 shows a network problem. A user in the Sales LAN can't get to Server B. You have the user run through the four basic troubleshooting steps and find that the host can communicate to the local network but not to the remote network. Find and define the IP addressing problem.

FIGURE 8.5 IP address problem 2

If you use the same steps used to solve the last problem, you can see first that the WAN link again provides the subnet mask to use— /29, or 255.255.255.248. You need to determine what the valid subnets, broadcast addresses, and valid host ranges are to solve this problem.

The 248 mask is a block size of 8 (256 – 248 = 8), so the subnets both start and increment in multiples of 8. By looking at the figure, you see that the Sales LAN is in the 24 subnet, the WAN is in the 40 subnet, and the Marketing LAN is in the 80 subnet. Can you see the problem yet? The valid host range for the Sales LAN is 25–30, and the configuration appears correct. The valid host range for the WAN link is 41–46, and this also appears correct. The valid host range for the 80 subnet is 81–86, with a broadcast address of 87 because the next subnet is 88. Server B has been configured with the broadcast address of the subnet.

Okay, now that you can figure out misconfigured IP addresses on hosts, what do you do if a host doesn't have an IP address and you need to assign one? What you need to do is look at other hosts on the LAN and figure out the network, mask, and default gateway. Let's take a look at a couple of examples of how to find and apply valid IP addresses to hosts.

You need to assign a server and router IP addresses on a LAN. The subnet assigned on that segment is 192.168.20.24/29, and the router needs to be assigned the first usable address and the server the last valid host ID. What are the IP address, mask, and default gateway assigned to the server?

To answer this, you must know that a /29 is a 255.255.255.248 mask, which provides a block size of 8. The subnet is known as 24, the next subnet in a block of 8 is 32, so the broadcast address of the 24 subnet is 31, which makes the valid host range 25–30:

Server IP address: 192.168.20.30

Server mask: 255.255.255.248

Default gateway: 192.168.20.25 (router's IP address)

As another example, let's take a look at Figure 8.6 and solve this problem.

Look at the router's IP address on Ethernet0. What IP address, subnet mask, and valid host range could be assigned to the host?

FIGURE 8.6 Find the valid host.

RouterA

E0: 192.168.10.33/27

HostA

Okay—the IP address of the router's Ethernet0 is 192.168.10.33/27. As you already know, a /27 is a 224 mask with a block size of 32. The router's interface is in the 32 subnet. The next subnet is 64, so that makes the broadcast address of the 32 subnet 63 and the valid host range 33–62:

Host IP address: 192.168.10.34–62 (any address in the range except for 33, which is assigned to the router)

Mask: 255.255.255.224

Default gateway: 192.168.10.33

Figure 8.7 shows two routers with Ethernet configurations already assigned. What are the host addresses and subnet masks of hosts A and B?

FIGURE 8.7   Find the valid host #2

RouterA has an IP address of 192.168.10.65/26 and RouterB has an IP address of 192.168.10.33/28. What are the host configurations? RouterA Ethernet0 is in the 192.168.10.64 subnet, and RouterB Ethernet0 is in the 192.168.10.32 network:

Host A IP address: 192.168.10.66–126

Host A mask: 255.255.255.192

Host A default gateway: 192.168.10.65

Host B IP address: 192.168.10.34–46

Host B mask: 255.255.255.240

Host B default gateway: 192.168.10.33

Just a couple more examples, and then this section is history. Hang in there!

Figure 8.8 shows two routers; you need to configure the S0/0 interface on RouterA. The network assigned to the serial link is 172.16.17.0/22. What IP address can be assigned?

First, you must know that a /22 CIDR is 255.255.252.0, which makes a block size of 4 in the third octet. Because 17 is listed, the available range is 16.1 through 19.254; so, for example, the IP address S0/0 could be 172.16.18.255 because that's within the range.

Okay, last one! You have one Class C network ID, and you need to provide one usable subnet per city while allowing enough usable host addresses for each city specified in Figure 8.9. What is your mask?

FIGURE 8.8   Find the valid host address #3

172.16.17.0/22

RouterA   RouterB

S0/0   S0/0

FIGURE 8.9   Find the valid subnet mask

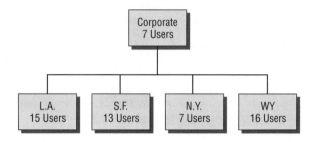

Corporate
7 Users

L.A.
15 Users

S.F.
13 Users

N.Y.
7 Users

WY
16 Users

Actually, this is probably the easiest thing you've done all day! I count 5 subnets needed, and the Wyoming office needs 16 users (always look for the network that needs the most hosts). What block size is needed for the Wyoming office? 32. (Remember, you cannot use a block size of 16 because you always have to subtract 2!) What mask provides you with a block size of 32? 224. Bingo! This provides 8 subnets, each with 30 hosts.

Introduction to Network Address Translation (NAT)

Similar to Classless Inter-Domain Routing (CIDR), the original intention for NAT was to slow the depletion of available IP address space by allowing many private IP addresses to be represented by some smaller number of public IP addresses.

Since then, it's been discovered that NAT is also a useful tool for network migrations and mergers, server load sharing, and creating "virtual servers." So in this section, I'm going to describe the basics of NAT functionality and the terminology common to NAT.

At times, NAT really decreases the overwhelming amount of public IP addresses required in your networking environment. And NAT comes in very handy when two companies that have duplicate internal addressing schemes merge. NAT is also great to have around when an organization changes its ISP and the networking manager doesn't want the hassle of changing the internal address scheme.

Here's a list of situations when it's best to have NAT on your side:

- You need to connect to the Internet, and your hosts don't have globally unique IP addresses.

- You change to a new ISP that requires you to renumber your network.

- You need to merge two intranets with duplicate addresses.

You typically use NAT on a border router. For an illustration of this, see Figure 8.10, where NAT would be configured on the Corporate router.

FIGURE 8.10 Where to configure NAT

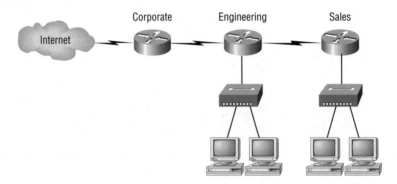

Now you may be thinking, "NAT's totally cool. It's the grooviest, greatest network gadget, and I just gotta have it." Well, hang on a minute. There are truly some serious snags related to NAT use. Oh, don't get me wrong: It really can save you sometimes, but there's a dark side you need to know about too. For a visual of the pros and cons linked to using NAT, check out Table 8.3.

TABLE 8.3 Advantages and disadvantages of implementing NAT

Advantages	Disadvantages
Conserves legally registered addresses.	Translation introduces switching path delays.
Reduces address overlap occurrences.	Loss of end-to-end IP traceability.
Increases flexibility when connecting to the Internet.	Certain applications will not function with NAT enabled.
Eliminates address renumbering as the network changes.	

Types of Network Address Translation

In this section, I'm going to go over the three types of NAT with you:

Static NAT (SNAT)   This type of NAT is designed to allow one-to-one mapping between local and global addresses. Keep in mind that the static version requires you to have one real Internet IP address for every host on your network.

Dynamic NAT   This version gives you the ability to map an unregistered IP address to a registered IP address from a pool of registered IP addresses. You don't have to statically configure your router to map an inside-to-an-outside-address as you would using static NAT, but you do have to have enough real, bona-fide IP addresses for everyone who's going to be sending packets to and receiving them from the Internet.

Overloading   This is the most popular type of NAT configuration. Understand that overloading really is a form of dynamic NAT that maps multiple unregistered IP addresses to a single registered IP address—many-to-one—by using different ports. Now, why is this so special? Well, because it's also known as Port Address Translation (PAT). And by using PAT (NAT Overload), you get to have thousands of users connect to the Internet using only one real global IP address—pretty slick, yeah? Seriously, NAT Overload is the real reason we haven't run out of valid IP address on the Internet. Really—I'm not joking.

NAT Names

The names we use to describe the addresses used with NAT are pretty simple. Addresses used after NAT translations are called *global* addresses. These are usually the public addresses used on the Internet, but remember, you don't need public addresses if you aren't going on the Internet.

   Local addresses are the ones we use before NAT translation. So, the inside local address is actually the private address of the sending host that's trying to get to the Internet, while the outside local address is the address of the destination host. The latter is usually a public address (web address, mail server, and so on) and is how the packet begins its journey.

   After translation, the inside local address is then called the *inside global address*, and the outside global address then becomes the name of the destination host. Check out Table 8.4, which lists all this terminology, for a clear picture of the various names used with NAT.

TABLE 8.4   NAT terms

Name	Meaning
Inside local	Name of the inside source address before translation
Outside local	Name of the destination host before translation
Inside global	Name of the inside host after translation
Outside global	Name of the outside destination host after translation

How NAT Works

Now it's time to look at how this whole NAT thing works. I'm going to start by using Figure 8.11 to describe the basic translation of NAT.

FIGURE 8.11   Basic NAT translation

In the example shown in Figure 8.11, host 10.1.1.1 sends an outbound packet to the border router configured with NAT. The router identifies the IP address as an inside local IP address destined for an outside network, translates the address, and documents the translation in the NAT table.

The packet is sent to the outside interface with the new translated source address. The external host returns the packet to the destination host, and the NAT router translates the inside global IP address back to the inside local IP address using the NAT table. This is as simple as it gets.

Let's take a look at a more complex configuration using overloading, or what is also referred to as PAT. I'll use Figure 8.12 to demonstrate how PAT works.

With overloading, all inside hosts get translated to one single IP address, hence the term *overloading*. Again, the reason we have not run out of available IP addresses on the Internet is because of overloading (PAT).

Take a look at the NAT table in Figure 8.12 again. In addition to the inside local IP address and outside global IP address, we now have port numbers. These port numbers help the router identify which host should receive the return traffic.

FIGURE 8.12   NAT overloading example (PAT)

Port numbers are used at the Transport layer to identify the local host in this example. If we had to use IP addresses to identify the source hosts, that would be called *static NAT*, and we would run out of addresses. PAT allows us to use the Transport layer to identify the hosts, which in turn allows us to use (theoretically) up to 65,000 hosts with one real IP address.

You're done, the diva has sung, the chicken has crossed the road...whew! Take a good break, and then come back and go through the written labs and review questions.

Summary

Did you read Chapter 7 and this chapter and understand everything on the first pass? If so, that is fantastic—congratulations! The thing is, you probably got lost a couple of times—and as I told you, that's what usually happens, so don't stress. Don't feel bad if you have to read each chapter more than once, or even 10 times, before you're truly good to go.

This chapter provided you with an important understanding of IP subnetting. After reading this chapter, you should be able to subnet IP addresses in your head.

You should also understand the basic troubleshooting methods. You must remember the four steps you take when trying to narrow down exactly where a network/IP addressing problem is and then know how to proceed systematically in order to fix it. In addition, you should be able to find valid IP addresses and subnet masks by looking at a network diagram.

I finished this chapter with an introduction to Network Address Translation. I discussed the difference between static and dynamic NAT and NAT overloading.

Exam Essentials

Remember the steps to subnet in your head.   Understand how IP addressing and subnetting work. First, determine your block size by using the 256-subnet mask math. Then, count your subnets and determine the broadcast address of each subnet—it is always the number right before the next subnet. Your valid hosts are the numbers between the subnet address and the broadcast address.

Understand the various block sizes.   This is an important part of understanding IP addressing and subnetting. The valid block sizes are always 4, 8, 16, 32, 64, 128, and so on. You can determine your block size by using the 256-subnet mask math.

Remember the four diagnostic steps.   The four simple steps for troubleshooting are ping the loopback address, ping the NIC, ping the default gateway, and ping the remote device.

You must be able to find and fix an IP addressing problem.   Once you go through the four troubleshooting steps, you should be able to determine the IP addressing problem by drawing out the network and finding the valid and invalid hosts addressed in your network.

Understand basic NAT terminology.   You want to know the difference between inside local and inside global. Inside local is before translation, and inside global is after translation. Inside global is defined as a registered address that represents an inside host to an outside network. You should also understand PAT and how it works by using different port numbers to map multiple private IP addresses to a single registered IP address.

Written Labs

Write the subnet, broadcast address, and valid host range for question 1 through question 6:

1. 192.168.100.25/30

2. 192.168.100.37/28

3. 192.168.100.66/27

4. 192.168.100.17/29

5. 192.168.100.99/26

6. 192.168.100.99/25

7. You have a Class B network and need 29 subnets. What is your mask?

8. What is the broadcast address of 192.168.192.10/29?

9. How many hosts are available with a Class C /29 mask?

10. What is the subnet for host ID 172.16.3.65/23?

You can find the answers in Appendix B.

Review Questions

You can find the answers in Appendix A.

1. What is the maximum number of IP addresses that can be assigned to hosts on a local subnet that uses the 255.255.255.224 subnet mask?

    A. 14

    B. 15

    C. 16

    D. 30

    E. 31

    F. 62

2. You have a Class A host of 10.0.0.110/25. It needs to communicate to a host with an IP address of 10.0.0.210/25. Which of the following devices do you need to use in order for these hosts to communicate?

    A. A Layer 2 switch

    B. Router

    C. DNS server

    D. Hub

3. What is the subnetwork address for a host with the IP address 200.10.5.68/28?

    A. 200.10.5.56

    B. 200.10.5.32

    C. 200.10.5.64

    D. 200.10.5.0

4. The network address of 172.16.0.0/19 provides how many subnets and hosts?

    A. 7 subnets, 30 hosts each

    B. 7 subnets, 2,046 hosts each

    C. 7 subnets, 8,190 hosts each

    D. 8 subnets, 30 hosts each

    E. 8 subnets, 2,046 hosts each

    F. 8 subnets, 8,190 hosts each

5. You receive a call from a user who is complaining that they cannot get on the Internet. You have them verify their IP address, mask, and default gateway. The IP address is 10.0.37.144, with a subnet mask of 255.255.254.0. The default gateway is 10.0.38.1. What is the problem?

   A. Incorrect DNS server address

   B. Invalid subnet mask

   C. Incorrect gateway IP

   D. IP address and mask not compatible

6. If a host on a network has the address 172.16.45.14/30, what is the subnetwork this host belongs to?

   A. 172.16.45.0

   B. 172.16.45.4

   C. 172.16.45.8

   D. 172.16.45.12

   E. 172.16.45.16

7. On a network, which mask should you use on point-to-point WAN links in order to reduce the waste of IP addresses?

   A. /27

   B. /28

   C. /29

   D. /30

   E. /31

8. On which of the following devices are you most likely to be able to implement NAT?

   A. Hub

   B. Ethernet switch

   C. Router

   D. Bridge

9. You have an interface on a router with the IP address of 192.168.192.10/29. Including the router interface, how many hosts can have IP addresses on the LAN attached to router interface?

   A. 6

   B. 8

   C. 30

   D. 62

   E. 126

10. When configuring the IP settings on a computer on one subnet to ensure that it can communicate with a computer on another subnet, which of the following is desirable?

    A. Configure the computer with the same default gateway as the other computer.

    B. Configure the computer with the same subnet mask as the other computer.

    C. Configure the computer with a default gateway that matches the IP address of the interface of the router that is attached to the same subnet as the computer.

    D. Configure the computer with a subnet mask that matches the IP address of the router's interface that is attached to the same subnet as the computer.

11. You have an interface on a router with the IP address of 192.168.192.10/29. What is the broadcast address the hosts will use on this LAN?

    A. 192.168.192.15

    B. 192.168.192.31

    C. 192.168.192.63

    D. 192.168.192.127

    E. 192.168.192.255

12. What is the highest usable address on the 172.16.1.0/24 network?

    A. 172.16.1.255

    B. 172.16.1.254

    C. 172.16.1.253

    D. 172.16.1.23

13. A network administrator is connecting two hosts directly through their Ethernet interfaces, as shown in the illustration. Ping attempts between the hosts are unsuccessful. What can be done to provide connectivity between the hosts? (Choose two.)

Straight-through Cable

IP Address: 192.168.1.20   IP Address: 192.168.1.201
Mask 255.255.255.240   Mask 255.255.255.240

    A. A crossover cable should be used in place of the straight-through cable.

    B. A rollover cable should be used in place of the straight-though cable.

    C. The subnet masks should be set to 255.255.255.192.

    D. A default gateway needs to be set on each host.

    E. The subnet masks should be set to 255.255.255.0.

14. If an Ethernet port on a router were assigned an IP address of 172.16.112.1/25, what would be the subnet address of this host?

    A. 172.16.112.0

    B. 172.16.0.0

    C. 172.16.96.0

    D. 172.16.255.0

    E. 172.16.128.0

15. Using the following illustration, what would be the IP address of E0 if you were using the eighth subnet? The network ID is 192.168.10.0/28, and you need to use the last available IP address in the range. The 0 subnet should not be considered valid for this question.

    A. 192.168.10.142

    B. 192.168.10.66

    C. 192.168.100.254

    D. 192.168.10.143

    E. 192.168.10.126

16. Using the illustration in question 15, what would be the IP address of E0 if you were using the first subnet? The network ID is 192.168.10.0/28, and you need to use the last available IP address in the range. Again, the zero subnet should not be considered valid for this question.

    A. 192.168.10.24

    B. 192.168.10.62

    C. 192.168.10.30

    D. 192.168.10.127

17. If you are forced to replace a router that has failed to the point that you are unable to access its current configuration to aid in setting up interface addresses on the new router, which of the following can you reference for assistance?

   A. The default-gateway settings on computers from each subnet that the old router interconnected.

   B. The router's configuration that was periodically cached on the DHCP server.

   C. The router's configuration that was periodically cached on the DNS server.

   D. The new router will auto-configure itself with the correct settings.

18. You have a network with a subnet of 172.16.17.0/22. Which of the following is a valid host address?

   A. 172.16.17.1 255.255.255.252

   B. 172.16.0.1 255.255.240.0

   C. 172.16.20.1 255.255.254.0

   D. 172.16.16.1 255.255.255.240

   E. 172.16.18.255 255.255.252.0

   F. 172.16.0.1 255.255.255.0

19. Your router has the following IP address on Ethernet0: 172.16.2.1/23. Which of the following can be valid host IDs on the LAN interface attached to the router? (Choose two.)

   A. 172.16.0.5

   B. 172.16.1.100

   C. 172.16.1.198

   D. 172.16.2.255

   E. 172.16.3.0

   F. 172.16.3.255

20. You have one IP address provided from your ISP with a /30 mask. However, you have 300 users that need to access the Internet. What technology will you use to implement a solution?

   A. PAT

   B. VPN

   C. DNS

   D. LANs

Chapter

9

Introduction to IP Routing

THE FOLLOWING COMPTIA NETWORK+ EXAM OBJECTIVES ARE COVERED IN THIS CHAPTER:

✓ **1.4 Explain the purpose and properties of routing and switching.**

- Link state vs. distance vector vs. hybrid
- Static vs. dynamic
- Next hop
- IGP vs. EGP
- Routing tables
- Convergence (steady state)

IP routing is the process of moving packets from one network to another network using routers. The IP routing process is a super-important subject to understand because it pertains to all routers and configurations that use IP.

Before you read this chapter, you need to understand the difference between a routing protocol and a routed protocol. A *routing protocol* is a tool used by routers to dynamically find all the networks in the internetwork as well as to ensure that all routers have the same routing table. Basically, a routing protocol determines the path of a packet through an internetwork. Examples of routing protocols are Routing Information Protocol (RIP), Routing Information Protocol version 2 (RIPv2), Enhanced Interior Gateway Routing Protocol (EIGRP), and Open Shortest Path First (OSPF).

Once all routers know about all networks, a *routed protocol* can be used to send user data (packets) through the established internetwork. Routed protocols are assigned to an interface and determine the method of packet delivery. Examples of routed protocols are Internet Protocol (IP) and Internet Protocol version 6 (IPv6).

In this chapter, I'm going to describe IP routing with routers. I will explain, in a step-by-step fashion, the IP routing process. I will also explain static and dynamic routing on a conceptual level, with more details about dynamic routing in Chapter 10, "Routing Protocols."

To find up-to-the-minute updates for this chapter, please see www.lammle.com/forum or the book's web site at www.sybex.com/go/netplus2e.

Routing Basics

Once you create an internetwork by connecting your wide area networks (WANs) and local area networks (LANs) to a router, you need to configure logical network addresses, such as IP addresses, to all hosts on the internetwork so that they can communicate via routers across that internetwork.

In IT, routing essentially refers to the process of taking a packet from one device and sending it through the network to another device on a different network. Routers don't really care about hosts—they care only about networks and the best path to each network. The logical network address of the destination host is used to get packets to a network through a routed network, and then the hardware address of the host is used to deliver the packet from a router to the correct destination host.

If your network has no routers, then it should be apparent that, well, no...you are not routing. But if you do have them, they're there to route traffic to all the networks in your internetwork. To be capable of routing packets, a router must know at least the following information:

- Destination address
- Neighbor routers from which it can learn about remote networks
- Possible routes to all remote networks
- The best route to each remote network
- How to maintain and verify routing information

The router learns about remote networks from neighbor routers or from an administrator. The router then builds a *routing table* (a map of the internetwork) that describes how to find the remote networks. If a network is directly connected, then the router already knows how to get to it.

If a network isn't directly connected to the router, the router must use one of two ways to learn how to get to it. One way is called *static routing*, which can be a ton of work because it requires someone to hand-type all network locations into the routing table. The other way is dynamic routing.

In *dynamic routing*, a protocol on one router communicates with the same protocol running on neighbor routers. The routers then update each other about all the networks they know about and place this information into the routing table. If a change occurs in the network, the dynamic routing protocols automatically inform all routers about the event. If static routing is used, the administrator is responsible for updating all changes by hand into all routers. Understandably, in a large network, it's common to find that a combination of both dynamic and static routing is being used.

Before we jump into the IP routing process, let's take a look at a simple example that demonstrates how a router uses the routing table to route packets out of an interface. We'll be going into a more detailed study of this process in a minute.

Figure 9.1 shows a simple two-router network. Lab_A has one serial interface and three LAN interfaces.

Looking at Figure 9.1, can you figure out which interface Lab_A will use to forward an IP datagram to a host with an IP address of 10.10.10.10?

By using the Cisco IOS command show ip route, we can see the routing table (map of the internetwork) that router Lab_A will use to make all forwarding decisions:

```
Router_A#show ip route
[output cut]
Gateway of last resort is not set
C    10.10.10.0/24 is directly connected, FastEthernet0/0
C    10.10.20.0/24 is directly connected, FastEthernet0/1
C    10.10.30.0/24 is directly connected, FastEthernet0/2
C    10.10.40.0/24 is directly connected, Serial 0/0
```

FIGURE 9.1   A simple routing example

The C in the routing table output means that the networks listed are "directly connected," and until we add a routing protocol—something like RIP, EIGRP, and so on—to the routers in our internetwork, or use static routes, we'll have only directly connected networks in our routing table.

So, let's get back to the original question: By looking at the figure and the output of the routing table, can you tell what Lab_A will do with a received packet that has a destination IP address of 10.10.10.10? If you answered, "The router will packet-switch the packet to interface FastEthernet 0/0, and this interface will then frame the packet and send it out on the network segment," you're right.

Just because we can, let's look at a different example. Based on the output of the next routing table, which interface will a packet with a destination address of 10.10.10.14 be forwarded from?

```
Router_A#sh ip route
[output cut]
Gateway of last resort is not set
C      10.10.10.16/28 is directly connected, FastEthernet0/0
C      10.10.10.8/29 is directly connected, FastEthernet0/1
C      10.10.10.4/30 is directly connected, FastEthernet0/2
C      10.10.10.0/30 is directly connected, Serial 0/0
```

First, you can see that the network is subnetted and that each interface has a different mask. And I have to tell you, you positively can't answer this question if you can't subnet—no way! Here's the answer: 10.10.10.14 would be a host in the 10.10.10.8/29 subnet connected to the FastEthernet 0/1 interface. Don't freak if this one left you staring vacantly. Instead, if you're struggling, go back and reread Chapter 8, "IP Subnetting, Troubleshooting IP, and Introduction to NAT," until you get it. This should then make perfect sense to you.

When the routing tables of all routers in the network are complete (because they include information about all the networks in the internetwork), they are considered *converged*, or in a steady state. This is covered in more detail in Chapter 10.

Now, let's get into this process in more detail.

The IP Routing Process

The IP routing process is actually pretty simple, and it doesn't change, regardless of the size of your network. I'm going to use Figure 9.2 to give you a picture of this step-by-step process. The question I'm asking is this: What happens when Host_A wants to communicate with Host_B on a different network? I'll go through how to answer that question by breaking down the process with headings to make it easier to understand. First, check out Figure 9.2.

FIGURE 9.2   IP routing example using two hosts and one router

Okay—here you can see that a user on Host_A pings Host_B's IP address. Routing doesn't get any simpler than this, but it still involves a lot of steps. Let's work through them.

A packet is created on the host:

1. Internet Control Message Protocol (ICMP) creates an echo request payload (which is just the alphabet in the data field).

2. ICMP hands that payload to IP, which then creates a packet. At a minimum, this packet contains an IP source address, an IP destination address, and a Protocol field with 01h. (Remember that Cisco likes to use *0x* in front of hex characters, so this could look like 0x01.) All of that tells the receiving host whom it should hand the payload to when the destination is reached. In this example, it's ICMP.

The packet is forwarded:

3. After the packet is created, IP determines whether the destination IP address is on the local network or a remote one.

4. Because IP has discovered that this is a remote request, the packet needs to be sent to the default gateway so the packet can be routed to the correct remote network. The Registry in Windows is parsed to find the configured default gateway.

5. The default gateway of host 172.16.10.2 (Host_A) is configured to 172.16.10.1. For this packet to be sent to the default gateway, the hardware address of the router's interface Ethernet 0 (configured with the IP address of 172.16.10.1) must be known. Why? So the packet can be handed down to the Data Link layer, framed, and sent to the router's interface that's connected to the 172.16.10.0 network. Because hosts only communicate via hardware addresses on the local LAN, it's important to recognize that for Host_A to communicate to Host_B, it has to send packets to the Media Access Control (MAC) address of the default gateway on the local network.

> MAC addresses are always local on the LAN and never go through and past a router.

6. The Address Resolution Protocol (ARP) cache of the host is checked to see whether the IP address of the default gateway has already been resolved to a hardware address. If it has, the packet is then free to be handed to the Data Link layer for framing. (The hardware-destination address is also handed down with that packet.) To view the ARP cache on your host, use the following command:

```
C:\>arp -a
Interface: 172.16.10.2 --- 0x3
   Internet Address      Physical Address       Type
   172.16.10.1           00-15-05-06-31-b0      dynamic
```

If the hardware address isn't already in the ARP cache of the host, an ARP broadcast is sent out onto the local network to search for the hardware address of 172.16.10.1. The router responds to that request and provides the hardware address of Ethernet 0, and the host caches this address.

7. After the packet and destination hardware address have been handed to the Data Link layer, the LAN driver is used to provide media access via the type of LAN being used (in this example, it's Ethernet). A frame is then generated, encapsulating the packet with control information. Within that frame are the hardware-destination and source addresses plus, in this case, an Ether-Type field that describes the Network layer protocol that handed the packet to the Data Link layer—in this instance, IP. At the end of the frame is something called a Frame Check Sequence (FCS) field that houses the result of the cyclic redundancy check (CRC). The frame would look something like what I've detailed in Figure 9.3. It contains Host_A's hardware (MAC) address and the hardware-destination address of the default gateway. It does not include the remote host's MAC address—remember that because it's important!

FIGURE 9.3   Frame used from Host_A to the Lab_A router when Host_B is pinged

Destination MAC (Routers E0 MAC Address)	Source MAC (Host_A MAC Address)	Ether-Type field	Packet	FCS (CRC)

8. When the frame is completed, it's handed down to the Physical layer to be placed onto the physical medium one bit at a time. In this example, the physical medium is twisted-pair wire.

The router receives the packet:

9. Every device within the collision domain receives these bits and builds the frame. They each run a CRC and check the answer in the FCS field. If the answers don't match, the frame is discarded. But if the CRC matches, then the hardware-destination address is checked to see if it matches too (in this example, it's the router's interface, Ethernet 0). If it's a match, then the Ether-Type field is checked to find the protocol used at the Network layer.

10. The packet is pulled from the frame, and what is left of the frame is discarded. The packet is then handed to the protocol listed in the Ether-Type field—it's given to IP.

The router routes the packet:

11. IP receives the packet and checks the IP destination address. Because the packet's destination address doesn't match any of the addresses configured on the receiving router's interfaces, the router will look up the destination IP network address in its routing table.

12. The routing table must have an entry for the network 172.16.20.0 or the packet will be discarded immediately and an ICMP message will be sent back to the originating device with a Destination Unreachable message.

13. If the router does find an entry for the destination network in its table, the packet is switched to the exit interface—in this example, interface Ethernet 1. The following output displays the Lab_A router's routing table. The C means "directly connected." No routing protocols are needed in this network because all networks (all two of them) are directly connected:

```
Lab_A>sh ip route
Codes:C - connected,S - static,I - IGRP,R - RIP,M - mobile,B -
    BGP, D - EIGRP,EX - EIGRP external,O - OSPF,IA - OSPF inter
    area, N1 - OSPF NSSA external type 1, N2 - OSPF NSSA external
type 2, E1 - OSPF external type 1, E2 - OSPF external type 2,
E - EGP,i - IS-IS, L1 - IS-IS level-1, L2 - IS-IS level-2, ia
    - IS-IS intearea * - candidate default, U - per-user static
    route, o - ODR P - periodic downloaded static route


Gateway of last resort is not set

     172.16.0.0/24 is subnetted, 2 subnets
C       172.16.10.0 is directly connected, Ethernet0
C       172.16.20.0 is directly connected, Ethernet1
```

14. The router packet-switches the packet to the Ethernet 1 buffer.

15. Now that the packet is in the Ethernet 1 buffer, IP needs to know the hardware address of the destination host and first checks the ARP cache. If the hardware address of Host_B has already been resolved and is in the router's ARP cache, then the packet and the hardware address are handed down to the Data Link layer to be framed. Let's take a look at the ARP cache on the Lab_A router by using the show ip arp command:

```
Lab_A#sh ip arp
Protocol  Address       Age(min)  Hardware Addr   Type   Interface
Internet  172.16.20.1   -         00d0.58ad.05f4  ARPA   Ethernet1
Internet  172.16.20.2   3         0030.9492.a5dd  ARPA   Ethernet1
Internet  172.16.10.1   -         0015.0506.31b0  ARPA   Ethernet0
Internet  172.16.10.2   12        0030.9492.a4ac  ARPA   Ethernet0
```

Okay—the dash (-) means that this is the physical interface on the router. From this output, we can see that the router knows the 172.16.10.2 (Host_A) and 172.16.20.2 (Host_B) hardware addresses. Cisco routers will keep an entry in the ARP table for 4 hours. But if the hardware address hasn't already been resolved, the router then sends an ARP request out E1 looking for the hardware address of 172.16.20.2. Host_B responds with its hardware address, and the packet and hardware-destination address are both sent to the Data Link layer for framing.

16. The Data Link layer creates a frame with the destination and source hardware address, Ether-Type field, and FCS field at the end. The frame is handed to the Physical layer to be sent out on the physical medium one bit at a time.

Finally, the remote host receives the packet:

17. Host_B receives the frame and immediately runs a CRC. If the result matches what's in the FCS field, the hardware-destination address is then checked. If the host finds a match, the Ether-Type field is then checked to determine the protocol that the packet should be handed to at the Network layer—IP, in this example.

18. At the Network layer, IP receives the packet and checks the IP destination address. Because there's finally a match made, the Protocol field is checked to find out whom the payload should be given to.

19. The payload is handed to ICMP, which understands that this is an echo request. ICMP responds to this by immediately discarding the packet and generating a new payload as an echo reply.

The destination host becomes a source host:

20. A packet is created, including the source and destination addresses, Protocol field, and payload. The destination device is now Host_A.

21. IP checks to see whether the destination IP address is a device on the local LAN or on a remote network. Because the destination device is on a remote network, the packet needs to be sent to the default gateway.

22. The default gateway IP address is found in the Registry of the Windows device, and the ARP cache is checked to see whether the hardware address has already been resolved from an IP address.

23. After the hardware address of the default gateway is found, the packet and destination hardware addresses are handed down to the Data Link layer for framing.

24. The Data Link layer frames the packet of information and includes the following in the header:

- The destination and source hardware addresses
- The Ether-Type field with 0x0800 (IP) in it
- The FCS field with the CRC result in tow

25. The frame is now handed down to the Physical layer to be sent out over the network medium one bit at a time.

Time for the router to route another packet:

26. The router's Ethernet 1 interface receives the bits and builds a frame. The CRC is run, and the FCS field is checked to make sure the answers match.

27. When the CRC is found to be okay, the hardware-destination address is checked. Because the router's interface is a match, the packet is pulled from the frame, and the Ether-Type field is checked to see which protocol at the Network layer the packet should be delivered to.

28. The protocol is determined to be IP, so it gets the packet. IP runs a CRC check on the IP header first and then checks the destination IP address.

IP does not run a complete CRC the way the Data Link layer does—it only checks the header for errors.

Because the IP destination address doesn't match any of the router's interfaces, the routing table is checked to see whether it has a route to 172.16.10.0. If it doesn't have a route over to the destination network, the packet will be discarded immediately. (This is the source point of confusion for a lot of administrators—when a ping fails, most people think the packet never reached the destination host. But as we see here, that's not *always* the case. All it takes is just one of the remote routers to be lacking a route back to the originating host's network and—*poof!*—the packet is dropped on the *return trip*, not on its way to the host.)

Just a quick note to mention that when (if) the packet is lost on the way back to the originating host, you will typically see a Request Timed Out message because it is an unknown error. If the error occurs because of a known issue, such as a route that is not in the routing table on the way to the destination device, you will see a Destination Unreachable message. This should help you determine if the problem occurred on the way to the destination or on the way back.

29. In this case, the router does know how to get to network 172.16.10.0—the exit interface is Ethernet 0—so the packet is switched to interface Ethernet 0.

30. The router checks the ARP cache to determine whether the hardware address for 172.16.10.2 has already been resolved.

31. Because the hardware address to 172.16.10.2 is already cached from the originating trip to Host_B, the hardware address and packet are handed to the Data Link layer.

32. The Data Link layer builds a frame with the destination and source hardware addresses and then puts IP in the Ether-Type field. A CRC is run on the frame, and the result is placed in the FCS field.

33. The frame is then handed to the Physical layer to be sent out onto the local network one bit at a time.

The original source host, now the destination host, receives the reply packet:

34. The destination host receives the frame, runs a CRC, checks the hardware destination address, and looks in the Ether-Type field to find out whom to hand the packet to.

35. IP is the designated receiver, and after the packet is handed to IP at the Network layer, IP checks the protocol field for further direction. IP finds instructions to give the payload to ICMP, and ICMP determines the packet to be an ICMP echo reply.

36. ICMP acknowledges that it has received the reply by sending an exclamation point (!) to the user interface. ICMP then attempts to send four more echo requests to the destination host.

You've just been introduced to "Todd's 36 easy steps to understanding IP routing." The key point to understand here is that if you had a much larger network, the process would be the *same*. In a really big internetwork, the packet just goes through more hops before it finds the destination host.

It's super important to remember that when Host_A sends a packet to Host_B, the destination hardware address used is the default gateway's Ethernet interface. Why? Because frames can't be placed on remote networks—only local networks. So packets destined for remote networks must go through the default gateway.

Let's take a look at Host_A's ARP cache now by using the arp -a command from the DOS prompt:

```
C:\ >arp -a
Interface: 172.16.10.2 --- 0x3
   Internet Address      Physical Address      Type
   172.16.10.1           00-15-05-06-31-b0     dynamic
   172.16.20.1           00-15-05-06-31-b0     dynamic
```

Did you notice that the hardware (MAC) address that Host_A uses to get to Host_B is the Lab_A E0 interface?

Hardware addresses are *always* local, and they never pass a router's interface. Understanding this process is as important to internetworking as breathing air is to you, so carve this into your memory!

Testing Your IP Routing Understanding

I want to make sure you understand IP routing because it's really that important. So, I'm going to use this section to test your understanding of the IP routing process by having you look at a couple of figures and answer some very basic IP routing questions.

Figure 9.4 shows a LAN connected to RouterA, which is, in turn, connected via a WAN link to RouterB. RouterB has a LAN connected with an HTTP server attached. Take a look.

FIGURE 9.4   IP routing example 1

The critical information you need to glean from this figure is exactly how IP routing will occur in this example. Okay—we'll cheat a bit. I'll give you the answer, but then you should go back over the figure and see if you can answer example 2 without looking at my answers:

1. The destination address of a frame, from HostA, will be the MAC address of the F0/0 interface of the RouterA router.

2. The destination address of a packet will be the IP address of the network interface card (NIC) of the HTTP server.

3. The destination port number in the segment header will have a value of 80.

That example was a pretty simple one, and it was also very to the point. One thing to remember is that if multiple hosts are communicating to the server using HTTP, they must all use a different source port number. That is how the server keeps the data separated at the Transport layer.

Let's mix it up a little and add another internetworking device into the network and then see if you can find the answers. Figure 9.5 shows a network with only one router but two switches.

What you want to understand about the IP routing process here is what happens when HostA sends data to the HTTPS server:

1. The destination address of a frame from HostA will be the MAC address of the F0/0 interface of the RouterA router.

2. The destination address of a packet will be the IP address of the NIC of the HTTPS server.

3. The destination port number in the segment header will have a value of 443.

FIGURE 9.5   IP routing example 2

Notice that neither switch was used as either a default gateway or another destination. That's because switches have nothing to do with routing. I wonder how many of you chose the switch as the default gateway (destination) MAC address for HostA? If you did, don't feel bad—just take another look with that fact in mind. It's very important to remember that the destination MAC address will always be the router's interface—if your packets are destined for outside the LAN, as they were in these last two examples.

Static and Dynamic Routing

How does a router send packets to remote networks when the only way it can send them is by looking at the routing table to find out how to get to the remote networks? And what happens when a router receives a packet for a network that isn't listed in the routing table? It doesn't send a broadcast looking for the remote network—the router just discards the packet. Period.

There are several ways to configure the routing tables to include all the networks so that packets will be forwarded. Understand that what's best for one network isn't necessarily what's best for another. Knowing about and being able to recognize the different types of routing will really help you come up with the best solution for your specific environment and business requirements.

Looking at Figure 9.6, we can see that we can configure a router either with static or dynamic routing. If we choose static routing, then we have to go to each router and type in each network and the path that IP will use to send packets. However, static routing does not scale well in large networks, but dynamic routing does because network routes are automatically added to the routing table via the routing protocol.

Dynamic routing protocols break up into many different categories or types of protocols, as shown in Figure 9.7. The first split in the dynamic protocol branch is the division of interior gateway protocols (IGPs) and exterior gateway protocols (EGPs). We are going to talk about each protocol and category in the next few sections, but for now the difference between IGP and EGP is interior or exterior routing of an autonomous system (AS).

FIGURE 9.6   Routing options

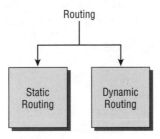

FIGURE 9.7   Dynamic routing options

An *autonomous system* is a collection of networks or subnets that are in the same administrative domain. This is another way of saying an administrative domain is within your company's network, and you control or administer all the subnets that are within it. You control and set the policy for what happens in the network or autonomous system. I hope you can now see that an IGP operates and routes within an AS and an EGP works outside or between more than one AS.

The most popular protocol for an EGP is Border Gateway Protocol (BGP), which is typically used by ISPs or really large corporations. As an administrator of a small to medium-size network, you'll probably never use BGP. (BGP will be discussed in Chapter 10.)

Now that we have that out of the way, let's talk about all the great things that dynamic routing protocols do for us. The thing that comes to mind first is the amount of time and energy we save configuring routers. We won't have to go to every single router and define for it, with a static route, what and where every destination network is. If that was the only way to configure routing, there would probably be a lot fewer of us interested in doing this for a living. Thankfully, we have routing protocols that do much of the work for us. We still have to know what the routing protocols are going to do and how they will do it, but the protocols will take care of most of the updating and sending information to each other.

That is the end of the EGP branch of the tree, but the IGP branch continues to split out as we go down further. Looking at Figure 9.8, with the IGP split, you can see that there are two primary categories: distance vector (DV) and link state (LS) routing protocols.

FIGURE 9.8 DV and LS routing protocols

No worries—I'm going to discuss all of these types of protocols in the next chapters. But in the distance vector category, for example, we have RIP and Interior Gateway Routing Protocol (IGRP). Under the link state category are the nonproprietary OSPF and Intermediate System-to-Intermediate System (IS-IS) that were designed to work in larger internetworks.

Now, in Figure 9.9, you can see from the diagram that there is a third category: the hybrid protocol category.

The only protocol under this category is EIGRP. It is Cisco proprietary and uses the features of both DV and LS.

Now that we have a handle on IP routing, let's move on to Chapter 10 and discuss the IGP routing protocols introduced in this chapter.

FIGURE 9.9 Hybrid routing

Summary

This chapter covered IP routing in detail. It's extremely important that you really understand the basics we covered in this chapter because everything that's done on a router typically will have some type of IP routing configured and running.

You learned in this chapter how IP routing uses frames to transport packets between routers and to the destination host. Understanding the process of how packets and frames traverse a network is critical to your fundamental understanding of IP routing.

After I covered the basics of IP routing, I went through some examples to test your understanding and to emphasize the importance of the IP routing fundamentals that you need. I finished the chapter with an introduction to static and dynamic routing and explained IGP and EGP as well as the difference between distance vector and link state routing protocols. In the next chapter, we'll continue with dynamic routing by discussing the various dynamic routing protocols.

Exam Essentials

Understand the basic IP routing process. You need to remember that the frame changes at each hop but that the packet is never changed or manipulated in any way until it reaches the destination device.

Understand that MAC addresses are always local. A MAC (hardware) address will only be used on a local LAN. It will never pass a router's interface.

Understand that a frame carries a packet to only two places. A frame uses MAC (hardware) addresses to send a packet on a LAN. The frame will take the packet to either a host on the LAN or a router's interface if the packet is destined for a remote network.

Remember the difference between static and dynamic routing. Static routing is where you, as the administrator, by hand, add every route into every routing table on every router on the network. This is as much work as it sounds like, which is why we use dynamic routing protocols that do the work for us. Of course, we'll discuss dynamic routing protocols more in the next chapter, but the main job of a routing protocol is to update routing tables.

Written Lab

Write the answers to the following questions:

1. True/False: RIPv2 is a hybrid routing protocol.

2. True/False: RIPv1 is a link state routing protocol.

3. True/False: EIGRP is a nonproprietary routing protocol.

4. An _____ _____ is a collection of networks or subnets that are in the same administrative domain.

5. You need a routing protocol that can be run in a very large network with routers from multiple vendors. What routing protocol would be your best choice?

6. Which type of routing are you performing if you have to go to each router and type in each network and the path that IP will use to send packets?

7. You are trying to reach a server on another subnet. What will be the destination hardware address of a frame sent from your host?

8. You are trying to reach a server on another subnet. What will be the destination IP address of a packet sent from your host?

9. A server has received a frame from your remote host. What will be the source hardware address of the frame?

10. A server has received a packet from your remote host. What will be the destination IP address of the packet?

You can find the answers in Appendix B.

Review Questions

You can find the answers in Appendix A.

1. Which is not a routing protocol?
   A. RIP
   B. RIPv2
   C. RIPv3
   D. EIGRP

2. Which of these best describes dynamic routing?
   A. All network addresses must be hand-typed into the routing table.
   B. Only a portion of the network address must be hand-typed into the routing table.
   C. Routing tables are updated automatically when changes occur in the network.
   D. A and B.

3. Which is true regarding dynamic routing?
   A. Static routes are best in large networks and thus better to use than dynamic routing protocols.
   B. Static routes are automatically added to the routing table but dynamic routes must be added by hand.
   C. You must use a DNS and WINS server when configuring dynamic routing.
   D. Dynamic routes are automatically added to the routing table.

4. Which of the following is true for MAC addresses?
   A. MAC addresses are never local on the LAN and always pass through a router.
   B. MAC addresses are always local on the LAN and never go through or past a router.
   C. MAC addresses will always be the IP address of Fa0/0 interface.
   D. None of the above.

5. What is it called when protocols update their forwarding tables after changes have occurred?
   A. Name resolution
   B. Routing
   C. Convergence
   D. ARP resolution

6. What command would be used to view the ARP cache on your host?

    A. `C:\ >show ip route`

    B. `C:\ >show ip arp`

    C. `C:\ >show protocols`

    D. `C:\ >arp -a`

7. What happens when a router receives a packet for a network that isn't listed in the routing table?

    A. It forwards the packet to the next available router.

    B. It holds the packet until the address is updated in the routing table.

    C. The router will use RIP to inform the host that it can't send the packet.

    D. None of the above.

8. Which of the following is not a distance vector protocol?

    A. RIPv1

    B. RIPv2

    C. OSPF

    D. IGRP

9. Which two of the following are link state protocols?

    A. RIPv1

    B. RIPv2

    C. OSPF

    D. IS-IS

    E. IGRP

10. Which of the following is a hybrid routing protocol?

    A. RIPv2

    B. EIGRP

    C. IS-IS

    D. IGRP

11. What does the acronym IGRP stand for?

    A. Interior Gateway Routing Protocol

    B. Inside Gateway Redundancy Protocol

    C. Interior Group Reliability Protocol

    D. Interior Gateway Redundancy Protocol

12. What EGP protocol is used on the Internet?

   A. GGP

   B. EGP

   C. BGP

   D. IGP

13. What are the two categories of IGP protocols?

   A. Link state

   B. Static

   C. Distance vector

   D. EGP

14. What two pieces of information does a router require to make a routing decision?

   A. Destination network (address)

   B. Destination MAC address

   C. Application layer protocol

   D. Neighbor router

15. Where does a frame have to carry a packet if it is destined for a remote network?

   A. Default gateway

   B. Neighbor host

   C. Switch

   D. Hub

16. Where along the IP routing process does a packet get changed?

   A. Router

   B. Host A

   C. Destination device

   D. Host B

17. When all routers in a network agree about the path from one point to another, the network is said to be what?

   A. Dynamic

   B. Static

   C. Secure

   D. Converged

18. What type of request must a client send if it does not know the destination MAC address?

    A. ARP broadcast

    B. Multicast

    C. ICMP redirect

    D. Reverse ARP

19. You need to perform maintenance on a router in your corporate office. It is important that the network does not go down. What can you do to accomplish your goal?

    A. Configure BGP on the router.

    B. Implement NAT on the router.

    C. Configure on the router a static route that temporarily reroutes traffic through another office.

    D. Implement convergence on the router.

20. When are you most likely to see a Request Timed Out message?

    A. When an unknown error has occurred

    B. When you have used the arp -a command incorrectly

    C. When a known error has occurred

    D. When you are using a hybrid routing protocol

Chapter

10

Routing Protocols

THE FOLLOWING COMPTIA NETWORK+ EXAM OBJECTIVES ARE COVERED IN THIS CHAPTER:

✓ **1.4 Explain the purpose and properties of routing and switching.**

- EIGRP

- OSPF

- RIP

- Routing metrics

    - Hop counts

    - MTU, bandwidth

    - Costs

    - Latency

- Next hop

- Routing tables

- Convergence (steady state)

✓ **2.1 Given a scenario, install and configure routers and switches.**

- Routing tables

Routing protocols are critical to a network's design. This chapter focuses on dynamic routing protocols. Dynamic routing protocols run only on routers that use them in order to discover networks and update their routing tables. Using dynamic routing is easier on you, the system administrator, than using the labor-intensive, manually achieved, static routing method, but it'll cost you in terms of router CPU processes and bandwidth on the network links.

The source of the increased bandwidth usage and CPU cycles is the operation of the dynamic routing protocol itself. A router running a dynamic routing protocol shares routing information with its neighboring routers, and it requires additional CPU cycles and additional bandwidth to accomplish that.

In this chapter, I'll give you all the basic information you need to know about routing protocols so you can choose the correct one for each network you work on or design.

To find up-to-the-minute updates for this chapter, please see www.lammle.com/forum or the book's web site at www.sybex.com/go/netplus2e.

Routing Protocol Basics

Because getting a solid visual can really help people learn, I'll get you started by combining the last few figures used in Chapter 9, "Introduction to IP Routing." This way, you can get the big picture and really understand how routing works. Figure 10.1 shows the complete routing tree that I broke up piece by piece at the end of Chapter 9.

As I touched on in Chapter 9, two types of routing protocols are used in internetworks: interior gateway protocols (IGPs) and exterior gateway protocols (EGPs). IGPs are used to exchange routing information with routers in the same *autonomous system (AS)*. An AS is a collection of networks under a common administrative domain, which simply means that all routers sharing the same routing table information are in the same AS. EGPs are used to communicate between multiple ASs. A nice example of an EGP would be Border Gateway Protocol (BGP), which really is beyond the scope of this book; I'll briefly describe it in this chapter anyway because there is a small objective about it on the exam. And no worries, we'll continue our discussion of IGPs too.

There are a few key points about routing protocols that I think it would be a good idea to talk over before getting deeper into the specifics of each one. First on the list is something known as an administrative distance.

FIGURE 10.1   Routing flow tree

Administrative Distances

The *administrative distance (AD)* is used to rate the trustworthiness of routing information received on one router from its neighboring router. An AD is an integer from 0 to 255, where 0 equals the most trusted route and 255 the least. A value of 255 essentially means, "No traffic is allowed to be passed via this route."

If a router receives two updates listing the same remote network, the first thing the router checks is the AD. If one of the advertised routes has a lower AD than the other, the route with the lower AD is the one that will get placed in the routing table.

If both advertised routes to the same network have the same AD, then routing protocol metrics like *hop count* or the amount of bandwidth on the lines will be used to find the best path to the remote network. And as it was with the AD, the advertised route with the lowest metric will be placed in the routing table. But if both advertised routes have the same AD as well as the same metrics, then the routing protocol will *load-balance* to the remote network. To perform load balancing, a router will send packets down each link to test for the best one.

Real World Scenario

Why Not Just Turn on All Routing Protocols?

Many customers have hired me because all their employees were complaining about the slow, intermittent network. Many times, I have found that the administrators did not truly understand routing protocols and just enabled them all on every router.

This may sound laughable, but it is true. When an administrator tried to disable a routing protocol, such as the Routing Information Protocol (RIP), they would receive a call that part of the network was not working. First, understand that because of default ADs, although every routing protocol was enabled, only the Enhanced Interior Gateway Routing Protocol (EIGRP) would show up in most of the routing tables. This meant that Open Shortest Path First (OSPF), Intermediate System-to-Intermediate System (IS-IS), and RIP would be running in the background but just using up bandwidth and CPU processes, slowing the routers almost to a crawl.

Disabling all the routing protocols except EGIRP (this would only work on an all-Cisco router network) improved the network at least 30 percent. In addition, finding the routers that were configured only for RIP and enabling EIGRP solved the calls from users complaining that the network was down when RIP was disabled on the network. Last, I replaced the core routers with better routers with more memory, enabling faster, more efficient routing and raising the network response time to a total of 50 percent.

Table 10.1 shows the default ADs that a router uses to decide which route to take to a remote network.

TABLE 10.1   Default administrative distances

Route source	Default AD
Connected interface	0
Static route	1
EIGRP	90
IGRP	100
OSPF	110
RIP	120

Route source	Default AD
External EIGRP	170
Unknown	255 (this route will never be used)

Understand that if a network is directly connected, the router will always use the interface connected to that network. Also good to know is that if you configure a static route, the router will believe that route to be the preferred one over any other routes it learns about dynamically. You can change the ADs of static routes, but by default, they have an AD of 1. That's only one place above zero, so you can see why a static route's default AD will always be considered the best by the router.

This means that if you have a static route, a RIP-advertised route, and an EIGRP-advertised route listing the same network, then by default, the router will always use the static route unless you change the AD of the static route.

Classes of Routing Protocols

The three classes of routing protocols introduced in Chapter 9, and shown in Figure 10.1, are as follows:

Distance vector   The *distance vector protocols* find the best path to a remote network by judging—you guessed it—distance. Each time a packet goes through a router, it equals something we call a *hop*. The route with the fewest hops to the network is determined to be the best route. The vector indicates the direction to the remote network. RIP, RIPv2, and Interior Gateway Routing Protocol (IGRP) are distance vector routing protocols. These protocols send the entire routing table to all directly connected neighbors.

Link State   Using *link state protocols*, also called *shortest path first protocols*, the routers each create three separate tables. One of these tables keeps track of directly attached neighbors, one determines the topology of the entire internetwork, and one is used as the actual routing table. Link state routers know more about the internetwork than any distance vector routing protocol. OSPF and IS-IS are IP routing protocols that are completely link state. Link state protocols send updates containing the state of their own links to all other routers on the network.

Hybrid   A *hybrid protocol* uses aspects of both distance vector and link state, and at this writing, there's only one—EIGRP. It happens to be a Cisco-proprietary protocol, meaning that it will run on only Cisco equipment. So if you have a multivendor environment, by default, this won't work for you.

I want you to understand that there's no one set way of configuring routing protocols for use in every situation. This is something you really have to do on a case-by-case basis. Even though this might seem a little intimidating, if you understand how each of the different routing protocols works, I promise you'll be capable of making good, solid decisions that will truly meet the individual needs of any business!

Distance Vector Routing Protocols

Okay, the distance vector routing algorithm passes complete routing table contents to neighboring routers, which then combine the received routing table entries with their own routing tables to complete the router's routing table. This is called *routing by rumor* because a router receiving an update from a neighbor router believes the information about remote networks without finding out for itself if it actually is correct.

It's possible to have a network that has multiple links to the same remote network, and if that's the case, the AD of each received update is checked first. As I said, if the AD is the same, the protocol will then have to use other metrics to determine the best path to use to get to that remote network.

Distance vector uses only hop count to determine the best path to a network. If a router finds more than one link with the same hop count to the same remote network, it will automatically perform what's known as *round-robin load balancing*.

It's important to understand what a distance vector routing protocol does when it starts up. In Figure 10.2, the four routers start off with only their directly connected networks in their routing table. After a distance vector routing protocol is started on each router, the routing tables are then updated with all route information gathered from neighbor routers.

FIGURE 10.2 The internetwork with distance vector routing

As you can see in Figure 10.2, each router has only the directly connected networks in each of its routing tables. Each router sends its complete routing table, which includes the network number, exit interface, and hop count to the network, out to each active interface.

Now, in Figure 10.3, the routing tables are complete because they include information about all the networks in the internetwork. They are considered *converged*. Usually, data transmission will cease while routers are converging—a good reason in favor of fast convergence time! In fact, one of the main problems with RIP is its slow convergence time.

FIGURE 10.3   Converged routing tables

As you can see in Figure 10.3, once all the routers have converged, the routing table in each router keeps information about three important things:

- The remote network number
- The interface that the router will use to send packets to reach that particular network
- The hop count, or metric, to the network

 Remember! Routing convergence time is the time required by protocols to update their forwarding tables after changes have occurred.

Let's start discussing dynamic routing protocols with one of the oldest routing protocols that is still in existence today.

Routing Information Protocol (RIP)

RIP is a true distance vector routing protocol. It sends the complete routing table out to all active interfaces every 30 seconds. RIP uses only one thing to determine the best way to a remote network—the hop count. And because it has a maximum allowable hop count of 15 by default, a hop count of 16 would be deemed unreachable. This means that although RIP works fairly well in small networks, it's pretty inefficient on large networks with slow WAN links or on networks populated with a large number of routers.

RIP version 1 uses only *classful routing*, which means that all devices in the network must use the same subnet mask. This is because RIP version 1 doesn't send updates with subnet mask information in tow. RIP version 2 provides something called *prefix routing* and does send subnet mask information with the route updates. Doing this is called *classless routing*.

RIP Version 2 (RIPv2)

Let's spend a couple of minutes discussing RIPv2 before we move into the advanced distance vector (also referred to as hybrid), Cisco-proprietary routing protocol EIGRP.

RIP version 2 is mostly the same as RIP version 1. Both RIPv1 and RIPv2 are distance vector protocols, which means that each router running RIP sends its complete routing tables out all active interfaces at periodic time intervals. Also, the timers and loop-avoidance schemes are the same in both RIP versions. Both RIPv1 and RIPv2 are configured with classful addressing (but RIPv2 is considered classless because subnet information is sent with each route update), and both have the same AD (120).

But there are some important differences that make RIPv2 more scalable than RIPv1. And I've got to add a word of advice here before we move on: I'm definitely not advocating using RIP of either version in your network. But because RIP is an open standard, you can use RIP with any brand of router. You can also use OSPF because OSPF is an open standard as well.

Table 10.2 discusses the differences between RIPv1 and RIPv2.

TABLE 10.2   RIPv1 vs. RIPv2

RIPv1	RIPv2
Distance vector	Distance vector
Maximum hop count of 15	Maximum hop count of 15
Classful	Classless
Broadcast based	Uses multicast 224.0.0.9
No support for VLSM	Supports VLSM networks
No authentication	Allows for MD5 authentication
No support for discontiguous networks	Supports discontiguous networks (covered in the next section)

RIPv2, unlike RIPv1, is a classless routing protocol (even though it is configured as classful, like RIPv1), which means that it sends subnet mask information along with the route updates. By sending the subnet mask information with the updates, RIPv2 can support Variable Length Subnet Masks (VLSMs), which are described in the next next section; in addition, network boundaries are summarized.

VLSM and Discontiguous Networks

VLSM allows classless routing, meaning that the routing protocol sends subnet-mask information with the route updates. The reason it's good to do this is to save address space. If we didn't use a routing protocol that supports VLSMs, then every router interface, every node (PC, printer, server, and so on), would have to use the same subnet mask.

As the name suggests, with VLSMs we can have different subnet masks for different router interfaces. Check out Figure 10.4 to see an example of why classful network designs are inefficient.

FIGURE 10.4   Typical classful network

Looking at this figure, you'll notice that we have two routers, each with two LANs and connected together with a WAN serial link. In a typical classful network design example (RIP or RIPv2 routing protocol), you could subnet a network like this:

192.168.10.0 = Network

255.255.255.240 (/28) = Mask

Our subnets would be (you know this part, right?) 0, 16, 32, 48, 64, 80, and so on. This allows us to assign 16 subnets to our internetwork. But how many hosts would be available on each network? Well, as you probably know by now, each subnet provides only 14 hosts. This means that with a /28 mask each LAN can support 14 valid hosts—one LAN requires 25 addresses, so a /28 mask doesn't provide enough addresses for the hosts in that LAN! Moreover the point-to-point WAN link also would consume 14 addresses when only two are required. It's too bad we can't just nick some valid hosts from that WAN link and give them to our LANs.

All hosts and router interfaces have the same subnet mask—again, this is called classful routing. And if we want this network to be more efficient, we definitely need to add different masks to each router interface.

But there's still another problem—the link between the two routers will never use more than two valid hosts! This wastes valuable IP address space, and it's the big reason I'm talking to you about VLSM networking.

Now let's take Figure 10.4 and use a classless design...which will become the new network shown in Figure 10.5. In the previous example, we wasted address space—one LAN didn't have enough addresses because every router interface and host used the same subnet mask. Not so good.

FIGURE 10.5 Classless network design

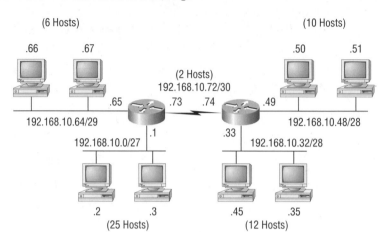

What would be good is to provide only the needed number of hosts on each router interface, meaning VLSMs.

So, if we use a /30 on our WAN links and a /27, /28, and /29 on our LANs, we'll get 2 hosts per WAN interface and 30, 14, and 6 hosts per LAN interface—nice! This makes a huge difference—not only can we get just the right number of hosts on each LAN, we still have room to add more WANs and LANs using this same network.

Remember, in order to implement a VLSM design on your network, you need to have a routing protocol that sends subnet-mask information with the route updates. This would be RIPv2, EIGRP, or OSPF. RIPv1 and IGRP will not work in classless networks and are considered classful routing protocols.

By using a VLSM design, you do not necessarily make your network run better, but you can save a lot of IP addresses.

Now, what's a discontiguous network? It's one that has two or more subnetworks of a classful network connected together by different classful networks. Figure 10.6 displays a typical discontiguous network.

The subnets 172.16.10.0 and 172.16.20.0 are connected together with a 10.3.1.0 network. By default, each router thinks it has the only 172.16.0.0 classful network.

It's important to understand that discontiguous networks just won't work with RIPv1 at all. They don't work by default on RIPv2 or EIGRP either, but discontiguous networks do work on OSPF networks by default because OSPF does not auto-summarize like RIPv2 and EIGRP.

EIGRP

EIGRP is a classless, Cisco proprietary, enhanced distance-vector protocol that possesses a real edge over another Cisco proprietary protocol, IGRP. That's basically why it's called Enhanced IGRP.

FIGURE 10.6 A discontiguous network

EIGRP uses the concept of an autonomous system to describe the set of contiguous routers that run the same routing protocol and share routing information. But unlike IGRP, EIGRP includes the subnet mask in its route updates. And as you now know, the advertisement of subnet information allows us to use VLSMs when designing our networks.

EIGRP is referred to as a *hybrid routing protocol* because it has characteristics of both distance vector and link state protocols. For example, EIGRP doesn't send link state packets as OSPF does; instead, it sends traditional distance vector updates containing information about networks plus the cost of reaching them from the perspective of the advertising router. But EIGRP has link state characteristics as well—it synchronizes routing tables between neighbors at startup and then sends specific updates only when topology changes occur. This makes EIGRP suitable for very large networks.

There are a number of powerful features that make EIGRP a real standout from RIP, RIPv2, and other protocols. The main ones are listed here:

- Support for IP and IPv6 (and some other useless routed protocols) via protocol-dependent modules
- Considered classless (same as RIPv2 and OSPF)
- Support for VLSM / Classless Inter-Domain Routing (CIDR)
- Support for summaries and discontiguous networks
- Efficient neighbor discovery
- Communication via Reliable Transport Protocol (RTP)
- Best path selection via Diffusing Update Algorithm (DUAL)

Another great feature of EIGRP is that it's simple to configure and turn on like a distance vector protocol, but it keeps track of more information than distance vector does. It creates and maintains additional tables instead of just one table as distance vector routing protocols do.

These tables are called the neighbor table, *topology table*, and routing table, as shown in Figure 10.7.

FIGURE 10.7 EIGRP tables

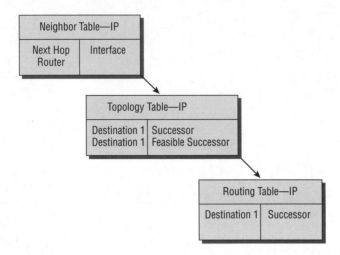

Neighbor table Each router keeps state information about adjacent neighbors. When a newly discovered neighbor is learned on a router interface, the address and interface of that neighbor are recorded, and the information is held in the neighbor table and stored in RAM. Sequence numbers are used to match acknowledgments with update packets. The last sequence number received from the neighbor is recorded so that out-of-order packets can be detected.

Topology table The topology table is populated by the neighbor table, and the best path to each remote network is found by running Diffusing Update Algorithm (DUAL). The topology table contains all destinations advertised by neighboring routers, holding each destination address and a list of neighbors that have advertised the destination. For each neighbor, the advertised metric, which comes only from the neighbor's routing table, is recorded. If the neighbor is advertising this destination, it must be using the route to forward packets.

Feasible successor (backup routes) A *feasible successor* is a path whose reported distance is less than the feasible (best) distance, and it is considered a backup route. EIGRP will keep up to six feasible successors in the topology table. Only the one with the best metric (the successor) is copied and placed in the routing table.

Successor (routes in a routing table) A successor route (think successful!) is the best route to a remote network. A successor route is used by EIGRP to forward traffic to a destination and is stored in the routing table. It is backed up by a feasible successor route that is stored in the topology table—if one is available.

By using the feasible distance and having feasible successors in the topology table as backup links, EIGRP allows the network to converge instantly and updates to any neighbor only consist of traffic sent from EIGRP. All of these things make for a very fast, scalable, fault-tolerant routing protocol.

Border Gateway Protocol (BGP)

In a way, you can think of Border Gateway Protocol (BGP) as the heavyweight of routing protocols. This is an external routing protocol (used between autonomous systems, unlike RIP or OSPF, which are internal routing protocols) that uses a sophisticated algorithm to determine the best route. In fact, it just happens to be the core routing protocol of the Internet. And it's not exactly breaking news that the Internet has become a vital resource in so many organizations, is it? No—but this growing dependence has resulted in redundant connections to many different ISPs.

This is where BGP comes in. The sheer onslaught of multiple connections would totally overwhelm other routing protocols like OSPF, which I am going to talk about in the next section. BGP is essentially an alternative to using default routes for controlling path selections. Default routes are configured on routers to control packets that have a destination IP address that is not found in the routing table. Please see *CCNA: Cisco Certified Network Associate Study Guide* (Sybex, 2011) for more information on static and default routing.

Because the Internet's growth rate shows no signs of slowing, ISPs use BGP for its ability to make classless routing and summarization possible. These capabilities help to keep routing tables smaller and more efficient at the ISP core.

BGP is used for IGPs to communicate ASs together in larger networks, if needed, as shown in Figure 10.8.

FIGURE 10.8   Border Gateway Protocol (BGP)

IGPs: RIP, IGRP, EIGRP, OSPF

EGPs: BGP

Autonomous System 1   Autonomous System 2

An autonomous system is a collection of networks under a common administrative domain. IGPs operate within an autonomous system, and EGPs connect different autonomous systems together.

So yes, very large private IP networks can make use of BGP. Let's say you wanted to join a number of large OSPF networks together. Because OSPF just couldn't scale up enough to handle such a huge load, you would go with BGP instead to connect the ASs together. Another situation in which BGP would come in really handy would be if you wanted to multi-home a network for better redundancy, either to a multiple access point of a single ISP or to multiple ISPs.

Internal routing protocols are employed to advertise all available networks, including the metric necessary to get to each of them. BGP is a personal favorite of mine because its routers exchange path vectors that give you detailed information on the BGP AS numbers, hop by hop (called an AS-Path), required to reach a specific destination network.

And BGP also tells you about any/all networks reachable at the end of the path. These factors are the biggest differences you need to remember about BGP. Unlike IGPs that simply tell you how to get to a specific network, BGP gives you the big picture on exactly what's involved in getting to an AS, including the networks located in that AS itself.

And there's more to that "BGP big picture"—this protocol carries information like the network prefixes found in the AS and includes the IP address needed to get to the next AS, (the next-hop attribute). It even gives you the history on how the networks at the end of the path were introduced into BGP in the first place, known as the origin code attribute.

All of these traits are what makes BGP so useful for constructing a graph of loop-free autonomous systems, for identifying routing policies, and for enabling us to create and enforce restrictions on routing behavior based upon the AS path—sweet!

Link State Routing Protocols

Link state protocols also fall into the classless category of routing protocols, and they work within packet-switched networks. OSPF and IS-IS are two examples of link state routing protocols.

Remember, for a protocol to be a classless routing protocol, the subnet-mask information must be carried with the routing update so that all neighbor routers know the cost of the network route that's being advertised. One of the biggest differences between link state and distance vector protocols is that link state protocols learn and maintain much more information about the internetwork than distance vector routing protocols do. Distance vector routing protocols maintain only a routing table with the destination routes in it. Link state routing protocols maintain two additional tables with more detailed information, with the first of these being the neighbor table. The neighbor table is maintained through the use of *hello packets* that are exchanged by all routers to determine which other routers are available to exchange routing data with. All routers that can share routing data are stored in the neighbor table.

The second table maintained is the topology table, which is built and sustained through the use of link state advertisements or packets (LSAs or LSPs, depending on the protocol). In the topology table, you'll find a listing for every destination network plus every neighbor (route) through which it can be reached. Essentially, it's a map of the entire internetwork.

Once all of that raw data is shared and each one of the routers has the data in its topology table, the routing protocol runs the Shortest Path First (SPF) algorithm to compare it all and determine the best paths to each of the destination networks.

Open Shortest Path First (OSPF)

Open Shortest Path First (OSPF) is an open-standard routing protocol that's been implemented by a wide variety of network vendors, including Cisco. OSPF works by using the *Dijkstra algorithm*. First, a shortest-path tree is constructed, and then the routing table is populated with the resulting best paths. OSPF converges quickly (although not as fast as EIGRP), and it supports multiple, equal-cost routes to the same destination. Like EIGRP, it supports both IP and IPv6 routed protocols, but OSPF must maintain a separate database and routing table for each, meaning you're basically running two routing protocols if you are using IP and IPv6 with OSPF.

OSPF provides the following features:

- Consists of areas and autonomous systems
- Minimizes routing update traffic
- Allows scalability
- Supports VLSM/CIDR
- Has unlimited hop count
- Allows multivendor deployment (open standard)

OSPF is the first link state routing protocol that most people are introduced to, so it's good to see how it compares to more traditional distance vector protocols like RIPv2 and RIPv1. Table 10.3 gives you a comparison of these three protocols.

TABLE 10.3   OSPF and RIP comparison

Characteristic	OSPF	RIPv2	RIPv1
Type of protocol	Link state	Distance vector	Distance vector
Classless support	Yes	Yes	No
VLSM support	Yes	Yes	No
Auto-summarization	No	Yes	Yes
Manual summarization	Yes	No	No
Discontiguous support	Yes	Yes	No
Route propagation	Multicast on change	Periodic multicast	Periodic broadcast
Path metric	Bandwidth	Hops	Hops
Hop-count limit	None	15	15
Convergence	Fast	Slow	Slow

TABLE 10.3   OSPF and RIP comparison   *(continued)*

Characteristic	OSPF	RIPv2	RIPv1
Peer authentication	Yes	Yes	No
Hierarchical network	Yes (using areas)	No (flat only)	No (flat only)
Updates	Event triggered	Route table updates	Route table updates
Route computation	Dijkstra	Bellman-Ford	Bellman-Ford

OSPF has many features beyond the few I've listed in Table 10.3, and all of them contribute to a fast, scalable, and robust protocol that can be actively deployed in thousands of production networks. One of the most noteworthy of its features is that after a network change (link up or down), OSPF converges (convergence is when all routers have been updated with the change) of any of the interior routing protocols we will discuss.

OSPF is supposed to be designed in a hierarchical fashion, which basically means that you can separate the larger internetwork into smaller internetworks called *areas*. This is definitely the best design for OSPF.

The following are reasons you really want to create OSPF in a hierarchical design:

- To decrease routing overhead
- To speed up convergence
- To confine network instability to single areas of the network

Pretty sweet benefits! But you have to earn them—OSPF is more elaborate and difficult to configure in this manner.

Figure 10.9 shows a typical OSPF simple design. Notice how each router connects to the backbone—called area 0, or the backbone area. OSPF must have an area 0, and all other areas should connect to this area. Routers that connect other areas to the backbone area within an AS are called area border routers (ABRs). Still, at least one interface of the ABR must be in area 0.

FIGURE 10.9   OSPF design example

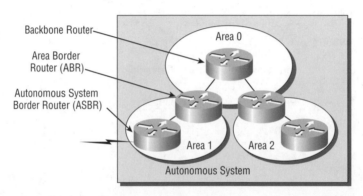

OSPF runs inside an autonomous system, but it can also connect multiple autonomous systems together. The router that connects these ASs is called an *autonomous system border router (ASBR)*. Typically, in today's networks, BGP is used to connect between ASs, not OSPF.

Ideally, you would create other areas of networks to help keep route updates to a minimum and to keep problems from propagating throughout the network. But that's beyond the scope of this chapter. Just make note of it for your future networking studies.

Intermediate System-to-Intermediate System (IS-IS)

IS-IS is an IGP, meaning that it's intended for use within an administrative domain or network, not for routing between ASs. That would be a job that an EGP (such as BGP, which we just covered) would handle instead.

IS-IS is a link state routing protocol, meaning it operates by reliably flooding topology information throughout a network of routers. Each router then independently builds a picture of the network's topology, just as OSPF does. Packets or datagrams are forwarded based on the best topological path through the network to the destination.

Figure 10.10 shows an IS-IS network and the terminology used with IS-IS.

FIGURE 10.10   IS-IS network terminology

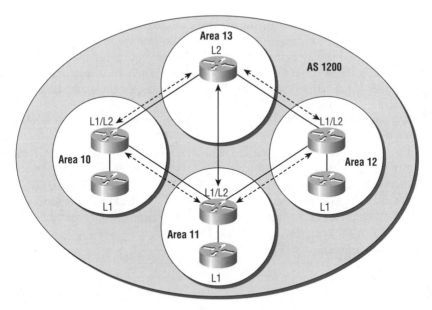

Here are the definitions for the terms used in the IS-IS network shown in Figure 10.10:

L1   Level 1 intermediate systems route within an area. When the destination is outside an area, they route toward a Level 2 system.

L2   Level 2 intermediate systems route between areas and toward other ASs.

The difference between IS-IS and OSPF is that IS-IS uses Connectionless Network Service (CLNS) to provide connectionless delivery of data packets between routers. OSPF uses IP to communicate between routers instead.

An advantage to having CLNS around is that it can easily send information about multiple routed protocols (IP and IPv6), and as I already mentioned, OSPF must maintain a completely different routing database for IP and IPv6, respectively, for it to be able to send updates for both protocols.

IS-IS supports the most important characteristics of OSPF and EIGRP because it supports VLSM and also because it converges quickly. Each of these three protocols has advantages and disadvantages, but it's these two shared features that make any of them scalable and appropriate for supporting the large-scale networks of today.

One last thing—even though it's not as common, IS-IS, although comparable to OSPF, is actually preferred by ISPs because of its ability to run IP and IPv6 without creating a separate database for each protocol as OSPF does. That single feature makes it more efficient in very large networks.

IPv6 Routing Protocols

Most of the routing protocols we've already discussed have been upgraded for use in IPv6 networks. Also, many of the functions and configurations that we've already learned will be used in almost the same way as they're used now. Knowing that broadcasts have been eliminated in IPv6, it follows that any protocols that use entirely broadcast traffic will go the way of the dodo—but unlike the dodo, it'll be good to say goodbye to these bandwidth-hogging, performance-annihilating little gremlins!

The routing protocols that we'll still use in version 6 got a new name and a facelift. Let's talk about a few of them now.

First on the list is RIPng (next generation). Those of you who have been in IT for a while know that RIP has worked very well for us on smaller networks, which happens to be the reason it didn't get whacked and will still be around in IPv6. And we still have EIGRPv6 because it already had protocol-dependent modules and all we had to do was add a new one to it for the IPv6 protocol. Rounding out our group of protocol survivors is OSPFv3— that's not a typo, it really is version 3. OSPF for IPv4 was actually version 2, so when it got its upgrade to IPv6, it became OSPFv3.

RIPng

To be honest, the primary features of RIPng are the same as they were with RIPv2. It is still a distance vector protocol, has a max hop count of 15, and still has the same loop avoidance mechanisms as well as using UDP port 521.

And it still uses multicast to send its updates too, but in IPv6, it uses FF02::9 for the transport address. This is actually kind of cool because in RIPv2, the multicast address was 224.0.0.9, so the address still has a 9 at the end in the new IPv6 multicast range. In fact, most routing protocols got to keep a little bit of their IPv4 identities like that.

But of course there are differences in the new version or it wouldn't be a new version, would it? We know that routers keep the next-hop addresses of their neighbor routers for every destination network in their routing table. The difference is that with RIPng, the router keeps track of this next-hop address using the link-local address, not a global address. So just remember that RIPng will pretty much work the same way as with IPv4.

EIGRPv6

As with RIPng, EIGRPv6 works much the same as its IPv4 predecessor does—most of the features that EIGRP provided before EIGRPv6 will still be available.

EIGRPv6 is still an advanced distance vector protocol that has some link state features. The neighbor-discovery process using hellos still happens, and it still provides reliable communication with a reliable transport protocol that gives us loop-free fast convergence using DUAL.

Hello packets and updates are sent using multicast transmission, and as with RIPng, EIGRPv6's multicast address stayed almost the same. In IPv4 it was 224.0.0.10; in IPv6, it's FF02::A (A = 10 in hexadecimal notation).

Last to check out in our group is what OSPF looks like in the IPv6 routing protocol.

OSPFv3

The new version of OSPF continues the trend of the routing protocols having many similarities with their IPv4 versions.

The foundation of OSPF remains the same—it is still a link state routing protocol that divides an entire internetwork or autonomous system into areas, making a hierarchy.

Adjacencies (neighbor routers running OSPF) and next-hop attributes now use link-local addresses, and OSPFv3 still uses multicast traffic to send its updates and acknowledgements, with the addresses FF02::5 for OSPF routers and FF02::6 for OSPF-designated routers, which provide topological updates (route information) to other routers. These new addresses are the replacements for 224.0.0.5 and 224.0.0.6, respectively, which were used in OSPFv2.

With all this routing information behind you, it's time to go through some review questions and then move on to learning all about switching in the next chapter.

Summary

This chapter covered the basic routing protocols that you may find on a network today. Probably the most common routing protocols you'll run into are RIP, OSPF, and EIGRP.

I covered RIP, RIPv2, the differences between the two RIP protocols, EIGRP, and BGP in the section on distance vector protocols.

I finished by discussing OSPF and IS-IS and when you would possibly see each one in a network.

Exam Essentials

Remember the differences between RIPv1 and RIPv2.   RIPv1 sends broadcasts every 30 seconds and has an AD of 120. RIPv2 sends multicasts (224.0.0.9) every 30 seconds and also has an AD of 120. RIPv2 sends subnet mask information with the route updates, which allows it to support classless networks and discontiguous networks. RIPv2 also supports authentication between routers, and RIPv1 does not.

Know EIGRP features.   EIGRP is a classless, advanced distance vector protocol that supports IP, IPX, AppleTalk, and now IPv6. EIGRP uses a unique algorithm called DUAL to maintain route information, and it uses RTP to communicate with other EIGRP routers reliably.

Compare OSPF and RIPv1.   OSPF is a link state protocol that supports VLSM and classless routing; RIPv1 is a distance vector protocol that does not support VLSM and supports only classful routing.

Written Lab

1. The default administrative distance of RIP is_____.

2. The default administrative distance of EIGRP is_____.

3. The default administrative distance of RIPv2 is_____.

4. What is the default administrative distance of a static route?

5. What is the version or name of RIP that is used with IPv6?

6. What is the version or name of OSPF that is used with IPv6?

7. What is the version or name of EIGRP that is used with IPv6?

8. When would you use BGP?

9. When could you use EIGRP?

10. Is BGP considered link state or distance vector?
    You can find the answers in Appendix B.

Review Questions

You can find the answers in Appendix A.

1. Which of the following protocols support VLSM, summarization, and discontiguous networking? (Choose three.)

   A. RIPv1

   B. IGRP

   C. EIGRP

   D. OSPF

   E. BGP

   F. RIPv2

2. Which of the following are considered distance vector routing protocols? (Choose two.)

   A. OSPF

   B. RIP

   C. RIPv2

   D. IS-IS

3. Which of the following are considered link state routing protocols? (Choose two.)

   A. OSPF

   B. RIP

   C. RIPv2

   D. IS-IS

4. Which of the following is considered a hybrid routing protocol?

   A. OSPF

   B. BGP

   C. RIPv2

   D. IS-IS

   E. EIGRP

5. Why would you want to use a dynamic routing protocol instead of using static routes?

   A. There is less overhead on the router.

   B. Dynamic routing is more secure.

   C. Dynamic routing scales to larger networks.

   D. The network runs faster.

6. Which of the following is a vendor-specific routing protocol?

    A. STP

    B. OSPF

    C. RIPv1

    D. EIGRP

    E. IS-IS

7. RIP has a long convergence time and users have been complaining of response time when a router goes down and RIP has to reconverge. Which can you implement to improve convergence time on the network?

    A. Replace RIP with static routes.

    B. Update RIP to RIPv2.

    C. Update RIP to OSPF using link state.

    D. Replace RIP with BGP as an exterior gateway protocol.

8. What is the administrative distance of OSPF?

    A. 90

    B. 100

    C. 110

    D. 120

9. Which of the following protocols will advertise routed IPv6 networks?

    A. RIP

    B. RIPng

    C. OSPFv2

    D. EIGRPv3

10. What is the difference between static and dynamic routing?

    A. You use static routing in large, scalable networks.

    B. Dynamic routing is used by a DNS server.

    C. Dynamic routes are added automatically.

    D. Static routes are added automatically.

11. Which routing protocol has a maximum hop count of 15?

    A. RIPv1

    B. IGRP

    C. EIGRP

    D. OSPF

12. Which of the following describes routing convergence time?

    A. The time it takes for your VPN to connect

    B. The time required by protocols to update their forwarding tables after changes have occurred

    C. The time required for IDS to detect an attack

    D. The time required by switches to update their link status and go into forwarding state

13. What routing protocol is typically used to connect ASs on the Internet?

    A. IGRP

    B. RIPv2

    C. BGP

    D. OSPF

14. RIPv2 sends out its routing table every 30 seconds just like RIPv1, but it does so more efficiently. What type of transmission does RIPv2 use to accomplish this task?

    A. Broadcasts

    B. Multicasts

    C. Telecast

    D. None of the above

15. Which routing protocols have an administrative distance of 120? (Choose two.)

    A. RIPv1

    B. RIPv2

    C. EIGRP

    D. OSPF

16. Which of the following routing protocols uses AS-Path as one of the methods to build the routing tables?

    A. OSPF

    B. IS-IS

    C. BGP

    D. RIP

    E. EIGRP

17. Which IPv6 routing protocol uses UDP port 521?

    A. RIPng

    B. EIGRPv6

    C. OSPFv3

    D. IS-IS

18. What EIGRP information is held in RAM and maintained through the usage of hello and update packets? (Select all that apply.)

    A. DUAL table

    B. Neighbor table

    C. Topology table

    D. Successor route

19. Which is true regarding EIGRP successor routes?

    A. Successor routes are saved in the neighbor table.

    B. Successor routes are stored in the DUAL table.

    C. Successor routes are used only if the primary route fails.

    D. A successor route is used by EIGRP to forward traffic to a destination.

20. Which of the following uses only hop count as a metric to find the best path to a remote network?

    A. RIP

    B. EIGRP

    C. OSPF

    D. BGP

Chapter

11

Switching and Virtual LANs

THE FOLLOWING COMPTIA NETWORK+ EXAM OBJECTIVES ARE COVERED IN THIS CHAPTER:

✓ **1.4 Explain the purpose and properties of routing and switching.**

- Spanning Tree Protocol

- VLAN (802.1q)

- Port mirroring

✓ **2.1 Given a scenario, install and configure routers and switches.**

- VLAN (trunking)

- Interface configurations

  - MAC filtering

- PoE

- VTP configuration

- QoS

- Port mirroring

Layer 2 switching is the process of using the hardware addresses of devices on a LAN to segment a network. Because you've got the basic ideas down, I'm now going to focus on the more in-depth particulars of Layer 2 switching and how it works.

You already know that switching breaks up large collision domains into smaller ones and that a collision domain is a network segment with two or more devices sharing the same bandwidth. A hub network is a typical example of this type of technology. But because each port on a switch is actually its own collision domain, you can create a much better Ethernet LAN network by simply replacing your hubs with switches!

Switches truly have changed the way networks are designed and implemented. If a pure switched design is properly implemented, it will result in a clean, cost-effective, and resilient internetwork. In this chapter, we'll survey and compare how networks were designed before and after switching technologies were introduced.

Routing protocols like RIP, which you learned about in Chapter 10, "Routing Protocols," employ processes for preventing network loops from occurring at the Network layer. This is all good, but if you have redundant physical links between your switches, routing protocols won't do a thing to stop loops from occurring at the Data Link layer. That's exactly the reason Spanning Tree Protocol was developed—to put a stop to loops taking place within a Layer 2 switched network. The essentials of this vital protocol, as well as how it works within a switched network, are some of the important subjects that we'll cover thoroughly in this chapter.

And to finish up this chapter, you're going to learn exactly what a VLAN is and how VLAN memberships are used in a switched network as well as how trunking is used to send information from all VLANs across a single link. Good stuff!

To find up-to-the-minute updates for this chapter, please see www.lammle.com/forum or the book's web site at www.sybex.com/go/netplus2e.

Networking Before Layer 2 Switching

Because knowing the history of something really helps with understanding why things are the way they are today, I'm going to go back in time a bit and talk about the condition of networks before switches and the part switches have played in the evolution of corporate

LANs by helping to segment them. For a visual of how a typical network design looked before LAN switching, check out the network in Figure 11.1.

FIGURE 11.1   A network before switching

The design in Figure 11.1 was called a *collapsed backbone* because all the hosts involved had to go to the corporate backbone in order to reach any network services—both LAN and mainframe.

Going back even further, before networks like the one shown in Figure 11.1 had physical segmentation devices such as routers and hubs, there was the mainframe network. This type of network comprised mainframe controllers made by IBM, Honeywell, Sperry, DEC, and so on and dumb terminals that connected into the controller(s). Any remote sites were connected to the mainframe with bridges.

And then the PC began its rise to stardom, and the mainframe was connected to an Ethernet or Token Ring LAN where the servers were installed. These servers were usually OS/2 or LAN Manager because this was "pre-NT." Each floor of a building ran either coax or twisted-pair wiring to the corporate backbone, which was then connected to a router. PCs ran an emulating software program that allowed them to connect to mainframe services, giving those PCs the ability to access services from the mainframe and LAN simultaneously. Eventually, the PC became robust enough to allow application developers to port applications more effectively than they ever could before—an advance that markedly reduced networking prices and enabled businesses to grow at a much faster rate.

Moving forward to when Novell rose to popularity in the late 1980s and early 1990s, OS/2 and LAN Manager servers were by and large replaced with NetWare servers. This made the Ethernet network even more popular because that's what Novell 3.*x* servers used to communicate with client-server software.

So basically, that's the story about how the network in Figure 11.1 came into being. But soon a big problem arose with this configuration. As the corporate backbone grew and grew, network services became slower and slower. A big reason for this was that at the same time this huge burst in growth was taking place, LAN services began to require even faster response times. This resulted in networks becoming totally saturated and over-whelmed. Everyone was dumping the dumb terminals used to access mainframe services in favor of those slick new PCs so they could more easily connect to the corporate backbone and network services.

And all this was taking place before the Internet's momentous popularity, so everyone in the company needed to access the corporate network's own, internal services. Without the Internet, all network services were internal, meaning that they were exclusive to the company network. As you can imagine, this situation created a screaming need to segment that single, humongous, and now plodding corporate network, which was connected together with slug-gish old routers.

How was this issue addressed? Well, at first, Cisco responded by simply creating faster routers (no doubt about that), but still more segmentation was needed, especially on the Ethernet LANs. The invention of Fast Ethernet was a very good and helpful thing, yet it too fell short of solving that network segmentation need. But devices called *bridges* did provide relief, and they were first used in the networking environment to break up colli-sion domains.

Sounds good, but only so much—bridges were sorely limited by the number of ports and other network services they could provide, and that's when Layer 2 switches came to the rescue. These switches saved the day by breaking up collision domains on each and every port—like a bridge—but switches could provide hundreds of ports! This early, switched LAN looked like the network pictured in Figure 11.2.

As you can see here, each hub was placed into a switch port—an innovation that vastly improved the network. So now, instead of each building being crammed into the same collision domain, each hub became its own separate collision domain. Yet still, as is too often the case, there was a catch—switch ports were still very new and therefore, super expensive. Because switches were so cost prohibitive, simply adding a switch into each floor of the building just wasn't going to happen—at least, not yet. But thanks to whomever you choose to thank for these things, the switch price tag has dropped dra-matically; now, having every one of your users plugged into a switch port is a really good solution, and cost-effective too!

So there it is—if you're going to create a network design and implement it, including switching services is a must.

A typical, contemporary, and complete switched network design/implementation would look something like Figure 11.3.

"But wait—there's still a router in there!" you say. Yes, it's not a mirage—there *is* a router in there. But its job has changed quite a bit. Instead of performing physical seg-mentation, it now creates and handles logical segmentation. Those logical segments are called VLANs, and no worries, I promise to explain them thoroughly throughout the rest of this chapter.

FIGURE 11.2   The first switched LAN

FIGURE 11.3   The typical switched network design

Switching Services

Bridges use software to create and manage a filter table, but switches use *application-specific integrated circuits (ASICs)* to accomplish this. Even so, it's still okay to think of a Layer 2 switch as a multiport bridge because their basic reason for being is the same: to break up collision domains.

Layer 2 switches and bridges are faster than routers because they don't take up time looking at the Network layer header information. Instead, they look at the frame's hardware addresses before deciding to forward, flood, or drop the frame.

Switches create private, dedicated collision domains and provide independent bandwidth on each port, unlike hubs. Figure 11.4 shows five hosts connected to a switch—all running 10Mbps half-duplex to the server. Unlike with a hub, each host has 10Mbps of dedicated communication to the server.

FIGURE 11.4   Switches create private domains.

Layer 2 switching provides the following benefits:

- Hardware-based bridging (ASIC)
- Wire speed
- Low latency
- Low cost

What makes Layer 2 switching so efficient is that no modification to the data packet takes place. The device reads only the frame encapsulating the packet, which makes the switching process considerably faster and less error prone than routing processes.

And if you use Layer 2 switching for both workgroup connectivity and network segmentation (breaking up collision domains), you can create a flatter network design with more network segments than you can with traditional routed networks.

Plus, Layer 2 switching increases bandwidth for each user because, again, each connection (interface) into the switch is its own collision domain. This feature makes it possible for you to connect multiple devices to each interface—very cool.

Coming up, we'll dive deeper into the Layer 2 switching technology.

Limitations of Layer 2 Switching

Because people usually toss Layer 2 switching into the same category as bridged networks, we also tend to think it has the same hang-ups and issues that bridged networks do. Keep in mind that bridges are good and helpful things if we design the network correctly, keeping our devices' features as well as their limitations in mind. To end up with a solid design that includes bridges, there are two really important things to consider:

- You absolutely have to break up the collision domains properly.
- A well-oiled, functional bridged network is one whose users spend 80 percent of their time on the local segment.

Okay—so bridged networks break up collision domains, but remember, that network is really still just one big broadcast domain. Neither Layer 2 switches nor bridges break up broadcast domains by default—something that not only limits your network's size and growth potential but can also reduce its overall performance!

Broadcasts and multicasts, along with the slow convergence time of spanning trees, can give you some major grief as your network grows. These are the big reasons Layer 2 switches and bridges just can't completely replace routers (Layer 3 devices) in the internetwork.

Bridging vs. LAN Switching

It's true—Layer 2 switches really are pretty much just bridges that give us a lot more ports. But the comparison doesn't end there. Here's a list of some significant differences and similarities between bridges and switches that you need to keep in mind:

- Bridges are software based, whereas switches are hardware based because they use ASIC chips to help make filtering decisions.
- A switch can be viewed as a multiport bridge.
- There can be only one spanning-tree instance per bridge, whereas switches can have many. (I'm going to tell you all about spanning trees in a bit.)
- Switches have a higher number of ports than most bridges.
- Both bridges and switches forward Layer 2 broadcasts.
- Bridges and switches learn MAC addresses by examining the source address of each frame received.
- Both bridges and switches make forwarding decisions based on Layer 2 addresses.

Three Switch Functions at Layer 2

There are three distinct functions of Layer 2 switching—you need to know these! They are as follows:

- Address learning
- Forward/filter decisions
- Loop avoidance

The next three sections cover these functions in detail.

Address Learning

Layer 2 switches and bridges are capable of *address learning*; that is, they remember the source hardware address of each frame received on an interface and enter this information into a MAC database known as a *forward/filter table*. But first things first—when a switch is initially powered on, the MAC forward/filter table is empty, as shown in Figure 11.5.

FIGURE 11.5   Empty forward/filter table on a switch

When a device transmits and an interface receives a frame, the switch places the frame's source address in the MAC forward/filter table, which allows it to remember the interface on which the sending device is located. The switch then has no choice but to flood the network with this frame out of every port except the source port because it has no idea where the destination device is actually located.

If a device answers this flooded frame and sends a frame back, then the switch will take the source address from that frame and place that MAC address in its database as well, thereby associating the newly discovered address with the interface that received the frame. Because the switch now has both of the relevant MAC addresses in its filtering table, the two devices can make a point-to-point connection. The switch doesn't need to flood the frame as it did the first time because now the frames can and will be forwarded only between the two devices recorded in the table. This is exactly the thing that makes Layer 2 switches better than hubs, because in a hub network, all frames are forwarded out all ports every time—no matter what. This is because hubs just aren't equipped to collect, store, and draw upon data in a table as a switch is. Figure 11.6 shows the processes involved in building a MAC database.

FIGURE 11.6 How switches learn hosts' locations

In this figure, you can see four hosts attached to a switch. When the switch is powered on, it has nothing in its MAC address forward/filter table (just as in Figure 11.6). But when the hosts start communicating, the switch places the source hardware address of each frame in the table along with the port that the frame's address corresponds to.

Let me give you a step-by-step example of how a forward/filter table becomes populated:

1. Host A sends a frame to Host B. Host A's MAC address is 0000.8c01.000A, and Host B's MAC address is 0000.8c01.000B.

2. The switch receives the frame on the E0/0 interface and places the source address in the MAC address table.

3. Because the destination address is not in the MAC database, the frame is forwarded out all interfaces—except the source port.

4. Host B receives the frame and responds to Host A. The switch receives this frame on interface E0/1 and places the source hardware address in the MAC database.

5. Host A and Host B can now make a point-to-point connection, and only the two devices will receive the frames. Hosts C and D will not see the frames, nor are their MAC addresses found in the database because they haven't yet sent a frame to the switch.

Oh, by the way, it's important to know that if Host A and Host B don't communicate to the switch again within a certain amount of time, the switch will flush their entries from the database to keep it as current as possible.

Forward/Filter Decisions

When a frame arrives at a switch interface, the destination hardware address is compared to the forward/filter MAC database and the switch makes a *forward/filter decision*. In other words, if the destination hardware address is known (listed in the database), the frame is only sent out the specified exit interface. The switch will not transmit the frame out any interface except the destination interface. Not transmitting the frame preserves bandwidth on the other network segments and is called *frame filtering*.

But as I mentioned earlier, if the destination hardware address isn't listed in the MAC database, then the frame is flooded out all active interfaces except the interface on which the frame was received. If a device answers the flooded frame, the MAC database is updated with the device's location—its particular interface.

So by default, if a host or server sends a broadcast on the LAN, the switch will flood the frame out all active ports except the source port. Remember, the switch creates smaller collision domains, but it's still one large broadcast domain by default.

In Figure 11.7, you can see Host A sending a data frame to Host D. What will the switch do when it receives the frame from Host A?

FIGURE 11.7 Forward/filter table

```
Switch#sh mac address-table
Vlan    Mac Address     Ports
----    -----------     -----
  1     0005.dccb.d74b  Fa0/4
  1     000a.f467.9e80  Fa0/5
  1     000a.f467.9e8b  Fa0/6
```

If you answered that because Host A's MAC address is not in the forward/filter table, the switch will add the source address and port to the MAC address table and then forward the frame to Host D, you're halfway there. If you also came back with, "If Host D's MAC address was not in the forward/filter table, the switch would have flooded the frame out all ports except for port Fa0/3," then congratulations—you nailed it!

Let's take a look at the output of a `show mac address-table` command as seen from a Cisco Catalyst switch (the MAC address table works pretty much exactly the same on all brands of switches):

```
Switch#sh mac address-table
Vlan    Mac Address       Type       Ports
----    --------------    -------    -----
  1     0005.dccb.d74b    DYNAMIC    Fa0/1
  1     000a.f467.9e80    DYNAMIC    Fa0/3
  1     000a.f467.9e8b    DYNAMIC    Fa0/4
  1     000a.f467.9e8c    DYNAMIC    Fa0/3
  1     0010.7b7f.c2b0    DYNAMIC    Fa0/3
  1     0030.80dc.460b    DYNAMIC    Fa0/3
  1     0030.9492.a5dd    DYNAMIC    Fa0/1
  1     00d0.58ad.05f4    DYNAMIC    Fa0/1
```

Okay—now suppose the preceding switch received a frame with the following MAC addresses:

Source MAC: **0005.dccb.d74b**

Destination MAC: **000a.f467.9e8c**

How will the switch handle this frame? The right answer is that the destination MAC address will be found in the MAC address table and the frame will be forwarded out Fa0/3 only. Remember that if the destination MAC address is not found in the forward/filter table, it will forward the frame out all ports of the switch looking for the destination device.

Now that you can see the MAC address table and how switches add hosts' addresses to the forward filter table, how do you stop switching loops if you have multiple links between switches? Let's talk about this possible problem in more detail.

Loop Avoidance

Redundant links between switches can be a wise thing to implement because they help prevent complete network failures in the event that one link stops working.

But it seems like there's always a downside—even though redundant links can be extremely helpful, they often cause more problems than they solve. This is because frames can be flooded down all redundant links simultaneously, creating network loops as well as other evils. Here are a few of the problems you can be faced with:

- If no loop avoidance schemes are put in place, the switches will flood broadcasts endlessly throughout the internetwork. This is sometimes referred to as a broadcast storm. (In real life, it's often referred to in less-polite ways that we're not permitted to repeat in print!) Figure 11.8 illustrates how a broadcast can be propagated throughout the network. Pay special attention to how a frame is continually being flooded through the internetwork's physical network media. One way to test the loop avoidance operations of your switch network is to plug one end of a cable into one port and the other end of the same cable into another port. If loop avoidance is not operational, this should cause a big broadcast storm!

FIGURE 11.8   Broadcast storm

- What you see here is that a device can receive multiple copies of the same frame because that frame can arrive from different segments at the same time. Figure 11.9 demonstrates how a whole bunch of frames can arrive from multiple segments simultaneously. The server in the figure sends a unicast frame to another device connected to Segment 1. Because it's a unicast frame, Switch A receives and forwards the frame, and Switch B provides the same service—it forwards the unicast. This is bad because it means that the destination device on Segment 1 receives that unicast frame twice, causing additional overhead on the network.

FIGURE 11.9   Multiple frame copies

- You may have thought of this one: The MAC address filter table could be totally confused about the device's location because the switch can receive the frame from more than one link. Worse, the bewildered switch could get so caught up in constantly updating the MAC filter table with source hardware address locations that it might fail to forward a frame! This is called *thrashing* the MAC table.

- One of the nastiest things that can happen is having multiple loops propagating throughout a network. This means you end up with loops occurring within other loops, and if a broadcast storm happened at the same time, the network wouldn't be able to perform frame switching at all—it's toast!

All of these problems spell disaster (or something like it) and are decidedly ugly situations that just must be avoided or at least fixed somehow. That's where the Spanning Tree Protocol comes into the game. It was developed to solve each and every one of the problems I just told you about.

Spanning Tree Protocol

Once upon a time, a company called Digital Equipment Corporation (DEC) was purchased and renamed Compaq. But before that happened, DEC created the original version of *Spanning Tree Protocol (STP)*. The IEEE later created its own version of STP called 802.1D. Yet again, it's not all clear skies—by default, most switches run the IEEE 802.1D version of STP, which isn't compatible with the DEC version. The good news is that there is a new industry standard called 802.1w, which is faster but not enabled by default on any switches.

To begin with, STP's main task is to stop network loops from occurring on your Layer 2 network (bridges or switches). It achieves this feat by vigilantly monitoring the network to find all links and making sure that no loops occur by shutting down any redundant ones. STP uses the *spanning-tree algorithm (STA)* to first create a topology database and then search out and destroy redundant links. With STP running, frames will be forwarded only on the premium, STP-picked links. Switches transmit Bridge Protocol Data Units (BPDUs) out all ports so that all links between switches can be found.

STP is a Layer 2 protocol that is used to maintain a loop-free switched network.

STP is necessary in networks such as the one shown in Figure 11.10.

FIGURE 11.10 A switched network with switching loops

In Figure 11.10, you see a switched network with a redundant topology (switching loops). Without some type of Layer 2 mechanism to stop network loops, we would fall victim to the problems I discussed previously: broadcast storms and multiple frame copies.

Understand that the network in Figure 11.10 would actually sort of work, albeit extremely slowly. This clearly demonstrates the danger of switching loops. And to make matters worse, it can be super hard to find this problem once it starts!

Spanning-Tree Port States

The ports on a bridge or switch running STP can transition through five different states:

Blocking   A blocked port won't forward frames; it just listens to BPDUs and will drop all other frames. The purpose of the blocking state is to prevent the use of looped paths. All ports are in blocking state by default when the switch is powered up.

Listening   The port listens to BPDUs to make sure no loops occur on the network before passing data frames. A port in listening state prepares to forward data frames without populating the MAC address table.

Learning   The switch port listens to BPDUs and learns all the paths in the switched network. A port in learning state populates the MAC address table but doesn't forward data frames. Forward delay means the time it takes to transition a port from listening to learning mode. It's set to 15 seconds by default.

Forwarding   The port sends and receives all data frames on the bridged port. If the port is still a designated or root port at the end of the learning state, it enters the forwarding state.

Disabled   A port in the disabled state (administratively) does not participate in the frame forwarding or STP. A port in the disabled state is virtually nonoperational.

Switches populate the MAC address table in learning and forwarding modes only.

Switch ports are usually in either the blocking or forwarding state. A forwarding port is one that has been determined to have the lowest (best) cost to the root bridge. But when and if the network experiences a topology change because of a failed link or when someone adds a new switch into the mix, you'll find the ports on a switch in the listening and learning states.

As I mentioned, blocking ports is a strategy for preventing network loops. Once a switch determines the best path to the root bridge, all other redundant ports will be in blocking mode. Blocked ports can still receive BPDUs—they just don't send out any frames.

If a switch determines that a blocked port should now be the designated, or root, port, say because of a topology change, it will respond by going into listening mode and check all the BPDUs it receives to ensure that it won't create a loop once the port goes back into forwarding mode.

STP Convergence

Convergence is what happens when all the ports on bridges and switches have transitioned to either forwarding or blocking modes. During this phase, no data will be forwarded until the convergence event is complete. Plus, before data can begin being forwarded again, all devices must be updated. Yes—you read that right: When STP is converging, all host data stops transmitting! So if you want to remain on speaking terms with your network's users (or remain employed for any length of time), you positively must make sure that your switched network is physically designed really well so that STP can converge quickly and painlessly.

Figure 11.11 demonstrates some really great ways to design and implement your switched network so that STP converges efficiently.

FIGURE 11.11   An optimal hierarchical switch design

Create core switch as STP root for fastest STP convergence.

Convergence is truly important because it ensures that all devices are in either the forwarding mode or the blocking mode. But as I've drilled into you, it does cost you some time. It usually takes 50 seconds to go from blocking to forwarding mode, and I don't recommend changing the default STP timers. (You can adjust those timers if you really have to.) By creating your physical switch design in a hierarchical manner, as shown in Figure 11.11, you can make your core switch the STP root. This makes everyone happy because it makes STP convergence happen fast.

Because the typical spanning-tree topology's time to convergence from blocking to forwarding on a switch port is 50 seconds, it can create time-out problems on your servers or hosts—like when you reboot them. To address this hitch, you can disable spanning tree on individual ports.

Rapid Spanning Tree Protocol 802.1w

How would you like to have a good STP configuration running on your switched network (regardless of the brand of switches) but instead of taking 50 seconds to converge, the switched network can converge in about 5 seconds, or maybe even less. How does that sound? Absolutely—yes, we want this! Well then, welcome to the world of *Rapid Spanning Tree Protocol (RSTP)*.

RSTP was not designed to be a "brand -new" protocol, but more of an evolution of the 802.1d standard, with faster convergence time when a topology change occurs. Backward compatibility was a must when 802.1w was created.

The 802.1w is defined in these different port states (compared to 802.1d):

- Disabled = Discarding
- Blocking = Discarding
- Listening = Discarding
- Learning = Learning
- Forwarding = Forwarding

Now that our switched networks have redundant links that are running properly with STP, let's break up broadcast domains in a Layer 2 switched network.

To verify the spanning-tree type running on your Cisco switch, use the following command:

```
S1#sh spanning-tree
VLAN0001
  Spanning tree enabled protocol ieee
  Root ID    Priority    32769
             Address     000d.29bd.4b80
             Cost        3012
             Port        56 (Port-channel1)
             Hello Time   2 sec  Max Age 20 sec  Forward Delay 15 sec

  Bridge ID  Priority    49153  (priority 49152 sys-id-ext 1)
             Address     001b.2b55.7500
             Hello Time   2 sec  Max Age 20 sec  Forward Delay 15 sec
             Aging Time 15
  Uplinkfast enabled
Interface        Role Sts Cost      Prio.Nbr Type
---------------- ---- --- --------- -------- ----------
Fa0/3            Desg FWD 3100      128.3    Edge Shr
Fa0/4            Desg FWD 3019      128.4    Edge P2p
Fa0/8            Desg FWD 3019      128.8    P2p
Po1              Root FWD 3012      128.56   P2p
```

Since the type output shows `Spanning tree enabled protocol ieee`, we know we are running the 802.1d protocol. If the output shows RSTP, then you know your switch is running the 802.1w protocol.

Virtual LANs

I know I keep telling you this, but I've got to be sure you never forget it, so here I go one last time: By default, switches break up collision domains and routers break up broadcast domains. Okay, I feel better! Now we can move on.

In contrast to the networks of yesterday, which were based on collapsed backbones, today's network design is characterized by a flatter architecture—thanks to switches. So now what? How do we break up broadcast domains in a pure switched internetwork? By creating a virtual local area network (VLAN), that's how!

A VLAN is a logical grouping of network users and resources connected to administratively defined ports on a switch. When you create VLANs, you gain the ability to create smaller broadcast domains within a Layer 2 switched internetwork by assigning the various ports on the switch to different subnetworks. A VLAN is treated like its own subnet or broadcast domain, meaning that frames broadcasted onto the network are only switched between the ports logically grouped within the same VLAN.

So, does this mean we no longer need routers? Maybe yes, maybe no—it really depends on what your specific goals and needs are. By default, hosts in a specific VLAN can't communicate with hosts that are members of another VLAN, so if you want inter-VLAN communication, the answer is yes, you still need a router.

VLAN Basics

Figure 11.12 shows how Layer 2 switched networks are typically designed—as flat networks. With this configuration, every broadcast packet transmitted is seen by every device on the network regardless of whether the device needs to receive that data or not.

FIGURE 11.12   Flat network structure

By default, routers allow broadcasts to occur only within the originating network, whereas switches forward broadcasts to all segments. Oh, and by the way, the reason it's called a *flat network* is because it's one *broadcast domain*, not because the actual design is physically flat. In Figure 11.12, you can see Host A sending out a broadcast and all ports on all switches forwarding it—all except the port that originally received it.

Now check out Figure 11.13. It pictures a switched network and shows Host A sending a frame with Host D as its destination. What's important to get out of this figure is that the frame is forwarded only out of the port where Host D is located. This is a huge improvement over the old hub networks, unless having one collision domain by default is what you really want. (I'm guessing not!)

FIGURE 11.13 The benefit of a switched network

Okay—you already know that the coolest benefit you gain by having a Layer 2 switched network is that it creates an individual collision domain segment for each device plugged into each port on the switch. But as is often the case, new advances bring new challenges with them. One of the biggest is that the greater the number of users and devices, the more broadcasts and packets each switch must handle.

And of course, the all-important issue of security and its demands also must be considered—while simultaneously becoming more complicated! VLANs present a security challenge because by default, within the typical Layer 2 switched internetwork, all users can see all devices. And you can't stop devices from broadcasting, plus you can't stop users from trying to respond to broadcasts. This means your security options are dismally limited to placing passwords on your servers and other devices.

To understand how a VLAN looks to a switch, it's helpful to begin by first looking at a traditional network. Figure 11.14 shows how a network used to be created using hubs to connect physical LANs to a router.

Here you can see that each network is attached with a hub port to the router (each segment also has its own logical network number, even though this isn't obvious looking at the figure). Each host attached to a particular physical network has to match that network's logical network number in order to be able to communicate on the internetwork. Notice that each department has its own LAN, so if we needed to add new users to, let's say, Sales, we would just plug them into the Sales LAN and they would automatically be part of the Sales collision and broadcast domain. This design actually did work well for many years.

FIGURE 11.14   Physical LANs connected to a router

But there was one major flaw: What happens if the hub for Sales is full and we need to add another user to the Sales LAN? Or, what do we do if there's no more physical space for a new employee where the Sales team is located? Hmmm, well, let's say there just happens to be plenty of room over in the Finance section of the building. That new Sales team member will just have to sit on the same side of the building as the Finance people, and we'll just plug the poor soul into the hub for Finance. Simple, right?

So wrong! Doing this obviously makes the new user part of the Finance LAN, which is very bad for many reasons. First and foremost, we now have a major security issue. Because the new Sales employee is a member of the Finance broadcast domain, the newbie can see all the same servers and access all network services that the Finance folks can. Second, for this user to access the Sales network services they need to get their job done, they would have to go through the router to log in to the Sales server—not exactly efficient.

Now, let's look at what a switch accomplishes for us. Figure 11.15 demonstrates how switches come to the rescue by removing the physical boundary to solve our problem. It also shows how six VLANs (numbered 2 through 7) are used to create a broadcast domain for each department. Each switch port is then administratively assigned a VLAN membership, depending on the host and which broadcast domain it's placed in.

So now, if we needed to add another user to the Sales VLAN (VLAN 7), we could just assign the port to VLAN 7 regardless of where the new Sales team member is physically located—nice! This illustrates one of the sweetest advantages to designing your network with VLANs over the old collapsed backbone design. Now, cleanly and simply, each host that needs to be in the Sales VLAN is merely assigned to VLAN 7.

Notice that I started assigning VLANs with VLAN number 2. The number is irrelevant, but you might be wondering what happened to VLAN 1. Well, that VLAN is an administrative VLAN, and even though it can be used for a workgroup, Cisco recommends that you use it for administrative purposes only. You can't delete or change the name of VLAN 1, and by default, all ports on a switch are members of VLAN 1 until you actually do change them.

FIGURE 11.15   Switches removing the physical boundary

Marketing	VLAN2	172.16.20.0/24
Shipping	VLAN3	172.16.30.0/24
Engineering	VLAN4	172.16.40.0/24
Finance	VLAN5	172.16.50.0/24
Management	VLAN6	172.16.60.0/24
Sales	VLAN7	172.16.70.0/24

Now, because each VLAN is considered a broadcast domain, it's got to also have its own subnet number (refer again to Figure 11.15). And if you're also using IPv6, then each VLAN must also be assigned its own IPv6 network number. So you don't get confused, just keep thinking of VLANs as separate subnets or networks.

Let's get back to that "because of switches, we don't need routers anymore" misconception. When looking at Figure 11.15, you can see that there are seven VLANs, or broadcast domains, counting VLAN 1. The hosts within each VLAN can communicate with each other but not with anything in a different VLAN because the hosts in any given VLAN "think" that they're actually in a collapsed backbone, illustrated in Figure 11.14.

So what handy little device do you think we need to enable the hosts in Figure 11.15 to communicate to a host or hosts on a different VLAN? You guessed it—a router! Those hosts absolutely need to go through a router, or some other Layer 3 device, just as they do when they're configured for internetwork communication (as shown in Figure 11.14). It works the same way it would if we were trying to connect different physical networks. Communication between VLANs must go through a Layer 3 device. So don't expect mass router extinction anytime soon!

Quality of Service

Before we dive in further into VLANs, I want to make sure that you have a fundamental understanding of QoS and why it is important. Chapter 20, "Management and Optimization," will provide more detail on QoS.

Quality of service (QoS) refers to the way the resources are controlled so that the quality of services is maintained. It's basically the ability to provide a different priority for one or more types of traffic over other levels; priority is applied to different applications, data flows, or users so that they can be guaranteed a certain performance level.

QoS methods focus on one of five problems that can affect data as it traverses network cable:

- Delay
- Dropped packets
- Error
- Jitter
- Out-of-order delivery

QoS can ensure that applications with a required bit rate receive the necessary bandwidth to work properly. Clearly, on networks with excess bandwidth, this is not a factor, but the more limited your bandwidth is, the more important a concept like this becomes.

To provide inter-VLAN communication (communication between VLANs), you need to use a router, or a Layer 3 switch.

VLAN Memberships

Most of the time, VLANs are created by a system administrator who proceeds to assign switch ports to each one. VLANs of this type are known as *static VLANs*. If you don't mind doing a little more work when you begin this process, assign all the host devices' hardware addresses into a database so your switches can be configured to assign VLANs dynamically anytime you plug a host into a switch. I hate saying things like "obviously," but obviously, this type of VLAN is known as a *dynamic VLAN*. I'll be covering both static and dynamic VLANs next.

Static VLANs

Creating static VLANs is the most common way to create a VLAN, and one of the reasons for that is because static VLANs are the most secure. This security stems from the fact that any switch port you've assigned a VLAN association to will always maintain it unless you change the port assignment manually.

Static VLAN configuration is pretty easy to set up and supervise, and it works really well in a networking environment where any user movement within the network needs to be controlled. It can be helpful to use network management software to configure the ports, but you don't have to use it if you don't want to.

In Figure 11.15, each switch port was configured manually with a VLAN membership based on which VLAN the host needed to be a member of—remember, the device's actual physical location doesn't matter one bit as long as the VLAN assignments are correctly configured. Which broadcast domain your hosts become members of is purely up to you. And again, remember that each host also has to have the correct IP address information. For instance, you must configure each host in VLAN 2 into the 172.16.20.0/24 network for them to become members of that VLAN. It's also a good idea to keep in mind that if you plug a host into a switch, you have to verify the VLAN membership of that port. If the membership is different than what's needed for that host, the host won't be able to gain access to the network services that it needs, such as a workgroup server.

 Static access ports are either manually assigned to a VLAN or assigned through a RADIUS server for use with IEEE 802.1x.

Dynamic VLANs

On the other hand, a dynamic VLAN determines a host's VLAN assignment automatically. Using intelligent management software, you can base VLAN assignments on hardware (MAC) addresses, protocols, or even applications that work to create dynamic VLANs.

For example, let's say MAC addresses have been entered into a centralized VLAN management application and you hook up a new host. If you attach it to an unassigned switch port, the VLAN management database can look up the hardware address and both assign and configure the switch port into the correct VLAN. Needless to say, this makes management and configuration much easier because if a user moves, the switch will simply assign them to the correct VLAN automatically. But here again, there's a catch—initially, you've got to do a lot more work setting up the database. It can be very worthwhile though!

And here's some more good news: You can use the VLAN Management Policy Server (VMPS) service to set up a database of MAC addresses to be used for the dynamic addressing of your VLANs. The VMPS database automatically maps MAC addresses to VLANs.

Identifying VLANs

Know that switch ports are Layer 2–only interfaces that are associated with a physical port. A switch port can belong to only one VLAN if it is an access port or all VLANs if it is a trunk port, as I'll explain in a minute. You can manually configure a port as an access or trunk port, or you can let the Dynamic Trunking Protocol (DTP) operate on a per-port basis to set the switch port mode. DTP does this by negotiating with the port on the other end of the link.

Switches are definitely pretty busy devices. As frames are switched throughout the network, they've got to be able to keep track of all the different port types plus understand what to do with them depending on the hardware address. And remember—frames are handled differently according to the type of link they're traversing.

There are two different types of links in a switched environment: access ports and trunk ports.

Access Ports

An access port belongs to and carries the traffic of only one VLAN. Anything arriving on an access port is simply assumed to belong to the VLAN assigned to the port. Any device attached to an *access link* is unaware of a VLAN membership—the device just assumes it's part of the same broadcast domain, but it doesn't have the big picture, so it doesn't understand the physical network topology at all.

Another good thing to know is that switches remove any VLAN information from the frame before it's forwarded out to an access-link device. Remember that access-link devices can't communicate with devices outside their VLAN unless the packet is routed. And you can only create a switch port to be either an access port or a trunk port—not both. So you've got to choose one or the other and know that if you make it an access port, that port can be assigned to one VLAN only.

Voice Access Ports

Not to confuse you, but all that I just said about the fact that an access port can be assigned to only one VLAN is really only sort of true. Nowadays, most switches will allow you to add a second VLAN to an access port on a switch port for your voice traffic; it's called the voice VLAN. The voice VLAN used to be called the auxiliary VLAN, which allowed it to be overlaid on top of the data VLAN, enabling both types of traffic through the same port. Even though this is technically considered to be a different type of link, it's still just an access port that can be configured for both data and voice VLANs. This allows you to connect both a phone and a PC device to one switch port but still have each device in a separate VLAN. If you are configuring voice VLANs, you'll want to configure Quality of Service (QoS) on the switch ports to provide a higher precedence to voice traffic over data traffic to improve sound quality.

 You plug a host into a switch port and users are unable to access any server resources. The two typical reasons this happens is because the port is configured in the wrong VLAN membership or STP has shut down the port because STP thought there was possibly a loop.

Trunk Ports

Believe it or not, the term *trunk port* was inspired by the telephone system trunks that carry multiple telephone conversations at a time. So it follows that trunk ports can similarly carry multiple VLANs at a time.

A *trunk link* is a 100Mbps or 1000Mbps point-to-point link between two switches, between a switch and router, or even between a switch and server, and it carries the traffic of multiple VLANs—from 1 to 4,094 at a time.

Trunking can be a real advantage because with it, you get to make a single port part of a whole bunch of different VLANs at the same time. This is a great feature because you can actually set ports up to have a server in two separate broadcast domains simultaneously so your users won't have to cross a Layer 3 device (router) to log in and access it. Another benefit of trunking comes into play when you're connecting switches. Information from multiple VLANs can be carried across trunk links, but by default, if the links between your switches aren't trunked, only information from the configured VLAN will be switched across that link.

Check out Figure 11.16. It shows how the different links are used in a switched network. All hosts connected to the switches can communicate to all ports in their VLAN because of the trunk link between them. Remember, if we used an access link between the switches, this would allow only one VLAN to communicate between switches. As you can see, these hosts are using access links to connect to the switch, so they're communicating in one VLAN only. That means that without a router, no host can communicate outside its own VLAN, but the hosts can send data over trunked links to hosts on another switch configured in their same VLAN.

FIGURE 11.16 Access and trunk links in a switched network

Trunk Link

Red VLAN   Blue VLAN   Green VLAN

VLANs can span across multiple switches by using trunk links, which carry traffic for multiple VLANs.

Red VLAN   Blue VLAN   Green VLAN

Okay—it's finally time to tell you about the VLAN identification methods.

VLAN Identification Methods

VLAN identification is what switches use to keep track of all those frames as they're traversing a switch fabric. All of our hosts connect together via a switch fabric in our switched network topology. It's how switches identify which frames belong to which VLANs, and there's more than one trunking method: ISL and 802.1q.

Inter-Switch Link (ISL)

Inter-Switch Link (ISL) is a way of explicitly tagging VLAN information onto an Ethernet frame. This tagging information allows VLANs to be multiplexed over a trunk link through an external encapsulation method (ISL), which allows the switch to identify the VLAN membership of a frame over the trunked link.

By running ISL, you can interconnect multiple switches and still maintain VLAN information as traffic travels between switches on trunk links. ISL functions at Layer 2 by encapsulating a data frame with a new header and cyclic redundancy check (CRC).

Of note is that this is proprietary to Cisco switches, and it's used for Fast Ethernet and Gigabit Ethernet links only. *ISL routing* is pretty versatile and can be used on a switch port, on router interfaces, and on server interface cards to trunk a server.

IEEE 802.1Q

Created by the IEEE as a standard method of frame tagging, IEEE 802.1Q actually inserts a field into the frame to identify the VLAN. If you're trunking between a Cisco switched link and a different brand of switch, you've got to use 802.1Q for the trunk to work.

And it works like this: You first designate each port that you want to be a trunk port with 802.1Q encapsulation. The ports must be assigned a specific management VLAN ID, which makes them part of the native VLAN in order for them to communicate. The ports that populate the same trunk create a group with this native VLAN, and each port gets tagged with an identification number reflecting that status, again the default being VLAN 1. The native VLAN allows the trunks to carry information that was received without any VLAN identification or frame tag.

VLAN Trunking Protocol

The basic goals of *VLAN Trunking Protocol (VTP)* are to manage all configured VLANs across a switched internetwork and to maintain consistency throughout that network. VTP allows you to add, delete, and rename VLANs—and information about those actions is then propagated to all other switches in the VTP domain.

Here's a list of some of the cool features VTP has to offer:

- Consistent VLAN configuration across all switches in the network
- Accurate tracking and monitoring of VLANs
- Dynamic reporting of added VLANs to all switches in the VTP domain
- Adding VLANs using Plug and Play

Very nice, but before you can get VTP to manage your VLANs across the network, you have to create a VTP server (really, you don't need to even do that since all switches default to VTP server mode, but just make sure you have a server). All servers that need to share VLAN information must use the same domain name, and a switch can be in only one domain at a time. So basically, this means that a switch can share VTP domain information with other switches only if they're configured into the same VTP domain. You can use a VTP domain if you have more than one switch connected in a network, but if you've got all your switches in only one VLAN, you just don't need to use VTP. Do keep in mind that VTP information is sent between switches only via a trunk port.

Switches advertise VTP management domain information as well as a configuration revision number and all known VLANs with any specific parameters. But there's also something called *VTP transparent mode*. In it, you can configure switches to forward VTP information through trunk ports but not to accept information updates or update their VTP databases.

If you've got sneaky users adding switches to your VTP domain behind your back, you can include passwords, but don't forget—every switch must be set up with the same password. And as you can imagine, this little snag can be a real hassle administratively!

Switches detect any added VLANs within a VTP advertisement and then prepare to send information on their trunk ports with the newly defined VLAN in tow. Updates are sent out as revision numbers that consist of summary advertisements. Anytime a switch sees a higher revision number, it knows the information it's getting is more current, so it will overwrite the existing VLAN database with the latest information.

You should know these requirements for VTP to communicate VLAN information between switches:

- The VTP management domain name of both switches must be set the same.
- One of the switches has to be configured as a VTP server.
- Set a VTP password if used.
- No router is necessary and a router is not a requirement.

Now that you've got that down, we're going to delve deeper into the world of VTP with VTP modes and VTP pruning.

VTP Modes of Operation

Figure 11.17 shows you all three different modes of operation within a VTP domain:

Server   This is the default mode for all Catalyst switches. You need at least one server in your VTP domain to propagate VLAN information throughout that domain. Also important: The switch must be in server mode for you to be able to create, add, and delete VLANs in a VTP domain. VLAN information has to be changed in server mode, and any change made to VLANs on a switch in server mode will be advertised to the entire VTP domain. In VTP server mode, VLAN configurations are saved in flash on the switch.

Client   In client mode, switches receive information from VTP servers, but they also receive and forward updates, so in this way, they behave like VTP servers. The difference is that they can't create, change, or delete VLANs. Plus, none of the ports on a client switch can be added to a new VLAN before the VTP server notifies the client switch of the new VLAN and the VLAN exists in the client's VLAN database. Also good to know is that VLAN information sent from a VTP server isn't stored in flash, which is important because it means that if the switch is reset or reloaded, the VLAN information will be deleted. Here's a hint: If you want a switch to become a server, first make it a client so it receives all the correct VLAN information, then change it to a server—so much easier!

Transparent   Switches in transparent mode don't participate in the VTP domain or share its VLAN database, but they'll still forward VTP advertisements through any configured trunk links. An admin on a transparent switch can create, modify, and delete VLANs because they keep their own database—one they keep secret from the other switches. Despite being kept in flash memory, the VLAN database in transparent mode is actually only locally significant. The whole purpose of transparent mode is to allow remote switches to receive the VLAN database from a VTP-server-configured switch through a switch that is not participating in the same VLAN assignments.

FIGURE 11.17   VTP modes

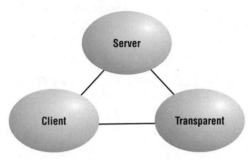

Server Configuration: Saved in NVRAM

Client Configuration: Not Saved in NVRAM   Transparent Configuration: Saved in NVRAM

Configuring VTP

All Cisco switches are configured to be VTP servers by default. To configure VTP, first you have to configure the domain name you want to use. And of course, once you configure the VTP information on a switch, you need to verify it.

When you create the VTP domain, you have a few options, including setting the domain name, password, operating mode, and pruning capabilities of the switch. Use the vtp global configuration mode command to set all this information. In the following example, I'll set the S1 switch to vtp server, the VTP domain to Lammle, and the VTP password to todd:

```
Switch#config t
Switch#(config)#vtp mode server
Device mode already VTP SERVER.
Switch(config)#vtp domain Lammle
Changing VTP domain name from null to Lammle
Switch(config)#vtp password todd
Setting device VLAN database password to todd
Switch(config)#do show vtp password
VTP Password: todd
Switch(config)#do show vtp status
```

```
VTP Version               : 2
Configuration Revision    : 0
Maximum VLANs supported locally : 255
Number of existing VLANs  : 8
VTP Operating Mode        : Server
VTP Domain Name           : Lammle
VTP Pruning Mode          : Disabled
VTP V2 Mode               : Disabled
VTP Traps Generation      : Disabled
MD5 digest                : 0x15 0x54 0x88 0xF2 0x50 0xD9 0x03 0x07
Configuration last modified by 192.168.24.6 at 3-14-93 15:47:32
Local updater ID is 192.168.24.6 on interface Vl1 (lowest numbered VLAN interface
found)
```

   Please make sure you remember that all switches are set to VTP server mode by default, and if you want to change and distribute any VLAN information on a switch, you absolutely must be in VTP server mode. After you configure the VTP information, you can verify it with the show vtp command as shown in the preceding output. The preceding switch output shows the VTP domain, the VTP password, and the switch's mode.

Two Additional Advanced Features of Switches

Switches really expand our flexibility when designing our networks. The features that we need to cover for the CompTIA Network+ objectives are as follows:

- Power over Ethernet (PoE)
- Port mirroring/spanning

Power over Ethernet

Power over Ethernet (PoE) technology describes a system for transmitting electrical power, along with data, to remote devices over standard twisted-pair cable in an Ethernet network. This technology is useful for powering IP telephones (Voice over IP, or VoIP), wireless LAN access points, network cameras, remote network switches, embedded computers, and other appliances—situations where it would be inconvenient, expensive, and possibly not even feasible to supply power separately. One reason for this is that the main wiring usually must be done by qualified and/or licensed electricians for legal and/or insurance mandates.

The IEEE has created a standard for PoE called 802.3af. This standard describes how a powered device is detected and also defines two methods of delivering Power over Ethernet to that particular powered device.

The IEEE has formed a new working group to develop the 802.3at standard, or PoE Plus, with the goal of boosting the amount of power that PoE can deliver.

This process happens one of two ways: either by receiving the power from an Ethernet port on a switch or other capable device or via a power injector. And you can't use both approaches to get the job done. This can lead to serious trouble, so be aware before connecting!

 Real World Scenario

PoE

It would be unusual for me not to design a network around PoE. Most of my consulting work is wireless networking, including large outdoor wireless networks. When I design the network, I order equipment based on the amount of power needed to run it, knowing I'll have only a few electrical outlets, or even no outlets if all my equipment is outside. This means that all my switches must run PoE to my access points and wireless bridges and must do this for long distances.

In order for me to accomplish this, I need to order the more expensive, large-scale, enterprise switches. If you have devices that need PoE but do not have long-distance connections, you can use lower-end switches, but you must verify that they provide the right amount of power. There was a customer who called me because their network access points were going up and down. The bottom line is that they had purchased less-expensive switches and the power was not enough to run the equipment. They ended up buying all new switches. So, before you buy a PoE switch, verify that the switch provides the right power for your environment.

Figure 11.18 shows an example of a switch that provides PoE to any PoE-capable device. As I just said, if you don't have a switch with PoE, then you can use a power injector. Figure 11.19 shows a picture of a typical power injector physically installed in a network.

Use caution when using an external power injector! Take the time to make sure the power injector provides the voltage level for which your device was manufactured.

FIGURE 11.18   Switched Ethernet ports can provide power to devices.

FIGURE 11.19   An external power injector used for PoE

Because most higher-end switches provide PoE, we don't need to worry about injectors, but if you are adding a wireless bridge into an existing network that has switches without PoE, you need to add a power injector. Figure 11.20 shows a power injector used for a wireless bridge.

Now, let's discuss how we would troubleshoot a network that has a switch in the LAN instead of a hub.

Port Mirroring/Spanning

Port mirroring, also called *Switch Port Analyzer (SPAN)*, allows you to sniff traffic on a network when using a switch. In Figure 11.21, you can see how a typical switch will read the forward/filter table and only send traffic out the destination port (this is the whole idea of using a switch, so this is good!).

FIGURE 11.20   Wireless-bridge power injector

FIGURE 11.21   Switches send frames out the destination port only.

All good, but a problem with this arises when you need to sniff traffic on the network. Figure 11.21 illustrates this issue and a solution to it. In Figure 11.21, you can see that the sniffer isn't seeing data coming from Host A to Host B. To solve this little snag, you can temporarily place a hub between Host A and Host B, as demonstrated in Figure 11.22.

This method will allow you to see the frames sent from Host A to Host B. The bad news, however, is that by doing this, you'll bring down the network temporarily.

FIGURE 11.22   Place a hub between two hosts to troubleshoot.

The port-mirroring option allows you to place a port in Span mode so that every frame from Host A is captured by both Host B and the sniffer, as shown in Figure 11.23. This would also be a helpful option to take advantage of if you were connecting an IDS or IPS to the switch as well.

FIGURE 11.23   Port mirroring

Do be careful when using port mirroring because it can cause a lot of overhead on the switch and possibly crash your network. So, it's a good idea to use this feature at strategic times and only for short periods if possible.

Summary

In this chapter, I talked about the differences between switches and bridges and how they both work at Layer 2 and create a MAC address forward/filter table in order to make decisions about whether to forward or flood a frame.

I also discussed problems that can occur if you have multiple links between bridges (switches) and how to solve these problems by using the Spanning Tree Protocol (STP).

This chapter also introduced you to the world of virtual LANs and described how switches can use them. We talked about how VLANs break up broadcast domains in a switched internetwork—a very important, necessary thing because Layer 2 switches only break up collision domains and, by default, all switches make up one large broadcast domain. I also described access links to you and went over how trunked VLANs work across a Fast Ethernet link.

Trunking is a crucial technology to understand well when you're dealing with a network populated by multiple switches that are running several VLANs.

Exam Essentials

Remember the three switch functions.   Address learning, forward/filter decisions, and loop avoidance are the functions of a switch.

Understand the main purpose of the Spanning Tree Protocol in a switched LAN.   The main purpose of STP is to prevent switching loops in a network with redundant switched paths.

Remember the states of STP. The purpose of the blocking state is to prevent the use of looped paths. A port in the listening state prepares to forward data frames without populating the MAC address table. A port in the learning state populates the MAC address table but doesn't forward data frames. A port in the forwarding state sends and receives all data frames on the bridged port. Last, a port in the disabled state is virtually nonoperational.

Remember to check a switch port's VLAN assignment when plugging in a new host. If you plug a new host into a switch, then you must verify the VLAN membership of that port. If the membership is different than what is needed for that host, the host will not be able to reach the needed network services, such as a workgroup server.

Understand what PoE provides. Power over Ethernet was created to provide power to devices that are connected to a switch port but that are not in a place that has a power outlet—for example, an access point in a ceiling.

Written Lab

Write the answers to the following questions:

1. VLANs break up _____ domains in a Layer 2 switched network.

2. Switches, by default, only break up _____ domains.

3. What does trunking provide?

4. You need to power a device such as an access point or IP phone. What protocol can provide power to these devices over an Ethernet cable?

5. You plug a host into a switch port and the host receives an IP address but the user can't get to the services it needs. What is probably the problem?

6. If a destination MAC address is not in the forward/filter table, what will the switch do with the frame?

7. What are the three switch functions at Layer 2?

8. If a frame is received on a switch port and the source MAC address is not in the forward/filter table, what will the switch do?

9. What is used at Layer 2 to prevent switching loops?

10. You need to implement a separate network for contractors and guests working at your office. Which technology should you implement?

    You can find the answers in Appendix B.

Review Questions

You can find the answers in Appendix A.

1. You want to improve network performance by increasing the bandwidth available to hosts and limiting the size of the broadcast domains. Which of the following options will achieve this goal?

   A. Managed hubs

   B. Bridges

   C. Switches

   D. Switches configured with VLANs

2. The types of ports that can be found on a switch are_____ and _____. (Choose two.)

   A. VLAN Trunk Protocol

   B. Access

   C. 802.1Q

   D. Trunk

3. Which switching technology reduces the size of a broadcast domain?

   A. ISL

   B. 802.1Q

   C. VLANs

   D. STP

4. Which of the following are IEEE versions of STP? (Choose two.)

   A. 802.1x

   B. VLANs

   C. 802.1d

   D. 802.11

   E. 802.1w

5. You connect a host to a switch port, but the new host cannot log into the server that is plugged into the same switch. What could the problem be? (Choose two.)

   A. The router is not configured for the new host.

   B. The STP configuration on the switch is not updated for the new host.

   C. The host has an invalid MAC address.

   D. The switch port the host is connected to is not configured to the correct VLAN membership.

   E. The STP shut down the port.

6. Which of the following are benefits of VLANs? (Choose three.)

   A. They increase the size of collision domains.

   B. They allow logical grouping of users by function.

   C. They can enhance network security.

   D. They increase the size of broadcast domains while decreasing the number of collision domains.

   E. They simplify switch administration.

   F. They increase the number of broadcast domains while decreasing the size of the broadcast domains.

7. Which of the following is a Layer 2 protocol used to maintain a loop-free network?

   A. VTP

   B. STP

   C. RIP

   D. CDP

8. What is the result of segmenting a network with a bridge (switch)? (Choose two.)

   A. It increases the number of collision domains.

   B. It decreases the number of collision domains.

   C. It increases the number of broadcast domains.

   D. It decreases the number of broadcast domains.

   E. It makes smaller collision domains.

   F. It makes larger collision domains.

9. You connect your host to a switch that is running network analyses software. However, you are not seeing any packets from the server. What do you need to implement on the switch to see all the packet information?

   A. VLANs

   B. STP

   C. Port mirroring

   D. Authentication

10. Which of the following features of a switch will allow two switches to pass VLAN network information?

   A. PoE

   B. VLANs

   C. Trunking

   D. STP

11. What are the distinct functions of Layer 2 switching that increase available bandwidth on the network? (Choose three.)

   A. Address learning

   B. Routing

   C. Forwarding and filtering

   D. Creating network loops

   E. Loop avoidance

   F. IP addressing

12. Which of the following statements is true?

   A. A switch creates a single collision domain and a single broadcast domain. A router creates a single collision domain.

   B. A switch creates separate collision domains but one broadcast domain. A router provides a separate broadcast domain.

   C. A switch creates a single collision domain and separate broadcast domains. A router provides a separate broadcast domain as well.

   D. A switch creates separate collision domains and separate broadcast domains. A router provides separate collision domains.

13. What does a switch do when a frame is received on an interface and the destination hardware address is unknown or not in the filter table?

   A. Forwards the switch to the first available link

   B. Drops the frame

   C. With the exception of the source port, floods the network with the frame looking for the device

   D. Sends back a message to the originating station asking for a name resolution

14. If a switch receives a frame, and the source MAC address is not in the MAC address table but the destination address is, what will the switch do with the frame?

   A. Discard it and send an error message back to the originating host

   B. Flood the network with the frame

   C. Add the source address and port to the MAC address table and forward the frame out the destination port

   D. Add the destination to the MAC address table and then forward the frame

15. When would you configure VTP on a switch?

    A. When you have hubs connected in your network

    B. When you have redundant links between switches

    C. When you have multiple hosts in multiple VLANs and you want to share all the data between hosts without a router

    D. When you have multiple switches with multiple VLANs and you want to share the VLAN database from one switch to all the others

16. When is STP said to be converged on the root bridge? (Choose two.)

    A. When all ports are in the forwarding state

    B. When all ports are in the blocking state

    C. When all ports are in the listening state

    D. When all ports are in the learning state

17. In which two states is the MAC address table populated with addresses?

    A. Blocked

    B. Listening

    C. Learning

    D. Forwarding

18. You have multiple departments all connected to switches, with cross-over cables connecting the switches together. However, response time on the network is still very slow even though you have upgraded from hubs to switches. What technology should you implement to improve response time on the networks?

    A. STP

    B. VLANs

    C. Convergence

    D. OSPF

19. If you are configuring voice VLANs, which of the following should you configure on the switch ports to provide a higher precedence to voice traffic over data traffic to improve sound quality?

    A. Access VLANs

    B. VTP

    C. QoS

    D. STP

20. What is a disadvantage of using port spanning?

    A. It breaks up broadcast domains on all ports.

    B. It can create overhead on the switch.

    C. It makes the switch one large collision domain.

    D. It makes the switch fast between only two ports instead of all ports.

Chapter

12

Wireless Networking

THE FOLLOWING COMPTIA NETWORK+ EXAM OBJECTIVES ARE COVERED IN THIS CHAPTER:

✓ **3.3 Compare and contrast different wireless standards.**

- 802.11 a/b/g/n standards
  - Distance
  - Speed
  - Latency
  - Frequency
  - Channels
  - MIMO
  - Channel bonding

✓ **3.7 Compare and contrast different LAN technologies.**

- Properties:
  - CSMA/CA

✓ **2.2 Given a scenario, install and configure a wireless network.**

- WAP placement
- Antenna types
- Interference
- Frequencies
- Channels
- Wireless standards
- SSID (enable/disable)
- Compatibility (802.11 a/b/g/n)

✓ **5.1 Given a scenario, implement appropriate wireless security measures.**

- Encryption protocols:
  - WEP
  - WPA
  - WPA2
  - WPA Enterprise
- MAC address filtering
- Device placement
- Signal strength

While you're sipping coffee at a café or hanging out in an airport until they finally fix the plane you're waiting to board, you are no longer limited to just reading actual papers and magazines. Now, you have the option to connect to the local wireless network and catch up on your emails, blog, do a little gaming—maybe even get some work done! It's come to the point that many of us wouldn't even think of checking into a hotel that doesn't offer this important little amenity. So clearly, those of us already in or wishing to enter the IT field better have our chops down regarding wireless network components and their associated installation factors, right? (Answer: a resounding YES!)

With that established, here's a great starting point...If you want to understand the basic wireless LANs (WLANs) most commonly used today, just think 10BaseT Ethernet with hubs. What this means is that our WLANs typically run half-duplex communication—everyone is sharing the same bandwidth, and only one user is communicating at a time. This isn't necessarily bad; it's just not good enough. Because most people rely upon wireless networks today, it's critical that they evolve faster than greased lightening to keep up with our rapidly escalating needs. The good news is that this is actually happening—and it even works securely!

The goal in this chapter is to introduce you to wireless networks and the technologies in use today. I'll also cover the various components used, the IEEE 802.11 standards, wireless installation, and of course, wireless security.

To find up-to-the-minute updates for this chapter, please see www.lammle.com/forum or the book's web site at www.sybex.com/go/netplus2e.

Introduction to Wireless Technology

Transmitting a signal using the typical 802.11 specifications works a lot like it does with a basic Ethernet hub: They're both two-way forms of communication, and they both use the same frequency to both transmit and receive, often referred to as *half-duplex* as mentioned in the chapter introduction. Wireless LANs (WLANs) use radio frequencies (RFs) that are radiated into the air from an antenna that creates radio waves. These waves can be absorbed, refracted, or reflected by walls, water, and metal surfaces, resulting in low signal strength. So because of this innate vulnerability to surrounding environmental factors, it's pretty apparent that wireless will never offer us the same robustness as a wired network can, but that still doesn't mean we're not going to run wireless. Believe me, we definitely will!

We can increase the transmitting power and we'd be able to gain a greater transmitting distance, but doing so can create some nasty distortion, so it has to be done carefully. By using higher frequencies, we can attain higher data rates, but this is, unfortunately, at the cost of decreased transmitting distances. And if we use lower frequencies, we get to transmit greater distances but at lower data rates. This should make it pretty clear to you that understanding all the various types of WLANs you can implement is imperative to creating the LAN solution that best meets the specific requirements of the unique situation you're dealing with.

Also important to note is the fact that the 802.11 specifications were developed so that there would be no licensing required in most countries—to ensure the user the freedom to install and operate without any licensing or operating fees. This means that any manufacturer can create wireless networking products and sell them at a local computer store or wherever. It also means that all our computers should be able to communicate wirelessly without configuring much, if anything at all.

Various agencies have been around for a very long time to help govern the use of wireless devices, frequencies, standards, and how the frequency spectrums are used. Table 12.1 shows the current agencies that help create, maintain, and even enforce wireless standards worldwide.

TABLE 12.1   Wireless agencies and standards

Agency	Purpose	Website
Institute of Electrical and Electronics Engineers (IEEE)	Creates and maintains operational standards	www.ieee.org
Federal Communications Commission (FCC)	Regulates the use of wireless devices in the US	www.fcc.gov
European Telecommunications Standards Institute (ETSi)	Chartered to produce common standards in Europe	www.etsi.org
Wi-Fi Alliance	Promotes and tests for WLAN interoperability	www.wi-fi.com
WLAN Association (WLANA)	Educates and raises consumer awareness regarding WLANs	www.wlana.org

Because WLANs transmit over radio frequencies, they're regulated by the same types of laws used to govern things like AM/FM radios. In the United States, it's the Federal Communications Commission (FCC) that regulates the use of wireless LAN devices, and the Institute of Electrical and Electronics Engineers (IEEE) takes it from there and creates standards based on what frequencies the FCC releases for public use.

The FCC has released three unlicensed bands for public use: 900MHz, 2.4GHz, and 5GHz. The 900MHz and 2.4GHz bands are referred to as the Industrial, Scientific, and Medical (ISM) bands, and the 5GHz band is known as the Unlicensed National Information Infrastructure (UNII) band. Figure 12.1 shows where the unlicensed bands sit within the RF spectrum.

FIGURE 12.1   Unlicensed frequencies

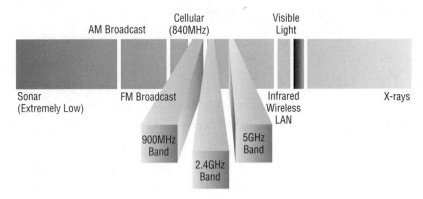

So it follows that if you opt to deploy wireless in a range outside of the three public bands shown in Figure 12.1, you need to get a specific license from the FCC to do so. Once the FCC opened the three frequency ranges for public use, many manufacturers were able to start offering myriad products that flooded the market, with 802.11b/g/n being the most widely used wireless network found today.

Figure 12.2 shows the WLAN history that is important to us. Although wireless transmissions date back many, many years, the type we really care about is wireless as related to WLANs starting in the 1990s. Use of the ISM band started in early 1990, and it's deployed today in multiple environments, including outdoor links, mesh networks, office buildings, healthcare facilities, warehouses, and homes.

FIGURE 12.2   Wireless LAN history

Speed	860Kbps	1 and 2Mbps	11Mbps	54Mbps
Network	Proprietary		Standards-Based	
Radio	900MHz	2.4GHz	5GHz	

IEEE 802.11 Drafting Begins	802.11 Ratified	802.11a, b Ratified	802.11g Ratified	802.11n Draft 2.0
1992	1997	1999	2003	2007

The Wi-Fi Alliance grants certification for interoperability among 802.11 products offered by various vendors. This certification provides a sort of comfort zone for the users purchasing the many types of products, although in my personal experience, it's just a whole lot easier if you buy all your access points from the same manufacturer.

In the current US WLAN market, there are several accepted operational standards and drafts created and maintained by the IEEE. We'll now take a look at these standards and then talk about how the most commonly used standards work.

The 802.11 Standards (WIRELESS)

Taking off from what you learned in Chapter 1, "Introduction to Networks," wireless networking has its own 802 standards group—remember, Ethernet's committee is 802.3. Wireless starts with 802.11, and there are various other up-and-coming standard groups as well, like 802.16 and 802.20. And even cellular networks are becoming huge players in our wireless experience. But for now, we're going to concentrate on the 802.11 standards committee and subcommittees.

IEEE 802.11 was the first, original standardized WLAN at 1Mbps and 2Mbps. It runs in the 2.4GHz radio frequency. It was ratified in 1997, although we didn't see many products pop up until around 1999 when 802.11b was introduced. All the committees listed in Table 12.2 made amendments to the original 802.11 standard except for 802.11f and 802.11t, which produced stand-alone documents.

TABLE 12.2 802.11 committees and subcommittees

Committee	Purpose
IEEE 802.11a	54Mbps, 5GHz standard
IEEE 802.11b	Enhancements to 802.11 to support 5.5Mbps and 11Mbps
IEEE 802.11c	Bridge operation procedures; included in the IEEE 802.1d standard
IEEE 802.11d	International roaming extensions
IEEE 802.11e	Quality of service
IEEE 802.11f	Inter-Access Point Protocol
IEEE 802.11g	54Mbps, 2.4GHz standard (backward compatible with 802.11b)
IEEE 802.11h	Dynamic Frequency Selection (DFS) and Transmit Power Control (TPC) at 5GHz
IEEE 802.11i	Enhanced security

Committee	Purpose
IEEE 802.11j	Extensions for Japan and US public safety
IEEE 802.11k	Radio resource measurement enhancements
IEEE 802.11m	Maintenance of the standard; odds and ends
IEEE 802.11n	Higher throughput improvements using multiple-input, multiple-output (MIMO) antennas
IEEE 802.11p	Wireless Access for the Vehicular Environment (WAVE)
IEEE 802.11r	Fast roaming
IEEE 802.11s	ESS Extended Service Set Mesh Networking
IEEE 802.11t	Wireless Performance Prediction (WPP)
IEEE 802.11u	Internetworking with non-802 networks (cellular, for example)
IEEE 802.11v	Wireless network management
IEEE 802.11w	Protected management frames
IEEE 802.11y	3650–3700 operation in the US

One type of wireless networking that doesn't get a whole lot of attention is infrared wireless. Infrared wireless uses the same basic transmission method as many television remote controls—that's right, infrared technology. Infrared is used primarily for short-distance, point-to-point communications, like those between a peripheral and a PC, with the most widely used for peripherals being the IrDA standard.

Okay, now let's discuss some important specifics of the most popular 802.11 WLANs.

2.4GHz (802.11b)

First on the menu is the 802.11b standard. It was the most widely deployed wireless standard, and it operates in the 2.4GHz unlicensed radio band that delivers a maximum data rate of 11Mbps. The 802.11b standard has been widely adopted by both vendors and customers who found that its 11Mbps data rate worked pretty well for most applications. But now that 802.11b has a big brother (802.11g), no one goes out and just buys an 802.11b card or access point anymore—why would you buy a 10Mbps Ethernet card when you can score a 10/100 Ethernet card for the same price?

An interesting thing about all 802.11 WLAN products is that they have the ability to data-rate-shift while moving. This allows the person operating at 11Mbps to shift to 5.5Mbps, then 2Mbps, and finally still communicate farthest from the access point at 1Mbps. And furthermore, this rate shifting happens without losing the connection and with no interaction from the user. Rate shifting also occurs on a transmission-by-transmission basis. This is important because it means that the access point can support multiple clients at varying speeds depending upon the location of each client.

The problem with all 802.11b communication lies in how the Data Link layer is dealt with. In order to solve problems in the RF spectrum, a type of Ethernet collision detection was created called *Carrier Sense Multiple Access with Collision Avoidance (CSMA/CA)*.

CSMA/CA also has an optional implementation called a *Request to Send, Clear to Send (RTS/CTS)* because of the way that hosts must communicate with the access point (AP). For every packet sent, an RTS/CTS and acknowledgment must be received, and because of this rather cumbersome process, it's kind of hard to believe it all actually works when you use this!

To get a clear picture of this, check out Figure 12.3.

FIGURE 12.3   802.11b CSMA/CA

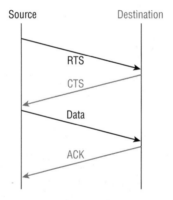

2.4GHz (802.11g)

The 802.11g standard was ratified in June 2003 and is backward compatible to 802.11b. The 802.11g standard delivers the same 54Mbps maximum data rate as you'll find in the 802.11a range but runs in the 2.4GHz range—the same as 802.11b.

Because 802.11b/g operates in the same 2.4GHz unlicensed band, migrating to 802.11g is an affordable choice for organizations with existing 802.11b wireless infrastructures. Just keep in mind that 802.11b products can't be "software upgraded" to 802.11g. This limitation is because 802.11g radios use a different chipset in order to deliver the higher data rate.

But still, much like Ethernet and Fast Ethernet, 802.11g products can be commingled with 802.11b products in the same network. Yet, for example, and completely unlike Ethernet, if you have four users running 802.11g cards and one user starts using an 802.11b card, everyone connected to the same access point is then forced to run the 802.11b CSMA/CA method—an ugly fact that really makes throughput suffer badly. So to optimize performance, it's recommended that you disable the 802.11b-only modes on all your access points.

To explain this further, 802.11b uses a *modulation technique* called *Direct Sequence Spread Spectrum (DSSS)* that's just not as robust as the *Orthogonal Frequency Division Multiplexing (OFDM)* modulation used by both 802.11g and 802.11a (modulation techniques will be discussed later in this chapter). 802.11g clients using OFDM enjoy much better performance at the same ranges as 802.11b clients do, but—and remember this—when 802.11g clients are operating at the 802.11b rates (11Mbps, 5.5Mbps, 2Mbps, and 1Mbps), they're actually using the same modulation 802.11b uses.

Figure 12.4 shows the 14 different channels (each 22Mhz wide) that the FCC released in the 2.4GHz range.

FIGURE 12.4   ISM 2.4GHz channels

In the United States, only 11 channels are configurable, with channels 1, 6, and 11 being non-overlapping. This allows you to have three access points in the same area without experiencing interference. You must be aware of the channels when installing APs in a large environment so you do not overlap channels. Make sure that each channel is not overlapping the same channel number! If you configure one AP with channel 1, then the next AP would be configured in channel 11, the channel farthest from that configured on the first AP.

5GHz (802.11a)

The IEEE ratified the 802.11a standard in 1999, but the first 802.11a products didn't begin appearing on the market until late 2001—and boy, were they pricey! The 802.11a standard delivers a maximum data rate of 54Mbps with 12 non-overlapping frequency channels. Figure 12.5 shows the UNII bands.

FIGURE 12.5 UNII 5GHz band has 12 non-overlapping channels (U.S.).

Operating in the 5GHz radio band, 802.11a is also immune to interference from devices that operate in the 2.4GHz band, like microwave ovens, cordless phones, and Bluetooth devices. 802.11a isn't backward compatible with 802.11b because they are different frequencies, so you don't get to just "upgrade" part of your network and expect everything to work together in perfect harmony. But no worries—there are plenty of dual-radio devices that will work in both types of networks. A definite plus for 802.11a is that it can work in the same physical environment without interference from 802.11b users.

Similar to the 802.11b radios, all 802.11a products also have the ability to data-rate-shift while moving. The 802.11a products allow the person operating at 54Mbps to shift to 48Mbps, 36Mbps, 24Mbps, 18Mbps, 12Mbps, and 9Mbps, and finally, still communicate farthest from the AP at 6Mbps.

There's also an extension to the 802.11a specification called 802.11h, which is described next.

5GHz (802.11h)

The FCC added 11 new channels in February 2004, and in 2008, we were finally able to begin using these channels based on manufacturers' releases of more 802.11a 5GHz products. This means that we gained access to up to 23 non-overlapping channels! And there are even two new features to the 5GHz radio that are part of the 802.11h specification: *Dynamic Frequency Selection (DFS)* and *Transmit Power Control (TPC)*.

Dynamic Frequency Selection (DFS) This cool feature continuously monitors a device's operating range for any radar signals that are allowed to operate in portions of the 5GHz band as well as 802.11a before transmitting. If DFS discovers any radar signals, it'll either abandon the occupied channel or mark it as unavailable to prevent interference from occurring on the WLAN.

Transmit Power Control (TPC) Even though it's been employed by the mobile phone industry for a long time, this technology has some handy new uses. You can set the client machine's adapter and the access point's transmit power to cover various size ranges—a feature that's useful for many reasons. For one, setting the access point's transmit power to 5mW reduces cell range, which works great if you've got a compact area with high-density usage.

Further advantages include the fact that TPC enables the client and the access point to communicate. This means the client machine can fine-tune its transmit power dynamically so it uses just enough energy to preserve its connection to the access point and conserve its battery power plus reduce interference on the neighboring WLAN cells—sweet!

2.4GHz/5GHz (802.11n)

802.11n builds on previous 802.11 standards by adding *multiple-input multiple-output (MIMO)*, which employs multiple transmitters and receiver antennas to increase data throughput. 802.11n can have up to eight antennas, but most of today's access points use four. These are sometimes referred to as *smart antennas*, and if you did have four of them, two would be used for transmitting simultaneously with the other two receiving simultaneously. This setup would allow for much higher data rates than 802.11a/b/g. In fact, the marketing people claim it will provide about 250Mbps, but personally, I'm not buying it. I just don't believe that's what our actual throughput levels can be, and even if what they're saying is true, exactly how would that help if all you've got is a 1Mbps or 2Mbps cable or DSL connection to the Internet?

This means that the products on the shelf today are proprietary, and they are called *pre-N* products. In some large, outdoor Cisco-proprietary networks that I'm currently working on, the Cisco "N" products work great. But keep in mind that all the devices are Cisco and the network won't tolerate other vendors' products working within it—at least, not today.

NOTE   802.11n allows for communication at both the 2.4Ghz and 5Ghz frequencies by using channel bonding.

Unlike 802.11a and 802.11 g, which are locked into using the 5.0 and 2.4 GHZ spectrums respectively, with 802.11n you can control which of the spectrums (or both) that you want to allow in your WLAN! Listed next are some additional components of 802.11n that give people reason to say 802.11n has greater reliability and predictability:

40Mhz channels   802.11g and 802.11a use 20Mhz channels, and tones on the sides of each channel are not used to protect the main carrier, which means that 11Mbps are unused or wasted. 802.11n aggregates two carriers to double the speed from 54Mbps to 108. Add the 11Mbps that we gain from not wasting the side tones and we have 119Mbps.

MAC Efficiency   802.11 protocols require acknowledgment of each and every frame. 802.11n can pass many packets before an acknowledgment is required, which saves you on overhead. This is called *block acknowledgment*.

So What Is Wi-Fi?

You may have seen products that are 802.11-compliant with a small sticker on them that says "Wi-Fi." You might be able to guess that this rather odd phrase stands for Wireless Fidelity, but you may not know what its implications are. Simply put, that sticker indicates that the product in question has passed certification testing for 802.11 interoperability by the Wi-Fi Alliance. This nonprofit group was formed to ensure that all 802.11a/b/g/n wireless devices would communicate seamlessly. So, Wi-Fi is a good thing.

Multiple-input, multiple-output (MIMO) Several frames are sent by several antennae over several paths and are then recombined by another set of antennae to optimize throughput and multipath resistance. This is called *spatial multiplexing*.

Comparing 802.11 Standards

Okay—before I move on to wireless installations, take at look at Figure 12.6, which lists, for each of the IEEE standards in use today, the year or ratification as well as the frequency, number of non-overlapping channels, physical layer transmission technique, and data rates.

FIGURE 12.6 Standards for spectrums and speeds

	802.11	802.11b	802.11a	802.11g		802.11n
Ratified	1997	1999	1999	2003		2010
Frequency Band	2.4GHz	2.4GHz	5GHz	2.4GHz		2.4GHz, 5GHz
No. of Channels	3	3	Up to 23	3		Varies
Transmission	IR, FHSS, DSSS	DSSS	OFDM	DSSS	OFDM	DSSS, CCK, OFDM
Data Rates (Mbps)	1, 2	1, 2, 5.5, 11	6, 9, 12, 18, 24, 36, 48, 54	1, 2, 5.5, 11	6, 9, 12, 18, 24, 36, 48, 54	100+

I mentioned earlier that 802.11b runs DSSS, whereas 802.11g and 802.11a both run the OFDM modulation technique. Let's take a closer look at these different modulation techniques used in today's networks.

Range Comparisons

Now let's take a look at Figure 12.7, which delimits the range comparisons of each 802.11 standard and shows these different ranges using an indoor open-office environment as a factor. (We'll be using default power settings.)

You can see that to get the full 54Mbps benefit of both 802.11a and 802.11g, you need to be between 50 feet and 100 feet (at the furthest) away and likely even less if there happen to be any obstructions between the client and the access point.

FIGURE 12.7 Range comparisons of 802.11 standards

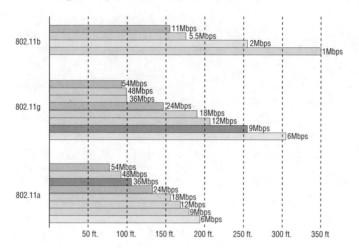

Wireless Network Components

Though it might not seem this way to you right now, wireless networks are less complex than their wired cousins because they require fewer components. To make a wireless network work properly, all you really need are two main devices: a wireless access point and a wireless NIC. This also makes it a lot easier to install a wireless network because, basically, you just need an understanding of these two components in order to do so.

Wireless Access Points

You'll find a central component—like a hub or switch—in the vast majority of wired networks that serves to connect hosts together and allow them to communicate with each other. It's the same idea with wireless networks. They also have a component that connects all wireless devices together, only that device is known as a *wireless access point (WAP)*, or just AP. Wireless access points have at least one antenna (sometimes two for better reception—a solution called *diversity*) and a port to connect them to a wired network. Figure 12.8 shows an example of a typical wireless access point.

You can even think of an AP as a bridge between the wireless clients and the wired network. In fact, an AP can be used as a wireless bridge (depending on the settings) to bridge two wired network segments together.

In addition to the stand-alone AP, there is another type of AP that includes a built-in router, which you can use to connect both wired and wireless clients to the Internet (the most popular home brand being Linksys). In summation, an AP can operate as a repeater, bridge (switch) or router, depending on its hardware and its implementation.

FIGURE 12.8   A wireless access point

These devices are usually known as (surprise) wireless routers. They're usually employed as Network Address Translation (NAT) servers by using the one ISP-provided global IP address to multiplex numerous local IP addresses that are generally doled out to inside clients by the wireless router from a pool within the 192.168.*x.x* range.

Wireless Network Interface Card

Every host that wants to connect to a wireless network needs a *wireless network interface card (NIC)* to do so. Basically, a wireless NIC does the same job as a traditional NIC, but instead of having a socket to plug some cable into, the wireless NIC has a radio antenna. In addition to the different types of wireless networking (I'll talk about those in a minute), wireless NICs (like other NICs) can also differ in the type of connection they use to connect to the host computer.

Figure 12.9 shows an example of a wireless NIC.

The wireless card shown in Figure 12.9 is used in a desktop PC. There are various options for laptops as well. Most new laptops have wireless cards built into the motherboard.

These days, it's pretty rare to use an external wireless client card because all laptops come with them built in, and desktops can be ordered with them too. But it's good to know that you can still buy the client card shown in Figure 12.9. Typically, you would use cards like the one shown in the figure for areas of poor reception because they can have a better range—depending on the antenna you use.

FIGURE 12.9   A wireless NIC

Wireless Antennas

Wireless antennas act as both transmitters and receivers. There are two broad classes of antennas on the market today: *Omni directional* (or point-to-multipoint) and *directional,* or *Yagi* (point-to-point). Yagi antennas usually provide greater range than Omni antennas of equivalent gain. Why? Because Yagis focus all their power in a single direction, whereas Omnis must disperse the same amount of power in all directions at the same time. A downside to using a directional antenna is that you've got to be much more precise when aligning communication points. This is why a Yagi is really only a good choice for point-to-point bridging of access points. It's also why most APs use Omnis, because often, clients and other APs could be located in any direction at any given moment.

To get a picture of this, think of the antenna on your car. Yes, it's a non-networking example, but it's still a good one because it clarifies the fact that your car's particular orientation doesn't affect the signal reception of whatever radio station you happen to be listening to. Well, most of the time, anyway. If you're in the boonies, you're out of range—something that also applies to the networking version of Omnis.

The television aerials that *some* of us are old enough to remember rotating into a specific direction for a certain channel are examples of Yagi antennas. (How many of you labeled your set-top antenna dial for the actual TV stations you could receive?) Believe it or not, they still look the same to this day!

Both Omnis and Yagis are rated according to their signal gain with respect to an actual or theoretical laboratory reference antenna. These ratings are relative indicators of the corresponding production antenna's range. Range is also affected by the bit rate of the underlying technology, with higher bit rates extending shorter distances. Remember, a Yagi will always have a longer range than an equivalently rated Omni, but as I said, the straight-line Yagi will be very limited in its coverage area.

Both antennas are also rated in units of decibel isotropic (dBi) or decibel dipole (dBd), based on the type of reference antenna (isotropic or dipole) of equivalent frequency that was initially used to rate the production antenna. A positive value for either unit of measure represents a gain in signal strength with respect to the reference antenna. *Webster's* defines *isotropic* as "exhibiting properties (as velocity of light transmission) with the same values when measured along axes in all directions." Isotropic antennas are not able to be produced in reality, but their properties can be engineered from antenna theory for reference purposes.

As a practical example, I'm going to use the Cisco Systems series of Aironet Access Point (indoor) and Bridge (outdoor) antennas. Table 12.3 describes the effect that gain ratings and attempted bit rates have on range limitations.

TABLE 12.3 Wireless antenna types and ranges

Model	Gain	Indoor range at 1Mbps	Indoor range at 11Mbps	Outdoor range at 2Mbps	Outdoor range at 11Mbps
AIR-ANT2410Y-R	10dBi	800ft	230ft	Not specified	Not specified
AIR-ANT1728	5.2dBi	497ft	142ft	Not specified	Not specified
AIR-ANT4941	2.2dBi	350ft	130ft	Not specified	Not specified
AIR-ANT2506	5.2dBi	Not specified	Not specified	5,000ft	1,580ft
AIR-ANT24120	12dBi	Not specified	Not specified	24,288ft	7,392ft

It's pretty much a given that antennas operating with frequencies below 1GHz are measured in dBd while those operating above 1GHz are measured in dBi. But because this rule doesn't always work definitively, sometimes we have to compare the strength of one antenna measured in dBd with another measured in numerically equivalent dBi in order to determine which one is stronger. This is exactly why it's important to know that a particular numerical magnitude of dBd is more powerful than the same numerical magnitude of dBi.

I know this sounds pretty complicated, but because the relationship between these two values is linear, it really makes the conversion a lot easier than you might think. Here's how it works: At the same operating frequency, a dipole antenna has about 2.2dB gain over a 0dBi theoretical isotropic antenna, which means you can easily convert from dBd to dBi by adding 2.2 to the dBd rating. Conversely, subtract 2.2 from the dBi rating and you get the equivalent dBd rating.

Armed with what you've learned about the difference between Omni and Yagi antennas and the difference between dBd and dBi gain ratings, you should be able to compare the relative range of transmission of one antenna with respect to another based on a combination of these characteristics. For example, the following four antenna ratings are given in relative order from greatest to least range:

- 7dBd Yagi (equivalent to a 9.2dBi Yagi)
- 7dBi Yagi (longer range than 7dBi Omni)
- 4.8dBd Omni (equivalent to a 7dBi Omni)
- 4.8dBi Omni (equivalent to a 2.6dBd Omni)

If you are having an intermittent problem with hosts connecting to the wireless network and varying signal strengthens at different locations, check your antennae location in the office or warehouse to make sure you are getting the best coverage possible.

So now that you understand the basic components involved in a wireless network, it's time to use what you learned about the standards we use in our everyday home and corporate wireless networks and the different ways that they're actually installed.

Installing a Wireless Network

Let's say you just bought a wireless NIC and a WAP for your laptop. What's next? Well, that all depends on the type of installation you want to create with your new toys. There are two main installation types, ad hoc and infrastructure mode, and each 802.11 wireless network device can be installed in one of these two modes, also called *service sets*.

Ad Hoc Mode: Independent Basic Service Set

This is the easiest way to install wireless 802.11 devices. In this mode, the wireless NICs (or other devices) can communicate directly without the need for an AP. A good example of this is two laptops with wireless NICs installed. If both cards were set up to operate in ad hoc mode, they could connect and transfer files as long as the other network settings, like protocols, were set up to enable this as well. We'll also call this an *independent basic service set (IBSS)*, which is created as soon as two wireless devices communicate.

Okay—to set up a basic ad hoc wireless network, all you need are two wireless NICs and two computers. First (assuming they aren't built in), install the cards into the computers according to the manufacturer's directions. During the software installation, you'll be asked if you want to set up the NIC in ad hoc mode or infrastructure mode. For an ad hoc network, you would obviously go with the ad hoc mode setting. Once that's done, all you've got to do is bring the computers within range (90m–100m) of each other, and voilà—they'll "see" each other and be able to connect to each other.

Figure 12.10 shows an example of an ad hoc wireless network. (Note the absence of an access point.)

FIGURE 12.10   A wireless network in ad hoc mode

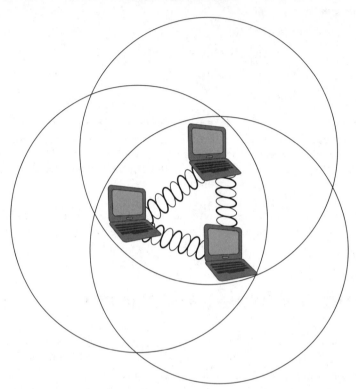

An ad hoc network would not scale well and really is not recommended due to collision and organization issues. With the low costs of APs, this type of network is just not needed today.

Infrastructure Mode: Basic Service Set

The most common use of wireless networking equipment is to give us the wireless equivalent of a wired network. To do this, all 802.11 wireless equipment has the ability to operate in what's known as infrastructure mode, also referred to as a *basic service set (BSS)*, which is provided by an AP. The term *basic service area (BSA)* is also used at times to define the area managed by the AP, but *BSS* is the most common term used to define the cell area.

In infrastructure mode, NICs communicate only with an access point instead of directly with each other as they do when they're in ad hoc mode. All communication between hosts, plus with any wired portion of the network, must go through the access point. A really important fact to remember is that in this mode, wireless clients actually appear to the rest of the network as though they were standard, wired hosts.

Figure 12.11 shows a typical infrastructure mode wireless network. Pay special attention to the access point and the fact that it's also connected to the wired network. This connection from the access point to the wired network is called the *distribution system (DS)*.

FIGURE 12.11   A wireless network in infrastructure mode

*DS = Distribution System

When you configure a client to operate in wireless infrastructure mode, you need to understand a couple of basic wireless concepts—namely, SSID and security. The *Security Set Identifier (SSID)* refers to the unique 32-character identifier that represents a particular wireless network and defines the basic service set. (By the way, a lot of people use the terms *SSID* and *BSS* interchangeably, so don't let that confuse you!) All devices involved in a particular wireless network must be configured with the same SSID.

Good to know is that if you set all your access points to the same SSID, mobile wireless clients can roam around freely within the same network. Doing this creates an *extended service set (ESS)* and provides more coverage than a single access point. Figure 12.12 shows two APs configured with the same SSID in an office, thereby creating the ESS network.

For users to be able to roam throughout the wireless network—from AP to AP without losing their connection to the network—all APs must overlap by 10 percent of their signal or more. To make this happen, be sure the channels on each AP are set differently. And remember, in an 802.11b/g network, there are only three non-overlapping channels (1, 6, 11), so careful design is super important here!

FIGURE 12.12   Extended service set (ESS)

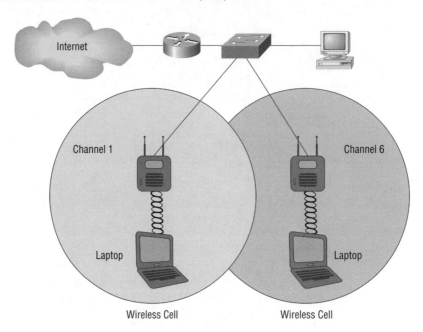

Signal Degradation

Something that's really important to consider when installing a wireless network is signal degradation. Because the 802.11 wireless protocols use radio frequencies, the signal strength varies according to many factors. The weaker the signal, the less reliable the network connection will be, and so the less usable as well. (Think dropped calls!) There are several key factors that affect signal strength:

Distance   This one is definitely on the obvious side—the farther away from the WAP you get, the weaker the signal you get. Most APs have a very limited maximum range that equals less than 100m for most systems. You can extend this range to some degree using amplifiers or repeaters or even by using different antennas.

Walls and other barriers   Also easy to imagine is the fact that the more walls and other office barriers a wireless signal has to pass through, the more attenuated (reduced) the signal becomes. Also, the thicker the wall, the more it interrupts the signal. So in an indoor office area with lots of walls, the range of your wireless network could be as low as 25 feet!

Protocols used   This one isn't so apparent, but it certainly is a factor that affects, and can even determine, the range of a wireless LAN. The various wireless 802.11 protocols have different maximum ranges. As discussed earlier, and illustrated in Figure 12.7, the maximum effective range varies quite a bit depending on the 802.11 protocol used. For example, if you have a client running the 802.11g protocol but it connects to an AP running only the 802.11b protocol, you'll only get a throughput of 11Mbps to the client.

Interference The final factor that affects wireless performance is outside interference. Because 802.11 wireless protocols operate in the 900MHz, 2.4GHz, and 5GHz ranges, interference can come from many sources. These include other wireless devices like Bluetooth, cordless telephones, cell phones, other wireless LANs, and any other device that transmits a radio frequency (RF) near the frequency bands that 802.11 protocols use. Even microwave ovens—a huge adversary of 802.11b and 802.11g—can be serious culprits!

Installing and Configuring Hardware

As I said earlier, installing 802.11 equipment is actually fairly simple—remember that there are really only two main types of components in 802.11 networks: APs and NICs. Wireless NIC installation is just like installing any other network card, but nowadays most, if not all, laptops have wireless cards preinstalled, and that's as easy as it gets! And just as with connecting an Ethernet card to a LAN switch, you need the wireless network card to connect to an access point.

The AP installation can be fairly simple as well. Take it out of the box, connect the antenna(e) if necessary, connect the power, and then place the AP where it can reach the highest number of clients. This last part is probably the trickiest, but it really just involves a little common sense and maybe a bit of trial and error. Knowing that walls obstruct the signal means that putting the AP out in the open—even indoors—works better. And you also know it should be placed away from sources of RF interference, so putting it next to the microwave or phone system is probably a really bad idea too. Near a metal filing cabinet is also not so good. So just experiment and move your AP around to find the spot that gives you the best signal strength for all the clients that need to use it.

Okay—now that you have the hardware installed, it's time to configure it, right? Let's get started.

No worries—configuring your AP and NIC to work together isn't as tricky as it sounds. Most wireless equipment is designed to work almost without configuration, so by default, you can pretty much turn things on and start working. The only things you need to configure are customization settings (name, network address, and so on) and security settings, and even these aren't required. But because I do highly recommend configuring them, I'll take you through that now.

NIC Configuration

Windows XP, Vista, and Windows 7 (as well as Windows Server 2003/2008) include software to automatically configure a wireless connection, and they do so automatically when you install a wireless NIC. Let's discuss both XP and Windows 7 installations. First, here are the steps for XP:

1. The first time you reboot an XP machine after the installation of the NIC, you'll see a screen like the one shown in Figure 12.13. (This is the Windows wireless configuration screen.) From this screen, you can see any available wireless networks and configure how a computer connects to them.

FIGURE 12.13   Windows XP wireless configuration screen

2. You can then configure several of the properties for how this wireless NIC connects to a particular wireless network, using the following options as shown on the wireless network configuration screen:

Use Windows to Configure My Wireless Network Settings   This check box determines whether Windows XP will configure the wireless settings. When it's unchecked, Windows XP will need an external program to configure how it connects to a wireless network, as is the case with some wireless NICs that have their own software program for this purpose. It is usually best to let Windows XP manage your wireless settings.

Available Networks   This list shows all of the wireless networks within range, with each network listed by its SSID. From this list, you can choose which network you wish to connect to, and you can then configure how your workstation connects by clicking the Configure button. If you don't see the wireless network you are looking for and you are in range, try clicking the Refresh button.

Preferred Networks   This list details any wireless networks you have connected to before and want to connect to again automatically. If there is more than one wireless network in range, this list determines the order in which the workstation will try to connect to them. You can change this order using the Move Up and Move Down buttons.

3. In addition to the general configuration, you may have to configure the encryption for the connection (if the wireless connection you are using requires it). To set up how your workstation uses encryption for a particular connection, from the screen shown in Figure 12.13, click the SSID of the wireless network you want to configure, and then click Configure. You will then see the screen shown in Figure 12.14.

FIGURE 12.14   Configuring encryption

Proceeding from this screen, you can configure several parameters for the specific connection:

Network Name (SSID)   If for some reason the SSID of the AP changes, you can change the name of the AP you're connecting to in this field. All you need to do is delete the old one and type in the new name. This is also the area where you add an SSID name if the AP is not broadcasting the name, so the client can find the AP.

Wireless Network Key (WEP)   This section contains all the parameters for configuring encryption for this particular connection. If the network you are connecting to uses *Wired Equivalent Privacy (WEP)* encryption, this is the section where you will click the check boxes and configure how the wireless connection uses WEP, the key it uses, and what type of key it is (I'll cover WEP in the section on security at the end of this chapter). The following parameters are in this section:

Data Encryption (WEP Enabled)   If a key is used to encrypt data sent over the network, you should definitely make sure this box is checked (even though it is by default). You'll then need to specify the key in the box labeled Network Key as well as specify what type of key it is (ASCII or hex) by selecting the appropriate item from the drop-down list.

Network Authentication (Shared Mode)   If your AP uses shared mode authentication, you've got to check this box to ensure that your workstation will authenticate to the AP using the shared key. The key can be provided automatically by the AP during the response to the initial request. If this is the case, you simply check the box labeled The Key Is Provided for Me Automatically, which happens to be the default. Otherwise, just uncheck it and enter the key and related information in the appropriate boxes.

This Is a Computer-to-Computer (Ad Hoc) Network Check this check box if you're connecting to another computer instead of an access point (not recommended, remember?).

4. Once you have changed any settings you need to, click OK to save the changes and finish the configuration.

Configuring a Windows 7 client is pretty simple unless, well, it doesn't work. Should this happen, you can indeed spend a long time searching for the answer!

1. To find a wireless network, in Control Panel, choose Network and Internet, then choose Network and Sharing Center, and finally, Connect to a network. If all is well, you'll get a screen similar to this one.

Now that was the long way around to get where we wanted to go. If you just go to the lower-right corner of your screen, click the signal strength bars with the yellow caution sign that I circled in the screen shot; you will receive the same results.

2. Double-click the network you want to join, and click Connect Anyway if it is an unsecured network. You'll then get a screen showing that it's trying to connect:

3. If you're using security, the AP will ask you for your credentials.

4. Check your TCP/IP settings to troubleshoot if you are not connected to the Internet.

AP Configuration

Once you've successfully configured your workstation(s), it's time to move on and configure the AP. There are literally hundreds of different APs out there, and of course, each uses a different method to configure its internal software. The good news is that for the most part, they all follow the same general patterns:

1. First of all, out of the box, the AP should come configured with an IP address that's usually something similar to 192.168.1.1. But check the documentation that comes with the AP to be sure. You can just take the AP out of its box, plug it into a power outlet, and connect it to your network, but in order to manage the AP, you've got to configure the AP's IP address scheme to match your network's.

2. Start by configuring a workstation on the wired network with an IP address (192.168.1.2 or similar) and subnet mask on the same subnet as the AP's. You should then be able to connect to the AP to begin the configuration progress. Usually, you do this via a web browser or with a manufacturer-supplied configuration program.

3. Once you have successfully connected to the AP, you then get to configure its parameters.

   Following are the minimum parameters common to APs that you should configure for your AP to work properly (remember, typically, an AP works right out of the box, but it is insecure too!).

   SSID   As I talked about earlier, this is the name of the wireless network that your AP will advertise. If this new AP is to be part of an existing wireless network, it needs to be configured with the same SSID as the existing network. In a network with only one AP, you can think of the SSID as the "name" of the AP.

   AP IP addresses   Remember, even though most APs come preconfigured with an IP address, it may not be one that matches the wired network's IP addressing scheme. So it follows that you should configure the AP's IP addresses (including the address, subnet mask, and default gateway addresses) to match the wired network you want it connected to. An AP does not need an IP address to work in your network. The IP address of the AP is used only to manage the AP.

   Operating mode (Access Point or Bridging)   Access points can operate in one of two main modes: *Access Point mode* or *Bridging mode*. Access Point mode allows the AP to operate as a traditional access point to allow a wireless client transparent access to a wired network. Alternatively, two APs set to Bridging mode provide a wireless bridge between two wired network segments.

   Password   Every access point has some kind of default password that's used to access the AP's configuration. For security reasons, it's a good idea to change this as soon as you can to connect to and configure the AP.

   Wireless channel   802.11 wireless networks can operate on different channels to avoid interference. Most wireless APs come set to work on a particular channel from the factory and you can change it if other networks in the area are using that channel but be aware that no particular channel is any more secure than another. Wireless stations do NOT use channel number as a faker when seeking a connection. They only pay attention to SSIDs!

WEP/WPA   Although it isn't a requirement per se, I definitely recommend enabling security right from the start as soon as you turn on the AP. WEP and Wi-Fi Protected Access (WPA) allow data to be encrypted before it's sent over the wireless connection, and all configuring it entails is to enable it and pick a key to be used for the connections. Simple, easy-to-configure security is certainly worth your time!

So here's what you do: First, you'll be asked to enter one or more human-readable passphrases called *shared keys*—secret passwords that won't ever be sent over the wire. After entering each one, you'll generally click a button to initiate a one-way hash to produce a WEP key of a size related to the number of bits of WEP encryption you want. Entering the same passphrase on a wireless client causes the hash (not the passphrase) to be sent from the wireless client to the AP during a connection attempt. Most configuration utilities allow you to create multiple keys in case you want to grant someone temporary access to the network, but you still want to keep the primary passphrase a secret. You can just delete the key you enabled to permit temporary access after you don't need it anymore without affecting access by any primary LAN participants.

Here's an example of connecting to a Linksys access point (not a Linksys wireless router, which is a different device):

1. The first screen shows that I've connected using HTTP to configure the device. The IP address of the Linksys AP is 192.168.1.245. If it was a Linksys wireless router instead—the typical home DSL/cable modem wireless connection device around today—than the address would be 192.168.1.1.

2. As you can see, there's no username required, and the password is just *admin*. As I mentioned, be sure not to leave this login configuration as the default! Once I click OK, I get taken to a screen where I can change my IP address.

3. It is not vitally important that an AP have an IP address, but it comes in handy for management purposes. But you can change the IP address as well as the device name from this screen if you want to. I clicked the Wireless tab on top and received this screen.

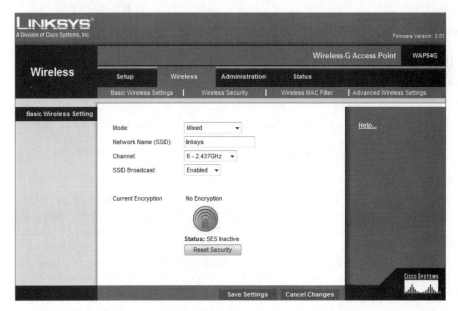

4. From here, you can set the device to run b/g or just g—even Mixed mode, which happens to be the default. You can also change the SSID from Linksys to another name, and I *highly* recommend doing this. The AP channel can be also be changed, and you can turn off the AP beacons as well—which, again, is recommended (if you do this, you have to set the new SSID name in each of your clients!). Last, you can see that by default, there's no encryption. Click the Wireless Security tab, and you'll get this screen.

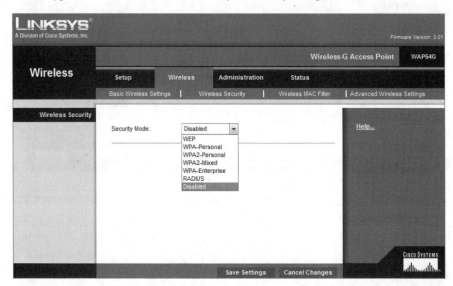

5. You can see from the pull-down menu that security is set to Disabled by default, but you can choose from various wireless security options.

I'll talk about security next.

Wireless Security

Okay, so wireless security is basically nonexistent on access points and clients. The original 802.11 committee just didn't imagine that wireless hosts would one day outnumber bounded media hosts, but that's actually where we're headed now. Also, unfortunately, just as with the IPv4 routed protocol, engineers and scientists didn't include security standards that are robust enough to work in a corporate environment. So we're left with proprietary solution add-ons to aid us in our quest to create a secure wireless network. And no—I'm not sitting here bashing the standards committees, because the security problems we're experiencing were also created by the US government because of export issues with its own security standards. Our world is a complicated place, so it follows that our security solutions would have to be as well.

⊕ **Real World Scenario**

War Driving

It's a fact—wireless networks are pretty much everywhere these days. You can get your hands on a wireless access point for less than $100.00, and they're flying off the shelves. You can find APs in public places like shopping malls, coffee shops, airports, and hotels, and in some cities, you can just hang out in a downtown area and zero in on a veritable menu of APs operating in almost every nearby business.

Predictably, this proliferation of APs has led to a new hobby for those with enough skill: It's called *war driving*. Not for the technologically challenged, war driving involves driving around in a car with a laptop, a wireless NIC, and a high-gain antenna, trying to locate open APs. If one with high-speed Internet access is found, it's like hitting the jackpot. People do this aided by various software programs and Global Positioning Systems (GPSs) to make their game even easier. But it's not always innocent—war drivers can be a serious security threat because they can potentially access anything on your wireless LAN as well as anything it's attached to! Even though they're not a sinister threat most of the time, realize that in the very least, they're consuming precious resources from your network. So, if you happen to notice unusually slow-moving vehicles outside your home or business—especially those with computer equipment inside—know that you're the potential target of a war driver.

A good place to start discussing Wi-Fi security is by talking about the standard basic security that was incorporated into the original 802.11 standards and why those standards are still way too flimsy and incomplete to help us create a secure wireless network relevant to today's challenges.

Open Access

All Wi-Fi Certified wireless LAN products are shipped in "open-access" mode, with their security features turned off. Although open access or no security may be appropriate and acceptable for public hot spots such as coffee shops, college campuses, and maybe airports, it's definitely not an option for an enterprise organization, and it's probably not even adequate for your private home network.

With what I've told you so far, I'm sure you agree that security needs to be enabled on wireless devices during their installation in enterprise environments. Yet surprisingly, many companies actually don't enable any WLAN security features. Obviously, the companies that do this are exposing their networks to tremendous risk.

The reason that the products are shipped with open access is so that any person who knows absolutely nothing about computers can just buy an access point, plug it into their cable or DSL modem, and voilà—they're up and running. It's marketing, plain and simple, and simplicity sells.

Service Set Identifiers, Wired Equivalent Privacy, and Media Access Control Address Authentication

What the original designers of 802.11 did to create basic security was to include the use of SSIDs, open or shared-key authentication, static WEP, and optional *Media Access Control (MAC) authentication*. Sounds like a lot, but none of these really offer any type of serious security solution—all they may be close to adequate for is use on a common home network. But we'll go over them anyway.

SSID is a common network name for the devices in a WLAN system that create the wireless LAN. An SSID prevents access by any client device that doesn't have the SSID. The thing is, by default, an access point broadcasts its SSID in its beacon many times a second. And even if SSID broadcasting is turned off, a bad guy can discover the SSID by monitoring the network and just waiting for a client response to the access point. Why? Because, believe it or not, that information, as regulated in the original 802.11 specifications, must be sent in the clear—how secure!

 If you cannot see an AP when trying to perform a site survey, verify that the AP has SSID beaconing enabled.

Two types of authentication were specified by the IEEE 802.11 committee: open and shared-key authentication. Open authentication involves little more than supplying the correct SSID—but it's the most common method in use today. With shared-key authentication, the access point sends the client device a challenge-text packet that the client must then encrypt with the correct WEP key and return to the access point. Without the correct key, authentication will fail and the client won't be allowed to associate with the access point. But shared-key authentication is still not considered secure because all an intruder has to do to get around this is detect both the clear-text challenge and the same challenge encrypted with a WEP key and then decipher the WEP key. Surprise—shared key isn't used in today's WLANs because of clear-text challenge.

With open authentication, even if a client can complete authentication and associate with an access point, the use of WEP prevents the client from sending and receiving data from the access point unless the client has the correct WEP key. A WEP key is composed of either 40 or 128 bits, and in its basic form, it's usually statically defined by the network administrator on the access point and all clients that communicate with that access point. When static WEP keys are used, a network administrator must perform the time-consuming task of entering the same keys on every device in the WLAN. Obviously, we now have fixes for this because tackling this would be administratively impossible in today's huge corporate wireless networks!

Last, client MAC addresses can be statically typed into each access point, and any of them that show up without that MAC address in the filter table will be denied access. Sounds good, but of course all MAC layer information must be sent in the clear—anyone equipped with a free wireless sniffer can just read the client packets sent to the access point and spoof their MAC address. If you have a small number of wireless clients and you don't want to deploy an encryption based access method, MAC address filters may be sufficient.

If you cannot connect to an AP and you've verified that your DHCP configuration and WEP key are correct, check the MAC address filtering on the AP.

WEP can actually work if administered correctly. But basic static WEP keys are no longer a viable option in today's corporate networks without some of the proprietary fixes that run on top of it.

So, what should you use today? The answer lies in the size of your wireless network and how tight your security needs to be. Let's discuss this further now.

Remote Authentication Dial In User Service

Remote Authentication Dial In User Service (RADIUS) is a networking protocol that offers us several security benefits: authorization, centralized access, and accounting supervision regarding the users and/or computers that connect to and access our network's services. Once RADIUS has authenticated the user, it allows us to specify the type of rights a user or workstation has plus control what it, or they, can do within the network. It also creates a record of all access attempts and actions. The provision of Authentication, Authorization, and Accounting is called AAA (spoken just like the automobile insurance company: Triple A).

RADIUS has risen to stardom because of its AAA features and is often employed by ISPs, web servers, wireless networks, and APs as well as network ports—basically, by anybody who wants or needs a AAA server. And these servers are only becoming more critically important in large corporate environments because they offer security for wireless networks. From the Linksys security screen shown earlier, you can see that RADIUS is an available option. If you choose it, you'll be asked for the IP address of the RADIUS server so the AP can send authentication packets.

Figure 12.15 shows how the AP becomes an authenticator when you choose the RADIUS authentication method.

Now, packets must pass through the AP until the user and/or host gets authenticated by the RADIUS server.

FIGURE 12.15   RADIUS authentication server

802.11 Network	Enterprise Edge	Enterprise Network
Supplicant	Authenticator	Authentication Server

802.1x Traffic Only

| Operates on client | Access point acts as authenticator | EAP plug-in goes in RADIUS server |

Temporal Key Integrity Protocol

Put up a fence, and it's only a matter of time until bad guys find a way over, around, and through it. And true to form, they indeed found ways to get through WEP's defenses, leaving our Wi-Fi networks vulnerable—stripped of their Data Link layer security! So someone had to come to the rescue. In this case, it happened to be the IEEE 802.11i task group and the Wi-Fi Alliance, joining forces for the cause. They came up with a solution called Temporal Key Integrity Protocol (TKIP). The Wi-Fi Alliance unveiled it back in late 2002 and introduced it as *Wi-Fi Protected Access (WPA)*. This little beauty even saved us lots of money because TKIP—say this like, "tee kip"—didn't make us upgrade all our legacy hardware equipment in order to use it. Then, in the summer of 2004, the IEEE put their seal of approval on its final version and added even more defensive muscle with goodies like 802.1x and AES-CCMP (AES-Counter Mode CBC-MAC Protocol) upon publishing IEEE 802.11i-2004. The Wi-Fi Alliance responded positively by embracing the now-complete specification and dubbing it WPA2 for marketing purposes.

A big reason that TKIP doesn't require buying new hardware to run is because it really just kind of wraps around the preexisting WEP encryption key (which was way too short) and upgrades it a whole lot to a much more impenetrable 128-bit encryption. Another reason for TKIP's innate compatibility is that both its encryption mechanism and the RC4 algorithm used to power and define WEP, respectively, remained the same.

But there are still significant differences that help make it the seriously tough shield it is, one of them being that it actually changes each packet's key. Let me explain…Packet keys are made up of three things: a base key, the transmitting device's MAC address, and the packet's serial number. It's an elegant design because, although it doesn't place a ton of stress on workstations and APs, it serves up some truly formidable cryptographic force. Here's how it works: Remember the packet serial number part of the transmission key? Well, it's not just your average serial number; it's special—very special.

TKIP-governed transmission ensures that each packet gets its very own 48-bit serial number, which is augmented with a sequence number whenever a new packet gets sent out and which not only serves as part of the key, but also acts as the initialization vector. And the good news doesn't end there—because each packet is now uniquely identified, the collision attacks that used to happen using WEP are also history. Plus, the fact that part of the packet's serial number is also the initialization vector prevents something called *replay attacks*. It takes an ice age for a 48-bit to repeat, so replaying packets from some past wireless connection is just not going to happen; those "recycled" packets won't be in sequence, but they will be identified, thus preventing the attack.

Now for what may be the truly coolest thing about TKIP keys: the base key. Because each base key that TKIP creates is unique, no one can recycle a commonly known key over and over again to gain access to a formerly vulnerable WEP wireless LAN. This is because TKIP throws the base key into the mix when it assembles each packet's unique key, meaning that even if a device has connected to a particular access point a bunch of times, it won't be permitted access again unless it has a completely new key granting it permission.

Even the base key itself is a fusion of something called *nonces*—an assortment of random numbers gleaned from the workstation, the access point, and each of these devices'

MAC addresses, so this should also be referred to as a *session secret*. So basically, if you've got IEEE 802.1x authentication working for you, rest assured that a session secret absolutely will be transmitted securely to each machine every time it initiates a connection to the wireless LAN by the authentication server—unless you're using pre-shared keys, that is, because if you happen to be using them, that important session secret always remains the same. Using TKIP with pre-shared keys is kind of like closing an automatically locking security door but not enabling its security settings and alarm—anyone who knows where the secret latch is can get right in!

Wi-Fi Protected Access or WPA 2 Pre-Shared Key

These are both essentially another form of basic security that's really just an add-on to the specifications. Even though you can totally lock the vault, as I mentioned in the previous section, WPA/WPA2 Pre-Shared Key (PSK) is a better form of wireless security than any other basic wireless security method I've talked about so far. And note that I did say basic! But if you are using only MAC address filters and/or WEP and you find that interlopers are still using your network and dragging down the performance, adding this layer of security should help tremendously since it's a better form of access control than either of those measures.

Wi-Fi Protected Access (WPA) is a standard developed by the Wi-Fi Alliance, formerly known as Wireless Ethernet Compatibility Alliance (WECA). WPA provides a standard for authentication and encryption of WLANs that's intended to solve known security problems. The standard takes into account the well-publicized AirSnort and man-in-the-middle WLAN attacks. So of course we use WPA2 to help us with today's security issues.

The PSK verifies users via a password or identifying code (also called a *passphrase*) on both the client machine and the access point. A client gains access to the network only if its password matches the access point's password. The PSK also provides keying material that TKIP or Advanced Encryption Standard (AES) uses to generate an encryption key for each packet of transmitted data.

Although more secure than static WEP, PSK still has a lot in common with static WEP in that the PSK is stored on the client station and can be compromised if the client station is lost or stolen (even though finding this key isn't all that easy to do). It's a definite recommendation to use a strong PSK passphrase that includes a mixture of letters, numbers, and non-alphanumeric characters. With WPA, it's still actually possible to specify the use of dynamic encryption keys that change each time a client establishes a connection.

 The benefit of WPA over a static WEP key is that WPA can change dynamically while the system is used.

WPA is a step toward the IEEE 802.11i standard and uses many of the same components, with the exception of encryption—802.11i (WPA2) uses AES-CCMP encryption. The IEEE 802.11i standard replaced WEP with a specific mode of AES known as the CCMP, as mentioned earlier. This allows AES-CCMP to provide both data confidentiality (encryption) and data integrity.

The highest level of wireless encryption you can run is WPA2-AES.

The following screen shows that if you choose WPA-2 Personal on the Linksys AP, you can then enter your passphrase—it's really called WPA2-Pre-Shared Key, but whatever.

You have a choice of TKIP or AES as the encryption, and by the way, you can choose up to a 64-character key—pretty tight!

WPA's mechanisms are designed to be implementable by current hardware vendors, meaning that users should be able to implement WPA on their systems with only a firmware/ software modification.

 The IEEE 802.11i standard has been sanctioned by WPA and is called WPA version 2.

Summary

Like rock 'n' roll, wireless technologies are here to stay. And for those of us who have come to depend on wireless technologies, it's actually pretty hard to imagine a world without wireless networks—what did we do before cell phones?

So we began this chapter by exploring the essentials and fundamentals of how wireless networks function.

Springing off that foundation, I then introduced you to the basics of wireless radio frequencies (RF) and the IEEE standards. We discussed 802.11 from its inception through its evolution to current and near future standards and talked about the subcommittees who create these standards.

All of this led into a discussion of wireless security—or, rather non-security for the most part—which we went over in detail.

We finished the chapter by bringing you up to speed on TKIP and WPA/WPA 2 security solutions—important tools used to protect the wireless LANs of today.

Exam Essentials

Understand the IEEE 802.11a specification.   802.11a runs in the 5GHz spectrum, and if you use the 802.11h extensions, you have 23 non-overlapping channels. 802.11a can run up to 54Mbps, but only if you are less than 50 feet from an access point.

Understand the IEEE 802.11b specification.   IEEE 802.11b runs in the 2.4GHz range and has three non-overlapping channels. It can handle long distances but with a maximum data rate of up to 11Mpbs.

Understand the IEEE 802.11g specification.   IEEE 802.11g is 802.11b's big brother and runs in the same 2.4GHz range, but it has a higher data rate of 54Mbps if you are less than 100 feet from an access point.

Remember the Wireless LAN modulation techniques.   Direct-Sequence Spread Spectrum (DSSS) is the most widely used modulation technique, but it has speeds only to 11Mbps. Frequency-Hopping Spread Spectrum (FHSS), although it is used in wireless devices like Bluetooth, isn't the technique of choice for either vendors or the 802.11 working group. To get the higher speeds needed in today's WLANs, we use Orthogonal Frequency Division Multiplexing (OFDM) in 802.11g and 802.11a networks.

Understand how WPA works in a WLAN.   Wi-Fi Protected Access (WPA) is the security of choice in today's home and corporate networks. It provides both authentication and encryption (either TKIP or AES); the latest version is WPA2.

Written Lab

Write the answers to the following wireless questions:

1. What is the maximum data rate of IEEE 802.11b?

2. What is the maximum data rate of IEEE 802.11g?

3. What is the maximum data rate of IEEE 802.11a?

4. What is the frequency range of IEEE 802.11b?

5. What is the frequency range of IEEE 802.11g?

6. What is the frequency range of IEEE 802.11a?

7. APs come set up with what type of security enabled by default?

8. Why would we use WPA instead of basic WEP?

9. Which IEEE committee has been sanctioned by WPA and is called WPA2?

10. The IEEE 802.11b/g basic standard has how many non-overlapping channels?
    You can find the answers to in Appendix B.

Review Questions

You can find the answers in Appendix A.

1. You need to install wireless Internet access in an open warehouse environment. After installing the equipment, the technician notices varying signal strengths throughout the warehouse. How do you make sure there is full coverage?

   A. Turn on broadcast key rotation.

   B. Change the encryption method used on all the APs.

   C. Change the antenna placement.

   D. Use channel bonding.

   E. Use channel shaping.

2. What is the frequency range of the IEEE 802.11a standard?

   A. 2.4Gbps

   B. 5Gbps

   C. 2.4GHz

   D. 5GHz

3. What is the frequency range of the IEEE 802.11g standard?

   A. 2.4Gbps

   B. 5Gbps

   C. 2.4GHz

   D. 5GHz

4. Which devices can interfere with the operation of a wireless network because they operate on similar frequencies? (Choose two.)

   A. Copier

   B. Microwave oven

   C. Toaster

   D. Cordless phone

   E. IP phone

   F. AM radio

5. Which wireless standard allows you to channel-bond to increase bandwidth and uses both the 2.4Ghz and 5Ghz frequencies?

   A. 802.11b

   B. 802.11g

   C. 802.11a

   D. 802.11n

6. How many non-overlapping channels are available with 802.11b?

   A. 3

   B. 12

   C. 23

   D. 40

7. How many non-overlapping channels are available with 802.11a?

   A. 3

   B. 12

   C. 23

   D. 40

8. What is the maximum data rate for the 802.11a standard?

   A. 6Mbps

   B. 11Mbps

   C. 22Mbps

   D. 54Mbps

9. You need to install wireless on multiple floors of a large building and maintenance area. What is your first concern before installing the APs?

   A. Authentication

   B. Encryption

   C. Channel overlap

   D. AP configuration

10. What is the maximum data rate for the 802.11b standard?

   A. 6Mbps

   B. 11Mbps

   C. 22Mbps

   D. 54Mbps

11. You connect a new host to your company's wireless network. The host is set to receive a DHCP address and the WEP key is entered correctly. However, the host cannot connect to the network. What can the problem be?

    A. DNS is not configured on the host.

    B. MAC filtering is enabled on the AP.

    C. The network has run out of wireless connections.

    D. The host is enabled to run 802.11b and 802.11g.

12. Which is the highest encryption that WPA2 can use?

    A. AES-CCMP

    B. PPK via IV

    C. PSK

    D. TKIP/MIC

13. Which additional configuration step is necessary in order to connect to an access point that has SSID broadcasting disabled?

    A. Set the SSID value in the client software to public.

    B. Configure open authentication on the AP and the client.

    C. Set the SSID value on the client to the SSID configured on the AP.

    D. Configure MAC address filtering to permit the client to connect to the AP.

14. Which spread-spectrum technology does the 802.11b standard define for operation?

    A. IR

    B. DSSS

    C. FHSS

    D. DSSS and FHSS

    E. IR, FHSS, and DSSS

15. Which wireless LAN design ensures that a mobile wireless client will not lose connectivity when moving from one access point to another?

    A. Using adapters and access points manufactured by the same company

    B. Overlapping the wireless cell coverage by at least 10 percent

    C. Configuring all access points to use the same channel

    D. Utilizing MAC address filtering to allow the client MAC address to authenticate with the surrounding APs

16. You have installed a point-to-point connection using wireless bridges and Omni-directional antennas between two buildings. The throughput is low. What can you do to improve the link?

  A. Replace the bridges with APs.

  B. Replace the Omni-directional antennas with Yagis.

  C. Configure 802.11a on the links.

  D. Install amps to boost the signal.

17. What does extended service set (ESS) ID mean?

  A. That you have more than one access point, and they are in the same SSID connected by a distribution system

  B. That you have more than one access point, and they are in separate SSIDs connected by a distribution system

  C. That you have multiple access points, but they are placed physically in different buildings

  D. That you have multiple access points, but one is a repeater access point

18. What is one reason that WPA encryption is preferred over WEP?

  A. A WPA key is longer and requires more special characters than the WEP key.

  B. The access point and the client are manually configured with different WPA key values.

  C. WPA key values remain the same until the client configuration is changed.

  D. The values of WPA keys can change dynamically while the system is used.

19. How wide are the channels used in 802.11n in order to gain the large bandwidth that the specification provides?

  A. 22MHz

  B. 20Mhz

  C. 40Mhz

  D. 100Mhz

20. 802.11n uses MIMO. How does this optimize throughput to gain the high speed advantage that 802.11n provides?

  A. By specifying an acknowledgment of each and every frame, 802.11n provides better overhead.

  B. Several frames are sent by several antennae over several paths and are then recombined by another set of antennae.

  C. One frame at a time is sent, but faster than in 802.11g because multiple antennas are used (multiple-in, multiple-out).

  D. MIMO packs smaller packets into a single unit, which improves throughput.

Chapter

13

Authentication and Access Control

THE FOLLOWING COMPTIA NETWORK+ EXAM OBJECTIVES ARE COVERED IN THIS CHAPTER:

✓ **5.2 Explain the methods of network access security.**

- ACL:
  - MAC filtering
  - IP filtering
  - Port filtering
- Tunneling and encryption:
  - SSL VPN
  - VPN
  - L2TP
  - PPTP
  - IPSec
  - ISAKMP
  - TLS
  - TLS1.2
  - Site-to-site and client-to-site
- Remote access:
  - RAS
  - RDP
  - PPPoE
  - PPP
  - ICA
  - SSH

✓ **5.3 Explain methods of user authentication.**

- ▪ PKI

- ▪ Kerberos

- ▪ AAA (RADIUS, TACACS+)

- ▪ Network access control (802.1x, posture assessment)

- ▪ CHAP

- ▪ MS-CHAP

- ▪ EAP

- ▪ Two-factor authentication

- ▪ Multifactor authentication

- ▪ Single sign-on

So far, you've learned a lot about networking standards and related technologies and even how to make computers and devices communicate so you can get a network up and running. But there's more—because network security is absolutely critical, I'm going to equip you with the knowledge you need to keep your network safe from intruders.

Yes, communication and accessing the information you need is all good, but knowing exactly who it is at the other end of the connection is vital. This means you need ways to confirm that the person or computer at the other end of the connection is really supposed to be accessing the resource it's trying to, and even whether the resources or entities that you're contacting are really who and what they appear to be. Seriously, if you don't have network security firmly in place, you're flying dangerously blind—you could be inadvertently exposing critical data to people who have no right to see that information and may even intend to exploit it in a big way! So, in this chapter, we'll focus on some very important pieces of the security puzzle; two of the first things on our list are security filtering and user authentication.

To find up-to-the-minute updates for this chapter, please see www.lammle.com/forum or the book's web site at www.sybex.com/go/netplus2e.

Security Filtering

How do we know who's really at the other end of our connections? The answer to that may seem simple enough because the computer or person on the other end has to identify him/her/itself, right? Wrong! That's just not good enough because people—especially hackers—lie, so it's totally naïve to assume that the person or computer on the other end of the line is who they're claiming to be. Sad but true: Hackers use the many tools out there today with the precise goal of convincing us they're someone else, and way too many of us have been, or know of someone who has been, a victim of identity theft thanks to bad guys with the right spoofing software in hand.

This means it's imperative to control who or what can get into our network by identifying the specific computers and individuals who have the right to gain access to it and its resources. But how do we do this? Well, for starters, I'm going to cover some basic ways to safely allow the computers you want to access into your network plus ways to keep out the ones you don't.

The first line of defense is something called *security filtering*, which broadly refers to ways to let people securely access your resources. This process is twofold and includes ensuring that only authorized computers get to enter your network and making sure data you're sending back and forth between networks is secured so it can't be intercepted and translated by bad guys.

Access Control Lists

It's rare to find a network around these days that isn't connected to the Internet. The Internet is clearly a public internetwork that anyone can connect to, but your company's or personal network is, and should definitely be, a private one. The catch here is that every time you connect to the Internet (where everyone is welcome) from a private network, you're instantly vulnerable to security break-ins. This is where something we call a *firewall* comes into play. Firewalls are basically tools that you can implement to prevent any unauthorized users roaming around on public networks from gaining access to your private network.

> I'll be covering the different types of firewalls, plus the skinny on exactly how they work, in Chapter 15, "Physical and Hardware Security." For now, understand that firewalls can be either stand-alone devices or combined with another hardware device like a server or a router. And although firewalls can use a lot of various technologies to restrict information flow, their primary weapon is known as an access control list (ACL).

Access control lists (ACLs) typically reside on routers to determine which packets are allowed to route through them based on the requesting device's source or destination Internet Protocol (IP) address. Oh, and just so you know, ACLs have been around for decades and have other uses apart from firewalls.

Figure 13.1 demonstrates how ACLs prevent users on Network B from accessing Network A.

FIGURE 13.1 Two networks with an ACL-enabled router

Okay, what we see here is that users in Network A can pass through the router into Network B. This means that an IP spoofing attack, when someone pretends to have a network address on the inside of a firewall to gain network access, can still happen if a user in Network

B pretends to be located in Network A. We'll go over things like IP spoofing more thoroughly in Chapter 14, "Network Threats and Mitigation," but for now, let's get back to ACLs.

You can create a wide array of ACLs, from the very simple to the highly complex, depending on exactly what you want to have them do for you. One example is placing separate inbound and outbound ACLs on a router to ensure that the data that's leaving your network comes from a different source than the data that's coming into it.

When configuring ACLs between the Internet and your private network to mitigate security problems, it's a good idea to include these four conditions:

- Deny any addresses from your internal networks.
- Deny any local host addresses (127.0.0.0/8).
- Deny any reserved private addresses.
- Deny any addresses in the IP multicast address range (224.0.0.0/4).

None of these addresses should ever be allowed to enter your internetwork. Interestingly enough, because of the way in-public IP addresses are issued, with some research you can create a filter that blocks a country, state or even locale based on IP addresses!

Most of the time, it's wise to configure ACLs so that they'll allow or deny access based on the IP address of the source or destination device. If your network is running a protocol other than Transmission Control Protocol/Internet Protocol (TCP/IP), you can filter traffic based on a Media Access Control (MAC), or hardware, address instead of an IP address. You can still use a MAC address–based ACL if you're running TCP/IP, but keep in mind that it's a lot easier to deal with IP addresses than MAC addresses. Another point to remember is that even though most firewalls and routers will allow you to create both IP-based and MAC-based ACLs, doing so can create an exceptionally ugly situation where access is denied when it really shouldn't be.

Port Filtering

ACLs can also be used to filter based on port numbers as well as IP addresses. In fact most firewalls default to allowing only the open ports that you specify. This is another version of the implicit deny (anything not allowed specifically is denied).

When managing a firewall it's important to know the port numbers of all traffic that needs to be allowed through the firewall, This means that for some of your applications you will need to read and learn the port numbers being used.

This also explains why it's a big deal to know the port numbers of security protocols like SSL and IPsec. Successful firewall management involves being aware of and allowing *only* the port required to keep things running.

Tunneling

Just thinking about the huge amount of sensitive data bouncing all over the Internet 24/7 makes me want to scream the word *security*! It's seriously clear that we need it almost as much as air. Worse, most of that data is sent out over the Internet without any encryption or security, but at least not the really sensitive stuff, which should be sent via one of several different security protocols available today—phew. These vital protocols are really sets of conditions or rules that define how a secure connection is maintained when we send sensitive data through an unsecure medium like the Internet or a wireless connection. Before talking about the security protocols that the Network+ exam is likely to quiz you on, I'd like to define a few terms.

The first is a concept called *tunneling*, which basically means encapsulating one protocol within another to ensure that a transmission is secure. Here's an example: The lion's share of us use IP, known as a *payload protocol*, which can be encapsulated within a *delivery protocol* like Internet Protocol Security (IPSec). If you took a look at these packets individually, you would see that they're encrypted. If you look at the process as a whole, it appears that a point-to-point tunnel is created on the Internet, as Figure 13.2 illustrates. (Make a note to yourself that usually, the tunneled protocol is running at a higher layer in the OSI model than the payload protocol, but not always.)

FIGURE 13.2 A tunnel through the Internet

Single Private Path or Tunnel
through the Internet

The Network+ exam will test your understanding of the following tunneling protocols:

- Virtual Private Network (VPN)
- Secure Sockets Layer (SSL)
- Secure Sockets Layer Virtual Private Network (SSL VPN)
- Layer 2 Tunneling Protocol (L2TP)
- Point-to-Point Tunneling Protocol (PPTP)
- Internet Protocol Security (IPSec)
- ISAKMP

Let's dig in and take a detailed look at each one now.

Virtual Private Network

No worries—VPNs aren't really that hard to understand. A VPN fits somewhere between a LAN and WAN and many times may seem just like a WAN link because your computer, on one LAN, connects to a different, remote LAN and uses its resources remotely. The key difference with VPNs is a big one—security! So the definition of connecting a LAN (or VLAN) to a WAN may sound the same, but a VPN is much more.

Here's the difference: A typical WAN connects two or more remote LANs together using someone else's network—like, say, your Internet service provider's (ISP's)—and a router. Your local host and router see these networks as remote networks and not as local networks or local resources. This would be a WAN in its most general definition. A VPN actually makes your local host part of the remote network by using the WAN link that connects you to the remote LAN. The VPN will make your host appear as though it's actually local on the remote network! This means that we now have access to the remote LANs resources and that access is very secure.

This may sound a lot like the VLAN definition I just used in Chapter 11, "Switching and Virtual LANs," and really, the concept is the same: "Take my host and make it appear local to the remote resources." Just remember that for networks that are physically local, using VLANs is a good solution, but for networks that are physically remote—those that span a WAN—we'd opt for using VPNs instead.

For a simple VPN example, let's use my home office in Boulder, Colorado. Here, I have my personal host, but I want it to appear as if it's on a LAN in my corporate office in Dallas, Texas, so I can get to my remote servers. VPN is the solution I use for this because I need the security it provides.

Figure 13.3 shows this example of my host using a VPN connection from Boulder to Dallas, which allows me to access the remote network services and servers as if my host is right there on the same VLAN as my servers.

FIGURE 13.3   Example of using a VPN network

Why is this so important? If you answered, "Because my servers in Dallas are secure, and only the hosts on the same VLAN are allowed to connect to them and use their resources," you nailed it! A VPN allows me to connect to these resources by locally attaching to the

VLAN through a VPN across the WAN. The other option is to open up my network and servers to everyone on the Internet or another WAN service, in which case my security goes poof! So you can see that it's a very good thing I have a VPN.

Types of VPNs are named based on the kind of role they play in a real-world business situation. There are three different categories of VPNs:

Remote-Access VPNs *Remote-access VPNs* allow remote users like telecommuters to securely access the corporate network wherever and whenever they need to. It is typical that users can connect to the Internet but not to the office via their VPN client because they don't have the correct VPN address and password. This is the most common problem and one you should always check first.

Site-to-Site VPNs *Site-to-site VPNs,* or intranet VPNs, allow a company to connect its remote sites to the corporate backbone securely over a public medium like the Internet instead of requiring more expensive wide area network (WAN) connections like Frame Relay. This is probably the BEST solution for connecting a remote office to a main company office.

Extranet VPNs *Extranet VPNs* allow an organization's suppliers, partners, and customers to be connected to the corporate network in a limited way for business-to-business (B2B) communications.

SSL and SSL VPN

Next on the list is *Secure Sockets Layer (SSL)*. This security protocol was developed by Netscape to work with its browser. It's based on Rivest, Shamir, and Adleman (RSA) public-key encryption and used to enable secure Session layer connections over the Internet between a web browser and a web server. SSL is service independent, meaning a lot of different network applications can be secured with it—a famous one being the ubiquitous HTTP Secure (HTTPS) protocol. As time marched on, SSL was merged with other Transport layer security protocols to form a new protocol called Transport Layer Security (TLS). The latest version of Transport Layer Security (TLS 2.0) provides a number of enhancements over earlier versions. The following are the most noteworthy:

- Several improvements in the operation of a central component, the MD5-SHA-1 hashing function. Hashing functions are used to ensure that the data is not changed or altered (also known as maintaining data integrity).

- More flexibility in the choice of hashing and encryption algorithms on the part of the client and the server.

- Enhanced support for the Advanced Encryption Standard (AES).

Figure 13.4 shows the SSL connection process.

SSL VPN is really the process of using SSL to create a virtual private network (VPN). A VPN is a secured connection between two systems that would otherwise have to connect to each other through a non-secured network. Here's what I mean: Even though I'd never really let this happen, let's just say I could connect to the servers in my corporate office through the Internet like, snap! You know by now that this would be a very bad thing because the Internet is far from secure, right? But if I connected to those servers using a VPN with a tunneling protocol instead, anything I send from my PC to my corporate office would be locked up nice and securely.

FIGURE 13.4 The SSL connection process

Plus, VPNs also come in handy for data that's being sent within a private network that you probably wouldn't want everyone on that network to be able to see. Maybe you want a few specific computers on the intranet to be able to communicate with each other securely—like say, the computers used by your top finance people. You wouldn't necessarily want that data just sent off in the clear to be viewed by the office gossip, now would you? No way. So, you can put those finance folks on a VPN that's just like having them on their own little private, secure subnetwork. Plus, what's even cooler about this setup is that the members of your intranet's VPN can still communicate with everyone else whenever they want; they just won't be doing that securely—nice solution!

L2TP

Next, we have the *Layer 2 Tunneling Protocol (L2TP)*, which was created by the Internet Engineering Task Force (IETF). It comes in handy for supporting non-TCP/IP protocols in VPNs over the Internet. L2TP is actually a combination of Microsoft's Point-to-Point Tunneling Protocol (PPTP) and Cisco's Layer 2 Forwarding (L2F) technologies. A nice L2TP feature is that because it works way down there at the Data Link layer (Layer 2) of the OSI model, it can support tons of protocols beyond just TCP/IP—a couple of biggies being Internetwork Packet Exchange (IPX) and AppleTalk. It's a really great tool to implement if you happen to have two non-TCP/IP networks that need to be connected via the Internet.

PPTP

I just mentioned *Point-to-Point Tunneling Protocol (PPTP)*, and even though I said it was Microsoft's PPTP, this security protocol was really developed jointly by Microsoft, Lucent Technologies, 3COM, and a few other companies. Oh, and it's not actually sanctioned by the IETF, but that doesn't mean it doesn't work. PPTP acts by combining an unsecured Point-to-Point Protocol (PPP) session with a secured session using the *Generic Routing Encapsulation (GRE) protocol.*

Because PPTP uses two different protocols, it actually opens up two different network sessions: So be warned, it can give you some grief when passing through a router. This is a big reason you won't find it around much nowadays. Another reason it's going the way of the dinosaurs is that it originally gained popularity because it was the first VPN protocol to be supported by Microsoft's dial-up networking services, and not too many of us depend on dial-up to get to the Internet anymore. As if these aren't reasons enough for PPTP's impending extinction, it's also not that secure. In fact, as you'd probably expect from a first-generation security protocol, it's now really vulnerable to spoofing attacks, which is why it's pretty much been replaced by L2TP and IPSec.

PPTP is a VPN protocol that runs over port 1723 and allows encryption to be done at the Application (data) level. It is important to remember for the CompTIA Network+ objectives that PPTP is a protocol that allows secure access to a VPN.

IPSec

On the other hand, IP Security (IPSec) was designed by the IETF for providing authentication and encryption over the Internet. It works at the Network layer of the OSI model (Layer 3) and secures all applications that operate in the layers above it. Because it's sanctioned by the IETF and designed to work with IPv4 and IPv6, it's got a huge amount of industry support, so it's the standard for VPNs on the Internet today.

The two major protocols you'll find working in IPSec are *Authentication Header (AH)* and *Encapsulating Security Payload (ESP)*. AH serves up authentication services only—no encryption—but ESP provides both authentication and encryption abilities. Both of these protocols can be used with either mode discussed in the following paragraphs.

The AH protocol within IPSec isn't compatible with networks running Network Address Translation (NAT).

IPSec works in two modes: transport mode and tunneling mode. Transport mode creates a secure tunnel between two devices end to end. This means that regardless of how many foreign networks (including the Internet) the packet traverses, it is protected. The data is protected by authentication and/or encryption. Figure 13.5 illustrates a TCP/IP packet and a TCP/IP packet in transport mode using AH. ESP can also be used with transport mode.

On the other hand, in tunnel mode, the tunnel is created between two endpoints, such as two routers or two gateway servers, protecting all traffic that goes through the tunnel. It is commonly used between two offices to protect all traffic going between the offices regardless of the source and destination. Figure 13.6 first shows a TCP/IP packet and then depicts one using ESP in tunnel mode. AH can also be used with tunnel mode.

You can see here that when data is tunneled in this way, hackers can't even see what transport protocol you're using, let alone decipher the data you're transmitting.

FIGURE 13.5   TCP/IP packet in IPSec transport mode with AH

FIGURE 13.6   TCP/IP packet in IPSec tunnel mode with ESP

ISAKMP

Internet Security Association and Key Management Protocol (ISAKMP) defines procedures and packet formats to establish, negotiate, modify, and delete security associations (SAs). SAs contain information required to execute security services, such as header authentication and payload encapsulation. ISAKMP's real value is its ability to provide a framework for safely transferring key and authentication data independent of the key generation technique, encryption algorithm, and authentication mechanism. ISAKMP is integrated into another security mechanism we have already discussed, IPSec.

Encryption

Sometimes, like it or not, sending out corporate financial and other types of sensitive data over the Internet just can't be avoided. This is why being able to hide or encode that data with encryption technologies is so vital for shielding it from the prying eyes of a company's competitors, identity thieves—anyone who wants to take a look. Without encryption, our sensitive files and information are essentially being paraded on full display as the data courses over the Internet.

Encryption works by running the data (which when encoded is represented as numbers) through a special encryption formula called a *key* that the designated sending and receiving devices both "know." When encrypted data arrives at its specified destination, the receiving device uses that key to decode the data back into its original form.

Back in 1979, the National Security Agency (NSA) classified encryption tools and their associated formulas as munitions, and the NSA has overseen their regulation ever since. The dangerous possibility that hostile nations, terrorists, and criminals may use encrypted communications to plan crimes and go undetected is the compelling reason for doing so. It's also the reason that we're only allowed to export weak encryption methods.

This brings up an important question: Exactly how do we measure an encryption algorithm's strength? One way to do that is to measure its bit strength. Until 1998, only software with 40-bit strength or less could be exported, but today, the bar has been raised to 64-bit strength. And by the way, exporting any software with a key length greater than 64 bits is subject to review by the Export Administration Regulations (EAR) required by the US Department of Commerce's Bureau of Industry and Security. This doesn't include exporting to every country because some—like most of those in Western Europe plus Canada, Australia, and Japan—are countries we trust with the technology. But if you happen to be curious or just want to be really careful, check out the current regulations at www.access.gpo.gov/bis/index.html. Remember, these regulations aren't there to make life a hassle; they're in place to protect us. The greater the number of bits that are encrypted, the tougher it is to crack the code.

 Clearly, the security of monetary transfers is extremely important. The NSA does allow US banks to use more secure encryption methods for this reason and to ensure that they communicate very securely with their overseas branches, customers, and affiliates.

Encrypting passwords being sent from a workstation to a server at login is the most basic need for internal networks, and it's done automatically by most network operating systems today. But legacy utilities like File Transfer Protocol (FTP) and Telnet don't have the ability to encrypt passwords. Most email systems also give users the option to encrypt individual (or all) email messages, and third-party software packages like Pretty Good Privacy (PGP)

are used by email systems that don't come with encryption abilities of their own. And you already know how critical encryption is for data transmission over VPNs. Last but not least, encryption capability is clearly very important for e-commerce transactions, online banking, and investing.

I mentioned this earlier, but I didn't tell you exactly what it is: An encryption key is essentially a random string of characters that is used in conjunction with the encryption algorithm. The algorithm is the same for all transactions but the key is unique to each transaction. Encryption keys come in two flavors: public and private. I'm going to tell you how each one is used next.

Symmetrical Encryption Keys

Using symmetrical key encryption, both the sender and receiver have the same key and use it to encrypt and decrypt all messages. The downside of this technique is that it becomes hard to maintain the security of the key. When the keys at each end are different, it is called symmetrical or public key. We'll talk about that right after we discuss some encryption standards.

The Data Encryption Standard (DES)

Kudos go to IBM for coming up with one of the most widely used standards: *Data Encryption Standard (DES)*. It was made a standard back in 1977 by the US government. If you want, you can look it up in the Federal Information Processing Standards Publication 46-2 (FIPS 46-2).

Basically, DES uses lookup and table functions, and it actually works much faster than more complex systems. It uses 56-bit keys. RSA Data Systems once issued a challenge to see if anyone could break the key. A group of Internet users worked together to attempt the task, with each member dealing with a portion of the 72 quadrillion possible combinations. They succeeded and cracked the key in June 1997, after searching only 18 quadrillion keys. Their prize? Knowing they had succeeded when they read a plain-text message that said, "Strong cryptography makes the world a safer place."

Back in the day, DES was a great security standard, but its 56-bit key length has proved to be too short. As I said, the key was first cracked in June 1997. A year later, one was cracked in just 56 hours, and in January 1999, a DES key was broken in a blazing 22 hours and 15 minutes! Not exactly secure, right? We definitely needed something stronger.

Triple Data Encryption Standard (3DES)

That's when *Triple Data Encryption Standard (3DES*, also referred to as TDES) came into its glory. Originally developed in the late 1970s, it became the recommended method of implementing DES encryption in 1999. As its name implies, 3DES is essentially three DES encryption methods combined into one.

So 3DES encrypts three times, and it allows us to use one, two, or three separate keys. Clearly, going with only one key is the most unsecure, and opting to use all three keys gives you the highest level of security. Three-key TDES has a key length of 168 bits (56 times 3), but due to a complex type of attack known as *meet-in-the-middle*, it really provides only 112 bits of security. It gets worse farther down the food chain—even though the two-key version has a key size of 112 bits, it actually arms you with only 80 bits of effective security.

Another problem with 3DES is that it's slow. No one likes that, so the National Institute of Standards and Technology (NIST) believes that 3DES will be an effective encryption standard only until sometime around 2030. Even now, it's being phased out in favor of faster methods like AES.

The Advanced Encryption Standard (AES)

The *Advanced Encryption Standard (AES*, also known as Rijndael) has been the "official" encryption standard in the United States since 2002. It specifies key lengths of 128, 192, or 256 bits.

The United States government has determined that 128-bit security is adequate for things like secure transactions and all materials deemed Secret, but all Top Secret information must be encoded using 192- or 256-bit keys.

The good news is that the AES standard has proven amazingly difficult to crack. Those who try use a popular method involving something known as a *side channel attack*. This means that instead of going after the cipher directly, they attempt to gather the information they want from the physical implementation of a security system. Hackers attempt to use power consumption, electromagnetic leaks, or timing information (like the number of processor cycles taken to complete the encryption process) to give them critical clues about how to break the AES system. Although it's true that attacks like these are possible to pull off, they're not really practical to clinch over the Internet.

Public Key Encryption

Public key encryption uses the *Diffie-Hellman algorithm*, which employs a public key and a private key to encrypt and decrypt data. It works like this: The sending machine's public key is used to encrypt a message that the receiving machine uses to decrypt the message with its private key. It's a one-way communication, but if the receiver wants to send a return message, it does so via the same process. If the original sender doesn't have a public key, the message can still be sent with a digital certificate that's often called a *digital ID*, which verifies the sender of the message.

Figure 13.7 shows public-key-encrypted communication between User X and User Y.

 Here's a cool factoid for you—*Diffie-Hellman* refers to all public-key algorithms. Whitfield Diffie and Martin Hellman from the Stanford Research Institute invented public-key encryption. They introduced the dual-key concept in their 1976 paper "New Directions in Cryptography."

RSA Data Security

Rivest, Shamir, and Adleman (RSA) encryption is a public-key algorithm named after the three scientists from MIT who created it. They formed a commercial company in 1977 to develop asymmetric keys and nailed several US patents. Their encryption software is used today in electronic commerce protocols.

FIGURE 13.7   Public-key encryption

For more information about RSA Data Security, go to www.rsa.com.

Pretty Good Privacy (PGP)

In the early 1990s, Phil Zimmerman (also from MIT) wrote most of the code for this freely available version of public-key encryption designed to encrypt data for email transmission. Zimmerman basically compared email to postcards, because anyone can read email messages traversing the Internet just as they can postcards traveling through the postal service. By contrast, he compared an encrypted message to a letter mailed inside an envelope. Figure 13.8 shows the PGP encryption system.

In Figure 13.8, the document is encrypted with a session key, which is then encrypted with the public key of the recipient. Then the ciphertext and the encrypted session key are sent to the recipient. Since the recipient is the only person with the matching private key, only they can decrypt the session key and then use it to decrypt the document.

Zimmerman distributed the software for personal use only, and as the name implies, it's really pretty good security.

RSA Data Security and the US federal government both had a problem with Zimmerman's product—the RSA complained about patent infringement, and the government actually decided to prosecute Zimmerman for exporting munitions-grade software. The government eventually dropped the charges, and now a licensing fee is paid to RSA, so today, PGP and other public-key-related products are readily available.

Don't let the name fool you! PGP is a highly secure encryption standard.

FIGURE 13.8   The PGP encryption system

Remote Access

Think of remote access as a telecommuting tool because it's used by companies to allow employees to connect to the internal network and access resources that aren't in the office. Remote access is great for users who work from home or travel frequently, but clearly, to a stalking hacker, using an unsecured remote-access connection is like stealing candy from a baby.

Using remote access requires a server configured to accept incoming calls and also requires remote-access software to be installed on the client. Microsoft Windows operating systems since Windows 95 have had remote-access client software built in, and there are many third-party remote-access clients available as well. Several different methods exist to create remote-access connections.

RAS

Remote Access Services (RAS) is not a protocol but refers to the combination of hardware and software required to make a remote-access connection. The term was popularized by

Microsoft when the company began referring to its Windows NT–based remote-access tools by this name. Users would dial in via a modem, be authenticated by the server, and then be asked for their username and password just as if they were on the local network. Once logged in, users had access to data on the internal network just as if they were logged in locally. Figure 13.9 gives you an idea of what this would look like.

FIGURE 13.9   A typical remote-access connection between a remote user and a server

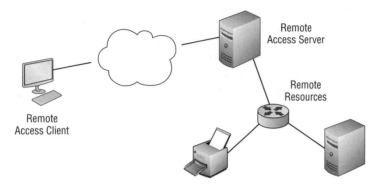

RAS itself was not secure; but there are options within RAS to include a secure protocol for tunneling, such as PPTP, and for authentication, such as Microsoft Challenge Handshake Authentication Protocol (MS-CHAP) and Extensible Authentication Protocol (EAP). RAS is versatile because it supports several other network protocols in addition to TCP/IP.

RDP

Remote Desktop Protocol (RDP) allows users to connect to a computer running Microsoft's Remote Desktop Services, but a remote computer must have the right kind of client software installed for this to happen. Most Windows-based operating systems include an RDP client, and so do most other major operating systems like Linux, Solaris, and Mac OS X. Microsoft's RDP client software is called either Remote Desktop Connection (RDC) or Terminal Services Client (TSC). Microsoft began calling all terminal services products *Remote Desktop* with Windows Server 2008 R2.

After establishing a connection, the user sees a *terminal window* that's basically a pre-configured window that looks like a Windows or other operating system's desktop. From there, the user on the client computer can access applications and files available to them by using the remote desktop.

The most current version of RDP is RDP 7.1, released in Windows 7 SP1 and Server 2008 R2 SP1. When logged in using RDP, clients are able to access local files and printers from the remote desktop just as if they were logged into the network. RDP offers 128-bit encryption using the RC4 encryption algorithm and also offers TLS 1.0 support.

PPP

Point-to-Point Protocol (PPP) is a Layer 2 protocol that provides authentication, encryption, and compression services to clients logging in remotely. ISPs use PPP a lot to authenticate clients dialing in with a modem or a DSL or cable modem. Many network servers that provide remote-access services (such as RAS) can also use PPP as an authentication protocol.

PPPoE

Point-to-Point Protocol over Ethernet (PPPoE) is an extension of PPP. Its purpose is to encapsulate PPP frames within Ethernet frames.

The need for PPPoE was born out of the need to deal with the massive increase in high-speed Internet connections. Service providers offering customers high-speed access using Asymmetric Digital Subscriber Line (ADSL) or cable modems needed a way to offer the authentication and encryption services of PPP. A Remote Authentication Dial In User Service (RADIUS) server—something I'll get into a bit later in this chapter—is commonly used to manage PPPoE connections.

PPPoE works in two stages: discovery and session. In the discovery phase, the MAC addresses of each of the connection's endpoints are given to each other so that a secure PPP connection can be made. During this phase, a session ID is also created that's used to facilitate further data transmission during the session. When the MAC addresses of each endpoint are known to each other, a point-to-point connection is created; the session stage begins at this time.

ICA

Independent Computing Architecture (ICA) is a protocol designed by Citrix Systems to provide communication between servers and clients. The most common application that uses ICA is Citrix's WinFrame, which administrators can use to set up Windows applications on a Windows-based server and then use to allow clients with virtually any operating system to access those applications. Client computers running Linux, Unix, or Mac OSs can access Windows-based applications with the help of WinFrame, giving network administrators all kinds of flexibility with client operating systems. But again, there's a downside—connections like these tend to be slow because of the huge amount of translation that's required to enable the client and server to communicate with each other properly.

SSH

Secure Shell is a network protocol that is designed as an alternative to command-based utilities such as Telnet that transmit requests and responses in clear text. It creates a secure channel between the devices and provides confidentiality and integrity of the data transmission. It uses public-key cryptography to authenticate the remote computer and allow the remote computer to authenticate the user, if necessary.

This public key is placed on any computer that must allow access to the owner of a matching private key (the owner keeps the private key in secret). The private key is never transferred through the network during authentication.

Managing User Account and Password Security

A whole bunch of authentication schemes are used today, and although it's important to know about these different schemes and how they work, all that knowledge doesn't equal power if your network's users aren't schooled on how to manage their account names and passwords correctly. This is because if bad guys get their hands on usernames and passwords, it gives them a way to get into your network. Worse, if a hacker gains the administrator account name and password for your network, it doesn't matter what authentication protocol or server you're using—that hacker isn't just going to get in, they're going to get in armed with the escalated rights that type of account allows, meaning they can do some serious damage.

With that in mind, let's get into some solid ways to manage user accounts and passwords and follow that up by talking about the key authentication methods in use today.

Usernames and passwords are vital to network security because their whole purpose is to control initial access to it. Even if the system administrator assigns individuals their usernames and passwords, users can and do often change them, so you need to make sure your network's users know the difference between a good password and a bad one and how to keep their passwords safe from theft.

I'll cover the important security issues related to user account and password management. Moreover, in the following sections, I'll discuss more secure methods of authentication (two-factor and multifactor authentication) and a widely used concept in the Enterprise networks: single sign-on.

Managing User Accounts

So, your first step in managing access to network resources is through user accounts and the rights you assign to the network resources. System administrators usually maintain user accounts on a daily basis, doing things like renaming accounts and setting the number of simultaneous connections. You can also specify where users can log in, how often, and when; plus, you can adjust how often their passwords expire and delimit when their accounts expire as well.

Disabling Accounts

This is important, so remember it—when a user leaves the organization, you have these three options:

- Leave the account in place.
- Delete the account.
- Disable the account.

The first option is not so good because if you just leave the account in place, anyone (including the user to whom it belonged) can still log in as that user if they know the password. This is clearly very bad security, but deleting the account presents its own set of problems too. If you delete an account and then create a new one, the numeric ID associated with that user (UID in UNIX, SID in Windows Servers) will be lost, and it's through this magic number that passwords and rights to network resources are associated with the user account. This can be a good thing—but if you create a new user account with the same name as the one you deleted, the identification number of the new account will be different from the old one, so none of its settings will be there for the new account.

This means that disabling an account until you've made a decision about what should happen to it is your best bet because you'll probably just want to rename the account when someone new is hired. When you disable an account, it still exists, but no one can use it to log in. Another good time to disable an account is when someone leaves for an extended period, like for maternity/paternity leave or other medical reasons, or goes on sabbatical.

Because it's really common for companies today to have contract and temporary employees, you need to know how to manage temporary accounts that will be used for only a short time and then disabled.

Managing these accounts is easy—you just set the account to expire on the employee's expected last day of work.

Setting Up Anonymous Accounts

Anonymous accounts allow only extremely limited access for a large number of users who all log in with the same username—for instance, *Anonymous* or *Guest*. These logins are frequently used to access FTP files; you gain access when you log in with the username *Anonymous* and enter your email address as the password.

 Sometimes people don't use their real email addresses. If you really want to know where a user is located on the Internet, use third-party software to verify IP addresses and Internet domain names.

It's obviously a very bad idea to use anonymous accounts for regular network access—you just can't track them. All Windows Server products from Windows NT on come with the anonymous account Guest disabled, and it's usually a good thing to leave it that way. When you want to enable that account, like at a public kiosk, make sure you carefully manage what it is able to access by implementing strict group policies.

Some web servers create an Internet user account to allow anonymous access to the website through which a user is allowed to access the web server over the network. The password is always blank, and you never see a request to log in to the server because it's done automatically. Without this kind of account, no one would be able to access your web pages.

 Do not rename the Internet user account or set a password because if you do so, the general public won't be able to view your website. If you want to secure documents, use a separate secure HTTP or Windows server.

Limiting Connections

There is a good reason to limit how many times a user can connect to the network. Users should normally be logged in to the network for one instance because they can only be in one place at a time. So if your system is telling you that someone is logged in from more than one place, it's probably because someone else is using their account. By limiting simultaneous connections to one, only a single user at a single workstation can gain access to the network using a specific user account. But there are times that some users need to log in multiple times to use certain applications or perform certain tasks, and you can allow that specific user to have multiple concurrent connections.

You may also want to limit the specific location from which a user logs in because most of the time, your users will be logging on to the network only from their own workstations. This makes sense, but this rule isn't usually enforced because sometimes users move around without taking their computers with them, or they log in at someone else's station to get their jobs done. So unless you require super tight security, imposing this rule can really complicate your job because it requires a lot of administration. Windows Server products can limit which station(s) a user is allowed to log in from, but they don't do so by default. Another Windows Server default feature is that average users aren't allowed to log in at the server console because they shouldn't be working directly on a server. They can do some serious damage accidentally!

Renaming the Maintenance Account

Network operating systems automatically give the network maintenance (or administration) account a default name. On Windows servers, it's (surprise) Administrator, and in UNIX it's Root. So it should be crystal clear that if you don't change this account name, bad guys already have half the information they need to break in to your network. The only thing they're missing is the password—yikes!

By all means, rename that account to something cool and creative that you'll remember but that would be really hard for someone to guess—and don't write it on a Post-it and stick it to the server. Here's a "do not use" list of names:

- Admin
- Administrator
- Analyst
- Audit
- Comptroller
- Controller
- Manager
- Root
- Super
- Superuser
- Supervisor

- Wizard
- Any variation on the above

Managing Passwords

Like any other aspect of network security, passwords must be managed, and doing that involves ensuring that all passwords for user accounts follow security guidelines so bad guys can't easily guess or crack them. You've also got to implement certain features of your network operating system to prevent unauthorized access.

Basically, a strong password is some combination of alphanumeric and special characters that's easy for you to remember but really hard for someone else to guess. Like server account names, they should never be written down on anything that is then put into your desk or stuck onto your computer. Unfortunately, this guideline is only followed in a perfect world. Users invariably try to make things easy on themselves by choosing passwords that are so simple to guess that they would have to be seriously mentally challenged not to be able to. Let's look at some characteristics of strong passwords.

Minimum Length

Strong passwords should be at least eight characters (the more, the merrier), but they shouldn't be any longer than 15 characters to make them easier to remember. You absolutely must specify a minimum length for passwords because a short password is easily cracked—after all, there are only so many combinations of three characters, right? The upper limit depends on the capabilities of your operating system and the ability of your users to remember complex passwords. Here's what I call "The Weak List" for passwords—never use them!

- The word *password* (not kidding—people actually do this!)
- Proper names
- Your pet's name
- Your spouse's name
- Your children's names
- Any word in the dictionary
- A license plate number
- Birth dates
- Anniversary dates
- Your username
- The word *server*
- Any text or label on the PC or monitor
- Your company's name
- Your occupation
- Your favorite color

- Any of the above with a leading number
- Any of the above with a trailing number
- Any of the above spelled backward

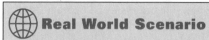

Real World Scenario

Security Audits

A great way to begin a basic security audit to get a feel for any potential threats to your network is to simply take a walk through the company's halls and offices. I've done this a lot, and it always pays off because invariably I happen upon some new and different way that people are trying to "beat the system" regarding security. This doesn't necessarily indicate that a given user is trying to cause damage on purpose; it's just that following the rules can be a little inconvenient—especially when it comes to adhering to strict password policies. Your average user just doesn't get how important their role is in maintaining the security of the network (maybe even their job security as well) by sticking to the network's security policy, so you have to make sure they do.

Think about it. If you can easily discover user passwords just by taking a little tour of the premises, so can a bad guy, and once someone has a username and a password, it's pretty easy to hack into resources. I wasn't kidding about people slapping sticky notes with their usernames and/or passwords right on their monitors—this happens a lot more than you would think. Some users, thinking they're actually being really careful, glue them to the back of their keyboards instead, but you don't have to be James Bond to think about looking there either, right? People wouldn't think of leaving their cars unlocked with the windows down and the keys in the ignition, but that's exactly what they're doing by leaving sensitive info anywhere on or near their workstations.

Even though it might not make you Mr. or Ms. Popularity when you search workspaces or even inside desks for notes with interesting or odd words written on them, do it anyway. People will try to hide these goodies anywhere. Or sometimes, not so much. I kid you not—I had a user who actually wrote his password on the border of his monitor with a Sharpie, and when his password expired, he just crossed it off and wrote the new one underneath it. Sheer genius! But my personal favorite was when I glanced at this one guy's keyboard and noticed that some of the letter keys had numbers written on them. All you had to do was follow the numbers that (surprise!) led straight to his password. Oh sure—he'd followed policy to the, ahem, letter by choosing random letters and numbers, but a lot of good that did—he had to draw himself a little map in plain sight on his keyboard to remember the password.

So, like it or not, you have to walk your beat to find out if users are managing their accounts properly. If you find someone doing things the right way, praise them for it openly. If not, it's time for more training—or maybe worse, termination.

There are more, but you get the idea, and these really are the most commonly used brainless passwords.

Using Characters to Make a Strong Password

The good news is that solid passwords don't have to be in ancient Mayan to be hard to crack. They just need to include a combination of numbers, letters, and special characters—that's it. Special characters aren't letters or numbers, but symbols like $ % ^ # @). Here's an example of a strong password: tqbf4#jotld. Looks like gibberish; but remember that famous sentence, "The quick brown fox jumped over the lazy dog"? Well, this particular password uses the first letter of each word in that sentence with a 4# thrown in the middle of it. Sweet—solid and easy to remember. You can do this with favorite quotes, song lyrics, and so on, with a couple of numbers and symbols stuck in the middle. Just make sure you don't sing the song or quote Shakespeare every time you log in!

If you want to test the strength of passwords to make sure they're nice and tight, you can use auditing tools like crack programs that try to guess passwords. Clearly, if that program has a really tough time or even fails to crack the password, you have a good one. By the way, don't just use a regular word preceded by or ending with a special character because good crack programs strip off the leading and trailing characters during decryption attempts.

Password-Management Features

All network operating systems include built-in features for managing passwords to help ensure that your system remains secure and that passwords cannot be easily hacked with crack programs. These features usually include automatic account lockouts and password expiration.

Automatic Account Lockouts

Hackers, and even people who forget their passwords, usually try to log in by guessing passwords. This is why most network operating systems will lock you out after a few unsuccessful attempts. Some will even disable the account. Once that happens, the user won't be able to log in to that account even if they enter the correct password. This feature prevents a potential hacker from running an automated script to crack account passwords by continuously attempting to log in using different character combinations.

When an account is on lockdown, guards—I mean, network staff—will have to unlock the account if the network operating system doesn't unlock it after a preset period. In any high-security network, it's a good idea to require an administrator to manually unlock every locked account instead of setting the network operating system to do it automatically. This way, the administrator will be sure to know about any possible security breaches.

WARNING   Be careful not to lock yourself out. With many network operating systems, only administrators can reset passwords, so if you happen to be the administrator and you lock yourself out, only another administrator can unlock your account. Embarrassing, yes, but what if you're the only administrator? You're in trouble then, because even though many network operating system vendors do have solutions to this humiliating little problem, the cost of those solutions isn't going to be cheap!

It's good to know that Windows-based servers allow you to configure accounts to be locked out after a number of bad login attempts, but the default Administrator account is exempt from this happening. This might sound convenient for you, but it's actually a security risk. You should definitely rename this account, and it's also a good idea not to use it for day-to-day administration. Create a new administrator account (with a different name, of course), and use it for administrative purposes instead.

Password Expiration and Password Histories

Unlike a good wine, even really good passwords don't age well over time; they just become more likely to be cracked. This is why it's good to set passwords so that they expire after a specific amount of time. Most organizations set up passwords to expire every 30 to 45 days, after which the network's users all must reset their passwords either immediately or during a preset grace period. The grace period is usually limited to a specific number of login attempts, or it may allow a couple of days.

 By default, each network operating system delimits a specific password-expiration period that bad guys usually know about. So make sure you reset that time period to something other than the default, in accordance with your security policy.

Older network operating systems allowed users to reset their passwords back to their original form after using an intermediary password for a while, but today's network operating systems prevent this by employing password histories that consist of a record of the past several passwords used by a specific user. This record prevents users from using any password that's stored in the password history. If they try, the password will fail, and the operating system will then request a password change. What this means to you, the system administrator, is that if your security policy dictates that passwords be reset every two weeks, you should make sure your password history can hold at least 20 passwords. This would prevent a user from reusing a password until the password is at least 10 months old (two changes per month). They'll forget that password by then!

By the way, your more experienced users know about this history feature, and because coming up with a really tight password takes a little thought, when savvy users create ones they really like, they may have a hard time letting go. Maybe they just want to avoid the hassle of creating a tight new password and remembering it, so they'll try to find ways to get out of doing that by getting around the password-history feature. For instance, I knew one guy who actually admitted that he just changed his password as many times as it took to defeat the history log and then changed it one last time to his beloved, original password—all of which took him only about five minutes to accomplish.

You can force users to change their passwords to ones that are unique because the latest operating systems require unique passwords and can, depending on the network operating system, store more than 20 passwords. This feature makes it a whole lot harder to revert to any previous passwords. But it's still possible for users to beat the system, so don't rely completely on it.

Single Sign-On

In today's modern enterprises, users can be overwhelmed by the number of points in the network where they may be challenged to identify themselves. Most users have to log onto the domain to have network access at all, and then there may be company websites that require an authentication process to access databases, SharePoint sites, secured drives, personal folders, and on and on!

When users must remember multiple passwords, as the number increases, they begin to resort to unsafe security practices such as writing passwords on sticky notes, hiding passwords in their drawers, and even sharing them with a coworkers. All of these practices undermine the security of the network.

Single sign-on addresses this problem. With single sign-on, when the users logs into the domain, the domain controller issues them an access token. This access token contains a list of all the resources (which can include folders, drives, websites, databases, and so on) to which they should have access. As a result, any time the user accesses a resource, the token is verified behind the scenes, and the users never needs to provide another password!

Multifactor Authentication

Multifactor authentication is designed to add an additional level of security to the authentication process by verifying more than one characteristic of a user before allowing access to a resource. Users can be identified in one of three ways:

- By something they know (password)
- By something they are (retinas, fingerprint, facial recognition)
- By something they possess (smart card)

Two-factor authentication is when two of the above factors are being tested while multifactor is when more than two of the above factors are being tested. An example of two-factor authentication would be requiring both a smart card and a PIN to log onto the network. The possession of either by itself would not be sufficient to authenticate. This protects against the loss and theft of the card as well as the loss of the password. An example of multifactor would be when three items are required such as a smart card, a PIN and a username and password.

This process can get as involved as the security requires. In an extremely high-security situation, you might require a smart card, a password, a retina scan, and a fingerprint scan. The trade-off to all the increased security is an inconvenient authentication process for the user and the high cost of biometric authentication devices.

User-Authentication Methods

There are a number of authentication systems in use today, but I'm going to focus on the ones you're likely to be confronted with on the Network+ exam.

Public Key Infrastructure (PKI)

Public Key Infrastructure (PKI) is a system that links users to public keys and verifies the user's identity by using a *certificate authority (CA)*. Think of a CA as an online notary public—an organization that's responsible for validating user IDs and issuing unique identifiers to confirmed individuals to certify that their identity can really be trusted. Figure 13.10 shows how the CA process works in relation to two users.

PKI allows people to communicate with each other with confidence that they're talking to who they think they are talking to. It is used to establish confidentiality and to ensure message integrity without knowing anything about the other party prior to the conversation. It's also used to verify the digital signature of a private key's owner.

Public-key encryption operates through asymmetric cryptography, meaning that a different key is used to encrypt and decrypt the message, respectively. Symmetric cryptography uses the same key to encrypt and decrypt, so it's a lot less secure. Here's how it works. If I sent you a message using PKI, I'd use your public key to encrypt the message. When you received the message, you would use your private key, which is theoretically the only thing that can be used to decrypt the message back into something readable by humans. If a digital signature was required, you would sign the document with your private key, and anyone with access to your public key would be able to verify that the signature was truly yours. So clearly, you should be the only one who has access to your private key. Figure 13.11 illustrates what I just described.

FIGURE 13.10   The certificate authority process

This type of authentication is used a lot in websites that perform transactions. You've probably experienced shopping online and having an error message pop up, notifying you that a certain site's certificate or key has expired and asking if you want to proceed with the transaction. If you do, it's time to rethink things—you're probably way too trusting. Just say no!

FIGURE 13.11   PKI in action

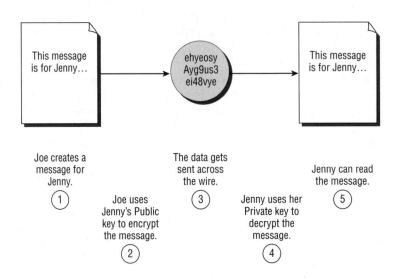

Public Key Encryption at Work

Joe creates a
message for
Jenny.
①

Joe uses
Jenny's Public
key to encrypt
the message.
②

The data gets
sent across
the wire.
③

Jenny uses her
Private key to
decrypt the
message.
④

Jenny can read
the message.
⑤

Kerberos

Kerberos, created at MIT, isn't just a protocol, it's an entire security system that establishes a user's identity when they first log on to a system that's running it. It employs strong encryption for all transactions and communication, and it's readily available. The source code for Kerberos can be freely downloaded from lots of places on the Internet.

Kerberos works by issuing tickets to users who log in, kind of like going to an amusement park—as long as you have your ticket to ride, you're good to go. Even though the tickets expire quickly, they're automatically refreshed as long as you remain logged in. Because of this refresh feature, all systems participating in a Kerberos domain must have synchronized clocks. This synchronicity is a bit complicated to set up. The real negative hits happen if you have only one Kerberos authentication server—if it goes down, no one can log in to the network. So when running Kerberos, having redundant servers is clearly vital. You should also know that because all users' secret keys are stored in one centralized database, if that's compromised, you have a security tsunami on your hands. Luckily these keys are stored in an encrypted state. Figure 13.12 shows Kerberos in action.

Authentication, Authorization, and Accounting (AAA)

In computer security speak, *AAA* (triple A, like the auto club) refers to authentication, authorization, and accounting. *AAAA* is a more robust version that adds auditing into the mix. AAA and AAAA aren't really protocols; instead, they're systematized, conceptual models for managing network security through one central location. Two common implementations of AAA are RADIUS and TACACS+.

FIGURE 13.12 The Kerberos authentication process

❶ Request for ticket granting ticket (TGT)	❹ Application ticket returned by ticket-granting service
❷ TGT returned by authentication service	❺ Request for service (authenticated with application ticket)
❸ Request for application ticket (authenticated with TGT)	

RADIUS

Although its name implies it, the *Remote Authentication Dial In User Service (RADIUS)* is not a dial-up server. Like pretty much everything else, it originated that way, but it's evolved into more of a verification service. Today, RADIUS is an authentication and accounting service that's used for verifying users over various types of links, including dial-up. Many ISPs use a RADIUS server to store the usernames and passwords of their clients in a central spot through which connections are configured to pass authentication requests. RADIUS servers are client-server-based authentication and encryption services maintaining user profiles in a central database.

RADIUS is also used in firewalls. Purposed this way, when a user wants to access a particular TCP/IP port, they must provide a username and a password. The firewall then contacts the RADIUS server to verify the credentials given. If successful, the user is granted access to that port.

RADIUS is an authentication server that allows for domain-level authentication on both wired and wireless networks.

TACACS+

The *Terminal Access Controller Access-Control System Plus (TACACS+)* protocol is also an AAA method and an alternative to RADIUS. Like RADIUS, it is capable of performing authentication on behalf of multiple wireless APs, RAS servers, or even LAN switches that are 802.1x capable. Based on its name, you would think it's an extension of the TACACS protocol (and in some ways it is), but the two definitely are not compatible.

Here are two major differences between TACACS+ and RADIUS:

- RADIUS combines user authentication and authorization into one profile, but TACACS+ separates the two.
- TACACS+ utilizes the connection-based TCP protocol, but RADIUS uses UDP instead.

Even though both are commonly used today, because of these two reasons TACACS+ is considered more stable and secure than RADIUS.

Figure 13.13 shows how TACACS+ works.

FIGURE 13.13   TACACS+ login and logout sequence

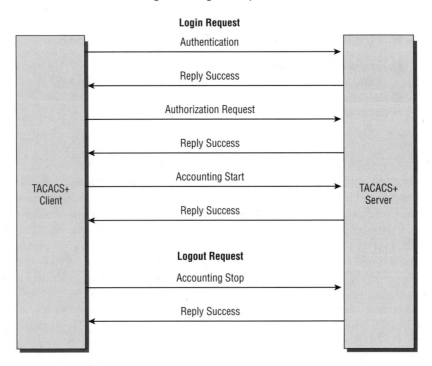

Okay—just to clarify things, in the IT world, *accounting* has nothing to do with money. Here's what I mean: When a TACACS+ session is closed, the information in the following list is logged, or accounted for. This isn't a complete list; it's just meant to give you an idea of the type of accounting information that TACACS+ gathers:

- Connection start time and stop time
- The number of bytes sent and received by the user
- The number of packets sent and received by the user
- The reason for the disconnection

The only time the accounting feature has anything to do with money is if your service provider is charging you based on the amount of time you've spent logged in or for the amount of data sent and received.

Network Access Control (NAC)

Network Access Control (NAC) is a method of securing network hosts before they're allowed to access the network. The most common implications for NAC are in wireless networking, where nodes are often added to and removed from the network freely. One of the most common forms of NAC is IEEE 802.1x.

Even the Institute of Electrical and Electronics Engineers (IEEE) recognizes the potential security holes in wireless networking, so it came up with the *IEEE 802.1x* standard as a way to authenticate wireless users. 802.1x is an open framework that's designed to support multiple authentication schemes. Before a client, called a *supplicant* in 802.1x-speak, can communicate on a wireless network, it asks the access point, or *authenticator*, for permission to join and then provides its credentials. The access point passes those credentials to a centralized authentication server that sends back an accept message to the access point if the authentication is accepted. Only then will the access point allow a user to connect to the wireless network.

Challenge Handshake Authentication Protocol (CHAP)

The *Challenge Handshake Authentication Protocol (CHAP)* is a secure authentication protocol because with CHAP, the username and password never cross the wire. Instead, both the client and server are configured with the same text phrase that's known as a *shared secret*. When a client sends out an authentication request, the server responds by sending a random value called a *nonce* plus an ID value back to the client. The client takes these two strings, sequences them with the shared secret, and then generates a one-way hash value using the Message-Digest algorithm 5 (MD5) encryption algorithm. This hash value is transmitted back to the server, which performs the same algorithm using the same values and shared secret. The server basically compares the hash value that it's received from the client with the hash value it has calculated, and if they match, the client gets to be authenticated. I know this sounds pretty complicated, so let me give you a visual demonstration of how CHAP works in Figure 13.14.

CHAP has replaced the older Password Authentication Protocol (PAP) because PAP sends usernames and passwords in clear text and CHAP does not.

MS-CHAP

Microsoft has its own variation of CHAP known as *Microsoft Challenge Handshake Authentication Protocol (MS-CHAP)*. It works basically the same way as CHAP, except that unlike CHAP, which requires the shared secret to be stored locally in clear text, MS-CHAP encrypts the secret locally. And whereas CHAP provides authentication of the client by the server only, MS-CHAP version 2 is capable of mutual authentication so that the client can be sure the server is legitimate as well. Also, the encryption method used to generate the one-way hash in MS-CHAP is DES. Finally, and predictably, MS-CHAP doesn't work on Linux or other platforms—it's a Windows proprietary protocol.

FIGURE 13.14   CHAP authentication process

Extensible Authentication Protocol (EAP)

Extensible Authentication Protocol (EAP) is an extension to PPP that provides a host of additional authentication methods for remote-access clients. Some examples include smart cards, certificates, Kerberos, and biometric schemes like retinal scans and fingerprint and voice recognition. Although EAP itself doesn't allow for mutual authentication, enhanced forms of the protocol do. For example, EAP-TLS and EAP-TTLS, a tunneled version of EAP-TLS, create a secure tunnel through which password-based versions like EAP-MD5 can run.

Summary

In this chapter, you learned about the two most basic security concerns: security filtering and user authentication. First, we talked about how to allow remote computers to join your network and how to specify the way traffic leaves your network using access control lists.

Then, you learned about various tunneling and encryption protocols like SSL, VPN, L2TP, PPTP, and IPSEC.

Moving on, we examined several of the ways used today to remotely access networks, including RAS, RDP, PPP, PPPoE, and ICA.

We wrapped things up by discussing solid user-account and password-management policies and why those policies are essential to maintaining tight security on your network. Finally, you learned about authentication methods like PKI, Kerberos, RADIUS, TACACS+, 802.1x, CHAP, MS-CHAP, and EAP—good stuff!

Exam Essentials

Know two ways you can filter traffic using an access control list.   Access control lists can filter traffic by IP address or MAC address.

Know which protocols can be used for tunneling and encryption of data.   Tunneling and encryption protocols include SSL, VPN, L2TP, PPTP, and IPSec.

Know which services allow you to remotely access computers across a network.   RAS, RDP, PPP, PPPoE, and ICA are remote-access services and protocols.

Know different user-authentication protocols used on networks.   User-authentication protocols and systems include PKI, Kerberos, RADIUS, TACACS+, 802.1x, CHAP, MS-CHAP, and EAP.

Written Lab

In this section, write the answers to the following authentication and access-control questions:

1. What two types of addresses can access control lists filter?

2. Which encryption protocol works with both IPv4 and IPv6?

3. Which encryption protocol or standard allows you to create a private network on an intranet?

4. Which user-authentication method uses a public key and private key pair?

5. In an authentication system that uses private and public keys, who should have access to the private key?

6. Which authentication method relies on tickets to grant access to resources?

7. In computer security, what does AAA stand for?

8. Which network access security method is commonly used in wireless networks?

9. Which user-authentication method is available only in an all-Windows environment?

10. Which user-authentication method utilizes the TCP protocol?

You can find the answers in Appendix B.

Review Questions

You can find the answers to the review questions in Appendix A.

1. To reduce the possibility of security break-ins from unauthorized users, which should be implemented?

   A. Packet sniffers

   B. Firewall

   C. Port scanners

   D. Intrusion detection system

2. What is the main difference between a private network and a public network?

   A. In a private network, everyone has access; in a public network, only authorized users have access.

   B. In a private network, only authorized users have access; in a public network, only authorized users have access.

   C. In a private network, only authorized users have access; in a public network, everyone that is connected has access.

   D. In a private network, everyone has access; in a public network, only the first 100 people have access.

3. You have a remote user who can connect to the Internet but not to the office via their VPN client. After determining the problem, which should be your next step?

   A. Have the client reboot their host.

   B. Make sure the user has the correct VPN address and password.

   C. Have the client reinstall their VPN software.

   D. Reboot the router at the corporate office.

4. Which IP address should you deny into your internetwork?

   A. 126.10.10.0/8

   B. 168.0.0.0/8

   C. 128.0.0.0/8

   D. 127.0.0.0/8

5. Which of the following is a tunneling protocol?

   A. Layer 2 Tunneling Protocol (L2TP)

   B. Internet Protocol Security (IPSec)

   C. Secure Sockets Layer (SSL)

   D. All of the above

6. Which tunneling protocol is based on RSA public-key encryption?

   A. SSL

   B. L2TP

   C. IPSec

   D. SSL VPN

7. What is the minimum number of characters you should use when creating a secure password?

   A. 6

   B. 7

   C. 8

   D. 15

8. Which layer of the OSI model does IPSec operate in?

   A. Physical

   B. Network

   C. Transport

   D. Application

9. Which protocol works in both the transport mode and tunneling mode?

   A. SSL

   B. L2TP

   C. PPTP

   D. IPSec

10. Companies that want to ensure that their data is secure during transit should use which of the following?

   A. Firewalls

   B. Encryption

   C. Data accounting

   D. Routing table

11. Which network utilities do not have the ability to encrypt passwords? (Select two.)

   A. FTP

   B. SSH

   C. Telnet

   D. SCP

12. To encode or read an encrypted message, what tool is necessary?

A. Routing table

B. Internet access

C. Encryption key

D. Email address

13. Which if the following is *not* an enhancement provided by TLS version1.2?

A. Improvements in the operation of the MD5-SHA-1 hashing function

B. Enhanced support for the Advanced Encryption Standard (AES)

C. Expansion of the use of TLS to VPNs

D. More flexibility in the choice of hashing and encryption algorithm

14. Which of the following is not a type of public-key encryption?

A. Diffie-Hellman algorithm

B. RSA Data Security

C. Pretty Good Privacy (PGP)

D. DES

15. Which of the following VPN protocols runs over port 1723, allows encryption to be done at the data level, and allows secure access?

A. RAS

B. Radius

C. PPPoE

D. PPTP

16. At which stage of PPPoE are the MAC addresses of each of the endpoints of the connection given to each other so that a PPP connection can be made?

A. Session

B. Discovery

C. Transport

D. Final

17. When utilizing multifactor authentication, which of the following is an example of verifying something you are?

A. Smart card

B. Password

C. Fingerprint

D. Certificate

18. Which of the following authentication methods allows for domain authentication on both wired and wireless networks?

   A. RADIUS

   B. TACACS+

   C. PKI

   D. RDP

19. Which user-client-server authentication software system combines user authentication and authorization into one central database and maintains user profiles?

   A. RADIUS

   B. TACACS+

   C. Kerberos

   D. PKI

20. Which of the following is not a Network Access Control method?

   A. CHAP

   B. 802.1x

   C. EAP

   D. ICA

Chapter 14

Network Threats and Mitigation

THE FOLLOWING COMPTIA NETWORK+ EXAM OBJECTIVES ARE COVERED IN THIS CHAPTER:

✓ **5.4 Explain common threats, vulnerabilities, and mitigation techniques.**

- ▪ Wireless:
    - ▪ War driving
    - ▪ War chalking
    - ▪ WEP cracking
    - ▪ WPA cracking
    - ▪ Evil twin
    - ▪ Rogue access point
- ▪ Attacks:
    - ▪ DoS
    - ▪ DDoS
    - ▪ Man in the middle
    - ▪ Social engineering
    - ▪ Virus
    - ▪ Worms
    - ▪ Buffer overflow
    - ▪ Packet sniffing
    - ▪ FTP bounce
    - ▪ Smurf
- ▪ Mitigation techniques:
    - ▪ Training and awareness
    - ▪ Patch management
    - ▪ Policies and procedures
    - ▪ Incident response

It's true…You're not paranoid if they really *are* out to get you. Although "they" probably aren't after you, personally, your network—no matter the size—is seriously vulnerable, so it's wise to be very concerned about keeping it secure. Unfortunately, it's also true that no matter how secure you think your network is, it's a good bet that there are still some very real threats out there that could breach its security and totally cripple your infrastructure!

I'm not trying to scare you; it's just that networks, by their very nature, are not secure environments. Think about it—the whole point of a having a network is to make resources available to people who aren't at the same physical location as the network's resources. Because of this, it follows that you've got to open access to those resources to users you may not be able to identify. One network administrator I know referred to a server running a much-maligned network operating system as "a perfectly secure server until you install the NIC." You can see the dilemma here, right?

Okay, with all this doom and gloom, what's a network administrator to do? Well, the first line of defense is to know about the types of threats out there because you can't do anything to protect yourself from something you don't know about. But once you understand the threats, you can then begin to design defenses to combat bad guys lurking in the depths of cyberspace just waiting for an opportunity to strike.

I'm going to introduce you to some of the more common security threats and teach you about the ways to mitigate them. I'll be honest—the information I'll be giving you in this chapter is definitely not exhaustive. Securing computers and networks is a huge task and there are literally hundreds of books on this subject alone. If you want to learn more about security on a much deeper level (and get another powerful certification in the process), get your hands on the *CompTIA Security+ Deluxe Study Guide,* by Emmett Dulaney (Sybex, 2008).

 To find up-to-the-minute updates for this chapter, please see www.lammle.com/forum or the book's web site at www.sybex.com/go/netplus2e.

Recognizing Security Threats

I'm not trying to freak you out, but I'm not exaggerating the dangers to your network security either. Here's an example: Recently, I hooked up a friend's computer to a high-speed network connection from his phone company. He had antivirus software but no personal firewall in place yet, and before I could get that firewall set up (which usually takes about 10 minutes), 15 virus alerts popped up!

Although viruses are common threats that we hear about all the time, there are many other nasty things out there as well. Bad guys who create threats to a network generally have one of two purposes in mind: destruction or reconnaissance. They're seeking to destroy data or deny access, and maybe even nick information that you definitely don't want them to have. Some types of attacks can accomplish both, but they're usually combinations of simpler forms. In the following sections, we'll look at several common approaches that bad guys use to breach the security of our precious networks.

Denial of Service

A *denial of service (DoS) attack* does exactly what it sounds like it would do—it prevents users from accessing the network and/or its resources. Today, DoS attacks are commonly launched against a major company's intranet and especially its websites. "Joe the Hacker" (formerly a plumber) thinks that if he can make a mess of, say, Microsoft's or Amazon's website, he's done that company some serious damage, and you know what? He's right!

Even though DoS attacks are nasty, strangely, hackers don't respect other hackers who execute them because they're really easy to deploy. It's true—even a pesky little 10-year-old can execute one and bring you to your knees. (That's just wrong!) This means that "real" bad guys have no respect for someone who uses DoS attacks, and they usually employ much more sophisticated methods of wreaking havoc on you instead. I guess it comes down to that "honor among thieves" thing. Still, know that even though a DoS-type attack won't gain the guilty party any esteemed status among "real" hackers, it's still not exactly a day at the beach to deal with.

Worse, DoS attacks come in a variety of flavors. Let's talk about some of them now.

The Ping of Death

Ping is primarily used to see whether a computer is responding to IP requests. Usually, when you ping a remote host, what you're really doing is sending four normal-sized Internet Control Message Protocol (ICMP) packets to the remote host to see if it's available. But during a *Ping of Death* attack, a humongous ICMP packet is sent to the remote host victim, totally flooding the victim's buffer and causing the system to reboot or helplessly hang there, drowning. It's good to know that patches are available for most operating systems to prevent a Ping of Death attack from working.

Smurf

Smurfs are happy little blue creatures that like to sing and dance, but a *Smurf attack* is far more nefarious. It's a version of a DoS attack that floods its victim with spoofed broadcast ping messages. I'll talk about spoofing in more detail later; for now, understand that it basically involves stealing someone else's IP address.

Here's how it works: The bad guy spoofs the intended victim's IP address and then sends a large number of pings (IP echo requests) to IP broadcast addresses. The receiving router responds by delivering the broadcast to all hosts in the subnet, and all the hosts respond with an IP echo reply—all of them at the same time. On a network with hundreds of hosts, this results in major network gridlock because all the machines are kept busy responding to each echo request. The situation is even worse if the routers have not been configured to keep these types of broadcasts confined to the local subnet. (Which thankfully they are by default!) Figure 14.1 shows a Smurf attack in process.

FIGURE 14.1 Smurf attack in progress

Fortunately, Smurf attacks aren't very common anymore because most routers are configured in a way that prevents them from forwarding broadcast packets to other networks. Plus, it's really easy to configure routers and hosts so they won't respond to ping requests directed toward broadcast addresses.

SYN Flood

A *SYN flood* is also a DoS attack that inundates the receiving machine with lots of packets that cause the victim to waste resources by holding connections open. In normal communications, a workstation that wants to open a Transmission Control Protocol/Internet Protocol (TCP/IP) communication with a server sends a TCP/IP packet with the SYN flag set to 1. The server automatically responds to the request, indicating that it's ready to start communicating with a SYN/ACK. In the SYN flood, the attacker send a SYN, the victim sends back a SYN/ACK, and the attacker leaves the victim waiting for the final ACK. While the server is waiting for the response, a small part of memory is reserved for it. As the SYNs continue to arrive, memory is gradually consumed.

Figure 14.2 shows an example of a simple DoS/SYN flood attack.

You can see that the preyed-upon machine can't respond to any other requests because its buffers are already overloaded, and it therefore rejects all packets requesting connections, even valid ones, which is the idea behind the attack. The good news is that patches to help guard against this type of attack are available for the various network operating systems today.

FIGURE 14.2   A sample DoS/SYN flood attack

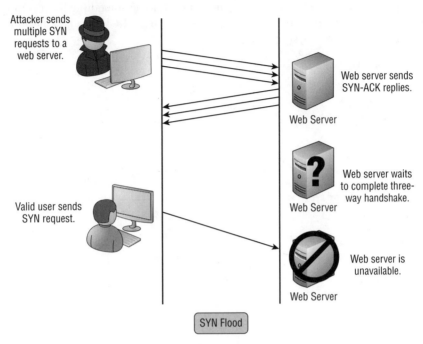

Tribe Flood Network and Tribe Flood Network 2000

These nasty assaults are a bit more complex because they initiate synchronized DoS attacks from multiple sources and can target multiple devices. Tribe Flood Network (TFN) and Tribe Flood Network 2000 (TFN2K) are called *distributed denial of service (DDos) attacks* and also make use of IP spoofing. Figure 14.3 shows what a DDos attack would look like.

Stacheldraht

This is actually a mélange of techniques that translates from the German word for *barbed wire*. It basically incorporates TFN and adds a dash of encryption to the mix. The nightmare begins with a huge invasion at the root level, followed with a DoS attack finale.

Viruses

Viruses with catchy names like Chernobyl, Michelangelo, Melissa, I Love You, and Love Bug are probably the best-known threats to your computer's security because they get a lot of media coverage as they proliferate and cause tons of damage to legions of people. In their simplest form, viruses are basically little programs that cause a variety of very bad things to happen on your computer, ranging from merely annoying to totally devastating. They can display a message, delete files, or even send out huge amounts of meaningless data over a network to block legitimate messages. A key trait of viruses is that they can't replicate themselves to other computers or systems without a user doing something like opening an executable attachment in an email to propagate them. Figure 14.4 shows how fast a virus can spread through an email system.

FIGURE 14.3 Distributed denial of service attack

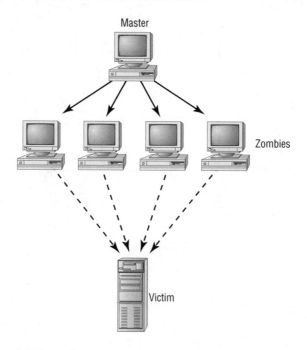

There are several different kinds of viruses, but the most popular ones are file viruses, macro (data file) viruses, and boot-sector viruses. Each type differs slightly in the way it works and how it infects your system. Predictably, many viruses attack popular applications like Microsoft Word, Excel, and PowerPoint because those programs are easy to use, so it's easy to create a virus for them. Unlike with DoS attacks, writing a unique virus is considered a programming challenge, so the scoundrel who's able to come up with it not only gains respect from the hacking community but also gets to bask in the glow of the media frenzy that results from their creation and relish their 15 minutes of fame. This is also a big reason why viruses are becoming more and more complex and harder to eliminate.

File Viruses

A *file virus* attacks executable application and system program files like those with filenames ending in .com, .exe, and .dll. These viruses do their damage by replacing some or all of the target program's code with their own. Only when the compromised file is executed can the virus do its dirty work. First, it loads itself into memory and waits to infect other executables, propagating its destructive effects throughout a system or network. A couple of well-known file viruses are Jerusalem and Nimda, the latter of which is actually an Internet worm that infects common Windows files and other files with filename extensions like .html, .htm, and .asp.

Don't fall into the trap of thinking that just because you have a Mac, you don't need to worry about viruses. It's a common misconception that Mac operating systems are immune to viruses, but they're not. Today's Macs are really BSD UNIX machines with a couple of proprietary programs running on top that provide users with a slick interface. And although it's true that more sophisticated programming skills are required to write viruses for Mac, BSD UNIX, and Linux operating systems than for DOS-based operating systems like Windows, all operating systems are vulnerable to attacks. True, it's a lot easier for a bad guy to write malicious code for Windows machines, but the real reason few programmers spend their time creating viruses for Sun workstations and Macs is that there aren't nearly as many people using them. On the other hand, Windows machines are everywhere, so viruses written for them will clearly infect multitudes, giving bad guys who want to infect as many computers as possible a lot more bang for their evil programming buck!

FIGURE 14.4   An email virus spreading rapidly

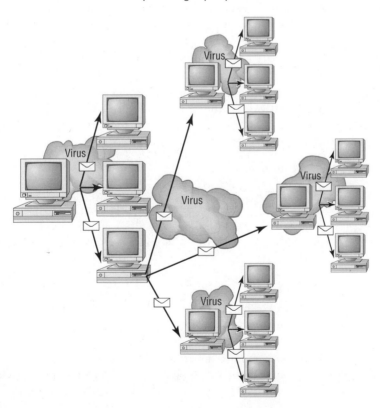

Macro Viruses

A macro is basically a script of commonly enacted commands used to automatically carry out tasks without requiring a user to initiate them. Some popular programs even give you the option of creating your own, personal scripts to perform tasks you do repeatedly in a single step instead of having to enter the individual commands one by one.

Similar to this, a *macro virus* uses something known as the Visual Basic macro-scripting language to perform nasty things in data files created with programs like those in the Microsoft Office Suite. Because macros are so easy to write, they're really common and usually fairly harmless, but they can be super annoying! People frequently find them infecting the files they're working on in Microsoft Word and PowerPoint. Suddenly you can't save the file even though the Save function is working, or you can't open a new document, only a template. As I said, these viruses won't crash your system, but they can ruin your day. Cap and Cap A are examples of macro viruses.

Boot-Sector Viruses

Boot-sector viruses work their way into the master boot record that's essentially the ground-zero sector on your hard disk where applications aren't supposed to live. When a computer boots up, it checks this area to find a pointer for its operating system. Boot-sector viruses overwrite your boot sector, making it appear as if there's no pointer to your operating system. You know you've got this type of virus when you power up the computer and get a Missing Operating System or Hard Disk Not Found error message. Monkey B, Michelangelo, Stoned, and Stealth Boot are a few examples of boot-sector viruses.

Multipartite Viruses

A multipartite virus is one that affects both the boot sector and files on your computer, making such a virus particularly dangerous and exasperatingly difficult to remove. Figure 14.5 gives you an idea of how a multipartite virus works. You can see that it is attacking the boot sector, memory, and the disk at once.

FIGURE 14.5   Multipartite virus

Anthrax and Tequila are both multipartite viruses. These viruses are so nasty that you might end up reformatting your computer if you get one. Although the Anthrax virus was more of a hoax then a real virus, what is really interesting about the Tequila virus is that it does nothing until the next reboot—it was no hoax!

Although many software companies can handle these, the best way to save your computer from a complete overhaul is to make sure you do not get a virus in the first place by using a good virus scan as well as Windows Defender (new on Vista and Server 2008).

Most of the viruses in one of these categories infect your system through something known as a *Trojan horse*. Troy was successfully invaded by troops hidden inside a giant horse; a Trojan virus hides within other programs and is launched when the program it's lurking in starts up.

Often viruses come as attachments to emails with double filename extensions to hide the true extension. DMSETUP.EXE and LOVE-LETTER-FOR-YOU .TXT.VBS are examples. Displaying filename extensions for known file types can help spot naming tricks like these, but they make up only a short list of the viruses out there. For a more complete inventory, see your antivirus software manufacturer's website.

Worms

Functionally, or not so much if your computer happens to have been infected with one, *worms* are a lot like viruses—only worse because they're much harder to stop. Worms can actively replicate without requiring you to do anything like open an infected file. Plus they can activate, propagate, and destroy all by themselves!

Buffer Overflow

When programs execute, they write commands into memory or to a *buffer*. Well-written programs allow a certain location and/or amount of memory space for these commands to execute. If a hacker is able to inject a command that overflows the amount of memory allocated and the command is able to execute with the proper security privileges, the hacker could execute commands that would not normally be allowed. He may be able to take control of the machine and create havoc.

A number of well-known exploits such as the Code Red worm employed buffer overflows to create their mayhem. The way to prevent buffer overflows is to include input validation into programs to mitigate the possibility of them occurring.

Wireless Threats

The proliferation of wireless communication has introduced a number of security challenges that are unique to the wireless environment. Some of these threats even take advantage of the security measures that have been created to protect wireless. Wireless threats such as WEP and WPA cracking (discussed in the following sections) remind us that network attackers never stop evolving their methods and that constant review and adaptation of security measures are required to maintain security in the network.

War Driving

War driving is one of the oldest wireless threats and perhaps one of the easiest to discourage (although you can't defeat it if the hacker is determined). The attacker simply drives around with a high-powered antenna connected to a wireless laptop scanning for networks. These networks will be listed by network name (SSID) in the wireless client software and, depending on the software, will also display the channel and security measures in use.

If the network is not secured, the attacker can connect to it. This is not just a matter of stealing bandwidth for Internet access. Once connected, the attacker may be able to proceed on into your wired network as well. They can then attempt other attacks, such as port scanning and peer-to-peer attacks. The point is that they have completed the first step in the hacking process, which is *penetration*.

War driving cannot be entirely prevented, but you can make it harder for an attacker. One of the simplest things you can do is limit the transmission power on the AP such that the signal does not go any further than the required! Additionally, if you set the access point to not broadcast the SSID, the name of the network will not appear in the display when they scan for networks. This means that to connect, they will have to know the SSID and create a wireless profile specifying it.

If an attacker is determined, however, they can learn the SSID by using a wireless protocol analyzer or sniffer to capture the raw packets. This is something you *cannot prevent* without turning off the AP. When you set the AP to not broadcast the SSID, it will remove the SSID from packets called *beacons* (these are the packets that populate the display when you scan for networks), but it will still be present in many other packet types.

In most cases, hiding the SSID will be sufficient because if an attacker doesn't see your network when scanning, they probably won't be motivated to use the sniffer.

War Chalking

War chalking is really just an extension of war driving. The hacker simply writes the SSID and security employed on the sidewalk or wall somewhere near your facility, sort of like advertising "here's a wireless network" to anyone who recognizes that code. Most of this type of activity has moved online where websites have sprung up that allow hackers to post and share these networks on maps indicating their location.

WEP Cracking

Wired Equivalent Privacy (WEP) is a security protocol created in the early years of 802.11 development that was designed to both authenticate users and encrypt the wireless data they transmitted. It uses the RC4 algorithm in the encryption process. Soon after its adoption as a security measure, it was discovered that due to a weakness in the way the algorithm was employed, programs that became widely available on the Internet could be used to crack the WEP key. Once the key was known, it could be used to decrypt the data. Because of this, WEP is no longer considered to be a sufficient security mechanism in any situation where the data is sensitive.

WPA Cracking

After the WEP cracking became known, the manufacturers of wireless equipment were faced with a problem. The IEEE was working on creating a new security standard (which became known as 802.11i) but were moving at their usual deliberate pace. In the meantime, companies were not deploying wireless because of security concerns. The Wi-Fi Alliance created a temporary solution called Wi-Fi Protected Access (WPA) that was an improvement on WEP.

Soon after WPA was rolled out, it was discovered that it also could be cracked. It required more effort than cracking WEP, and it required what is called a dictionary file (a file of words that could possibly be used as a password). It also required that the passphrase or password be a word in the dictionary. Finally, it required capturing a large number of wireless frames and the cracking process took a lot of time.

But the point is that if the hackers had good reason to believe they were capturing valuable data, it could be done. Therefore, WPA is not considered good security unless it is employed as WPA-2, which is based in the secure 802.11i architecture.

Rogue Access Points

Rogue access points are access points that you do not control and manage. There are two types, those that are connected to your wired infrastructure and those that are not. The ones that are connected to your wired network present a danger to your wired and wireless network. They may be placed there by your own users without your knowledge, or they may purposefully be put there by a hacker to gain access to the wired network. In either case, they allow access to your wired network. Wireless Intrusion Prevention System (IPS) devices are usually used to locate them and to alert administrators of their presence.

Rogue access points that are not connected to your wired infrastructure are usually used as a part of a highjacking attack, which is discussed in the next section.

Evil Twin

An evil twin is an AP that is not under your control but is used to perform a highjacking attack. A highjacking attack is one in which the hacker gets one or more of your users' computers connected to their network for the purpose of a peer-to-peer attack.

The attack begins with the introduction of an access point that is under the hacker's control. This access point will be set to use the same network name or SSID as your network, and it will be set to require no authentication (which is called an open network). Moreover, this access point will be set to use a different channel than the access point under your control.

To understand how the attack works, you must understand how wireless stations (laptops, PDAs, and so on) choose an access point with which to connect. It is done by SSID and not by channel. The hacker will "jam" the channel on which your access point is transmitting. When a station gets disconnected from an access point, it scans the area for another access point with the same SSID. The stations will find the hacker's access point and will connect to it.

Once the station is connected to the hacker's access point, it will receive an IP address from a DHCP server running on the access point and the user will now be located on the same network as the hacker. At this point, the hacker is free to commence a peer-to-peer attack.

Attackers and Their Tools

The old adage "never talk to strangers" applies here because you can't spot a hacker by looking at one. That quiet 15-year-old kid next door or the head of the PTA could secretly be a criminal hacker (or *cracker*, in nerd-speak)—you just never know. But instead of living your life being suspicious of everyone you meet, it's much better to understand the ways and strategies bad guys use to infiltrate your defenses.

The interaction between a hacker and a network administrator can be anything from a harmless game of cat and mouse to a terrorist attack on national security. Either way, there's someone out there trying to break into or crash your system, and it's up to you to track and prevent the attacks.

Network attacks executed by an actual hacker are called *directed attacks*. For instance, a bad guy can use the WinNuke utility, which I'll describe soon, to generate a packet and send it to a specific machine. On the other hand, viruses aren't usually directed attacks—instead they're just blindly copied from user to user.

I'll start by telling you about some common network attacks and then move on to cover the techniques used to prevent them from happening to you.

IP Spoofing

IP spoofing is the process of sending packets with a fake source address that makes it look like those packets actually originate from within the network that the hacker is trying to attack. This means that even a packet-filtering router is going to treat this packet as validly coming from within the network and pass it on. You need a firewall in place to prevent this type of packet from passing into your network. Figure 14.6 shows a hacker attempting an IP spoof and the spoofed IP address being denied access to the network by the firewall.

FIGURE 14.6 IP spoofing

Hacker attempts to get in pretending to have the IP address of Server A.

Firewall

Hacker denied access by Firewall

Client expecting data from Server A

Server A

🌐 **Real World Scenario**

Do We Really Need Firewalls?

Believe it or not, the honor system used to apply to the Internet, and it pretty much worked, so firewalls just weren't needed. Now, nothing could be further from the truth! Today, multitudes of companies have their entire corporate intranets connected to the Internet; plus, a legion of e-commerce sites like eBay and Amazon transfer seriously sensitive personal and financial data over the Internet. Corporate espionage and identity theft are currently the fastest-growing crimes worldwide—evil deeds pulled off by bad guys lurking on the Net. So, we all need to practice "Safe Net," and one popular way to do that is by implementing firewalls on our networks.

Application-Layer Attacks

Application-layer attacks usually zero in on well-known holes in software that's running on our servers. Favorite targets include FTP, sendmail, and HTTP because the permissions level granted to these accounts is often privileged. This means that bad guys who break in not only gain access to your network but also get the added bonus of having privileged status while they're in there—yikes!

ActiveX Attacks

A fairly new form of attack makes its way to your computer through ActiveX and Java programs (applets). These are miniature programs that run on a web server or that you download to your local machine. Most ActiveX and Java applets are safe, but some contain viruses or snoop or spyware programs. Snoop or spyware programs allow a hacker to look at everything on your hard drive from a remote location without you knowing about it, which is really bad, so be sure you properly configure the on-access component of your antivirus software to check and clean for these types of attacks.

Autorooters

You can think of autorooters as a kind of hacker automaton. Hackers use something called a *rootkit* to probe, scan, and then capture data on a strategically positioned computer that's poised to give them "eyes" into entire systems automatically. This is clearly very bad for you and your data. Note that this is typically how a cracker can attack a Mac or Unix box.

Backdoors

Backdoors are simply paths leading into a computer or network. From simple invasions to elaborate Trojan horses, villains can use their previously placed inroads into a specific host or a network whenever they want to. That is, unless you can detect them and stop them in their tracks.

Network Reconnaissance

Before breaking into a network, bad guys gather all the information they can about it because the more they know about the network, the better they can compromise it. This is called *network reconnaissance*. Hackers accomplish their objectives through methods like port scans, Domain Name Service (DNS) queries, and ping sweeps—even social engineering, or *phishing*, which I'll cover in a bit.

Packet Sniffers

A *packet sniffer* is a software tool that can be incredibly effective in troubleshooting a problematic network but that can also be a hacker's friend. Here's how it works. A network adapter card is set to promiscuous mode so it will send all packets snagged from the network's Physical layer through to a special application to be viewed and sorted out. A packet sniffer can nick some highly valuable, sensitive data including, but not limited to, passwords and usernames, making such a tool a prize among identity thieves.

Port Scanners

Port scanners are programs that ping every port on the target to identify which ports are open. It does this by pinging the IP address of the target with the port number appended after a colon. If an answer is received, the port is open. Open ports are potential services the hacker can exploit.

FTP Bounce

This attack is a variation of the port scan in that the attacker uses the FTP PORT command to request access to ports indirectly through the use of the victim machine as a middleman for the request. This cloaks the identity of the device performing the port scan.

Password Attacks

Password attacks come in many flavors. Even though they can be achieved via more sophisticated types of attacks like IP spoofing, packet sniffing, and Trojan horses, their sole purpose is to (surprise!) discover user passwords so the thief can pretend they're a valid user and then access that user's privileges and resources.

Brute-Force Attacks

A brute-force attack is another software-oriented attack that employs a program that is running on a targeted network and tries to log in to some type of shared network resource like a server. It attempts combinations of characters until it hits the correct one. For the hacker, it's ideal if the accessed accounts have a lot of privileges because then the bad guys can form backdoors to use for gaining access later and bypass the need for passwords entirely. Modern password policy systems prevent this by only allowing a small number of incorrect password attempts before an account is locked out.

Port-Redirection Attacks

A port-redirection attack requires a host machine the hacker has broken into and uses to get wonky traffic that normally wouldn't be allowed passage through a firewall. The attacker gains access to a trusted computer that is outside the firewall and installs software on the machine. They then redirect traffic bound for a particular port on the trusted yet now compromised host to their machine.

Trust-Exploitation Attacks

Trust-exploitation attacks happen when someone exploits a trust relationship in your network. The attacker gains control of a host that is outside the firewall yet is trusted by hosts that are inside the firewall. Once compromised, the host outside the firewall can be used as a platform to exploit the fact it is trusted by those inside the firewall.

Man-in-the-Middle Attacks

Interception! But it's not a football, it's a bunch of your network's packets—your precious data. A man-in-the-middle attack happens when someone intercepts packets intended for one computer and reads the data. A common guilty party could be someone working for your very own ISP using a packet sniffer and augmenting it with routing and transport protocols. Rogue ATM machines and even credit-card swipers are tools that are also increasingly used for this type of attack. Figure 14.7 shows a man-in-the-middle attack.

FIGURE 14.7 Man-in-the-middle attack

Client   Man in the Middle   Server

Social Engineering (Phishing)

Hackers are more sophisticated today than they were 10 years ago, but then again, so are network administrators. Because most of today's sys admins have secured their networks well enough to make it pretty tough for an outsider to gain access, hackers decided to try an easier route to gain information: They just asked the network's users for it.

Social engineering, or *phishing*, refers to the act of attempting to illegally obtain sensitive information by pretending to be a credible source. Common phishing tactics include emails, phone calls, or even starting up a conversation in person.

Some email phishing scams have made the news. There was this case where bad guys sent out a mass email that was all dressed up to appear as though the message actually came from a real bank. The email said that the bank had an issue with one of its servers, so it now required you to confirm your user-account information to verify that none of your data was lost. All you needed to do was click the link provided in the email, enter your information, and snap—your identity went poof! If you possess a working brain and someone you didn't know phoned and asked for your bank-account number, you certainly wouldn't give it to them, right? No way—but the same request, coming in the form of a really legitimate-looking email, seems more believable for some reason. This has become a popular phishing tool, notoriously used to separate people from anything from a few bucks to their entire identity. Be careful!

Oh, and speaking of phone calls…Let's say you get a call to your desk at work from "Joe" in IT. He says he's noticed some unusual activity on your network account and wants to check it out, but for security purposes, he needs your permission first. So he proceeds to confirm your login, and then he tells you he needs to enter your password into the network tracker. He asks, "What's your password?" To protect yourself from this one, all you need to do is confirm *his* information and verify it with your IT department *before* you give him any of your data. You know by now that just because "Joe" knows your login doesn't mean he's on the up-and-up; even if "Joe" hangs up on you, you should still report the call to IT.

How did Joe get your login and telephone number? Remember network reconnaissance? First, because company phone directories are often on the Web, getting your phone number was easy. Even if it isn't published, maybe Joe did some earlier phishing by calling one of your coworkers and, pretending to be a colleague at another site, asked for your phone number. But what about the username? On most networks, your username is the same as your email address because that makes things easier for your sys admin. This means that knowing that information is probably just a good guess on the attacker's part. Maybe Joe the Hacker has gotten an email from someone at your company and knows what your email format is, and he may have some other information to help him figure out your network login. And even if the number on your caller ID when Joe called was an internal phone number, it doesn't mean a thing—remember IP spoofing? Well, you can do that with phone numbers too.

The golden rule is don't ever give any of your information or anyone else's to anyone you're not absolutely sure should have it. And if they are someone who should have it, they probably already do, and they shouldn't be contacting you for it!

Understanding Mitigation Techniques

To be honest, I'm not going to go into detail about how to mitigate each and every one of the security threats I just talked about, not only because that would be outside the scope of this book, but also because the methods I am going to teach you will truly protect you from being attacked in general. You'll learn enough tricks to make all but the most determined bad guys give up on you and search for easier prey. Basically, think of this as a section on how to practice "Safe Net."

Safe networking techniques fall into three major categories: policies and procedures, training, and patches and upgrades. But before we go there, let's cover some of those general defense techniques I just referred to.

Okay—first know that there are three main ways to detect an intruder and defend yourself against one:

- Active detection, which involves constantly scanning the network for possible break-ins
- Passive detection, which involves logging all network events to a file
- Proactive defense methods, which involve using tools to shore up your network walls against attack

Active Detection

Active detection is analogous to a security guard walking the premises, rattling doors to make sure they're locked, and checking for intruders and any unusual activity. Similarly, there's special network software that searches for hackers attempting known attack methods and scans for the kind of suspicious activity and weird network traffic that hackers leave behind as they travel over the network. Some sophisticated active systems go a step further and take action by doing things like shutting down the communications sessions a bad guy is using as well as emailing or paging you. Some security packages will even go as far as trying to cripple the computer the hacker is attacking from! Cisco's NetRanger, Memco's Session Wall, and Snort are all forms of active intrusion-detection software.

Passive Detection

Using video cameras is a good example of using a passive intrusion-detection system. Their counterparts in networking are files that log events that occur on the network. Tripwire for Unix systems is one of the earliest programs of this variety. It identifies changes in files using checksums. Changes in files indicate that someone has accessed them. Passive detection systems work by examining files and data and then calculating the checksums for each. The checksums are stored in a log file so that if the sys admin notices that a security breach has occurred on the network, they can access the log files to find clues about it.

Proactive Defense

A proactive defense is something you do or implement to ensure that your network is impenetrable. You can accomplish a lot through solid research and vigilant maintenance—you absolutely must stay current regarding any known security holes relevant to your type of network and the devices that populate it. You can also use tools like the unfortunately dubbed Security Administrator Tool for Analyzing Networks (SATAN) to find the holes in your security walls and plug them with software patches.

Clearly, before you can patch a hole, you've got to know it's there, right? This is why I said it's so important to stay current. Even better, stay a step ahead of bad guys by knowing your enemy's strategies because the war against attackers is ever evolving—as soon as one hole is patched, bad guys will search for and find another vulnerability to exploit. And because patches usually take some time to develop, you can lose your shirt to a hacker in the interim.

This is a big reason I'm saying it's a better idea for you to know thy enemy than to rely on patches and the like.

Incident Response

Often when an attack or security breach occurs in the network, valuable time and information are lost in the critical first minutes and hours after the incident occurs. In some cases, evidence is inadvertently destroyed, making prosecution of the offending party impossible. In other cases, attacks that could have been interrupted and prevented before damage occurs are allowed to continue.

An incident response policy is designed to prevent this by establishing in advance the procedures that should be followed when an attack occurs. It may categorize incidents in such a way that certain event types (such as an active port scan) may require a response (such as disabling certain services) within 10 minutes while other events (such as an attempt to access a file without proper credentials) may only require a notation and follow-up in the next few days. The point is to establish these rules ahead of time to ensure that events are handled in a way that minimizes damage and preserves evidence.

There is a host of great shareware and freeware available on the Internet today, including Windows Defender, Spybot Search & Destroy, and Ad-Aware as well as Windows Update.

Policies and Procedures

Every company should have written policies to effectively enable security on their computer networks. These policies should have the approval of the highest-ranking security or IT officer within the company, and they should address all aspects of the company network. Procedures should also be in place to determine the appropriate course of action in the event that there is a security breach. And all network administrators absolutely need to be thoroughly trained on all policies and procedures—no weak links.

All of this might sound a bit militaristic in nature, but it's truly necessary. Speaking of the military, though, the US Department of Defense (DoD) has some really good standards that it wouldn't hurt you to keep in mind when setting up the security policies for your own network.

You can find the evaluation criteria for the DoD computer standards at www.niap-ccevs.org/cc-scheme/. In the past, this was known as the Rainbow Series (found at https://www.securecomputing.com/WBT/wbt-61/csec0001_r/module3/3mandatory.sb.html) because of the color of the books, but that's been replaced by the much less colorful Common Criteria Evaluation and Validation Scheme (CCEVS).

Security Policies

So what, exactly, is a *security policy*? Ideally, it should precisely define how security is to be implemented within an organization and include physical security, document security, and network security. Plus, you have to make sure these forms of security are implemented completely and solidly because if they aren't, your security policy will be a lot like a block of Swiss cheese—some areas are covered, but others are full of holes.

Before a network can be truly secure, the network support staff should post the part of the security policy that applies to employee conduct on bulletin boards. It should, for example, forbid posting any company and/or employee information that's not absolutely necessary—like, believe it or not, sticking Post-its with usernames and passwords on computer screens. Really clean desks, audits, and recording email communications and, in some cases, phone calls, should also be requirements. And don't forget to also post the consequences of not complying with the security policy.

Security Audit

Let me take a minute to explain all this a little more, beginning with security audits. A *security audit* is a thorough examination of your network that includes testing all its components to make sure everything is secure. You can do this internally, but you can also contract an audit with a third party if you want the level of security to be certified. A valid and verified consultant's audit is a good follow-up to an internal audit. One reason for having your network's security certified like this is that government agencies usually require it before they'll grant you contract work, especially if that work is considered Confidential, Secret, or Top Secret.

Clean-Desk Policy

That clean-desk policy doesn't just end with "get rid of the crumbs from your last snack." It means requiring that all potentially important documents like books, schematics, confidential letters, notes to self, and so on aren't left out in the open when someone's away from their desk. Instead, they're locked away, securely out of sight. And make sure it's clear that this rule applies to users' PC desktops too. Policies like this apply to offices, laboratories, and workbenches as well as desks, and it's really important for employees who share workspaces and/or workstations.

It's super easy to nick something off someone's desk or screen. Because most security problems involve people on the inside, implementing and enforcing a clean-desk policy is a simple way to guard against security breaches.

> The International Computer Security Association (ICSA, www.icsa.net) reports that as many as 80 percent of all network break-ins occur from within the company and are carried out by employees, so protecting your data with a firewall is just the beginning of establishing network security.

It might sound really nitpicky, but for a clean-desk policy to be effective, users have to clean up their desks every time they walk away from them—without exception. The day someone doesn't, will be the very day when some prospective tenant is being shown the building's lay-out and a sensitive document suddenly disappears. You should make sure workstations are locked to desks and do random spot checks once in a while to help enforce the policy. For obvious reasons, before company picnics and parties and before "bring your child to work day" are good times to do this.

 The ICSA is a vendor-neutral organization that certifies the functionality of security products as well as makes recommendations on security in general.

Recording Equipment

Recording equipment—such as tape recorders, cell phones, and small memory devices like USB flash memory keychains—can contain sensitive, confidential information, so a good security policy should prohibit their unauthorized presence and use.

Just walk into almost any large technology company and you'll be immediately confronted with signs. A really common one is a camera with a circle surrounding it and a slash through the center of the circle. Read the text below the sign and you'll be informed that you can't bring any recording devices onto the premises.

Here's a good example. The NSA has updated its policy to include prohibiting Furby dolls on government premises because they have reasonably sophisticated computers inside them, complete with a digital recording device. The doll repeats what it hears at a certain interval of time, which is either cute or creepy but pretty much harmless—maybe even protective—in a children's daycare center. Not so much at the NSA, though—no recording conversations there. Maybe, at least in some locations, it's not such a good idea for your company either.

Other Common Security Policies

So you get the idea—security policies can cover literally hundreds of items. Here are some common ones:

Notification   Security policies aren't much good if no one knows about them, right? So make sure you give users a copy of the security policy when you give them their usernames and passwords. It's also a good idea to have computers display a summarized version of the policy when any user attempts to connect. Here's an example: "Unauthorized access is prohibited and will be prosecuted to the fullest extent of the law." Remember—your goal is to close loopholes. One hacker actually argued that because a computer didn't tell him otherwise, anyone was free to connect to and use the system!

Equipment access   Disable all unused network ports so that any nonemployees who happen to be in the building can't connect a laptop to an unused port and gain access to the network. And don't forget to place all network equipment under lock and key.

Wiring   Your network's wires should never run along the floor where they can be easily accessed (or tripped over, getting you sued). Routers, switches, and concentrators should live in locked closets or rooms, with access to those rooms controlled by anything ranging from a good lock to a biometric access system, depending on the level of security your specific network and data require.

Door locks/swipe mechanisms   Be sure that only authorized people know the combination to the cipher lock on your data-center doors or that only the appropriate people have badges that allow access to the data center. Change lock combinations often, and never ever leave server room doors open or unlocked.

Badges   Require everyone to wear an ID badge, including contractors and visitors, and assign appropriate access levels to everyone.

Tracking   Require badge access to all entrances to buildings and internal computer rooms. Track and record all entry to and exits from these rooms.

Passwords   Reset passwords at least every month. Train everyone on how to create strong passwords. Set BIOS passwords on every client and server computer to prevent BIOS changes.

Monitor viewing   Place computer monitors strategically so that visitors or people looking through windows can't see them, and make sure unauthorized users/persons can't see security-guard stations and server monitors. Use monitor privacy screens if necessary.

Accounts   Each user should have their own, unique user account, and employees should never share user accounts. Even temporary employees should have their own account. Otherwise, you won't be able to isolate a security breach.

Testing   Review and audit your network security at least once a year.

Background checks   Do background checks on all network support staff. This may include calling their previous employers, verifying their college degrees, requiring a drug test, and checking for a criminal background.

Firewalls   Use a firewall to protect all Internet connections, and use the appropriate proxies and dynamic-packet-filtering equipment to control access to the network. Your firewall should provide as much security as your company requires and your budget allows.

Intrusion Detection   Use intrusion-detection and logging software to discover security breaches, and be sure you're logging the events you want to monitor.

Cameras   Cameras should cover all entrances to the building and the entire parking lot. Be sure that cameras are in weather-proof and tamper-proof housings, and review the output at a security-monitoring office. Record everything on extended-length tape recorders.

Mail servers   Provide each person with their own email mailbox, and attach an individual network account to each mailbox. If several people need to access a mailbox, don't give all of them the password to a single network account. Instead, assign individual privileges to each person's network account so you can track activity down to a single person, even with a generic address like `info@mycompany.com`.

DMZ   Use a demilitarized zone (DMZ) for all publicly viewable servers, including web servers, FTP servers, and email relay servers. Figure 14.8 shows a common DMZ setup.

FIGURE 14.8   A common DMZ configuration

It is not advisable to put a DMZ outside the firewall because any servers outside your firewall defeat the whole purpose having one. However, it is possible that you may see a DMZ outside the firewall in some networks.

Mail relay   Mail servers relay to other email servers by design. When the email server relays from any server that requests it, it is called *open relay.* Hackers use this feature to forward spam. Modern email systems allow you to control which servers your email server will relay for, which helps to prevent this.

Patches   Make sure the latest security updates are installed after being properly tested on a nonproduction computer.

Backups   Store backup tape cartridges securely, not on a shelf or table within reach of someone working at the server. Lock tapes in a waterproof, fireproof safe, and keep at least some of your backups off site.

Modems   Do not ever allow desktop modems because they can be used to get to the Internet without your knowledge. Restrict modem access to approved server-based modem pools.

Guards   If you need security guards, they shouldn't patrol the same station all the time. As people become familiar with an environment and situation, they tend to become less observant about that environment, so rotating guards to keep their concentration at the highest possible level makes a lot of sense. Clearly, guards are people who need breaks to ensure alertness, but make sure that all patrol areas are covered during shift changes, rotations, and breaks. Guards should also receive periodic training and testing to make sure they can recognize a threat and take appropriate action.

WARNING Believe it or not, covering all these bases still won't guarantee that your network or facility is secure. All of this is really just a starting point that's meant to point you in the right direction.

Breaking Policy

You know that for your policy to be effective it's got to be enforced consistently and completely. Nobody is so special that they don't have to adhere to it. And people have to understand the consequences of breaking policy too. Your network users need to have a clearly written document, called a *security policy*, that fully identifies and explains what's expected of them and what they can and can't do. Plus, people must be made completely aware of the consequences of breaking the rules, and penalties have to match the severity of the offense and be carried out quickly, if not immediately, to be effective.

Let's take a minute and talk about those penalties. As far back as the mid-1980s, employees were immediately terminated for major technology policy infractions. For example, one guy from a large computer company immediately got his pink slip when pornography was found on his computer's hard drive. The situation was handled decisively—his manager informed him that he was being immediately terminated and that he had one hour to vacate the premises. A security guard stood watch while he cleaned out his desk to make sure the employee only touched personal items—no computer equipment, including storage media—and when he had finished gathering his personal things, the guard then escorted him from the building.

Downloading and installing software from the Internet to your PC at work is not as major (depending on where you work), but from the things we've been over so far, you know that doing that can compromise security. Beta products, new software, and patches need to be tested by the IT department before anyone can use them, period! Here's an example: After an employee installed the untested beta release of a web browser and rebooted their PC, the production Windows NT server at a national telephone company crashed. The resulting action was to revoke that employee's Internet FTP privileges for three months.

The Exit Interview

Sometimes, the importance of an employee's position and the amount of knowledge they have about the company and its systems justifies requiring an exit interview when they're terminated. It's done to minimize the risk of that employee being disgruntled and to attempt to ensure that they're leaving under the most favorable circumstances possible. The interview can include the IT manager, a human resources representative, a sys admin, and sometimes even security personnel.

When an employee leaves the company—whether they're quitting to move on to another job or being terminated—all company property needs to be turned in and logged. This includes things like company cell phones, pagers, toolkits, keys, badges, security tokens, models, and, obviously, all company documents.

And clearly, IT needs to disable all accounts immediately, including those for network access and voicemail, and remaining employees should be informed that the employee is leaving at this time. This is especially important when that employee has access to sensitive documents because even if they're leaving under favorable conditions, they could still log in and copy data to take with them for their own use. For instance, salespeople can easily hurt a company by taking client information with them, and it has happened—a salesperson accessed his former company's voicemail system and stole sales leads. So it's not just the obviously disgruntled ex–network administrator who could demolish your website after leaving that you need to be concerned about.

Security Procedures

A *security procedure* defines how to respond to any security event that happens on your network. Here's a short list of items you might include:

- What to do when someone has locked themselves out of their account
- How to properly install or remove software on servers
- What to do if files on the servers suddenly appear to be "missing" or altered
- How to respond when a network computer has a virus
- Actions to take if it appears that a hacker has broken into the network
- Actions to take if there is a physical emergency such as a fire or flood

Security Training

This brings us to the human element of network security. It's true that most of your users want to do the right thing to protect the company—and their jobs—from the prying eyes of hackers, but the problem is that people don't always know the right thing to do. That's why training is so vital. It can include classroom sessions and/or web-based training, but experience has shown me that actual classroom-based instruction works the best. It's also a good idea to have separate training classes for IT personnel and end users.

End-User Training

End-user training is pretty easy—it can take just an hour or so to bring employees up to speed. The "keep it short and simple" rule applies here or you'll just end up with nap time. This is a great time to include detailed security protocol training. But if you see eyes beginning to glaze over or hear anyone snoring, you might want to make security protocol training a separate session because, as I said, it's really important for the effectiveness of your security policy for everyone to know about and understand it. You can even use a year-end bonus or something else cool as a motivational reward for the employees who complete their training and test well on it.

And you have to back up your training by providing your end users with hard-copy, printed reference manuals in case they forget something (which they will). Include things like the following items:

- Recommended policies for creating safe passwords
- The number to call if they've locked themselves out of their accounts

- What to do if they think someone is phishing for information
- What to do if they think their computer has a virus

Clearly, new employees to the company or division should be required to go through training, but requiring that everybody attend refresher courses is also a good idea. And don't hesitate to call a meeting if new threats arise or any sudden changes occur to keep everyone up-to-date.

Administrator Training

Obviously, training sessions for your IT personnel have to be a lot more in depth because they'll be the ones who set up and configure policies, and they'll also be the first responders to any security emergency.

It's important to cover every aspect of your security policy with these people. And be sure they understand the correct ways to escalate issues in case of an emergency. Reacting to a security emergency is pretty stressful, and you don't want your administrators to panic or feel isolated if one occurs. Making sure they know where their lifelines are and how to reach them quickly if they need backup will relieve a lot of pressure when something nasty happens.

Patches and Upgrades

The operating systems and applications we use today are really just gigantic collections of computer code. Windows Vista has about 50 million lines of code, and Windows XP has 35 to 40 million lines of code. And if you look at the subsystems within Windows, you'll find that there are more than 50 dependency layers—processes that depend on other processes. Experts who work on developing Windows say that it typically takes someone about five years to fully learn two or three of these layers. So it's pretty easy to imagine that with that much code being created by a couple of thousand different people, sometimes a few things get mixed up—and that's the reason why there always seems to be a few holes, glitches, and bugs to fix.

The good news is, as operating systems and applications are released, their developers have a chance to catch and repair the problems they uncover. In addition, as hackers find and take advantage of vulnerabilities, software developers work to plug those holes. The repairs are usually released to the public as *patches* or *hotfixes*. To address large-scale issues or add major features and components to the program, companies release complete upgrades instead.

Here's where we get into the software side of security, which includes things like applying patches, hotfixes, and upgrades, plus how to choose and install the right third-party software to protect yourself against viruses.

Ensuring that your software is up-to-date is one of the best ways to protect against bad guys exploiting the security holes on your network.

Automatic Updates through Windows Update

It's really easy to get updates for Windows-based operating systems from Windows 2000 on via Windows Update—a utility that's usually automatically installed when you install Windows. If you need to get more information, go to www.microsoft.com.

To ensure that Windows Update is enabled, open your System Properties dialog (right-click My Computer and then choose Properties). You will see a screen similar to the one shown in Figure 14.9.

FIGURE 14.9   Automating Windows Update

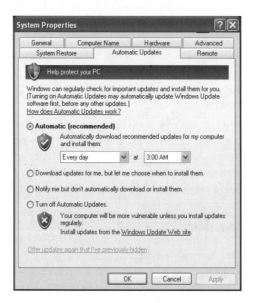

If you have Windows Update installed, it will periodically scan your system for the version of Windows components you already have installed and compare them to the most current versions available from Microsoft. If your software is out-of-date, a Windows Update dialog box will appear, asking if you want to install the software updates. If you click Continue, the installation will proceed in the background; you'll still be able to work in the foreground without skipping a beat.

Downloading Patches and Hotfixes

If you don't have automatic updates set up, you can download patches and hotfixes manually. A hotfix is just like a patch that updates software, but this term is reserved for a solution to potentially serious issues that could compromise your network and hosts. When a company like Microsoft has created a whole bunch of patches, hotfixes, and upgrades, it will put them together in a larger bundle called a *service pack*. For instance, you can download Windows 7 Service Pack 1 (SP1) or Windows Server 2008 Pack 2 (SP2), which will update lots of components and address security, performance, and stability issues all at the same time. For the latest service pack for your Windows-based operating system or application, visit support.microsoft.com.

But let's say you think you have a smaller, specific issue and you only want to download a patch for that particular problem. Maybe you're dealing with an issue with IPSec and you want to know about creating IPSec security filters in Windows XP. After surfing

Microsoft's support site, you come across article KB914841 (`support.microsoft.com/default.aspx?kbid=914841`). (KB stands for Knowledge Base, and it's one way Microsoft organizes its support documents.) This article will give you background information as well as allow you to download hotfixes for the operating system you're running.

Updating Antivirus Components

A typical antivirus program consists of two components:

- The definition files
- The engine

The definition files list the various viruses, their types, and their footprints and tell you how to remove them. More than 100 new viruses are found in the wild each month, so it's easy to see that an antivirus program would be totally useless if it didn't keep up with all those emerging viruses.

The engine accesses the definition files (or database), runs virus scans, cleans the files, and notifies the appropriate people and accounts. Eventually, viruses become so sophisticated that a new engine, or even a whole new technology, is required to combat them effectively.

Heuristic scanning is a technology that allows an antivirus program to search for a virus even if there's no definition for it yet. The engine looks for suspicious activity of the kind that usually indicates the presence of a virus. But use such a tool with caution—if it's turned on, this scanning technique can mistake harmless or even necessary code for suspicious code, and that can give you some major grief.

For your antivirus program to work for you, you have to upgrade, update, and scan in a specific order:

1. Upgrade the antivirus engine.
2. Update the definition files.
3. Create an antivirus emergency boot disk.
4. Configure and run a full on-demand scan.
5. Schedule monthly full on-demand scans.
6. Configure and activate on-access scans.
7. Make a new antivirus emergency boot disk monthly.
8. Get the latest update when fighting a virus outbreak.
9. Repeat all steps when you get a new engine.

I'm going to cover only the steps in this list that map to objectives of the Network+ exam, but looking into the others won't hurt and will give you some worthwhile knowledge.

Upgrading an Antivirus Engine

An antivirus engine is the core program that runs the scanning process and virus definitions are keyed to an engine version number. For example, a 3.*x* engine won't work with 4.*x* definition files. When the manufacturer releases a new engine, consider both the cost to upgrade and how much you'll benefit before buying it.

> Before installing new or upgraded software, back up your entire computer system, including all your data.

Updating Definition Files

I recommend that you update your list of known viruses—called the *virus definition files*—no less than weekly. You can do this manually or automatically through the manufacturer's website, and you can use a staging server within your company to download and distribute the updates or set up each computer to download updates individually.

Scanning for Viruses

An *antivirus scan* is the process that an antivirus program deploys to examine a computer suspected of having a virus, identify the virus, and then get rid of it. There are three types of antivirus scans, and to really make sure your system is clean, you should use a combination of the types I'm covering in this section:

On-demand scan   An *on-demand scan* is a virus scan initiated by you or an administrator that searches a file, a directory, a drive, or an entire computer but only checks the files you're currently accessing. I recommend doing this at least monthly, but you'll also want to do an on-demand scan when the following occurs:

- You first install the antivirus software

- You upgrade the antivirus software engine

- You suspect a virus outbreak

> Before you initiate an on-demand scan, be sure you have the latest virus definitions.

On-access scan   An on-access scan runs in the background when you open a file or use a program in situations like these:

- Inserting a floppy disk or thumb drive

- Downloading a file with FTP

- Receiving email messages and attachments

- Viewing a web page

This kind of scan slows down the processing speed of other programs, but it's worth the inconvenience.

Emergency scan   During an emergency scan, only the operating system and the antivirus program are running. You initiate one of these scans when a virus has totally invaded your system and taken control of the machine. In this situation, insert your antivirus emergency boot disk and boot the infected computer from it. Then, scan and clean the entire computer. If you don't have your boot disk, go to another, uninfected machine and create one from it. Another possibility is to use an emergency scan website like `housecall.trendmicro.com`, which allows you to scan your computer via a high-speed Internet access without using an emergency disk.

Fixing an Infected Computer

So what do you do if you know you have a virus? First, you want to make sure to scan all potentially affected hard disks plus any external disks that could be infected. Establish a cleaning station, and quarantine the infected area. You'll have a really hard time doing this if anyone continues to use the computer while it is infected, so make sure all users in the infected area stop using their computers.

Then, remove all external memory devices from all disk drives and perform a scan and clean at the cleaning station. Update the virus definitions of any computers that are still operational. For the ones that aren't, or the ones that are still working but are infected, boot to an antivirus emergency boot disk. After you've done that, run a full scan and clean the entire system on all computers in the office space. With luck, you will be done before your users return from lunch.

WARNING   It's frustrating, but a lot of programs won't install unless you disable the on-access portion of your antivirus software. Clearly, this is dangerous if the program has a virus. If you want to be really safe, do an on-demand scan of the software before installing it. If things are all good, go ahead and disable on-access scanning during installation, and then reactivate it when the installation is complete.

Summary

Whew—this was a long chapter with a lot of good information in it. We talked about the dark side of computer networking: bad guys and the threats and attacks they use to victimize our systems and networks. You learned a lot about tactics like denial of service attacks, viruses, worms, social engineering, and other devious methods that hackers use. After that, you learned about ways to mitigate these threats and protect yourself by establishing policies and procedures, providing training, and ensuring that all your software is up-to-date. You also learned what to do about the ubiquitous problem of viruses. It's a lot to remember, I know, but believe me, you'll be really glad you're armed with this knowledge because unfortunately, you'll probably deal with these threats sooner or later.

Exam Essentials

Know what types of threats can adversely affect your network.   Threats include denial of service attacks, viruses, worms, rogue access points, phishing, and various other attack methods employed by hackers.

Understand how attackers attempt to get information about your network.   Attackers have various methods they can use to gather information. Some of the most common reconnaissance tools are packet sniffers and social engineering.

Know how to keep your systems automatically updated.   Programs such as Windows Update can keep your operating systems current, which will reduce opportunities for attackers to exploit your computers and network.

Know where to go to find downloadable software updates.   Check the manufacturer's website for the most current security information, patches, and updates.

Written Lab

In this section, write the answers to the following wireless questions:

1. The Ping of Death and SYN floods are examples of what types of attack?

2. How often should you update your virus definitions in your antivirus software?

3. What type of attack injects a command that overflows the amount of memory allocated and executes commands that would not normally be allowed?

4. What type of virus attacks executable programs?

5. What kind of tool could a hacker use to intercept traffic on your network?

6. What type of virus uses Microsoft's Visual Basic scripting language?

7. What is it called when someone intercepts traffic on your network that's intended for a different destination computer?

8. If someone installed a wireless router on your network without your knowledge, that would be called _____.

9. What software application can help automatically ensure that your Windows-based computers have the most current security patches?

10. The two different types of virus scans are _____.

You can find the answers in Appendix B.

Review Questions

You can find the answers in Appendix A.

1. Which of the following is a type of denial of service attack?

    A. Ping of Death

    B. Stacheldraht

    C. SYN flood

    D. All of the above

2. Which is not a type of threat that can affect your network?

    A. Worm

    B. Phishing

    C. Access control list

    D. Rogue access point

3. Which type of virus impacts files with the filename extensions `.com`, `.exe`, and `.dll`?

    A. File viruses

    B. SYN flood

    C. Smurf

    D. Tribe Flood Network

4. In which type of attack does the attacker scan for networks using a high-powered antenna connected to a wireless laptop?

    A. War driving

    B. Evil twin

    C. WEP cracking

    D. WPA cracking

5. Monkey B, Michelangelo, Stoned, and Stealth Boot are examples of which type of virus?

    A. IP spoofing

    B. Multipartite

    C. Macro

    D. Boot sector

6. Which type of virus affects both the boot sector and files on a computer?

    A. Mulipartite

    B. Macro

    C. Tribe Flood Network 2000 (TFN2K)

    D. Smurf

7. What is the main difference between a worm and a virus?

   A. Worms require user action for replication.

   B. Viruses do not require user intervention for replication.

   C. Worms can replicate without user intervention.

   D. None of the above.

8. What kind of attack involves the hacker attempting all combinations of characters for a password to gain access?

   A. Packet sniffers

   B. Brute-force attack

   C. Worm

   D. Backdoor

9. What type of security threat allows an attacker to learn your password through the use of an email or phone call?

   A. Phishing

   B. Trust-exploration attack

   C. Man-in-the-middle attack

   D. Rogue access point

10. Which type of policy should be implemented to secure important company documents and materials when employees leave their workstations?

    A. Clean housekeeping

    B. Clean desk

    C. Security audit

    D. Proactive defense

11. If you implement a set of policies and procedures that define corporate information as confidential and then train employees on these procedures, what type of attack can you prevent?

    A. DoS

    B. Man-in-the-middle attacks

    C. Smurf

    D. Social engineering

12. What type of wireless frame populates the display when someone is scanning for wireless networks?

    A. Probe response

    B. Beacon

    C. SSID

    D. Discovery

13. What defines the appropriate response to a security event on a network?

    A. Implementing security procedures

    B. Installing a new router

    C. Turning off the network

    D. Implementing an HR policy for dress code

14. Which of the following security mechanisms has been compromised?

    A. WEP

    B. 802.11i

    C. WPA-2

    D. RADIUS

15. What process allows you to update your Windows-based operating system?

    A. Technet

    B. Windows Update

    C. Text message

    D. Hotfix

16. Why is it important to keep your system patched and up-to-date?

    A. To completely stop your need for security

    B. To increase the functionality of your applications

    C. To fix system vulnerabilities

    D. To make Windows completely safe and worry free

17. Which value does a wireless station use to choose an access point?

    A. Signal-to-noise ratio

    B. MAC address

    C. SSID

    D. Channel number

18. Which type of scanning allows an antivirus program to search for a virus even if there is no definition for it?

   A. Update scan

   B. Signature-file scan

   C. Database scan

   D. Heuristic scan

19. What type of files need to be updated in order for your antivirus program to have the latest information about attacks and viruses?

   A. Definition files

   B. Email files

   C. DOC (.doc) files

   D. EXE (.exe) files

20. What type of scan can be done by an antivirus program?

   A. Emergency

   B. In-demand

   C. On-access

   D. All of the above

Chapter

15

Physical and Hardware Security

THE FOLLOWING COMPTIA NETWORK+ EXAM OBJECTIVES ARE COVERED IN THIS CHAPTER:

✓ **5.5 Given a scenario, install and configure a basic firewall.**

- Types:
  - Software and hardware firewalls
- Port security
- Stateful inspection vs. packet filtering
- Firewall rules:
  - Block/allow
  - Implicit deny
  - ACL
- NAT/PAT
- DMZ

✓ **5.6 Categorize different types of network security appliances and methods.**

- IDS and IPS:
  - Behavior based
  - Signature based
  - Network based
  - Host based
- Vulnerability scanners:
  - NESSUS
  - NMAP
- Methods:
  - Honeypots
  - Honeynets

Finding a corporate network that isn't connected to the Internet would be pretty tough these days. Being connected allows for a huge increase in productivity, and not having an online presence is akin to sheer oblivion in today's business environment. But as is often the case, advantages, even big ones, have a downside to them, and being hooked up to the Internet is no exception. Connecting our private networks to a huge public one exposes us to some really major security risks, so we absolutely have to protect our networks from the very real threats of intrusion, corporate espionage, data and identity theft, and exploitation in general. To succeed, our networks need one or more security devices to control any traffic coming into and flowing out from them. We need things like firewalls and intrusion detection and/or prevention systems as much as we need any other form of security in our businesses and daily lives today—period.

These vital security methods are going to be the focus of this chapter. In it, I'll be covering the ins and outs of the protective networking measures and devices designed to shield and secure our network traffic, zooming in on the all-important firewalls because they're a ubiquitous and critical line of defense against the exploits of the all-too-common hackers who seek to compromise our corporate and personal network security.

I'll end this important chapter by going over the specific issues that can and do affect device security on your network. I'll discuss things you can do physically and logically to implement tight security, right down to choosing the best protocols to use for safe communication to the outside world.

To find up-to-the-minute updates for this chapter, please see www.lammle.com/forum or the book's web site at www.sybex.com/go/ netplus2e.

Using Hardware and Software Security Devices

This heading may be a little misleading because it makes it sound like I'm going to discuss the differences between hardware and software security devices. But I'm not, because even though many firewalls and routers that contain proxy and/or firewall services brand themselves as hardware or software solutions, the fact is, most of these devices are really a combination of the two. For instance, there's software embedded within a hardware ROM chip to make the software harder to attack, but it still actually functions as software. So instead of focusing on the type of device, it makes a lot more sense to delve into exactly what it is that a device does and how it does it.

In medium to large enterprise networks, strategies for security usually include some combination of internal and perimeter routers plus firewall devices. Internal routers provide added security by screening traffic to the more vulnerable parts of a corporate network through a wide array of strategic *access lists*. You can see where each of these devices is found within a typical network in Figure 15.1.

FIGURE 15.1   A typical secured network

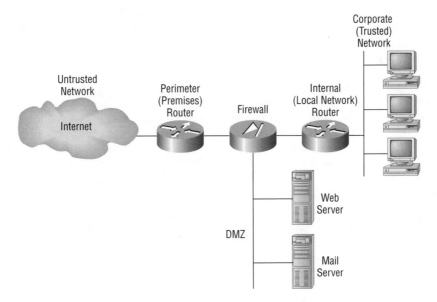

I'll use the terms *trusted network* and *untrusted network* throughout this chapter, so it's important that you can see where they are found in a typical secured network. The demilitarized zone (DMZ) can be global (real) Internet addresses or private addresses, depending on how you configure your firewall, but this is typically where you'll find the HTTP, Domain Name Service (DNS), email, and other Internet-type corporate servers. The DMZ is used to create a security zone that allows public traffic but the traffic is isolated from the company private network.

Instead of having routers, we can also use virtual local area networks (VLANs) with switches on the inside trusted network. Multilayer switches containing their own security features can sometimes replace internal (LAN) routers to provide higher performance in VLAN architectures.

Next, I'll show you how these devices go about directing traffic between your *private network* that only authorized users have access to and the *public network* part of the network that everyone connects to.

Defining Firewalls

Firewalls are usually a combination of hardware and software. The hardware part is usually a router, but it can also be a computer or a dedicated piece of hardware called a *black box* that has two Network Interface Cards (NICs) in it. One of the NICs connects to the public side, and the other one connects to the private side. The software part is configured to control how the firewall actually works to protect your network by scrutinizing each incoming and outgoing packet and rejecting any suspicious ones.

Firewalls generally allow only packets that pass specific security restrictions to get through; they can also permit, deny, encrypt, decrypt, and proxy all traffic that flows through, either between the public and private parts of a network or between different security domains, or zones, on a private network. The system administrator decides on and sets up the rules a firewall follows when deciding to forward data packets or reject them.

 Just so you know, a Network+ certified system administrator rarely has the sophisticated knowledge required to design, install, and manage a firewall. The information I'm imparting to you here will give you the tools you need to understand the basic ways firewalls work and to help you to work effectively in an environment where a firewall is already installed.

Firewalls can be placed on top of an existing operating system or be self-contained. Conversely, black-box systems are proprietary and have external controls that aren't controlled by the operating system itself. If you opt to use a general-purpose server operating system to run your firewall, you can do that with Unix and Windows because both support third-party firewall products.

 For networks with multiple Windows-based computers, firewalls should be installed on a router that connects the private network to the Internet or to a Windows server like Windows Server 2008 rather than on clients like Windows 7.

Clearly, if your firewalls aren't configured properly, they're not going to do you much good. Most of them are configured as default-deny, meaning that the only network connections allowed are the ones that have been specified to be permitted. A proficient system administrator has to do this, and trust me, with the multitude of applications and ports involved in internal-external network communication, it's not all that easy! To make life easier, some people resort to trusting the default-allow option, where all traffic is allowed to pass through unless it's been specifically blocked. But doing this isn't exactly tight because it makes inadvertent network connections and security breaches much more likely to happen. Even though it might ease a little administrative pain, I don't recommend going with this method—ever.

Network-Based Firewalls

A *network-based firewall* is what companies use to protect their private network from public networks. The defining characteristic of this type of firewall is that it's designed to protect an entire network of computers instead of just one system, and it's usually a combination of hardware and software.

As you can imagine, protecting an entire network of computers from malicious attacks is quite the challenge. Most of the firewall features that I'm going to cover in this chapter are designed with this goal in mind, although the technology is certainly applicable to host-based firewalls too.

Host-Based Firewalls

In contrast to a network-based firewall, a *host-based firewall* is implemented on a single machine so it protects only that one machine. This type of firewall is usually a software implementation because you don't need any additional hardware in your personal computer to run it. All current Windows client operating systems come with Windows Firewall, which is a great example of a host-based solution.

If you hear someone say that host-based software solutions just aren't as secure as a separate hardware-based solution, they're pretty much right. This is because if you're running a dedicated black-box firewall and someone manages to hack in and disable it, your best-case scenario is a blown black box and a ruined firewall. Believe it or not, even if that happens, all the data on your internal network may still be safe if the bad guy wasn't able to get past everything. But if they were able to get all the way in, you could have some ugly consequences to deal with; if the hacker makes it through the often relatively flimsy software firewall running on your local computer, they could not only view and/or nick your files but also trash your entire system—yikes!

Still, it all comes down to how much security you really require. Unless you're the director of the CIA or something, you probably don't need to go the extra mile and shell out for a dedicated black box if all you want to do is protect your personal computer from someone who's trying to hack their way in through your high-speed Internet connection.

Firewall Technologies

There's a whole bunch of firewall technologies, and they all differ in the way that they restrict information flow. Things like access control lists and dynamic packet filtering are often used as firewalls in their own right, or they can be implemented along with proxies and DMZs and other firewall technologies to build a serious, formidable system fortress.

Access Control Lists

The first line of defense for any network that's connected to the Internet is what we call *access control lists (ACLs)*. These reside on your routers and determine by IP addresses which machines are allowed to use those routers and in what direction. ACLs have been around for decades and have some other really cool uses apart from being used as firewalls. Figure 15.2 gives you a great demonstration of how ACLs can work to prevent users on Network B from accessing Network A.

FIGURE 15.2   Two networks with an ACL-enabled router

An important thing to note here is that data from users in Network A can still pass through the router into Network B. This means that a hacker executing an IP spoofing attack that makes it appear as though they're an IP address originating from inside the firewall can still gain access to Network B by pretending to be a valid user in Network A.

ACLs are essentially lists of conditions that categorize packets, so you can imagine how helpful they can be in helping you gain control over the network's traffic. One of the most common and easiest-to-understand ways that ACLs are used is for filtering unwanted packets when you're implementing security policies. You can set up the ACLs to make very specific decisions about regulating traffic patterns so that they'll allow only certain hosts to access web resources on the Internet while restricting others. With a solid combination of ACLs, network managers can arm themselves like Rambo and powerfully enforce pretty much any security policy they need to.

Chapter 14 discussed some of the security threats that ACLs can help mitigate. Those threats include the following:

- IP address spoofing, inbound
- IP address spoofing, outbound
- Denial of service (DoS) TCP SYN attacks
- DoS Smurf attacks

Mitigations include the following:

- Using TCP intercept to address DoS TCP SYN attacks
- Filtering ICMP messages, inbound
- Filtering ICMP messages, outbound
- Filtering Traceroute

You can even employ ACLs for situations that don't necessarily involve blocking packets—like using them to control which networks will or won't be advertised by dynamic routing protocols. The way you configure your ACL to do that is the same; you just apply it to a routing protocol instead of an interface. The only other difference here is that an ACL applied to a protocol is referred to as a *distribution list*, and it doesn't stop routing advertisements, it just controls their content. You can also use ACLs to categorize and queue packets for applications that require quality of service (QoS) and for controlling the types of traffic that can activate a pricey backup link.

So, how do you go about creating an ACL? Well, it's really a lot like programming a series of if-then statements: If a given condition is met, then a specific action happens; but if that explicit condition isn't met, nothing happens except that the next statement in the list is evaluated. Access-list statements are basically packet filters that packets are compared against, categorized by, and then acted on accordingly as directed. Once your list is built, it can be applied to either inbound or outbound traffic on any interface, causing the router to analyze every packet crossing that interface in the specified direction and take the appropriate action.

There are a few important rules by which packets are processed when being compared with an ACL:

- They're always compared with each line of the ACL in sequential order, always beginning with the first line, then proceeding to line 2, then line 3, and so on.

- They'll be compared with subsequent lines of the list until a match is made. Once the packet matches the condition on a line of the ACL, the packet is acted upon and no further comparisons take place.

- There is an implicit "deny" at the end of each ACL that says that if a packet doesn't match the condition on any of the lines in the ACL, it will be discarded.

Each of these rules has some powerful implications for filtering IP packets with ACLs, which is why creating effective ACLs truly takes some practice!

There are two main types of ACLs:

Standard ACLs   These use only the source IP address in an IP packet as the condition test, so all decisions regarding a packet will be based on the source IP address. This means that standard ACLs basically permit or deny an entire suite of protocols without distinguishing between any of the myriad types of IP traffic like web, Telnet, UDP, and so on.

Extended ACLs   Extended ACLs go the distance and evaluate lots of the other fields in the Layer 3 and 4 headers of an IP packet. They can evaluate source and destination IP addresses, the protocol field in the Network layer header, and the port number at the Transport layer header. This gives extended ACLs the ability to enforce highly specific network traffic control conditions.

Once you create an ACL, it doesn't do much of anything until you apply it. Yes, it's there on the router, but it's inactive until you tell that router what to do with it. To use an ACL as a packet filter, you've got to apply it to the interface on the router exactly where you want the traffic filtered, and you've also got to specify the traffic's direction—inbound or outbound.

This is because you probably want different controls in place for traffic leaving your network that's destined for the Internet than you want for traffic coming into your network from the Internet. Here's the difference:

Inbound ACLs   When an ACL is applied to inbound packets on an interface, those packets are processed through the ACL before being routed to the outbound interface. Any packets that are denied won't be routed because they'll be discarded before the routing process is completed.

Outbound ACLs   When an ACL is applied to outbound packets on an interface, those packets are routed to the outbound interface and then processed through the ACL before being queued.

Creating ACLs is great, but don't forget to apply them to an interface or they're not going to filter traffic. With that in mind, here's a list of rules to live by when configuring ACLs on interfaces from the Internet into your production network:

- Deny any addresses from your internal networks.
- Deny any local host addresses (127.0.0.0/8).
- Deny any reserved private addresses.
- Deny any addresses in the IP multicast address range (224.0.0.0/4).

These addresses should never, ever be allowed to enter your internetwork.

Port Security

While firewalls can be used to protect access to the network at Layer 3 (IP addresses), there are cases where security needs to be maintained between users within the network. This can be done by implementing port security on the switches in the network. When you do this, you are enforcing security at Layer 2 (MAC addresses).

This can be used in several ways. First, you can use port security to define a set of MAC addresses that are allowed to access a port where a sensitive device is located. Another use is to set unused ports to only be available to a preconfigured set of MAC addresses. The second example could help to prevent unauthorized persons from plugging into a wall outlet (connected to a secured switch port) and accessing the network.

Demilitarized Zone

Most firewalls in use today implement something called a *demilitarized zone (DMZ)*, which, as its name implies, is a network segment that isn't public or local but halfway between the two. People outside your network primarily access your web servers, File Transfer Protocol (FTP) servers, and mail relay servers, and because bad guys tend to go after these servers first, it's a good idea to place them in the DMZ.

A standard DMZ setup typically (but not always) has two or three network cards in the firewall computer. The first goes to the Internet, the second one goes to the network segment where the commonly targeted servers exist (the servers I recommended be placed in the DMZ), and the third connects to your intranet. As you can see in Figure 15.3, the email server, the FTP server, and web server are all in the DMZ, so all critical servers live inside the firewall.

Understand that it is very possible to have a DMZ outside the firewall. Figure 15.3 shows an example of having the DMZ inside the firewall. Both options are available when building your intranets.

FIGURE 15.3   A firewall with a DMZ

If you set things up like this, hackers who break into servers in the DMZ will only get to see public information—meaning your entire corporate network won't be compromised. Understand that email messages are still fairly vulnerable, but only the relay server can be accessed because all messages are stored and viewed on email servers inside the network.

It is important to understand and remember that you need to administer your DMZ. This is not a device you buy at the store and just connect, turn on, and forget—you need to permit and deny the ports you want. If your company uses custom port numbers, you need to verify that the DMZ is allowing these ports through your server. This is easy to do by telneting to the DMZ server using the custom port number. If the server responds, you're good!

Protocol Switching

Protocol switching protects data on the inside of a firewall, and because Transmission Control Protocol/Internet Protocol (TCP/IP) is what the Internet runs on, most external attacks take direct aim at this protocol stack. In days gone by, protocol switching used to be pretty popular, but not so much anymore due to the greatly intensified power of firewall technology and the fact that TCP/IP is now the protocol of choice for all network communications. But if you did want to implement protocol switching, here are the two best ways to do it:

▪ Use a protocol other than TCP/IP on the internal network inside the firewall. IP-based attacks aimed at your development server just can't work if you use Internetwork Packet Exchange (IPX) on the internal-network side of a router, which gives you an automatic firewall.

▪ Use TCP/IP on the internal network and use a different protocol like IPX in a dead zone between the internal network and the Internet. Basically, you'll have things set up to switch from IP to IPX in that dead zone and switch back to IP again once inside your network (IPv6 would work in this example as well, but IPX is a good example because no one would expect it).

Figure 15.4 demonstrates both of these strategies. Focus on the dead zone between two of the routers, and also notice that the only protocol on the inside of either router is IPX. This means that any TCP/IP packets coming in from the Internet can't pass through into the local network because of the difference in protocols used by each network.

FIGURE 15.4   Protocol switching with and without a dead zone

Both of these methods protect only the Internal network. You still need a firewall to guard against attacks on your network's access point and protocol-switching device.

Dynamic Packet Filtering

Packet filtering refers to the ability of a router or a firewall to discard packets that don't meet the right criteria. Firewalls use *dynamic packet filtering* to ensure that the packets they forward match sessions initiated on their private side by something called a *dynamic state list* or *state table*, which keeps track of all communication sessions between stations from inside and outside the firewall. This list changes dynamically as sessions are added and deleted.

So with dynamic packet filtering, only packets for valid and current sessions are allowed to pass. Anyone trying to play back a communication session—for instance, a login to gain access—won't be able to do that if your firewall is using dynamic packet filtering with a dynamic state list because the data they send isn't part of a currently valid session. The firewall will respond to an event like this by dropping all packets that don't correspond to a current session via the information in the dynamic state list. Let me clarify this: Say a computer in Network A requests a Telnet session with a server in Network B. The firewall in between the two keeps a log of the communication packets that are sent each way, and only packets that belong to the current session will be allowed back into Network A through that firewall.

Figure 15.5 depicts a failed attempt to infiltrate a network protected with a dynamic state list. Can you see that the hacker attempts to insert a packet into the communication stream but can't because they don't have the correct packet number? This is because the firewall was waiting for a specific order of packets, and the hacker's packet is out of sequence.

FIGURE 15.5   A hacker denied by a dynamic state list

State List

Session between A & B:
Last packet #1238
Next packet #1239

Server sending
packet #1239

Firewall

Client expecting
packet #1239

Hacker attempts
to get in using
packet #1211.

Hacker is denied access because the
state list says the firewall should expect
packet #1239 next, but instead it is
receiving #1211, so it rejects the packet.

Proxy Services

Firewalls can also implement something called *proxy services*, which actually makes them *proxy servers*, or proxies for short. Proxies act on behalf of the whole network to completely separate packets from internal hosts and external hosts. Let's say an internal client sends a request to an external host on the Internet. That request will get to the proxy server first, where it will be examined, broken down, and handled by an application that will create a new packet requesting information from the external server. Figure 15.6 demonstrates this process. Make a note to self that this exchange occurs between applications at the Application layer of the OSI model.

FIGURE 15.6   A packet going to a proxy

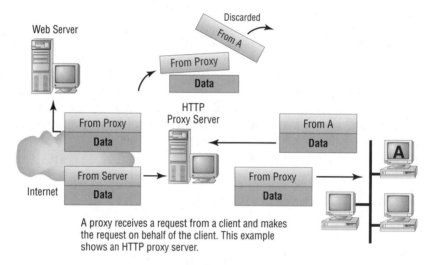

A proxy receives a request from a client and makes the request on behalf of the client. This example shows an HTTP proxy server.

Proxies make good firewalls because they dissect the entire packet so that each section of it can be scrutinized for invalid data at each and every layer of the OSI model; proxies look at everything from information in the packet header to the actual contents of the message. They can even examine attachments for viruses. As if all that isn't cool enough, proxies can also search messages for keywords that can indicate the source of a packet. That last little goodie is vital because you can use this type of searching to prevent sensitive information from escaping your organization along with the outbound data stream. If your sensitive documents contain a header or footer that includes something like *MyCompanyName Confidential*, you can set up your proxy server software to search for it. The only downside is that all that analysis will definitely degrade overall performance because it requires a lot more time than just checking state lists.

There are many types of proxy servers:

IP proxy   An *IP proxy* hides the IP addresses of all the devices on the internal network by exchanging its IP address for the address of any requesting station. This is good because you definitely don't want a hacker to know any IP addresses specific to your internal network, right? Even Internet web servers won't be able to determine the specific IP address from which they receive a request because any and all communications appear to have originated from the proxy server—nice! These proxies are sometimes called *Network Address Translation (NAT)* proxies.

Web (HTTP) proxy   *Web proxies*, also called HTTP proxies, handle HTTP requests on behalf of the sending workstation. When these are implemented correctly, a client's web browser asks a web server on the Internet for a web page using an HTTP request. Because the browser is configured to make HTTP requests using an HTTP proxy, the browser sends the request to the proxy server. The proxy server changes the From address of the HTTP request to its own network address and sends it to the Internet web server. The response to the HTTP request goes directly to the proxy (because it replaced the sender's address with its own). The proxy server then replaces its address with the address of the original sender, and the response is delivered to the original sender.

The most popular implementation of a web proxy is a *proxy cache server*. This server receives an HTTP request from a web browser and then makes the request on behalf of the sending workstation. When the requested page is returned, the proxy server caches a copy of the page locally. The next time someone requests the same web page or Internet information, the page can be delivered from the local cache instead of the proxy server having to formulate a new request to the web server on the Internet. This speeds up web surfing for commonly accessed pages. Web proxies can also increase network security by filtering out content that is considered insecure, such as executables, scripts, or viruses.

FTP proxy   FTP proxies handle the uploading and downloading of files from a server on behalf of a workstation. An FTP proxy operates in a fashion similar to a web proxy. As with web proxies, FTP proxies can filter out undesirable content (viruses and the like).

SMTP proxy   SMTP proxies handle Internet email. Here, the actual contents of the packet and mail can be automatically searched. Any packets or messages that contain material that is not considered secure can be blocked. Many SMTP proxies allow network virus protection software to scan inbound mail.

 Not every firewall falls into a simple category. Although firewalls are used to typically work in one arena, today's firewalls offer multiple solutions within one box or software program. Firewalls that perform more than one type of filtering service are sometimes referred to as *hybrid firewalls*.

Firewalls at the Application Layer vs. the Network Layer

By now, you know all about the OSI model and remember that the Application layer is at the top of the heap and the Network layer is third up from the bottom. And as a rule of thumb, the higher you get in the OSI model, the more complex the interactions become.

This rule holds true for discussions of firewalls that work at the Application layer versus those that work at the Network layer.

The first firewalls that were developed functioned solely at the Network layer, and the earliest of these were known as *packet-filter firewalls*. I covered packet filtering a bit earlier in this chapter; as a refresher, all it means is that the firewall looks at an incoming packet and applies it against the set of rules in the ACL(s). If the packet passes, it gets sent on. If not, the packet is dropped.

This type of filtering is pretty basic because all the firewall considers is the individual packet. All that matters are the source and destination addresses, protocol, and port number. The firewall doesn't care whether that packet is stand-alone or part of another data stream. This process works fairly well for common protocols such as TCP and User Datagram Protocol (UDP), which communicate on predefined port numbers. People generally refer to two types of Network layer firewalls: stateful and stateless.

Stateful vs. Stateless Network Layer Firewalls

As I said in the last section, a basic packet filter doesn't care about whether the packet it is examining is stand-alone or part of a bigger message stream. That type of packet filter is said to be *stateless*, in that it does not monitor the status of the connections passing through it. Again, these work pretty well, but the firewall has no idea whether a packet is legitimate or possibly a rogue packet trying to sneak by. These types of firewalls tended to be susceptible to various DoS attacks and IP spoofing.

The one big advantage that a stateless firewall has over its stateful counterparts is that it uses less memory. Today, stateless firewalls are best used on an internal network where security threats are lower and there are few restrictions.

In contrast to a stateless firewall, a *stateful* firewall is one that keeps track of the various data streams passing through it. If a packet that is a part of an established connection hits the firewall, it's passed through. New packets are subjected to the rules as specified in the ACL. These types of firewalls are better at preventing network attacks that look to exploit existing connections, or DoS attacks.

A stateful firewall works by using the TCP three-way handshake. First, the client sends a packet with the SYN bit set to the firewall. The firewall interprets this as a new connection and passes the request to the appropriate service provider on the internal network. Next, the service responds with a packet that has both the SYN and ACK bits set. Finally, the client responds with a packet with only the ACK bit set. At that point, the connection is considered established and the firewall will only allow packets in that have the same connection identification. The established connection is logged in the *state table*.

If there is no data on the connection for a specified period of time, the connection will time out in the state table. Any new communication will need to be reestablished based on the ACL rules.

Stateful firewalls tend to be a bit slower at establishing connections than stateless ones because there is more to do. After the connection is established, though, stateful firewalls are usually faster because they just have to check the state table for the connection instead of comparing the packet against all the relevant ACLs. This is done via *stateful packet inspection*. Most stateful firewalls can also keep track of connections using connectionless protocols such as UDP.

In a common DoS attack, the SYN flood, the attacker attempts to overload a firewall by spamming it with inordinate numbers of SYN requests. The firewall by default will keep sending SYN/ACKs back, thereby preventing it from responding to legitimate connection requests. An additional problem for the firewall is that it maintains memory space for every SYN/ACK its send out and the attacker never answers with a final ACK, so memory gets used up. Many of today's firewalls can circumvent this problem by not responding to multiple SYN requests from the same host.

 Real World Scenario

Firewall Challenges

You were just given a firewall for your network and that firewall was appropriated from a different part of your company. You want to make sure hackers can't get in through that firewall on random ports. Fortunately for you, the firewall is default deny, so you don't have too many worries. You open up the ports for legitimate traffic, such as 80 for HTTP, 161 for Simple Network Management Protocol (SNMP), 21 for FTP, and so on. But users complain that they are unable to download files from the extranet using FTP. What happened?

FTP does work on port 21, but it also establishes connections on arbitrary high-number ports to complete its work. If those ports are not opened, FTP won't work. This is where a stateful firewall is handy. When FTP goes to open the new port number, the firewall will see that the data intended for the new port is part of the existing FTP connection and let the data pass through. Yet another reason why stateful firewalls are so much better than stateless ones!

Application Layer Firewalls

Although stateful firewalls are more powerful and secure than stateless ones, Application layer firewalls are even better. They work by inspecting more than just data in the IP header: They read data at the Application layer. In other words, they will know whether a packet is FTP, SNMP, HTTP, or whatever Application layer protocol it is. The one major drawback is speed. Because these devices have to read more information than their Network layer counterparts, they do tend to be a bit slower. It's generally not enough that you'll notice, though, unless you have the reaction time of Superman.

One nice feature of Application layer firewalls is that they let you set proxy rules for multiple applications on the same firewall. As a proxy, the firewall processes all data between the two endpoints and drops all packets that are suspicious. In theory, a rogue packet will never reach the system on your internal network. Application layer firewalls also handle complex protocols such as H.323, which is used for Voice over IP (VoIP), much better than their Network layer counterparts.

Scanning Services and Other Firewall Features

Most firewalls are capable of performing *scanning services*, which means that they scan different types of incoming traffic in an effort to detect problems. For example, firewalls can scan incoming HTTP traffic to look for viruses or spyware, or they can scan email looking for spam. You can often set scanning rules that will prevent users from downloading files over a certain size. On Cisco routers, scanning is administered by the Content Security Control (CSC) and Security Services Module (SSM). Two categories of content are typically scanned: mail and web.

Table 15.1 shows some key default scanning settings within CSC SSM.

TABLE 15.1 Default scanning settings

Category	Protocol	Function
Mail	SMTP and POP3	Scans all scannable files in the email
Mail	SMTP and POP3	Rejects all messages larger than 15MB
Mail	SMTP	Rejects messages addressed to more than 100 recipients
Mail	SMTP	Cleans emails or attachments containing malware, and attaches a notification that the malware was deleted
Web	HTTP	Scans all file downloads
Web	HTTP	Scans web mail sites for AOL, MSN, Google, and Yahoo!
Web	FTP	Scans all file transfers
Web	HTTP and FTP	Skips scanning of files larger than 50MB; can also enable deferred scanning
Web	HTTP and FTP	Cleans files in which malware is detected; deletes files that cannot be cleaned

The defaults give you a pretty good level of protection, but there may be instances where you want to change settings. For example, if you are concerned about bandwidth, then you can limit the size of files transferred via FTP or HTTP. If mail storage is an issue, then you can set the firewall to reject mail larger than 10MB.

Keep in mind, though, that by changing some settings, you are increasing your security risk. If you offer deferred scanning for large files, it will allow you to begin viewing the data without a prolonged wait while the entire body of information is scanned. However, the unscanned portion of information can introduce a security risk.

If you are having problems with large file transfers timing out on your network, it's possible that it's partially caused by the firewall scanning the files immediately. Offering deferred scanning can help fix the problem, but you also need to weigh the additional security risk.

Content Filtering

Content filtering is very closely related to scanning services, and on Cisco routers it's also provided by the CSC SSM. Specifically, *content filtering* means blocking data based on the content of the data rather than the source of the data. Most commonly, this is used to filter email and website access.

The reasons for using content filtering seem pretty obvious. Most companies have a zero-tolerance policy against hateful material or pornography. If a user on a company network uses that network to spread hate mail or porn, the company could be liable for damages in a lawsuit if they didn't take measures to prevent such actions. It's not only a moral issue, it's a legal issue too.

Content filtering is also important in places like schools. It's doubtful that parents want their kids to be able to stumble upon a porn site in the school library while researching a school project. Content filtering can block that site from being accessed so the problem never occurs. You can also find several parental-control software packages for home use that employ content filtering.

There are several ways to filter content; here are some of the more common categories used:

- Attachment (blocking attachments of a certain type, such as EXE files)
- Bayesian
- Content-encoding
- Email headers
- Language
- Phrases
- Proximity of words to each other
- URLs

Nearly all filtering methods use a combination of filters to protect users from improper content.

Signature Identification

Firewalls can also stop attacks and problems through a process called *signature identification*. Viruses that are known will have a signature, which is a particular pattern of data, within them. Firewalls (and antivirus programs) can use signatures to identify a virus and remove it. The same holds true for other software bugs such as worms and spyware.

Numerous network attacks have signatures as well. For example, if your router starts getting hit by large numbers of SYN requests, you may be at the beginning of a SYN flood attack. The inundation of SYN traffic is a signature of a SYN flood.

Zones

A *zone* is an individual area of the network that has been configured with a specific trust level. Firewalls are ideal devices to regulate the flow of traffic between zones. If you look back at Figure 15.3, this provides a good example of how zone levels could work. The Internet would be a zone with no trust or a low level of trust. The DMZ, located between the Internet and the internal network, could have a medium level of trust. The computers on the intranet would all be within a high trust zone. The higher the trust level, the less scrutiny you place on data coming from a computer in that zone.

Another way to look at zones is to understand how Internet Explorer deals with them. Figure 15.7 shows you what the Internet Options Security tab looks like. On this tab, you can see that there are four zones for which you can configure security levels: Internet, Local Intranet, Trusted Sites, and Restricted Sites. There are three default security levels for the Internet: High, Medium, and Low. Don't get this confused with the trust levels I talked about in the previous paragraph—they are basically opposites. If the security level is set to High, it means you have low trust.

FIGURE 15.7   Internet Options Security tab

A good way to ensure some security through your browser is to set the security level to Medium-High or High and leave it there. If there are sites that you download from frequently and that you trust, then you can put those sites into the Trusted Sites zone. Click Trusted Sites and then click the Sites button to get to the screen shown in Figure 15.8.

FIGURE 15.8   Adding a trusted site

Finally, you can customize the security level of any of the zones by clicking the Custom Level button near the bottom of the Internet Options window. This will take you to a screen similar to the one shown in Figure 15.9.

FIGURE 15.9   Custom security settings

Within the custom settings, you can specify behavior for .NET framework components, ActiveX controls and plug-ins, downloads, scripting, user authentication, and several other options. Most of the options have choices to disable, enable, or prompt you if you want to continue with the operation.

WARNING

Although Internet Explorer security options can help protect your computer, do not think of them as a replacement for a firewall. The best security systems are multifaceted. You should have a firewall solution in place and then augment that with solid security measures on your local computer as well.

Intrusion Detection and Prevention Systems

If someone has broken into your network, how would you know? I mean, it's not like you're going to find broken windows or the door left wide open, right? Although it's true that you won't be dusting for prints, bad guys who break into networks still leave clues behind that can help you sleuth out their identities as well as how they gained access. A great tool for doing network detective work is known as an *intrusion detection system (IDS)*.

Firewalls are designed to block nasty traffic from entering your network, but an IDS is more of an auditing tool: It keeps track of all activity on your network so you can see if someone has been trespassing. Because IDSs are a fairly new technology, people are busy developing ways to combine IDS technology with existing firewalls.

WARNING

An intrusion detection system does *not* replace a firewall on your network!

There are two ways IDS systems can detect attacks or intrusions. The first is based on the signature of an intrusion, often referred to as a *misuse-detection IDS (MD-IDS)*, and it works by looking for fingerprints. That's right—I said fingerprints, which in this case means strange or abusive use of the network. The IDS sends up an alarm only if it recognizes the fingerprints typical of attackers. The second approach looks for anomalies in network activity, or an *anomaly-detection IDS (AD-IDS)*. An AD-IDS basically watches for anything out of the ordinary; if it discovers fingerprints where there shouldn't be any, it will send out an alert. And a really cool feature is that it's known as a *smart system* because it learns on the go by keeping track of and building a history of network activity for norms to which you can compare unusual activity. Most IDSs today are a combination the two types of detection systems. Figure 15.10 shows an MD-IDS in action.

NOTE

An intrusion detection system cannot detect attacks within encrypted traffic.

FIGURE 15.10   An MD-IDS system in action

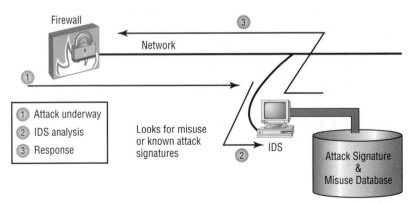

An IDS is a system made up of several components, including one or more sensors to detect events, a console to control and configure the sensors and monitor events, and a database that records the events. These three elements can all be on the same device, or they can be implemented on multiple devices.

The two most common types of IDS implementations are network based and host based.

Network-Based IDS

By far the most common implementation of a detection system is a *network-based IDS (NIDS)*, where the IDS is a separate device attached to the network via a machine like a switch or directly via a tap. Some IDSs are even capable of attaching to the network both outside and inside the firewall; this gives you the best security because you can see what is happening out in the wild and really nail exactly what's getting through your defenses. Figure 15.11 gives you an example of what this setup can look like.

FIGURE 15.11   An IDS connected to the network

When your IDS detects an intrusion, it will respond to it either passively or actively. Passive responses are the easiest to configure and include the following:

Logging   All activity to the intrusion is logged. The information gathered can be used to foil future attacks of the same type. Intrusions should always be logged.

Notification   When an attack occurs, an IDS can send an alert to one or more administrators.

Shunning   I'm not kidding about this one—you can sometimes just ignore the attack because it's possible it won't affect your network. For instance, if someone launches an attack designed to cripple a Microsoft Exchange email server at a network that's running Lotus Notes, you're all good, so why waste time doing anything about it? I would recommend recording the event though.

Active responses mean taking immediate action. When an IDS moves to prevent an attack, it's often called a reactive system or an *intrusion protection system (IPS)*. Here are three common active responses:

Changing network configuration   Let's say an attack comes in on port 21. Your IDS can close the port either temporarily or permanently. The downside is that if the IDS closes ports, legitimate traffic can't get through either, but it will definitely stop the attack. Figure 15.12 shows an example of closing port 80 (HTTP) for 60 seconds.

FIGURE 15.12   Shutting down port 80 for 60 seconds to stop an attack

Terminating sessions   When the IDS detects an attack, it can force all sessions to close and restart, which will affect and delay legitimate traffic too, but not for long.

Deceiving the attacker   This one's the most fun because it tricks the bad guy into thinking their attack is really working when it's not. The system logs information, trying to pinpoint who's behind the attack and which methods they're using. This response requires something called a *honeypot*, typically a server or group of servers (called honeynets) or maybe even access points, to which the hacker is directed; it's intended to keep their interest long enough to gather enough information to identify them and their attack method so you can prevent another attack in the future. Figure 15.13 demonstrates this.

FIGURE 15.13   Deceiving an attacker with a honeypot

I am not endorsing using honeypots, just explaining the concept and how they work.

Host-Based IDS

In a *host-based IDS (HIDS)*, software runs on one computer to detect abnormalities on that system alone by monitoring applications, system logs, and event logs—not by directly monitoring network traffic.

Systems like these are typically implemented on servers because they're a bear to manage if spread across several client computers on a network. Plus, if the IDS database is on the local computer and its data becomes compromised by an attack, the IDS data could be corrupted too.

 Other types of IDSs are protocol based (PIDS), which monitor traffic for one protocol on one server; application protocol based (APIDS), which monitor traffic for a group of servers running the same application (such as SQL); and hybrid IDS, which combine one or more IDS technologies.

Vulnerability Scanners

One of the most effective ways to determine if security holes exist in the network is to think like an attacker and attack your own network. In that case, why not use the same tools that the hacker might use to identify your weaknesses? For example, if I wanted to verify the proper application of some ACLs to a firewall, I could do so with with scanning services supplied by a vulnerability scanner. In the following sections, I'll cover two of the most widely known and effective programs that can be used for this purpose.

NESSUS

NESSUS is a propriety vulnerability scanning program that requires a license to use commercially yet is the single most popular scanning program in use. It normally is executed from the command line because it can thus be included in batch files that can automate its operation on a schedule. Its output can be reported in a variety of formats, including plain text, HTML, and XML.

It operates by performing a port scan and then follows up with more specific tests and scans based on the ports open. It can identify a wide array of weaknesses, including the following:

- Unsecured access to sensitive data on a system
- Misconfigurations like open mail relay and missing patches
- Password issues such as the use of default passwords, common passwords, and blank passwords on system accounts

It can also perform an active attack such as denial of service or a dictionary attack.

NMAP

Network Mapper (NMAP) was originally intended to simply identify devices on the network for the purpose of creating a network diagram. Its functionality has evolved however, and now it can also do the following:

- Perform port scanning
- Identify versions of network services in operation on the network
- Identify operating systems

It can be used from the command line as with NESSUS, but it also can be used with web-based interfaces to be controlled remotely.

VPN Concentrators

A *VPN concentrator* is a device that creates remote access for virtual private networks (VPNs) either for users logging in remotely or for a large site-to-site VPN. In contrast to standard remote-access connections, remote-access VPNs often allow higher data throughput and provide encryption. Cisco produces VPN concentrators that support anywhere from 100 users up to 10,000 simultaneous remote-access connections.

Encryption for a remote-access VPN through a concentrator is usually handled by Internet Protocol Security (IPSec) or by Secure Sockets Layer (SSL), and user authentication can be achieved via Microsoft's Active Directory; Kerberos; Remote Authentication Dial In User Service (RADIUS); Rivest, Shamir, and Adleman (RSA); and digital certificates. Many VPN concentrators also have a built-in authentication server and allow ACLs to be implemented through them. In Figure 15.14, you can see where VPN concentrators are usually placed within a network setup.

FIGURE 15.14   VPN concentrator in a network

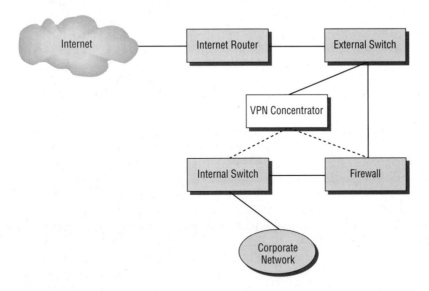

The dotted line indicates that you can opt to run your remote-access clients through the firewall before they're granted internal access, or you can just let the concentrator handle the security.

Understanding Problems Affecting Device Security

Throughout this whole chapter, I've been going on and on about the myriad devices we use to secure traffic coming into our networks and devices and the things we depend on to detect and prevent attacks on them. It's an important subject and one that you must solidly understand in order to be effective in networking. Knowing how to implement a tight security program requires working knowledge of these devices, but it doesn't end there because there's always more you can know.

There happen to be a few more really significant and valuable concepts you should have a good grasp of when setting up and managing the security on your network. So that's the direction in which we're going to head for the remainder of this chapter—we'll cover key issues you need to be aware of, including physical security and corresponding logical security structures, restricting access, and the types of protocols you should and should not use on your network.

Physical Security

Over the years, I've visited lots of different companies, large and small, public and private, and analyzed, advised, troubleshot, designed, and implemented their networks. Without fail, the system administrators I've met along the way have been really eager to tell me all about the security systems they have in place. "Look at this awesome firewall setup!" "Check out the cool Group Policy structure we have!" "Watch how quickly our fault tolerance springs into action!" They're very proud, and rightly so, of what they've worked so hard to set up, because doing that isn't easy.

But interestingly, one of the things few people brag about is physical security—like it's some kind of afterthought. Maybe the server room has a locked door, maybe it doesn't. Maybe the badges that open that door are owned by the right people, or maybe they aren't. I guess that on a subconscious level, we tend to inherently trust the people working within the walls and focus our fears, suspicions, and ammo on mysterious outside forces that we're sure are incessantly trying to break in, steal data, or totally murder our networks. Some of the sharpest, most talented, and savvy system administrators I've ever met still have a tendency to neglect inside security and fail to reasonably monitor things going on within the building.

And there are some seriously vital things to nail down on the inside. For instance, does it really matter if your network has a secured subnet for the servers, with its own dedicated internal firewall? Definitely—I've actually found servers in racks like sitting ducks in a hallway right across from the lunch room. When I pointed out the fact that this was not so good, I was assured that it was only temporary until the server room construction was complete. I don't know about you, but for some reason, that didn't cut it and didn't make me feel anywhere near okay with the situation. At another company, I found the door to the server room propped open because otherwise "it got too hot in there." Because that toasty server room didn't exactly have a guard posted, anyone could just walk in and do whatever; the backup tapes were clearly marked and sitting there on a shelf—yikes! And don't even get me started about the heat. The bottom line is that if your system is not physically secured, you're basically sending out an open invitation to a Pandora's box of problems without even realizing it.

 Real World Scenario

Beware the Big Gulp

Several years ago when I was teaching a networking class, one of my best students issued me a challenge. He was proud of the security configuration on his server computer in the classroom and went so far as to tell me there was no way I could get to or damage any files on his system. He was really sure about that. Well, it just so happens I like a good challenge...

The students went off to lunch, and I stayed behind to work on a few things. While they were gone, I got out my handy Partition Magic diskette (I said this was a while ago) and popped it into his system. One reset button push later, I was in business. I wiped out the partitions on his hard drive and shut down the system.

When he came back from lunch, he looked a bit confused. He clearly remembered leaving his computer on, and upon booting up and playing around for a minute, he realized that his hard drive was gone. At first, he was more than a little angry at me for doing that, but then I asked him to give me a chance to prove a point—an important one. That is, when someone has access to your computer, they can do whatever they want. Yes, they might not be able to read your files (although I could have done that too), but they can still do a lot of damage. My tool of destruction was a partitioning program, but going back to that "servers out in the open across from the lunch room" situation, all it would take is a spilled soft drink to cause mass destruction. In any case, the data clearly was not safe, so physical security needs to be a top priority.

Physical Barriers

Your first objective is to keep people from physically getting to your equipment. Clearly, end users need to be able to get to their workstations, but only authorized personnel should be anywhere near your servers. The best way to do this is to have a dedicated, two-stage, air-conditioned server room with really secure doors and locks. Even better, your data center should have more than one form of physical security—preferably three. We call that a *multiple barrier system*. For instance, you could have a perimeter security system controlling access to the building as your first line of defense. The second would be a secured door to the computer room, and the third would be another security door to the server room itself. This is illustrated in Figure 15.15.

FIGURE 15.15   A three-layer security model

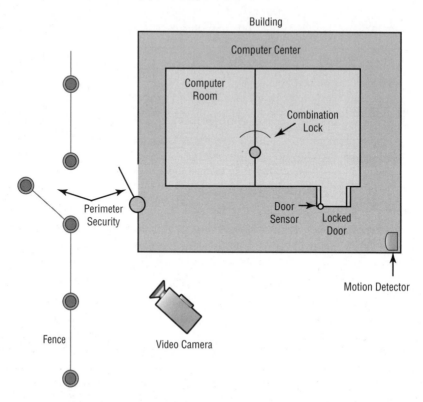

Security Zones

Your network probably has different security zones. Let's say your servers are in one zone and the clients are in another. Maybe your engineering department has its own zone. So why not have the same zones for physical access to the computers? Many companies today use magnetically encoded badges to control where employees are allowed to go inside the building. You may need a safety clearance and/or certification before you can go in the room where the pilot production machine lives. People should be cleared and certified before they're allowed in the server room as well.

Logical Security Configurations

Now that you have your physical network locked down tight, it's time to review the security configuration of your network. The same concepts that apply to physical security apply here too. First, you want to ensure that your network has an outside barrier and/or a perimeter defense. This is usually achieved by having a solid firewall, and it's best to have an IDS or IPS of some sort as well. Figure 15.16 shows what this might look like.

FIGURE 15.16 Network perimeter defense

That may be enough for your network, but maybe not. Let's say that your network serves several distinct departments at your company. The engineering, accounting, and sales groups all have their own unique needs. What you can now do is divide up your internal network into smaller administrative zones by creating VLANs and using a DMZ. Maybe your network would logically look like the one shown in Figure 15.17.

FIGURE 15.17 Network divided into security zones

Finally, your network might be similar to the one shown in Figure 15.16, but just larger. Maybe traffic is heavy and you need to break up physical segments. Perhaps different groups are in different buildings or on different floors of a building and you want to effectively segment them. There could be any number of reasons for you to "physically" separate your network into different groups, effectively partitioning your network by using multiple routers as shown in Figure 15.18.

FIGURE 15.18 Using routers to divide a network into security zones

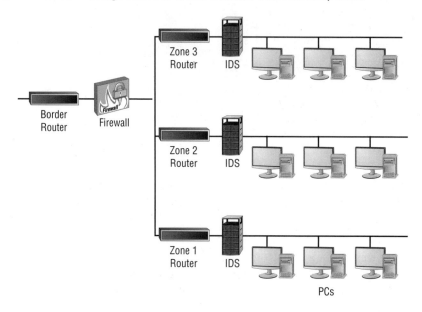

Summary

In this chapter, you learned a lot about physical and hardware security. We dove into this increasingly important subject by looking at one of the most useful network protection devices around: firewalls. You found out the differences between network-based versus host-based firewalls and then learned the specific ways that firewalls work to protect our data and networks by using access control lists (ACLs). You also learned about other key firewall topics like demilitarized zones (DMZs), protocol switching, packet filtering, and proxy services. I talked about how firewalls can operate at the Network layer or the Application layer of the OSI model. For those operating at the Network level, there are stateful firewalls that keep track of the established connections passing through them and stateless firewalls that don't. Firewalls also provide services like scanning, signature identification, content filtering, and breaking your network up into security zones.

We then moved on and discussed two other vital hardware devices: intrusion detection and prevention systems and VPN concentrators. You learned that IDS devices can be network or host based, just like firewalls, but unlike firewalls, which block traffic based on specific rules, IDS and IPS systems allow traffic in and then initiate a reaction if any problems are detected. I also talked about something called an IPS, which is an IDS that can generate an active response when an intrusion is detected. We then covered VPN concentrators, which are specifically designed to allow several hundred—even several thousand—users to remotely access your network either through a secure connection or by setting up a virtual secure network between two locations.

Finally, you discovered some often-overlooked aspects of physical security that can seriously affect your network. You now know that beyond a doubt, if people can get to your hardware, they can do damage to your infrastructure, intentionally or not.

Exam Essentials

Understand the difference between a network-based firewall and a host-based firewall. A network-based firewall is a hardware device on the network or on a router that protects a group of computers. A host-based firewall is software installed on one individual machine, and it protects only that machine.

Understand how a firewall determines which traffic can pass through it. Firewalls use access control lists (ACLs), which are sets of rules, to determine which traffic is allowed to pass through.

Remember where a DMZ can be placed. A demilitarized zone (DMZ) can be located outside a firewall, connected directly to the Internet. However, it can also be placed after the firewall. You need to remember that it can be placed in either location.

Understand what a proxy server is and what types of proxying are common. A proxy server is a computer that makes and fulfills requests on behalf of another computer. Many firewalls can act as proxies. Common proxy services include IP proxy, web proxy, FTP proxy, and mail (SMTP) proxy.

Know on which levels of the OSI model various security devices operate. Firewalls work at the Application Layer or the Network layer. Port security on switches operates at the Data Link layer.

Understand the difference between stateful and stateless firewalls. A stateful firewall keeps track of the established connections passing through it. When another packet is received that's part of an existing connection (part of a current state), the packet is passed without checking the ACLs. A stateless firewall examines each packet individually and does not track existing states. This makes it a bit slower and more susceptible to network attacks.

Know what types of services firewalls can provide. Most firewalls provide scanning services, content filtering, signature identification, and the ability to segregate network segments into separate security zones.

Know the difference between an IDS and an IPS. An intrusion detection system (IDS) monitors network traffic, looking for signs of an intrusion. Intrusions are detected by matching activity versus known signatures within the IDS's database. If an intrusion is detected, a passive response such as logging or notifying a network administrator is executed. An intrusion prevention system (IPS) is like an IDS, but with two key differences. First, it learns what is "normal" on the network and can react to abnormalities even if they're not part of the signature database. Second, it can issue an active response such as shutting down a port, resetting connections, or attempting to lull the attacker into a trap.

Written Lab

In this section, write the answers to the following security questions:

1. Which type of security device employs a redirection device known as a honeypot?

2. Which type of firewall keeps track of existing connections passing through it?

3. If you wanted to ensure that your firewall could block inflammatory email, which type of service would you look for?

4. A firewall's list of rules that it uses to block traffic is called _____.

5. If you wanted to allow remote access to 500 users, which type of device is recommended?

6. If data from one of your subnets should be restricted from entering another subnet, the subnets should be configured as different _____.

7. What type of internal security is implemented at Layer 2?

8. How does an ACL treat any traffic type by default?

9. What is a group of servers used to lure attackers called?

10. Logging, notification, and shunning are what types of reactions from what type of security device?

    You can find the answers in Appendix B.

Review Questions

You can find the answers in Appendix A.

1. In general, firewalls work by _____.

    A. Rejecting all packets regardless of security restrictions

    B. Forwarding all packets regardless of security restrictions

    C. Allowing only packets that pass security restrictions to be forwarded

    D. None of the above

2. In which layer of the OSI model do software firewalls operate? (Choose all that apply.)

    A. Application

    B. Presentation

    C. Physical

    D. Network

3. What is the main difference between a network-based firewall and a host-based firewall?

    A. A network-based firewall protects the Internet from attacks.

    B. A network-based firewall protects a network, not just a single host.

    C. A network-based firewall protects the network wires.

    D. A network-based firewall protects a CD from data loss.

4. What is one advantage that a stateless firewall has over its stateful counterparts?

    A. It uses less power.

    B. It utilizes less memory.

    C. It's better at preventing network attacks.

    D. It works better on external networks.

5. Which if the following items cannot be identified by the NESSUS program?

    A. Default password use

    B. Incorrect IP addresses

    C. Unsecured data

    D. Missing security patches

6. What is the benefit of using a firewall?

   A. Protects external users

   B. Protects external hardware

   C. Protects LAN resources

   D. Protects hardware from failure

7. IDS systerms can identify attackers by their _____.

   A. Port number

   B. Signature

   C. Timing

   D. IV

8. Which device can limit traffic on a network and allow access onto specific TCP/IP port numbers when security is a concern?

   A. Hub

   B. Firewall

   C. DNS

   D. Modem

9. Which is not a type of access control list (ACL)?

   A. Standard

   B. Extended

   C. Referred

   D. Outbound

10. What is it called when the firewall ignores an attack?

    A. Logging

    B. Shunning

    C. Notification

    D. False negative

11. What is the function of a DMZ?

    A. To separate a security zone for an IPS and IDS server

    B. To create a security zone for VPN terminations

    C. To create a security zone that allows public traffic but is isolated from the private inside network

    D. To create a security zone that allows private traffic but is isolated from the public network

12. Which of the following are types of services that firewalls can provide?

    A. Content filtering

    B. Segregate network segments

    C. Signature identification

    D. Scanning services

    E. All of the above

13. Which type of security device monitors network traffic, looking for signs of an intrusion?

    A. Intrusion detection system

    B. Demilitarized zone (DMZ)

    C. Firewall

    D. VPN concentrator

14. Which of the following is a vulnerability scanner?

    A. Network Monitor

    B. NESSUS

    C. Traceroute

    D. Tripwire

15. Which of the following is NOT a function of NMAP?

    A. Perform port scanning

    B. Identify operating systems

    C. Collect passwords

    D. Identify versions of network services in operation on the network

16. Changing network configurations, terminating sessions, and deceiving the attacker are actions that can be taken from what type of security device?

    A. Access control list (ACL)

    B. Content filtering

    C. Security zones

    D. Intrusion prevention system (IPS)

17. _____act on behalf of the whole network to completely separate packets from internal hosts and external hosts.

    A. Honeypots

    B. IDSs

    C. IPSs

    D. Proxies

18. Which of the following cannot be identified by NESSUS?

   A. Unsecured access to sensitive data on a system

   B. IP address conflicts

   C. Misconfigurations like open mail relay

   D. Password issues

19. A _____ firewall keeps track of the established connections passing through it.

   A. Hardware

   B. Software

   C. Stateful

   D. Network

20. A(n) _____ learns what is "normal" on the network and can react to abnormalities even if they're not part of the signature database.

   A. IDS

   B. Firewall

   C. IPS

   D. VPN concentrator

Chapter

16

Wide Area Networks

THE FOLLOWING COMPTIA NETWORK+ EXAM OBJECTIVES ARE COVERED IN THIS CHAPTER:

✓ **3.4 Categorize WAN technology types and properties.**

- Types:
    - T1/E1
    - T3/E3
    - DS3
    - OCx
    - SONET
    - SDH
    - DWDM
    - Satellite
    - ISDN
    - Cable
    - DSL
    - Cellular
    - WiMAX
    - LTE
    - HSPA+
    - Fiber
    - Dialup
    - PON
    - Frame relay
    - ATMs

- Properties:
  - Circuit switch
  - Packet switch
  - Speed
  - Transmission media
  - Distance

So what, exactly, is it that makes something a wide area network (WAN) instead of a local area network (LAN)? Well, there's obviously the distance thing, but these days, wireless LANs can cover some serious turf. What about bandwidth? Here again, some really big pipes can be had for a price in many places, so that's not it either. What the heck is it then?

One of the main ways a WAN differs from a LAN is that whereas you generally own a LAN infrastructure, you usually lease WAN infrastructure from a service provider. To be honest, modern technologies even blur this definition, but it still fits neatly into the context of CompTIA's Network+ exam objectives. Anyway, I've already talked about the data link that you usually own (Ethernet), but now we're going to find out about the kind you usually don't own—the type most often leased from a service provider.

You may already be familiar with T-series connections, which are leased line connections that reserve or dedicate lines that provide paths between network segments. In addition to these, I'll cover broadband services, including the various flavors of digital subscriber line (DSL) and cable modem connectivity that most of us use to connect to the Internet from home. Another new home option is the passive optical network (fiber to the premises). We'll take a look at that as well.

Cellular technologies have evolved over the years and may become the connection of choice for many to the Internet. In addition to HSPA+, WiMAX, and LTE, we'll briefly discuss the evolution of 1G, 2G, 3G, and 4G.

We'll also talk about the different kinds of WAN connectivity achieved through other kinds of links and over different transmission media. WAN technologies run the gamut from short-range *Bluetooth* to the seriously long-distance coverage available through satellite transmissions. And not to be forgotten are the WAN protocols that are basically sets of rules that delimit how long-distance communication and connectivity should happen. I'll tell you about the not-so-modern technologies like *Integrated Services Digital Networks (ISDN)*, *Frame Relay*, and *Asynchronous Transfer Mode (ATM)*, and I'll talk about the legacy phone-company network and some of its terminology as well. You'll also learn everything you'll need to know about different speed links—including T1s and E1s, SONET fiber links, and the plain old telephone service (POTS) lines that connect us to the Public Switched Telephone Network (PSTN)—to arm you with the knowledge you need to meet the CompTIA Network+ objectives.

For up-to-the-minute updates for this chapter, please see www.lammle.com/forum or the book's web site at www.sybex.com/go/netplus2e.

What's a WAN?

As local area networks grew and developed, it became necessary to be able to connect their resources together over long distances—not just locally. At first, we achieved this goal via the phone company network known as the Public Switched Telephone Network (PSTN). And so, the first successful network that could establish voice communications over disparate locations was born.

Because few of us remember back to a time when there was no such thing as phone service, PSTN was an obvious solution because it was already a fully operational circuit-switching network, where every phone call established a unique circuit from one endpoint (phone) to another through a path of switches. So, instead of reinventing the wheel to design LANs, early network planners used packet switching as their communications-delivery method. And clearly, the task of wiring these packet-switched networks to enable communication over vast locales wasn't exactly something that could be done quickly, so early wide area networks (WANs) also used the existing phone company network. But this solution wasn't all that great because it was costly and imposed some ugly limitations on networks trying to transfer their data to each other.

So there's the history for you. Today's WANs are communications networks that cover broad geographic areas that still frequently use phone companies (service providers) along with their circuit-switched networks to connect LANs together. Competition can be great, and with the Internet entering the playing field and giving us an alternative way to connect LANs, we benefit tremendously from the resulting reduction in the cost of our connectivity. These new connection options, along with their related protocols and technologies can greatly reduce the cost of a WAN's infrastructure, and lowered transport costs are a huge relief for network administrators and designers.

Anyway, remember that WAN protocols and technologies all occupy the lower three layers of the OSI model—the Physical layer, Data Link layer, and sometimes the Network layer. The various types of connections, technologies, topologies, and devices used with WANs as well as creating WAN connections using different transmission media like air (wireless), space (satellite), and both copper and glass fiber for wired connections will all be covered in this chapter. But before we go there, you need to know some basic WAN terms.

Defining WAN Terms

Before you run out and order a WAN service type from a provider, it would be a really good idea to understand the following terms that service providers typically use:

Customer premises equipment (CPE) *Customer premises equipment (CPE)* is equipment that's owned by the service provider but located on the subscriber's (your) property.

CSU/DSU *Channel service unit/data service unit (CSU/DSU)* is a Layer 1 device that connects your serial ports on your router to the provider's network and connects directly to the *demarcation point* (demark) or location. These devices can be external, as shown a little later in Figure 16.1, or they can be internal cards on the router. The CSU/DSU provides clocking of the line to the CPE (your router, in this case) and provides other important options, like voltage regulation.

Demarcation point   The demarc is the precise spot where the service provider's (local exchange carrier) responsibility ends and the CPE begins. It's generally a device in a telecommunications closet owned and installed by the telecommunications company (telco). It's your responsibility to cable—a task called *extended demark*—from this box to the CPE, which is usually a connection to a CSU/DSU or ISDN interface.

Local loop   A cable consisting of a pair of copper wires called the *local loop* connects the demarc to the closest switching office, known as a *central office (CO)*.

Central office (CO)   A phone company building that connects the customer's network to the provider's switching network. It is good to know that a CO is sometimes referred to as a *point of presence (POP)*.

Toll network   The *toll network* is a trunk line inside a WAN provider's network. This network is a collection of switches and facilities owned by the ISP.

With all this being said, let's take a look at Figure 16.1, which uses all these items to describe a typical WAN connection.

FIGURE 16.1   A typical wide area network

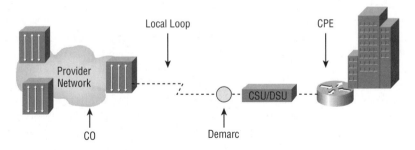

You would find the typical WAN as shown in Figure 16.1 when you order a T1 or Frame Relay circuit. Definitely familiarize yourself with these terms because they're crucial to understanding WAN technologies.

The Public Switched Telephone Network

The portion of the PSTN that runs from your house to the rest of the world is known as *plain old telephone service (POTS)*, and it's a popular method for connecting remote users to a local network because of its simplicity, low cost, and easy installation. But connecting to PSTN via ISDN, DSL, a cable modem, or even your cellular service is becoming all the rage today.

Two key concepts to keep in mind about PSTN are public and switched. *Public* basically means that, for a fee, anyone can lease the use of the network without having to deal with running any cabling, and *switched* explains how the phone system works. Even though one or more wires are actually connected to your home and/or office, all of them aren't always online, being used. But the wires are still available to you in their offline state so you can get online and join the network pretty much whenever you want. Think of it like a standing reservation, and your phone number is used as an ID to access it. Because you initiate the connection by dialing a certain phone number, it's easy to imagine how technically impractical it would be—even impossible—for this method to work if every phone number stayed connected all the time. If they did, the resulting backbone cabling requirements and problems would essentially be insurmountable.

Take, for instance, the US and worldwide telephone systems. The actual numbering sequence varies in other countries, but the concept is identical. The phone company runs the local loop from the demarc to the CO. All the pairs from all the local loop cables within a small regional area come together at a central point a lot like a patch panel in a LAN based on unshielded twisted-pair (UTP) cable.

This centralized point has a piece of equipment attached called a *switch*, which opens a communications session when it's initiated by a user who's dialed the phone number of the receiver and keeps it open until the "conversation" ends, when the switch closes it. On one side of the switch is the neighborhood wiring, and on the other side are lines that connect to either another switch or a local set of wiring.

Let me make this really clear. When you want to make a call, you pick up the phone, which completes a circuit that in most cases gives you a dial tone. The tone is the switch's way of saying, "I'm ready." When you don't get that dial tone, it means that either there's a break in the equipment chain or the switch is too busy processing other requests. In many areas of the world, you hear a fast on-and-off tone (somewhat like a fast busy signal) after giving a command string (phone number) to the local switch. This means that other switches the local switch is attempting to communicate with are too busy at that time.

Recently, this tone thing has been replaced with a voice recording saying something like, "We're sorry. All circuits are busy. Please try your call later." Sometimes you even get offered the shady-sounding "For only 99 cents, you can interrupt this call" added to the message. This happens frequently on holidays or during natural disasters because the local area's phone company uses only the minimum number of wires, called *trunk lines*, required to handle the norms of usage capacity plus a few auxiliary lines for peak usage. They keep equipment to a minimum because wiring and switches are really expensive; it's essentially a trade-off between providing 100 percent uptime and keeping the costs of leasing the connection from the phone company reasonably affordable.

WAN Connection Types

With all that in mind, it's time to go over the various types of WAN connections you'll find on the market today. Figure 16.2 shows the different WAN connection types that can be used to connect your LANs together.

FIGURE 16.2   WAN connection types

Okay—let me explain the different WAN connection types you see pictured here:

Dedicated (leased) lines   These are usually referred to as a *point-to-point* or dedicated connections. A dedicated *leased line* is a preestablished WAN communications path that goes from the CPE through the DCE switch and then over to the CPE of the remote site. The CPE enables DTE networks to communicate at any time with no cumbersome setup procedures to muddle through before transmitting data. When you've got plenty of cash, this is the way to go because it uses synchronous serial lines up to 45 Mbps. High-Level Data Link Control (HDLC) and Point-to-Point Protocol (PPP) encapsulations are frequently used on leased lines, and I'll go over them with you in detail in a bit.

Circuit switching   When you hear the term *circuit switching*, think phone call. The big advantage is cost—you only pay for the time you actually use. No data can transfer before an end-to-end connection is established. Circuit switching uses dial-up modems or ISDN and is used for low-bandwidth data transfers. I know what you're thinking: "Modems? Did he say modems? Aren't those only in museums by now?" After all, with all the wireless technologies available, who uses modems these days? Well, some people do have ISDN: It's still viable, and there are many places on Earth where you still need a modem to get yourself dialed in. Plus, circuit switching can be used in some of the newer WAN technologies as well.

Packet switching   This is a WAN switching method that allows you to share bandwidth with other companies to save money. *Packet switching* can be thought of as a network that's designed to look like a leased line yet charges you more like circuit switching does. But less isn't always more—there's definitely a downside, and if you need to transfer data constantly, just forget about this option. Instead, get yourself a leased line. Packet switching will only work for you if your data transfers are the bursty type—that is, not continuous. Frame Relay and the super-old X.25 are packet-switching technologies with speeds that can range from 56Kbps up to T3 (45Mbps).

LANs use packet switching with the source and destination addresses in the packet header to let the network move the packet closer and closer to the destination in the same way the post office takes your letter and keeps it moving closer and closer to its destination. This method avoids the necessity of establishing an actual contiguous electrical circuit from one end to the other, which is the method phone companies use to facilitate a phone call in their circuit-switched network.

Most WAN connections work on the phone company's circuit-switched network where the point-to-point nature of most connections eliminates the need for addressing because there's only one possible destination between endpoints. But you still need a proper addressing scheme within your LAN to ensure that data packets reach their correct destinations.

Bandwidth or Speed

Satisfying the need for speed involves moving large volumes of data, voice, and video loaded packets across vast distances to communicate. As companies' volume requirements have grown, so has the appetite for ever bigger, faster connections. Speed or bandwidth is measured in bits per second or multiples of bits per second, such as kilobits (thousands of bits) per second, for example.

The winner of the "slowest type of WAN connection" prize is (surprise) the much-maligned dial-on-demand dial-up connection. Modern dial-up modems typically have a maximum theoretical transfer speed of 56Kbps, although in most cases 40 to 50Kbps is the norm. Factors such as phone-line noise as well as the quality of the modem itself play a large part in determining connection speeds. Modems are required to *modulate/demodulate* the signal, which means translating the analog signal our ears hear into a digital stream for transfer across a digital network. Some connections may be as slow as 20 Kbps in extremely "noisy" environments like hotel rooms where phone lines are shared with an abundant number of extensions.

Megabyte (MB) and *gigabyte (GB)* usually refer to the amount of storage capacity available, whereas *bandwidth* and *speed* refer to units that measure how much data (bits) can be sent per second. In the networking world, speed is essentially the measurement of how fast the data flows (Hz) and also refers to how fast data flows within memory systems. Sometimes the terms bandwidth and speed are used interchangeably.

T-Series Connections

The basic, first level in bandwidth or speed for leased lines that provide synchronous connections between sites is known as the T1 line. It serves up 24 Digital Signal 0 (DS0)

64 Kbps channels in our country, Japan, and South Korea. A slightly bigger/faster version with 30 DS0 channels is available in Europe; it's called the E1 or E carrier line.

T1s use Digital Signal 1 (DS1) bit patterns to transmit packets; DS1 has to do with the service to be sent over a T1 --originally, 24 digitized voice channels. The terms T1 (which came from the carrier letter or part number assigned by AT&T to the technology) and DS1 have become synonymous and include a bunch of different services from voice to data to clear-channel pipes. The line speed is always consistent at 1.544 Mbps (millions of bits per second), but the payload can vary greatly.

That Doesn't Add Up!

Twenty-four of these channels is a composite of 1.536 Mbps, not 1.544 Mbps! Why is there a difference? The reason is that after a byte (8 bits) of data is sent from each channel (24×8 = 192 bits), there is an extra bit used for synchronizing called a frame bit. Hence, 193 bits are sent, and this increase of 1 bit per 192 causes the speed to increase to 1.544 Mbps.

T-series connections are digital connections that you can lease from the telephone company. They can use copper pairs like regular phone lines, or they can be brought in as part of a backbone (also called a trunk line). At this point, T-series connections use time-division multiplexing (TDM) to divide the bandwidth into channels of equal bit rate.

T-series connection types are denoted by the letter T plus a number. Each connection type differs in its speed and in the signal used to multiplex the channels. Table 16.1 lists some of the T-series connections and their maximum data rates. The most commonly used T-series lines are T1 and T3.

TABLE 16.1 T-series connections

Connection	Maximum speed
T1	1.544 Mbps
T1C	3.152 Mbps
T2	6.312 Mbps
T3	44.736 Mbps
T4	274.176 Mbps

The T1 Connection

As I said, a T1 is a 1.544 Mbps digital connection that's typically carried over two pairs of copper wires. This 1.544 Mbps connection uses DS1 and aggregates 24 discrete, 64 Kbps channels that use DS0 (which refers to the timeslots within a channel). Each channel can carry either voice or data. In the POTS world, T1 lines are used to convert and bundle analog phone conversations over great distances due to the better quality of a digital signal and the use of much less wiring than would be needed if each pair carried only one call. This splitting into independent channels also allows a company to combine voice and data over one T1 connection or to use the T1 as if it were an unchannelized 1.544 Mbps pipe. You can also order a fractional T1 (FT1) circuit that's delivered on a T1 but doesn't allow the use of all 24 channels.

The European version of the T1 is the E1, which operates at 2.048 Mbps and uses 30 64 Kbps channels (30 DS0s). It was designed later, based on T1s—they just made theirs a little bigger. You'll also find the J1, which is the Japanese version of the T1 and which operates at 1.544 Mbps, just like the T1.

 Real World Scenario

What Is a Good Speed for a Business?

Many of you who happen to be in charge of setting up your company's Internet connection may think that a T1 is the best speed for your business. Unfortunately, however, T1 connections to the Internet can be really pricey. If you're in the business of selling Internet connections as an ISP is, you can justify spending the big bucks on large bandwidth pipes. Another example of when it would make sense for you to opt for a T1 is if you have loads of users on your network—at least 50 or more.

But even if you've got bunches of users on your network, it could be worth it to check out alternative solutions for your business that offer similar speeds at lower costs, like DSL or a cable modem. You can always use a virtual private network (VPN) if you need the security. And there are inexpensive wireless connection options out there as well that provide good bandwidth. It's always a good idea to do your research before buying.

The T3 Connection

A T3 line works similarly to a T1 connection but carries a whopping 44.736 Mbps. This is equivalent to 28 T1 circuits (or a total of 672 DS0 channels), and it uses a signal known as Digital Signal 3 (DS3) that's definitely not the same as the DS1 signal and is generally delivered over fiber-optic cable. Many local ISPs have T3 connections to their next-tier ISPs. (Again, the math doesn't work out because of the frame bits.) Also, very large multinational companies use T3 connections to send voice and data between their major regional offices.

As with the T1, the T3 has a European counterpart (the E3), which operates at 34.368 Mbps. And the Japanese Digital Hierarchy specifies the J3 circuit, which operates at 32.064 Mbps.

That Doesn't Add Up!

Why does an E1 have more capacity than a T1 but a T3 has more capacity than an E3? E and T lines are incremented differently. A T1 is 28 T1s, while an E3 is 16 E1s.

Transmission Media

Another aspect of WAN technologies that can have a big effect on the speed, bandwidth, and the volume of data that can be transferred is the type of transmission media. Wireless transmissions use air as a transmission media. This not only creates a bit of challenge concerning security, it also presents us with signal degradation—the further the signal has to travel from the original source, the weaker it gets. A solution to this last hang-up comes through using microwave repeaters that retransmit signals through the air and bolster them. This approach is a lot more efficient because it can preserve signal strength over much greater distances.

The most far-reaching technology uses the air and even empty space to send electromagnetic signals to satellites from which they are then resent to distant geographic locations.

Wired Connections

Back on Earth, wired connections use either copper wire or glass fiber to carry bits as voltages or light pulses, respectively. That attenuation issue I just talked about under wireless technology, where the signal gradually weakens over distances, also relates to copper wire transmissions and limits the length of wire you can use. Fiber gives us a lot more bandwidth and is a lot less susceptible to noise, but it costs more to buy and install. In the United States, the standard for synchronous data transmission on optical fiber is called *Synchronous Optical Network (SONET)*, and the international equivalent of SONET is Synchronous Digital Hierarchy (SDH). SONET defines a base data rate, or *throughput*, of 51.84 Mbps, and multiples of this rate are known as optical carrier (OC) levels like OC-3, OC-12, and so on. Table 16.2 depicts common OC levels and their associated data rates.

TABLE 16.2   Common optical carrier levels (OC-*x*)

Level	Data rate
OC-1	51.84 Mbps
OC-3	155.52 Mbps
OC-12	622.08 Mbps
OC-48	2.488 Gbps
OC-192	9.953 Gbps

Regardless of the media used to carry WAN traffic, the growing volume of voice and video traversing data networks has led to new traffic problems. Regular data traffic can arrive out of order and be reassembled back into its original order on the receiving end, but voice and video data require real-time delivery to be understandable. Clearly, this makes regular data a lot less vulnerable to congestion or busy traffic conditions that delay voice and video communications and seriously mess them up. The explosion in the popularity and amount of multimedia being sent over data networks is a big reason why the never-ending quest for greater bandwidth and speed to avoid traffic jams on WAN links is so vital today.

Dense Wavelength Division Multiplexing

Wavelength Division Multiplexing (WDM) is a technology that multiplexes several optical carriers on a single optical fiber by using different wavelengths. Remember, fiber-optic signals are light, so using different wavelengths of the light spectrum is somewhat like using different frequencies in a radio wave.

Dense Wavelength Division Multiplexing (DWDM) multiplexes within a specific band (1550 nm), allowing for the use of erbium-doped fiber amplifiers (EDFAs) that boost the signal. This allows for upgrading the bit rate of a single strand line by simply replacing equipment at either end of the line. The system consists of the following:

- DWDM terminal multiplexer
- Intermediate line repeater (every 80–100 km)
- Intermediate terminal multiplexer (remote amplification site)
- DWDM terminal de-multiplexer

Passive Optical Network

Passive Optical Network (PON), also called *fiber to the premises*, is a new option for connecting homes and business to the Internet. It is point-to-multipoint technology with a single fiber strand used for multiple premises (typically 16–28). Unpowered optical splitters are used in the process (thus the term *passive*).

The system consists of an optical line termination (OLT) at the telco's office and a number of optical network units (ONUs) near end users. These systems typically have downlink speeds of 155 to 655 Mbps and uplink bursts to 155 Mbps.

Wireless Technologies

Now let's get back to that distance issue. You know that different technologies offer different distance ranges and that optical fiber carries signals much further than copper cabling can. You also know that fiber comes with a much higher price tag to match its higher capacity and that it's much harder to install.

But we haven't covered *Bluetooth*, which is a type of wireless technology that's only used for short-distance wireless transmissions. Bluetooth is actually a wireless protocol that creates *personal area networks (PANs)*. It utilizes a short-range communications technology enabling data transmission between fixed and/or mobile devices. It's not exactly a news bulletin that most of us have mobile phones, and on some of them we can even get our email. Some states, with more surely to follow soon, have passed laws making it illegal not to use a wireless headset while driving and talking. Those headsets use Bluetooth technology, as do wireless keyboards and mice, for example.

Bluetooth uses a radio technology called frequency hopping spread spectrum that chops up the data being sent and transmits chunks of it through the air on up to 75 different frequencies. The transmitter and receiver change frequencies or channels in a prearranged pattern. Getting all of our wireless toys to play nicely with each other and synch up can be a challenge, and meeting that need is exactly what the people who created Bluetooth intended to do—develop a single digital wireless protocol, capable of connecting multiple devices and overcoming problems arising from trying to synchronize them. Bluetooth achieves this goal.

Microwave radio relay is a technology for transmitting digital and sometimes even analog signals between two locations on a line-of-sight radio path through the atmosphere. During microwave radio relay, radio waves are transmitted between the two locations with directional antennas that form a fixed radio connection between them. A really long connected series of links can form line-of-sight transcontinental communication systems. (If this sounds familiar, it should—you read an entire chapter on wireless—remember Chapter 12, "Wireless Technologies"?) Anyway, although having a dedicated microwave connection is still common because it allows you to purchase your own frequency range from the FCC to ensure that you don't get any interference, a much less costly installation is the wireless 802.11 specification (also discussed in Chapter 12), which provides us with long-distance solutions and a healthy amount of bandwidth too.

A *communications satellite (comsat)* is an artificial satellite stationed in space for telecommunications purposes. Modern communications satellites use a variety of orbits. Here's a list of them:

- Geostationary orbits
- Molniya orbits, named after a series of communications satellites from Russia. (*Molniya* means lightning in Russian.)
- Low-polar and non-polar Earth orbits from which the satellite can first boost communications signals and then send them back to earth

There are other elliptical orbits too, but I'm not going to go into them in this book because you're not reading this to help you get your FCC license. Instead, you want to pass the CompTia Network+ exam, and to do that, you do need to understand point-to-multipoint services and how communications satellites provide a microwave radio-relay technology, as shown in Figure 16.3.

FIGURE 16.3   An example of a satellite point-to-multipoint

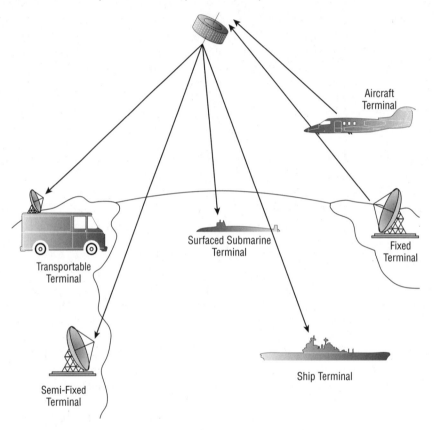

This technology is also used for mobile applications like GPS communications to ships, vehicles, planes, and handheld terminals as well as for fun stuff like watching football on satellite HDTV and radio broadcasting. These all require capabilities that are impractical or impossible to use with other technologies like cable.

Broadband Services

Now, before I get into telling you all about the WAN protocols required to meet the CompTIA objectives, I've got to talk about cable modems and DSL as solutions for connecting to WANs.

I think it will really help you understand the practical differences between DSL and cable-modem networking, and they happen to be CompTIA objectives as well.

Dedicated broadband services include transmissions over media in a broad range of frequencies. The various forms of *digital subscriber line (DSL)* services are broadband in the sense that digital information is sent over a high-bandwidth channel above the baseband voice channel on a single pair of wires. Ethernet digital signals sent over a *cable modem* from your local cable television service provider are a competitor for DSL service.

Although it's true that DSL and cable Internet services do indeed have a lot in common, they still have some basic, essential differences that are really important for you to understand:

Speed Most would tell you that cable is faster than DSL Internet, but cable doesn't always win the race in the real world.

Security DSL and cable are based on different network-security models, and until recently, cable has been the reputed loser in this contest. But now it's pretty much a toss-up, and both offer adequate security that meets the needs of most users. And when I say adequate, I mean that there are still some very real security issues relating to both alternatives, no matter what your ISP says.

Popularity Cable Internet is definitely "best in show" in the United States, but DSL is beginning to catch up.

Customer satisfaction Here, the reverse is true—in the United States, DSL is top dog. Still, do you really know anyone who's satisfied with their ISP?

Figure 16.4 shows how a connection can terminate from modems to either a PC directly or to a router. The two devices that lie between the router and the cloud and between the computer and the cloud represent the cable or DSL modem. Typically, your router would run Dynamic Host Configuration Protocol (DHCP) on that interface as well as Point-to-Point Protocol over Ethernet (PPPoE), which we discussed back in Chapter 13, "Authentication and Access Control."

FIGURE 16.4 Broadband access using cable or DSL

Both DSL and cable high-speed Internet services are available to millions of residential and business consumers worldwide, but in some areas, only one (sometimes neither) service is available. Surprisingly, some of the differences between DSL and cable modem have nothing to do with the actual technologies—it comes down to the individual ISP. All other things being equal, issues like cost, reliability, and quality of customer support for both installation and maintenance vary significantly from one provider to the next.

DSL Technology and *x*DSL

DSL is not a complete end-to-end solution. It is really a Physical layer transmission technology like dial-up, cable, or wireless. DSL connections are deployed in the *last-mile* of a local telephone network or local loop. The term *last-mile* has been used quite a bit in the last few years with broadband-type connections. It basically means the same thing as local loop and defines the physical connection from the customer to the first aggregation device of the provider network.

A DSL connection is set up between a pair of modems on either end of a copper wire that is between the CPE and the digital subscriber line access multiplexer (DSLAM). A DSLAM is the device located at the providers' CO that concentrates connections from multiple DSL subscribers.

xDSL is really a family of technologies that have become popular for data transmission over phone lines because *x*DSL uses regular PSTN phone wires to transmit digital signals and is extremely inexpensive compared with other digital communications methods. The *x* in *x*DSL represents the various letters that refer to different DSL flavors. *x*DSLs use high-frequency signals, whereas regular phone calls use low-frequency signals over the same lines.

Communicating via *x*DSL requires an interface to a PC. All *x*DSL configurations require a DSL modem called an *endpoint* and a network interface card (NIC) in your computer. The NIC can be connected directly to the DSL modem using a straight-through Ethernet UTP patch cord with standard RJ-45 connectors on each end. But if there are other connecting devices between the computer and the cable modem, you'll need either a special switchable port or an Ethernet crossover cable for things to work well.

Are These Really Modems?

Actually, neither ISDN nor cable modems are actually modems in the sense that no analog to digital signal modulation is occurring. But the industry has come to call them modems anyway!

A nice feature of *x*DSL implementations is that they cost tens of dollars instead of the hundreds (possibly thousands) that you would have to pony up for a dedicated, digital point-to-point link like a T1. These cost-effective implementations include the following:

High bit-rate digital subscriber line (HDSL)   HDSL was the first DSL technology to use a higher-frequency spectrum of copper twisted-pair cables. HDSL was developed in the United States as a better technology for high-speed, synchronous circuits. It was typically used to interconnect local-exchange carrier systems and to carry high-speed corporate data links and voice channels using T1 lines.

Symmetric digital subscriber line (SDSL)   Symmetric (same rate in both directions) digital subscriber line (SDSL) provides T1/E1 type speeds symmetrically for both uploading and downloading data but doesn't allow low-frequency phone calls on the same line as asymmetric digital subscriber line (ADSL) does. How much it will set you back ranges between the cost of ADSL and T1s. It's typically used by small to medium-sized businesses that don't require the higher performance of a leased line for connecting to a server.

Very high bit-rate digital subscriber line (VDSL)   VDSL, or very high bitrate DSL (VHDSL), provides faster data transmission over single, flat, untwisted or twisted pairs of copper wires. This capacity for blazingly fast speeds mean that VDSL is capable of supporting high-bandwidth applications like HDTV and telephone services like the popular Voice over IP (VoIP) as well as general Internet access over a single connection. VDSL is deployed over existing wiring used for POTS and lower-speed DSL connections. Second-generation VDSL2 systems utilize bandwidths of up to 30 MHz to provide data rates exceeding 100 Mbps simultaneously in both the upstream and downstream directions. The maximum available bit rate is achieved at a range of about 300 meters with the signal performance degrading as the loop attenuation increases.

Asymmetric digital subscriber line (ADSL)   Asymmetric (meaning different upload and download speeds) DSL has become the most popular *x*DSL because it focuses on providing reasonably fast upstream transmission speeds (768 Kbps) and very fast downstream transmission speeds (up to 9 Mbps, although usually slower). This makes downloading graphics, audio, video, and data files from any remote computer a snap. The majority of web traffic is downstream. The best part is that ADSL works on a single phone line without losing voice call capability. This is accomplished with something called a *splitter* that enables the use of multiple frequencies on your POTS line.

Cable Modem

Cable is a great cost-effective connection for a small office or home office (SOHO)—yes, there is an acronym for everything. Even in larger organizations, cable, or even DSL, can be great to have around as a backup link.

Here are a few cable network terms:

Headend   This is where all cable signals are received, processed, and formatted. The signals are then transmitted over the distribution network from the headend.

Distribution network   These are relatively small service areas that usually range in size from 100 to 2,000 customers. They're typically composed of a mixed, fiber-coaxial, or hybrid fiber-coaxial (HFC) architecture, with optical fiber substituting for the distribution network's trunk portion. The fiber forms both the connection from the headend and an optical node that changes light to radio frequency (RF) signals that are then distributed through a coaxial cable throughout the specific service area, that is, your home or office.

Data over cable service interface specification (DOCSIS)   This specification provides the interface requirements for a data over cable system, including that of high-speed data transfer to an existing cable TV system. All cable modems and similar devices have to measure up to this standard.

Figure 16.5 shows where you would be likely to find the various types of networks and how the terms I just listed would be used in a network diagram. The area on the right where coaxial cable is in use is the distribution network and the box labeled Node is the optical node where light is converted to RF signals for use on the coaxial cable.

FIGURE 16.5   Cable network

The problem with this is that ISPs often use a fiber-optic network that extends from the cable operator's master headend—sometimes even to regional headends—out to a neighborhood's hubsite and finally arrives at a fiber-optic node that services anywhere from 25 to 2,000 or more homes. I'm really not picking on cable, but here's another issue: If you have cable, open your PC's command prompt, type **ipconfig**, and check out your subnet mask. It's probably a /20 or /21 Class B address—yikes! You already know that translates to either 4,094 or 2,046 hosts per cable network connection. Definitely not good.

When we say *cable*, we really mean using coax (coaxial) cable for transmission. Community antenna television (CATV) is now used as a means to offer cost-effective broadcasting to subscribers. Cable is able to provide voice and data, plus analog and digital video, without requiring you to cough up your whole paycheck.

Your average cable connection gives you a maximum download speed of 2 Mbps. And remember—you have to share that bandwidth with all the other subscribers. As if that weren't enough, there are other things like overloaded web servers and plain old network congestion that factor into the mix as well. But your email-checking neighbors really aren't making that much of a difference. So who or what is? Well, if you're an online gamer, you will likely notice a bit more lag during peak periods, which could be a matter of virtual life and death. And if somebody in your neighborhood is uploading a large amount of data, like, say, an entire collection of pirated *Star Wars* movies, it could definitely max out the entire connection and bring everyone's browser to crawl speed.

Cable-modem access may or may not be faster or easier to install than DSL, and your mileage will vary, depending on where you live plus a variety of other factors. But it's usually more available and a tad less pricey, making it a winner by a nose. But no worries; if cable access isn't available in your neighborhood, DSL is okay—anything is better than dial-up.

Wireless WAN Technologies

At one time, it was taken as gospel that wireless technologies, especially WAN technologies, could never be completely acceptable, especially when compared to terrestrial technologies. Today, that given is being challenged with a number of new technologies that can provide acceptable Internet and even multimedia performance without a landline. In this section, we'll look at some of the cellular WAN technologies and see how far we've really come in this regard.

Cellular WAN

Cellular technologies have evolved since their introduction in the late 1970s. Terms like 1G (first generation) 2G, 3G, and 4G are often used to describe significant advances in the technology. In this section I'll first give you a quick overview of the major developments and then we'll look more closely at a couple of the newer technologies specifically and what these technologies bring to the table and what they may promise for the future.

First generation cellular (1G) was a voice-only analog network. The second generation (2G) marked the switch to digital, which allowed voice and for the first time, simple data, such as a text message. Third generation (3G), which is the most widely used globally at the time of this writing (things change quickly), allows high-speed voice and data, even Internet. This is the type of network supporting most of your smartphones.

Fourth generation (4G) is a still emerging technology that has two variants, LTE and WiMAX. An organization called the Third Generation Partnership Project 2 (3GPP2) has set specific requirements for a system to call itself 4G. At this point in time, LTE and WiMAX meet these requirements.

The goal of 4G is to provide data rates way beyond what is available today. Having said that, uplinks (from the mobile device to the tower) will always be much slower, and actual performance in the real world remains to be seen. Some figures are listed in the following sections. 4G systems should be backward compatible with 3G systems (though not always, as you will see), and to fully achieve the performance discussed here, the device itself must be 4G capable.

HSPA+

Evolved High Speed Packet Access (HSPA+) is really considered a 3.5 generation technology. It does include an optional all-IP architecture (one of the requirements of 4G), and it has greatly improved data rates over its predecessor HSPA. Its use of all-IP architecture indicates that it could eventually develop into a true 4G technology. It has downlink speeds of 3 Mbps to 4 Mbps and uplink of 1 Mbps to 2 Mbps.

WiMAX

World Wide Interoperability for Microwave Access (WiMax) is considered a true 4G technology. It is based on the IEEE 802.16 standard. It supports fixed (tower to tower) and mobile applications. It was originally designed as a last-mile technology to deliver Internet to locations where landlines were not possible as an alternative to DSL and cable.

The challenges for WiMAX are that it is not compatible with 2G and 3G technologies and it has high cost and power needs. It also lags behind LTE with regard to speed. It has downlink speeds of 5 Mbps to 6 Mbps and uplink speeds of 2 Mbps to 3 Mbps.

LTE

Long Term Evolution (LTE) is the most promising of the emerging 4G technologies. It uses an all-IP-based core, has the highest data rates, and is compatible not only with 3G but with WiMAX. It also has the best indoor coverage and maintains high data rates all the way to the edge of a coverage cell. And it accommodates more devices in an area while maintaining performance. It has data rates of 7 Mbps to 12 Mbps on the downlink and 3 Mbps to 5 Mbps on the uplink.

WAN Protocols

I'm going to focus on the following technologies in this section:

- ISDN
- Frame Relay
- ATM

Integrated Services Digital Network

ISDN is a digital, point-to-point WAN technology capable of maximum transmission speeds of about 2 Mbps (Primary Rate Interface [PRI]), although speeds of 128 Kbps (Basic Rate Interface [BRI]) are more common in a SOHO environment.

Because it's capable of much higher data rates at a relatively low cost, ISDN is becoming a viable remote-user connection method—especially for those who work out of their homes. ISDN uses the same UTP wiring as POTS, yet it can transmit data at much higher speeds. But that's where the similarity ends. What makes ISDN different from a regular POTS line is how it uses the copper wiring. Instead of carrying an analog (voice) signal, it carries digital signals. This is the reason behind several key differences.

First, a computer connects to the 128 Kbps ISDN line via an ISDN *terminal adapter (TA)* that's often incorrectly referred to as an ISDN modem. An ISDN TA is not a modem because it doesn't convert a digital signal from the computer to an analog signal on the subscriber line—ISDN signals are digital on the subscriber line. A TA is technically an ISDN-compatible device that has one or more non-ISDN ports for devices like computer serial interfaces and RJ-11 analog phones, giving these non-ISDN devices access to the ISDN network.

Second, an ISDN line has two types of channels. The data is carried on special *Bearer channels*, or *B channels*, each of which can carry 64 Kbps of data. A BRI ISDN line has 2 B channels, and a PRI has 23 64 Kbps channels. One channel can be used for a voice call while the other can be used for data transmissions, and this is made possible by time-division multiplexing (TDM) on one pair of copper wires.

The other type of channel in ISDN is also multiplexed onto only one copper pair. It's used for call setup and link management and is known as the *signaling channel*, *D channel*, or *Delta channel*. This channel has only 16 Kbps of bandwidth in BRI and 64 Kbps in PRI.

To maximize throughput, the two B channels are often combined into one data connection for a total bandwidth of 128 Kbps. This is known as *Bandwidth on Demand Interoperability Group* (BONDING) or *inverse multiplexing*.

This still leaves the D channel free for signaling purposes. In rare cases, you may see user data, such as credit-card verification, on the D channel. This was introduced as an additional feature of ISDN, but it hasn't caught on.

Some of the main advantages of ISDN are as follows:

- It has a fast connection.
- It offers higher bandwidth than POTS. BONDING yields 128 Kbps bandwidth.
- There is no conversion from digital to analog.

ISDN disadvantages include these:

- It's more expensive than POTS.
- Specialized equipment is required at the phone company and at the remote computer.
- Not all ISDN equipment can connect to every other type of equipment.
- Why use ISDN if you can get DSL or cable?

Remember that ISDN is a type of dial-up connection that must be initiated.

So, you now know that ISDN is another form of high-speed Internet access that delivers digital services (on 64 Kbps channels) over conditioned telephone copper pairs. As I mentioned earlier, the device you must hook up to your computer to access ISDN services is properly known as an ISDN terminal adapter, which doesn't change from digital to analog as a modem does. It just changes between digital transmission formats.

The box itself is about the size of a modem and happens to look pretty similar to one. And also like DSL modems, it has a phone jack and an Ethernet jack. You connect a phone cord from the phone jack to the wall jack where your ISDN services are being delivered, and then you connect an Ethernet cable from your PC to the ISDN TA's Ethernet jack. Older, less-capable TAs used an Electronic Industries Association/Telecommunications Industry Alliance (EIA/TIA) 232 serial port for PC connectivity. These similarities are why people confuse ISDN TAs with standard modems.

Frame Relay Technology

Frame Relay is a WAN technology in which variable-length packets are transmitted by switching. *Packet switching* involves breaking messages into chunks at the sending device. Each packet can be sent over any number of routes on its way to its destination. The packets are then reassembled in the correct order at the receiver. Because they are packet-switched and the exact path is unknown, a cloud is used when creating a diagram to illustrate how data travels throughout this service.

From everything you've learned so far, just telling you that Frame Relay is a packet-switched technology should make you immediately realize a couple of things about it:

- Frame Relay doesn't work like a point-to-point leased line (although it can be made to look and act like one).

- Frame Relay is usually less expensive than leased lines are, but there are some sacrifices to make to get that savings.

So, why would you even consider using Frame Relay? Take a look at Figure 16.6 to get an idea of what a network looked like before Frame Relay.

FIGURE 16.6   Before Frame Relay

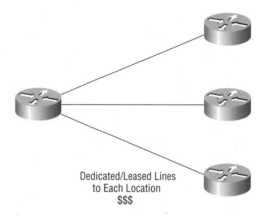

Dedicated/Leased Lines
to Each Location
$$$

Now check out Figure 16.7. You can see that there's now only one connection between the Corporate router and the Frame Relay switch. That saves some major cash.

Let's say you need to add seven remote sites to the corporate office and you have only one free serial port on your router. Frame Relay to the rescue! Of course, I should probably mention that you now also have one single point of failure, which is not so good. But Frame Relay is used to save money, not to make a network more resilient.

Coming up, I'm going to cover the Frame Relay technology information you need to know about when studying for the CompTIA Network+ exam.

Committed Information Rate

Frame Relay provides a packet-switched network to many different customers at the same time. This is a really good thing because it spreads out the cost of the switches among many customers. But remember, Frame Relay is based on the assumption that all customers won't need to transmit data constantly—or even all at the same time.

FIGURE 16.7 After Frame Relay

Statistically multiplexing
multiple logical circuits over a
single physical connection

Frame Relay works by providing a portion of dedicated bandwidth to each user, and it also allows the user to exceed their guaranteed bandwidth if resources on the telco network happen to be available. So basically, Frame Relay providers allow customers to buy a lower amount of bandwidth than they really use. There are two separate bandwidth specifications with Frame Relay:

Access rate   The maximum speed at which the Frame Relay interface can transmit.

Committed information rate (CIR)   The maximum bandwidth of data guaranteed to be delivered. In reality, it's the average amount that the service provider will allow you to transmit, based on what you purchased.

If these two values are the same, the Frame Relay connection is pretty much just like a leased line. But they can also be set to different values. Here's an example: Let's say that you buy an access rate of T1 (1.544 Mbps) and a CIR of 256 Kbps. By doing this, you're guaranteed that the first 256 Kbps of traffic you send will be delivered. Anything beyond that is called a *burst*—a transmission that exceeds your guaranteed 256 Kbps rate and can total any amount up to the T1 access rate (if that amount is in your contract). If your combined committed burst (the basis for your CIR) and excess burst sizes, known as the maximum burst rate (MBR), exceed the access rate, you can pretty much say goodbye to your additional traffic. It will most likely be dropped, although this happening depends on the subscription level of a particular service provider.

In a perfect world, this always works beautifully—but remember that little word *guarantee*—as in guaranteed rate, of 256 Kbps to be exact? This means any burst of data you send that exceeds your guaranteed 256 Kbps rate will be delivered on something called a "best effort" delivery basis. Or maybe not—if your telco's equipment doesn't have the capacity to deliver it at the time you transmitted, then your frames will be discarded and the DTE will be notified. Timing is everything—you can scream data out at six times your guaranteed rate of 256 Kbps (T1) *only if* your telco has the capacity available on its equipment at that moment.

Virtual Circuits

Frame Relay operates using *virtual circuits* as opposed to the actual circuits that leased lines use. These virtual circuits are what link together the thousands of devices connected to the provider's "cloud." Frame Relay provides a virtual circuit between your two DTE devices, making them appear to be connected via a circuit when in reality they're dumping their frames into a large, shared infrastructure. You never see the complexity of what's actually happening inside the cloud because you only have a virtual circuit.

And on top of all that, there are two types of virtual circuits—permanent and switched. Permanent virtual circuits (PVCs) are by far the most common type in use today. What *permanent* means here is that the telco creates the mappings inside its gear and as long as you pay the bill, they'll remain in place.

Switched virtual circuits (SVCs) are more like phone calls. The virtual circuit is established when data needs to be transmitted, and it's taken down when the data transfer is complete.

I have never seen a Frame Relay service using SVCs offered by a telco in North America. It's used mainly in private Frame Relay networks.

Data Link Connection Identifiers

Frame Relay PVCs are identified to DTE end devices by *Data Link Connection Identifiers (DLCIs)*. A Frame Relay service provider typically assigns DLCI values, which are used on Frame Relay interfaces to distinguish between different virtual circuits. Because many virtual circuits can be terminated on one multipoint Frame Relay interface, many DLCIs are often affiliated with it.

Let me explain. Suppose you have a central HQ with three branch offices. If you were to connect each branch office to HQ using a T1, you would need three serial interfaces on your router at HQ, one for each T1. Simple, right? Well, suppose you use Frame Relay PVCs instead. You could have a T1 at each branch connected to a service provider and only a *single* T1 at HQ. There would be three PVCs on the single T1 at HQ, one going to each branch. And even though you'd have only a single interface and a single CSU/DSU, the three PVCs would function as three separate circuits. Remember what I said about saving money? How much for two additional T1 interfaces and a pair of CSU/DSUs? Answer: A lot! So, why not go ahead and ask for a percentage of the savings in your bonus?

Asynchronous Transfer Mode

Asynchronous Transfer Mode (ATM), not to be confused with automated teller machines, first emerged in the early 1990s. ATM was designed to be a high-speed communications protocol that does not depend on any specific LAN topology. It uses a high-speed cell-switching technology that can handle data as well as real-time voice and video. The ATM protocol breaks up transmitted data into 53-byte cells. A *cell* is analogous to a packet or frame, except that an ATM cell is always fixed in length and is relatively small and fast, whereas a frame's length can vary.

ATM is designed to switch these small cells through an ATM network very quickly. It does this by setting up a virtual connection between the source and destination nodes; the cells may go through multiple switching points before ultimately arriving at their final destination. The cells may also arrive out of order, so the receiving system may have to reassemble and correctly order the arriving cells. ATM, like Frame Relay, is a connection-oriented service in contrast to most Data Link protocols, which are best-efforts delivery services and do not require virtual circuits to be established before transmitting user data.

Data rates are scalable and start as low as 1.5 Mbps, with speeds of 25 Mbps, 51 Mbps, 100 Mbps, 155 Mbps, and higher. The common speeds of ATM networks today are 51.84 Mbps and 155.52 Mbps; both of them can be used over either copper or fiber-optic cabling. An ATM with a speed of 622.08 Mbps is also becoming common but is currently used exclusively over fiber-optic cable. ATM supports very high speeds because it's designed to be routed by hardware rather than software, which makes faster processing speeds possible.

Fiber-based service-provider ATM networks are running today at data rates of 10 Gbps, and they're becoming more and more common. These fast speeds make real-time payloads like voice and video travel with data on an ATM network and arrive without too much delay, or *latency*. The small size of the payload, compared to the size of each cell's header, makes ATM less efficient than other WAN technologies. In other words, ATM networks are fast, but they get bad gas mileage.

Summary

In this chapter, you learned about the important issues involved in providing WAN connectivity between geographically separated network locations. You learned about the different kinds of WAN connections, including point-to-point connections, circuit-switched service provider networks, and packet-switched service provider networks.

You also learned about the impact different transmission media and different distance parameters made with WAN connections. In addition, you learned about different choices for leased-line connections along with broadband technologies such as xDSL and cable modems.

You studied the different WAN protocols and technologies used in connecting today's high-speed WANs, including ISDN, Frame Relay, ATM, and MPLS.

Exam Essentials

Be able to differentiate the kinds of WAN technologies.   You must be able to tell the speeds and capacities of the different remote-access and WAN technologies as well as the media over which they are implemented.

Identify the basic characteristics of various Internet access technologies.   These include DSL, broadband cable, POTS, and fiber to the premises (PON). It is important to know the differentiating features of these access technologies. Know their advantages and disadvantages so you can identify the best use of each.

Be knowledgeable about the differences between circuit-switched and packet-switched technologies, and know which protocols use either.   Frame Relay is a packet-switched technology, and ISDN is a circuit-switched digital solution. ATM is considered to be a cell-switched technology because it incorporates a 53-byte cell. Both MPLS and ATM are considered connection-oriented technologies because the connection is set up first.

Be clear about the differences involving speed and distance between different media and between different WAN protocols.   The use of both wireless and fiber is growing, and their standards are facilitating faster speeds and coverage of greater distances.

Be able to differentiate cellular WAN technologies like HSPA+, WiMAX, and LTE.   HSPA+ is considered 3.5G, while LTE and WiMAX are considered true 4G.

Be able to differentiate between the different WAN protocols and technologies, their relative costs and speeds, and the types of implementations for which each would serve as a best solution.   ISDN is rarely used nowadays in its BRI configuration except for small home or office solutions. Frame Relay is relatively inexpensive, but service providers have overbooked their Frame Relay clouds, resulting in poor performance. ATM is fast but inefficient, and MPLS is fast and more efficient but complicated to administer.

Written Lab

1. What is the greatest advantage of PSTN (POTS)?

2. Which technology uses the term *HFC*?

3. You have one serial port on your router but need to connect many remote sites. What WAN protocol could you consider as an option?

4. What is the maximum speed for T1?

5. What does the acronym DSL stand for?

6. Which WAN technologies are considered packet-switching networks?

7. Which cellular technologies are considered 4G?

8. Which WAN technology is considered a cell-switching network?

9. What are the different flavors of *x*DSL?

10. What is another name for PON?

    You can find the answers in Appendix B.

Review Questions

You can find the answers in Appendix A.

1. Which of the following is not a WAN protocol or technology?

   A. ATM

   B. ISDN

   C. MPLS

   D. RIP

2. What OSI model layers do WAN protocols operate in?

   A. Layer 6, Layer 4, Layer 2

   B. Transport, Data Link, Network

   C. Physical, Data Link, Network

   D. Application, Data Link, Network

3. If you have a device in a telecommunications closet owned and installed by the telecommunications company (telco) and it's your responsibility to cable from this box to the CPE, which term should you use to refer to the device?

   A. Customer premises equipment

   B. Demarcation point

   C. Toll network

   D. Central office

4. You have an E1. How many DS0s are used in this point-to-point connection?

   A. 24

   B. 25

   C. 30

   D. 32

5. Where does the local exchange carrier responsibility end and your responsibility begin on a WAN link?

   A. POP

   B. Central office

   C. Demarc

   D. Smart jack

6. You have a small office, home office environment. What WAN technology would most likely be used?

   A. T1

   B. T3

   C. Frame Relay

   D. Cable Modem

7. Which type of communication has a line speed of 1.544 Mbps (millions of bits per second)?

   A. T3

   B. T1C

   C. T1

   D. T4

8. Which cellular WAN technology has the best data rate?

   A. HSPA

   B. HSPA+

   C. LTE

   D. WiMAX

9. Which is not a common optical carrier level (OC-*x*)?

   A. OC-1

   B. OC-4

   C. OC-12

   D. OC-192

10. Which wireless protocol utilizes a short-range communications technology facilitating data transmission from fixed and/or mobile devices, creating wireless personal area networks (PANs)?

    A. Bluetooth

    B. Microwave radio relay

    C. Comsat

    D. Point-to-multipoint

11. What does the *x* in *x*DSL represent?

    A. Wire type

    B. Transmission speed

    C. DSL type

    D. Download speed

12. Which is not a type of *x*DSL?

  A. ADSL

  B. HDSL

  C. SONET

  D. SDSL

13. What is the acronym DOCSIS stand for?

  A. Data over cable service interface spectrum

  B. Data over cable systems Internet specification

  C. Data over cable service Internet specification

  D. Data over cable service interface specification

14. What is the bandwidth for OC-12?

  A. 1.544 Mbps

  B. 45 Mbps

  C. 622 Mbps

  D. 1000 Mbps

15. Which WAN protocol utilizes cell-switching technology?

  A. Frame Relay

  B. ISDN

  C. ATM

  D. RIP

16. Which WAN protocol utilizes packet-switched technology?

  A. Frame Relay

  B. ISDN

  C. ATM

  D. RIP

17. What is the CIR in Frame Relay?

  A. Virtual circuit that is established when data needs to be transmitted

  B. Maximum speed at which the Frame Relay interface can transmit

  C. Rate at which the Frame Relay switch guarantees to transfer data

  D. Rate at which the Frame Relay switch agrees to receive data

18. What does the acronym ATM stand for?

   A. Automated Teller Machine

   B. Asynchronous Transfer Mode

   C. Asynchronous Transfer Method

   D. Autonomous Transfer Mode

19. Which WAN has a transfer rate of 44.7 Mbps?

   A. T1

   B. T3

   C. E1

   D. E3

20. How does DWDM put multiple transmissions on a single strand?

   A. Different frequencies

   B. Different polarizations

   C. Different wavelengths

   D. Different time slots

Chapter

17

Troubleshooting Tools

THE FOLLOWING COMPTIA NETWORK+ EXAM OBJECTIVES ARE COVERED IN THIS CHAPTER:

✓ **4.3 Given a scenario, use appropriate software tools to troubleshoot connectivity issues.**

- Protocol analyzer
- Throughput testers
- Connectivity software
- Ping
- Tracert/traceroute
- Dig
- Ipconfig/ifconfig
- Nslookup
- Arp
- Nbtstat
- Netstat
- Route

Most of us are running Transmission Control Protocol/Internet Protocol (TCP/IP) version 4 on our networks these days, so we absolutely need a way to test IP connectivity. But we also need to be able to test and verify IPv6 networks. The reason for this is that even though Microsoft makes the majority of client platforms, a lot of the commands used to test IP connectivity are really platform independent, and most of them can now use both IPv4 and IPv6. Even so, keep in mind that the Network+ exam focuses on the basic concepts of the function and use of the TCP/IP utilities that come with Windows.

You can use several utilities, both command line and GUI, to verify TCP/IP function on Windows workstations, and most of them are listed in the chapter objectives. But there are a few others that I'm going to discuss with you because they're really important for anyone working in the networking field to know about. Here's a list of them:

- Traceroute (`tracert` in Microsoft)
- `ipconfig`/`winipcfg` (`ifconfig` in UNIX)
- `ping`
- `arp`
- `nslookup` (`dig` in UNIX)
- `Mtr`
- `route`
- `nbtstat`
- `netstat`
- `ftp`
- `telnet`

And by the way…it's very important that you don't just blow through the output that I've supplied for each command. Instead, pay serious attention to it because to meet the Network+ objectives, you'll be required to correctly identify each command's output.

So, let's cut right to the chase and take a look at some of these commands and their output. Oh, and do try and have fun with it!

 To find up-to-the-minute updates for this chapter, please see www.lammle.com/forum or the book's web site at www.sybex.com/go/netplus2e.

Protocol Analyzers

Protocol analyzers, also called sniffers or network monitors, are used to capture packets in their raw format as they cross the network. Windows desktop operating systems before Windows Vista came with a built-in protocol analyzer called Network Monitor, but that is no longer the case, although you can download one for free that will work with the newer operating systems.

The Network Monitor tool that comes with these operating systems will capture only packets that are sourced from or destined to the computer on which the tool is running. Commercial sniffers like Wireshark or OmniPeek can capture any packets because they set the NIC to operate in promiscuous mode, which means the NIC processes all packets that it sees.

Protocol analyzers can be used to determine the type of traffic that you have in your network, and depending on the product and the bells and whistles contained therein, you may be able to sort the results based on port numbers, protocols, and so on. Another use of a sniffer is to examine the traffic that should be occurring on the network when something is not working to aid in troubleshooting. These devices can capture and display all packets involved in the connection setup including, for example, request and response headers to a web server.

For example, earlier in the book we discussed the operation of DHCP, and you learned that there are a series of four packet types that must occur for a DHCP client to receive an IP configuration from the server. As a review, those packets are as follows:

- DHCPDISCOVER
- DHCPOFFER
- DHCPREQUEST
- DHCPACK

If you turned on the analyzer and then executed the `ipconfig/release` and `ipconfig/renew` commands on the client (more on those commands later in this chapter), you should see these four packets in the analyzer's capture file. The packets would be interspersed with the hundreds and perhaps thousands of other packet types that would be captured, but by using the display filtering options in the software, you can easily segregate out the DHCP traffic. An example of the DHCP process as seen in a capture is shown in Figure 17.1.

FIGURE 17.1   DHCP capture

If all you saw in the capture were the DHCDISCOVER packets with no DHCPOFFER packets, you could reasonably assert that the DHCP server is not receiving the DHCPDISCOVER packets (perhaps it is located in another broadcast domain or perhaps it is not on). Additionally, you could examine fields in the DHCPOFFER packets that may tell you that the DHCP server is out of addresses. The point is that the tool can be used to troubleshoot the issue.

Throughput Testers

Users of a network often complain about the speed of the network. Network "speed" is in some ways a personal perception because some people have more patience than others. To determine when a network slowdown is real as opposed to perceived, you need to actually measure the throughput. That's what throughput testers are used for.

These devices, typically software based, work much like a protocol analyzer in that they measure the traffic seen on the network and can also classify the types of traffic that are eating up your bandwidth (which is probably what you really need to know). Figure 17.2 shows one version of this software by Tamosoft.

This software is installed on a server and also on a client. In the figure the software is measuring traffic between the client and a server. It shows the throughput for traffic in real time and in this shot is breaking that traffic up by unicast (TCP) and broadcast (UDP) types and by direction.

FIGURE 17.2   Throughput

Earlier in this book, I discussed the importance of baselines, and this is another area where they are important. Network throughput figures mean little without a baseline with which comparisons can be made. How do you know what is abnormal when you don't know what normal is? Baselines should be taken when the network is operating well, but also they should be taken when the traffic load is normal.

Connectivity Software

There are times when you need to make a remote connection to a machine to perform troubleshooting but you are miles away. Connectivity software is designed to allow you to make a connection to the machine, see the desktop, and perform any action you could perform if you were sitting in front of it.

Microsoft has made what it calls Remote Desktop software available for free with Windows products since Windows NT. When this software is installed (installed by default in later versions) on both source and destination computers, a remote desktop connection can be made.

Commercial tools are also available that (of course) claim to have more functionality, and they probably do have a few extra bells and whistles. These include LogMein.com, GoToMyPC, and others. Figure 17.3 shows the session window for a LogMein.com session.

The advantages of these connectivity tools are obvious. With these tools, you can do anything you need to on the machine as long as you can connect. They also allow you to see what a user is actually doing when they encounter a problem rather than having to rely on what they tell you they are doing. You can even show a user what they are doing wrong. Most of these tools allow for chat sessions and for either end of the connection to take control of the machine. You can also transfer files to them if required (maybe a DLL got deleted, for example).

FIGURE 17.3   Logmein

Using *Traceroute*

For starters, let's pose these questions: Where do all those packets really go when we send them over the Internet? And, how do all the packets actually get to their destinations? Well, we can use the TCP/IP traceroute (tracert with Windows) command-line utility to help us answer both questions because its output will show us every router interface a TCP/IP packet passes through on the way to its destination.

Traceroute (trace for short) displays the path a packet takes to get to a remote device in all its glory by using something we call IP Packet Time-To-Live (TTL), time-outs, and Internet Control Message Protocol (ICMP) error messages. And it's also a handy tool for troubleshooting an internetwork because we can use it to figure out which router along a path through that internetwork happens to be causing a network failure when a certain destination machine or network is, or suddenly becomes, unreachable.

To use tracert, at a Windows command prompt, type **tracert**, a space, and the Domain Name Service (DNS) name or IP address of the host machine to which you want to find the route. The tracert utility will respond with a list of all the DNS names and IP addresses of the routers that the packet is passing through on its way. Plus, tracert uses TTL to indicate the time it takes for each attempt.

Following is the tracert output from my workstation in Boulder, Colorado, to my Lammle.com server in Dallas, Texas:

```
C:\Users\tlammle>tracert www.lammle.com


Tracing route to lammle.com [206.123.114.186]
over a maximum of 30 hops:


   1     1 ms    <1 ms    <1 ms   dslmodem.domain.actdsltmp [192.168.0.1]
   2    53 ms    52 ms    52 ms   hlrn-dsl-gw36-228.hlrn.qwest.net
[207.225.112.228]
   3    52 ms    53 ms    52 ms   hlrn-agw1.inet.qwest.net [71.217.189.25]
   4    75 ms    75 ms    74 ms   dal-core-01.inet.qwest.net [67.14.2.53]
   5    76 ms    76 ms    76 ms   dap-brdr-01.inet.qwest.net [205.171.225.49]
   6    76 ms    76 ms    76 ms   205.171.1.110
   7    75 ms    76 ms   106 ms   xe-0-0-0.er2.dfw2.us.above.net [64.125.26.206]
   8    76 ms    76 ms    76 ms   209.249.122.74.available.above.net
[209.249.122.74]
   9    76 ms    76 ms    76 ms   65.99.248.250
  10    76 ms    76 ms    76 ms   pageuppro.pageuppro.com [206.123.114.186]
Trace complete.
```

Okay, were you able to see that the packet bounces through several routers before arriving at its destination? Good! This utility is useful if you are having problems reaching a web server on the Internet and you want to know if a wide area network (WAN) link is down or if the server just isn't responding. What this means to you is that, basically, wherever the trace stops is a great place to start troubleshooting. No worries here, though—the previous output shows that every router is up and responding. Last, notice in the output the ms. This is the latency of each hop, meaning the delay. Tracert (or traceroute) is a great troubleshooting tool you can use to find out where your network bottlenecks are.

If you use traceroute or tracert and receive an asterisk, this indicates that the attempt to reach that router took longer than the default time-out value. This is very good to know because it can mean that either the router is extremely busy or that a particular link is slow. Another reason for getting an asterisk could be that the administrator has disabled ICMP on the router that the packet is trying to hop through.

Why would someone want to do that? For security reasons, that's why. It happens to be a typical strategic move done on the routers that interface to the ISP to conceal their actual location so bad guys can't hack into them and therefore into your internetwork. It's a good idea, and I highly recommend doing it.

> If you are running traceroute and see repeating addresses and TTL time-outs, you probably have a routing loop.

Using *ipconfig* and *ifconfig*

The utilities known as ipconfig (in Windows) and ifconfig (in UNIX/Linux/Mac) will display the current configuration of TCP/IP on a given workstation—including the current IP address, DNS configuration, Windows Internet Naming Service (WINS) configuration, and default gateway. In the following sections, I will show you how to use both.

Using the *ipconfig* Utility

With the new Mac, Windows Vista, Windows 7, and Windows Server 2008 operating systems, you can see now the IPv6 configuration because IPv6 is enabled by default. The output of the ipconfig command provides the basic routed protocol information on your machine. From a DOS prompt, type **ipconfig**, and you'll see something like this:

```
C:\Users\tlammle>ipconfig
Windows IP Configuration
Ethernet adapter Local Area Connection:
    Connection-specific DNS Suffix  . : domain.actdsltmp
    Link-local IPv6 Address . . . . . : fe80::2836:c43e:274b:f08c%11
    IPv4 Address. . . . . . . . . . . : 192.168.0.6
```

```
   Subnet Mask . . . . . . . . . . . : 255.255.255.0
   Default Gateway . . . . . . . . . : 192.168.0.1

Wireless LAN adapter Wireless Network Connection:
   Connection-specific DNS Suffix  . : qwest.net
   Link-local IPv6 Address . . . . . : fe80::20e7:7fb8:8a00:832b%10
   IPv4 Address. . . . . . . . . . . : 10.0.1.198
   Subnet Mask . . . . . . . . . . . : 255.255.255.0
   Default Gateway . . . . . . . . . : fe80::21b:63ff:fef3:3694%10
                                       10.0.1.1


Tunnel adapter Local Area Connection* 6:
   Media State . . . . . . . . . . . : Media disconnected
   Connection-specific DNS Suffix  . :


Tunnel adapter Local Area Connection* 7:
   Media State . . . . . . . . . . . : Media disconnected
   Connection-specific DNS Suffix  . :
 [output cut for brevity]
```

Wow, there sure are a lot of options in this output compared to the output for earlier versions of Windows! First, what's up with all these interfaces showing? I only have two—one Ethernet and one wireless. You can see that my Ethernet adapter shows up first, and it has an IP address, a mask, and a default gateway plus an IPv6 address and a DNS suffix. The next configured interface is the wireless local area network (LAN) adapter, which has an IP address, a mask, a default gateway, an IPv6 address, and the IPv6 default gateway as well. This IPv6 default gateway address is simply my router advertising that it runs IPv6 and saying, "I am the way out of the local LAN!"

The next adapters are disconnected because they are logical interfaces and I'm not using them—my machine actually shows eight, but I cut the output because it provides no new information. They're automatically inserted because IPv6 is installed and running on my machine, and these adapters allow me to run IPv6 over an IPv4-only network.

But just in case the ipconfig command doesn't provide enough information for you, try the ipconfig /all command—talk about details. Here's the beginning of that output:

```
C:\Users\tlammle>ipconfig /all
Windows IP Configuration
   Host Name . . . . . . . . . . . . : globalnet-todd
   Primary Dns Suffix  . . . . . . . : globalnet.local
   Node Type . . . . . . . . . . . . : Hybrid
   IP Routing Enabled. . . . . . . . : No
   WINS Proxy Enabled. . . . . . . . : No
```

```
    DNS Suffix Search List. . . . . . : globalnet.local
                                        domain.actdsltmp
                                        qwest.net

Ethernet adapter Local Area Connection:
    Connection-specific DNS Suffix  . : domain.actdsltmp
    Description . . . . . . . . . . . : Intel(R) 82566MM Gigabit Network
Connection
    Physical Address. . . . . . . . . : 00-1E-37-D0-E9-35
    DHCP Enabled. . . . . . . . . . . : Yes
    Autoconfiguration Enabled . . . . : Yes
    Link-local IPv6 Address . . . . . : fe80::2836:c43e:274b:f08c%11(Preferred)
    IPv4 Address. . . . . . . . . . . : 192.168.0.6(Preferred)
    Subnet Mask . . . . . . . . . . . : 255.255.255.0
    Lease Obtained. . . . . . . . . . : Monday, October 20, 2008 9:08:36 AM
    Lease Expires . . . . . . . . . . : Tuesday, October 21, 2008 9:08:39 AM
    Default Gateway . . . . . . . . . : 192.168.0.1
    DHCP Server . . . . . . . . . . . : 192.168.0.1
    DNS Servers . . . . . . . . . . . : 192.168.0.1
                                        205.171.3.65
    NetBIOS over Tcpip. . . . . . . . : Enabled

Wireless LAN adapter Wireless Network Connection:
    Connection-specific DNS Suffix  . : qwest.net
    Description . . . . . . . . . . . : Intel(R) Wireless WiFi Link 4965AGN
    Physical Address. . . . . . . . . : 00-1F-3B-3F-4A-D9
    DHCP Enabled. . . . . . . . . . . : Yes
    Autoconfiguration Enabled . . . . : Yes
    Link-local IPv6 Address . . . . . : fe80::20e7:7fb8:8a00:832b%10(Preferred)
    IPv4 Address. . . . . . . . . . . : 10.0.1.198(Preferred)
    Subnet Mask . . . . . . . . . . . : 255.255.255.0
    Lease Obtained. . . . . . . . . . : Monday, October 20, 2008 10:43:53 AM
    Lease Expires . . . . . . . . . . : Monday, October 20, 2008 2:43:53 PM
    Default Gateway . . . . . . . . . : fe80::21b:63ff:fef3:3694%10
                                        10.0.1.1
    DHCP Server . . . . . . . . . . . : 10.0.1.1
    DNS Servers . . . . . . . . . . . : 10.0.1.1
    NetBIOS over Tcpip. . . . . . . . : Enabled

Tunnel adapter Local Area Connection* 6:
```

```
   Media State . . . . . . . . . . . : Media disconnected
   Connection-specific DNS Suffix  . :
   Description . . . . . . . . . . . : isatap.globalnet.local
   Physical Address. . . . . . . . . : 00-00-00-00-00-00-00-E0
   DHCP Enabled. . . . . . . . . . . : No
   Autoconfiguration Enabled . . . . : Yes

Tunnel adapter Local Area Connection* 7:
   Media State . . . . . . . . . . . : Media disconnected
   Connection-specific DNS Suffix  . :
   Description . . . . . . . . . . . : isatap.{9572A79F-3A58-4E9B-9BD0-
8F6FF2F058FC}
   Physical Address. . . . . . . . . : 00-00-00-00-00-00-00-E0
   DHCP Enabled. . . . . . . . . . . : No
   Autoconfiguration Enabled . . . . : Yes
[output cut]
```

As you can see, it's more of the same—a whole lot more. The most important thing I want you to notice is that I've received the hardware information about each interface, including the Media Access Control (MAC) address. Also significant is that I can see the Dynamic Host Configuration Protocol (DHCP) lease times and DNS addresses now.

But why stop here? There are two more valuable options you need to use with the ipconfig command. They are /release and /renew.

When you change networks, you need to get the IP address of that subnet and/or virtual LAN (VLAN). Vista and Windows 7 work most of the time without doing anything, but sometimes I do have to renew the IP configuration when changing networks. But that's easy—just type **ipconfig /renew** from a command prompt, and if you're connected to a DHCP server that's available, you'll then magically receive an IP address.

Now, if it still doesn't work, you'll need to release and renew your TCP/IP settings. To release your current DHCP TCP/IP information, you must elevate your command prompt or you'll get this warning:

```
C:\Users\tlammle>ipconfig /release
The requested operation requires elevation.
C:\Users\tlammle>
```

Should this happen to you, choose Start ➢ All Programs ➢ Accessories ➢ Command Prompt, right-click, and choose Run As Administrator. (Of course, you'll have to enter your name and password to do this if you are using Vista or Windows 7. But we love Vista and Windows 7, right? Okay, maybe not always.) Figure 17.4 shows how I did this.

Once your command prompt has been duly elevated, you can use the ipconfig / release command and then the ipconfig /renew command to get new TCP/IP information for your host.

FIGURE 17.4   Elevating your command prompt

Using the *ifconfig* Utility

There is a utility in Linux/UNIX/Mac that will give you information similar to what ipconfig shows. It's called ifconfig (short for *interface configuration*). Although ipconfig and ifconfig show similar information, there are major differences between these two utilities. The ipconfig utility is mainly used to view the TCP/IP configuration for a computer. You can use ifconfig to do the same thing, but ifconfig can also be used to configure a protocol or a particular network interface.

The general syntax of the ifconfig command is as follows:

```
ifconfig interface [address [parameters]]
```

The *interface* parameter equals the UNIX name of the interface, such as eth0. If the optional *address* parameter is specified, the ifconfig command sets the IP address for the interface to the address you've specified. When the ifconfig command is used by itself with no parameters, all configured interfaces will be reported on. But if only the interface name is specified, you'll get output that looks like this:

```
# ifconfig eth0
eth0  Link encap 10Mbps Ethernet  HWaddr 00:00:C0:90:B3:42
```

```
inetaddr 172.16.0.2 Bcast 172.16.0.255 Mask 255.255.255.0 UP BROADCAST RUNNING
MTU 1500  Metric 0
   RX packets 3136 errors 217 dropped 7 overrun 26
   TX packets 1752 errors 25 dropped 0 overrun 0
```

Looking at this, we can see that the eth0 interface is a 10Mbps Ethernet interface. The interface's MAC and IP address information is displayed in this output as well. And, although not shown in the output, the ifconfig tool can show you the DNS information configured on the host.

Using the *ping* Utility

ping is the most basic TCP/IP utility, and it's included with most TCP/IP stacks for most platforms. Windows, again, is no exception. In most cases, ping is a command-line utility, although there are many GUI implementations available. You use the ping utility for two primary purposes:

- To find out if a host is responding
- To find out if you can reach a host

Here's the syntax:

```
Ping hostname or IP address
```

If you ping any station that has an IP address, the ICMP that's part of that particular host's TCP/IP stack will respond to the request. The ICMP test and response looks something like this:

```
ping 204.153.163.2

Pinging 204.153.163.2 with 32 bytes of data:

Reply from 204.153.163.2: bytes=32 time<10ms TTL=128
Reply from 204.153.163.2: bytes=32 time=1ms TTL=128
Reply from 204.153.163.2: bytes=32 time<10ms TTL=128
Reply from 204.153.163.2: bytes=32 time<10ms TTL=128
```

Because I've received a reply from the destination station (204.153.163.2, in this case), I know that I can reach the host and that it's responding to basic IP requests. Don't forget that you can use name resolution and ping to a name, such as ping www.sybex.com, and as long as that name can be resolved, you're golden.

Most versions of ping work the same way, but there are some switches you can use to specify certain information, like the number of packets to send, how big a packet to send, and so on. And if you're running the Windows command-line version of ping, just use the /? or -? switch to display a list of the available options like this:

```
C:\Users\tlammle>ping /?
```

```
Usage: ping [-t] [-a] [-n count] [-l size] [-f] [-i TTL] [-v TOS]
            [-r count] [-s count] [[-j host-list] | [-k host-list]]
            [-w timeout] [-R] [-S srcaddr] [-4] [-6] target_name
```

The command will also output a table showing what each of the options does, presented here in Table 17.1.

TABLE 17.1   Options for ping switches

Option	Description
-t	Pings the specified host until stopped. To see statistics and continue, press Ctrl+Break; to stop, press Ctrl+C.
-a	Resolves addresses to hostnames.
-n count	Specifies the number of echo requests to send.
-l size	Sends the buffer size.
-f	Sets the Don't Fragment flag in the packet (IPv4-only).
-i TTL	Specifies the time to live of the packet.
-v TOS	Specifies the type of service (IPv4-only).
-r count	Records the route for count hops (IPv4-only).
-s count	Specifies the timestamp for count hops (IPv4-only).
-j host-list	Uses a loose source route along the host-list (IPv4-only).
-k host-list	Uses a strict source route along host-list (IPv4-only).
-w timeout	Specifies the time-out to wait for each reply in milliseconds.
-R	Uses the routing header to test the reverse route also (IPv6-only).
-S srcaddr	Specifies the source address to use.
-4	Forces using IPv4.
-6	Forces using IPv6.

You can ping your local TCP/IP interface by typing **ping 127.0.0.1** or **ping localhost**. Understand that both addresses represent the local interface. Really, you can use any address in the 127.0.0.0 network range to provide a loopback test.

As you can see, there's a plethora of options you can use with the ping command from a Windows DOS prompt. But I really want you to focus on a few from the previous output. (I'm going to go over only a few of them, but you can get on your host machine and play with all the options.)

The -a switch is very cool because if you have name resolution (such as a DNS server), you can see the name of the destination host even if you only know its IP address. The -n switch sets the number of echo requests to send, where four is the default, and the -w switch allows you to adjust the time-out in milliseconds. The default ping time-out is 1 second (1000ms).

The -6 is also nice if you want to ping an IPv6 host. By the way, unless you really love typing 128-bit addresses, this is a wonderful example of how important name resolution is. And then there's -t, which keeps the ping running. Here's an example of a ping to an IPv6 address:

```
C:\Users\tlammle>ping -6 fe80::1063:16af:3f57:fff9

Pinging fe80::1063:16af:3f57:fff9 from fe80::1063:16af:3f57:fff9%25
with 32 bytes of data:
Reply from fe80::1063:16af:3f57:fff9: time<1ms
Reply from fe80::1063:16af:3f57:fff9: time<1ms
Reply from fe80::1063:16af:3f57:fff9: time<1ms
Reply from fe80::1063:16af:3f57:fff9: time<1ms

Ping statistics for fe80::1063:16af:3f57:fff9:
Packets: Sent = 4, Received = 4, Lost = 0 (0% loss),
Approximate round trip times in milli-seconds:
Minimum = 0ms, Maximum = 0ms, Average = 0ms
C:\Users\tlammle>
```

And if I want to have a continuous ping, I just use that -t option like this:

```
C:\Users\tlammle>ping -t 192.168.0.1

Pinging 192.168.0.1 with 32 bytes of data:
Reply from 192.168.0.1: bytes=32 time=7ms TTL=255
Reply from 192.168.0.1: bytes=32 time=1ms TTL=255
Reply from 192.168.0.1: bytes=32 time=1ms TTL=255
Reply from 192.168.0.1: bytes=32 time=1ms TTL=255
```

```
Reply from 192.168.0.1: bytes=32 time=1ms TTL=255
Reply from 192.168.0.1: bytes=32 time=1ms TTL=255

Ping statistics for 192.168.0.1:
Packets: Sent = 6, Received = 6, Lost = 0 (0% loss),
Approximate round trip times in milli-seconds:
Minimum = 1ms, Maximum = 7ms, Average = 2ms
Control-C
^C
C:\Users\tlammle>
```

This ping will just keep going and going like the Energizer Bunny until you press Ctrl+C. And by the way, it's an awesome tool for troubleshooting links.

Using the Address Resolution Protocol

The *Address Resolution Protocol (ARP)* is part of the TCP/IP protocol stack. It's used to translate TCP/IP addresses to MAC addresses using broadcasts. When a machine running TCP/IP wants to know which machine on an Ethernet network is using a certain IP address, it will send an ARP broadcast that says, in effect, "Hey...exactly who is IP address xxx.xxx.xxx.xxx?" The machine that owns the specific address will respond with its own MAC address, supplying the answer. The machine that made the inquiry will respond by adding the newly gained information to its own ARP table.

In addition to the normal usage, the ARP designation refers to a utility in Windows that you can use to manipulate and view the local workstation's ARP table.

The Windows ARP Table

The *ARP table* in Windows includes a list of TCP/IP addresses and their associated physical (MAC) addresses. This table is cached in memory so that Windows doesn't have to perform ARP lookups for frequently accessed TCP/IP addresses like those of servers and default gateways. Each entry contains an IP address and a MAC address plus a value for TTL that determines how long each entry will remain in the ARP table.

Remember that the ARP table contains two kinds of entries:

- Dynamic
- Static

Dynamic ARP table entries are created whenever the Windows TCP/IP stack performs an ARP lookup but the MAC address isn't found in the ARP table. When the MAC address of the requested IP address is finally found, or *resolved*, that information is then added into the ARP table as a dynamic entry. Whenever a request to send a packet to the host is sent to the Data

Link layer, the ARP cache is checked first before an ARP broadcast is sent out. Remember, the ARP request is broadcast on the local segment—it does not go through a router.

 The ARP table is cleared of dynamic entries whose TTL has expired to ensure that the entries are current.

Static ARP table entries serve the same function as dynamic entries but are made manually using the arp utility.

Using the *arp* Utility

You now know that ARP is a protocol included in the TCP/IP suite. You also understand that ARP is used by IP to determine the MAC address of a device that exists on the same subnet as the requesting device. When a TCP/IP device needs to forward a packet to a device on the local subnet, it first looks in its own table, called an *ARP cache*, for an association between the known IP address of the destination device on the local subnet and that same device's MAC address. The cache is called that because the contents are periodically weeded out.

If no association that includes the destination IP address can be found, the device will then send out an ARP broadcast that includes its own MAC and IP information as well as the IP address of the target device and a blank MAC address field. Filling in that blank is the object of the whole operation—it's the unknown value that the source device is requesting to be returned to it in the form of an ARP reply. Windows includes a utility called arp that allows us to check out the operating system's ARP cache. To view this, from a Windows DOS prompt, use the arp command like this:

```
C:\Uses\tlammle>arp

Displays and modifies the IP-to-Physical address translation tables used
by address resolution protocol (ARP).

ARP -s inet_addr eth_addr [if_addr]
ARP -d inet_addr [if_addr]
ARP -a [inet_addr] [-N if_addr] [-v]
```

Table 17.2 describes the various options that you can use with the arp command.

TABLE 17.2 arp options

Option	Description
-a	Displays current ARP entries by interrogating the current protocol data. If inet_addr is specified, the IP and physical addresses for only the specified computer are displayed. If more than one network interface uses ARP, entries for each ARP table are displayed.

Option	Description
-a	Displays current ARP entries by interrogating the current protocol data. If inet_addr is specified, the IP and physical addresses for only the specified computer are displayed. If more than one network interface uses ARP, entries for each ARP table are displayed.
-g	Same as -a.
-v	Displays current ARP entries in verbose mode. All invalid entries and entries on the loopback interface will be shown.
inet_addr	Specifies an Internet address.
-N	Displays the ARP entries for the network interface specified by if_addr.
-d	Deletes the host specified by inet_addr. inet_addr. May be wildcarded with * to delete all hosts.
-s	Adds the host, and associates the Internet address inet_addr with the physical address eth_addr. The physical address is given as six hexadecimal bytes separated by hyphens. The entry is permanent.
eth_addr	Specifies a physical address.
if_addr	If present, specifies the Internet address of the interface whose address translation table should be modified. If not present, the first applicable interface will be used.

Sheesh. Looking at that output really makes me wish we were all just running IPv6 because, as you already should know, IPv6 doesn't need ARP as well as many other annoying features and protocols required when running IPv4.

Of note, the Windows arp utility is primarily useful for resolving duplicate IP addresses. For example, let's say your workstation receives its IP address from a DHCP server but it accidentally receives the same address that some other workstation gets. And so, when you try to ping it, you get no response. Your workstation is basically confused—it's trying to determine the MAC address, and it can't because two machines are reporting that they have the same IP address. To solve this little snag, you can use the arp utility to view your local ARP table and see which TCP/IP address is resolved to which MAC address.

To display the entire current ARP table, use the arp command with the –a switch, like so:

```
C:\Users\tlammle>arp -a

Interface: 192.168.0.6 --- 0xb
Internet Address      Physical Address       Type
```

```
192.168.0.1          00-15-05-06-31-b0    dynamic
192.168.0.255        ff-ff-ff-ff-ff-ff    static
224.0.0.22           01-00-5e-00-00-16    static
224.0.0.252          01-00-5e-00-00-fc    static
239.255.255.250      01-00-5e-7f-ff-fa    static
255.255.255.255      ff-ff-ff-ff-ff-ff    static

Interface: 10.100.10.54 --- 0x10
Internet Address     Physical Address     Type
10.100.10.1          00-15-05-06-31-b0    dynamic
10.100.10.255        ff-ff-ff-ff-ff-ff    static
224.0.0.22           01-00-5e-00-00-16    static
224.0.0.252          01-00-5e-00-00-fc    static
239.255.255.250      01-00-5e-7f-ff-fa    static
```

By the way, the −g switch will produce the same result.

Now, from this output, you can tell which MAC address is assigned to which IP address. Then, for static assignments, you can tell which workstation has a specific IP address and if it's indeed supposed to have that address by examining your network documentation—you do have that record, right?

For DHCP-assigned addresses, you can begin to uncover problems stemming from multiple DHCP scopes or servers doling out identical addresses and other common configuration issues. And remember that under normal circumstances, you shouldn't see IP addresses in the ARP table for a given interface that aren't members of the same IP subnet as the interface.

If the machine has more than one network card (as may happen in Windows servers and on laptops with both Ethernet and wireless cards), each interface will be listed separately.

It's good to know that in addition to displaying the ARP table, you can use the arp utility to manipulate the table itself. To add static entries to the ARP table, you use the arp command with the −s switch. These static entries will stay in the ARP table until the machine is rebooted. A static entry essentially hardwires a specific IP address to a specific MAC address so that when a packet needs to be sent to that IP address, it will automatically be sent to that MAC address. Here's the syntax:

```
arp −s [IP Address] [MAC Address]
```

Simply replace the *[IP Address]* and *[MAC Address]* sections with the appropriate entries, like so:

```
arp -s 204.153.163.5 00-a0-c0-ab-c3-11
```

Now, take a look at your new ARP table by using the `arp -a` command. You should see something like this:

```
Internet Address          Physical Address          Type
204.153.163.5             00-a0-c0-ab-c3-11          static
```

Finally, if you want to delete entries from the ARP table, you can either wait until the dynamic entries time out or use the –d switch with the IP address of the static entry you'd like to delete, like this:

```
arp -d 204.153.163.5
```

Doing so effectively deletes the entry from the ARP table in memory.

> The arp utility doesn't confirm successful additions or deletions (use arp -a or arp -g for that), but it will give you an error message if you use incorrect syntax.

Using the *nslookup* Utility

Whenever you're configuring a server or a workstation to connect to the Internet, you've got to start by configuring DNS if you want name resolution to happen (that is, if you want to be able to type **www.sybex.com** instead of an IP address). When configuring DNS, it's a very good thing to be able to test what IP address DNS is returning to ensure that it's working properly. The nslookup utility allows you to query a name server and quickly find out which name resolves to which IP address.

> The UNIX dig (short for *domain information groper*) utility does the exact same thing as nslookup. It's primarily a command-line utility that allows you to perform a single DNS lookup for a specific entity, but it can also be employed in batch mode for a series of lookups. Detailed information on this command is beyond the scope of this study guide, but you can find more information on the Web by searching for "unix dig."

The nslookup utility comes with Windows NT and later as well as most versions of UNIX and Linux, but not with Windows 95/98. You can run it from a Windows command prompt. At the command prompt, you can start the nslookup utility by typing **nslookup** and pressing Enter. When you're inside this utility, the command prompt will change from something similar to C:\> sign to a shorter > sign. It will also display the name and IP address of the default DNS server you will be querying (you can change it, if necessary). Then you can start using nslookup. The following output gives you a sample of the display after the nslookup command has been entered at the C:\> prompt.

```
C:\Users\tlammle>nslookup
Default Server:  gnt-corpdc1.globalnet.local
Address:  10.100.36.12

>
```

The primary job of nslookup is to tell you the many different features of a particular domain name, the names of the servers that serve it, and how they're configured. To get that, just type in a domain name at the > prompt, and the nslookup utility will then return this information:

```
> lammle.com
Server:  dslmodem.domain.actdsltmp
Address:  192.168.0.1

Non-authoritative answer:
Name:    lammle.com
Address:  206.123.114.186
```

What this tells you is that the server that returned the information is not responsible (authoritative) for the zone information of the domain for which you requested an address and that the name server for the domain lammle.com is located at the IP address 206.123.114.186.

You can also ask nslookup for other information by setting a different option within nslookup. Just type **set** *option* at the > prompt and replace *option* with the actual option you want to use—for example, use >set type=mx to determine the IP address of your email server. If you can't decide which one you want, use the question mark (?) at the greater than sign (>) to see all available options.

If you type in **nslookup** and receive the reply

```
NS request timed out.
    timeout was 2 seconds.
***Can't find server name for address 206.123.114.186: Timed out
Default Server:  UnKnown
Address:  fec0:0:0:ffff::1
```

then you know your DNS servers are not answering. You need to get over to the DNS server stat!

Resolving Names with the Hosts Table

The Hosts table is really a lot like DNS, except its entries are static for each and every host and server. Within the Hosts table, you'll find a collection of hostnames that devices reference for name-resolution purposes. And even though it works in both IPv4 and IPv6 environments, it's unlikely you will use it these days because the Hosts table is a way-ancient relic left over from old UNIX machines.

But just because it's museum quality doesn't mean you won't run into it now and then, which is the main reason I'm showing it to you. You can find the Hosts table in C:\Windows\System32\drivers\etc. Just double-click the file, and then choose to open the file in Notepad or another text editor. Here's the default information—it's really nothing more than an explanation of how to use it and the local hosts for both IP and IPv6:

```
# Copyright (c) 1993-2006 Microsoft Corp.
#
# This is a sample HOSTS file used by Microsoft TCP/IP for Windows.
#
# This file contains the mappings of IP addresses to host names. Each
# entry should be kept on an individual line. The IP address should
# be placed in the first column followed by the corresponding host name.
# The IP address and the host name should be separated by at least one
# space.
#
# Additionally, comments (such as these) may be inserted on individual
# lines or following the machine name denoted by a '#' symbol.
#
# For example:
#
#      102.54.94.97     rhino.acme.com          # source server
#       38.25.63.10     x.acme.com              # x client host

127.0.0.1       localhost
::1             localhost
```

Any information entered to the right of a pound sign (#) in a Hosts file is ignored, so you can use this space for comments.

Because it's a plain ASCII text file, you add the IP address under the local hosts and then the name to which you want to resolve the IP address. It's a pretty simple configuration, and again, one I don't recommend using because you have to type in the names of every host on every machine in your network. DNS is definitely the name resolution of choice for networks today.

Do not get the Hosts table confused with the hostname command. The hostname command doesn't do much but display the name of your host, as shown:

```
C:\Users\tlammle>hostname /?

Prints the name of the current host.

hostname

C:\Users\tlammle>hostname
globalnet-todd
```

Using the *Mtr* Command

Mtr, or My traceroute, is a computer program that combines the functions of the traceroute and ping utilities in a single network diagnostic tool. It also adds round-trip time and packet loss to the output—very cool.

Mtr probes routers on the route path by limiting the number of hops individual packets are allowed to traverse and listening to news of their termination. It will regularly repeat this process (usually once per second) and keep track of the response times of the hops along the path.

Mtr is great if you have Linux or UNIX, but by default, it's not installed on Windows devices. Third-party applications of Mtr are available to install on Windows, but Microsoft did respond with its own version of Mtr—it's called pathping and provides the same functions as Mtr. Here's a look at the output and the options:

```
C:\Users\tlammle>pathping

Usage: pathping [-g host-list] [-h maximum_hops] [-i address] [-n]
                [-p period] [-q num_queries] [-w timeout]
                [-4] [-6] target_name
```

Table 17.3 lists the options of the Windows pathping command.

TABLE 17.3 pathping options

Option	Description
-g *host-list*	Uses a loose source route along the *host-list*.
-h *maximum_hops*	Specifies the maximum number of hops to search for the target.

Option	Description
-i *address*	Uses the specified source address.
-n	Does not resolve addresses to hostnames.
-p *period*	Waits *period* milliseconds between pings.
-q *num_queries*	Specifies the number of queries per hop.
-w *timeout*	Waits *timeout* milliseconds for each reply.
-4	Forces using IPv4.
-6	Forces using IPv6.

The Mtr utility is basically the same as traceroute and ping, but it does give you some additional output that can help you troubleshoot your network.

Using the *route* Command

I went over static routing in Chapter 9, "Introduction to IP Routing," so you know that Windows devices like routers perform routing. Most of the time, it's a good idea to leave Windows alone, but it's still good to know how to add and delete routes on your Windows machines.

Probably the biggest reason for manipulating the routing table on a Windows server is to create a firewall. For instance, let's say we're running an Application layer firewall on a Windows server located between the demilitarized zone (DMZ) and the internal network. This scenario would mean the routing that's happening on the server or hosts located in the DMZ wouldn't be able to reach the internal network's hosts and vice versa.

To circumvent this problem, we would need to employ both static and default routing because Windows Vista, Windows 7, and Server 2008 don't support routing protocols—running routing protocols on hosts and servers wouldn't be a good solution for today's networks, and Microsoft knows that.

To view the routing table on a Windows device, use the route print command, as shown in Figure 17.5.

In this output, you can see that each of the routes was added automatically when the system booted up. (This is all based on the configuration of your IP stack.) To see all the options available with the route command, type the route command and then press Enter. To add a route to your routing table, use the following syntax:

route [**-f**] [**-p**] [*Command* [*Destination*] [**mask** *Netmask*] [*Gateway*] [**metric** *Metric*]] [**if** *Interface*]]

FIGURE 17.5 route print output

Using the *route* Command Options

Let's start with the switches you can use:

-f Using this command with any of the options like add, change, or delete will clear the routing table of all entries that aren't host routes (routes with the subnet mask 255.255.255.255), the loopback network route(s) (routes with a destination of 127.0.0.0 and the subnet mask 255.0.0.0), and any multicast routes (those with a destination of 224.0.0.0 and the subnet mask 240.0.0.0).

-p If you use this with the add command, the individual route will be added to the Registry and then used to initialize the IP routing table whenever TCP/IP is started. Important to remember is that by default, the routes you've statically added won't remain in the routing table the next time TCP/IP boots. And if you use -p with the print command, you'll get shown a list of the persistent routes that are stored in the Registry location of HKEY_LOCAL_MACHINE\SYSTEM\CurrentControlSet\Services\ Tcpip\Parameters\PersistentRoutes.

Now, let's take a look at how and when you would use the route command. Table 17.4 shows the command options available and what they do when you are using the route command with them.

TABLE 17.4 route command options

Command	Purpose
add	Adds a route
change	Modifies an existing route
delete	Deletes a route(s)
print	Prints a route(s)

Here's a description of some other tasks you can accomplish via the rest of the command's options:

destination This will give you the network destination of a given route. If the host bits of the network address are set to 0, it will be depicted with the destination's IP network address, an IP address for a specific host route, or the default route of 0.0.0.0.

mask netmask This will provide you with the *netmask*—often referred to as the *subnet mask*—that's associated with the destination network. The default destination subnet mask is 0.0.0.0, and typically you'll see 255.255.255.255 representing a host route. It's really important to remember that the destination address can't be more specific than its corresponding subnet mask. What I'm saying is that there absolutely can't be a bit set to 1 in the destination address if the equivalent bit in the subnet mask is a 0.

gateway The gateway also depends on the network address and subnet mask, but it's even more specific and delimits what's called the *next-hop IP address*. For routes located on a local subnet, the gateway address maps directly to a particular interface. If the destination is on a remote network, the gateway IP address will direct packets to the neighboring router.

metric metric *Metric* refers to the cost of a given route from the sending to the receiving device, and it's a value between 1 and 9999. Devices use this value to choose the best, or most efficient, routes among those in its routing table—the route with the lowest value wins. This decision can also include factors like the number of hops, the speed, reliability, and available bandwidth of the path being considered plus the various administrative aspects associated with it.

if interface   This tool depends on information from the gateway address and determines the interface index for the specific interface that needs to receive the data. You can get a list of interfaces along with their relevant interface indexes by typing the **route print** command.

/?   Using this will allow you to view help at the command prompt.

Some Examples of the *route* Command

Even though the finer points of the route command demand that you use caution when deploying some of the options, I'll still list the basics of the route command because it can be really useful. I highly recommend that you spend some time practicing them on a non-production server, though—especially at first.

- To display the entire IP routing table, type **route print**.

- To add a default route with the default gateway address 192.168.10.1, type **route add 0.0.0.0 mask 0.0.0.0 192.168.10.1**.

- To add a route to the destination 10.1.1.0 with the subnet mask 255.255.255.0 and the next-hop address 10.2.2.2, type **route add 10.1.1..0 mask 255.255.255.0 10.2.2.2**.

- If you want to, let's say, add a persistent route to the destination 10.100.0.0 with the subnet mask 255.255.0.0 and the next-hop address 10.2.0.1, type **route -p add 10.100.0.0 mask 255.255.0.0 10.2.0.1**. If you want to delete the route to the destination 10.100.0.0 with the subnet mask 255.255.0.0, enter **route delete 10.100.0.0 mask 255.255.0.0**.

- And finally, if you want to change the next-hop address of a route with the destination 10.100.0.0 and the subnet mask 255.255.0.0 from 10.2.0.1 to 10.7.0.5, type **route change 10.100.0.0 mask 255.255.0.0 10.7.0.5**.

Okay, let's move on to some other important Windows utilities.

Using the *nbtstat* Utility

Microsoft Windows uses an interface called Network Basic Input/Output System (NetBIOS), which relates names with workstations and is an upper-layer interface that requires a transport protocol—usually, TCP/IP. But IPv6 can be used as well. Deploying the nbtstat utility will achieve these three important things:

- Track NetBIOS over TCP/IP statistics
- Show the details of incoming and outgoing NetBIOS over TCP/IP connections
- Resolve NetBIOS names

Understand that because NetBIOS name resolution is primarily a Windows network utility, the nbtstat command is available only in Windows-based operating systems.

To display a basic description of **nbtstat** and its associated options, type **nbtstat** at the command line. Then, use these options to get a display of information about NetBIOS over TCP/IP hosts. Here are some of the tools, or *switches*, you can use:

−a	−A
−c	−n
−r	−R
−S	−s

−a	**−A**
−c	−n
−r	−R
−S	−s

 All nbtstat switches are case sensitive. Generally speaking, lowercase switches deal with NetBIOS names of hosts, and the uppercase ones deal with the TCP/IP addresses of hosts.

The *−a* Switch

Making use of the −a switch will get you a remote machine's NetBIOS name table consisting of a list of every NetBIOS name the machine from which you've deployed the switch knows of. The −a switch produced the output from server S1 shown in Figure 17.6.

FIGURE 17.6   Sample output of the nbtstat −a command

```
C:\>nbtstat -a s1


      NetBIOS Remote Machine Name Table

      Name              Type        Status
      ---------------------------------------
      S1            <20> UNIQUE    Registered
      S1            <00> UNIQUE    Registered
      ACME          <00> GROUP     Registered
      ACME          <1C> GROUP     Registered
      ACME          <1B> UNIQUE    Registered
      S1            <03> UNIQUE    Registered
      ACME          <1E> GROUP     Registered
      ACME          <1D> UNIQUE    Registered
      .._MSBROWSE__.<01> GROUP     Registered
      INet~Services <1C> GROUP     Registered
      IS~S1........ <00> UNIQUE    Registered

      MAC Address = 00-A0-C9-D4-BC-DC
```

So, using this switch arranges the NetBIOS name-table information in table form with output in four columns. The Name column displays the NetBIOS name entry for the remote host machine.

The next column gives you a unique two-digit hexadecimal identifier for the NetBIOS name. This identifier represents the last byte of the NetBIOS name depicted in the Name column, and it's important because the same name could actually be used several times for the same machine. Plus, it identifies the specific service on the particular host that the name is referencing. Table 17.5 and Table 17.6 list the hexadecimal identifiers for unique and group hostnames.

TABLE 17.5   Last-byte identifiers for unique names

Hex ID	Description
00	General name for the computer.
03	Messenger service ID used to send messages between a WINS server and a workstation. This is the ID registered with a WINS server.
06	Remote Access Server (RAS) server service ID.
20	File-serving service ID.
21	RAS client.
53	DNS.
123	Network Time Protocol (NTP).
1B	Domain master browser ID. A NetBIOS name with this ID indicates the domain master browser.
1F	Network Dynamic Data Exchange (NetDDE) service ID.
BE	Network monitor agent ID.
BF	Network monitor utility ID.

TABLE 17.6   Last-byte identifiers for group names

Hex ID	Description
01	Master browser for a domain to other master browsers.
20	Internet group name ID. This ID is registered with the WINS server to indicate which computers are used for administrative purposes.

Hex ID	Description
1C	Domain group name ID.
1D	Master browser name.
1E	Normal group name.

The Type column refers to (surprise) the type of NetBIOS name being referenced. Unique NetBIOS names refer to individual hosts, and group names refer to logical groupings of workstations—either domains or workgroups.

The Status column gives you information about the status of a host's NetBIOS even if it hasn't been registered with the rest of the network.

The –A Switch

The –A switch works just like the –a switch and will give you the same output, but the syntax of the command is different. Obviously, you use an uppercase A instead of a lowercase one, and you also have to include the host's IP address instead of its NetBIOS name. To use it, type **nbtstat** followed by **–A** and finally the IP address of the specific host whose NetBIOS table you want to check out:

```
nbtstat –A 199.153.163.2
```

The –c Switch

Use the –c switch to display the local NetBIOS name cache on the workstation it's running on. Figure 17.7 shows sample output of the nbtstat –c command.

FIGURE 17.7   Sample output of the nbtstat –c command

```
Node IpAddress: [204.153.163.4] Scope Id: []

        NetBIOS Remote Cache Name Table

    Name            Type       Host Address    Life [sec]
-----------------------------------------------------------
S1          <00>  UNIQUE      204.153.163.2       420
```

Each entry in this display shows the NetBIOS name, the hex ID for the service that was accessed, the type of NetBIOS name (unique or group), the IP address that the name resolves to, and its life. The Life value shows how many seconds each entry will live in the cache. When this time expires, the entry will be deleted.

Sometimes, deploying nbtstat to display the cache will get you the response "No names in the cache" because all entries in the cache have expired. This is what happens if you don't regularly access machines or services with NetBIOS names.

The *–n* Switch

The –n switch will give you the local NetBIOS name table on a Windows device. Figure 17.8 shows output that's similar to the output of the –a switch except for one important thing: What you're seeing is the NetBIOS name table for the machine you're running the command on instead of that of another host. Check it out.

FIGURE 17.8   Sample output of the nbtstat –n command

```
C:\NBTSTAT -n

Node IpAddress: [204.153.163.4] Scope Id: []

            NetBIOS Local Name Table

    Name              Type        Status
---------------------------------------------
DEFAULT        <00>  UNIQUE   Registered
WORKGROUP      <00>  GROUP    Registered
DEFAULT        <03>  UNIQUE   Registered
DEFAULT        <20>  UNIQUE   Registered
WORKGROUP      <1E>  GROUP    Registered
WORKGROUP      <1D>  UNIQUE   Registered
.._MSBROWSE__.<01>  GROUP    Registered
ADMINISTRATOR  <03>  UNIQUE   Registered
```

The *–r* Switch

This switch is probably the one you'll use most often when you want to get ahold of NetBIOS over TCP/IP (NBT) statistics because it tells you exactly how many NetBIOS names have been resolved to TCP/IP addresses. Figure 17.9 shows sample output of the nbtstat –r command.

FIGURE 17.9   Sample output of the nbtstat –r command

```
C:\>nbtstat -r


NetBIOS Names Resolution and Registration Statistics
----------------------------------------------------------

Resolved By Broadcast     = 2
Resolved By Name Server   = 0

Registered By Broadcast   = 12
Registered By Name Server = 0

    NetBIOS Names Resolved By Broadcast
---------------------------------------------------
    ACME            <1B>
    ACME            <00>
```

What you can see here is that the statistics are divided into two categories. First, there are the NetBIOS names resolution and registration statistics. This is how many names have been resolved or registered either by broadcasts on the local segment or via lookup from a WINS name server.

Next you have the NetBIOS unique and group names and their associated hex IDs that were resolved or registered. In Figure 17.9, you can see that there's a distinct lack of information regarding names resolved by a name server. What this means is that the output is telling you that there's no WINS server operating—instead, all NetBIOS names were resolved by broadcast only.

> The −r switch comes in handy when you want to determine how a workstation is resolving NetBIOS names and whether WINS is configured correctly. If WINS isn't configured correctly or it's simply not being used, the numbers in the Resolved By Name Server and Registered By Name Server categories will always be zero.

The −*R* Switch

Unlike the −a and −A switches, -r and -R use the same letter but do *not* have anything in common.

Here's an example. Let's say you have a bad name in the NetBIOS name cache but the right name is in the LMHOSTS file instead. (The LMHOSTS file contains NetBIOS names of stations and their associated IP addresses.) Because the cache is consulted before the LMHOSTS file is, that bad address will remain in the cache until it expires.

This command is used when you want to purge the NetBIOS name table cache and reload the LMHOSTS file into memory. You do that using the nbtstat command with the −R switch, like so:

nbtstat −R

You can practice this nbtstat −R command on your host to purge the NBT remote cache table.

The −*S* Switch

Using the -S switch will display the NetBIOS sessions table that lists all NetBIOS sessions to and from the host from which you issued the command. The −S switch displays both workstation and server sessions but lists remote addresses by IP address only.

Figure 17.10 shows sample output of the nbtstat −S command.

Here you can see the NetBIOS name being displayed along with its hex ID and the status of each session. An entry in the In/Out column determines whether the connection has been initiated from the computer on which you're running nbtstat (outbound) or whether another computer has initiated the connection (inbound). The numbers in the Input and Output columns indicate in bytes the amount of data transferred between the stations.

FIGURE 17.10   Sample output of the nbtstat –S command

```
C:\NBTSTAT -S
                  NetBIOS Connection Table
Local Name             State      In/Out  Remote Host           Input   Output
-------------------------------------------------------------------------------
S1            <00>     Connected    Out    204.153.163.4         256B    432B
S1            <03>     Listening
```

The *–s* Switch

As with the –A and –a switches, the lowercase –s switch is similar to its uppercase sibling. The nbtstat –s command produces the same output as nbtstat –S except that it will also attempt to resolve remote-host IP addresses into hostnames. Figure 17.11 shows sample output from the nbtstat –s command.

FIGURE 17.11   Sample output of the nbtstat –s command

```
C:\NBTSTAT -s
                  NetBIOS Connection Table
Local Name             State      In/Out  Remote Host           Input   Output
-------------------------------------------------------------------------------
S1            <00>     Connected    Out    DEFAULT       <20>    256B    432B
S1            <03>     Listening
```

Note the similarities between Figure 17.10 and Figure 17.11.

As with the netstat command, with the nbtstat command you can place a number for an interval at the end to direct it to deploy once every so many seconds until you press Ctrl+C.

Using the *netstat* Utility

Using netstat is a great way to check out the inbound and outbound TCP/IP connections on your machine. You can also use it to view packet statistics like how many packets have been sent and received, the number of errors, and so on.

When used without any options, netstat produces output similar to the following, which shows all the outbound TCP/IP connections. This utility is a great tool to use to determine the status of outbound web connections. Take a look:

C:\Users\tlammle>**netstat**

Active Connections

Proto	Local Address	Foreign Address	State
TCP	10.100.10.54:49545	gnt-exchange:epmap	TIME_WAIT
TCP	10.100.10.54:49548	gnt-exchange:epmap	TIME_WAIT
TCP	10.100.10.54:49551	gnt-exchange:1151	ESTABLISHED
TCP	10.100.10.54:49557	gnt-exchange:1026	ESTABLISHED
TCP	10.100.10.54:49590	gnt-exchange:epmap	TIME_WAIT
TCP	127.0.0.1:49174	globalnet-todd:62514	ESTABLISHED
TCP	127.0.0.1:62514	globalnet-todd:49174	ESTABLISHED
TCP	192.168.0.6:2492	blugro2relay:2492	ESTABLISHED
TCP	192.168.0.6:2492	blugro3relay:2492	ESTABLISHED
TCP	192.168.0.6:49170	64.12.25.26:5190	ESTABLISHED
TCP	192.168.0.6:49171	oam-d05c:5190	ESTABLISHED
TCP	192.168.0.6:49473	205.128.92.124:http	CLOSE_WAIT
TCP	192.168.0.6:49625	64-190-251-21:ftp	ESTABLISHED
TCP	192.168.0.6:49628	210-11:http	ESTABLISHED
TCP	192.168.0.6:49629	varp1:http	ESTABLISHED
TCP	192.168.0.6:49630	varp1:http	ESTABLISHED
TCP	192.168.0.6:49631	varp1:http	ESTABLISHED
TCP	192.168.0.6:49632	varp1:http	ESTABLISHED
TCP	192.168.0.6:49635	199.93.62.125:http	ESTABLISHED
TCP	192.168.0.6:49636	m1:http	ESTABLISHED
TCP	192.168.0.6:49638	spe:http	ESTABLISHED

The Proto column lists the protocol being used. You can see that I'm connected to my Exchange server and an FTP server and that I have some HTTP sessions open; by the way, all of them use TCP at the Transport layer.

The Local Address column lists the source address and the source port (source socket). The Foreign Address column lists the address of the destination machine (the hostname if it's been resolved) plus the fact that the destination port is a TCP port. If the destination port is known, it will show up as the well-known port. In the previous output, you see http instead of port 80 and ftp instead of port 21.

The State column indicates the status of each connection. This column shows statistics only for TCP connections because User Datagram Protocol (UDP) establishes no virtual circuit to the remote device. Usually, this column indicates ESTABLISHED when a TCP connection between your computer and the destination computer has been established. All sessions eventually time out and then close, and you can see that I have all of these listed in my netstat output.

If the address of either your computer or the destination computer can be found in the HOSTS file on your computer, the destination computer's name, rather than the IP address, will show up in either the Local Address or Foreign Address column.

The output of the `netstat` utility depends on the switch. By using the `netstat /?` command, we can see the options available to us.

`C:\Users\tlammle>`**`netstat /?`**

All of the `netstat` switch options are listed in Table 17.7.

TABLE 17.7 netstat options

Option	Description
-a	Displays all connections and listening ports.
-b	Displays the executable involved in creating each connection or listening port. In some cases, well-known executables host multiple independent components, and in these cases the sequence of components involved in creating the connection or listening port is displayed. In this case, the executable name is in [ ] at the bottom; on top is the component it called, and so forth, until TCP/IP was reached. Note that this option can be time consuming and will fail unless you have sufficient permissions.
-e	Displays Ethernet statistics. This may be combined with the –s option.
-f	Displays fully qualified domain names (FQDNs) for foreign addresses.
-n	Displays addresses and port numbers in numerical form.
-o	Displays the owning process ID associated with each connection.
-p *proto*	Shows connections for the protocol specified by *proto*; *proto* may be TCP, UDP, TCPv6, or UDPv6. If used with the –s option to display per-protocol statistics, *proto* may be IP, IPv6, ICMP, ICMPv6, TCP, TCPv6, UDP, or UDPv6.
-r	Displays the routing table.
-s	Displays per-protocol statistics. By default, statistics are shown for IP, IPv6, ICMP, ICMPv6, TCP, TCPv6, UDP, and UDPv6; the -p option may be used to specify a subset of the default.
-t	Displays the current connection offload state. Redisplays selected statistics, pausing interval seconds between each display. Press Ctrl+C to stop redisplaying statistics. If -t is omitted, `netstat` will print the current configuration information once.

Simply type **netstat** followed by a space and then the particular switch you want to use. Some switches have options, but no matter what, the syntax is basically the same.

Note that with UNIX-type switches, the hyphen absolutely must be included. This is common in Microsoft operating systems for TCP/IP utilities that originate from UNIX systems. I'm not going to exhaustively go over each and every switch, but make sure you practice all of these on your own Windows machine.

The *–a* Switch

When you use the –a switch, the netstat utility displays all TCP/IP connections and all UDP connections. Figure 17.12 shows sample output produced by the netstat –a command.

FIGURE 17.12   Sample output of the netstat –a command

```
C:\ NETSTAT -a

Active Connections

Proto      Local Address        Foreign Address       State
TCP        default:1026         204.153.163.2:80      ESTABLISHED
TCP        default:1027         204.153.163.2:80      ESTABLISHED
TCP        default:1028         204.153.163.2:80      ESTABLISHED
TCP        default:1029         204.153.163.2:80      ESTABLISHED
UDP        default:nbname       *:*
UDP        default:nbdatagram   *:*
```

The last two entries in Figure 17.12 show that the protocol is UDP and give the source-port nicknames nbname and nbdatagram. These are the well-known port numbers of 137 and 138, respectively. These port numbers are commonly seen on networks that broadcast the NetBIOS name of a workstation on the TCP/IP network. You can tell that this is a broadcast because the destination address is listed as *:* (meaning "any address, any port").

The State column in Figure 17.12 has no entry because UDP is not a connection-oriented protocol and, therefore, has no connection state.

The most common use for the –a switch is to check the status of a TCP/IP connection that appears to be hung. You can determine if the connection is simply busy or is actually hung and no longer responding.

The –*e* Switch

The -e switch displays a summary of all the packets that have been sent over the Network Interface Card (NIC) as of that instant. The Received and Sent columns show packets coming in as well as being sent:

```
C:\Users\tlammle>netstat -e
Interface Statistics

                         Received              Sent

Bytes                     7426841           7226953
Unicast packets             25784             35006
Non-unicast packets          1115             12548
Discards                        0                 0
Errors                          0                71
Unknown protocols               0
```

You can use the –e switch to display the following categories of statistics:

Bytes   The number of bytes transmitted or received since the computer was turned on. This statistic is useful for finding out if data is actually being transmitted and received or if the network interface isn't doing anything at all.

Unicast packets   The number of packets sent from or received at this computer. To register in one of these columns, the packet must be addressed directly from one computer to another and the computer's address must be in either the source or destination address section of the packet.

Non-unicast packets   The number of packets that weren't directly sent from one workstation to another. For example, a broadcast packet is a non-unicast packet. The number of non-unicast packets should be smaller than the number of unicast packets. If the number of non-unicast packets is as high or higher than that of unicast packets, too many broadcast packets are being sent over your network. Definitely find the source of these packets and make any necessary adjustments to optimize performance.

Discards   The number of packets that were discarded by the NIC during either transmission or reception because they weren't assembled correctly.

Errors   The number of errors that occurred during transmission or reception. (These numbers may indicate problems with the network card.)

Unknown protocols   The number of received packets that the Windows networking stack couldn't interpret. This statistic only shows up in the Received column because if the computer sent them, they wouldn't be unknown, right?

Unfortunately, statistics don't mean much unless they can be colored with time information. For example, if the Errors column shows 71 errors, is that a problem? It might be if the computer has been on for only a few minutes. But 71 errors could be par for the course if the computer has been operating for several days. Unfortunately, the netstat utility doesn't have a way of indicating how much time has elapsed for these statistics.

The *–r* Switch

You use the –r switch to display the current route table for a workstation so that you can see exactly how TCP/IP information is being routed. This will give you the same output as the route print command that we covered earlier in this chapter.

The *–s* Switch

Using the –s switch displays a variety of TCP, UDP, IP, and ICMP protocol statistics. But be warned—the output you'll get is really long, which may or may not be okay for you. For this book, it's way too long for me to insert. With that in mind, we can add another modifier called the -p switch.

The *–p* Switch

Like the –n switch, the -p switch is a modifier that's usually used with the –s switch to specify which protocol statistics to list in the output (IP, TCP, UDP, or ICMP). For example, if you want to view only ICMP statistics, you use the –p switch like so:

```
netstat -s -p ICMP
```

The netstat utility then displays the ICMP statistics instead of the entire gamut of TCP/IP statistics that the –s switch will typically flood you with. For a different example, let's use the -s and -p switches to retrieve some IPv6 information:

```
C:\Users\tlammle>netstat -s -p IPV6

IPv6 Statistics

    Packets Received            = 1400
    Received Header Errors      = 0
    Received Address Errors     = 6
    Datagrams Forwarded         = 0
    Unknown Protocols Received  = 0
    Received Packets Discarded  = 451
    Received Packets Delivered  = 10441
    Output Requests             = 24349
    Routing Discards            = 0
    Discarded Output Packets    = 3575
    Output Packet No Route      = 41
```

```
Reassembly Required              = 0
Reassembly Successful            = 0
Reassembly Failures              = 0
Datagrams Successfully Fragmented = 0
Datagrams Failing Fragmentation  = 0
Fragments Created                = 0


C:\Users\tlammle>
```

Nice! Gets right to the point. Now, let's see the TCP connections my host has:

```
C:\Users\tlammle>netstat -s -p tcp

TCP Statistics for IPv4

    Active Opens                 = 7832
    Passive Opens                = 833
    Failed Connection Attempts   = 1807
    Reset Connections            = 2428
    Current Connections          = 11
    Segments Received            = 1391678
    Segments Sent                = 1340994
    Segments Retransmitted       = 6246

Active Connections

    Proto  Local Address         Foreign Address          State
    TCP    10.100.10.54:54737    gnt-exchange:1151        ESTABLISHED
    TCP    10.100.10.54:54955    gnt-exchange:1026        ESTABLISHED
    TCP    10.100.10.54:55218    gnt-exchange:epmap       TIME_WAIT
    TCP    127.0.0.1:2492        globalnet-todd:54840     ESTABLISHED
    TCP    127.0.0.1:54516       globalnet-todd:62514     ESTABLISHED
    TCP    127.0.0.1:54840       globalnet-todd:2492      ESTABLISHED
    TCP    127.0.0.1:62514       globalnet-todd:54516     ESTABLISHED
    TCP    192.168.0.6:2492      blugro2relay:2492        ESTABLISHED
    TCP    192.168.0.6:2492      blugro3relay:2492        ESTABLISHED
    TCP    192.168.0.6:54527     64.12.25.26:5190         ESTABLISHED
    TCP    192.168.0.6:54531     oam-d05c:5190            ESTABLISHED
    TCP    192.168.0.6:55163     207.123.44.123:http      CLOSE_WAIT


C:\Users\tlammle>
```

This kind of efficiency is exactly why it's good you to use the -p modifier with the -s switch.

 Because the Network+ exam doesn't cover them, we won't go into detail about what all these statistics mean for most of these commands. You can probably figure out most of them—for instance, Packets Received. For more details, go to Microsoft's support website at www.support.microsoft.com.

The *–n* Switch

The -n switch is a modifier for the other switches. When used with them, it reverses the natural tendency of netstat to use names instead of network addresses. In other words, when you use the –n switch, the output always displays network addresses instead of their associated network names. Following is output from the netstat command used with the netstat -n command. It's showing the same information but with IP addresses instead of names:

```
C:\Users\tlammle>netstat

Active Connections

  Proto  Local Address            Foreign Address          State
  TCP    10.100.10.54:54737       gnt-exchange:1151        ESTABLISHED
  TCP    10.100.10.54:54955       gnt-exchange:1026        ESTABLISHED
  TCP    127.0.0.1:2492           globalnet-todd:54840     ESTABLISHED
  TCP    127.0.0.1:54516          globalnet-todd:62514     ESTABLISHED
  TCP    127.0.0.1:54840          globalnet-todd:2492      ESTABLISHED
  TCP    127.0.0.1:62514          globalnet-todd:54516     ESTABLISHED
  TCP    192.168.0.6:2492         blugro2relay:2492        ESTABLISHED
  TCP    192.168.0.6:2492         blugro3relay:2492        ESTABLISHED
  TCP    192.168.0.6:54527        64.12.25.26:5190         ESTABLISHED
  TCP    192.168.0.6:54531        oam-d05c:5190            ESTABLISHED
  TCP    192.168.0.6:55163        207.123.44.123:http      CLOSE_WAIT

C:\Users\tlammle>netstat -n

Active Connections

  Proto  Local Address            Foreign Address          State
  TCP    10.100.10.54:54737       10.100.36.13:1151        ESTABLISHED
  TCP    10.100.10.54:54955       10.100.36.13:1026        ESTABLISHED
  TCP    127.0.0.1:2492           127.0.0.1:54840          ESTABLISHED
```

```
TCP   127.0.0.1:54516        127.0.0.1:62514        ESTABLISHED
TCP   127.0.0.1:54840        127.0.0.1:2492         ESTABLISHED
TCP   127.0.0.1:62514        127.0.0.1:54516        ESTABLISHED
TCP   192.168.0.6:2492       65.55.239.100:2492     ESTABLISHED
TCP   192.168.0.6:2492       65.55.248.110:2492     ESTABLISHED
TCP   192.168.0.6:54527      64.12.25.26:5190       ESTABLISHED
TCP   192.168.0.6:54531      205.188.248.163:5190   ESTABLISHED
TCP   192.168.0.6:55163      207.123.44.123:80      CLOSE_WAIT
```

C:\Users\tlammle>

 Real World Scenario

Uses for netstat

You might be saying to yourself, "Okay. Fine…I can use lots of cool switches with netstat, but really, what for?" I'm always finding uses for netstat. For instance, once I found a particularly nasty worm on my PC using netstat. I just happened to run netstat for giggles one day and noticed a very large number of outbound connections to various places on the Internet. My PC was sending out SYN packets to a large number of hosts (an indication that my computer was involved—unknowingly—in a large-scale denial of service attack). Upon further examination, I noticed that this activity would start shortly after bootup.

I tried running netstat after bootup and noticed that the first outbound connection was to TCP port 6667, some Internet Relay Chat (IRC) server I'd never heard of—I didn't even have an IRC client on my machine at the time. The worm was particularly nasty to try to get rid of while active, so I turned off port 6667 on my firewall. That prevented the initial connection to the IRC server and, as I found out later, nicely prevented the worm from getting its instructions from the IRC server. I was then able to simply remove it. I would've never found out that this worm was working without netstat. Even my antivirus program missed it.

Using the File Transfer Protocol

Okay, you already know that *File Transfer Protocol (FTP)* is a subset of TCP/IP and that FTP is used for the transfer of files. In recent years, FTP has become a truly cross-platform protocol for transferring files. Because Internet (and thus TCP/IP) use has skyrocketed, almost every client and server platform has implemented FTP. Windows is no exception. Its TCP/IP stack comes with a command-line ftp utility.

To start the ftp utility, enter **ftp** at a command prompt. The result is an ftp command prompt:

```
C:\Users\tlammle>ftp
ftp>
```

From this prompt, you can open a connection to an FTP server and upload and download files as well as change the way FTP operates. To display a list of all the commands you can use at the ftp command prompt, type **help** or **?** and press Enter. To get help on a specific command, type **help**, a space, and then the name of the command. Here is some output from the help command:

```
ftp>help
Commands may be abbreviated.   Commands are:

!             delete        literal       prompt        send
?             debug         ls            put           status
append        dir           mdelete       pwd           trace
ascii         disconnect    mdir          quit          type
bell          get           mget          quote         user
binary        glob          mkdir         recv          verbose
bye           hash          mls           remotehelp
cd            help          mput          rename
close         lcd           open          rmdir
ftp>
```

In the following sections, I'll give you an introduction to uploading and downloading files because every network technician and administrator positively needs to know how to do this. As they come up, I'll go over the specific commands necessary to perform those two operations as well as any commands that relate to those processes. But first, let's look at how to begin the process.

Third-party applications are available that provide a GUI interface for FTP, which is easier to use than a command line.

Starting FTP and Logging In to an FTP Server

Of the two FTP file operations (download and upload), the ability to download files is definitely the more crucial for you to have down as a network technician or sys admin. The reason it's so important for you to master is that network and client operating system drivers and patches are located on FTP servers all over the Internet.

The first steps in starting an FTP download session are to determine the address of the FTP site and start the `ftp` utility. The FTP site typically has the same name as the website except that the first three characters are `ftp` instead of www. For example, Microsoft's website is www.microsoft.com. Its FTP site, on the other hand, is `ftp.microsoft.com`. We'll use my personal FTP site as an example for the rest of this section because it works, so I can actually log in to it.

First, start the `ftp` utility as demonstrated earlier, and then follow these steps:

1. At the `ftp` command prompt, type **open**, a space, and the name of the FTP server, like this:

```
C:\Users\tlammle>ftp
ftp>open ftp.lammle.com
Connected to ftp.lammle.com.
220---------- Welcome to Pure-FTPd [TLS] ----------
220-You are user number 1 of 50 allowed.
220-Local time is now 11:45. Server port: 21.
220-IPv6 connections are also welcome on this server.
220 You will be disconnected after 15 minutes of inactivity.
User (ftp.lammle.com:(none)):enter
230 Anonymous user logged in
ftp>
```

As shown here, if the FTP server is available and running, you'll receive a response welcoming you to the server and asking you for a username. Right now, I just have *Anonymous* as the username (enabled by default on the FTP server), which means that anyone can log in to it. (By the way, don't bother trying this on my server because I disabled it for obvious reasons as soon as I finished writing this section.)

You can also start an FTP session by typing **ftp**, a space, and the address of the FTP server (for example, **ftp ftp.globalnettraining.com**). This allows you to start the `ftp` utility and open a connection in one step. Here's an example:

```
C:\Users\tlammle>ftp ftp.globalnettraining.com
Connected to ftp.globalnettraining.com.
220 Microsoft FTP Service
User (ftp.globalnettraining.com:(none)):todd
331 Password required for todd.
Password:not shown when typed
230 User todd logged in.
ftp>quit
```

2. Enter a valid username, and press Enter.

3. Enter your password, and press Enter. (The password won't show up when you type it.)

Most Internet web servers that allow just about anyone to download files also allow the username *anonymous*, as I demonstrated. In addition to *anonymous*, you can use the username *ftp* to gain access to a public FTP server. They are both anonymous usernames. Remember that FTP (and UNIX) usernames are case sensitive.

All good, but if you want to access a private FTP server, as I'll demonstrate in a minute, you'll need to use the username and password given to you by the site's administrator. Oh, and sometimes you can use your email address as a password when accessing a public FTP server with a username like *anonymous*.

You don't have to enter your entire email address to log in with the *anonymous* username. Most of the time, FTP server software doesn't actually verify the actual email address, only that it is, in fact, an email address. To do this, it checks for an @ sign and two words separated by a period. You just need to enter a very short email address to bypass the password (like u@me.com). This is especially helpful if you have a long email address, and it's a really good idea if you don't want to get a ton of junk email.

If you enter the wrong username and/or password, the server will tell you so by displaying the following and leaving you at the `ftp` command prompt:

```
530 Login Incorrect
Login failed.
```

This means you've got to try again and must start the login process over. If you're successful, the FTP server will welcome you and drop you back at the `ftp` command prompt. You're now ready to start uploading or downloading files.

Downloading Files

After you log in to the FTP server, you'll navigate to the directory that contains the files you want. Thankfully, the FTP command-line interface is similar to the DOS command-line interface. This is no surprise because DOS is based on UNIX, and FTP is a UNIX utility. Table 17.8 lists and describes the common navigation commands for FTP. (Remember that these are also case sensitive.)

After you navigate to the directory and find the file you want to download, it's time to set the parameters for the type of file. Files come in two types:

- ASCII, which contains text
- Binary, which is all other files

If you set `ftp` to the wrong type, the file you download will contain gibberish. So if you're in doubt, set `ftp` to download files as binary files. Check out Table 17.8.

TABLE 17.8   Common FTP navigation commands

Command	Description
Ls	Short for *list*. Displays a directory listing. Very similar to the DIR command in MS-DOS.
Cd	Short for *change directory*. Works almost identically to the MS-DOS CD command. Use it to change to a different directory and navigate the server's directory structure.
Pwd	Short for *print working directory*. Displays the current directory on the server. Useful if you forget where you are when changing to several locations on the server.
Lcd	Short for *local change directory*. Displays and changes the current directory on the local machine. Useful when you are downloading a file and aren't in the directory where you want to put the file.

To set the file type to ASCII, type **ascii** at the ftp command prompt. ftp will respond by telling you that the file type has been set to A (ASCII):

```
ftp>ascii
Type set to A
```

To set the file type to binary, type **binary** at the ftp command prompt. ftp will respond by telling you that the file type has been set to I (binary):

```
ftp>binary
Type set to I
```

To download the file, just use the get command like this:

```
ftp>get lammlepress.exe
200 PORT command successful.
150 Opening BINARY mode data connection for 'scrsav.exe'
(567018 bytes).
```

The file will start downloading to your hard drive. Unfortunately, with its default settings, the ftp utility doesn't give you any indication of the progress of the transfer. When the file has downloaded, the ftp utility will display the following message and return you to the ftp command prompt:

```
226 Transfer complete.
567018 bytes received in 116.27 seconds (4.88 Kbytes/sec)
```

You can download multiple files by using the mget command. Simply type **mget**, a space, and then something known as a *wildcard* that specifies the files you want to get. For example, to download all the text files in a directory, type **mget** *.**txt**.

Uploading Files

To upload a file to an FTP server, you've got to have rights on that specific server. These rights are assigned on a directory-by-directory basis. To upload a file, log in and then follow these steps:

1. At the ftp command prompt, type **lcd** to navigate to the directory on the local machine where the file resides.

2. Type **cd** to navigate to the destination directory.

3. Set the file type to ASCII or binary.

4. Use the put command to upload the file.

   The syntax of the put command looks like this:

```
ftp>put local file destination file
```

Let's say you want to upload a file called 1.txt on the local server but you want it to be called my.txt on the destination server. To accomplish that, use the following command:

```
ftp>put 1.txt my.txt
```

You'll get the following response:

```
200 PORT command successful.
150 Opening BINARY mode data connection for collwin.zip
226 Transfer complete.
743622 bytes sent in 0.55 seconds (1352.04 Kbytes/sec)
```

You can upload multiple files using the mput command. Simply type **mput**, a space, and then a wildcard that specifies the files. For example, to upload all the text files in a directory, type **mput** *.**txt**.

When you're finished with the ftp utility, just type **quit** to return to the command prompt.

Using the *Telnet* Utility

Part of the TCP/IP protocol suite, *telnet* is a virtual terminal protocol utility that allows you to make connections to remote devices, gather information, and run programs. Telnet was originally developed to open terminal sessions from remote UNIX workstations to UNIX servers. Although it's still used for that purpose, we now use it as a troubleshooting tool as well. Figure 17.13 shows the basic Telnet interface as it's being used to start a terminal session on a remote UNIX host.

FIGURE 17.13 The Telnet utility

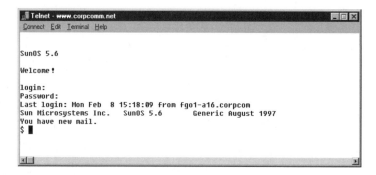

In today's Windows environments, Telnet is a basic command-line tool for testing TCP connections. You can telnet to any TCP port to see if it's responding—something that's especially useful when checking Simple Mail Transfer Protocol (SMTP) and HTTP (web) ports.

As you learned back in Chapter 6, "Introduction to the Internet Protocol," each upper-layer service in a TCP stack has a number for its address. And by default, each network service that uses a particular address will respond to a TCP request on that specific port.

How to Enable Telnet in Vista

Because most people have Vista or Windows 7 operating systems running on their PCs these days, it's good to know that, by default, these operating systems install without Telnet available. But there's a way around that one—if you really must have a Telnet client enabled in these operating systems, here's how to do it:

1. Open Control Panel.

2. Select Programs And Features.

3. In the left column, select Turn Windows Features On Or Off (get ready for the annoying User Account Control [UAC] prompt, and then enter your name and password).

4. Select the Telnet check box (and any other obscure services you may want enabled), and wait while Vista or Windows 7 thinks for a while and then reboots.

Nice—now you can go to Start and then type **telnet** in the Start search box to get a Telnet window to open for you. You can also open a DOS prompt and just type **telnet** from there. Here are the options that Windows provides with Telnet:

```
Microsoft Telnet> ?
Commands may be abbreviated. Supported commands are:

c    - close              close current connection
d    - display            display operating parameters
o    - open hostname [port]   connect to hostname (default port 23).
q    - quit               exit telnet
set  - set                set options (type 'set ?' for a list)
sen  - send               send strings to server
st   - status             print status information
u    - unset              unset options (type 'unset ?' for a list)
?/h  - help               print help information
```

Now that we've finished talking about Telnet, my personal recommendation is that you never use it again. What? Yes, you read that right, and here's why…

Don't Use Telnet, Use Secure Shell

What? I just told you how to use Telnet, and now I am telling you not to use it. That's right, don't use Telnet! Telnet is totally insecure because it sends all data in crystal-clear text—including your name and password. And I'm pretty sure you know that's a really bad thing these days. If Microsoft doesn't even enable it on its latest OSs, than you know it really must be insecure.

So if you shouldn't use Telnet, what should you use instead? Secure Shell (SSH) is your answer. It provides the same options as Telnet, plus a lot more; but most important, it doesn't send any data in clear text. The thing is, your servers, routers, and other devices need to be enabled with SSH, and it's not configured by default on most devices.

Some configuration is usually necessary if you want things to work as they really should, and yes, sometimes it's a little painful to get everything running smoothly, but it's all worth it in the long run. Personally, I disable Telnet on all my routers and use SSH exclusively. No lie—I never use Telnet any more if I can help it. Even so, you should still understand Telnet and get in some practice with it in case you do ever need it.

In my Sybex book *Cisco CCNA Study Guide*, I get into the skinny on how to configure SSH on all Cisco devices and use an SSH client, but because SSH is not among the Network+ objectives, I'm not going to do that here. Still, keep this all in mind when building your networks.

Summary

In this chapter, you learned about many of the utilities for using and troubleshooting TCP/IP. These utilities include GUI tools like protocol analyzers, throughput testers, and connectivity software like Remote Desktop, and they include command-line utilities like `tracert`, `ping`, `arp`, `netstat`, `nbtstat`, `ipconfig`, `ifconfig`, and `nslookup`.

You also learned how these utilities are used, including their various options and switches and how they all affect the use of the utilities. Finally, you learned about how these utilities work within the TCP/IP suite.

Exam Essentials

Describe some of the GUI tools available to assist in testing and troubleshooting. These include protocol analyzers, throughput testers, and connectivity software. Understand each product's purpose and how to use it.

Know how to describe and use the troubleshooting information and statistics that `arp`, `nbtstat`, and `netstat` provide for you. The `arp` utility shows whether an IP address is being resolved to your MAC address (or someone else's, in case of conflicts). The `netstat` utility produces TCP/IP statistics, and `nbtstat` produces NetBIOS over TCP/IP statistics.

Know how to diagnose a network by using TCP/IP's troubleshooting commands. The `ping` command echoes back if a machine is alive and active on a network. The `tracert` command shows the path that the ping packets take from source to target. And `telnet` enables a user to participate in a remote text-based session.

Know what the `tracert` utility does. The `tracert` utility finds the route from your computer to any computer on a network.

Know what the `ping` utility does. `ping` determines whether a particular IP host is responding.

Know what the `ftp` utility does. The `ftp` utility allows you to reliably download and upload files from and to an FTP server across the Internet.

Know what the `ipconfig` and `ifconfig` utilities do. The `ipconfig` utility displays TCP/IP configuration information for Windows NT and later operating systems. The `ifconfig` utility performs a similar function in UNIX environments, in addition to performing certain interface-configuration tasks.

Know what the `nslookup` and `dig` utilities do. The `nslookup` and `dig` utilities allow you to look up DNS resolution information.

Written Lab

Write the answers to the following questions about command-line tools:

1. What command can you type from a command prompt to see the hops a packet takes to get to a destination host?

2. What tool would you use to verify a complaint about a slow network?

3. You need your IP address, subnet mask, default gateway, and DNS information. What command will you type from a Windows command prompt?

4. You need to log in as a dumb terminal to a server or UNIX host and run programs. What application will you use?

5. You need to add a route to your Windows server's routing table. What command will you use?

6. You want to log in to a server and transfer files. What application will you use?

7. You need to check your name-resolution information on your host. What command will you type from the command prompt?

8. You want to use `netstat`, but you want to see only the IP address, not the names of the hosts. Which modifier will you use?

9. You want the IP configuration on a UNIX host. What command will you type at the command prompt?

10. Which Windows command will show you the routing table of your host or server?

    You can find the answers in Appendix B.

Review Questions

You will find the answers in Appendix A.

1. Which TCP/IP utility is most often used to test whether an IP host is up and functional?

   A. ftp

   B. telnet

   C. ping

   D. netstat

2. Which TCP/IP utility will produce the following result?
   ```
   Interface: 199.102.30.152
   Internet Address    Physical Address    Type
   199.102.30.152      A0-ee-00-5b-0e-ac   dynamic
   ```

   A. arp

   B. netstat

   C. tracert

   D. nbtstat

3. Which Windows utility can you use to connect to a machine 50 miles away to troubleshoot?

   A. Remote desktop

   B. netstat

   C. arp

   D. Wireshark

4. Which TCP/IP utility might produce the following output?
   ```
   Pinging 204.153.163.2 with 32 bytes of data:
   Reply from 204.153.163.2: bytes=32 time=1ms TTL=128
   Reply from 204.153.163.2: bytes=32 time=1ms TTL=128
   Reply from 204.153.163.2: bytes=32 time=1ms TTL=128
   Reply from 204.153.163.2: bytes=32 time<10ms TTL=128
   ```

   A. tracert

   B. ping

   C. WINS

   D. ipconfig

5. Which utility can you use to find the MAC and TCP/IP addresses of your Windows workstation?

    A. `ping`

    B. `ipconfig`

    C. `ipconfig /all`

    D. `tracert`

    E. `telnet`

6. Which `ping` commands will verify that your local TCP/IP interface is working? (Choose all that apply.)

    A. `ping 204.153.163.2`

    B. `ping 127.0.0.1`

    C. `ping localif`

    D. `ping localhost`

    E. `ping iphost`

7. Which switch for the Windows `nbtstat` utility will display all NetBIOS name-resolution statistics?

    A. `-r`

    B. `/r`

    C. `-R`

    D. `/R`

8. You need to find a NIC's specific MAC address and IP address. Which command-line tool can you use to find this information without physically going to the computer?

    A. `ping`

    B. `nbtstat`

    C. `arp`

    D. `netstat`

    E. `ftp`

9. Which `nbtstat` utility switch will purge and reload the remote NetBIOS name table cache?

    A. `-r`

    B. `-R`

    C. `/r`

    D. `/R`

10. Wireshark is an example of a _____?

   A. Throughput tester

   B. Protocol analyzer

   C. Remote connection tool

   D. Port scanner

11. Which utility produces output similar to the following?

```
1  110 ms   96 ms   107 ms fgo1.corpcomm.net [209.74.93.10]
2   96 ms  126 ms    95 ms someone.corpcomm.net [209.74.93.1]
3  113 ms  119 ms   112 ms Serial5-1-1.GW2.MSP1.alter.net
[157.130.100.185]
4  133 ms  123 ms   126 ms 152.ATM3-0.XR2.CHI6.ALTER.NET
[146.188.209.126]
5  176 ms  133 ms   129 ms 290.ATM2-0.TR2.CHI4.ALTER.NET    [146.188.209.10]
6  196 ms  184 ms   218 ms 106.ATM7-0.TR2.SCL1.ALTER.NET    [146.188.136.162]
7  182 ms  187 ms   187 ms 298.ATM7-0.XR2.SJC1.ALTER.NET    [146.188.146.61]
8  204 ms  176 ms   186 ms 192.ATM3-0-0.SAN-JOSE9- GW.ALTER.NET
[146.188.144.133]
9  202 ms  198 ms   212 ms atm3-0-622M.cr1.sjc.globalcenter.net [206.57.16.17]
10 209 ms  202 ms   195 ms pos3-1-155M.br4.SJC.globalcenter.net
[206.132.150.98]
11 190 ms    *       191 ms pos0-0-0-155M.hr3.SNV.globalcenter.net [206.251.5.93]
12 195 ms  188 ms   188 ms pos4-1-0-    155M.hr2.SNV.globalcenter.net
[206.132.150.206]
13 198 ms  202 ms   197 ms www10.yahoo.com [204.71.200.75]
```

   A. arp

   B. tracert

   C. nbtstat

   D. netstat

12. You are the network administrator. A user calls you, complaining that the performance of the intranet web server is sluggish. When you try to ping the server, it takes several seconds for the server to respond. You suspect that the problem is related to a router that is seriously overloaded. Which workstation utility could you use to find out which router is causing this problem?

   A. netstat

   B. nbtstat

   C. tracert

   D. ping

   E. arp

13. Which `ipconfig` switch will display the most complete listing of IP configuration information for a station?

    A. `/all`

    B. `/renew`

    C. `/release`

    D. `/?`

14. Which utility will display a list of all the routers that a packet passes through on the way to an IP destination?

    A. `netstat`

    B. `nbtstat`

    C. `tracert`

    D. `ping`

    E. `arp`

15. Which Windows TCP/IP utility could you use to find out whether a server is responding on TCP port 21?

    A. `tcp`

    B. `port`

    C. `ping`

    D. `nbtstat`

    E. `telnet`

16. Which arp command can you use to display the currently cached ARP entries?

    A. `arp`

    B. `arp -all`

    C. `arp /a`

    D. `ipconfig /arp`

    E. `arp /ipconfig`

17. Which command-line tool would best be used to verify DNS functionality?

    A. `netstat`

    B. `nbtstat`

    C. `dig`

    D. `icmp`

    E. `arp`

18. Which of the following arp utility switches perform the same function? (Choose all that apply.)

 A. -g

 B. -A

 C. -d

 D. -a

19. Which command would you use at a workstation prompt to see the DNS servers that are configured to use? (Choose three.)

 A. arp

 B. nslookup

 C. netstat

 D. nbtstat

 E. ipconfig/all

 F. ifconfig

20. Which nbtstat switch displays a list of all the NetBIOS sessions currently active on the local workstation?

 A. -a

 B. -r

 C. -s

 D. -I

Chapter

18

Software and Hardware Tools

THE FOLLOWING COMPTIA NETWORK+ EXAM OBJECTIVES ARE COVERED IN THIS CHAPTER:

✓ **4.2 Given a scenario, use appropriate hardware tools to troubleshoot connectivity issues.**

- ▪ Cable tester
- ▪ Cable certifier
- ▪ Crimper
- ▪ Butt set
- ▪ Toner probe
- ▪ Punch down tool
- ▪ Protocol analyzer
- ▪ Loopback plug
- ▪ TDR
- ▪ OTDR
- ▪ Multimeter
- ▪ Environmental monitor

Specialized tasks require specialized tools, and installing network components is no exception. We use some of these tools, like network scanners, on an everyday basis, but most of the hardware tools I'll be covering in this chapter are used mainly in the telecommunications industry.

Still, in order to meet the CompTIA Network+ objectives, and also because you're likely to run across them in today's networking environments, it's very important that you're familiar with them.

For up-to-the-minute updates for this chapter, please see www.lammle.com/forum or www.sybex.com/go/netplus2e.

Understanding Network Scanners

Network scanner has become a broad term often referring to a family of tools used to analyze our networks, but the CompTIA Network+ objectives are much less vague. So with regard to those critical objectives, know that *network scanners* refer to these three tools:

- Packet sniffers
- Intrusion detection system / intrusion prevention system (IDS/IPS) software
- Port scanners

Packet Sniffers

Unlike port scanners, *packet sniffers* actually look inside every packet on a network segment. Packet sniffers come in many flavors, and some of them, like Microsoft's Network Monitor (NetMon), are even free today. Even though NetMon comes in more complex versions that are, well, not exactly free, the version that comes bundled with Windows Server does allow you to analyze network communications traffic. The full version will give you statistics on network utilization and packet traffic data as well as capture individual frames for analysis. These abilities really mean that NetMon is both a packet sniffer and a *network analyzer*, and it's common for these to be combined and referred to as one and the same.

All good, but personally, I use Wireshark instead. It's also free, and you can easily download it from www.wireshark.org. A nice feature of Wireshark is that it runs from Windows,

OS X, Linux, and Unix platforms. It easily captures data on all my interfaces, including my wireless and virtual private network (VPN) connections, and looks at all traffic on the network segment. There are tons of packet sniffers available, and to get your hands on most of them, you'll have to pony up some cash. Sometimes they're worth it, though, because these higher-end products can even provide solutions to problems you find on your network—nice.

Anyway, free or not, the basic purpose of packet sniffers (or network analyzers) is to collect and analyze each individual packet that is captured on a specific network segment to determine if problems like bottlenecks, retransmissions, and security breaches are happening. Packet sniffers are a must have for every network administrator to troubleshoot and find problems or security holes in a network. For example, you may discover that users are using an application on the network with usernames and passwords being sent unencrypted over the network.

You can also use packet sniffers to see if there is too much traffic on a segment, or even if a broadcast storm has been created by a bad Network Interface Card (NIC). And remember—I do mean on a network segment—you can't use them to catch packets passing through routers. Yes, they can help you find a hacker stalking around in there, but you'd really have to be looking closely and constantly to discover this. For that level of monitoring, you'd be better off using a tool known as IDS/IPS. It can really help you track and even defeat hackers. (We'll talk about IDS/IPS software in the next section.) The more expensive network sniffers can help find anomalies in your network, like a hack, and even alert you of these problems. Figure 18.1 shows output from a packet sniffer. Notice that you can identify both the IP addresses and the MAC addresses associated with any of the packets captured as well as identify the protocol in use.

FIGURE 18.1   Output from a packet sniffer

You can definitely see that a packet sniffer can provide you with huge amounts of information. This means you really need something to narrow things down and help you to more readily find the needle in the haystack that you're looking for, right?

In this case, help comes in the form of some handy built-in filters that can be used to gather information from just one specific host or server; without them, you'd have to go through possibly thousands of packets to find the problem. For the packet I've highlighted, you can see that there's a probable User Datagram Protocol (UDP) checksum error. And by the way, because UDP is connectionless, this is a pretty common error.

You should download and start working with a network sniffer right away. As I mentioned, you can download Wireshark at www.wireshark.org for free, so what are you waiting for? Go for it!

Now comes the fun stuff—let's take a look at ways we can find and stop hackers dead in their tracks.

Intrusion Detection and Prevention Software

An IDS detects unwanted attempts to manipulate network systems and/or environments, and an IPS is a computer-security device that monitors network and/or system activities for any strange or malicious behavior. It can react in real time to prevent and even block nasty activities. An IDS identifies, detects, and reports attempts of unauthorized access to the network as well as any suspicious activity, and an IDS is the best software type for identifying an attack. However, if you want to stop the attack in its tracks, you need to add an IPS device. So, unlike IDSs, which can identify an attack and report it, an IPS can stop the attack by shutting down ports or dropping certain types of packets.

A bunch of different IDS/IPS software packages are available on the market, and a lot of them are free. Again, predictably, the best ones aren't, and they can be a bit pricey. These high-powered versions run on Linux or other proprietary hardware. But there are still many IDS/IPS software applications available for Windows.

Snort is one of the most popular IDS/IPS software products around. It runs on both Linux and Windows, and it's a free, open-source platform, which happens to be a big reason for its popularity. But that's not the only reason—just because it is free doesn't mean it doesn't offer up some pretty cool features. On the other hand, if you're dealing with a large, corporate environment, you need some serious weaponry, and Cisco offers an Adaptive Security Appliance (ASA) as an enterprise solution that's powerful but definitely far from free. It's worth it, though.

Figure 18.2 shows a picture of the stack of Cisco ASA boxes I use in my security classes.

Personally, I think the Cisco box is the best IDS/IPS box on the market today. Still, Snort isn't bad; so if cost is an issue, rest assured you can use it, as well as several other tools, and be much better equipped than you would be without them working on your network to help you keep it secure.

Figure 18.3 shows where you'd find a typical IDS/IPS in a internetwork.

FIGURE 18.2   A stack of Cisco ASAs

FIGURE 18.3   IDS/IPS placement in an internetwork

Okay...to be honest, this is a relatively simplistic view of an IDS/IPS working within a network because of the device's complexity and the many different physical configurations possible. The important thing I want you to pay attention to is the fact that you would typically find the IDS/IPS software positioned between your internal router and the firewall to the outside network (Internet). If you're using Snort, just add the software to a Linux box, and connect this box between the firewall and the router. This area would typically be your demilitarized zone (DMZ). The Basic Analysis and Security Engine (BASE) displays and reports intrusions and attacks logged in the Snort database in a web browser for convenient analysis.

Port Scanners

A *port scanner* is a software tool designed to search a host for open ports. Those of us administering our networks use port scanners to ensure their security, but bad guys use them to find a network's vulnerabilities and compromise them. To *port scan* means to scan for TCP and UDP open ports on a single target host either to legitimately connect to and use its services for business and/or personal reasons or to find and connect to those ports and subsequently attack the host and steal or manipulate it for nefarious reasons.

In contrast, *port sweeping* means scanning multiple hosts on a network for a specific listening TCP or UDP port, like SQL. (SQL injection attacks are super common today.) This just happens to be a favorite approach used by hackers when trying to invade your network. They port sweep in a broad manner, and then, if they find something—in this case, SQL—they can port scan the particular host they've discovered with the desired service available to exploit and get what they're after. This is why it's a really good idea to turn off any unused services on your servers and routers and to run only the minimum services required on every host machine in your network. Do yourself a big favor and make sure this is in your security policy.

Remember that three-way handshake I discussed in Chapter 6 "Introduction to the Internet Protocol"? Well, it just so happens that a SYN scan is the most popular form of TCP scanning. Rather than use the operating system's network functions, the port scanner actually generates raw IP packets itself and monitors for responses. This scan type is also known as *half-open scanning* because it never really opens a full TCP connection. The port scanner generates a SYN packet, and if the targeted port is open, it will respond with a SYN-ACK packet. The scanner host responds with an RST (reset) packet, closing the connection before the handshake is completed.

WARNING   Never use the tools I'm telling you about on computers belonging to any businesses or government agencies without their permission. It's against the law in a big way, and they do monitor and prosecute! Know that I am not exaggerating here, so please do yourself a favor and use the following tools only to test your own network for vulnerabilities.

Although a free program named Network Mapper (Nmap) can be used as a port scanner, you can use it to do so much more. I give it two thumbs up and recommend that you download Nmap (`http://nmap.org`) and play with this cool program.

Nmap, like Snort, is open source. But Nmap runs on all platforms and can provide port-scanning ability, check all the open services running on each host, find firewalls, and even help tremendously with network management.

Figure 18.4 shows Nmap running on a Windows Vista platform, performing a Domain Name Service (DNS) resolution and then a port scan to the host being monitored (Zenmap is the name of the GUI interface it uses). Pretty chill, right?

Nmap is very flexible and, again, I really encourage you to check it out. One of the other nice features of Nmap is its documentation capacity. It comes with a complete set of instructions and equips you with documentation to help you troubleshoot and map your network.

FIGURE 18.4   Nmap in action

Even though Nmap is pretty simple, there are even simpler tools out there—a whole lot of them. Angry IP is a program I also use that provides both IP-scanning and port-scanning abilities. It's definitely not as complex as Nmap, but because it's extremely easy to use, you might want to try out this free, open-source program as well. Figure 18.5 illustrates port scanning with Angry IP.

FIGURE 18.5   Angry IP port scanning

You can see right away that this is a much simpler program than some of the other sniffing and port mapping tools we've discussed, but simple doesn't mean it isn't powerful. Angry IP slowed the PC I was scanning way down when I performed a full port scan on the host using this program. Check it out at www.angryziber.com/w/Home.

 Real World Scenario

Hacked and Blamed!

I've already mentioned that you shouldn't port scan on hosts that are not yours, but you need to be careful that someone else does not use your hosts or servers to port scan someone else's servers as well. A few years ago, I had a server at an ISP, and some crackers had hacked into my server and were using it to port scan the Department of Defense (DoD) servers. I received a letter from the DoD informing me of this issue. They were very professional and even mentioned that it probably wasn't me that was doing the port scanning, but they said that if it happened again, they would prosecute me. They told me that I was responsible for my server and that if I did not stop the attackers, I would be liable.

I was terribly embarrassed, and I was a little freaked out too! After looking at the server logs, I realized that the crackers were from France and that they had been in my server for three months. Instead of just locking down the ports and getting rid of the hackers, I formatted the server. Why? Because crackers/hackers are notorious for creating many backdoors once they are in a system, in case they get caught, so just locking them out would not have solved the problem. If this happens to you, a format is typically what you need to do. I also upgraded to the latest server operating system, which helped with some of the security issues.

After you've downloaded all the software tools I just went over with you and practiced honing your skills with them (*only* on your own network, right?), you'll be ready to move on and explore the hardware tools that you need to be familiar with to meet the CompTIA Network+ objectives.

Identifying Hardware Tools

A great example of when the hardware tools and testers I'm about to cover would come in really handy is if you're dealing with failed fiber links between structures. As a system administrator running a network with a server, routers, and switches, it's entirely possible you'll never find yourself in a situation that calls for these tools. But if you're in network design or a field that requires installing cabling, then these hardware tools are going to be really valuable to you. Unlike the software tools we just talked about, none of these goodies are free, but they do come in a variety of flavors that run the gamut from real bargains to "You're joking—how much?" Some of them can indeed free you of thousands of dollars!

Cable testers are the most widely used hardware tool in today's LANs, so let's start with them.

Cable Testers

The best way to deal with a faulty cable installation is to avoid the problem in the first place by purchasing high-quality components and installing them carefully. Still, this isn't a perfect world—no matter how careful you are, problems are bound to arise anyway. The tools that I'm going to cover can be used to test cables at the time of their installation and afterward, if and when you need to troubleshoot cabling problems. Cable-testing tools can range from simple, inexpensive mechanical devices to elaborate electronic testers that automatically supply you with a litany of test results in an easy-to-read pass/fail format. Figure 18.6 shows an example of an inexpensive cable tester for twisted-pair wiring testing.

FIGURE 18.6   An inexpensive cable tester

This little box can verify the connection through the cable and tell you if the cable is straight-through or crossover. It can also identify problems such as grounding issues as well. Sometimes the problem is not a complete lack of connectivity. Sometimes performance is slow, which can also be a cabling issue that a cable tester can identify. This tool is as cheap as they come.

Let's focus on the types of tools available for both copper and fiber-optic cable testing. This is not to say that you need all of the tools listed here. In fact, I'll try to steer you away from certain types of tools. Sometimes you'll get lucky and have the luxury of choosing between high-tech and low-tech devices that perform roughly the same function. You can choose which ones you prefer according to the requirements of your network, your operational budget, even your temperament and time constraints. Some of the tools are extremely complicated and

require extensive training to use effectively, whereas others can be used by pretty much anybody equipped with a functioning brain.

Other important considerations to keep in mind when selecting the types of tools you
need are based on the descriptions of cable tests given earlier in this chapter, the test results
required by the standards you're using to certify your network, and the capabilities of the
people who will be doing the actual work. And don't forget the potentially painful cost of
some of them.

Loopback Plug

A loopback test is a diagnostic procedure in which a signal is transmitted and returned to the
sending device after passing through all or a portion of a network or circuit. The returned
signal is compared with the transmitted signal to evaluate the integrity of the equipment or
transmission path. A computer needs a loopback plug that is inserted into a port in order to
perform a loopback test.

Loopback plugs are made for both Ethernet and fiber applications. Figure 18.7 shows an
Ethernet loopback plug and Figure 18.8 shows a plug for fiber applications.

FIGURE 18.7   Ethernet loopback plug

FIGURE 18.8   Fiber loopback plugs

Wire-Map Testers

A *wire-map tester* is a device that transmits signals through each wire in a copper twisted-pair
cable to determine if it's connected to the correct pin at the other end. Wire mapping is the

most basic test for twisted-pair cables because the eight separate wire connections involved in each cable run are a common source of installation errors. Wire-map testers detect transposed wires, opens (broken or unconnected wires), and shorts (wires or pins improperly connected to each other). All of these problems can render a cable run completely inoperable.

Wire-map testing is nearly always included in multifunction cable testers, but sometimes it's just not worth spending serious cash on a comprehensive device. Dedicated wire-map testers that run about two to three hundred bucks are relatively inexpensive options that enable you to test your installation for the most common faults that occur during installations and afterward. If, say, you're installing voice-grade cable, a simple wire-mapping test is probably all that's needed.

A wire-map tester essentially consists of a remote unit that you attach to the far end of a connection and a battery-operated, handheld main unit that displays the results. Typically, the tester displays various codes that indicate the specific type of fault that it finds. You can also purchase a tester with multiple remote units that are numbered so that one person can test several connections without constantly traveling back and forth from one end of the connections to the other to move the remote unit.

WARNING The one wiring fault that is not detectable by a dedicated wire-map tester is something known as *split pairs*. This fault flies under the radar because even though the pinouts are incorrect, the cable is still wired straight through. To detect split pairs, you must use a device that tests the cable for the near-end crosstalk that split pairs cause.

Continuity Testers

A *continuity tester* is an even simpler and less-expensive device than a wire-map tester; it's designed to check a copper cable connection for basic installation problems like opens, shorts, and crossed pairs. It will set you back only a few dollars, but such a device usually can't detect the more complicated twisted-pair wiring faults. It's still a nice option for basic cable testing, especially for coaxial cables that have only two conductors and so don't easily confuse whoever is installing them.

Like a wire-map tester, a continuity tester consists of two separate units that you connect to each end of the cable you want to test. Most of the time, the two units can snap together for storage and easy testing of patch cables.

Protocol Analyzer

A *protocol analyzer* is often confused with a packet sniffer because some products really are both. Remember—a packet sniffer looks at all traffic on a network segment. On the other hand, a protocol analyzer (surprise!) analyzes protocols. These tools come in both software and hardware versions, but compared to the products I listed earlier in this chapter, a network analyzer is likely to give you more information and help than a sniffer will. This is because a bona fide protocol analyzer can actually help you troubleshoot problems, whereas most sniffers just provide information for you to have a ball deciphering.

A network protocol analyzer can perform the following functions:

- Help troubleshoot hard-to-solve problems
- Help you detect and identify malicious software (malware)
- Help gather information, such as baseline traffic patterns and network-utilization metrics
- Help you identify unused protocols so that you can remove them from the network
- Provide a traffic generator for penetration testing
- Possibly even work with an IDS

And last and perhaps most important for you, they can really help you learn about networking in general. This means if you just want to find out why a network device is functioning in a certain way, you can use a protocol analyzer to sniff (there's that word again) the traffic and expose the data and protocols that pass along the wire.

 I've found a whole bunch of network analyzers you can use for free at the following location:

`www.snapfiles.com/freeware/network/fwpacketsniffer.html`

But understand that there's no way I can verify the validity of this link after this book is published. Again, the terms *sniffer* and *analyzer* are used to define the same product found at this link. Both Microsoft's NetMon and Wireshark are called sniffers and analyzers, and they both are—at least to some degree.

Certifiers

Certification testers—or *certifiers*—are used to determine whether your network meets specific International Organization for Standardization (ISO) or TIA standards (Cat 5e, Cat 6, or Cat 7). They are the only option for you in this case. Also, if your network is wired with both copper and fiber, you really must use a certification tester.

Basically, a certifier is a combination cable tester and network analyzer, only better, because it comes with more options. This is wonderful because it makes your job easier and makes you seem smarter to everyone around you—you're only as good as your tools, right? A good certifier will test the performance and response times of network resources like web, file, email, and even DNS and Dynamic Host Configuration Protocol (DHCP) servers. And, at the same time, it will certify your full Category 6 cable installation. After it finishes all this, you can provide your boss with a detailed network test report complete with dazzling, colorful graphics to make it simple to explain and understand—voilà! You're instantly the genius of the day.

To get these smarts, all you need is a lot of money. These products are not for the small office, home office (SOHO) market because they cost literally thousands of dollars, starting at about $5,000.

Time-Domain Reflectometer

A *time-domain reflectometer (TDR)* is a tool that finds and describes faults in metallic cables like twisted wire pairs and coaxial cables. The equivalent device for optical fiber is an optical time-domain reflectometer (OTDR), which I'll talk about in a minute.

A TDR works in the same basic way that radar does. It transmits a short rise time pulse along the conductor, and if it turns out to be of a uniform impedance and properly terminated, the entire transmitted pulse is absorbed in the far-end termination; no signal is reflected back to the TDR. Any impedance interruptions will cause some of the incident signal to be sent back toward the source, letting you know all is not well.

So basically, any increases in the impedance create a reflection that reinforces the original pulse and decreases the impedance, thereby creating a reflection that opposes the original pulse. The resulting reflected pulse that's measured at the output/input to the TDR is displayed or plotted in measures of time. And because the speed of signal propagation is pretty consistent for a given type of transmission medium, the reading can also tell you about the cable length.

Because of this sensitivity to any variation in impedance, you can use a TDR to verify these things:

- Speed and condition of the cable
- How long it takes to send a signal down a cable and how long it takes to come back
- Cable impedance characteristics
- Splice and connector locations and their associated loss amounts
- Estimated cable lengths

Now, let's take a look at a device that tests fiber-optic cables.

Optical Time-Domain Reflectometer

An *optical time-domain reflectometer (OTDR)* is an optoelectronic instrument used to give you the skinny on optical fibers. It works by putting out a series of optical pulses into the specific fiber you want to test. From the same end from which these impulses were sent, it collects and measures the light that is scattered and reflected along the length of the fiber. It then records the change in the amount of refraction at various points. From the same end from which these impulses were sent, it collects and measures the light that is scattered and reflected along the length of the fiber. It then records the change in the amount of refraction at various points. This is a lot like the way an electronic TDR measures reflections caused by impedance changes in a cable that you're testing. The strength of the return pulses is incorporated into a measure of time, which also conveniently gives you the fiber's length.

We use OTDRs to give us the following information:

- The fiber's estimated length
- Its overall attenuation, including splice and mated-connector losses
- The location faults, such as breaks

Figure 18.9 shows the output from an OTDR testing a fiber connection.

The spike shows where a splice in the fiber is located, which has resulted in the signal being degraded. This is a very typical output. As the signal attenuates, you see a gradual but quick drop in decibels (db). Any connector will actually show a reflection, which, as mentioned, shows up as a spike in the OTDR output. The connector then creates more attenuation and loss of more db. The more splices, the less distance you can run with fiber.

FIGURE 18.9   Sample OTDR output

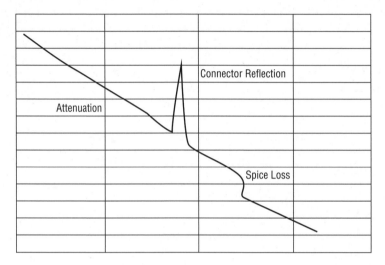

Multimeter

A *multimeter* or a multitester (also called a volt/ohm meter [VOM]) is a multitasking electronic measuring instrument. Your average multimeter typically includes features like the ability to measure voltage, current, and resistance. Multimeters come in analog and digital versions, and they range from basic handheld devices useful for simple fault-finding and field-service work to more complex bench instruments that will give you measurements with a very high degree of accuracy.

They can be used to troubleshoot electrical problems in a wide array of electrical devices like batteries, motor controls, appliances, power supplies, and wiring systems. Figure 18.10 shows the multimeter that I use to help troubleshoot my networks.

Multimeters come in lots of flavors with different ranges of features and prices. Cheap ones cost less than 10 bucks, but the top-of-the-line models can set you back up to 5 thousand.

Toner Probe

A *toner probe*, also called a tone generator, is a simple copper cable tester that is simple to use and can be used to trace a wire in a wall. It is a two-piece unit that's basically a tone generator and probe, sometimes called a "fox and hound" wire tracer. This type of device consists of one part that you connect to a cable with a standard jack—or to an individual wire with alligator clips that transmit a signal over the cable or wire—and another part that's a penlike probe that emits an audible tone when it touches the other end of the cable, the wire, or even its insulating sheath.

Most often, you will use a toner probe to locate a specific connection in a punch-down block because (annoyingly) some installers run all the cables for a network to the central punch-down block without labeling them. They (or you, if you're unlucky enough) then have to use a tone generator to identify which block is connected to which wall plate and label the punch-down block accordingly. This tool can identify a particular cable at any point between the two ends, and because the probe can detect the cable containing the tone signal through its sheath, it can help you to locate one specific cable out of a massive cable-spaghetti bundle in a ceiling conduit or other type of raceway.

FIGURE 18.10   A multimeter

Just connect the tone generator to one end, and touch the probe to each cable in the bundle until you hear the tone. Figure 18.11 shows a picture of my toner and the probe I use to find the tone on the other end of the cable.

Also, by testing the continuity of individual wires using alligator clips, you can use a tone generator and probe to find opens, shorts, and miswires. An open wire won't produce a tone at the other end, a short will produce a tone on two or more wires at the other end, and an improperly connected wire will produce a tone on the wrong pin at the other end.

Sound like fun to you? Well, not so much—it takes a really long time, and it's super tedious. Worse, the whole process is almost as prone to errors as the cable installation itself. You have to either continually travel from one end of the cable to the other to move the tone generator unit or use a partner to test each connection, keeping in close contact using radios or some other means of communication to avoid confusion. So, considering the time and effort involved, investing in a wire-map tester is just a much more practical solution unless you're numbingly bored or really easily amused.

FIGURE 18.11 A toner probe

Butt Set

A *butt set* is essentially a portable telephone that allows you to test analog wet or dry lines and is used to monitor those lines. The most common type, shown in Figure 18.12, can both monitor and transmit.

You see these all the time with telco guys up on the telephone poles. They use their butt sets to connect to telephone lines, test them, and even make phone calls.

Another handy tool that will take the place of a butt set is a *hound*. This noncanine device is nothing more than an inductively coupled amplifier with a small speaker in a handheld tool. It's used to monitor the audio on a given line to verify that you have the right pair before connecting it and typically is used with a toner probe. It will also monitor for noise.

Punch-Down Tool

Most networks today are built using twisted-pair cable of some sort. This cable is usually terminated in wiring closets using a tool known as a *punch-down tool*. It's called that because that's exactly what the tool does—punch down the wire into some kind of insulation displacement connector (IDC).

FIGURE 18.12   A butt set

There are different types of punch-down tools. The most common is a punch down with replaceable blades for the different types of connectors (either 66 or 110). Figure 18.13 shows an example of this type of punch-down tool.

FIGURE 18.13   An example of a punch-down tool

IDCs make contact by cutting through, or displacing, the insulation around a single conductor inside a twisted-pair cable.

As shown in Figure 18.14, the punch-down tool pushes a conductor between the sides of a V inside an IDC, in this example a 110 block, allowing the small metal blade inside the connector to make contact with the inner conductor deep inside the wire.

FIGURE 18.14   Using a punch-down tool on a small 110 block

Now let's take a look at how to put a cable end together.

Cable Stripper/Snips

A *wire crimper*, often simply called a crimper, is a handy tool found in most network technicians' tool bags. Crimpers are primarily used for attaching ends onto different types of network cables via a process known as—that's right—*crimping*. Crimping involves using your hands to apply a certain amount of force to press some kind of metal teeth into the inner conductors of a cable. Before you can crimp a connector onto the end, you've got to strip the cable with a type of *cable stripper* (or snips) and then properly put the wires into the connector.

Figure 18.15 shows what a cable stripper and snip looks like (this particular tool also includes a crimper).

Often, network technicians will make patch cables with a crimper. They'll take a small piece of Category 5e unshielded twisted-pair (UTP), strip the cable, and crimp two RJ-45 ends onto it to create the cable. Snips will create the type of cable needed to connect a host to a wall jack connection, for example. There are strippers and crimpers for the other types of cable as well—even specialized crimpers for fiber-optic ends.

Voltage Event Recorder

Alternating current (AC) is basically the food that PCs and other network devices require in specific amounts to function properly. In the United States, it's normally 110 volts and changes polarity 60 times a second (60 hertz). These values are referred to as *line voltage*. Any deviation from these values can create some major problems for your PC or other electronics—like death.

FIGURE 18.15   A combination cable stripper, crimper, and snippers

This is why we have *surge protectors*. These little saviors use a special electronic circuit that monitors the incoming voltage level and trips a circuit breaker when the voltage level reaches critical mass which is known as the *overvoltage threshold*. Even though having a surge protector is definitely better than nothing, they too can fall victim to overvoltage events—I'm reminded of a friend whose home was struck by lightning during a thunderstorm and he found his surge protectors literally melted into the carpet! But they're still cool because even though they're really only somewhat protective, they are multiple-outlet strips that give us a lot more places to plug in our stuff.

By contrast, a quality *voltage event recorder* can troubleshoot and even provide preventative maintenance on your entire electrical system, whether it's a home or a huge factory. Although they do big things, they're typically small devices that just plug into a wall and record, over time, the power quality of a given circuit. You would typically use a voltage event recorder for the following applications:

Recording voltage   The voltage event recorder monitors and records the supply voltage and checks whether the socket outlet is providing voltage within specifications.

Measuring distortion   The device measures frequency and harmonics, and it checks whether your uninterruptible power supply (UPS) system is functioning correctly.

Measuring flicker   It checks the switching loads on lighting systems.

Capturing voltage transients   It can help you find intermittent, momentary events that may be affecting your equipment; the full waveform is captured with date, time stamp, and duration.

But you still have to do more to ensure the vitality of your electronic devices because they're very sensitive to temperature as well. This means you also need a way to monitor the temperature of the place(s) where your equipment is stored.

Environmental Monitors

Environmental monitors are designed to monitor the temperate, humidity, and air flow in an area or in a device. Temperature and humidity are both critical factors in the health of computing equipment. High temperatures lead to CPU overheating and shortly thereafter systems start rebooting.

High humidity cannot be tolerated because it leads to corrosion of electrical parts followed by shorts and other failures. Low humidity sounds good on paper, but with it comes static electricity buildup in the air, which can fry computer parts if it reaches them. Both of these conditions should be monitored.

A *temperature and humidity monitor* can save you and your precious devices from a total meltdown. By their very nature, networks often include lots of machines placed close together in one or several location(s)—like server rooms. Clearly, these devices, all humming along at once, generate quite a bit of heat.

Just like us, electronics need to "breathe," and they're also pretty sensitive to becoming overheated, which is why you'll often need a jacket in a chilly server room. It's also why we need to set up and use temperature-monitoring devices. Twenty years ago or so, these devices didn't send alerts or give off any kind of alarms; they were just little plastic boxes that had pieces of round graph paper to graph temperature. The paper was good for a month, and for that duration, it would just spin around in a circle being drawn on by a pen attached to the temperature coil. As the temperature moved up or down, the pen moved in or out, leaving a circle line around the paper. All of this allowed you to manually monitor the temperature modulation in the server room over time. Although intended to "alert" you when and if there were climate changes, it usually did so after the fact, and therefore, too late.

Today, these temperature/humidity systems can provide multiple sensors feeding data to a single control point—nice. Now we can much more accurately track the temperature in our server rooms dynamically in real time. The central control point is usually equipped with HTTP software that can send alerts and provide alarms via a browser should your server room experience a warming event.

Temperature/humidity monitors also come in a variety of flavors. They vary in size and cost and come in hardware and/or software varieties. The kind you need varies and is based on the size of the room and the number of devices in it. You can even get one that will just monitor your PC's internal heat.

What type of indication or other problems will indicate you have a temperature problem in your server room? When you install new servers in a rack and you have network instability and other issues across all the servers in the rack but the power resources and bandwidth have been tested, this would be a good time to check your temperature monitor and verify that the servers are staying cool enough. Another red flag when it comes to environmental issues is a problem that occurs every day at the same time. This could be the time of day when the room temperature reaches the problematic stage.

Summary

You need network tools, and you need to know how to use them. And as I said, you can get your hands on many of them for free; so download them and use them as soon as possible to get the experience you'll need to pass the CompTIA Network+ exam.

This chapter covered network scanners, including packet sniffers, IDS and IPS software, and port scanners. I also covered hardware tools, which are rarely free. The good news is that you don't need many of them yourself, but the company that owns all the equipment definitely does. Even though I've used all of the tools I talked about in this chapter, I don't own most of them personally—only the ones that are free or relatively inexpensive.

In the hardware tools section, I covered cable testers, analyzers, certifiers, TDR/OTDRs, and other critical tools that help you test the cables and devices in your network, monitor them, and keep them up and running smoothly.

Exam Essentials

Understand what network scanners are and how to use each one.   Network scanners are described as packet sniffers, IDS/IPS software, and port scanners. These devices can help you both troubleshoot and fix your network as well as find and stop hackers in their tracks.

Remember the basic purpose of a packet sniffer.   The basic purpose of packet sniffers or network analyzers is to collect and analyze each individual packet that is captured on a specific network segment to determine if problems are happening.

Remember the main purpose of IDS/IPS software.   The IDS detects unwanted attempts to manipulate network systems and/or environment, and the IPS is a computer security device that monitors network and/or system activities for malicious behavior and can react in real time to stop attacks.

Understand what an OTDR is used for.   An optical time-domain reflectometer (OTDR) is an optoelectronic instrument used to test fiber-optic cabling. You can learn the cable's estimated length and attenuation (loss in db) and the location of faults.

Understand the difference between cable testers and certifiers. Cable testers simply tell you if the cable will function. Cable certifiers run much more sophisticated tests that determine if the cable performs according to specifications called for in the standard.

Understand the value of temperature and humidity monitors. These devices can monitor environmental conditions and alert you if either the temperature or the humidity in a server room or area falls below or rises above the prescribed range of safe values.

Written Lab

Answer the following questions about software and hardware tools:

1. True/False: An IDS box can find and fix a problem as the attack occurs.

2. True/False: A TDR is used to test fiber connections.

3. True/False: An IDS box will report an attack but not fix it.

4. True/False: An OTDR is used to test fiber connections.

5. True/False: A network analyzer will see every packet on every segment of your network at the same time.

6. What type of device determines if a cable meets standards specifications?

7. True/False: It is okay to scan the DoD network servers with a port scanner.

8. You need to monitor the temperature of your server room. What device should you use?

9. You want to monitor your UPS systems and make sure they are functioning correctly. What device should you use?

10. What type of device is used to put an RJ-45 end on a Cat 5e cable?

    You can find the answers in Appendix B.

Review Questions

You can find the answers in Appendix A.

1. Which is a tool in the network scanner category?

   A. Packet sniffers

   B. IDS/IPS software

   C. Port scanners

   D. All of the above

2. What is the purpose of packet sniffers?

   A. Discarding frames

   B. Sending transmissions from one port to another port

   C. Looking inside every packet on a network segment

   D. Stopping malicious behavior on the network

3. You need to trace cables in multiple pair wiring. What tool will you use?

   A. Toner probe

   B. IDS

   C. Cable tester

   D. Butt set

4. What tool would you use to both find a break in a fiber-optic connection and test the fiber connectivity on the network?

   A. Multimeter

   B. OTDR

   C. Butt set

   D. Toner probe

5. You need to create a cable that will connect your host to a wall jack connection. Which of the following will you use?

   A. IDS/IPS

   B. Snips

   C. Coax cable strippers

   D. Multimeter

6. Where is the IDS/IPS software typically placed within a network?

    A. Between the internal router and the firewall connected to the ISP

    B. Between the printer and the router connected to the ISP

    C. Between the computer and the switch configured with VLANs

    D. Between the firewall and the router connected to the email server

7. What is the purpose of a port scanner?

    A. Scan UDP for closed ports

    B. Sweep TCP for closed ports

    C. Search the network host for open ports

    D. None of the above

8. What is the purpose of wire-map testers?

    A. Check copper cable for crossed pairs only

    B. Analyze protocols in software

    C. Help find unused protocols and remove them from the network

    D. Detect transposed wires, opens, and shorts in twisted-pair cables

9. Which of the following can check the speed and condition of the signal on a cable, measure the time it takes to send a signal down the wire and back, and find the exact location of a break?

    A. Multimeter

    B. TDR

    C. Tone generator

    D. Event recorder

10. Which device should be used if you need to determine whether your network meets ISO or TIA standards?

    A. Angry IP

    B. Certifiers

    C. Nmap

    D. Routing table

11. Which software tool is used to view network traffic at the frame level?

    A. TDR

    B. Multimeter

    C. Port scanner

    D. Packet sniffer

12. Which of the following options is not a function of a TDR?

   A. Estimate cable lengths

   B. Find splice and connector locations and their associated loss amounts

   C. Display unused services

   D. Determine cable-impedance characteristics

   E. Send a signal down a cable and measure how long it takes to come back

13. Which device would be used to measure voltage?

   A. Multimeter

   B. OTDR

   C. Butt set

   D. Toner probe

14. Which device would most likely be used to locate a specific connection in an unlabeled punch-down block?

   A. VOM

   B. Certifier

   C. TDR

   D. Toner probe

15. Which tool would be used to connect wire between two punch-down block blades?

   A. Punch-down tool

   B. Crimper

   C. Snips

   D. Strippers

16. Which tool is used to attach an RJ-45 connector to a Cat 5 cable?

   A. Punch-down tool

   B. Crimper

   C. Snips

   D. Strippers

17. Which of the following would a technician use a punch-down tool on?

   A. RJ-45 connector

   B. CSU/DSU

   C. 110 block

   D. Fiber ST connector

18. Which device monitors incoming voltage levels and overvoltage thresholds?

    A. Repeater

    B. Toner probe

    C. VOM

    D. Surge protector

19. Which of the following tools can test a port on a device?

    A. Cable certifier

    B. Loopback plug

    C. Butt set

    D. Toner probe

20. You install new switches in your server room and are now experiencing network instability and other issues across all servers in the rack. Which device would be used to alert you of a system overheating?

    A. Voltage event recorder

    B. Temperature monitor

    C. Surge protector

    D. Probe

Chapter

19

Network Troubleshooting

THE FOLLOWING COMPTIA NETWORK+ EXAM OBJECTIVES ARE COVERED IN THIS CHAPTER:

✓ **1.8 Given a scenario, implement the following network troubleshooting methodology:**

- Identify the problem:
  - Information gathering
  - Identify symptoms
  - Question users
  - Determine if anything has changed
- Establish a theory of probable cause:
  - Question the obvious
- Test the theory to determine cause:
  - Once theory is confirmed determine next steps to resolve problem.
  - If theory is not confirmed, re-establish new theory or escalate.
- Establish a plan of action to resolve the problem and identify potential effects
- Implement the solution or escalate as necessary
- Verify full system functionality and if applicable implement preventative measures
- Document findings, actions, and outcomes

✓ **2.4 Given a scenario, troubleshoot common wireless problems.**

- Interference
- Signal strength
- Configurations
- Incompatibilities
- Incorrect channel
- Latency
- Encryption type
- Bounce
- SSID mismatch
- Incorrect switch placement

✓ **2.5 Given a scenario, troubleshoot common router and switch problems.**

- Switching loop
- Bad cables/improper cable types
- Port configuration
- VLAN assignment
- Mismatched MTU/MUT black hole
- Power failure
- Bad/missing routes
- Bad modules (SFPs, GBICs)
- Wrong subnet mask
- Wrong gateway
- Duplicate IP address
- Wrong DNS

✓ **3.6 Given a scenario, troubleshoot common physical connectivity problems.**

- Cable problems:
  - Bad connectors
  - Bad wiring

- Open, short
- Split cables
- DB loss
- TXRX reversed
- Cable placement
- EMI/Interference
- Distance
- Cross-talk

There is no way around it. Troubleshooting computers and networks is a combination of art and science, and the only way to get really good at it is by doing it—a lot! So its practice, practice, and practice with the basic yet vitally important skills you'll attain in this chapter. Of course, I'm going to cover all the troubleshooting topics you'll need to sail through the Network+ exam, but I'm also going to add some juicy bits of knowledge that will really help you to tackle the task of troubleshooting successfully in the real world.

First, you'll learn to check quickly for problems in the "super simple stuff" category, and then we'll move into a hearty discussion about a common troubleshooting model that you can use like a checklist to go through and solve a surprising number of network problems. We'll finish the chapter with a good briefing about some common troubleshooting resources, tools, tips, and tricks to keep up your sleeve and equip you even further.

I won't be covering any new networking information in this chapter because you've gotten all the foundational background material you need for troubleshooting in the previous chapters. But no worries. I'll go through each of the issues described in this chapter's objectives, one at a time, in detail, so that even if you've still got a bit of that previous material to nail down yet, you'll be good to get going and fix some networks anyway.

To find up-to-the-minute updates for this chapter, please see www.lammle .com/forum or the book's web site at www.sybex.com/go/netplus.2e.

Narrowing Down the Problem

When initially faced with a network problem in its entirety, it's easy to get totally overwhelmed. That's why it's a great strategy to start by narrowing things down to the source of the problem. To help you achieve that goal, it's always wise to ask the right questions. You can begin doing just that with this list of questions to ask yourself:

- Did you check the super simple stuff (SSS)?

- Is hardware or software causing the problem?

- Is it a workstation or server problem?

- Which segments of the network are affected?

Are There Any Cabling Issues? Did You Check the Super Simple Stuff?

Yes—it sounds like a snake's hiss (appropriate for a problem, right?), but exactly what's on the SSS list that you should be checking first, and why? Well, as the saying goes, "All things being equal, the simplest explanation is probably the correct one," so you probably won't be stunned and amazed when I tell you that I've had people call me in and act like the sky is falling when all they needed to do was check to make sure their workstation was plugged in or powered on. (I didn't say "super simple stuff" for nothing!) Your SSS list really does include things that are this obvious—sometimes so obvious, no one thinks to check for them. Even though anyone experienced in networking has their own favorite "DUH" events to tell about, almost everyone can agree on a few things that should definitely be on the SSS list:

- Check to ensure login procedures and rights.
- Look for link lights and collision lights.
- Check all power switches, cords, and adapters.
- Look for user errors.

The Correct Login Procedure and Rights

You know by now that if you've set up everything correctly, your network's users absolutely have to follow the proper login procedure to the letter (or number, or symbol) in order to successfully gain access to the network resources they're after. If they don't do that, they will be denied access, and considering that there are truly tons of opportunities to blow it, it's a miracle, or at least very special, that anyone manages to log in to the network correctly at all.

Think about it. First, a user must enter their username and password flawlessly. Sounds easy, but as they say, "in a perfect world…" In this one, people mess up, don't realize it, and freak out at you about the "broken network" or the imaginary IT demon that changed their password on them while they went to lunch and now, they can't log in. (The latter could be true—you may have done exactly that. If you did, just gently remind them about that memo you sent about the upcoming password-change date and time that they must have spaced about due to the tremendous demands on them.)

Anyway, it's true. By far, the most common problem is bad typing—people accidentally enter the wrong username or password, and they do that a lot. With some operating systems, a slight brush of the Caps Lock key is all it takes: The user's username and password are case sensitive, and suddenly, they're trying to log in with what's now all in uppercase instead—oops.

Plus, if you happen to be running one of the shiny new operating systems around today, you can also restrict the times and conditions under which users can log in, right? So, if your user spent an unusual amount of time in the bathroom upon returning from lunch, or if they got distracted and tried to log in from their BFF's workstation instead of their own, the network's operating system would've rejected their login request even though they still can type impressively well after two martinis.

And remember—you can also restrict how many times a user can log in to the network simultaneously. If you've set that up, and your user tries to establish more connections than you've allowed, access will again be denied. Just know that most of the time, if a user is denied access to the network and/or its resources, they're probably going to interpret that as a network problem even though the network operating system is doing what it should.

 Real World Scenario

Can the Problem Be Reproduced?

The first question to ask anyone who reports a network or computer problem is, "Can you show me what 'not working' looks like?" This is because if you can reproduce the problem, you can identify when it happens, which may give you all the information you need to determine the source of the problem and maybe even solve it in a snap. The hardest problems to solve are those of the random variety that occur intermittently and can't be easily reproduced.

Let's pause for a minute to outline the steps to take during any user-oriented network problem-solving process:

1. Make sure the username and password is being entered correctly.
2. Check that Caps Lock key.
3. Try to log in yourself from another workstation, assuming that doing this doesn't violate the security policy. If it works, go back to the user-oriented login problems, and go through them again.
4. If none of this solves the problem, check the network documentation to find out whether any of the aforementioned kinds of restrictions are in place; if so, find out whether the user has violated any of them.

 Remember, if intruder detection is enabled on your network, a user will get locked out of their account after a specific number of unsuccessful login attempts. If this happens, either they'll have to wait until a predetermined time period has elapsed before their account will unlock and give them another chance or you'll have to go in and manually unlock it for them.

The Link and Collision Lights

The link light is that little light-emitting diode (LED) found on both the Network Interface Card (NIC) and the hub. It's typically green and labeled Link or some abbreviation of that.

If you're running 10BaseT, a link light indicates that the NIC and hub are making a logical (Data Link layer) connection. If the link lights are lit up on both the workstation's NIC and the hub port to which the workstation is connected, it's usually safe to assume that the workstation and hub are communicating just fine.

The link lights on some NICs don't activate until the driver is loaded. So, if the link light isn't on when the system is first turned on, you'll just have to wait until the operating system loads the NIC driver. But don't wait forever!

The *collision light* is also a small LED, but it's typically amber in color, and it can usually be found on both Ethernet NICs and hubs. When lit, it indicates that an Ethernet collision has occurred. If you've got a busy Ethernet network on which collisions are somewhat common, understand that this light is likely to blink occasionally; if it stays on continuously, though, it could mean that there are way too many collisions happening for legitimate network traffic to get through. Don't assume this is really what's happening without first checking that the NIC, or other network device, is working properly because one or both could simply be malfunctioning.

Don't confuse the collision light with the network-activity or network-traffic light (which is usually green) because that light just indicates that a device is transmitting. This particular light *should* be blinking on and off continually as the device transmits and receives data on the network.

The Power Switch

Clearly, to function properly, all computer and network components must be turned on and powered up first. Obvious, yes, but if I had a buck for each time I've heard, "My computer is on, but my monitor is all dark," I'd be rolling in money by now.

When this kind of thing happens, just keep your cool and politely ask, "Is the monitor turned on?" After a little pause, the person calling for help will usually say, "Ohhh… ummmm…thanks," and then hang up ASAP. The reason I said to be nice is that, embarrassing as it is, this, or something like it, will probably happen to you too eventually.

Most systems include a power indicator (a Power or PWR light). The power switch typically has an On indicator, but the system or device could still be powerless if all the relevant power cables aren't actually plugged in—including the power strip.

Remember that every cable has two ends, and both must be plugged in to something. If you're thinking something like, "Sheesh—a four-year-old knows that," you're probably right. But again, I can't count the times this has turned out to be the root cause of a "major system failure."

The best way to go about troubleshooting power problems is to start with the most obvious device and work your way back to the power-service panel. There could be a number of power issues between the device and the service panel, including a bad power cable, bad outlet, bad electrical wire, tripped circuit breaker, or blown fuse, and any of these things could be the actual cause of the problem that appears to be device-death instead.

Operator Error

Or, the problem may be that you've got a user who simply doesn't know how to be one. Maybe you're dealing with someone who doesn't have the tiniest clue about the equipment they're using or about how to perform a certain task correctly—in other words, the problem may be due to something known as *operator error (OE)*. Here's a short list of the most common types of OEs and their associated acronyms:

- Equipment exceeds operator capability (EEOC)
- Problem exists between chair and keyboard (PEBCAK)
- ID Ten T error (an ID10T)

A word of caution here, though—assuming that all your problems are user related can quickly make an ID10T error out of you.

Although it can be really tempting to take the easy way out and blow things off, remember that the network's well-being and security are ultimately your responsibility. So, before you jump to the operator-error conclusion, ask the user in question to reproduce the problem in your presence, and pay close attention to what they do. Understand that doing this can require a great deal of patience, but it's worth your time and effort if you can prevent someone who doesn't know what they're doing from causing serious harm to pricey devices or leaving a gaping hole in your security. You might even save the help desk crew's sanity from the relentless calls of a user with the bad habit of flipping off the power switch without following proper shutdown procedures. You just wouldn't know they always do that if you didn't see it for yourself, right?

And what about finding out that that pesky user was, in fact, trained really badly by someone, and that they aren't the only one? This is exactly the kind of thing that can turn the best security policy to dust and leave your network and its resources as vulnerable to attack as that goat in *Jurassic Park*.

The moral here is, always check out the problem thoroughly. If the problem and its solution aren't immediately clear to you, try the procedure yourself, or ask someone else at another workstation to do so. Don't just leave the issue unsettled or make the assumption that it is user error or a chance abnormality because that's exactly what the bad guys out there are hoping you'll do.

This is only a partial list of super simple stuff. No worries. Rest assured you'll come up with your own expanded version over time.

Is Hardware or Software Causing the Problem?

A hardware problem often rears its ugly head when some device in your computer skips a beat and/or dies. This one's pretty easy to discern because when you try to do something requiring that particular piece of hardware, you can't do it and instead get an error telling you that you can't do it. Even if your hard disk fails, you'll probably get warning signs before it actually kicks, like a Disk I/O error or something similar.

Other problems drop out of the sky and hit you like something from the wrong end of a seagull. No warning at all—just splat! Components that were humming along fine a second ago can and do suddenly fail, usually at the worst possible time, leaving you with a mess of lost data, files, everything—you get the idea.

Solutions to hardware problems usually involve one of three things:

- Changing hardware settings
- Updating device drivers
- Replacing dead hardware

If your hardware has truly failed, it's time to get out your tools and start replacing components. If this isn't one of your skills, you can either send the device out for repair or replace it. Your mantra here is "backup, backup, backup," because in either case, a system could be down for a while—anywhere from an hour to several days—so it's always good to keep backup hardware around. And I know everyone and your momma has told you this, but here it is one more time: Back up all data, files, hard drive, everything, and do so on a regular basis.

Software problems are muddier waters. Sometimes you'll get General Protection Fault messages, which indicate a Windows or Windows program (or other platform) error of some type, and other times the program you're working in will suddenly stop responding and hang. At their worst, they'll cause your machine to randomly lock up on you. When this type of thing happens, I'd recommend visiting the manufacturer's support website to get software updates and patches or searching for the answer in a knowledge base.

Sometimes you get lucky and the ailing software will tell the truth by giving you a precise message about the source of the problem. Messages saying the software is missing a file or a file has become corrupt are great because you can usually get your problem fixed fast by providing that missing file or by reinstalling the software. Neither solution takes very long, but the downside is that whatever you were doing before the program hosed will probably be at least partially lost; so again, back up your stuff, and save your data often.

Please reread Chapter 17, "Troubleshooting Tools," and Chapter 18, "Software and Hardware Tools," and use the software and hardware tools discussed in those two chapters to help you troubleshoot network problems.

Okay—it's time for you to learn how to troubleshoot your workstations and servers.

Is It a Workstation or a Server Problem?

The first thing you've got to determine when troubleshooting these kinds of problems is whether it's only one person or a whole group that's been affected. If the answer is only one person, think workstation—more than that, and it's probably part of the network (a segment) that's giving you grief.

So what do you do about it? Well, if it's the single-user situation, your first line of defense is to try to log in from another workstation within the same group of users. If you can do that, the problem is definitely the user's workstation, so look for things like cabling faults, a bad NIC, power issues, and OSs.

But if a whole department can't access a specific server, take a good, hard look at that particular server, and start by checking all user connections to it. If everyone is logged in correctly, the problem may have something to do with individual rights or permissions; if no one can log in to that server, including you, the server probably has a communication problem with the rest of the network. And if the server has totally crashed, you'll either see messages regarding this nasty fact on the server's monitor, or you'll find its screen completely blank—screaming indications that the server is no longer running. All good, but it's important to keep in mind that these symptoms vary among network operating systems.

Which Segments of the Network Are Affected?

Figuring this one out can be a little tough. If multiple segments are affected, you may be dealing with a network-address conflict. If you're running Transmission Control Protocol/Internet Protocol (TCP/IP), remember that IP addresses must be unique across an entire network. So, if two of your segments have the same static IP subnet addresses assigned, you'll end up with duplicate IP errors—an ugly situation that can be a real bear to troubleshoot and can make it tough to find the source of the problem.

If all of your network's users are experiencing the problem, it could be a server everyone accesses. Thank the powers that be if you nail it down to that because if not, other network devices like your main router or hub may be down, making network transmissions impossible and usually meaning a lot more work on your part to fix.

Adding wide area network (WAN) connections to the mix can complicate matters exponentially, and you don't want to go there if you can avoid it, so start by finding out if stations on both sides of a WAN link can communicate. If so, get the champagne—your problem isn't related to the WAN—woo hoo! But if those stations can't communicate, it's not your lucky day: You've got to check everything between the sending station and the receiving one, including the WAN hardware, to find the culprit. The good news is that most of the time, WAN devices have built-in diagnostics that tell you whether a WAN link is working okay, which really helps you determine if the failure has something to do with the WAN link itself or with the hardware involved instead.

Is It Bad Cabling?

Back to hooking up correctly. After you've figured out whether your plight is related to one workstation, a network segment, or the whole tamale (network), you must then examine the relevant cabling. Are the cables properly connected to the correct port? More than once, I've seen a digital subscriber line (DSL) modem connection to the wall cabled all wrong—it's an easy mistake to make and an easy one to fix.

And you know that nothing lasts forever, so check those patch cables running between a workstation and a wall jack. Just because they don't come with expiration dates written on them doesn't mean they don't expire. They do go bad—especially if they get moved, trampled, or tripped over a lot. (I did tell you that it's a bad idea to run cabling across the office floor, didn't I?) Connection problems are the tell here—if you check the NIC and there is no link light blinking, you may have a bad patch cable to blame.

It gets murkier if your cable in the walls or ceiling is toast or hasn't been installed correctly. Maybe you've got a user or two telling you the place is haunted because they only have problems with their workstations after dark when the lights go on. Haunted? No...Some genius probably ran a network cable over a fluorescent light, which is something that just happens to produce lots of electromagnetic interference (EMI), which can really mess up communications in that cable.

Next on your list is to check the medium dependent interface/medium dependent interface-crossover (MDI/MDI-X) port setting on small, workgroup hubs and switches. This is a potential source of trouble that's often overlooked, but it's important because this port is the one that's used to uplink to a switch on the network's backbone.

First, understand that the port setting has to be set to either MDI or MDI-X depending on the type of cable used for your hub-to-hub or switch-to-switch connection. For instance, the crossover cables I talked about way back in Chapter 3, "Networking Topologies, Connectors, and Wiring Standards," require that the port be set to MDI, and a standard network patch cable requires that the port be set to MDI-X. You can usually adjust the setting via a regular switch or a dual inline package (DIP) switch, but to be sure, if you're still using hubs, check out the hub's documentation. (You did keep that, right?)

Other Important Cable Issues You Need to Know About

They may be basic, but they're still vital—understanding the physical issues that can happen on a network when a user is connected via cable (usually Ethernet) is critical information to have in your troubleshooting repertoire.

Because most of today's networks still consist of large amounts of copper cable, they suffer from the same physical issues that have plagued networking since the very beginning. Newer technologies and protocols have helped to a degree, but they haven't made these issues a thing of the past yet. Some physical issues that still affect networks are listed and defined next:

Crosstalk   Again, harkening back to Chapter 3, remember that crosstalk is what happens when there's signal bleed between two adjacent wires that are carrying a current. Network designers minimize crosstalk inside network cables by twisting the wire pairs together, putting them at a 90-degree angle to each other. The tighter the wires are twisted, the less the crosstalk you have, and newer cables like Cat 6 cable really make a difference. But like I said, not completely—crosstalk still exists and affects communications, especially in high-speed networks.

Nearing or near-end crosstalk This is a specific type of crosstalk measurement that has to do with the EMI bled from a wire to adjoining wires where the current originates. This particular point has the strongest potential to create crosstalk because the crosstalk signal itself degrades as it moves down the wire; if you have an issue with it, it's probably going to show up in the first part of wire where it's connected to a switch or a NIC.

Attenuation/DB loss As a signal moves through any medium, the medium itself will degrade the signal—a phenomenon known as *attenuation* that's common in all kinds of networks. True, signals traversing fiber-optic cable don't attenuate as fast as those on copper cable, but they still do eventually. You know that all copper twisted-pair cables have a maximum segment distance of 100 meters before they'll need to be amplified or *repeated* by a hub or a switch, but single-mode fiber-optic cables can sometimes carry signals for miles before they begin to attenuate (degrade). If you need to go big, use fiber, not copper.

Collisions A network *collision* happens when two devices try to communicate on the same physical segment at the same time. Collisions like this were a big problem in the early Ethernet networks, and a tool known as *Carrier Sense Multiple Access with Collision Detection* (CSMA/CD) was used to detect and respond to them in Ethernet_II. Nowadays, we use switches in place of hubs because they can separate the network into multiple collision domains, learn the Media Access Control (MAC) addresses of the devices attached to them, create a type of permanent virtual circuit between all network devices, and prevent collisions.

Shorts Basically, a *short circuit*, or *short*, happens when the current flows through a different path within a circuit than it's supposed to; in networks, they're usually caused by some type of physical fault in the cable. You can find shorts with circuit-testing equipment, but because sooner is better when it comes to getting a network back up and running, replacing the ailing cable until it can be fixed (if it can be) is your best option.

Open impedance mismatch (echo) Open impedance on cable-testing equipment tells you that the cable or wires connect into another cable and there is an impedance mismatch. When that happens, some of the signal will bounce back in the direction it came from, degrading the strength of the signal, which ultimately causes the link to fail.

Interference/cable placement EMI and *radio frequency interference (RFI)* occur when signals interfere with the normal operation of electronic circuits. Computers happen to be really sensitive to sources of this, such as TV and radio transmitters, which create a specific radio frequency as part of their transmission process. Two other common culprits are two-way radios and cellular phones.

Your only way around this is to use shielded network cables like shielded twisted-pair (STP) and coaxial cable (rare today) or to run EMI/RFI-immune but pricey fiber-optic cable throughout your entire network.

Split pairs A split pair is a wiring error where two connections that are supposed to be connected using the two wires of a twisted pair are instead connected using two wires from different pairs. Such wiring causes errors in high-rate data lines. If you buy your cables precut, you won't have this problem.

Unbounded Media Issues (Wireless)

Now let's say your problem-ridden user is telling you they only use a wireless connection. Well, you can definitely take crosstalk and shorts off the list of suspects, but don't get excited because with wireless, you've got a whole new bunch of possible Physical layer problems to sort through.

Wireless networks are really convenient for the user but not so much for administrators. They can require a lot more configuration, and understand that with wireless networks, you don't just get to substitute one set of challenges for another—you pretty much add all those fresh new issues on top of the wired challenges you already have on your plate.

The following list includes some of those new wireless challenges:

Interference   Because wireless networks rely on radio waves to transmit signals, they're more subject to interference, even from other wireless devices like Bluetooth keyboards, mice, or cell phones that are all close in frequency ranges. Any of these—even microwave ovens!—can cause signal bleed that can slow down or prevent wireless communications. Factors like the distance between a client and a wireless access point (WAP) and the stuff between the two can also affect signal strength and even intensify the interference from other signals. So, careful placement of that WAP is a must.

Configurations   Mistakes in the configuration of the wireless access point or wireless router or inconsistencies between the settlings on the AP and the stations can also be the source of problems. This section describes some of the main sources of configuration problems.

> **Incorrect encryption**   You know that wireless networks can use encryption to secure their communications and that different encryption flavors are used for wireless networks, like Wired Equivalent Privacy (WEP) and Wi-Fi Protected Access 2 (WPA2) with Advanced Encryption Standard (AES). To ensure the tightest security, configure your wireless networks with the highest encryption protocol that both the WAP and the clients can support. Oh, and make sure the AP and its clients are configured with same type of encryption. This is why it's a good idea to disable security before troubleshooting client problems, because if the client can connect once you've done that, you know you're dealing with a security configuration error.

> **Incorrect channel**   Wireless networks use many different frequencies within the 2.4GHz or 5Ghz band, and I'll bet you didn't know that these frequencies are sometimes combined to provide greater bandwidth for the user. You actually do know about this—has anyone heard of something called a *channel*? Well, that's exactly what a channel is, and it's also the reason some radio stations come in better than others—they have more bandwidth because their channel has more combined frequencies. You also know what happens when the AP and the client aren't quite matching up. Have you ever hit the scan button on your car's radio and only kind of gotten a station's static-ridden broadcast? That's because the AP (radio station) and the client (your car's radio) aren't quite on the same channel. Most of the time, wireless networks use channel 1, 6, or 11, and because clients auto-configure themselves to any channel the AP is broadcasting on, it's not usually a configuration issue unless someone has forced a client onto an incorrect channel.

Incorrect frequency   Okay—so setting the channel sets the frequency or frequencies that wireless devices will use. But some devices, such as an AP running 802.11g and a, allow you to tweak those settings and choose a specific frequency such as 2.4Ghz or 5Ghz. As with any relationship, it works best if things are mutual. So if you do this on one device, you've got to configure the same setting on all the devices with which you want to communicate, or they won't—they'll argue, and you don't want that. Incorrect-channel and frequency-setting problems on a client are rare, but if you have multiple APs and they're in close proximity, you need to make sure they're on different channels/frequencies to avoid potential interference problems.

ESSID mismatch   When a wireless device comes up, it scans for Service Set Identifiers (SSIDs) in its immediate area. These can be Basic Service Set Identifiers (BSSIDs) that identify an individual access point or Extended Service Set Identifiers (ESSIDs) that identify a set of APs. In your own wireless LAN, you clearly want the devices to find the ESSID that you're broadcasting, which isn't usually a problem: Your broadcast is closer than the neighbor's, so it should be stronger—unless you're in an office building or apartment complex that has lots of different APs assigned to lots of different ESSIDs because they belong to lots of different tenants in the building. This can definitely give you some grief because it's possible that your neighbor's ESSID broadcast is stronger than yours, depending on where the clients are in the building. So if a user reports that they're connected to an AP but still can't access the resources they need or authenticate to the network, you should verify that they are, in fact, connected to your ESSID and not your neighbor's. This is very typical in an open security wireless network. You can generally just look at the information tool tip on the wireless software icon to find this out. However, you can easily solve this problem today by making the office SSID the preferred network in the client software.

Standard mismatch   As you found out in Chapter 12, "Wireless Technologies," wireless networks have many standards that have evolved over time, like 802.11a, 802.11b, 802.11g, and 802.11n. Standards continue to develop that make wireless networks even faster and more powerful. The catch is that some of these standards are backward compatible and others aren't. For instance, most devices you buy today can be set to 802.11a/b/g, which means they can be used to communicate with other devices of all three standards. So, make sure the standards on the AP match the standards on the client, or that they're at least backward compatible. It's either that or tell all your users to buy new cards for their machines.

Distance/signal strength   Location, location, location. You've got only two worries with this one: Your clients are either not far enough away or they're too far from the AP. If your AP doesn't seem to have enough power to provide a connectivity point for your clients, you can move it closer to them, increase the distance that the AP can transmit by changing the type of antenna it uses, or use multiple APs connected to the same switch or set of switches to solve the problem. If the signal is too strong, and it reaches out into the parking area or further out to other buildings and businesses, place the AP as close as possible to the center of the area it's providing service for. And don't forget to verify that you've got the latest security features in place to keep bad guys from authenticating to and using your network.

Latency   When wireless users complain that the network is slow (latency) or that they are losing their connection to applications during a session, it is usually a capacity or distance issue. Remember, 802.11 is a shared medium, and as more users connect, all user throughput goes down. If this becomes a constant problem as opposed to the occasional issue where 20 guys with laptops gather for an every six-month meeting in the conference room, it may be time to consider placing a second AP in the area. When you do this, place the second AP on a different non-overlapping channel from the first and make sure the second AP uses the same SSID as the first. In the 2.4 Ghz frequency (802.11b and 802.11g), the three non-overlapping channels are 1,6, and 11. Now the traffic can be divided between them and users will get better performance. It is also worth noting that when clients move away from the AP, the data rate drops until at some point it is insufficient to maintain the connection.

Bounce   For a wireless network spanning large geographical distances, you can install repeaters and reflectors to bounce a signal and boost it to cover about a mile. This can be a good thing, but if you don't tightly control signal bounce, you could end up with a much bigger network than you wanted. To determine exactly how far and wide the signal will bounce, make sure you conduct a thorough wireless site survey. However, bounce can also refer to multipath issues, where the signal reflects off objectives and arrives at the client degraded because it is arriving out of phase. The solution is pretty simple. APs use two antennas that both sample the signal and use the strongest signal and ignore the out-of-phase signal. However, 802.11n takes advantage of multipath and can combine the out-of-phase signals to increase the distance hosts can be from the AP.

Incorrect antenna/switch placement   Most of the time, the best place to put an AP and/or its antenna is as close to the center of your wireless network as possible. But you can position some antennas a distance from the AP and connect to it with a cable—a method used for a lot of the outdoor installations around today. If you want to use multiple APs, you've also got to be a little more sophisticated about deciding where to put them all; you can use third-party tools like the packet sniffers Wireshark and AirMagnet on a laptop to survey the site and establish how far your APs are actually transmitting. You can also hire a consultant to do this for you—there are many companies that specialize in assisting organizations with their wireless networks and the placement of antennas and APs. This is important because poor placement can lead to interference and poor performance, or even no performance at all.

Now that you know all about the possible physical network horrors that can befall you on a typical network, it's a good time for you to memorize the troubleshooting steps that you've got to know to ace the CompTIA Network+ exam.

Troubleshooting Steps

In the Network+ troubleshooting model, there are seven steps you've got to have dialed in:

1. Identify the problem.
2. Establish a theory of probable cause.

3. Test the theory to determine cause.

4. Establish a plan of action to resolve the problem and identify potential effects.

5. Implement the solution or escalate as necessary.

6. Verify full system functionality, and if applicable, implement preventative measures.

7. Document findings, actions, and outcomes.

To get things off to a running start, let's assume that the user has called you yet again, but now they're almost in tears because they can't connect to the server on the intranet and they also can't get to the Internet. (By the way, this happens a lot, so pay attention—it's only a matter of time before it happens to you!)

Absolutely, positively make sure you memorize this seven-step troubleshooting process in the right order when studying for the Network+ exam!

Step 1: Identify the Problem

Before you can solve the problem, you've got to figure out what it is, right? Again, asking the right questions can get you far along this path and really help clarify the situation. Identifying the problem involves steps that together constitute *information gathering*.

Question Users

A good way to start is by asking the user the following questions:

- Exactly which part of the Internet can't you access? A particular website? A certain address? A type of website? None of it at all?

- Can you use your web browser?

- If the hitch has to do with an internal server to the company, ask the user if they can ping the server and talk the them through doing that.

- Ask the user to try to telnet or FTP to an internal server to verify local network connectivity; if they don't know how, talk them through it.

Here's another really common trouble ticket that just happens to build on the last scenario: Now let's say you've got a user who's called you at the help desk. By asking the previous questions, you found out that this user can't access the corporate intranet or get out to any sites on the Internet. You also established that the user can use their web browser to access the corporate FTP site, but only by IP address, not by the FTP server name. This information tells you two important things: that you can rule out the host and the web browser (application) as the source of the problem and that the physical network is working.

Determine If Anything Has Changed

Moving right along, if you can reproduce the problem, your next step is to verify what has changed and how. Drawing on your knowledge of networking, you ask yourself and your user questions like these:

Were you ever able to do this?   If not, then maybe it just isn't something the hardware or software is designed to do. You should then tell the user exactly that, as well as advise them that they may need additional hardware or software to pull off what they're trying do.

If so, when did you become unable to do it?   If, once upon a time, the computer was able to do the job and then suddenly could not, whatever conditions surrounded and were involved in this turn of events become extremely important. You have a really good shot at unearthing the root of the problem if you know what happened right before things changed. Just know that there's a high level of probability that the cause of the problem is directly related to the conditions surrounding the change when it occurred.

Has anything changed since the last time you could do this?   This question can lead you right to the problem's cause. Seriously—the thing that changed right before the problem began happening is almost always what caused it. It's so important that if you ask it, and your user tells you, "Nothing changed...it just happened," you should rephrase the question and say something like, "Did anyone add anything to your computer?" or "Are you doing anything differently from the way you usually do it?"

Were any error messages displayed?   These are basically arrows that point directly at the problem's origin; error messages are designed by programmers for the purpose of pointing them to exactly what it is that isn't working properly in computer systems. Sometimes error messages are crystal clear, like Disk Full, or they can be cryptically annoying little puzzles in and of themselves. If you pulled the short straw and got the latter variety, it's probably best to hit the software or hardware vendor's support site, where you can usually score a translation from the "programmerese" in which the error message is written into plain English so you can get back to solving your riddle.

Are other people experiencing this problem?   You've got to ask this one because the answer will definitely help you target the cause of the problem. First, try to duplicate the problem from your own workstation because if you can't, it's likely that the issue is related to only one user or group of users—possibly their workstations. (A solid hint that this is the case is if you're being inundated with calls from a bunch of people from the same workgroup.)

Is the problem always the same?   It's good to know that when problems crop up, they're almost always the same each time they occur. But their symptoms can change slightly as the conditions surrounding them change. A related question would be, "If you do x, does the problem get better or worse?" For example, ask a user, "If you use a different file, does the problem get better or worse?" If the symptoms lighten up, it's an indication that the problem is related to the original file that's being used.

Understand that these are just a few of the questions you can use to get to the source of a problem.

Okay, so let's get back to our sample scenario. So far, you've determined that the problem is unique to one user, which tells you that the problem is specific to this one host. Confirming that is the fact that you haven't received any other calls from other users on the network.

And when watching the user attempt to reproduce the problem, you note that they're typing the address correctly. Plus, you've got an error message that leads you to believe that the problem has something to with Domain Name Service (DNS) lookups on his host. Time to go deeper...

Identify Symptoms

I probably don't need to tell you that computers and networks can be really fickle—they can hum along fine for months, suddenly crash, and then continue to work fine again without ever seizing in that way again. That's why it's so important to be able to reproduce the problem and identify the affected area to narrow things down so you can cut to the chase and fix the issue fast. This really helps—when something isn't working, try it again, and write down exactly what is and is not happening.

Most users' knee-jerk reaction is to straight up call the help desk the minute they have a problem. This is not only annoying but also inefficient, because you're going to ask them exactly what they were doing when the problem occurred and most users have no idea what they were doing with the computer at the time because they were focused on doing their jobs instead. This is why if you train users to reproduce the problem and jot down some notes about it *before* calling you, they'll be much better prepared to give you the information you need to start troubleshooting it and help them.

So with that, here we go. The problem you've identified results in coughing out an error message to your user when they try to access the corporate intranet. It looks like this.

And when this user tries to ping the server using the server's hierarchical web name, it fails too.

```
Command Prompt
Microsoft Windows [Version 6.0.6001]
Copyright (c) 2006 Microsoft Corporation.  All rights reserved.

C:\Users\tlammle>ping internal.lammle.com
Ping request could not find host internal.lammle.com. Please check the name and
try again.

C:\Users\tlammle>
```

You're going to respond by checking to see whether the server is up by pinging the server by its IP address.

```
Command Prompt

Microsoft Windows [Version 6.0.6001]
Copyright (c) 2006 Microsoft Corporation.  All rights reserved.

C:\Users\tlammle>ping 206.123.114.186

Pinging 206.123.114.186 with 32 bytes of data:
Reply from 206.123.114.186: bytes=32 time=75ms TTL=56
Reply from 206.123.114.186: bytes=32 time=75ms TTL=56
Reply from 206.123.114.186: bytes=32 time=74ms TTL=56
Reply from 206.123.114.186: bytes=32 time=75ms TTL=56

Ping statistics for 206.123.114.186:
    Packets: Sent = 4, Received = 4, Lost = 0 (0% loss),
Approximate round trip times in milli-seconds:
    Minimum = 74ms, Maximum = 75ms, Average = 74ms

C:\Users\tlammle>
```

Nice—that worked, so the server is up, but you could still have a server problem. Just because you can ping a host, it doesn't mean that host is 100 percent up and running, but in this case, it's a good start.

And you're in luck because you've been able to re-create this problem from this user's host machine. By doing that, you now know that the URL name is not being resolved from Internet Explorer, and you can't ping it by the name either. But you can ping the server IP address from your limping host, and when you try this same connection to the `internal.lammle.com` server from another host nearby, it works fine, meaning the server is working fine. So, you've succeeded in isolating the problem to this specific host—yes!

 TIP   It is a huge advantage if you can watch the user try to reproduce the problem themselves because then you know for sure whether the user is performing the operation correctly. It's a really bad idea to assume the user is typing in what they say they are.

Great—now you've nailed down the problem. This leads us to step 2.

Step 2: Establish a Theory of Probable Cause

After you observe the problem and identify the symptoms, next on the list is to establish its most probable cause. (If you're stressing about now, don't, because though you may feel overwhelmed by all this, it truly does get a lot easier with time and experience.)

You must come up with at least one possible cause, even though it may not be completely on the money. And you don't always have to come up with it yourself. Someone else in the group may have the answer. Also, don't forget to check online sources and vendor documentation.

Again, let's get back to our scenario, in which you've determined the cause is probably an improperly configured DNS lookup on the workstation. The next thing to do is to verify the configuration and probably reconfigure DNS on the workstation; we'll get to this solution later, in step 4.

Understand that there are legions of problems that can occur on a network—and I'm sorry to tell you this, but they're typically not as simple as the example we've been using.

They can be, but I just don't want you to expect them to be. Always consider the physical aspects of a network, but look beyond them into the realm of logical factors like the DNS lookup issue we've been using.

Question the Obvious

The probable causes that you've got to thoroughly understand to meet the Network+ objectives are as follows:

- Port speed
- Port duplex mismatch
- Mismatched MTU
- Incorrect virtual local area network (VLAN)
- Incorrect IP address
- Wrong gateway
- Wrong DNS
- Wrong subnet mask

Let's talk about these logical issues, which can cause an abundance of network problems. Most of these happen because a device has been improperly configured:

Port speed   Because networks have been evolving for many years, there are various levels of speed and sophistication mixed into them—often within the same network. Most of the newest NICs can be used at 10Mbps, 100Mbps, and 1000Mbps. Most switches can support at least 10Mbps and 100Mbps, and an increasing number of switches can also support 1,000Mbps. Plus, many switches can also autosense the speed of the NIC that's connected and use different speeds on various ports. As long as the switches are allowed to autosense the port speed, it's rare to have a problem develop that results in a complete lack of communication. But if you decide to set the port speed manually, make positively sure to set the same speed on both sides of a link.

Port duplex mismatch   There are generally three duplex settings on each port of a network switch: full, half, and auto. In order for two devices to connect effectively, the duplex setting has to match on both sides of the connection. If one side of a connection is set to full and the other is set to half, they're mismatched. More elusively, if both sides are set to auto but the devices are different, you can also end up with a mismatch because the device on one side defaults to full and the other one defaults to half.

Duplex mismatches can cause lots of network errors and even the lack of a network connection. This is partially because setting the interfaces to full duplex disables the CSMA/CD protocol. This is definitely not a problem in a network that has no hubs (and therefore no shared segments in which there could be collisions), but it can make things really ugly in a network where hubs are still being used. This means the settings you choose are based on the type of devices you have populating your network. If you have all switches and no hubs, feel free to set all interfaces to full duplex, but if you've got hubs in the mix, you have shared networks, so you're forced to keep the settings at half duplex. With all new switches produced today, leaving the speed and duplex setting to auto (the default on both switches and hosts) is the recommended way to go.

Mismatched MTU   Ethernet LANs enforce what is called a maximum transmission unit (MTU). This is the largest size packet that is allowed across a segment. In most cases this is 1,500 bytes. Left alone this is usually not a problem, but it is possible to set the MTU on a router interface, which means it is possible for a mismatch to be present between two router interfaces. This can cause problems with communications between the routers, resulting in the link failing to pass traffic. To check the MTU on an interface, execute the command show interface.

Incorrect VLAN   Switches can have multiple VLANs each, and they can be connected to other switches using trunk links. As you now know, VLANs are often used to represent departments or the occupations of a group of users. This makes the configurations of security policies and network access lists much easier to manage and control. On the other hand, if a port is accidentally assigned to the wrong VLAN in a switch, it's as if that client was magically transported to another place in the network. If that happens, the security policies that should apply to the client won't anymore, and other policies will be applied to the client that never should have been. The correct VLAN port assignment of a client is as important as air; when I'm troubleshooting a single-host problem, this is the first place I look.

It's pretty easy to tell if you have a port configured with a wrong VLAN assignment. If this is the case, it won't be long before you'll get a call from some user screaming something at you that makes the building shake, like, "I can get to the Internet but I can't get to the Sales server, and I'm about to lose a huge sale. DO SOMETHING!" When you check the switch, you will invariably see that this user's port has a membership in another VLAN like Marketing, which has no access to the Sales server.

Incorrect IP address   The most common addressing protocol in use today is IPv4, which provides a unique IP address for each host on a network. Client computers usually get their addresses from Dynamic Host Configuration Protocol (DHCP) servers. But sometimes, especially in smaller networks, IP addresses for servers and router interfaces are statically assigned by the network's administrator. An incorrect address on a client will keep that client from being able to communicate and may even cause a conflict with another client on the network, and a bad address on a server or router interface can be disastrous and affect a multitude of users. This is exactly why you need to be super careful to set up DHCP servers correctly and also when configuring the static IP addresses assigned to servers and router interfaces.

Wrong gateway   A *gateway*, sometimes called a *default gateway* or an *IP default gateway*, is a router interface's address that's configured to forward traffic with a destination IP address that's not in the same subnet as the device itself. Let me clarify that one for you: If a device compares where a packet wants to go with the network it's currently on and finds that the packet needs to go to a remote network, the device will send that packet to the gateway to be forwarded to the remote network. Because every device needs a valid gateway to obtain communication outside of its own network, it's going to require some careful planning when considering the gateway configuration of devices in your network.

> If you're configuring a static IP address and default gateway, you need to verify the router's address. Not doing so is a really common "wrong gateway" problem that I see all the time.

Wrong DNS   DNS servers are used by networks and their clients to resolve a computer's hostname to its IP addresses and to enable clients to find the server they need to provide the resources they require, like a domain controller during the login and authentication process. Most of the time, DNS addresses are automatically configured by a DHCP server, but sometimes these addresses are statically configured instead. Because lots of applications rely on hostname resolution, a botched DNS configuration usually causes a computer's network applications to fail just like the user's applications in our example scenario.

> If you can ping a host using its IP address but not its name, you probably have some type of name-resolution issue. It's probably lurking somewhere within a DNS configuration.

Wrong subnet mask   When network devices look at an IP address configuration, they see a combination of the IP address and the subnet mask. The device uses the subnet mask to establish which part of the address represents the network address and which part represents the host address. So clearly, a subnet mask that is configured wrong has the same nasty effect as a wrong IP address configuration does on communications. Again, a subnet mask is generally configured by the DHCP server; if you're going to enter it manually, make sure the subnet mask is tight or you'll end up tangling with the fallout caused by the entire address's misconfiguration.

With all that in mind, let's move on with our troubleshooting steps.

Step 3: Test the Theory to Determine Cause

Let's look into the matter by first checking the IP configuration of the host that just happens to include DNS information. You use the `ipconfig /all` command to show the IP configuration. The `/all` switch will give you the DNS information you need.

```
Administrator: Command Prompt

Ethernet adapter Local Area Connection:

   Connection-specific DNS Suffix  . : domain.actdsltmp
   Description . . . . . . . . . . . : Intel(R) 82566MM Gigabit Network Connecti
on
   Physical Address. . . . . . . . . : 00-1E-37-D0-E9-35
   DHCP Enabled. . . . . . . . . . . : Yes
   Autoconfiguration Enabled . . . . : Yes
   Link-local IPv6 Address . . . . . : fe80::2836:c43e:274b:f08c%11(Preferred)
   IPv4 Address. . . . . . . . . . . : 192.168.0.6(Preferred)
   Subnet Mask . . . . . . . . . . . : 255.255.255.0
   Lease Obtained. . . . . . . . . . : Friday, November 14, 2008 7:21:34 AM
   Lease Expires . . . . . . . . . . : Sunday, November 16, 2008 2:39:01 PM
   Default Gateway . . . . . . . . . : 192.168.0.1
   DHCP Server . . . . . . . . . . . : 192.168.0.1
   DNS Servers . . . . . . . . . . . : 1.1.1.1
                                       2.2.2.2
   NetBIOS over Tcpip. . . . . . . . : Enabled
```

Check out the DNS entries: 1.1.1.1 and 2.2.2.2. Is this right? What are they supposed to be? You can find this out by checking the addresses on a working host, but let's check the settings on your troubled host's adapter first. Click Start, then Control Panel, then Network And Sharing Center, and then Manage Network Connections on the left side of the screen, which will take you to this screen.

Now, click the interface in question, and click Properties. You receive this screen.

From here, you highlight Internet Protocol Version 4, and click Properties (or just double-click). From the next screen, do you see what may be causing the problem?

As I said, you're using DHCP right? But DNS is statically configured on this host. Interesting enough, when you set a static DNS entry on an interface, it will override the DHCP-provided DNS entry.

Step 4: Establish a Plan of Action to Resolve the Problem and Identify Potential Effects

Now that you've identified some possible changes, you've got to follow through and test your solution to see if you really solved the problem. In this case, you ask the user to try to access the intranet server (because that's what they called about). Basically, you just ask the user to try doing whatever it was they couldn't do when they called you in the first place. If it works—sweet—problem solved. If not, try the operation yourself.

Now you can test the proposed solution on the computer of the user who is still waiting for a solution. To do that, you need to check the DNS configuration on your host. But first, let me point out something about the neglected user's network. All hosts are using DHCP, so it's really weird that a single user is having a DNS resolution issue.

So, to fix the problem and get your user back in the game, just click Obtain DNS Server Address Automatically, and then click OK. Voilà!

Let's take a look at the output of `ipconfig /all` and see if you received new DNS server addresses.

```
Windows IP Configuration

    Host Name . . . . . . . . . . . . : globalnet-todd
    Primary Dns Suffix  . . . . . . . : globalnet.local
    Node Type . . . . . . . . . . . . : Hybrid
    IP Routing Enabled. . . . . . . . : No
    WINS Proxy Enabled. . . . . . . . : No
    DNS Suffix Search List. . . . . . : globalnet.local

Ethernet adapter Local Area Connection 3:

    Connection-specific DNS Suffix  . : globalnet.local
    Description . . . . . . . . . . . : Cisco Systems VPN Adapter
    Physical Address. . . . . . . . . : 00-05-9A-3C-78-00
    DHCP Enabled. . . . . . . . . . . : No
    Autoconfiguration Enabled . . . . : Yes
    Link-local IPv6 Address . . . . . : fe80::6cd5:2e37:bd94:1004%21(Preferred)
    IPv4 Address. . . . . . . . . . . : 10.100.10.58(Preferred)
    Subnet Mask . . . . . . . . . . . : 255.255.255.0
    Default Gateway . . . . . . . . . :
    DNS Servers . . . . . . . . . . . : 10.100.36.12
                                        10.100.36.13
    Primary WINS Server . . . . . . . : 10.100.36.13
    NetBIOS over Tcpip. . . . . . . . : Enabled
```

All good; you did. And you can test the host by trying to use HTTP to connect to a web page on the intranet server and even pinging by hostname. Congratulations on solving your first trouble ticket!

If things hadn't worked out so well, you would go back to step 2, select a new possible cause, and redo step 3. If this happens, keep track of what worked and what didn't so you don't make the same mistakes twice.

It's pretty much common sense that you should change settings like this only when you fully understand the effect your changes will have, or when you're asked to by someone who does. The incorrect configuration of these settings will disable the normal operation of your workstation, and, well, it seems that someone (the user, maybe?) did something they shouldn't have or you wouldn't have had the pleasure of solving this problem.

> You have to be super careful when changing settings and always check out a troubled host's network settings. Don't just assume that because they're using DHCP, someone has screwed up the static configuration.

Step 5: Implement the Solution or Escalate as Necessary

Although it's true that CompTIA doesn't expect you to fix every single network problem that could possibly happen in the universe, they actually do expect you to get pretty close to determining exactly what the problem is. And if you can't fix it, you'll be expected to know how to escalate it and to whom. You are only as good as your resources—be they your own skill set, a book like this one, other more reference-oriented technical books, the Internet, or even a guru at a call center.

I know it seems like I talked to death physical and logical issues that cause problems in a network, but trust me, with what I've taught you, you're just getting started. There's a galaxy of networking evils that we have not even touched on because they're far beyond the objectives for Network+ certification and, therefore, the scope of this book. But out there in the real world, you'll get calls about them anyway, and because you're not yet equipped to handle them yourself, you need to escalate these nasties to a senior network engineer who has the additional experience and knowledge required to resolve the problems.

Some of the calamities that you should escalate are as follows:

- Switching loops
- Missing routes
- Routing loops
- Routing problems
- MTU black hole
- Bad modules
- Proxy Address Resolution Protocol (ARP)
- Broadcast storms

> After you escalated the problem, you are done with the seven-step troubleshooting model and you now need to meet with the emergency response team to determine the next step.

And just as with other problems, you have to be able to identify these events because if you can't do that, how else will you know that you need to escalate them?

Switching loops   Today's networks often connect switches with redundant links to provide for fault tolerance and load balancing. Protocols such as Spanning Tree Protocol (STP) prevent switching loops and simultaneously maintain fault tolerance. If STP fails, it takes some expertise to reconfigure and repair the network, so you just need to be concerned with being able to identify the problem so you can escalate it. Remember, when you hear users complaining that the network works fine for a while, then unexpectedly goes down for about a minute, and then goes back to being fine, it's definitely an STP convergence issue that's pretty tough to find and fix. Escalate this problem ASAP!

Missing routes   Routers must have routes either configured or learned to function. There are a number of issues that can prevent a router from learning the routes that it needs. To determine if a router has the route to the network in question, execute the `show ip route` command and view the routing table. This can save a lot of additional troubleshooting if you can narrow the problem to a missing route.

Routing loops   Routing protocols are often used on networks to control traffic efficiently while preventing routing loops that happen when a routing protocol hasn't been configured properly or network changes didn't get the attention they deserved. Routing loops can also happen if you or the network admin blew the static configuration and created conflicting routes through the network. This evil event affects the traffic flow for all users, and because it's pretty complicated to fix, again, it's up, up, and away with this one. You can expect routing loops to occur if your network is running old routing protocols like Routing Information Protocol (RIP) and RIPv2. Just upgrading your routing protocol to Enhanced Interior Gateway Routing Protocol (EIGRP), Open Shortest Path First (OSPF), or Intermediate System-to-Intermediate System (IS-IS) will usually take care of the problem once and for all. Anyway, escalate this problem to the router group—which hopefully is soon to be you.

Routing problems   Routing packets through the many subnets of a large enterprise while still maintaining security can be a tremendous challenge. A router's configuration can include all kinds of stuff like access lists, Network Address Translation (NAT), Port Address Translation (PAT), and even authentication protocols like Remote Authentication Dial In User Service (RADIUS) and Terminal Access Controller Access-Control System (TACACS). Particularly diabolical, errant configuration changes can trigger a domino effect that can derail traffic down the wrong path or even cause it to come to a grinding halt and stop traversing the network completely. To identify routing problems, check to see if someone has simply set a wrong default route on a router. This can easily create routing loops. I see it all the time. These configurations can be highly complex and specific to a particular device, so they need to be escalated to the top dogs—get the problem to the best sys admin in the router group.

MTU black hole   On a WAN connection, communication routes may fail if an intermediate network segment has an MTU that is smaller than the maximum packet size of the communicating hosts—and if the router does not send an appropriate Internet Control Message Protocol (ICMP) response to this condition. If ICMP traffic is allowed, the routers will take care of this problem using ICMP messages. However, as ICMP traffic is increasingly being blocked, this can create what is called a black hole. This will probably be an issue you will escalate.

Bad modules   Some multilayer switches and routers have slots available to add new features. The hardware that fits in these slots is called modules. These modules can host fiber connections, wireless connections, and other types as well. A common example is the Cisco Small Form-Factor Pluggable (SFP) Gigabit Interface Ethernet Converter (GBIC). This is an input-output device that plugs into an existing Gigabit Ethernet port or slot providing a variety of additional capabilities to the device hosting the slot or port. Conversion examples include from Ethernet to fiber. Like any piece of hardware made by humans, the modules can fail. It is always worth checking if there are no other reasons a link is not functioning.

Proxy ARP   Address Resolution Protocol (ARP) is a service that resolves IP addresses to MAC addresses. Proxy ARP is just wrong to use in today's networks, but hosts and routers still have it on by default. The idea of Proxy ARP was to solve the problem of a host being able to have only one configured default gateway. To allow redundancy, Proxy ARP running on a router will respond to an ARP broadcast from a host that's sending a packet to a remote network—but the host doesn't have a default gateway set. So the router responds by being the proxy for the remote host, which in turn makes the local host think the remote host is really local; as a result, the local host sends the packets to the router, which then forwards the packets to the remote host. Most of the time, in today's networks, this does not work well, if at all. Disable Proxy ARP on your routers, and make sure you have default gateways set on all your hosts. If you need router redundancy, there are much better solutions available than Proxy ARP! This is another job for the routing group.

Broadcast storms   When a switch receives a broadcast, it will normally flood the broadcast out all the ports except for the one the broadcast came in on. If STP fails between switches or is disabled by an administrator, it's possible that the traffic could continue to be flooded repeatedly throughout the switch topology. When this happens, the network can get so busy that normal traffic can't traverse it—an event referred to as a *broadcast storm*. As you can imagine, this is a particularly gruesome thing to have to troubleshoot and fix because you need to find the one bad link that is causing the mess while the network is probably still up and running—but at a heavily congested crawl. Escalate ASAP to experts!

Step 6: Verify Full System Functionality and If Applicable Implement Preventative Measures

A trap that any network technician can fall into is solving one problem and thinking it's all fixed without stopping to consider the possible consequences of their solution. The cure can be worse than the disease, and it's possible that your solution falls into this category. So before you fully implement the solution to a problem, make sure you totally understand the ramifications of doing so—clearly, if it causes more problems than it fixes, you should toss it and find a different solution that does no harm.

Many people update a router's operating system or firmware just because a new version of code is released from the manufacturer. Do not do this on your production routers—just say no! Always test any new code before upgrading your production routers: Like a bad solution, sometimes the new code provides new features but creates more problems, and the cons outweigh the pros.

Step 7: Document Findings, Actions, and Outcomes

I can't stress enough how vital network documentation is. Always document problems and solutions so that you have the information at hand when a similar problem arises in the future. With documented solutions to documented problems, you can assemble your own database of information that you can use to troubleshoot other problems. Be sure to include information like the following:

- A description of the conditions surrounding the problem
- The OS version, the software version, the type of computer, and the type of NIC
- Whether you were able to reproduce the problem
- The solutions you tried
- The ultimate solution

 Real World Scenario

Network Documentation

I don't know how many times I've gone into a place and asked where their documentation was only to be met with a blank stare. I was recently at a small business that was experiencing network problems. The first question I asked was, "Do you have any kind of network documentation?" I got the blank stare. So, we proceeded to search through lots of receipts and other paperwork—anything we could find to help us understand the network layout and figure out exactly what was on the network. It turned out they had recently bought a WAP, and it was having trouble connecting—something that would've taken me five minutes to fix instead of searching through a mess for a couple hours!

Documentation doesn't have to look like a sleek owner's manual or anything—it can consist of a simple three-ring binder with an up-to-date network map; receipts for network equipment; a pocket for owner's manuals; and a stack of loose-leaf paper to record services, changes, network-addressing assignments, access lists, and so on. Just this little bit of documentation can save lots of time and money and prevent grief, especially in the critical first few months of a new network install.

Troubleshooting Tips

Now that you've got the basics of network troubleshooting down pat, I'm going to go over a few really handy troubleshooting tips for you to arm yourself with even further in the quest to conquer the world's networking evils.

Don't Overlook the Small Stuff

The super simple stuff (SSS) I referred to at the beginning of this chapter should never be overlooked—ever! Here's a quick review: Just remember that problems are often caused by little things like a bad power switch; a power switch in the wrong position; a card or port that's not working, indicated by a link light that's not lit; or simply operator error (OE). Even the most experienced system administrator has forgotten to turn on the power, left a cable unplugged, or mistyped a username and password—not me, of course, but others...

And make sure that users get solid training for the systems they use. An ounce of prevention is worth a pound of cure, and you'll experience dramatically fewer ID10T errors this way.

Prioritize Your Problems

Being a network administrator or technician of even a fairly small network can keep you hopping, and it's pretty rare that you'll get calls for help one at a time and never be interrupted by more coming in. Closer to reality is receiving yet another call when you already have three people waiting for service. So, you've got to prioritize.

You start this process by again asking some basic questions to determine the severity of the problem being reported. Clearly, if the new call is about something little and you already have a huge issue to deal with, you should put the new call on hold or get their info and get back to them later. If you establish a good set of priorities, you'll make much better use of your time. Here's an example of the rank you probably want to give to networking problems, from highest priority to lowest:

- Total network failure (affects everyone)
- Partial network failure (affects small groups of users)
- Small network failure (affects a small, single group of users)
- Total workstation failure (single user can't work at all)
- Partial workstation failure (single user can't do most tasks)
- Minor issue (single user has problems that crop up now and then)

Mitigating circumstances can, of course, change the order of this list. For example, if the president of the company can't retrieve email, you'd take the express elevator to their office as soon as you got the call, right? And even a minor issue can move up the ladder if it's persistent enough.

Don't fall prey to thinking that simple problems are easier to deal with because even though you may be able to bring up a crashed server in minutes, a user who doesn't know how to make columns line up in Microsoft Word could take a chunk out of your day. You'd want to put the latter problem toward the bottom of the list because of the time involved—it's a lot more efficient to solve problems for a big group of people than to fix this one user's problem immediately.

Some network administrators list all network-service requests on a chalkboard or a whiteboard. They then prioritize them based on the previously discussed criteria. Some larger companies have written support-call tracking software whose only function is to track and prioritize all network and computer problems. Use whatever method makes you comfortable, but prioritize your calls.

Check the Software Configuration

Often, network problems can be traced to software configuration, like our DNS configuration scenario; so when you're checking for software problems, don't forget to check types of configurations:

- DNS configuration
- WINS configuration
- HOSTS file
- The Registry

Software-configuration settings love to hide in places like these and can be notoriously hard to find (especially in the Registry).

Also, look for lines that have been commented out either intentionally or accidentally in text-configuration files—another place for clues. A command such as REM or REMARK, or asterisk or semicolon characters, indicates comment lines in a file.

 In the HOSTS file, a pound sign (#) is used to indicate a comment line.

Don't Overlook Physical Conditions

You want to make sure that from a network-design standpoint, the physical environment for a server is optimized for placement, temperature, and humidity. When troubleshooting an obscure network problem, don't forget to check the physical conditions under which the network device is operating. Check for problems like these:

- Excessive heat
- Excessive humidity (condensation)
- Low humidity (leads to electrostatic discharge [ESD] problems)
- EMI/RFI problems
- ESD problems
- Power problems
- Unplugged cables

Don't Overlook Cable Problems

Cables, generally speaking, work fine once they are installed properly. If the patch cable isn't the problem, use a cable tester (not a tone generator and locator) to find the source of the problem.

One of the easiest mistakes to make, especially if cables are not labeled, is to use a crossover cable where a straight through cable should be used or vice-versa. In either case, when you do this it causes TXRX reversal. What's that? That when the Transmit wire is connected to Transmit and the Receive wire to Receive. That sounds good, but it needs to be Transmit to Receive. See more about this issue in Chapter 3, "Networking Topologies, Connectors, and Wiring Standards."

Wires that are moved can be prone to breaking or shorting, and a short can happen when the wire conductor comes in contact with another conductive surface, changing the path of the electrical signal. The signal will go someplace else instead of to the intended recipient. You can use cable testers to test for many types of problems:

- Broken cables
- Incorrect connections
- Interference levels
- Total cable length (for length restrictions)
- Cable shorts
- Connector problems

As a matter of fact, cable testers are so sophisticated that they can even indicate the exact location of a cable break, accurate to within 6 inches or better.

Check for Viruses

People overlook scanning for viruses because they assume that the network's virus-checking software has already picked them off. But to be effective, the software must be kept up-to-date, and updates are made available pretty much daily. You've got to run the virus-definition update utility to keep the virus-definition file current.

If you are having strange, unusual, irreproducible problems with a workstation, try scanning it with an up-to-date virus-scan utility. You'd be surprised how many times people have spent hours and hours troubleshooting a strange problem only to run a virus-scan utility, find and clean out one or more viruses, and have the problem disappear like magic.

Summary

In this chapter, you learned about all things troubleshooting, and you now know how to sleuth out and solve a lot of network problems. You learned to first check all the SSS and about how to approach problem resolution by eliminating what the problem is *not*. You learned how to narrow the problem down to its basics and define it.

Next, you learned a systematic approach using a seven-step troubleshooting model to troubleshoot most of the problems you'll run into in networking. And you also learned about some resources you can use to help you during the troubleshooting process. In addition, you learned how important documentation is to the health of your network.

Finally, I gave you a bunch of cool tips to further equip you, tips about prioritizing issues, checking for configuration issues, environmental factors—even hunting down viruses. As you venture out into the real world, keep these tips in mind; along with your own personal experience, they'll really help make you into an expert troubleshooter.

Exam Essentials

Know the seven troubleshooting steps, in order.   The steps, in order, are as follows:

1. Identify the problem.
2. Establish a theory of probable cause.
3. Test the theory to determine cause.
4. Establish a plan of action to resolve the problem and identify potential effects.
5. Implement the solution or escalate as necessary.
6. Verify full system functionality, and if applicable, implement preventative measures.
7. Document findings, actions, and outcomes.

Be able to identify a link light.   A link light is the small, usually green LED on the back of a network card. This LED is typically found next to the media connector on a NIC and is usually labeled Link.

Understand how proper network use procedures can affect operation of a network.   If a user is not following a network use procedure properly (for example, not logging in correctly), that user may report a problem where none exists. A good network troubleshooter should know how to differentiate between a network hardware/software problem and a "lack of user training" problem.

Know how to narrow down a problem to one specific area or cause. Most problems can be traced to one specific area or cause. You must be able to determine if a problem is specific to one user or a bunch of users, specific to one computer or a bunch of computers, and related to hardware or software. The answers to these questions will give you a very specific problem focus.

Know how to detect cabling-related problems. Generally speaking, most cabling-related problems can be traced by plugging the suspect workstation into a known, working network port. If the problem disappears (or at the very least changes significantly), it is related to the cabling for that workstation.

Written Lab

In this section, write the answers to the following questions:

1. What is step 3 of the seven-step troubleshooting model?

2. What is step 7 of the seven-step troubleshooting model?

3. How is crosstalk minimized in twisted-pair cabling?

4. If you plug a host into a switch port and the user cannot get to the server or other services they need to access despite a working link light, what could the problem be?

5. What is it called when a cable has two wires of a twisted pair connected to two wires from a different pair?

6. When a signal moves through any medium, the medium itself will degrade the signal. What is this called?

7. What is step 4 of the seven-step troubleshooting model?

8. What is step 5 of the seven-step troubleshooting model?

9. What are some of the problems that, if determined, should be escalated?

10. What cable issues should you know and understand for network troubleshooting?

    You can find the answers in Appendix B.

Review Questions

You can find the answers in Appendix A.

1. Which of the following are not steps in the Network+ troubleshooting model? (Choose all that apply.)

   A. Reboot the servers.

   B. Identify the problem.

   C. Test the theory to determine the cause.

   D. Implement the solution or escalate as necessary.

   E. Document findings, actions, and outcomes.

   F. Reboot all the routers.

2. You have a user who cannot connect to the network. What is the first thing you could check to determine the source of the problem?

   A. Workstation configuration

   B. Connectivity

   C. Patch cable

   D. Server configuration

3. When wireless users complain that they are losing their connection to applications during a session, what is the source if the problem?

   A. Incorrect SSID

   B. Latency

   C. Incorrect encryption

   D. MAC address filter

4. Several users can't log in to the server. Which action would help you to narrow the problem down to the workstations, network, or server?

   A. Run `tracert` from a workstation.

   B. Check the server console for user connections.

   C. Run `netstat` on all workstations.

   D. Check the network diagnostics.

5. A user can't log in to the network. She can't even connect to the Internet over the LAN. Other users in the same area aren't experiencing any problems. You attempt to log in as this user from your workstation with her username and password and don't experience any problems. However, you cannot log in with either her username or yours from her workstation. What is a likely cause of the problem?

   A. Insufficient rights to access the server

   B. A bad patch cable

   C. Server down

   D. Wrong username and password

6. A user is experiencing problems logging in to a Unix server. He can connect to the Internet over the LAN. Other users in the same area aren't experiencing any problems. You attempt logging in as this user from your workstation with his username and password and don't experience any problems. However, you cannot log in with either his username or yours from his workstation. What is a likely cause of the problem?

   A. The Caps Lock key is pressed.

   B. The network hub is malfunctioning.

   C. You have a downed server.

   D. You have a jabbering NIC.

7. You receive a call from a user who is having issues connecting to a new VPN. Which is the first step you should take?

   A. Find out what has changed.

   B. Reboot the workstation.

   C. Document the solution.

   D. Identify the symptoms and potential causes.

8. A workstation presents an error message to a user. The message states that a duplicate IP address has been detected on the network. After establishing what has changed in the network, what should be the next step using the standard troubleshooting model?

   A. Test the result.

   B. Select the most probable cause.

   C. Create an action plan.

   D. Identify the results and effects of the solution.

9. You have gathered information on a network issue and determined the affected areas of the network. What is your next step in resolving this issue?

   A. You should implement the best solution for the issue.

   B. You should test the best solution for the issue.

   C. You should check to see if there have been any recent changes to this affected part of the network.

   D. You should consider any negative impact to the network that might be caused by a solution.

10. A user calls you, reporting a problem logging in to the corporate intranet. You can access the website without problems using the user's username and password. At your request, the user has tried logging in from other workstations but has been unsuccessful. What is the most likely cause of the problem?

    A. The user is logging in incorrectly.

    B. The network is down.

    C. The intranet server is locked up.

    D. The server is not routing packets correctly to that user's workstation.

11. You have just implemented a solution and you want to celebrate your success. But what should you do next before you start your celebration?

    A. Gather more information about the issue.

    B. Document the issue and the solution that was implemented.

    C. Test the solution and identify other effects it may have.

    D. Escalate the issue.

12. You can ping the local router and web server that a local user is trying to reach, but you cannot reach the web page that resides on that server. From step 2 of the troubleshooting model, what is a possible problem that would lead to this situation?

    A. Your network cable is unplugged.

    B. There is a problem with your browser.

    C. Your NIC has failed.

    D. The web server is unplugged.

13. When troubleshooting an obscure network problem, what physical conditions should be reviewed to make sure the network device is operating correctly?

    A. Excessive heat

    B. Low/excessive humidity

    C. ESD problems

    D. All of the above

14. Which of the following is not a basic physical issue that can occur on a network when a user is connected via cable?

A. Crosstalk

B. Shorts

C. Open impedance mismatch

D. DNS configurations

15. You are troubleshooting a LAN switch and have identified the symptoms. What is the next step you should take?

A. Escalate the issue.

B. Create an action plan.

C. Implement the solution.

D. Determine the scope of the problem.

16. A user calls you, complaining that he can't access the corporate intranet web server. You try the same address, and you receive a Host Not Found error. Several minutes later, another user reports the same problem. You can still send email and transfer files to another server. What is the most likely cause of the problem?

A. The hub is unplugged.

B. The server is not routing protocols to your workstation.

C. The user's workstation is not connected to the network.

D. The web server is down.

17. You have implemented and tested a solution and identified any other effects the solution may have. What is your next step?

A. Create an action plan.

B. Close the case and head home for the day.

C. Reboot the Windows server.

D. Document the solution.

18. Users are reporting that they can access the Internet but not the internal company website. Which of the following is the most likely problem?

A. The DNS entry for the server is non-authoritative.

B. The intranet server is down.

C. The DNS address handed out by DHCP is incorrect.

D. The default gateway is incorrect.

19. Several users have complained about the server's poor performance as of late. You know that the memory installed in the server is sufficient. What could you check to determine the source of the problem?

    A. Server's NIC link light

    B. Protocol analyzer

    C. Performance-monitoring tools

    D. Server's system log file

20. You lose power to your computer room and the switches in your network do not come back up when everything is brought online. After you have identified the affected areas, established the cause, and escalated this problem, what do you do next?

    A. Start to implement a solution to get those users back online ASAP.

    B. Create an action plan and solution.

    C. Meet with the emergency response team to determine the next step.

    D. Copy all the working routers' configurations to the nonworking switches.

Chapter

20

Management, Monitoring, and Optimization

THE FOLLOWING COMPTIA NETWORK+ EXAM OBJECTIVES ARE COVERED IN THIS CHAPTER:

✓ **4.4 Given a scenario, use the appropriate network monitoring resource to analyze traffic.**

- SNMP
- SNMPv2
- SNMPv3
- Syslog
- System logs
- History logs
- General logs
- Traffic analysis
- Network sniffer

✓ **4.5 Describe the purpose of configuration management documentation.**

- Wire schemes
- Network maps
- Documentation
- Cable management
- Asset management
- Baselines
- Change management

✓ **4.6 Explain different methods and rationales for network performance optimization.**

- Methods:
  - QoS
  - Traffic shaping
  - Load balancing
  - High availability
  - Caching engines
  - Fault tolerance
  - CARP
- Reasons:
  - Latency sensitivity
  - High bandwidth applications (VoIP, video applications, unified communications)
  - Uptime

✓ **1.9 Identify virtual network components.**

- Virtual switches
- Virtual desktops
- Virtual servers
- Virtual PBX
- Onsite vs. offsite
- Network as a Service (NaaS)

If you didn't just skip to the end of this book, you've trekked through enough material to know that without a doubt, the task of designing, implementing, and maintaining a state-of-the-art network doesn't happen magically. Ending up with a great network requires some really solid planning before you buy even one device for it. And planning includes thoroughly analyzing your design for potential flaws and optimizing configurations everywhere you can to maximize the network's future throughput and performance. If you blow it in this phase, trust me—you'll pay dearly later in bottom-line costs and countless hours consumed troubleshooting and putting out the fires of faulty design.

Start planning by creating an outline that precisely delimits all goals and business requirements for the network, and refer back to it often to ensure that you don't deliver a network that falls short of your client's present needs or fails to offer the scalability to grow with those needs. Drawing out your design and jotting down all the relevant information really helps in spotting weaknesses and faults. If you have a team, make sure everyone on it gets to examine the design and evaluate it, and keep that network plan up throughout the installation phase. Hang on to it after implementation has been completed as well because having it is like having the keys to the kingdom—it will enable you to efficiently troubleshoot any issues that could arise after everything is in place and up and running.

High-quality documentation should include a baseline for network performance because you and your client need to know what "normal" looks like in order to detect problems before they develop into disasters. Don't forget to verify that the network conforms to all internal and external regulations and that you've developed and itemized solid management procedures and security policies for future network administrators to refer to and follow.

I'll begin this chapter by going over the fundamentals of things like plans, diagrams, baselines, rules, and regulations and then move on to cover critical hardware and software utilities you should have in your problem resolution arsenal, like packet sniffers, throughput testers, connectivity packages, and even different types of event logs on your servers. And because even the best designs usually need a little boost after they've been up and running for a while, I'll wrap things up by telling you about some cool ways you can tweak things to really jack up a network's performance, optimize its data throughput, and, well, keep it all humming along as efficiently and smoothly as possible.

To find up-to-the-minute updates for this chapter, please see www.lammle.com/forum or the book's web site at www.sybex.com/go/netplus2e.

Managing Network Documentation

I'll admit it—creating network documentation is one of my least favorite tasks in network administration. It just isn't as exciting to me as learning about the coolest new technology or tackling and solving a challenging problem. Part of it may be that I figure I know my networks well enough—after all, I installed and configured them, so if something comes up, it should be easy to figure it out and fix it, right? And most of the time I can do that, but as networks get bigger and more complex, it gets harder and harder to remember it all. Plus, it's integral part of the service I provide for my clients to have seriously solid documentation in hand to refer to after I've left the scene and turned their network over to them. So while I'll admit that creating documentation isn't something I get excited about, I know from experience that having it around is critical when problems come up—for myself and for my clients' technicians and administrators, who may not have been part of the installation process and simply aren't familiar with the system.

Using SNMP

In Chapter 6, "Introduction to the Internet Protocol," I introduced you to Simple Network Management Protocol (SNMP), which is used to gather information from and send settings to devices that are SNMP compatible. (Don't forget to review the differences between version 1, 2, and 3 that we discussed there!) Remember, I told you it gathers data by polling the devices on the network from a management station at fixed or random intervals, requiring them to disclose certain information. Consequently, SNMP can help simplify the process of gathering information of your entire internetwork.

SNMP uses UDP to transfer messages back and forth between the management system and the agents running on the managed devices. Inside the UDP packets (called *datagrams*) are commands from the management system to the agent. These commands can be used to either get information from the device about its state (SNMP GetRequest) or to make a change in the device's configuration (SetRequest). If a GetRequest command has been sent, the device will respond with an SNMP response. If there is an item of information of particular interest to an administrator about the device, the administrator can set what is called a *trap* on the device.

So, no whining! Begrudgingly or not, we're going to create some sweet documentation. Because you probably don't want to redo it, it's a really good idea to keep it safe in at least three forms:

- An electronic copy that you can easily modify after configuration changes
- A hard copy in a binder of some sort, stored in an easily accessible location
- A copy on an external drive to keep in a really safe place (even off site) in case something happens to the other two or the building or part of it burns to the ground

Why the hard copy, you ask? Well, what if the computer storing the electronic copy crashes and burns just when a major crisis develops? Good thing you have the paper on hand! Plus, sometimes you'll be troubleshooting on the run—maybe literally, as in running down the hall to the disaster's origin. Having that binder containing key configuration information on board could save you a lot of time and trouble; plus, it's also handy for making notes to yourself as you troubleshoot. And depending on the size of the intranet and the amount of people staffing the IT department, you may even need to have several hard copies. Just always make sure they're checked out only by staff who are cleared to have them, and that they're all returned to a secure location at the end of each shift. You definitely don't want that information in the wrong hands.

Now that I have (I hope) got you totally convinced that you need to have documentation, let's take a look into the different documentation types so you can learn how to assemble it. Network documentation basically falls into three categories:

- Schematics and diagrams
- Baselines
- Policies, procedures, and regulations

Schematics and Diagrams

No, reading network documentation can't exactly compete with racing your friends on jet skis, but it's really not that bad. It's better than eating canned spinach, and sometimes it's actually interesting to check out schematics and diagrams—especially when they describe innovative, elegant designs or when you're hunting down clues needed to solve an intricate problem with an elusive solution. I can't tell you how many times, if something isn't working between point A and point B, a solid diagram of the network that precisely describes exactly what exists between point A and point B has totally saved the day. Other times these tools come in handy is when you need to extend your network and you want a clear picture of how the expanded version will look and work. Will the new addition cause one part of the network to become bogged down while another remains underutilized? You get the idea.

Diagrams can be simple sketches created while brainstorming or troubleshooting on the fly, or they can be highly detailed, refined illustrations created with some of the flashy software packages available today, like Microsoft Visio, SmartDraw, and a host of computer-aided design (CAD) programs. Some of the more complex varieties, especially CAD programs, are super pricey. But whatever tool you use to draw pictures about your networks, they basically fall into these three groups:

- Wiring diagrams/schematics
- Physical network diagrams
- Logical network diagrams

Wiring Schematics

Wireless is definitely the wave of the future, but for now even the most extensive wireless networks have a wired backbone they rely on to connect them to the rest of humanity.

That skeleton is made up of cabled physical media like coax, fiber, and twisted pair. Surprisingly, it is the latter—specifically, unshielded twisted pair (UTP)—that screams to be pictured in a diagram. You'll see why in a minute. To help you follow me, let's review what we learned in Chapter 3, "Networking Topologies, Connectors, and Wiring Standards." Let's start by checking out Figure 20.1 (a diagram!) that pictures the fact that UTP cables use an RJ-45 connector (*RJ* stands for *registered jack*).

FIGURE 20.1   RJ-45 connector

What we see here is that pin 1 is on the left and pin 8 is on the right, so clearly, within your UTP cable, you need to make sure the right wires get to the right pins. No worries if you got your cables premade from the store, but if you make them yourself because it saves money and allows you to customize cable lengths (wise), this is really important. Table 20.1 matches the colors for the wire associated with each pin, based on the Electronic Industries Association and the Telecommunications Industry Alliance (EIA/TIA) 568B wiring standard.

TABLE 20.1   Standard EIA/TIA 568B wiring

Pin	Color
1	White/Orange
2	Orange
3	White/Green
4	Blue
5	White/Blue
6	Green
7	White/Brown
8	Brown

Standard drop cables or *patch cables* have the pins in the same order on both connectors. If you're connecting a computer to another computer directly, you should already know that you need a *crossover cable* that has one connector with flipped wires—specifically, pins 1 and 3 and pins 2 and 6 get switched to ensure that the send port from one computer's Network

Interface Card (NIC) gets attached to the receive port on the other computer's NIC. Crossover cables were also used to connect older routers, switches, and hubs through their uplink ports. Figure 20.2 shows you what this would look like.

FIGURE 20.2   Two ends of a crossover cable

End 1 (Standard)		End 2 (Crossed over)	
1	White and Orange	1	White and Green
2	Orange	2	Green
3	White and Green	3	White and Orange
4	Blue	4	Blue
5	White and Blue	5	White and Blue
6	Green	6	Orange
7	White and Brown	7	White and Brown
8	Brown	8	Brown

The crossover cable shown in Figure 20.2 is for connections up to 100BaseTX. If you are using 1000BaseT4, all four pairs of wires get crossed at the opposite end, meaning pins 4 and 7 and pins 5 and 8 get crossed as well. The Automatic MDI/MDI+ Configuration standard (an optional feature of the 1000BaseT standard) makes the need for crossover cables between gigabit-capable interfaces a thing of the past.

This is where having a diagram is as good as gold. Let's say you're troubleshooting a network and discover connectivity problems between two hosts. Because you've got the map, you know the cable running between them just happens to be a brand-new custom-made one, so you go there immediately knowing that cable probably wasn't made well and is causing the snag.

Another reason it's so important to diagram all things wiring is that all wires have to plug in somewhere, and it's really good to know where that is. Whether it's into a hub, a switch, a router, a workstation, or the wall, you positively need to know the who, what, where, when, and how of the way the wiring is attached.

After adding a new cable segment on your network, you need to update the wiring schematics.

For medium to large networks, devices like hubs, switches, and routers are rack-mounted and would look something like the switches in Figure 20.3.

FIGURE 20.3 Rack-mounted switches

Knowing someone or something's name is important because it helps us differentiate between people and things—especially when communicating with each other. If you want to be specific, you can't just say, "You know that router in the rack?" This is why coming up with a good naming system for all the devices living in your racks will be invaluable for ensuring that your, err, wires don't get crossed (sorry!). Figure 20.3 displays switches with labels taped on them to designate them Sales and Marketing (names not displayed in the picture), which indicates they're located in Sales and Marketing, respectively. Last, you can see on some of the cables that they are marked X/O for crossover.

Okay, I know it probably seems like we're edging over into obsessive-compulsive disorder territory, but stay with me here; in addition to labeling, well, everything so far, you should really label both ends of your cables too. If something happens (earthquake, tsunami, temper tantrum, even repairs) and more than one cable gets unplugged at the same time, it can get messy scrambling to reconnect them from memory—fast.

Physical Network Diagrams

A *physical network diagram* contains all the physical devices and connectivity paths on your network and should accurately picture how your network physically fits together in detail. Again, I know it seems like overkill, but ideally, your network diagram should list and map everything you would need to rebuild your network from scratch if you had to. This is actually what this type of diagram is designed for. However, another example of a physical network diagram is one that includes the firmware revision on all the switches and access points in your network. Besides having your physical network detailed, you need to understand the connections, types of hardware, and their firmware revisions. This document is very helpful in troubleshooting.

⊕ **Real World Scenario**

Avoiding Confusion

Naming your network devices is no big deal, but for some reason, coming up with systems for naming devices and numbering connections can really stress people out.

Let me ease the pain. Let's say your network has two racks of switches, creatively named Block A and Block B. (Sounds like a prison, I know, but it's just to keep things simple for this example. In the real world, you can come up with whatever naming system works for you.)

Anyway, I'm going to use the letters *FETH* for Fast Ethernet; and because each rack has six switches, I'm going to number them (surprise!) 1 through 6. Because we read from left to right, it's intuitive to number the ports on each switch that way too.

Having a solid naming system makes thing so much more efficient—even if it's a bit of a hassle to create. For instance, if you were the system administrator in this example and suddenly all computers connected to FETHB-3 couldn't access any network resources, you would have a pretty good idea of where to look first, right?

If you can't diagram everything, at least make sure all network devices are listed. As I said, physical network diagrams can run from simple, hand-drawn models to insanely complex monsters created by software packages like SmartDraw, Visio, and AutoCAD. Figure 20.4 shows a simple diagram that most of us could draw by hand.

FIGURE 20.4   Simple network physical diagram

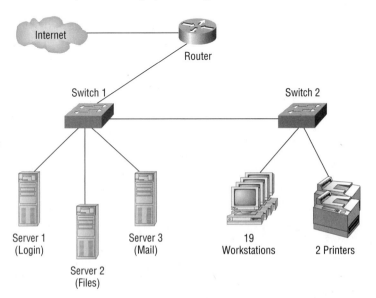

For the artistically impaired, or if you just want a flashier version, Figure 20.5 exhibits a more complex physical diagram. This is an actual sample of what SmartDraw can do for you, and you can get it at www.smartdraw.com. In addition, Microsoft Visio provides many or possibly more of these same functions.

My last example, also courtesy of SmartDraw, includes diagrams of hardware racks, as revealed in Figure 20.6.

Don't throw anything at me, but I need to bring up one last thing: Never forget to mirror any changes you make to your actual network in the network's diagram. Think of it like an updated snapshot. If you give the authorities your college buddy's baby picture after he goes missing, will that really help people recognize him? Not without the help of some high-tech, age-progression software, that's for sure—and they don't make that for networks, so it's better to just keep things up-to-date.

FIGURE 20.5   Network diagram with firewalls from SmartDraw

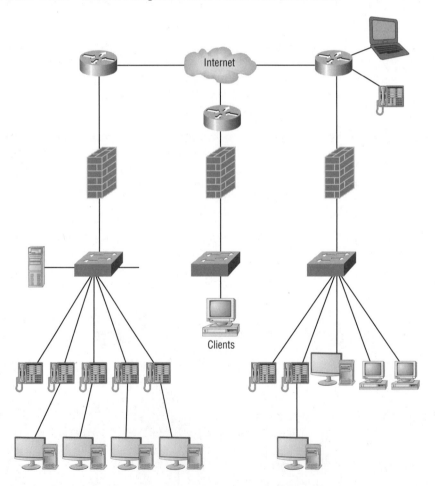

Reproduced with permission from SmartDraw.com (www.smartdraw.com).

FIGURE 20.6   Hardware-rack diagram from SmartDraw

Rack Diagram

Reproduced with permission from SmartDraw.com (www.smartdraw.com).

Logical Network Diagrams

Physical diagrams depict how data physically flows from one area of your network to the next, but a *logical network diagram* includes things like protocols, configurations, addressing schemes, access lists, firewalls, types of applications, and so on—all things that apply logically to your network. Figure 20.7 shows what a logical network diagram could look like.

And just as you mirror any physical changes you make to the network (like adding devices or even just a cable) on your physical diagram, you map logical changes (like creating a new subnet, VLAN, or security zone) on your logical network diagram. It is important that you keep this oh-so-important document up-to-date.

Baselines

In networking, *baseline* can refer to the standard level of performance of a certain device or to the normal operating capacity for your whole network. For instance, a specific server's baseline describes norms for factors like how busy its processors are, how much of the memory it uses, and how much data usually goes through the NIC at a given time.

FIGURE 20.7 Logical network diagram

Reproduced with permission from SmartDraw.com (www.smartdraw.com).

A network baseline delimits the amount of bandwidth available and when. For networks and networked devices, baselines include information about four key components:

- Processor
- Memory
- Hard-disk (or other storage) subsystem
- Network adapter or subsystem

After everything is up and running, it's a good idea to establish performance baselines on all vital devices and your network in general. To do this, measure things like network usage at three different strategic times to get an accurate assessment. For instance, peak usage usually happens around 8:00 a.m. Monday through Friday, or whenever most people log in to the network in the morning. After hours or on weekends is often when usage is the lowest. Knowing these values can help you troubleshoot *bottlenecks* or determine why certain system resources are more limited than they should be. Knowing what your baseline is can even tell you if someone's complaints about the network running like a slug are really valid—nice!

It's good to know that you can use network-monitoring software to establish baselines. Even some server operating systems come with software to help with network monitoring, which can help find baselines as well.

In my experience, it's wise to re-baseline network performance at least once a year. And always pinpoint new performance baselines after any major upgrade to your network's infrastructure.

Policies, Procedures, and Regulations

It's up to us, individually and corporately, to nail down exactly what solid guidelines there should be for *policies* and *procedures* for network installation and operation. Some organizations are bound by regulations that also affect how they conduct their business, and that kind of thing clearly needs to be involved in their choices. But let me take a minute to make sure you understand the difference between policies and procedures.

Policies govern how the network is configured and operated as well as how people are expected to behave on it. They're in place to direct things like how users access resources and which employees and groups get various types of network access and/or privileges. Basically, policies give people guidelines as to what they are expected to do. Procedures are precise descriptions of the appropriate steps to follow in a given situation, such as what to do when an employee is terminated or what to do in the event of a natural disaster. They often dictate precisely how to execute policies.

Of note, one of the most important aspects of any policy or procedure is that it's given high-level management support, because neither will be very effective if there aren't any consequences for not following the rules.

Policies

I talked extensively about security policies in Chapter 14, "Network Threats and Mitigation," so if you're drawing a blank, you can go back there for details. Here's a summary list of factors that most policies cover:

Security policies　These are policies applied to users to help maintain security in the network:

- Clean-desk policies
- Network access (who, what, and how)
- Acceptable-use policy

Change management　These policies ensure a consistent approach to managing changes to network configurations:

- Disposal of network equipment
- Use of recording equipment
- How passwords are managed (length and complexity required, and how often they need to be changed)
- Types of security hardware in place
- How often to do backups and take other fault-tolerant measures
- What to do with user accounts after an employee leaves the company

Procedures

These are the actions to be taken in specific situations:

- Disciplinary action to be taken if a policy is broken
- What to do during an audit
- How issues are reported to management
- What to do when someone has locked themselves out of their account
- How to properly install or remove software on servers
- What to do if files on the servers suddenly appear to be "missing" or altered
- How to respond when a network computer has a virus
- Actions to take if it appears that a hacker has broken into the network
- Actions to take if there is a physical emergency like a fire or flood

So you get the idea, right? For every policy on your network, there should be a credible related procedure that clearly dictates the steps to take in order to fulfill it. And you know that policies and procedures are as unique as the wide array of companies and organizations that create and employ them. But all this doesn't mean you can't borrow good ideas and plans from others and tweak them a bit to meet your requirements.

An example of a network access policy is a time of day restriction on logging into the network.

Regulations

In contrast, *regulations* are rules imposed on your organization by an outside agency, like a certifying board or a government entity, and they're usually totally rigid and nonmutable. The list of possible regulations that your company could be subjected to is so exhaustively long there's no way I can include it in this book. Different regulations exist for different types of organizations depending on if they're corporate, nonprofit, scientific, educational, legal, governmental, and so on, and they also vary by where that organization is located.

For instance, US governmental regulations vary by county and state, federal regulations are piled on top of those, and many other countries have multiple regulatory bodies as well. The Sarbanes-Oxley Act of 2002 (Sar-Ox) is an example of a regulation system imposed on all publicly traded companies in the United States. Its main goal was to ensure corporate responsibility and sound accounting practices, and although that may not sound like it would have much of an effect on your IT department, it does, because a lot of the provisions in this act target the retention and protection of data. Believe me, something as innocent sounding as deleting old emails could get you in trouble—if any of them could've remotely had a material impact on the company's financial disclosures, deleting them could actually be breaking the law. All good to know—be aware, and be careful.

I'm not going to give you a laundry list of regulations for you to memorize here, but I will tell you that IT regulations center around something known as the CIA triad:

- Confidentiality: Only authorized users have access to the data.
- Integrity: The data is accurate and complete.
- Availability: Authorized users have access to the data when access is needed.

One of the most commonly applied regulations is the ISO/IEC 27002 standard for information security, previously known as ISO 17799 and renamed in 2007. It was developed by the International Organization for Standardization (ISO) and the International Electrotechnical Commission (IEC), and it is based on British Standard (BS) 7799-1:1999.

The official title of ISO/IEC 27002 is *Information technology - Security techniques - Code of practice for information security management.* Although it's beyond our scope to get into the details of this standard, know that it covers 12 main areas:

- Risk assessment
- Security policy
- Organization of information security
- Asset management
- Human-resources security
- Physical and environmental security
- Communications and operations management
- Access control
- Information systems acquisition, development, and maintenance
- Information security incident management
- Business-continuity management
- Compliance

So, what do you take with you from this? Your mission is clear. Know the regulations your company is expected to comply with, and make sure your IT policies and procedures are totally in line with any regulations so it's easy for you to comply with them. No sense getting hauled off to jail because you didn't archive an email, right?

Monitoring the Network and Optimizing Its Performance

We've talked about how important creating a good plan for your network design is to its ultimate success, but I still have to tell you that no matter how much time and energy you put into your plan, it's not going to be perfect. To be real, you'll still probably go through a challenge, or five. Not to discourage you—working thoroughly through the planning stage definitely pays off big-time; it's just not possible to foresee everything. Plus, things can always get better, right? There will always be ways to improve and optimize your network's performance.

And those two things are exactly what we're going to focus on next. First, I'll show you some cool ways to monitor your network and nail its problem areas through using a variety of logs on your servers. After that, we'll get into the skinny on how to optimize your system's performance.

Network Monitoring and Logging

There are a lot of ways to find out what's really going on within your network. Most administrators opt to directly keep tabs on network performance by looking at important factors like data rates and available bandwidth, using the many tools on the market designed to help with that. Another good strategy for assessing a network's health and well-being is via the more indirect route of monitoring the logs that your server operating systems keep. These can help you spot problems on your physical network as well as services or applications that aren't running properly and could eventually bring the network or its resources down and make your users really unhappy.

Syslog

Syslog is a standard for logging program messages. It is somewhat like SNMP in that it provides devices that would otherwise be unable to communicate with a means to notify administrators of problems or performance. These messages are usually logged to a Syslog server. It is supported by a wide variety of devices (such as printers and routers) and can integrate log data from many different types of systems into a central repository.

Network Monitoring

Some key network-monitoring tools and diagnostic utilities around today are software additions that run on an existing server operating system like Windows Server 2008 or Unix. Others are stand-alone hardware devices that you plug into your network, but both are basically the packet sniffers we talked about back in Chapter 14. Although it's true that hackers can and do use sniffers to capture network traffic and gather data for an attack, we make good use of them too. And strange but true, being a bit of a hacker yourself can make you a much better sys admin—knowing your enemies and their methods can help you find the same holes they would use for evil, and you can use that knowledge to plug security holes and even optimize your network's performance.

Packet sniffers allow you to examine network traffic down to details of individual packets. You can put the packet's header under the microscope: It contains vital information about the protocol being used to encapsulate it, plus the source and destination IP addresses. This is super-valuable information—if I'm seeing the speed of traffic on a specific segment grind to a crawl, one of first the things I'll look for is only one IP address that's spewing tons of data. If so, it could mean that I've got a failing network adapter because a common symptom of a dying NIC is to become extremely "chatty" by sending out broadcast packets and clogging things to the point that legitimate traffic can't get through. It's like getting a deluge of junk mail and being forced to read every last bit of it; a broadcast packet is technically addressed to everyone, meaning that all the other NICs on the segment have to stop and read their junk—not so good.

> Good news—routers are, by default, configured to prevent broadcasts from going from one segment to another. Most switches sold today are also able to prevent broadcasts from spreading to multiple network segments, but not by default.

When you hear people refer to things like *load testing*, *connectivity testing*, and *throughput testing*, they're really talking about network monitoring. You'll also hear network monitors referred to as *protocol analyzers*. Microsoft has a graphical utility called Network Monitor that can be used to capture network traffic. The current version is 3.4, and it's supported by Windows Vista, Windows 7, Server 2003, and Server 2008. You can download it from Microsoft's website, but for it to work, your network adapter must be able to work in promiscuous mode (yes, you read that right!). Several third parties specialize in producing network monitors, such as, for example, Fluke Networks, which makes some cool tools like the OptiView Network Analyzer.

Server Logs

Windows Server 2003 and 2008 (and most other Windows operating systems) come with a tool called Event Viewer that provides you with several logs containing vital information about events happening on your computer. Other server operating systems have similar logs, and many connectivity devices like routers and switches also have graphical logs that gather statistics on what's happening to them. These logs can go by various names, like *history logs*, *general logs*, or *server logs*. Figure 20.8 shows an Event Viewer system log display from a Windows Server 2003 machine.

On Windows servers, a minimum of three separate logs hold different types of information:

Application   Contains events triggered by applications or programs determined by their programmers. Example applications include LiveUpdate, the Microsoft Office suite, and SQL and Exchange servers.

Security   Contains security events like valid or invalid logon attempts and potential security problems. By default, it's not enabled, so you've got to set it up manually.

System   Contains events generated by Windows system components, including drivers and services that started or failed to start.

The basic "Big Three" can give us lots of juicy information about who's logging on, who's accessing the computer, and which services are running properly (or not). If you want to find out whether your Dynamic Host Configuration Protocol (DHCP) server started up its DHCP service properly, just check out its system log. Because the computer depicted in Figure 20.8

is configured as a domain controller, its Event Viewer serves up three more logs: Directory Service, DNS Server, and File Replication Service, for a total of six.

FIGURE 20.8   Windows Event Viewer system log

Windows 2000 Server and Windows Server 2003 came with System Monitor—another graphical tool used to create network baselines, provide performance logs, and identify bottlenecks. Windows Server 2008 R2 offers an optional new monitoring and optimization tool called System Center Operations Manager 2010.

Reasons to Optimize Your Network's Performance

So why do we have networks, anyway? I don't mean this in a historical sense; I mean pragmatically. The reason they've become such precious resources is that as our world has become smaller and more connected, we need a way to keep in touch like never before. Networks make accessing resources easy for people who can't be in the same location as the resources they need—including other people.

In essence, networks of all types are really complex tools we use to facilitate communication from afar and to allow lots of us to access the resources we need to keep up with the demands imposed on us in today's lightning paced world. And use them we do—a lot. And when you have many, many people trying to access one resource like a valuable file server or a shared database, our systems can get as bogged down and clogged as a freeway at rush hour. Just as road rage can result from driving on one of those not-so-expressways, frustrated people can direct some serious hostility at you if the same thing happens when they're trying to get somewhere using a network that's crawling along at snail speed.

This is why optimizing performance is in everyone's best interest—it keeps you and you network's users happily humming along. Optimization includes things like splitting up network segments, stopping unnecessary services on servers, offloading one server's work onto another, and upgrading outmoded hardware devices to newer, faster models. I'll get to exactly how to make that happen coming up soon, but in this next section, I'm going to talk about the theories behind performance optimization and even more about the reasons why you want to make sure performance is at its best.

In a perfect world, there would be unlimited bandwidth, but in reality, you're more likely to find Bigfoot. So, it's helpful to have some great strategies up your sleeve.

If you look at what computers are used for today, there's a huge difference between the files we transfer now versus those transferred even three to five years ago. Now we do things like watch movies online without them stalling, and we can send humongous email attachments. Video teleconferencing is more common than Starbucks locations—well, almost. The point is that the files we transfer today are really huge compared to what we sent back and forth just a few years ago. And although bandwidth has increased to allow us to do what we do, there are still limitations that cause network performance to suffer miserably. Let's start with a few reasons why you need to carefully manage whatever amount of precious bandwidth you've got.

Latency Sensitivity

Most of us have clicked to open an application or clicked a web link only to have the computer just sit there staring back at us, helplessly hanging. That sort of lag comes when the resources needed to open the program or take us to the next page are not fully available. That kind of lag on a network is called *latency*—the time between when data is requested and the moment it actually gets delivered. The more latency, the longer the delay and the longer you have to stare blankly back at your computer screen, hoping something happens soon.

Latency affects some programs more than others. If you are sending an email, it may be annoying to have to wait a few seconds for the email server to respond, but that type of delay isn't likely to cause physical harm to you or a loved one. Applications that are adversely affected by latency are said to have high *latency sensitivity*. A common example of this is online gaming. Although it may not mean actual life or death, playing certain online games with significant delays can mean the untimely demise of your character—and you won't even know it. Worse, it can affect the entire experience for those playing with you, which can get you booted from some game servers. On a much more serious level, applications like remote surgery also have high latency sensitivity.

High-Bandwidth Applications

Many of the applications we now use over the network would have been totally unservice-able in the past because of the high amount of bandwidth they consume. And even though technology is constantly improving to give us more bandwidth, developers are in hot pursuit, developing new applications that gobble up that bandwidth as soon as it becomes—even in advance of it becoming—available. A couple of good examples of high-bandwidth applications are VoIP and video streaming:

VoIP   *Voice over Internet Protocol (VoIP)* describes several technologies that work to deliver voice communications over the Internet or other data networks. In many cases, VoIP includes not only voice but video transmissions as well. VoIP allows us to send voice, video, and data all over the same connection to another location. Its most common application is video teleconferencing.

Many companies are investing in VoIP systems to reduce travel costs. Ponying up for pricey plane tickets, lodging, and rental cars adds up fast, so investing in a good VoIP system that allows the company to have virtual conferences with people in another state or country pays for itself in no time.

But sadly, VoIP installations can be stressed heavily by things like really low bandwidth, latency issues, packet loss, jitter, security flaws, and reliability concerns. And in some cases, routing VoIP through firewalls and routers using address translation can prove pretty problematic as well.

Video applications   Watching real-time video on the Internet today is great if you have a decent high-speed connection. You can watch the news, sports, movies, and pretty much anything else that you watch on television. Although viewing digital media online is so common that anyone born after the year 2000 won't be able to remember a time when you needed to watch videos on anything other than a computer, again, this requires lots of bandwidth, and excessive use can cause traffic problems even on robust networks.

Uptime

Uptime is the amount of time the system is up and accessible to your end users, so the more uptime you have, the better. And depending on how critical the nature of your business is, you may need to provide four-nine or five-nine uptime on your network—that's a lot. Why is this a lot? Because you write out four-nine as 99.99%, or better, you write out five-nine as 99.999%! Now that is some serious uptime!

How to Optimize Performance

You now know that bandwidth is to networking as water is to life, and you're one of the lucky few if your network actually has an excess of it. Cursed is the downtrodden administrator who can't seem to find enough, and more fall into this category than the former. At times, your very sanity may hinge upon ensuring that your users have enough available bandwidth to get their jobs done on your network, and even if you've got a 1Gbps connection, it doesn't mean all your users have that much bandwidth at their fingertips. What it really means is that they get a piece of it, and they share the rest with other users and network processes. Because it's your job to make sure as much of that 1Gbps as possible is there to use when needed, I'm going to discuss some really cool ways to make that happen for you.

Quality of Service

Quality of service (QoS) refers to the way the resources are controlled so that the quality of services is maintained. It's basically the ability to provide a different priority to one or more types of traffic over other levels for different applications, data flows, or users so that they can be guaranteed a certain performance level.

QoS methods focus on one of five problems that can affect data as it traverses network cable:

Delay Data can run into congested lines or take a less-than-ideal route to the destination, and delays like these can make some applications, such as VoIP, fail. This is the best reason to implement QoS when real-tine applications are in use in the network—to prioritize delay-sensitive traffic.

Dropped packets Some routers will drop packets if they receive a packet while their buffers are full. If the receiving application is waiting for the packets but doesn't get them, it will usually request that the packets be retransmitted—another common cause of a service(s) delay.

Error Packets can be corrupted in transit and arrive at the destination in an unacceptable format, again requiring retransmission and resulting in delays.

Jitter Not every packet takes the same route to the destination, so some will be more delayed than others if they travel through a slower or busier network connection. The variation in packet delay is called *jitter*, and this can have a nastily negative impact on programs that communicate in real time.

Out-of-Order delivery Out-of-order delivery is also a result of packets taking different paths through the network to their destinations. The application at the receiving end needs to put them back together in the right order for the message to be completed, so if there are significant delays or the packets are reassembled out of order, users will probably notice degradation of an application's quality.

QoS can ensure that applications with a required bit rate receive the necessary bandwidth to work properly. Clearly, on networks with excess bandwidth, this is not a factor, but the more limited your bandwidth is, the more important a concept like this becomes.

Applications that generally require some level of QoS include online gaming, VoIP, streaming multimedia, and safety-critical applications like remote surgery. There are eight levels of QoS priorities. The lowest level, 0, is called "best effort" but doesn't really mean that—it actually means something more like "your data will get there when it gets there." The highest level, 5, is used for things like remote surgery when data needs to get there in real time or else! (Levels 6 and 7 are reserved for network control traffic.) Table 20.2 displays the eight QoS levels.

TABLE 20.2 Eight levels of QoS

Level	Description
0	Best effort
1	Background
2	Standard (spare)
3	Excellent load (business-critical applications)
4	Controlled load (streaming media)
5	Voice and video (interactive voice and video, less than 100ms latency and jitter)
6	Layer 3 Network Control Reserved Traffic (less than 10ms latency and jitter)
7	Layer 2 Network Control Reserved Traffic (lowest latency and jitter)

QoS levels are established per call, per session, or in advance of the session by an agreement known as a service level agreement (SLA).

Traffic Shaping

Traffic shaping, or packet shaping, is another form of bandwidth optimization. It works by delaying packets that meet a certain criteria to guarantee usable bandwidth for other applications. Traffic shaping is basically traffic triage—you're really just delaying attention to some traffic so other traffic gets A-listed through. Traffic shaping uses *bandwidth throttling* to ensure that certain data streams don't send too much data in a specified period of time as well as *rate limiting* to control the rate at which traffic is sent.

Most often, traffic shaping is applied to devices at the edge of the network to control the traffic entering the network, but it can also be deployed on devices within an internal network. The devices that control it have what's called a *traffic contract* that determines which packets are allowed on the network and when. You can think of this kind of like the stoplights on busy freeway on-ramps, where only so much traffic is allowed onto the road at one time, based on predefined rules. Even so, some traffic (like carpools and emergency vehicles) is allowed on the road immediately. Delayed packets are stored in the managing device's first-in, first-out (FIFO) buffer until they're allowed to proceed per the conditions in the contract. If you're the first car at the light, this could happen immediately. If not, you get to go after waiting briefly until the traffic in front of you is released.

Load Balancing

Load balancing refers to a technique used to spread work out to multiple computers, network links, or other devices.

Using load balancing, you can provide an active/passive server cluster in which only one server is active and handling requests. For example, your favorite Internet site might actually consist of 1 of 20 servers that all appear to be the same exact site because that site's owner wants to ensure that its users always experience quick access. You can accomplish this on a network by installing multiple, redundant links to ensure that network traffic is spread across several paths and to maximize the bandwidth on each link.

Think of this as like having two or more different freeways that will both get you to your destination equally well—if one is really busy, just take the other one.

High Availability

High availability is a system-design protocol that guarantees a certain amount of operational uptime during a given period of time. The design attempts to minimize unplanned downtime—the time users are unable to access resources. In almost all cases high availability is provided through the implementation of duplicate equipment (multiple servers, multiple NIC etc.). Organizations that serve critical functions obviously need this; after all, you really don't want to blaze your way to a hospital ER only to find that they can't treat you because their network is down!

There's a difference between planned downtime and unplanned downtime. Planned downtime is good—it's occasionally scheduled for system maintenance and routine upgrades. Unplanned downtime is bad: It's a lack of access due to system failure, which is exactly the issue high-availability resolves.

One of the highest standards in uptime is the ability to provide five-nine availability, which I spoke of earlier. This actually means the network is accessible 99.999% of the time—way impressive! Think about this. In one non-leap year, there are 31,536,000 seconds. If you are available 99.999% of the time, it means you can be down only .001% of the time, or a total of 315.36 seconds, or 5 minutes and 15.36 seconds per year—wow!

There's a difference between uptime and availability. Your servers may be up but not accessible if a cable gets cut or something, and that outage would definitely count against your availability time.

Caching Engines

A *cache* is a collection of data that duplicates key pieces of original data. Computers use caches all the time to temporarily store information for faster access, and processors have both internal and external caches available to them, which speeds up their response times.

A *caching engine* is basically a database on a server that stores information people need to access fast. The most popular implementation of this is with web servers and proxy servers, but caching engines are also used on internal networks to speed up access to things like database services.

Fault Tolerance

Fault tolerance means that even if one component fails, you won't lose access to the resource it provides. To implement fault tolerance, you need to employ multiple devices or connections that all provide a way to access the same resource(s).

A familiar form of fault tolerance is configuring an additional hard drive to be a mirror image of another so that if either one fails, there's still a copy of the data available to you. In networking, fault tolerance means that you have multiple paths from one point to another. What's really cool is that fault-tolerant connections can be configured to be available either on a standby basis only or all the time if you intend to use them used as part of a load-balancing system.

Common Address Redundancy Protocol

Common Address Redundancy Protocol (CARP) provides IP-based redundancy, allowing a group of hosts on the same network segment (referred to as a *redundancy group*) to share an IP address. One host is designated the *master* and the rest as *backups*. The master host responds to any traffic or ARP requests directed toward it. Each host may belong to more than one redundancy group at a time.

One of its most common uses is to provide redundancy for devices such as firewalls or routers. The virtual IP address (this is another name for the shared group IP address) will be shared by a group of routers or firewalls.

The client machines use the virtual IP address as their default gateway. In the event that the master router suffers a failure or is taken offline, the IP will move to one of the backup routers and service will continue. Other protocols that use similar principles are Virtual Router Redundancy Protocol and the Hot Standby Router Protocol.

Virtual Networking

Over the last few years, one of the most significant developments helping to increase the efficient use of computing resources—leading to an increase in network performance without an increase in spending on hardware—has been the widespread adoption of virtualization technology. You can't read an industry publication without coming across the term *cloud computing* within 45 seconds!

The concept of virtualization is quite simple. Instead of dedicating a physical piece of hardware to every server, run multiple instances of the server operating system, each in its own "virtual environment" on the same physical piece of equipment. This saves power, maximizes the use of memory and CPU resources, and can even help to "hide" the physical location of each virtual server.

Virtual computing solutions come from a number of vendors. The following are some of the more popular currently:

- VMware vSphere
- Microsoft Hyper-V
- Citrix XenServer

All of these solutions work on the same basic concept but each has its own unique features, and of course all claim to be the best solution. In the following sections, I will discuss the building blocks of virtualization rather than the specific implementation from any single vendor.

Onsite vs. Offsite

Often you hear the terms *public cloud* and *private cloud. Clouds* can be thought of as virtual computing environments where virtual servers and desktops live and can be accessed by users. A private cloud is one in which this environment is provided to the enterprise by a third party for a fee. This is a good solution for a company that has neither the expertise nor the resources to manage their own cloud yet would like to take advantage of the benefits that cloud computing offers:

- Increased performance
- Increased fault tolerance
- Constant availability
- Access from anywhere

These types of clouds might be considered offsite or public. On the other hand, for the organization that has the expertise and resources, a private or onsite solution might be better and might be more secure. This approach will enjoy the same benefits as a public cloud and may offer more precise control and more options to the organization.

Virtual Networking Components

Virtualization can be deployed in several different ways to deliver cost-effective solutions to different problems. Each of the following components can have its place in the solution:

Virtual servers Virtual servers can perform all the same functions as physical servers but can enjoy some significant advantages. By clustering a virtual server with other virtual servers located on different hosts, you can achieve fault tolerance in the case of a host failure. Increased performance can also be derived from this approach.

The virtualization software can allow you to allocate CPU and memory resources to the virtual machines (VMs) dynamically as needed to ensure that the maximum amount of computing power is available to any single VM at any moment while not wasting any of that power on an idle VM. In fact, in situations where VMs have been clustered, they may even be suspended or powered down in times of low demand in the cluster.

Virtual switches   Virtual switches are software versions of a Layer 2 switch that can be used to create virtual networks. They can be used for the same purposes as physical switches. VLANs can be created, virtual servers can be connected to the switches, and the virtual network can be managed all while residing on the same physical box. These switches can also span multiple hosts (the physical machines that house multiple virtual servers, desktops, and switches are called hosts).

Distributed virtual switches are those switches that span multiple hosts, and they are what link the VMs that are located on different hosts yet members of the same cluster together.

Figure 20.9 shows the relationship between a physical server and the virtual servers and virtual switches that it hosts. The virtual servers called virtual machines (VMs) have virtual network cards (vNICs) that connect to the virtual switch. Keep in mind that all three of these components are software running on the same physical server. Then the virtual switch makes a software connection to the physical NIC on the physical host, which makes a physical connection to the physical switch in the network.

It is interesting to note and important to be aware that the IP address of the physical NIC in Figure 20.9 will actually be transmitting packets from multiple MAC addresses since each of the virtual servers will have a unique virtual MAC address.

FIGURE 20.9   Virtualization

Virtual desktops   Using operating system images for desktop computers is not a new concept. Delivering these desktop images to users from a virtual environment when they start their computer is. This allows for the user desktop to require less computing power, especially if the applications are also delivered virtually and those applications are ruining in a VM in the cloud rather than in the local desktop eating up local resources. Another benefit of using virtual desktops is the ability to maintain a consistent user environment (same desktop, applications etc.) when can enhance user support.

Thin computing takes this a step further. In this case, all of the computing is taking place on the server. A *thin client* is simply displaying the output from the operating system running in the cloud and the keyboard is used to interact with that operating system in the cloud. Does this sound like dumb terminals with a GUI to anyone yet? Back to the future indeed! The thin client needs very little processing power for this job.

Virtual PBX   Virtual PBX is an example of what is called *software as a service* (SaaS). A hosting company manages the entire phone system for the company, freeing the organization from the need to purchase and manage the physical equipment that would be required otherwise to provide the same level of service. To the outside world, the company appears to have a professional phone system while everything is actually being routed through the hosting company's system.

Network as a Service (NaaS)   Now that you know what SaaS is you can probably guess what NaaS is. You guessed it: a network hosted and managed by a third party on behalf of the company. For many enterprises, it makes more sense to outsource the management of the network to a third party when it is not cost effective to maintain a networking staff.

An example of this is the Cisco OpenStack cloud operating system, which is an open-source platform that provides computers and storage.

Summary

In this chapter, I talked a lot about the documentation aspects of network administration. I started off discussing physical diagrams and schematics and moved on to the logical form as well as configuration-management documentation. You learned about the importance of these diagrams as well as the simple to complex forms they can take and the tools used to create them—from pencil and paper to high-tech AutoCAD schematics. You also found out a great deal about creating performance baselines. After that, I delved deep into a discussion of network policies and procedures and how regulations can affect how you manage your network.

   Next, you learned about network monitoring and optimization and how monitoring your network can help you find issues before they develop into major problems. You learned that server operating systems and intelligent network devices have built-in graphical monitoring tools to help you troubleshoot your network. Also covered was how to check logs on servers or network devices to find out what's been happening on them, such as who has logged in or how much traffic has passed through them.

   We got into performance optimization and the many theories and strategies you can apply to optimize performance on your network. All of them deal with controlling the traffic in some way and include methods like QoS, traffic shaping, load balancing, high availability, and the use of caching servers. We discussed how Common Address Redundancy Protocol (CARP) can be used to increase availability of gateways and firewalls. You also learned how important it is to ensure that you have plenty of bandwidth available for any applications that vitally need it, like critical service operations, VoIP, and real-time multimedia streaming.

Finally we discussed cloud computing, or virtualization. We looked at its benefits, including increased performance and fault tolerance, increased availability, and the ability to access cloud services from anywhere. You also learned about some of its major components, such as virtual servers, virtual switches, virtual desktops, and an example of software as a service (SaaS), virtual PBX.

Exam Essentials

Understand the difference between a physical network diagram and a logical network diagram.   A physical diagram shows all of the physical connections and devices and in many cases the cables or connections between the devices. It's a very detail-oriented view of the hardware on your network. A logical network diagram takes a higher-level view, such as your subnets and which protocols those subnets use to communicate with each other.

Understand the difference between policies, procedures, and regulations.   A policy is created to give users guidance as to what is acceptable behavior on the network. Policies also help resolve problems before they begin by specifying who has access to what resources and how configurations should be managed. Procedures are steps to be taken when an event occurs on the network, such as what to do when a user is fired or how to respond to a natural disaster. Regulations are imposed on your organization; you are required to follow them, and if you don't, you may be subject to punitive actions.

Know how your servers and network devices can help you monitor your network.   Most servers and network devices have monitoring tools built in that are capable of tracking data and events on your network. These include graphical tools as well as log files.

Understand several theories of performance optimization.   There are several ways to manage traffic on your network to speed up access and in some cases guarantee available bandwidth to applications. These include QoS, traffic shaping, load balancing, high availability, and using caching servers.

Know some examples of bandwidth-intensive applications.   Two examples of high-bandwidth applications are Voice over IP (VoIP) and real-time video streaming.

Describe the major building blocks of virtualization.   Understand how virtual servers, virtual switches, and virtual desktops are used to supply the infrastructure to deliver cloud services. Differentiate onsite or private clouds from offsite or public cloud services. Identify services that can be provided such as network as a service (NaaS) and software as a service (SaaS).

Written Lab

In this section, write the answers to the following management questions:

1. In which type of network diagram do you typically list the IP addresses of your servers and router ports?

2. Which network-performance optimization technique uses a contract to determine which data can get on to the network?

3. The lowest level of QoS is called _____.

4. The variation in packet delay on a network is called _____.

5. Spreading network traffic across multiple connections is called _____.

6. A standard of normal network performance is called _____.

7. If you need to connect two PCs directly together using their network adapters, what type of cable do you need?

8. What is another name for using virtualization to provide services?

9. List at least three major components of virtualization.

10. The steps you should take when, for example, a network user is fired, are called _____.

    You can find the answers in Appendix B.

Review Questions

You can find the answers in Appendix A.

1. UTP cables use which type of connector?

   A. RJ-11

   B. RJ-25

   C. RJ-45

   D. BCN

2. Which type of cable will have the pins in the same order on both connectors?

   A. Crossover cable

   B. Straight-through cable

   C. Console cable

   D. Telephone cable

3. Which pins are switched in a crossover cable?

   A. 1 and 2, 3 and 4

   B. 1 and 3, 2 and 6

   C. 2 and 4, 5 and 7

   D. 1 and 4, 5 and 8

4. UTP cable has specific colors for the wire associated with each pin. Based on the TIA/EIA 568B wiring standard, what is the correct color order, starting with pin 1?

   A. White/Orange, Orange, Blue, White/Green, White/Blue, Green, White/Brown, Brown

   B. Orange, White/Orange, White/Green, Blue, White/Blue, White/Brown, Brown, Green

   C. White/Orange, Orange, White/Green, Blue, White/Blue, Green, White/Brown, Brown

   D. White/Green, Green, White/Orange, Blue, White/Blue, Orange, White/Brown, Brown

5. A baseline contains information about which resources on a network component? (Choose all that apply.)

   A. Hard disk

   B. Memory

   C. Processor

   D. Network adapter

6. Which of the following govern how the network is configured and operated as well as how people are expected to behave on the network?

   A. Baselines

   B. Laws

   C. Policies

   D. Procedures

7. You have upgraded the firmware on your switches and access points. What documentation do you need to update?

   A. Baselines and configuration documentation

   B. Physical network diagram

   C. Logical network diagram

   D. Wiring schematics

8. A user reports slowness on a network. The network administrator can begin to monitor the system by using what to look into the problem?

   A. IPS

   B. Load balancing

   C. Packet sniffing

   D. Regulations

9. Load testing, connectivity testing, and throughput testing are all examples of what?

   A. Load balancing

   B. Network monitoring

   C. Packet sniffer

   D. Traffic shaping

10. Which type of Windows server log will give information about specific programs?

    A. Application

    B. Security

    C. System

    D. None of the above

11. Which type of Windows server log will give you information about drivers and services?

    A. Application

    B. Security

    C. System

    D. None of the above

12. What can provide different priority levels to different applications, data flows, or users to help guarantee performance levels?

    A. 1Gbps connection

    B. Bandwidth

    C. Uptime

    D. Quality of service

13. Which of the following provides increased availability to firewalls and gateways?

    A. DHCP

    B. CARP

    C. SaaS

    D. NaaS

14. You have added a new cable segment to your network. You need to make sure you document this for troubleshooting purposes. What should you update?

    A. The disaster recovery plan

    B. The wiring schematics

    C. The router connections document

    D. The baseline document

15. What is the basic purpose of QoS? (Choose two.)

    A. Block access to certain websites

    B. Make your entire network run faster

    C. Provide priority of one of more types of traffic over others

    D. Block access to web resources for just certain users or groups

    E. Prioritize delay-sensitive traffic

16. Which network-performance optimization technique can delay packets that meet certain criteria to guarantee usable bandwidth for other applications?

    A. Traffic shaping

    B. Jitter

    C. Logical

    D. Load balancing

17. Which of the following is neither a virtualization component nor a service made available through virtualization?

    A. Virtual servers

    B. SaaS

    C. CARP

    D. Virtual switches

18. Which of the following are reasons to optimize network performance? (Choose all that apply.)

   A. Maximizing uptime

   B. Minimizing latency

   C. Using VoIP

   D. Using video applications

   E. B and D

   F. All of the above

19. What term describes technologies that can deliver voice communications over the Internet?

   A. Jitter

   B. Uptime

   C. Voice over Internet Protocol

   D. None of the above

20. To optimize performance on your network, which of the following control traffic in some way?

   A. QoS

   B. Traffic shaping

   C. Load balancing

   D. Caching services

   E. All of the above

Appendix
A

Answers to Review Questions

Chapter 1: Introduction to Networks

1. C. A client-server logical topology allows you to have a centralized database of users so that authentication is provided in one place.

2. C. To install a physical topology that provides ease of scalability, use a star network. This is a hub or switch device, and this is the most common LAN network today.

3. D. Only a mesh physical topology has point-to-point connections to every device, so it has more connections and is not a popular LAN technology.

4. B. In a star topology, each workstation connects to a hub, switch, or similar central device but not to other workstations. The benefit is that when connectivity to the central device is lost, the rest of the network lives on.

5. C. MultiProtocol Label Switching has many advantages as a LAN protocol. When labels are used, voice can have priority over basic data, for example.

6. B. A logical grouping of hosts is called a LAN, and you typically group them by connecting them to a switch.

7. C. It is easy to relax about security in a peer-to-peer environment. Because of the trouble it takes to standardize authentication, a piecemeal approach involving users' personal preferences develops. There are no dedicated servers in a peer-to-peer network, and such a network can be created with as few as two computers.

8. A. When a central office, such as a headquarters, needs to communicate directly with its branch offices, but the branches do not require direct communication with one another, the point-to-multipoint model is applicable. The other scenarios tend to indicate the use of a point-to-point link between sites.

9. D. LANs generally have a geographic scope of a single building or smaller. They can range from simple (two hosts) to complex (with thousands of hosts).

10. B. The only disadvantage mentioned is the fact that there is a single point of failure in the network. However, this topology makes troubleshooting easier; if the entire network fails, you know where to look first. The central device also ensures that the loss of a single port and the addition of a new device to an available port do not disrupt the network for other stations attached to such a device.

11. D. A typical WAN connects two or more remote LANs together using someone else's network (your ISP's) and a router. Your local host and router see these networks as remote networks and not as local networks or local resources. Routers use proprietary serial connections for WANs.

12. D. MultiProtocol Label Switching provides logical links between sites, so branch offices can be easily and quickly added.

13. A. In a peer-to-peer network, all computers are considered equals. It is up to the computer that has the resource being requested to perform a security check for access rights to its resources.

14. D. In client-server networks, requests for resources go to a main server that responds by handling security and directing the client to the resource it wants instead of the request going directly to the machine with the desired resource (as in peer-to-peer).

15. A. The best answer to this question is an Ethernet switch, which uses a star physical topology with a logical bus technology.

16. D. Routers break up broadcast domains and are used to connect different networks together.

17. D. In the mesh topology, there is a path from every connection to every other one in the network. A mesh topology is used mainly because of the robust fault tolerance it offers— if one connection goes on the blink, computers and other network devices can simply switch to one of the many redundant connections that are up and running.

18. A. As its name implies, in a point-to-point topology you have a direct connection between two routers, giving you one communication path. The routers in a point-to-point topology can either be linked by a serial cable, making it a physical network, or be far away and only connected by a circuit within a Frame Relay network, making it a logical network.

19. B. A hybrid topology is a combination of two or more types of physical or logical network topologies working together within the same network.

20. A, B, C, D. Each topology has its own set of pros and cons regarding implementation, so it's important to ask the right questions and consider cost, ease of installation, maintenance, and fault tolerance.

Chapter 2: The Open Systems Interconnection Specifications

1. C. A connection-oriented session is set up using what is called a three-way hand-shake. The transmitting host sends a SYN packet, the receiving host sends a SYN-ACK, and the transmitting host replies with the last ACK packet. The session is now set up.

2. D. TCP and UDP are Transport layer protocols. The Transport layer is Layer 4 of the OSI model.

3. A. The top layer of the OSI model gives applications access to the services that allow network access.

4. A. If the remote server is busy or does not respond to your web browser request, this is an Application layer problem.

5. B. The Presentation layer makes data "presentable" for the Application layer.

6. C. Bridges, like switches, are Data Link layer devices. Hubs, like repeaters, are Physical layer devices. Routers are Network layer devices.

7. D. The Physical layer's job is to convert data into impulses that are designed for the wired or wireless medium being used on the attached segment.

8. D. A receiving host can control the transmitter by using flow control (TCP uses win-dowing by default). By decreasing the window size, the receiving host can slow down the transmitting host so the receiving host does not overflow its buffers.

9. C, D. Not that you really want to enlarge a single collision domain, but a hub (multi-port repeater) will provide this functionality for you.

10. D. The Transport layer receives large data streams from the upper layers and breaks these up into smaller pieces called segments.

11. C. The encapsulation order is data, segment, packet, frame, bits.

12. B, C. Bridges and switches break up collision domains, which allow more bandwidth for users.

13. C. A reliable Transport layer connection uses acknowledgments to make sure all data is received reliably. A reliable connection is defined by the use of acknowledgments, sequencing, and flow control, which is characteristic of the Transport layer (Layer 4).

14. A, C, D. When using sequencing and acknowledgments, the segments delivered are acknowledged back to the sender upon their reception. At this point, any segments not acknowledged are retransmitted, and segments are sequenced back into their proper order upon arrival at their destination.

15. C. Flow control allows the receiving device to control the pace of the transmitting device so the receiving device's buffer does not overflow.

16. B. IP is a Network layer protocol. TCP is an example of a Transport layer protocol, Ethernet is an example of a Data Link layer protocol, and T1 can be considered a Physical layer protocol.

17. D. The Presentation layer is the sixth layer of the model. Only the Application layer is higher, but it is not listed. Session is Layer 5, Transport is Layer 4, and Network is Layer 3.

18. C. A router is specified at the Network layer and a router routes packets. Routers can also be called Layer 3 switches.

19. C. The phrase "Please Do Not Throw Sausage Pizza Away" contains the first letters of the layers in order from Layer 1 through Layer 7. "All People Seem To Need Data Processing" works from the top down, but that's not exactly how the option that looks similar reads. The other options have all the right letters, just not completely in the right order.

20. B. The 802.3 standard, commonly associated with Ethernet, specifies the media-access method used by Ethernet, which is known as Carrier Sense Multiple Access with Collision Detection (CSMA/CD).

Chapter 3: Networking Topologies, Connectors, and Wiring Standards

1. B, C. Plenum-rated means that the cable's coating doesn't begin burning until a much higher temperature of heat, doesn't release as many toxic fumes as PVC when it does burn, and is rated for use in air plenums that carry breathable air, usually as nonenclosed fresh-air return pathways that share space with cabling.

2. D. UTP is commonly used in twisted-pair Ethernet like 10BaseT, 100BaseTX, 1000BaseTX, and so on.

3. D. Unshielded twisted-pair has standards from Category 2 through 6 for use on Ethernet networks. There is no Category 8 defined.

4. C. UTP usually connects with RJ-45. You use a crimper to attach an RJ connector to a cable.

5. A. Single-mode fiber allows for the maximum cable run distances.

6. B. You would use a straight-through cable to connect a host to a switch, and the typical pin-out is called 568A.

7. C. Fiber-optic cable transmits digital signals using light impulses rather than electricity; therefore, it is immune to EMI and RFI.

8. B. Remember that fiber-optic cable transmits a digital signal using light impulses. Light is carried on either a glass or a plastic core.

9. B. The difference between single-mode fibers and multimode fibers is in the number of light rays (and thus the number of signals) they can carry. Generally speaking, multimode fiber is used for shorter-distance applications and single-mode fiber for longer distances. —

10. C. Standards limit UTP to a mere 100 meters. Different fiber-optic types have different maximum lengths, but fiber-optic is the only cable type that can extend well beyond 100 meters.

11. B, D, E. There are many different types of fiber-optic connectors. SC, ST, LC, and MT-RJ are some of the more typical connectors in use today.

12. B. To connect two devices for voice on a vertical connect, the minimum cable you can use is Category 5.

13. B. In half-duplex communication, a device can either send communication or receive communication, but it cannot do both at the same time.

14. B. Fiber-optic cable transmits only light (not electricity like UTP), so EMI has zero effect on it.

15. C. Full-duplex communication requires a point-to-point configuration because the collision-avoidance circuit is disabled.

16. B. Both wiring standards for UTP (568A and 568B) utilize only pins 1, 2, 3, and 6.

17. D. All devices that are pinned the same for transmit and receive require a crossover cable to communicate directly.

18. A. A T1 cable uses T568B pairs 1 and 2, so to connect two T1 CSU/DSU devices back-to-back requires a crossover cable that swaps these pairs. Specifically, pins 1, 2, 4, and 5 are connected to 4, 5, 1, and 2, respectively.

19. D. The demarcation point, or demarc, is the point at which the operational control or ownership changes from your company to a service provider. This is often at the MDF in relation to telephone connections and the CSU/DSU in regard to WAN connections.

20. B. A 568B is an RJ-45 wiring standard and this type of cable uses two pairs of wires.

Chapter 4: The Current Ethernet Specifications

1. B. On an Ethernet network, the MAC address (hardware address) is used for one host to communicate with another.

2. B. 100BaseTX uses CAT 5e and can run 200Mbps when using full duplex.

3. D. When one device sends a packet out on a network segment, all other devices on the same physical network segment must wait and let it be transmitted.

4. B. 100BaseTF means that you have an Ethernet over fiber cable implementation.

5. B. Carrier Sense Multiple Access with Collision Detection (CSMA/CD) helps packets that are transmitted simultaneously from different hosts share bandwidth evenly.

6. B. A 10GBaseSR cable can have a maximum distance of 990 feet (302 meters).

7. B. With half duplex, you are using only one wire pair with a digital signal either transmitting or receiving.

8. A. Full-duplex Ethernet uses two pairs of wires at the same time.

9. C. A 10GBaseLR implementation can go a distance of up to 6 miles.

10. B. Double up! You can get 20Mbps with a 10Mbps Ethernet running full duplex or 200Mbps for Fast Ethernet.

11. B. Full-duplex communication cannot be used with a hub because a hub is a half-duplex single communication device. A host, switch, and router have the ability to process traffic (frames), whereas a hub is a multiport repeater.

12. B. 11000000 is 192, 10101000 is 168, 00110000 is 48, and 11110000 is 240.

13. A. Bonding can increase bandwidth and provide redundancy for devices that have multiple links connected together.

14. C. Nibble values are 8 + 4 + 2 + 1, giving us a maximum value of 15. If we have a decimal value of 10, that means the 8 bit and the 2 bit are turned on.

15. D. The 128, 64, 32, and 8 bits are on, so just add the values:
128 + 64 + 32 + 8 = 232.

16. B. The first 10 hexadecimal digits (0–9) are the same values as the decimal values. We already know the binary value for the number 10 is 1010—in hex, the number 10 needs to be displayed as a single character. To display double-digit numbers as a single character, we substitute letters. In our example, 10 is A.

17. C. A MAC, or hardware, address is a 48-bit (6-byte) address written in hexadecimal format.

18. A. 100BaseT and 1000BaseT both have a maximum distance of 100 meters, or 328 feet.

19. B. The FCS can detect frames in the sequence by calculating the cyclic redundancy check (CRC), which verifies that all the bits in the frame are unchanged.

20. C. The 100 means 100Mbps. The *Base* means *baseband*, which refers to baseband technology—a signaling method for communication on the network.

Chapter 5: Networking Devices

1. C. NICs are the physical network connections for a computer but are not one of the devices or mediums used to provide Internet access in a SOHO setting.

2. C. Like a hub, a switch connects multiple segments of a network together, with one important difference. Whereas a hub sends out anything it receives on one port to all the others, a switch recognizes frame boundaries and pays attention to the destination MAC address of the incoming frame as well as the port on which it was received.

3. When we say segment, we mean to create multiple collision or broadcast domains. Hubs don't segment a network; they just connect network segments together. Repeaters don't segment the network; they repeat a signal and allow the distance covered to be increased. So the only correct option is B, a switch.

4. A. The primary function of a bridge is to keep traffic separated on both sides of the bridge, breaking up collision domains.

5. A. Hubs create one collision domain and one broadcast domain.

6. B. By allowing full duplex operation on each port, a switch provides extra bandwidth to each port.

7. B. A switch is typically just a Layer 2 device segmenting the network by using MAC addresses. However, some higher-end switches can provide Layer 3 services.

8. D. Remember that DHCP servers assign IP addresses to hosts. Thus DHCP allows easier administration than providing IP information to each host by hand (called static IP addressing).

9. B. Multilayer switches (also called Layer 3 switches) don't have any fewer features, less bandwidth, or fewer ports than a normal switch; they just allow routing functions between subnets.

10. B. A load balancer uses a little trickery and sends incoming packets to one or more machines that are hidden behind a single IP address. Modern load-balancing routers can use different rules to make decisions about where to route traffic, which can be based on least load, fastest response times, or simply balancing requests.

11. A. DNS translates human names to IP addresses for routing your packet through the Internet. Hosts can receive the IP address of this DNS server and then resolve host names to IP addresses.

12. C. Routers, switches, and bridges are all devices that help break up big networks into a number of smaller ones—also known as network segmentation. Hubs don't segment networks—they just connect network segments together.

13. A. Web cache, of course! Most proxy programs provide a means to deny access to certain URLs in a blacklist, thus providing content filtering, usually in corporate environments.

14. D. Options A, B, and C all aid in boosting network performance, so the only option left is broadcast storms. Increased traffic will increase LAN congestion.

15. B. If the DHCP server has stopped functioning, it will not hand out IP addresses to hosts that are restarted. However, the hosts that were not shut down still have an IP addresses because the lease time has not expired.

16. D. A proxy server can be used to prevent external traffic from reaching your internal network directly and can also be used to filter the sites to which your users are allowed to connect.

17. C. Switches create separate collision domains but a single broadcast domain. Remember that routers provide a separate broadcast domain for each interface.

18. A. Using appliances to offload functions such as encryption, content filtering and VPN concentration can decrease the workload of other systems and add functionality that may be present in these dedicated devices.

19. C. A DNS server uses many types of records. An "A" record is a hostname to IP address record and a pointer record is an IP address to hostname record.

20. D. A proxy server can provide many functions. A proxy server can use a caching engine so repeated access requests for web information would accelerate repeated access for users, and they can also limit the availability of web sites.

Chapter 6: Introduction to the Internet Protocol

1. D. SMTP resides at the Application layer of the OSI and DoD models.

2. D. HTTPS, or Secure HTTP, uses port 443 by default.

3. C. Dynamic Host Configuration Protocol (DHCP) is used to provide IP information to hosts on your network. DHCP can provide a lot of information, but the most common is IP address, subnet mask, default gateway, and DNS information.

4. B. Address Resolution Protocol (ARP) is used to find the hardware address from a known IP address.

5. B. Secure Shell (SSH) allows you to remotely administer router, switches, and even servers securely.

6. C. The problem is with DNS, which uses both TCP and UDP port 53.

7. A, B. A client that sends out a DHCP Discover message in order to receive an IP address sends out a broadcast at both Layer 2 and Layer 3. The Layer 2 broadcast is all *F*s in hex, or FF:FF:FF:FF:FF:FF. The Layer 3 broadcast is 255.255.255.255, which means all networks and all hosts. DHCP is connectionless, which means it uses User Datagram Protocol (UDP) at the Transport layer, also called the Host-to-Host layer.

8. E. Telnet uses TCP at the Transport layer with a default port number of 23.

9. C, D. Internet Control Message Protocol (ICMP) is used to send error messages through the network, but ICMP does not work alone. Every segment or ICMP payload must be encapsulated within an IP datagram (or packet).

10. B, D, E. SMTP, FTP, and HTTP use TCP.

11. A, C, F. DHCP, SNMP, and TFTP use UDP. SMTP, FTP, and HTTP use TCP.

12. C, D, E. Telnet, File Transfer Protocol (FTP), and Trivial FTP (TFTP) are all Application layer protocols. IP is a Network layer protocol. Transmission Control Protocol (TCP) is a Transport layer protocol.

13. C. SMTP is used by a client to send mail to its server and by that server to send mail to another server. POP3 and IMAP are used by clients to retrieve their mail from the server that stores it until it is retrieved. HTTP is only used with web-based mail services.

14. C. Remote Desktop Protocol (RDP) allows you to connect to a remote computer and run programs, as Telnet does. However, the large advantage that RDP has over Telnet is that RDP allows you to have a GUI interface connection.

15. B. Simple Network Management Protocol is typically implemented using version 3, which allows for a connection-oriented service, authentication and secure polling of network devices, and alerts and reports on network devices.

16. B, E. Secure Copy Protocol (SCP) and File Transfer Protocol (FTP) can be used to transfer files between two systems.

17. B. The four layers of the IP stack (also called the DoD model) are Application/Process, Host-to-Host, Internet, and Network Access. The Host-to-Host layer is equivalent to the Transport layer of the OSI model.

18. C. Network Time Protocol will ensure a consistent time across network devices on the network.

19. A. Through the use of port numbers, TCP and UDP can establish multiple sessions between the same two hosts without creating any confusion. The sessions can be between the same or different applications, such as multiple web-browsing sessions or a web-browsing session and an FTP session.

20. D. DNS uses TCP for zone exchanges between servers and UDP when a client is trying to resolve a hostname to an IP address.

Chapter 7: IP Addressing

1. D. The addresses in the range 172.16.0.0 through 172.31.255.255 are all considered private, based on RFC 1918. Use of these addresses on the Internet is prohibited so that they can be used simultaneously in different administrative domains without concern for conflict. Some experts in the industry believe these addresses are not routable, which is not true.

2. B. APIPA uses the link-local private address range of 169.254.0.0 through 169.254.255.255 and a subnet mask of 255.255.0.0 (see RFC 3330). APIPA addresses are used by DHCP clients that cannot contact a DHCP server and have no static alternate configuration. These addresses are not Internet routable and cannot, by default, be used across routers on an internetwork.

3. C. Private IP addresses are not routable over the Internet, as either source or destination addresses. Because of that fact, any entity that wishes to use such addresses internally can do so without causing conflicts with other entities and without asking permission of any registrar or service provider. Despite not being allowed on the Internet, private IP addresses are fully routable on private intranets.

4. D. The Class A range is 1 through 126 in the first octet/byte, so this makes option B incorrect. Only option D is a valid Class A address.

5. C. The Class B range is 128 through 191 in the first octet/byte. Only option C is a valid Class B address.

6. B. If you turned on all host bits (all of the host bits are 1s), this would be a broadcast address for that network.

7. B. A Layer 2 broadcast is also referred to as a MAC address broadcast, which is in hexadecimal and is FF.FF.FF.FF.FF.FF.

8. C. A default class C subnet mask is 255.255.255.0, which means that the first three octets, or first 24 bits, are the network number.

9. A. Packets addressed to a unicast address are delivered to a single interface. For load balancing, multiple interfaces can use the same address.

10. C. I wonder how many of you picked APIPA address as your answer? An APIPA address is 169.254.*x.x*. The host address in this question is a public address. Somewhat of a tricky question if you did not read carefully.

11. B. An IPv6 address is 128 bits in size.

12. B. Packets addressed to a multicast address are delivered to all interfaces identified by the multicast address, the same as in IPv4. A multicast address is also called a one-to-many address. You can tell multicast addresses in IPv6 because they always start with *FF*.

13. C. Anycast addresses identify multiple interfaces, which is the same as multicast; however, the big difference is that the anycast packet is delivered to only one address: the first one it finds defined in terms of routing distance. This address can also be called one-to-one-of-many.

14. A, C. The loopback address with IPv4 is 127.0.0.1. With IPv6, that address is ::1.

15. B, D. In order to shorten the written length of an IPv6 address, successive fields of zeros may be replaced by double colons. In trying to shorten the address further, leading zeros may also be removed. Just as with IPv4, a single device's interface can have more than one address; with IPv6 there are more types of addresses and the same rule applies. There can be link-local, global unicast, and multicast addresses all assigned to the same interface.

16. C, D. IPv4 addresses are 32 bits long and are represented in decimal format. IPv6 addresses are 128 bits long and represented in hexadecimal format.

17. D. Only option D is in the Class C range of 192 through 224. It might look wrong because there is a 255 in the address, but this is not wrong—you can have a 255 in a network address.

18. C, E. The Class A private address range is 10.0.0.0 through 10.255.255.255. The Class B private address range is 172.16.0.0 through 172.31.255.255, and the Class C private address range is 192.168.0.0 through 192.168.255.255.

19. B. The private address range is 10.0.0.0 through 10.255.255.255, 172.16.0.0 through 172.31.255.255, and 192.168.0.0 through 192.168.255.255. Also, 224.0.0.0 through 239.255.255.255 is reserved for multicast addressing.

20. C. Option C is a multicast address and cannot be used to address hosts.

Chapter 8: IP Subnetting, Troubleshooting IP, and Introduction to NAT

1. D. A /27 (255.255.255.224) is 3 bits on and 5 bits off. This provides 8 subnets, each with 30 hosts. Does it matter if this mask is used with a Class A, B, or C network address? Not at all. The number of host bits would never change.

2. B. Don't freak because this is a Class A. What is your subnet mask? 255.255.255.128. Regardless of the class of address, this is a block size of 128 in the fourth octet. The subnets are 0 and 128. The 0 subnet host range is 1–126, with a broadcast address of 127. The 128 subnet host range is 129–254, with a broadcast address of 255. You need a router for these two hosts to communicate because they are in different subnets.

3. C. This is a pretty simple question. A /28 is 255.255.255.240, which means that our block size is 16 in the fourth octet (0, 16, 32, 48, 64, 80, and so on). The host is in the 64 subnet.

4. F. A CIDR address of /19 is 255.255.224.0. This is a Class B address, so that is only 3 subnet bits, but it provides 13 host bits, or 8 subnets, each with 8,190 hosts.

5. C. The host ID of 10.0.37.144 with a 255.255.254.0 mask is in the 10.0.36.0 subnet (yes, you need to be able to subnet in this exam!). Do not stress that this is a class A, what we care about is that the third octet has a block size of 2, so the next subnet is 10.0.38.0, which makes the broadcast address 10.0.37.255. The default gateway address of 10.0.38.1 is not in the same subnet as the host. Even though this is a Class A address, you still should easily be able to subnet this because you look more at the subnet mask and find your interesting octet, which is the third octet in this question. 256 − 254 = 2. Your block size is 2.

6. D. A /30, regardless of the class of address, has a 252 in the fourth octet. This means we have a block size of 4 and our subnets are 0, 4, 8, 12, 16, and so on. Address 14 is obviously in the 12 subnet.

7. D. A point-to-point link uses only two hosts. A /30, or 255.255.255.252, mask provides two hosts per subnet.

8. C. Devices with Layer 3 awareness, such as routers and firewalls, are the only ones that can manipulate the IP header in support of NAT.

9. A. A /29 (255.255.255.248), regardless of the class of address, has only 3 host bits. Six hosts is the maximum number of hosts on this LAN, including the router interface.

10. C. A computer should be configured with an IP address that is unique throughout the reachable internetwork. It should be configured with a subnet mask that matches that of all other devices on its local subnet, but not necessarily one that matches the mask used on any other subnet. It should also be configured with a default gateway that matches its local router's interface IP address.

11. A. A /29 (255.255.255.248) has a block size of 8 in the fourth octet. This means the subnets are 0, 8, 16, 24, and so on. 10 is in the 8 subnet. The next subnet is 16, so 15 is the broadcast address.

12. B. A 24-bit mask, or prefix length, indicates that the entire fourth octet is used for host identification. In a special case, such as this, it is simpler to visualize the all-zeros value (172.16.1.0) and the all-ones value (172.16.1.255). The highest usable address, the last one before the all-ones value, is 172.16.1.254.

13. A, E. First, if you have two hosts directly connected, as shown in the graphic, then you need a crossover cable. A straight-through cable won't work. Second, the hosts have different masks, which puts them in different subnets. The easy solution is just to set both masks to 255.255.255.0 (/24).

14. A. A /25 mask is 255.255.255.128. Used with a Class B network, the third and fourth octets are used for subnetting with a total of 9 subnet bits: 8 bits in the third octet and 1 bit in the fourth octet. Because there is only 1 bit in the fourth octet, the bit is either off or on—which is a value of 0 or 128. The host in the question is in the 0 subnet, which has a broadcast address of 127 because 128 is the next subnet.

15. A. A /28 is a 255.255.255.240 mask. Let's count to the ninth subnet (we need to find the broadcast address of the eighth subnet, so we need to count to the ninth subnet). We start at 16 (remember, the question stated that we will not use subnet 0, so we start at 16, not 0): 16, 32, 48, 64, 80, 96, 112, 128, 144. The eighth subnet is 128, and the next subnet is 144, so our broadcast address of the 128 subnet is 143. This makes the host range 129–142. 142 is the last valid host.

16. C. A /28 is a 255.255.255.240 mask. The first subnet is 16 (remember that the question stated not to use subnet 0), and the next subnet is 32, so our broadcast address is 31. This makes our host range 17–30. 30 is the last valid host.

17. A. The best method here is to check the configuration of devices that were using the old router as a gateway to the rest of the internetwork. Routers do not periodically cache their configurations to servers of any sort. You might have copied the old router's configuration to a TFTP server or the like, but failing that, you will have to rebuild the configuration from scratch, which might well be much more than interface addresses. Therefore, keeping a copy of the router's current configuration somewhere other than on the router is a wise choice. Routers don't auto-configure themselves; we wouldn't want them to.

18. E. A Class B network ID with a /22 mask is 255.255.252.0, with a block size of 4 in the third octet. The network address in the question is in subnet 172.16.16.0 with a broadcast address of 172.16.19.255. Only option E has the correct subnet mask listed, and 172.16.18.255 is a valid host.

19. D, E. The router's IP address on the E0 interface is 172.16.2.1/23, which is a 255.255.254.0. This makes the third octet a block size of 2. The router's interface is in the 2.0 subnet, and the broadcast address is 3.255 because the next subnet is 4.0. The valid host range is 2.1 through 3.254. The router is using the first valid host address in the range.

20. A. Network Address Translation can allow up to 65,000 hosts to get onto the Internet with one IP address by using Port Address Translation (PAT).

Chapter 9: Introduction to IP Routing

1. C. Yup, you got it. RIP, RIPv2, and EIGRP are all examples of routing protocols.

2. C. In dynamic routing, routers update each other about all the networks they know about and place this information into the routing table. This is possible because a protocol on one router communicates with the same protocol running on neighbor routers. If changes occur in the network, a dynamic routing protocol automatically informs all routers about the event.

3. D. Dynamic routing scales well in large networks and routes are automatically added into the routing table. Static routing is done by hand, one route at a time into each router.

4. B. Media Access Control (MAC) addresses are always local on the LAN and never go through and past a router.

5. C. Routing convergence is the time required by the routing protocols to update the routing tables (forwarding tables) on all routers in the network.

6. D. The arp -a command will show the ARP cache on your host.

7. D. Hope you answered D! A router will not send a broadcast looking for the remote network—the router will discard the packet.

8. C. RIPv1 and 2 and IGRP are all distance vector (DV) protocols. Routers using a DV protocol send all or parts of their routing table in a routing-update message at a regular interval to each of their neighbor routers.

9. C, D. Open Shortest Path First (OSPF) and Intermediate System-to-Intermediate System (IS-IS) are link state (LS) routing protocols.

10. B. The only protocol you could select is Enhanced Interior Gateway Routing Protocol (EIGRP).

11. A. Interior Gateway Routing Protocol is a DV interior gateway protocol.

12. C. Border Gateway Protocol (BGP) is the most popular choice for ISPs or really large corporations.

13. A, C. Distance vector (DV) and link state (LS) are the two routing protocols to remember.

14. A, D. A frame uses MAC addresses to send a packet on the LAN. The frame will take the packet to either a host on the LAN or a router's interface if the packet is destined for a remote network.

15. A. I hope you said A! Packets specifically have to be carried to a router in order to be routed through a network.

16. C. Remember that the frame changes at each hop but that the packet is never changed in any way until it reaches the destination device.

17. D. When the routing tables are complete because they include information about all networks in the internetwork, they are considered converged.

18. A. This is step 6 in the IP routing process. If the hardware address isn't in the ARP cache of the host, an ARP broadcast is sent out onto the local network to search for the hardware address.

19. C. The best answer would be to reroute traffic using a temporary static route until the maintenance is complete on the router.

20. A. You are most likely to see a Request Timed Out message when (if) a packet is lost on the way back to the originating host for an unknown error. Remember, if the error occurs because of a known issue, you are likely to see a Destination Unreachable message.

Chapter 10: Routing Protocols

1. C, D, F. RIPv1 and IGRP are true distance vector routing protocols and can't do much, really—except build and maintain routing tables and use a lot of bandwidth! RIPv2, EIGRP, and OSPF build and maintain routing tables, but they also provide classless routing, which allows for VLSM, summarization, and discontiguous networking.

2. B, C. RIP and RIPv2 are distance vector routing protocols. OSPF and IS-IS are link state.

3. A, D. RIP and RIPv2 are distance vector routing protocols. OSPF and IS-IS are link state.

4. E. RIP and RIPv2 are distance vector routing protocols. OSPF and IS-IS are link state. EIGRP uses qualities from both distance vector and link state to create a hybrid routing protocol.

5. C. Dynamic routing is typically used in today's networks because it scales to larger networks and takes less administrative work.

6. D. EIGRP is called a hybrid routing protocol because it uses the characteristics of both distance vector and link state routing protocols. However, EIGRP can be run only on Cisco routers and is not vendor neutral.

7. C. Static routes may be a good solution, but remember that they are not dynamic and if a piece of equipment goes down, new routes to remote networks will not automatically update, so OSPF is the best answer. It dynamically will update the routing tables with faster convergence then RIP.

8. C. The administrative distance (AD) is a very important parameter in a routing protocol. The lower the AD, the more trusted the route. If you have IGRP and OSPF running, by default IGRP routes would be placed in the routing table because IGRP has a lower AD of 100. OSPF has an AD of 110. RIPv1 and RIPv2 both have an AD of 120, and EIGRP is the lowest at 9.

9. B. The routing protocols that have been upgraded to advertise IPv6 routes are RIPng, OSPFv3, and EIGRPv6. IS-IS can advertise IPv6 routes as well, but no upgrade was needed for IS-IS.

10. C. Dynamic routing protocols, like RIP, EIGRP and OSPF, automatically add route updates to the routing table. Static routes must be added by hand.

11. A. The distance vector protocols RIPv1 and RIPv2 both have a maximum hop count of 15 (remember, 16 is unreachable). IGRP and EIGRP have a hop count of 255, and OSPF doesn't have a maximum hop count.

12. B. Routing convergence time happens in many protocols, for many devices, but routing convergence time is the time for all routers to update their routing tables (forwarding tables).

13. C. BGP is used to connect autonomous systems together on the Internet for its ability to make classless routing and summarization possible. These capabilities help to keep routing tables smaller and more efficient at the ISP core.

14. B. RIPv1 sends broadcasts every 30 seconds and has an AD of 120. RIPv2 sends multicasts (224.0.0.9) every 30 seconds and also has an AD of 120. RIPv2 sends subnet-mask information with the route updates, which allows it to support classless networks and discontiguous networks. RIPv2 also supports authentication between routers; RIPv1 does not.

15. A, B. Both RIPv1 and RIPv2 have an AD of 120. EIGRP has an AD of 90.

16. C. Border Gateway Protocol (BGP) attributes include the IP address to get to the next AS (the next-hop attribute) as well as an indication of how the networks at the end of the path were introduced into BGP (the origin code attribute). The AS path information is useful to construct a graph of loop-free autonomous systems and is used to identify routing policies so that restrictions on routing behavior can be enforced based on the AS path.

17. A. RIPng has many of the same features as RIPv2: It's a distance vector protocol; it has a max hop count of 15; and it uses split horizon, poison reverse, and other loop-avoidance mechanisms. And it still uses multicast to send its updates too, but in IPv6, it uses FF02::9 for the transport address. For RIPv2, the multicast address was 224.0.0.9, so the address still has a 9 at the end in the new IPv6 multicast range.

18. B, C. EIGRP holds three tables in RAM: neighbor, topology, and routing. The neighbor and topology tables are built and also maintained with the use of hello packets.

19. D. A successor route is used by EIGRP to forward traffic to a destination and is stored in the routing table. It is backed up by a feasible successor route that is stored in the topology table—if one is available. Remember that all routes are in the topology table.

20. A. RIP and RIPv2 use only hop count as a metric, with a maximum of 15 hops, to find the best path to a remote network.

Chapter 11: Switching and Virtual LANs

1. D. By creating and implementing VLANs in your switched network, you can break up broadcast domains at Layer 2. For hosts on different VLANs to communicate, you must have a router or Layer 3 switch.

2. B, D. Hosts are connected to a switch and are members of one VLAN. This is called an access port. Trunk links connect between switches and pass information about all VLANs.

3. C. Virtual LANs break up broadcast domains in Layer 2 switched internetworks.

4. C, E. Both 802.1d and 802.1w are IEEE STP versions, with 802.1w being the latest and greatest version.

5. D, E. The best answers are that the VLAN membership for the port is configured incorrectly and that STP shut down the port.

6. B, C, F. VLANs break up broadcast domains in a switched Layer 2 network, which means smaller broadcast domains. They allow configuration by logical function instead of physical location and can create some security if configured correctly.

7. B. The Spanning Tree Protocol is used to stop switching loops in a switched network with redundant paths.

8. A, E. Bridges break up collision domains, which would increase the number of collision domains in a network and also make smaller collision domains.

9. C. In order to see all frames that pass through the switch and read the packets with a network analyzer, you need to enable port mirroring on the port your diagnostic host is plugged into.

10. C. Trunking allows switches to pass information about many or all VLANs configured on the switches.

11. A, C, E. Layer 2 features include address learning, forwarding and filtering of the network, and loop avoidance.

12. B. Switches break up collision domains, and routers break up broadcast domains.

13. C. With the exception of the source port, switches flood all frames that have an unknown destination address. If a device answers the frame, the switch will update the MAC address table to reflect the location of the device.

14. C. Because the source MAC address is not in the MAC address table, the switch will add the source address and the port it is connected to into the MAC address table and then forward the frame to the outgoing port.

15. D. Virtual Trunk Protocol (VTP) is a Cisco-proprietary method of having a single VLAN database advertised to all other switches in your network. This allows for ease of VLAN management in a larger network. Option C is not a possible configuration, by the way; I made that up.

16. A, B. The sequence of steps for STP convergence is, by default, disabled, blocking, listening, learning, and forwarding. When all ports are in either the blocking or forwarding state, STP is converged.

17. C, D. In the blocked and listening states, the MAC address table is not learning. Only in the learning and forwarding states is the MAC address table learning MAC addresses and populating the MAC address table.

18. B. Switches break up collision domains by default, but the network is still one large broadcast domain. In order to break up broadcast domains in a Layer 2 switched network, you need to create virtual LANs.

19. C. If you are configuring voice VLANs, you'll want to configure Quality of Service (QoS) on the switch ports to provide a higher precedence to voice traffic over data traffic to improve quality of the line.

20. B. Be careful when using port mirroring/spanning on a switch because it can cause a lot of overhead on the switch and possibly crash your network. So it's a good idea to use this feature at strategic times and only for short periods if possible.

Chapter 12: Wireless Networking

1. C. It is imperative that a good site survey is completed before installing your wireless network. Trying various types of antennas and their placements is the key to covering the whole wireless area.

2. D. The IEEE 802.11a standard runs in the 5GHz RF range.

3. C. The IEEE 802.11b and IEEE 802.11g both run in the 2.4GHz RF range.

4. B, D. If you are running 802.11b/g frequency, which most networks are, then you can receive interference from microwave ovens and cordless phones.

5. D. 802.11n uses channel bonding of both the 2.4Ghz range and the 5Ghz range to get increased bandwidth of over 100Mbps.

6. A. The IEEE 802.11b and g standards provide three non-overlapping channels.

7. B. The IEEE 802.11a standard provides up to 12 non-overlapping channels, or up to 23 if you add the 802.11h standard.

8. D. The IEEE 802.11a standard provides a maximum data rate of up to 54Mbps.

9. C. If you have a large area to cover with wireless, you need to be concerned with channel overlap.

10. B. The IEEE 802.11b standard provides a maximum data rate of up to 11Mbps.

11. B. If everything is correctly configured on the host, then MAC filtering would stop the host from connecting to the AP. If you try to connect and can't, check the AP's settings.

12. A. The IEEE 802.11i standard replaced Wired Equivalent Privacy (WEP) with a specific mode of the Advanced Encryption Standard (AES) known as the Counter Mode Cipher Block Chaining-Message Authentication Code (CBC-MAC) protocol. This allows AES-CCMP (AES-Counter Mode CBC-MAC Protocol) to provide both data confidentiality (encryption) and data integrity.

13. C. If you disable SSID broadcasting, which you should, then you must configure the SSID name on the clients that need to connect to the AP.

14. B. The IEEE 802.11b standard uses Direct Sequence Spread Spectrum (DSSS). If you are running 802.11g, it uses Orthogonal Frequency Division Multiplexing (OFDM).

15. B. If you are running an extended service set (meaning more than one AP with the same SSID name), you need to overlap the cell coverage by 10 percent or more so clients will not drop out while roaming.

16. B. You need to use directional antennas, like a Yagi, in order to get the best signal between antennas.

17. A. Extended service set ID means that you have more than one access point, they all are set to the same SSID, and they are all connected together in the same VLAN or distribution system so users can roam.

18. D. WPA is cool because it is easy to configure and works great. Type in a passphrase (assuming you're using Pre-Shared Key), and you're done. Plus, you have great security because the keys change dynamically.

19. C. 802.11n uses two 20MHz-wide channels to create a 40Mhz-wide channel, which provides over 100Mbps wireless.

20. B. 802.11n MIMO sends multiple frames by several antennae over several paths. The frames are then recombined by another set of antennae to optimize throughput and multipath resistance. This is called spatial multiplexing.

Chapter 13: Authentication and Access Control

1. B. A firewall protects a private network from unauthorized users on a public network.

2. C. On a private network, only authorized users have access to the data, versus a public network where everyone connected has access to the data.

3. B. After determining that the user has local network access, your next step would be to verify the VPN address and password.

4. D. To have good security on your network, deny any addresses from your internal networks, deny any local host addresses (127.0.0.0/8), deny any reserved private addresses, and deny any addresses in the IP multicast address range (224.0.0.0/4).

5. D. Tunneling is encapsulating one protocol within another protocol to complete a secure transmission. Options A, B, and C are all tunneling protocols you should be aware of, as well as Secure Sockets Layer Virtual Private Network (SSL VPN) and Point-to-Point Tunneling Protocol (PPTP).

6. A. SSL is based on RSA public-key encryption and is used to provide secure Session layer connections over the Internet between a web browser and a web server.

7. C. The minimum length should be 8, and the maximum length should be 15. A strong password is a combination of alphanumeric and special characters that is easy for you to remember but difficult for someone else to guess.

8. B. IPSec works at the Network layer of the OSI model (Layer 3) and secures all applications that operate above it (Layer 4 and above). Additionally, because it was designed by the IETF and designed to work with IPv4 and IPv6, it has broad industry support and is quickly becoming the standard for VPNs on the Internet.

9. D. IPSec works in both transport mode and tunneling mode. In transport mode, a secure IP connection between two hosts is created. Data is protected by authentication or encryption (or both). Tunnel mode is used between network endpoints to protect all data going through the tunnel.

10. B. Companies that want to ensure their data is secure during transit should encrypt their data before transmission. Encryption is the process that encodes and decodes data.

11. A, C. Some older network utilities such as FTP and Telnet don't have the ability to encrypt passwords.

12. C. To encode a message and decode an encrypted message, you need the proper encryption key or keys. The encryption key is the table or formula that defines which character in the data translates to which encoded character.

13. C. TLS was available for use with VPNs in the earlier version of TLS.

14. D. The Data Encryption Standard (DES) is not a type of public-key encryption.

15. D. PPTP is a VPN protocol that was created by Microsoft and uses port 1723 to encrypt data at the Application level.

16. B. PPPoE has only two stages: discovery and session. In the discovery phase, the MAC addresses of each of the endpoints of the connection are given to each other so that a secure PPP connection can be made.

17. C. A fingerprint is an example of something you are. Other examples are retina scans and facial recognition.

18. A. RADIUS servers provide both authentication and encryption services and can combine these into one service. RADIUS can be used for allowing or denying access on both wired and wireless access at the domain level.

19. A. RADIUS combines user authentication and authorization into one centralized database and maintains user profiles.

20. D. Independent Computing Architecture (ICA) is a protocol designed by Citrix Systems to provide communication between servers and clients. ICA is a remote-access method.

Chapter 14: Network Threats and Mitigation

1. D. A denial of service (DoS) attack prevents users from accessing the system. All of the options are possible denial of service attacks.

2. C. Worms, phishing, and rogue access points are all threats that may adversely affect a network.

3. A. Options B, C, and D are all DoS attacks, so the only real option is a file virus. A file virus attacks executable application and system program files.

4. A. In war driving, the attacker simply drives around with a high-powered antenna connected to a wireless laptop scanning for networks.

5. D. These are all examples of boot-sector viruses that get into the master boot record. A boot-sector virus will overwrite the boot sector, thereby making it look as if there is no pointer to your operating system. When you power up the computer, you will see a Missing Operating System or Hard Disk Not Found error message.

6. A. A multipartite virus is one that affects both the boot sector and files on your computer.

7. C. A worm can actively replicate itself without user intervention, whereas a virus can be activated and spread only if a user opens an application.

8. B. A brute-force attack is a software-related attack that employs a program that is running on a targeted network and tries to log in to some type of shared network resource like a server.

9. A. Social engineering, or phishing, refers to the act of attempting to illegally obtain sensitive information by pretending to be a credible source. Phishing usually takes one of two forms: an email or a phone call.

10. B. A clean-desk policy means that all important documents, such as books, schematics, confidential letters, and the like, are removed from the desk (and locked away) when employees leave their workstations.

11. D. It is important to train all employees by informing them that people may try to call and email them to gather information to attack the company. This is called phishing or social engineering.

12. B. When you set the AP to not broadcast the SSID, it will remove the SSID from packets called beacons (these are the packets that populate the display when you scan for networks) but it will still be present in many other packet types.

13. A. A security procedure defines the appropriate response to a security event on your network.

14. A. Soon after its adoption as a security measure, it was discovered that due to a weakness in the way the algorithm was employed, programs that became widely available on the Internet could be used to crack the WEP key.

15. B. Windows Update is a utility that is typically automatically installed when you install Windows. The update engine will periodically scan your system for the version of Windows components you have installed and compare them to the most current versions available from Microsoft. If your software is out-of-date, a Windows Update dialog box will appear, asking if you want to install the software updates.

16. C. With so much code written for applications and operating systems, developers go back after the initial release to fix any problems that are uncovered. These fixes are released as hotfixes or patches.

17. C. Wireless stations (laptops, PDAs, and so on) choose an access point with which to connect by SSID and not by channel, MAC address, or signal-to-noise ratio.

18. D. Heuristic scanning allows for this type of scanning. The engine looks for suspicious activity that might indicate a virus.

19. A. Every week, you need to update your list of known viruses—called the virus definition files. You can do this manually or automatically through the manufacturer's website. You can use a staging server within your company to download and then distribute the updates, or you can set up each computer to download updates.

20. D. An antivirus program examines the computer suspected of being infected and eradicates any viruses it finds using any of these methods.

Chapter 15: Physical and Hardware Security

1. C. Firewalls work by allowing only packets that pass security restrictions to be forwarded through the firewall. A firewall can also permit, deny, encrypt, decrypt, and proxy all computer traffic that flows through it; this can be between a public and private network or between different security domains (or zones) on a private network. You as the administrator set up the rules by which a firewall decides to forward or reject packets of data.

2. A, D. Firewalls work at the Application layer or the Network layer.

3. B. A *network-based firewall* is what companies use to protect their private network from public networks. The defining characteristic of this type of firewall is that it's designed to protect an entire network of computers as opposed to just one system. This is usually a combination of hardware and software. A *host-based firewall* is implemented on one machine and is designed to protect that machine only. Most often, this is implemented as software; no additional hardware is required in your personal computer to run a host-based firewall.

4. B. The one big advantage that a stateless firewall has over its stateful counterparts is that it uses less memory. Today, stateless firewalls are best if used on an internal network where security threats are lower and there are few restrictions.

5. B. NESSUS cannot identify an incorrect IP addresses.

6. C. One of the benefits of using a firewall is that it helps protect LAN resources from unwanted attacks.

7. B. An intrusion detection system (IDS) monitors network traffic, looking for signs of an intrusion. Intrusions are detected by an attack signature.

8. B. Firewalls, which use access lists, can permit or deny connections and types of traffic in or out of the network.

9. C. Standard, extended, and outbound are all types of ACL. Referred is not.

10. B. You can sometimes just ignore the attack because it's possible it won't affect your network. This is called shunning.

11. C. A DMZ can be set up many different ways, but the best explanation is the DMZ is used to separate and secure your inside network from the Internet, while still allowing hosts on the Internet to access your servers.

12. E. Most firewalls provide content filtering, signature identification, and the ability to segregate network segments into separate security zones. Most firewalls are also capable of performing scanning services, which means that they scan different types of incoming traffic in an effort to detect problems.

13. A. An intrusion detection system (IDS) monitors network traffic, looking for signs of an intrusion. Intrusions are detected by matching activity versus known signatures within the IDS's database. If an intrusion is detected, a passive response such as logging or notifying a network administrator is executed. An intrusion prevention system (IPS) is like an IDS, but with two key differences. First, it learns what is "normal" on the network and can react to abnormalities even if they aren't part of the signature database. Second, it can issue an active response such as shutting down a port, resetting connections, or attempting to lull the attacker into a trap.

14. B. NESSUS is a propriety vulnerability scanning program that requires a license for commercial use yet is the single most popular scanning program in use.

15. C. NESSUS does not collect passwords.

16. D. Changing network configurations, terminating sessions, and deceiving the attacker are all actions that can be taken by an IPS device.

17. D. Proxies act on behalf of the whole network to completely separate packets from internal hosts and external hosts.

18. B. NESSUS operates by performing a port scan and then follows up with more specific tests, but it cannot identify IP address conflicts.

19. C. A stateful firewall keeps track of the established connections passing through it. When another packet is received that's part of an existing connection (part of a current state), the packet is passed without checking the ACLs.

20. C. An intrusion prevention system (IPS) is like an IDS, but with two key differences. First, it learns what is "normal" on the network and can react to abnormalities even if they're not part of the signature database. Second, it can issue an active response such as shutting down a port, resetting connections, or attempting to lull an attacker into a trap.

Chapter 16: Wide Area Networks

1. D. Routing Information Protocol (RIP) is not a WAN protocol but a routing protocol used in internetworks.

2. C. These different protocols and technologies all occupy the lower three layers of the OSI model: the Physical layer, the Data Link layer, and sometimes the Network layer. Most WAN protocols work only at the Physical layer and Data Link layer.

3. B. The demarcation point is the precise spot where the service provider's responsibility ends and the CPE begins.

4. C. The European version of the T1 is the E1, which operates at 2.048Mbps and uses 30 64Kbps channels (30 DS0s).

5. C. The demarc is the precise spot where the service provider's (local exchange carrier) responsibility ends and the CPE begins. It's generally a device in a telecommunications closet owned and installed by the telecommunications company (telco).

6. D. Cable is a great cost-effective connection for a small office or home office (SOHO).

7. C. A T1 has a line speed of 1.544Mbps. This 1.544Mbps connection uses Digital Signal 1 (DS1) and aggregates 24 discrete 64Kbps channels that use Digital Signal 0 (DS0). Other T-series connections have greater maximum connection speeds.

8. C. LTE is true 4G and has the best data rates.

9. B. OC-1, OC-3, OC-12, OC-48, and OC-192 are the normal service offerings. OC-1 has the lowest data rate at 51.84Mbps, and OC-192 is the highest at 9.953Gbps.

10. A. Bluetooth uses a radio technology called frequency hopping spread spectrum. It chops up the data being sent and transmits chunks of it through the air on up to 75 different frequencies.

11. C. The *x* in *x*DSL represents the different letters that refer to the DSL flavors. *x*DSLs use high-frequency signals, whereas regular phone calls use low-frequency signals over the same lines.

12. C. ADSL, HDSL, SDSL, VDSL or VHDSL, and VDSL2 are all common *x*DSL types. Synchronous Optical Network (SONET) is the standard for synchronous data transmission on optical fiber.

13. D. DOCSIS stands for data over cable service interface specification. All cable modems and like devices have to measure up to this standard.

14. C. Optical carrier 12 has speeds up to 622Mbps.

15. C. ATM uses a high-speed cell-switching technology that can handle data as well as real-time voice and video. The ATM protocol breaks up transmitted data into 53-byte cells.

16. A. Frame Relay is the frame WAN technology in which variable-length packets are transmitted by switching.

17. C. The committed information rate (CIR) is the rate, in bits per second, at which the Frame Relay switch guarantees to transfer data.

18. B. We're thinking in terms of a WAN, so B is obviously the correct choice. Asynchronous Transfer Mode was designed to be a high-speed communications protocol that does not depend on any specific LAN topology.

19. B. A T3 line works similarly to a T1 connection but carries a whopping 44.736Mbps. This is equivalent to 28 T1 circuits (or a total of 672 DS0 channels), and it uses a signal known as Digital Signal 3 (DS3).

20. C. Wavelength Division Multiplexing (WDM) is a technology that multiplexes multiple optical carriers on a single optical fiber by using different wavelengths.

Chapter 17: Troubleshooting Tools

1. C. The program Packet Internet Groper (`ping`) is used to find out if a host has the IP stack initialized.

2. A. The `arp` utility is used to display the contents of the ARP cache, which tracks the resolution of IP addresses to physical (MAC) addresses and will produce the displayed output.

3. A. Microsoft has made what it calls Remote Desktop software available for free with Windows products since Windows NT. When this software is installed (installed by default in later versions) on both source and destination computers, a remote desktop connection can be made.

4. B. The purpose of the `ping` utility is to test the communications channel between two IP hosts as well as how long it takes the packets to get from one host to another.

5. C. The `ipconfig /all` utility will display the current configuration of TCP/IP on a given workstation—including the current IP address, DNS configuration, WINS configuration, and default gateway.

6. B, D. The address 127.0.0.1 is the special IP address designated for the local TCP/IP interface. The hostname localhost is the hostname given to the local interface. Therefore, pinging either the IP address or the hostname for the local interface will tell you whether the local interface is working.

7. A. The command `nbtstat –r` displays all the name resolutions performed by the local client as well as their associated IP addresses. The –R switch will reload the cache.

8. C. The `arp` utility will show you the resolved MAC to IP address of all hosts on your network segment. Remember, this will work for only local hosts, not remote hosts.

9. B. To purge and reload the remote NetBIOS name cache, you must use `nbtstat -R`. Remember that the R must be uppercase and that it will not work correctly without the hyphen before it.

10. B. Commercial sniffers like Wireshark or OmniPeek can capture any packets because they set the NIC to operate in promiscuous mode, which means the NIC processes all packets that it sees.

11. B. The `tracert` utility will give you that output. The `tracert` command (or `trace` for short) traces the route from the source IP host to the destination host.

12. C. The `tracert` utility will tell you which router is having the performance problem and how long it takes to move between each host. `tracert` can be used to locate problem areas in a network.

13. A. The `ipconfig /all` switch will display the most complete listing of TCP/IP configuration information, also displaying the MAC address, DHCP lease times, and the DNS addresses.

14. C. The `tracert` utility returns the names and addresses of all router through which a packet passes on its way to a destination host.

15. E. The `telnet` utility can be used to test if a particular IP host is responding on a particular TCP port.

16. C. The `arp /a` command will display the current contents of the ARP cache on the local workstation.

17. C. `Dig` is an old unix command that will show you DNS server information.

18. A, D. The `arp` utility's –a and –g switches perform the same function. They both show the current ARP cache.

19. B, E, F. The `nslookup`, `ipconfig`, and `ifconfig` commands will show you the DNS servers that a computer is configured to use.

20. C. The command `nbtstat -s` will display pre-protocol statistics for IP, IPv6, ICMP, ICMPv6, TCP, TCPv6, UDP, and UDPv6.

Chapter 18: Software and Hardware Tools

1. D. Yup, all of the above. The CompTIA Network+ objectives cover all three in regard to tools used to analyze today's networks.

2. C. The basic purpose of packet sniffers or network analyzers is to collect and analyze each individual packet that is captured on a specific network segment to determine whether problems are happening. You can also use them to see if there is too much traffic on a segment.

3. A. A toner probe sends a signal down a pair of wires so that the wires can be traced. Typically, a butt set is used to find this signal, but toner probe is the best answer to this question.

4. B. An optical time-domain reflectometer (OTDR) is an optoelectronic instrument used to give you the skinny on optical fibers. It works by putting out a series of optical pulses into the specific fiber you want to test and can tell you if a break in the fiber has occurred and where.

5. B. To create a patch cable (568A) to connect your host to a jack in the wall, you need to use a snips.

6. A. Remember that firewalls are the first line of defense for an Internet-connected network. If a network was directly connected to the Internet without a firewall, an attacker could theoretically gain direct access to the computers and servers on that network with little effort. The IDS/IPS software is usually positioned between your internal router and the firewall to the outside network (Internet).

7. C. Hope you answered C! A port scanner is just a piece of software designed to search a network for open hosts. Administrators of networks use port scanners to ensure security and bad guys use them to compromise it.

8. D. Wire-map testing is the most basic test for twisted-pair cables. It detects transposed wires, opens (broken or unconnected wires), and shorts (wires or pins improperly connected to each other).

9. B. A time-domain reflectometer (TDR) is a tool that finds and describes faults in metallic cables like twisted wire pairs and coaxial cables. The equivalent device for optical fiber is an optical time-domain reflectometer (OTDR). A TDR can also check the speed and condition of the signal on the cable.

10. B. A certifier is a combination cable tester and network analyzer, only better. It can test the performance and response times of network resources and certify your full Category 6 cable installation at the same time.

11. D. Unlike port scanners, packet sniffers actually look inside every packet on a network segment at the frame level.

12. C. Due to sensitivity to any variation and impedance, options A, B, D, and E are all reasons you'd use a TDR.

13. A. A multimeter or a volt/ohm meter (VOM) is used to measure voltage, current, and resistance.

14. D. Otherwise known as a "fox and hound" wire tracer, a toner probe would be useful in this situation. A toner probe will emit an audible tone when it touches the other end of the cable.

15. A. I hope you said A! A punch-down tool would be used if you needed to connect wire to a punch-down block. Most networks today have wiring closets, and to terminate the cables, you're certain to need a punch-down tool.

16. B. A wire crimper or crimper is used for attaching ends onto different types of network cables.

17. C. A punch-down tool is used to punch down an RJ-45 cable to an insulation displacement connector, typically a 110 block.

18. D. An everyday surge protector monitors the incoming voltage level and trips a circuit breaker when the when the voltage reaches a certain level, known as the overvoltage threshold.

19. B. A loopback test is a diagnostic procedure in which a signal is transmitted and returned to the sending device after passing through all or a portion of a network or circuit. A loopback plug makes this test possible.

20. B. Electronic devices are prone to overheating, which is why you should use a temperature monitor.

Chapter 19: Network Troubleshooting

1. A, F. Rebooting servers and routers are not part of the troubleshooting model.

2. B. You need to check basic connectivity. The link light indicates that the network card is making a basic-level connection to the rest of the network. It is a very easy item to check, and if the link light is not lit, it is usually a very simple fix (like plugging in an unplugged cable).

3. B. When wireless uses complain that the network is slow (latency) or that they are losing their connection to applications during a session, it is usually latency arising from a capacity issue.

4. B. Although all of these are good tests for network connectivity, checking the server console for user connections will tell you whether other users are able to log into the server. If they can, the problem is most likely related to one of those users' workstations. If they can't, the problem is either the server or network connection. This helps narrow down the problem.

5. B. Because of all the tests given and their results, you can narrow the problem down to the network connectivity of that workstation. And because no other users in her area are having the same problem, it can't be the hub or server. You can log in as the user from your workstation, so you know it isn't a rights issue or username/password issue. The only possible answer listed is a bad patch cable.

6. A. Because other users in the same area aren't having a problem, it can't be a downed server, network hub, or jabbering NIC. And because both you and the user can't log in, more than likely it's a problem specific to that workstation. The only one that would affect your ability to log in from that station is the Caps Lock key being pressed. That will cause the password to be in all uppercase (which most server operating systems treat as a different password), and thus it will probably be rejected.

7. D. Since this is a new connection, you need to start by troubleshooting and identify the symptoms and potential causes.

8. B. According to the Network+ troubleshooting model, the next step would be step 2, establishing the most probable cause.

9. C. After determining the affected area, you need to find out if any changes have taken place.

10. A. Because the user can't log in correctly from any machine, more than likely he is using the wrong procedure for logging in. Because no one else is having that problem (including yourself), the problem must be related to that user.

11. C. After you have implemented a solution, you need to test if the solution works and identify other effects it may have.

12. B. Because you cannot reach the web page that resides on the server, the problem is most likely related to a problem with your browser.

13. D. From a design standpoint, the physical environment for a server should be optimized for items such as placement, temperature, and humidity. When troubleshooting, don't forget to check the physical conditions under which the network device is operating. Check for problems such as those mentioned here as well as EMI/RFI problems, power problems, and unplugged cables.

14. D. Because most of today's networks still consist of large amounts of copper cable, networks can suffer from the physical issues that have plagued all networks since the very beginning of networking (and the answers here are not a complete list). Newer technologies and protocols have lessened these issues but have not resolved them completely.

15. A. Once you have determined that the switch is the problem or the configuration of the switch is the problem, you need to escalate the issue.

16. D. Because other people are experiencing the problem, most likely it is either network or server related. Because you can transfer files to and from another server, it can't be the network. Thus, the problem is related to the web server.

17. D. After investigating the problem thoroughly and successfully testing and resolving an issue, you need to document the solution.

18. B. Since users can get to the Internet, this means the DNS server is working and they have the correct default gateway. The intranet server is probably down.

19. C. Performance-monitoring tools can give you an idea of how busy the server and the rest of the network are. These tools use graphs to indicate how much traffic is going through the server.

20. C. Once you escalate the problem, you are done with the seven-step model. Meet with the escalation team to determine the next step.

Chapter 20: Management, Monitoring, and Optimization

1. C. UTP cables use an RJ-45 connector. RJ-11 and RJ-25 are often used for terminating telephone lines.

2. B. Straight-through cables, known as drop cables or patch cables, will have the pins in the same order on both connectors.

3. B. On a crossover cable, one connector has flipped the wires. Specifically, pins 1 and 3 get switched, and pins 2 and 6 get switched.

4. C. If you are going to make your own UTP cables (drop/patch cables) to customize length, you need to make sure that the right wires get to the right pins.

5. A, B, C, D. A baseline is the standard level of performance of a network component or a system of components. For networks and networked devices, the four key components are hard disk, memory, processor, and network adapter.

6. C. Policies govern how the network is configured and operated as well as how people are expected to behave on the network, such as how users are able to access resources and which types of employees get network access.

7. A. A physical network diagram contains all the physical devices and connectivity paths on your network and should accurately picture how your network physically fits together in detail. This document will also have the firmware revision on all the switches and access points in your network.

8. C. A good choice here would be to use a packet sniffer. Packet sniffers allow you to examine network traffic down to details of individual packets. The key piece that network administrators are usually looking for is the packet header, or the beginning of each packet. The packet header will contain the protocol being used as well as the source and destination IP addresses.

9. B. Network monitoring can have several names, including load testing, connectivity testing, and throughput testing. You will also hear network monitors referred to as protocol analyzers.

10. A. The application log contains events triggered by applications or programs. These events are determined by the programmers. Examples of software that provide application logs are LiveUpdate, the Microsoft Office suite, and SQL and Exchange servers.

11. C. The system log contains events generated by Windows system components. It includes events such as drivers and services starting or failing to start.

12. D. QoS provides different priority levels to different applications, data flows, or users so that they can be guaranteed a certain performance level.

13. B. Common Address Redundancy Protocol (CARP) can be used to increase availability of gateways and firewalls.

14. B. If you add a new cable segment to the network, you need to update the wiring schematics document.

15. C, E. Quality of service (QoS) is basically the ability to provide different priority to one or more types of traffic over other levels for different applications, data flows, or users so that they can be guaranteed a certain performance level.

16. A. Traffic shaping, also known as packet shaping, is a form of bandwidth optimization. It delays packets that meet a certain criteria to guarantee usable bandwidth for other applications. Essentially, with traffic shaping, you're delaying some traffic so other traffic can get through. Traffic shaping uses bandwidth throttling to ensure that certain data streams don't send too much data in a specified period of time.

17. C. Common Address Redundancy Protocol (CARP) can be used to increase availability of gateways and firewalls. It is not related to virtualization.

18. F. There are many bandwidth-intensive programs, like VoIP and video streaming. These are just a few of the reasons why it's necessary to try to optimize network performance.

19. C. Voice over Internet Protocol (VoIP) is a general term that describes several technologies that are able to deliver voice communications over the Internet or other data networks.

20. E. There are many theories and strategies you can apply to optimize performance on your network. All of them deal with controlling the traffic in some way. Strategies include QoS, traffic shaping, load balancing, high availability, and the use of caching servers. You want to ensure that you have plenty of bandwidth available for those applications that need it, such as critical service operations, VoIP, and real-time multimedia streaming.

Appendix
B

Answers to Written Labs

Chapter 1: Introduction to Networks

1. Bus, ring, and star
2. Multiprotocol Label Switching (MPLS)
3. Server
4. Client-server
5. Point-to-point
6. Hub
7. MultiProtocol Label Switching
8. Wide area network
9. A segment
10. Bus

Chapter 2: The Open Systems Interconnection Specifications

1. The Application layer is responsible for finding the network resources broadcast from a server and adding flow control and error control (if the application developer chooses).
2. The Physical layer takes frames from the Data Link layer and encodes the 1s and 0s into a digital signal for transmission on the network medium.
3. The Network layer provides routing through an internetwork and logical addressing.
4. The Presentation layer makes sure that data is in a readable format for the Application layer.
5. The Session layer sets up, maintains, and terminates sessions between applications.
6. Protocol Data Units (PDUs) at the Data Link layer are called frames. As soon as you see *frame* in a question, you know the answer.

7. The Transport layer uses virtual circuits to create a reliable connection between two hosts.

8. The Network layer provides logical addressing, typically IP addressing, and routing.

9. The Physical layer is responsible for the electrical and mechanical connections between devices.

10. The Data Link layer is responsible for the framing of data packets.

Chapter 3: Networking Topologies, Connectors, and Wiring Standards

1. Category 6

2. Demarcation point or demarc

3. Crossover

4. RG-6

5. Category 5e

6. Straight-through

7. To connect two CSU/DSUs

8. 1, 2, 3, and 6

9. 1 to 3 and 2 to 6

10. It is completely immune to EMI and RFI and can transmit up to 40 kilometers (about 25 miles).

Chapter 4: The Current Ethernet Specifications

1. Convert from decimal IP address to binary format.

   Complete the following table to express 192.168.10.15 in binary format.

Decimal	128	64	32	16	8	4	2	1	Binary
192	1	1	0	0	0	0	0	0	11000000
168	1	0	1	0	1	0	0	0	10101000
10	0	0	0	0	1	0	1	0	00001010
15	0	0	0	0	1	1	1	1	00001111

Complete the following table to express 172.16.20.55 in binary format.

Decimal	128	64	32	16	8	4	2	1	Binary
172	1	0	1	0	1	1	0	0	10101100
16	0	0	0	1	0	0	0	0	00010000
20	0	0	0	1	0	1	0	0	00010100
55	0	0	1	1	0	1	1	1	00110111

Complete the following table to express 10.11.12.99 in binary format.

Decimal	128	64	32	16	8	4	2	1	Binary
10	0	0	0	0	1	0	1	0	00001010
11	0	0	0	0	1	0	1	1	00001011
12	0	0	0	0	1	1	0	0	00001100
99	0	1	1	0	0	0	1	1	01100011

2. Convert the following from binary format to decimal IP address.

Complete the following table to express 11001100.00110011.10101010.01010101 in decimal IP address format.

Binary	128	64	32	16	8	4	2	1	Decimal
11001100	1	1	0	0	1	1	0	0	204
00110011	0	0	1	1	0	0	1	1	51
10101010	1	0	1	0	1	0	1	0	170
01010101	0	1	0	1	0	1	0	1	85

Complete the following table to express 11000110.11010011.00111001.11010001 in decimal IP address format.

Binary	128	64	32	16	8	4	2	1	Decimal
11000110	1	1	0	0	0	1	1	0	198
11010011	1	1	0	1	0	0	1	1	211
00111001	0	0	1	1	1	0	0	1	57
11010001	1	1	0	1	0	0	0	1	209

Complete the following table to express 10000100.11010010.10111000.10100110 in decimal IP address format.

Binary	128	64	32	16	8	4	2	1	Decimal
10000100	1	0	0	0	0	1	0	0	132
11010010	1	1	0	1	0	0	1	0	210
10111000	1	0	1	1	1	0	0	0	184
10100110	1	0	1	0	0	1	1	0	166

3. Convert the following from binary format to hexadecimal.

Complete the following table to express 11011000.00011011.00111101.01110110 in hexadecimal.

Binary	128	64	32	16	8	4	2	1	Hexadecimal
11011000	1	1	0	1	1	0	0	0	D8
00011011	0	0	0	1	1	0	1	1	1B
00111101	0	0	1	1	1	1	0	1	3D
01110110	0	1	1	1	0	1	1	0	76

Complete the following table to express 11001010.11110101.10000011.11101011 in hexadecimal.

Binary	128	64	32	16	8	4	2	1	Hexadecimal
11001010	1	1	0	0	1	0	1	0	CA
11110101	1	1	1	1	0	1	0	1	F5
10000011	1	0	0	0	0	0	1	1	83
11101011	1	1	1	0	1	0	1	1	EB

Complete the following table to express 10000100.11010010.01000011.10110011 in hexadecimal.

Binary	128	64	32	16	8	4	2	1	Hexadecimal
10000100	1	0	0	0	0	1	0	0	84
11010010	1	1	0	1	0	0	1	0	D2
01000011	0	1	0	0	0	0	1	1	43
10110011	1	0	1	1	0	0	1	1	B3

Chapter 5: Networking Devices

Description	Device or OSI Layer
This device sends and receives information about the Network layer.	Router
This layer creates a virtual circuit before transmitting between two end stations.	Transport
A Layer 3 switch, or multilayer switch	Router
This device uses hardware addresses to filter a network.	Bridge or switch
Ethernet is defined at these layers.	Data Link and Physical
This layer supports flow control and sequencing.	Transport
This device can measure the distance to a remote network.	Router
Logical addressing is used at this layer.	Network
Hardware addresses are defined at this layer.	Data Link (MAC sublayer)
This device creates one big collision domain and one large broadcast domain.	Hub
This device creates many smaller collision domains, but the network is still one large broadcast domain.	Switch or bridge
This device can never run full duplex	Hub
This device breaks up collision domains and broadcast domains.	Router

Chapter 6: Introduction to the Internet Protocol

1. The most likely problem is that a rogue DHCP server has been introduced into the network and is handing this device an incorrect lease.
2. FTP uses both TCP ports 20 and 21 for the data channel and the control channel, respectively.

3. A DNS server uses TCP port 53 for zone transfers and UDP port 53 for name resolutions.

4. ICMP uses IP directly to build error-reporting packets that are transmitted back to the originating source host when issues arise during the delivery of data packets. ICMP is also used during ping and some Traceroute operations.

5. Quite simply, the service might not be running currently on that server. Another possibility might be that a firewall between the client and the server has blocked the protocol in question from passing.

6. Most ISPs have their own mail servers. When you switch service, you might need to point your mail application to the servers provided by the new service provider.

7. The Unix command `rlogin` functions similarly to Telnet.

8. ICMP is the protocol that the `ping` and `tracert` commands rely on. If you're having trouble getting pings and Traceroutes through a router, you might need to check if ICMP is being allowed thorough.

9. TFTP servers respond to UDP messages sent to port 69.

10. SMTP uses TCP port 25, POP3 uses TCP port 110, RDP uses TCP port 3389, and IMAP4 uses TCP port 143.

Chapter 7: IP Addressing

1. The class C private range is 192.168.0.0 through 192.168.255.255.

2. IPv6 has the following characteristics, among others, that make it preferable to IPv4: more available addresses, simpler header, options for authentication and other security.

3. Automatic Private IP Addressing (APIPA) is the technology that results in hosts automatically configuring themselves with addresses that begin with 169.254.

4. An IP address assigned to an interface

5. One-to-many address

6. A MAC address, sometimes called a hardware address or even a burned-in address

7. The fact that it has 128-bit (16-octet) addresses, compared to IPv4's 32-bit (4-octet) addresses

8. 172.16.0.0 through 172.31.255.255

9. 192–223, 110$xxxxx$

10. Loopback or diagnostics

Chapter 8: IP Subnetting, Troubleshooting IP, and Introduction to NAT

1. 192.168.100.25/30. A /30 is 255.255.255.252. The valid subnet is 192.168.100.24, broadcast is 192.168.100.27, and valid hosts are 192.168.100.25 and 26.

2. 192.168.100.37/28. A /28 is 255.255.255.240. The fourth octet is a block size of 16. Just count by 16s until you pass 37. 0, 16, 32, 48. The host is in the 32 subnet, with a broadcast address of 47. Valid hosts are 33–46.

3. 192.168.100.66/27. A /27 is 255.255.255.224. The fourth octet is a block size of 32. Count by 32s until you pass the host address of 66. 0, 32, 64. The host is in the 64 subnet, broadcast address of 95. The valid host range is 65–94.

4. 192.168.100.17/29. A /29 is 255.255.255.248. The fourth octet is a block size of 8. 0, 8, 16, 24. The host is in the 16 subnet, broadcast of 23. Valid hosts are 17–22.

5. 192.168.100.99/26. A /26 is 255.255.255.192. The fourth octet has a block size of 64. 0, 64, 128. The host is in the 64 subnet, broadcast of 127. Valid hosts are 65–126.

6. 192.168.100.99/25. A /25 is 255.255.255.128. The fourth octet is a block size of 128. 0, 128. The host is in the 0 subnet, broadcast of 127. Valid hosts are 1–126.

7. A default Class B is 255.255.0.0. A Class B 255.255.255.0 mask is 256 subnets, each with 254 hosts. We need fewer subnets. If we use 255.255.240.0, this provides 16 subnets. Let's add one more subnet bit. 255.255.248.0. This is 5 bits of subnetting, which provides 32 subnets. This is our best answer, a /21.

8. A /29 is 255.255.255.248. This is a block size of 8 in the fourth octet. 0, 8, 16. The host is in the 8 subnet, and broadcast is 15.

9. A /29 is 255.255.255.248, which is 5 subnet bits and 3 host bits. This is only 6 hosts per subnet.

10. A /23 is 255.255.254.0. The third octet is a block size of 2. 0, 2, 4. The host is in the 16.2.0 subnet; the broadcast address is 16.3.255.

Chapter 9: Introduction to IP Routing

1. False. RIP and RIPv2 are both distance vector protocols.

2. False. RIP and RIPv2 are both distance vector protocols.

3. False. EIGRP is a Cisco-proprietary routing protocol.

4. Autonomous system

5. RIP does not work well in large networks, so OSPF would be the best answer, and both RIP and OSPF are nonproprietary.

6. Static routing

7. The MAC address of your default gateway (router)

8. The IP address of the server

9. The MAC address of the router sending the frame to the server

10. The IP address of the server

Chapter 10: Routing Protocols

1. 120

2. 90

3. 120

4. 1

5. RIPng (Next Generation). I wonder how many of you answered RIPv3.

6. OSPFv3

7. EIGRPv6

8. When you need to connect two autonomous systems (ASs) together

9. When all your routers are Cisco routers

10. Distance vector

Chapter 11: Switching and Virtual LANs

1. Broadcast

2. Collision

3. Trunking allows you to send information about many or all VLANs through the same link. Access ports allow information about only one VLAN transmitted.

4. Power over Ethernet (PoE)

5. The VLAN port membership is set wrong.

6. Flood the frame out all ports except the port on which it was received.

7. Address learning, filtering, and loop avoidance

8. It will add the source MAC address to the forward/filter table.

9. Spanning Tree Protocol (STP)

10. Create a VLAN for contractors and another VLAN for guests.

Chapter 12: Wireless Networking

1. 11Mbps
2. 54Mbps
3. 54Mbps
4. 2.4GHz
5. 2.4GHz
6. 5GHz
7. None
8. The values of WPA keys can change dynamically while the system is being used.
9. The IEEE 802.11i standard has been sanctioned by WPA and is called WPA version 2.
10. Three

Chapter 13: Authentication and Access Control

1. IP addresses and MAC addresses
2. IPSec
3. SSL VPN
4. PKI
5. Only the owner of the key
6. Kerberos
7. Authentication, Authorization, and Accounting
8. 802.1x
9. MS-CHAP
10. TACACS+

Chapter 14: Network Threats and Mitigation

1. Denial of service (DoS)
2. Once per a week
3. Buffer Overflow
4. A file virus
5. Packet sniffer
6. A macro virus
7. Man-in-the-middle attack
8. A rogue access point
9. Windows Update
10. On-demand and on-access virus scans

Chapter 15: Physical and Hardware Security

1. Intrusion prevention system
2. Stateful
3. Content filtering
4. An access control list (ACL)
5. A VPN concentrator
6. Security zones
7. Port security
8. Deny
9. Honeynet
10. Passive reactions from an IDS

Chapter 16: Wide Area Networks

1. It is readily available.

2. Cable. In a modern network, hybrid fiber coaxial (HFC) is a telecommunications industry term for a network that incorporates both optical fiber and coaxial cable to create a broadband network.

3. Frame Relay. Although Frame Relay is not available in many markets today, it is a possible solution for the problem presented.

4. 1.544Mbps

5. Digital Subscriber Line

6. Frame Relay and X.25

7. LTE and WiMAX

8. ATM

9. HDSL, SDSL, VDSL, ADSL

10. Fiber to the premises

Chapter 17: Troubleshooting Tools

1. `traceroute` or `tracert`

2. Throughput tester

3. `ipconfig /all`

4. Telnet

5. `route`

6. FTP

7. `nslookup`

8. `-n`

9. `ifconfig`

10. `route print`

Chapter 18: Software and Hardware Tools

1. False
2. False
3. True
4. True
5. False. A typical network analyzer can see only one segment at a time.
6. Cable certifier
7. False. Unless you don't mind prison.
8. A temperature monitor
9. A voltage event recorder
10. A cable stripper/crimper

Chapter 19: Network Troubleshooting

1. Test the theory to determine cause.
2. Document findings, actions, and outcomes.
3. Network designers minimize crosstalk inside network cables by twisting the wire pairs together, putting them at a 90 degree angle to each other.
4. The port has the wrong VLAN assignment.
5. Split pairs
6. Attenuation
7. Establish a plan of action to resolve the problem and identify potential effects.
8. Implement the solution or escalate as necessary.
9. Switching loops, routing loops, routing problems, Proxy ARP, broadcast storms
10. Crosstalk, attenuation, collisions, shorts, open impedance mismatch, interference

Chapter 20: Management, Monitoring, and Optimization

1. Logical
2. Traffic shaping
3. Best effort
4. Jitter
5. Load balancing
6. A baseline
7. Crossover
8. Cloud computing
9. Virtual servers, virtual switches, virtual desktops, software as a service (SaaS) and network as a service (NaaS)
10. Procedures

Appendix C

Subnetting Class A

Class A subnetting is not performed any differently than subnetting with Classes B and C, but there are 24 bits to play with instead of the 16 in a Class B address and the 8 in a Class C address.

Let's start by listing all the Class A masks:

255.0.0.0	(/8)		
255.128.0.0	(/9)	255.255.240.0	(/20)
255.192.0.0	(/10)	255.255.248.0	(/21)
255.224.0.0	(/11)	255.255.252.0	(/22)
255.240.0.0	(/12)	255.255.254.0	(/23)
255.248.0.0	(/13)	255.255.255.0	(/24)
255.252.0.0	(/14)	255.255.255.128	(/25)
255.254.0.0	(/15)	255.255.255.192	(/26)
255.255.0.0	(/16)	255.255.255.224	(/27)
255.255.128.0	(/17)	255.255.255.240	(/28)
255.255.192.0	(/18)	255.255.255.248	(/29)
255.255.224.0	(/19)	255.255.255.252	(/30)

That's it. You must leave at least 2 bits for defining hosts. And I hope you can see the pattern by now. Remember, we're going to do this the same way as with a Class B or C subnet. It's just that, again, we simply have more host bits and we use the same subnet numbers we used with Class B and Class C, but we start using these numbers in the second octet.

Subnetting Practice Examples: Class A Addresses

When you look at an IP address and a subnet mask, you must be able to distinguish the bits used for subnets from the bits used for determining hosts. This is imperative. If you're still struggling with this concept, please reread Chapter 6 "Introduction to the Internet Protocol." It shows you how to determine the difference between the subnet and host bits and should help clear things up.

Practice Example #1A: 255.255.0.0 (/16)

Class A addresses use a default mask of 255.0.0.0, which leaves 22 bits for subnetting since you must leave 2 bits for host addressing. The 255.255.0.0 mask with a Class A address is using 8 subnet bits.

- *Subnets?* 2^8 = 256.
- *Hosts?* 2^{16} − 2 = 65,534.
- *Valid subnets?* What is the interesting octet? 256 − 255 = 1. 0, 1, 2, 3, etc. (all in the second octet). The subnets would be 10.0.0.0, 10.1.0.0, 10.2.0.0, 10.3.0.0, etc., up to 10.255.0.0.
- *Broadcast address for each subnet?*
- *Valid hosts?*

The following table shows the first two and last two subnets, valid host range, and broadcast addresses for the private Class A 10.0.0.0 network:

Subnet	10.0.0.0	10.1.0.0	...	10.254.0.0	10.255.0.0
First host	10.0.0.1	10.1.0.1	...	10.254.0.1	10.255.0.1
Last host	10.0.255.254	10.1.255.254	...	10.254.255.254	10.255.255.254
Broadcast	10.0.255.255	10.1.255.255	...	10.254.255.255	10.255.255.255

Practice Example #2A: 255.255.240.0 (/20)

255.255.240.0 gives us 12 bits of subnetting and leaves us 12 bits for host addressing.

- *Subnets?* 2^{12} = 4096.
- *Hosts?* 2^{12} − 2 = 4094.
- *Valid subnets?* What is your interesting octet? 256 − 240 = 16. The subnets in the second octet are a block size of 1 and the subnets in the third octet are 0, 16, 32, etc.
- *Broadcast address for each subnet?*
- *Valid hosts?*

The following table shows some examples of the host ranges—the first three and the last three subnets:

Subnet	10.0.0.0	10.0.16.0	10.0.32.0	...	10.255.240.0
First host	10.0.0.1	10.0.16.1	10.0.32.1	...	10.255.240.1
Last host	10.0.15.254	10.0.31.254	10.0.47.254	...	10.255.255.254
Broadcast	10.0.15.255	10.0.31.255	10.0.47.255	...	10.255.255.255

Practice Example #3A: 255.255.255.192 (/26)

Let's do one more example using the second, third, and fourth octets for subnetting.

- *Subnets?* 2^{18} = 262,144.
- *Hosts?* $2^6 - 2$ = 62.
- *Valid subnets?* In the second and third octet, the block size is 1, and in the fourth octet, the block size is 64.
- *Broadcast address for each subnet?*
- *Valid hosts?*

The following table shows the first four subnets and their valid hosts and broadcast addresses in the Class A 255.255.255.192 mask:

Subnet	10.0.0.0	10.0.0.64	10.0.0.128	10.0.0.192
First host	10.0.0.1	10.0.0.65	10.0.0.129	10.0.0.193
Last host	10.0.0.62	10.0.0.126	10.0.0.190	10.0.0.254
Broadcast	10.0.0.63	10.0.0.127	10.0.0.191	10.0.0.255

The following table shows the last four subnets and their valid hosts and broadcast addresses:

Subnet	10.255.255.0	10.255.255.64	10.255.255.128	10.255.255.192
First host	10.255.255.1	10.255.255.65	10.255.255.129	10.255.255.193
Last host	10.255.255.62	10.255.255.126	10.255.255.190	10.255.255.254
Broadcast	10.255.255.63	10.255.255.127	10.255.255.191	10.255.255.255

Subnetting in Your Head: Class A Addresses

This sounds hard, but as with Class C and Class B, the numbers are the same; we just start in the second octet. What makes this easy? You only need to worry about the octet that has the largest block size (typically called the interesting octet; one that is something other than 0 or 255)—for example, 255.255.240.0 (/20) with a Class A network. The second octet has a block size of 1, so any number listed in that octet is a subnet. The third octet is a 240 mask, which means we have a block size of 16 in the third octet. If your host ID is 10.20.80.30, what is your subnet, broadcast address, and valid host range?

The subnet in the second octet is 20 with a block size of 1, but the third octet is in block sizes of 16, so we'll just count them out: 0, 16, 32, 48, 64, 80, 96...voilà! (By the way, you can count by 16s by now, right?) This makes our subnet 10.20.80.0, with a broadcast of 10.20.95.255 because the next subnet is 10.20.96.0. The valid host range is 10.20.80.1 through 10.20.95.254. And yes, no lie! You really can do this in your head if you just get your block sizes nailed!

Okay, let's practice on one more, just for fun!

Host IP: 10.1.3.65/23

First, you can't answer this question if you don't know what a /23 is. It's 255.255.254.0. The interesting octet here is the third one: 256 − 254 = 2. Our subnets in the third octet are 0, 2, 4, 6, etc. The host in this question is in subnet 2.0, and the next subnet is 4.0, so that makes the broadcast address 3.255. And any address between 10.1.2.1 and 10.1.3.254 is considered a valid host.

Written Lab 1

Given a Class B network and the net bits identified (CIDR), complete the following table to identify the subnet mask and the number of host addresses possible for each mask.

Classful Address	Subnet Mask	Number of Hosts per Subnet ($2^x - 2$)
/16		
/17		
/18		
/19		
/20		
/21		
/22		
/23		
/24		
/25		
/26		
/27		
/28		
/29		
/30		

Written Lab 2

Given the decimal IP address, write in the address class, number of subnet and host bits, number of subnets, and number of hosts for each IP address.

Decimal IP Address	Address Class	Number of Subnet and Host Bits	Number of Subnets (2^x)	Number of Hosts ($2^x - 2$)
10.25.66.154/23				
172.31.254.12/24				
192.168.20.123/28				
63.24.89.21/18				
128.1.1.254/20				
208.100.54.209/30				

Answers to Written Lab 1

Classful Address	Subnet Mask	Number of Hosts per Subnet ($2^x - 2$)
/16	255.255.0.0	65,534
/17	255.255.128.0	32,766
/18	255.255.192.0	16,382
/19	255.255.224.0	8,190
/20	255.255.240.0	4,094
/21	255.255.248.0	2,046
/22	255.255.252.0	1,022
/23	255.255.254.0	510
/24	255.255.255.0	254
/25	255.255.255.128	126
/26	255.255.255.192	62
/27	255.255.255.224	30

/28	255.255.255.240	14
/29	255.255.255.248	6
/30	255.255.255.252	2

Answers to Written Lab 2

Decimal IP Address	Address Class	Number of Subnet and Host Bits	Number of Subnets (2^x)	Number of Hosts ($2^x - 2$)
10.25.66.154/23	A	15/9	32768	510
172.31.254.12/24	B	8/8	256	254
192.168.20.123/28	C	4/4	16	14
63.24.89.21/18	A	10/14	1,024	16,382
128.1.1.254/20	B	4/12	16	4094
208.100.54.209/30	C	6/2	64	2

Appendix D

About the Additional Study Tools

IN THIS APPENDIX:

✓ Additional Study Tools

✓ System requirements

✓ Using the Study Tools

✓ Troubleshooting

Additional Study Tools

The following sections are arranged by category and summarize the software and other goodies you'll find on the companion website. If you need help with installing the items, refer to the installation instructions in the "Using the Study Tools" section of this appendix.

 NOTE The additional study tools can be found at www.sybex.com/go/netplus2e. Here, you will get instructions on how to download the files to your hard drive.

Sybex Test Engine

The files contain the Sybex test engine, which includes two bonus practice exams.

Electronic Flashcards

These handy electronic flashcards are just what they sound like. One side contains a question or fill-in-the-blank question, and the other side shows the answer.

PDF of Glossary of Terms

We have included an electronic version of the Glossary in .pdf format. You can view the electronic version of the Glossary with Adobe Reader.

Adobe Reader

We've also included a copy of Adobe Reader so you can view PDF files that accompany the book's content. For more information on Adobe Reader or to check for a newer version, visit Adobe's website at www.adobe.com/products/reader/.

System Requirements

Make sure your computer meets the minimum system requirements shown in the following list. If your computer doesn't match up to most of these requirements, you may have problems using the software and files. For the latest and greatest information, please refer to the ReadMe file located in the downloads.

- A PC running Microsoft Windows 98, Windows 2000, Windows NT4 (with SP4 or later), Windows Me, Windows XP, Windows Vista, or Windows 7
- An Internet connection

Using the Study Tools

To install the items, follow these steps:

1. Download the .ZIP file to your hard drive, and unzip to the appropriate location. Instructions on where to download this file can be found here: www.sybex.com/go/netplus2e.

2. Click the Start.EXE file to open up the study tools file.

3. Read the license agreement, and then click the Accept button if you want to use the study tools.

The main interface appears. The interface allows you to access the content with just one or two clicks.

Troubleshooting

Wiley has attempted to provide programs that work on most computers with the minimum system requirements. Alas, your computer may differ, and some programs may not work properly for some reason.

The two likeliest problems are that you don't have enough memory (RAM) for the programs you want to use or you have other programs running that are affecting installation or running of a program. If you get an error message such as "Not enough memory" or "Setup cannot continue," try one or more of the following suggestions and then try using the software again:

Turn off any antivirus software running on your computer. Installation programs sometimes mimic virus activity and may make your computer incorrectly believe that it's being infected by a virus.

Close all running programs. The more programs you have running, the less memory is available to other programs. Installation programs typically update files and programs; so if you keep other programs running, installation may not work properly.

Have your local computer store add more RAM to your computer. This is, admittedly, a drastic and somewhat expensive step. However, adding more memory can really help the speed of your computer and allow more programs to run at the same time.

Customer Care

If you have trouble with the book's companion study tools, please call the Wiley Product Technical Support phone number at (800) 762-2974, or email them at `http://sybex.custhelp.com/`.

Index

Note to the reader: Throughout this index **boldfaced** page numbers indicate primary discussions of a topic. *Italicized* page numbers indicate illustrations.

Symbols and Numbers

/?, route, 540
* (asterisk), wildcard, *559*
- (dash), IP routing, 260
(pound sign), Hosts table, 535
2.4 GHz, **341–343**, *343*
2.4 GHz/5 GHz, **345–346**
-4, 527, 537
5GHz, **343–345**
-6, 527, 537
10Base2. *See* thinnet
10Base5. *See* thicknet
10BaseFL, 105
10BaseT, 92, 102, 105
10GBaseER, 106
10GBaseEW, 104, 106
10GBaseGR, 104
10GBaseLR, 104, 106
10GBaseLW, 104, 106
10GBaseSR, 104, 105
10GBaseSW, 104, 106
10GBaseT, 60, 104, 105
25-pair cable, **79**
40 MHz, 345
100BaseFX, 103, 105
100BaseTX, 103, 105
100-Megabit Ethernet, 58
110 block, **79**
568A, *73*, **73–74**, *74*
568B, **73–74**
1000BaseCX, 103, 105
1000BaseLX, 103, 105
1000BaseSX, 103, 105
1000BaseT, 103

A

-A, 543
-a, 531, **541–543**, 549

AAA. *See* authentication, authorization, and accounting
ABRs. *See* area border routers
AC. *See* alternating current
access control lists (ACLs), *378*, **378–379**
    firewalls, **453–456**
    port numbers, 379
    stateful firewalls, 462
access links, 319
access lists, 451
Access Point mode, WAP, 359
access points (AP), **347–348**, *348*, 355, **359–362**
    configuration, 359–362
    DHCP, 365
    installing, 355
    rogue, 423
access ports, 319
accounts
    anonymous, 394
    automatic account lockouts, 398–399
    security policy, 433
    user, **393–396**
ACK (acknowledgment), 34, **37–39**, 462
ACLs. *See* access control lists
active detection, **429**
ActiveX attacks, **425**
AD. *See* administrative distance
ad hoc mode, wireless networks, **351–352**, *352*
add, 539
address learning, 304–306, *305*
Address Resolution Protocol (ARP), 90, *176*, **176–177**, **529–533**
    IP routing, 258
    Proxy ARP, 622
AD-IDS. *See* anomaly-detection IDS
administrative distance (AD), **275–277**, 280
administrator training, **437**
ADSL. *See* Asymmetric Digital Subscriber Line
Advanced Encryption Standard (AES), 382, 388, 607
AES-Counter Mode CBC-MAC Protocol (AES-CCMP), 366, 367

agents, 163
aggregate rate, 93
AH. *See* Authentication Header
alias record, 133
alternating current (AC), 587
Angry IP, *575*, 575–576
anomaly-detection IDS (AD-IDS), 468
anonymous accounts, 394
antenna
    troubleshooting, 609
    wireless, **349–351**
antivirus engine, **440**
antivirus programs, **439–441**
antivirus scan, **440–441**
anycast, 202, 204
AP. *See* access points
APIPA. *See* Automatic Private IP Addressing
applications
    bandwidth, **653–654**
    server logs, 651
Application layer, OSI, **31–32**
    firewalls, **463–464**
application server, 6, 39
application-layer attacks, **425**
application-specific integrated circuit (ASIC),
    130, 144, 302
area border routers (ABRs), 288
ARP. *See* Address Resolution Protocol
arp, **530–533**
arp -a, 236
ARPAnet, 157–158
AS. *See* autonomous system
ASBR. *See* autonomous system border router
ASIC. *See* application-specific integrated circuit
Asymmetric Digital Subscriber Line (ADSL),
    392, 501
Asynchronous Transfer Mode (ATM), 487,
    508–509
Attachment Unit Interface (AUI), 102–103
attenuation, 71, 102, 606
AUI. *See* Attachment Unit Interface
authentication, **400–406**
    authorization, and accounting (AAA),
        402–403
    CHAP, 405, *406*
    EAP, 391, **406**
    FTP, 161
    Kerberos, **402**, *403*
    MAC, 364
    MS-CHAP, 391, **405–406**

NAC, **405**
PKI, **401**
RADIUS, **403**
RIPv2, 280
TACACS+, **403–405**, *404*
    wireless networks, 357
Authentication Header (AH), 384
authenticator, 405
auto-detect mechanism, 93
automatic account lockouts, 398–399
Automatic Private IP Addressing (APIPA), 168,
    197–198
autonomous system (AS), 264–265, 274,
    287, 289
    BGP, 285, 286
    EIGRP, 283
autonomous system border router (ASBR), 289
autorooters, **425**

B

backbone
    collapsed, 299
    networks, *20*, **20–21**
    OSPF, 288
backdoors, **425**
background checks, 433
backups, 434
badges, 433
bandwidth, 492, **653–654**
Bandwidth on Demand Interoperability Group
    (BONDING), 505
BASE. *See* Basic Analysis and Security Engine
baselines, 163, **645–647**
Basic Analysis and Security Engine (BASE),
    573
Basic Rate Interface (BRI), 504
basic service area (BSA), 352
basic service set (BSS), 352
Basic Service Set Identifiers (BSSIDs), 608
beacons, 422
Bearer channels, 505
Berkeley Software Distribution (BSD), 158
BGP. *See* Border Gateway Protocol
binary numbers, **94–98**
bit, 94, 190
black box, 452
black hole, 621

block acknowledgment, 345
blocking state, 310
Bluetooth, 487, 497
BNC. *See* British Naval Connector
BONDING. *See* Bandwidth on Demand
    Interoperability Group
boot-sector viruses, **420**
Border Gateway Protocol (BGP), 265, *285*,
    285–286
bottlenecks, 646
bounce, **426**, 609
BPDUs. *See* Bridge Protocol Data Units
BPL. *See* Broadband over Power Line
BRI. *See* Basic Rate Interface
bridges, **120**, 300, 303
    collision domain, *120*
    Layer 2, **144–145**
    multicast packets, 142
Bridge Protocol Data Units (BPDUs), 309
Bridging mode, WAP, 359
British Naval Connector (BNC), 57, *57*, 63, 102
Broadband over Power Line (BPL), **67–68**, *68*
broadband services, **498–503**, *499*
broadcasts, 40, 41, 203–204, 303, 651
    Layer 2, IPv4, 198
    Layer 3, IPv4, 198–199
broadcast address, 191
broadcast domains, 138, 140, 303
    Ethernet, **90**
    VLAN, 143, 314
broadcast storm, 307, *308*, 622
brute-force attacks, **426**
BSA. *See* basic service area
BSD. *See* Berkeley Software Distribution
BSS. *See* basic service set
BSSIDs. *See* Basic Service Set Identifiers
buffer, 35
Buffer Full, 175
buffer overflow, **421**
burst, 507
bus topology, **12**, *13*
butt set, **584**
byte, 94, 95, 190, 550

cables. *See also specific cable types*
    properties, **71–72**
    troubleshooting, **604–609**
    wiring standards, **72–78**
cable modem, 499, *499*, **501–503**
cable stripper/snips, **586**
cable testers, 77, *577*, **577–579**
caching engines, **657–658**
caching proxy server, 135
call setup, 168
cameras, security policy, 433
canonical name (CNAME), 133
CARP. *See* Common Address Redundancy
    Protocol
Carrier Sense Multiple Access with Collision
    Detection (CSMA/CD), *91*, **91–92**, 118,
    343, 606
Category 2 twisted-pair cable, 59
Category 3 twisted-pair cable, 59
Category 4 twisted-pair cable, 59
Category 5 twisted-pair cable, 59, 103
Category 5e twisted-pair cable, 59, *60*,
    62, 103
Category 6 twisted-pair cable, 59, 103
Category 6a twisted-pair cable, 59
CATV. *See* community antenna television
CCEVS. *See* Common Criteria Evaluation and
    Validation Scheme
Cd, *558*
cellular WAN, **503**
central office (CO), 489
central processing unit (CPU), 5, 274
centralized WAN, 9
certificate authority (CA), 401, *401*
certifiers, 580, *580*
Challenge Handshake Authentication Protocol
    (CHAP), **405**, *406*
change, 539
change management, 647
channels, 505
    EtherChannel, 101
    side channel attack, 388
    T-series connections, 493–495
    WAP, 359
    wireless networks, 607
channel bonding, *101*, **101**, *101*, **101**
channel service unit/data service unit (CSU/
    DSU), 44, 76, 79, 488–489
CHAP. *See* Challenge Handshake
    Authentication Protocol

C

-c, 543–544
CA. *See* certificate authority

CIDR. *See* Classless Internet Domain Routing
CIR. *See* committed information rate
circuit switching, 491
cladding, 63
Class A network address, **193–194**, 215, 217
Class B network address, **194–195**, 215, 216, **226–234**
Class C network address, **195–196**, 215, **217–226**, *219*, 220–221, *221*
Class D network address, **196**
Class E network address, **196**
classful routing, 279, *281*
Classless Internet Domain Routing (CIDR), 197, **215–217**, 287
    IPv6, 200
    NAT, 241
    subnet mask, 225
classless routing, 279, *282*
clean-desk policy, **431–432**
client machines, **5**
client mode, VTP, 322, *323*
client-server, **11**, *11*
CLNS. *See* Connectionless Network Service
cloud computing, *658–659*
CNAME. *See* canonical name
CO. *See* central office
coaxial cable, **55–58**, 67
collapsed backbone, 299
collisions, 40, 606
collision domains, 94, *120*, 300
    Ethernet, **90**
    routers, 143
    switches, *138*, 140, 143, 302
collision events, 90
collision light, **600–601**
.com, 131, 418
committed information rate (CIR), **506**
Common Address Redundancy Protocol (CARP), **658**
Common Criteria Evaluation and Validation Scheme (CCEVS), 430
communication satellite (comsat), 497–498, *498*
community antenna television (CATV), 57, 502
compression, **33**
comsat. *See* communication satellite
Connectionless Network Service (CLNS), 290
connectionless protocol, 170
connection-oriented communication, **34–35**, *35*
connectivity software, **519**

connectivity testing, 651
content filtering, 136–137, *137*, **465**
Content Security Control (CSC), 464
continuity testers, 579
convergence, 257, 303
    routing tables, 278, *279*
    Spanning Tree Protocol, 311, *311*
CPE. *See* customer premises equipment
CPU. *See* central processing unit
CRC. *See* cyclic redundancy check
crossover cable, 74, **75–76**, *76*, 640, *641*
crosstalk, 58, 605–606
CSC. *See* Content Security Control
CSMA/CD. *See* Carrier Sense Multiple Access with Collision Detection
CSU/DSU. *See* channel service unit/data service unit
customer premises equipment (CPE), 488
cyclic redundancy check (CRC), 179
    frames, 182
    IP routing, 258, 259, 261

D

-d, 531
D channel, 505
DA. *See* Destination Address
data communication equipment (DCE), 44
Data Encryption Standard (DES), 387
data frame, 42
Data Link Connection Identifiers (DLCIs), 508
Data Link layer, OSI, *42*, **42–44**
    encapsulation, 179
    Ethernet, **94–101**
    frames, 181
    IP routing, 258, 260, 261, 262
data over cable service interface specification (DOCSIS), 502
data packets, 40, 100
data steam, 180–181
data terminal equipment (DTE), 44, 507
datagrams, 179
DB-9, 69
dBi. *See* decibel isotropic
DCE. *See* data communication equipment
DDos. *See* distributed denial of service attacks
decibel isotropic (dBi), 350
decimal numbers, **94–98**

decompression, **33**
decryption, **33**
dedicated lines, 491
de-encapsulation, 179
default gateway
    DHCP, 166
    incorrect, 615–616
    IP routing, 257–258, 261
    ping, 235–236
default routes, 285
delay, 655
delete, 539
delivery protocol, 380
demarc, **79–80**, 489
demarc extension, **79–80**
demilitarized zone (DMZ), 125, *125*, 451
    firewalls, **456–457**, *457*
    IDS/IPS, 573
    route, 537
    security policy, 433–434, *434*
denial of service attack (DoS), **415**
    ACLs, 454
    DDos, 417, *418*
    DoS/SYN flood attack, 416, *417*, 454
    firewalls, 463
Dense Wavelength Division Multiplexing
    (DWDM), **496**
Department of Defense (DoD), 159, 430
    OSI, 158–159, *159*
    port scanners, 576
    TCP/IP, **158–159**, *160*
DES. *See* Data Encryption Standard
destination, 539
Destination Address (DA), 99–100
Destination Unreachable, 175, 259, 261
DFS. *See* Dynamic Frequency Selection
DHCP. *See* Dynamic Host Configuration
    Protocol
Diffie-Hellmann algorithm, 388
Diffusing Update Algorithm (DUAL), 283, 291
dig, 533
Digital, Intel, and Xerox (DIX), 101
digital certificates, 473
digital ID, 388
Digital Signal 0 (DS0), 492–493
Digital Signal 1 (DS1), 493
Digital Signal 3 (DS3), 494
digital subscriber line (DSL), 61, 487, 499, *499*,
    500–501. *See also specific DSL types*

digital subscriber line access multiplexer
    (DSLAM), 500
Dijkstra algorithm, 287
DIP. *See* dual inline package
Direct Sequence Spread Spectrum (DSSS), 343
directional antennas, 349–351
Directory Service, 652
disabled state, Spanning Tree Protocol, 310
discontiguous networks, **280–282**, *283*
distance vector (DV), 266, *266*, 278, *278*
    EIGRP, 283
    RIPv2, 280
    routing protocols, 277, **278–286**
distributed denial of service attacks (DDos),
    417, *418*
distributed WAN, 9
distribution list, 455
distribution network, 501
distribution system (DS), 352
diversity, 347
DIX. *See* Digital, Intel, and Xerox
DLCIs. *See* Data Link Connection Identifiers
.dll, 418
DMZ. *See* demilitarized zone
DNS. *See* Domain Name Service
DNS Server, 652
DOCSIS. *See* data over cable service interface
    specification
DoD. *See* Department of Defense
Domain Name Service (DNS), 89, **130–135**,
    132, *134*, **165–166**
    certifiers, 580
    DHCP, 166
    DMZ, 451
    incorrect, 616
    IP address, 236
    ipconfig, 524
    network reconnaissance, 426
    port scanners, 574
    tracert, 520
door locks, 433
DoS. *See* denial of service attack
DOS commands, 236–237
DoS/SYN flood attack, 416, *417*, 454
dropped packets, 655
DS. *See* distribution system
DS0. *See* Digital Signal 0
DS1. *See* Digital Signal 1
DS3. *See* Digital Signal 3

DSL. *See* digital subscriber line

DSLAM. *See* digital subscriber line access multiplexer

DSSS. *See* Direct Sequence Spread Spectrum

DTE. *See* data terminal equipment

DTP. *See* Dynamic Trunking Protocol

DUAL. *See* Diffusing Update Algorithm

dual inline package (DIP), 605

dumb terminals, **7**

DV. *See* distance vector

DWDM. *See* Dense Wavelength Division Multiplexing

dynamic ARP table entries, 529

dynamic DNS, 135

Dynamic Frequency Selection (DFS), 344

Dynamic Host Configuration Protocol (DHCP), 125, *126*, **126–129**, *128*, *129*, **166–168**, *167*

   APIPA, 198

   certifiers, 580

   DSL, 499

   evil twin, 424

   ipconfig, 524

   Parameter Request List, 127–128, *128*

   protocol analyzers, *517*, 517–518

   Scope Options, 127, *127*

   server logs, 651

   WAP, 365

dynamic IP routing, 255, **264–266**, *265*

dynamic NAT, 243

dynamic packet filtering, **459**

dynamic state list, *459*, *459*

Dynamic Trunking Protocol (DTP), 318

dynamic VLAN, 318

E

-e, 550–551

EAP. *See* Extensible Authentication Protocol

EAR. *See* Export Administration Regulations

echo, 606

echo request payload, 257

.edu, 131

EEOC. *See* equipment exceeds operator capability

EGPs. *See* exterior gateway protocols

EIA/TIA. *See* Electronic Industries Association/Telecommunications Industry Alliance

EIGRP. *See* Enhanced Interior Gateway Routing Protocol

electromagnetic interference (EMI), 71–72, 104, 355, 605

Electronic Industries Association/Telecommunications Industry Alliance (EIA/TIA), 60, 102, 505, 640

email server, 580

email virus, *419*, 451

emergency virus scan, 441

EMI. *See* electromagnetic interference

Encapsulating Security Payload (ESP), 384

encapsulation, 98–99

   IP, **178–182**, *179*

   OSI, *45*, **45**

encryption

   AES, 382, 388

   DES, 387

   devices, *136*, **136–137**

   OSI Presentation layer, **33**

   passwords, 386–387

   PGP, 386–387, 389, *390*

   public key, 388, *389*

   security filtering, **386–389**

   SSL, 382

   symmetrical key, 387

   3DES, 387–388

   VPN concentrator, 473

   wireless networks, 607

   wireless NICs, 356–358, *357*

endpoints, 500

end-user training, **436–437**

Enhanced Interior Gateway Routing Protocol (EIGRP), 40, 266, **282–284**, 621

   AD, 275

   DV, 266

   IP routing, 254

   IS-IS, 290

   LS, 266

   multicast, 199

   RIPv2, 280

   v6, **291**

   VLSM, 282

environment, **146–147**, 337

environmental monitors, **588–589**

equipment access, 432

equipment exceeds operator capability
    (EEOC), 602
ESP. *See* Encapsulating Security Payload
ESS. *See* extended service set
ESSIDs. *See* Extended Service Set Identifiers
eth_addr, 531
EtherChannel, 101
Ethernet. *See also specific Ethernet types*
    addressing, **98**
    broadcast domain, **90**
    channel bonding, *101*, **101**
    collision domain, **90**
    CSMA/CD, *91*, **91–92**
    frames, **98–100**, *99*
    full duplex, **92–94**
    half duplex, **92–94**
    MMF, *66*, **66–67**
    OSI
        Data Link layer, 42–43, **94–101**
        Physical layer, **101–106**, *102*
    RJ-45, 102
    SMF, *66*, **66–67**
    specifications, **87–114**
    switches, 120–121, *121*
    Type, 100, 259–262
    UTP, 102
        crossover cable, 75
ETSi. *See* European Telecommunications
    Standards Institute
European Telecommunications Standards
    Institute (ETSi), 338
Event Viewer, 652, *652*
evil twin, **423–424**
Evolved High Speed Packet Access (HSPA+),
    503–504
.exe, 418
exit interviews, **435–436**
expansion slots, 118–119
Export Administration Regulations (EAR), 386
extended ACLs, **455–456**
extended demark, 489
extended service set (ESS), 353, *354*
Extended Service Set Identifiers (ESSIDs), 608
Extensible Authentication Protocol (EAP),
    391, **406**
exterior gateway protocols (EGPs), **264–266**,
    265, 274
extranet VPN, 382

F

-f, 527, 538
F connector, *56*
Fast Ethernet, 93, 103
fault tolerance, 13, 15, 284, **658**
fax server, 6
FCC. *See* Federal Communications
    Commission
FCS. *See* Frame Check Sequence
feasible successor, 284
Federal Communications Commission (FCC),
    338–339
FEP. *See* fluoroethylenepropylene
fiber to premises, 496
fiber-optic cable, **61–66**, *63*, *67*
FIFO. *See* first-in, first-out
File Replication Service, 652
file server, 6, 580
File Transfer Protocol (FTP), **160–161**
    application-layer attacks, 425
    bounce, **426**
    DMZ, 456–457
    DNS, 133
    firewalls, 463
    OSI Application layer, 32
    password encryption, 386
    proxy, 461
    troubleshooting, **554–559**
file viruses, **418–419**
firewalls, **125–126**, 425, **452–468**
    ACLs, **453–456**
    DMZ, **456–457**, *457*
    IP spoofing attacks, 378
    OSI
        Application layer, **463–464**
        Network layer, **461–463**
    protocol switching, **457–458**
    scanning services, **464–468**
    security policy, 433
    technologies, **453–461**
first-in, first-out (FIFO), 656
flat network, 314
flow control, **35–36**, *36*
fluoroethylenepropylene (FEP, Teflon), 55
forward/filter decisions, 306–307
forward/filter table, 304, *304*, *306*, 326
forwarding state, 310

FQDN. *See* fully qualified domain name
fractional T1 (FT1), 494
frames
    CRC, 182
    Ethernet, **98–100**, *99*
    IP routing, 259
    OSI
        Data Link layer, 179, 181
        Physical layer, 182
    Spanning Tree Protocol, 309
    switches, 306
Frame Check Sequence (FCS), 100, 179,
    259, 260
frame filtering, 306
Frame Relay, 16, 487, **506–508**
frequency, 72
FT1. *See* fractional T1
FTP. *See* File Transfer Protocol
ftp, 555
FTP PORT, 426
full duplex, 71
    Ethernet, **92–94**
    OSI Session layer, 33
    TCP, 168
fully qualified domain name (FQDN), 165–166

G

-g, 531
-g *host-list*, 536
gateway, 539
gateways, 7, 39. *See also* default gateway;
    specific gateway protocols
    BPL, 68
    encryption, 136–137
    incorrect, 615–616
GB. *See* gigabyte
Generic Routing Encapsulation (GRE), 383
GetRequest, 638
Gigabit Ethernet, 101, 104
gigabyte (GB), 492
G/L. *See* Global/Local bit
global address, NAT, 243
global unicast address, IPv6, 204
Global/Local bit (G/L), 98
.gov, 131
GRE. *See* Generic Routing Encapsulation
guards, 434

H

-h *maximum_hops*, 536
H.323, 464
half duplex, 71
    Ethernet, **92–94**
    NICs, 123
    OSI Session layer, 33
    switches, 302
    wireless networks, 337
handshake
    CHAP, **405**, *406*
    MS-CHAP, 391, **405–406**
    three-way handshake, 34, 36, 168
hardware address, 88, 174, 254, 258,
    260, 262
hardware broadcasts. *See* Layer 2
hashing functions, 382
HDLC. *See* High-Level Data Link Control
HDSL. *See* high bit-rate digital subscriber line
headend, 501
hello packets, 286, 291
heuristic scanning, 439
hexadecimal numbers, **94–98**
HFC. *See* hybrid fiber-coaxial
HIDS. *See* host-based IDS
hierarchical addressing, **191–198**
high availability, **657**
high bit-rate digital subscriber line (HDSL),
    500–501
High Speed Serial Data Connector
    (HSSDC), 103
High-Level Data Link Control (HDLC), 491
honeynets, 471
honeypot, 471, *471*
hops, 175
hop count, 40, 275, 290
    DV, 278
    OSPF, 287
    RIP, 279
    RIPv2, 280
hosts
    duplex, 93
    networks, 7, 39
    VLSM, 281
    workstations, **5**
host address, 192
host-based firewalls, **453**
host-based IDS (HIDS), **471–472**

hostname, 536
Hosts table, **535–536**
Host-to-Host layer, DoD model, 159,
    168–173
hotfixes, **437–439**
HSPA+. *See* Evolved High Speed Packet Access
HSSDC. *See* High Speed Serial Data Connector
HTML, 32
HTTP. *See* Hypertext Transfer Protocol
HTTPS. *See* Hypertext Transfer Protocol
    Secure
hubs, 39, *118*, **118**, *146*
    collision domains, 300
    full duplex, 93
    LAN, 4
    OSI Physical layer, **145–146**
    switches, 143
humidity, 147, 588–589
hybrid fiber-coaxial (HFC), 501
hybrid IP routing, 266, *266*, 277, 283
hybrid mesh topology, 15
hybrid topology, **18**, *18*
Hypertext Transfer Protocol (HTTP), 6, **164**
    application-layer attacks, 425
    DMZ, 451
    DNS, 131
    firewalls, 463
    IP routing, 263
    IPv6, 202
    netstat, 547
    OSI Application layer, 32
    port numbers, 263
    proxy, 461
    Telnet, 560
Hypertext Transfer Protocol Secure (HTTPS),
    164, 263, 382

I

-i *address*, 537
-i *TTL*, 527
IBSS. *See* independent basic service set
ICA. *See* Independent Computing Architecture
ICMP. *See* Internet Control Message Protocol
ICSA. *See* International Computer Security
    Association
ID Ten T error (ID10T), 602
IDC. *See* insulation displacement connector

IDF. *See* intermediate distribution frame
IDS. *See* intrusion detection system
IE. *See* Internet Explorer
IEC. *See* International Electrotechnical
    Commission
IEEE. *See* Institute of Electrical and Electronics
    Engineers
IETF. *See* Internet Engineering Task Force
if, 540
if_addr, 531
ifconfig, **525–526**
I/G. *See* Individual/Group bit
IGMP. *See* Internet Group Management
    Protocol
IGPs. *See* interior gateway protocols
IGRP. *See* Interior Gateway Routing Protocol
IMAP. *See* Internet Message Access Protocol
inbound ACLs, 456
incident response, **430**
independent basic service set (IBSS), 351
Independent Computing Architecture
    (ICA), **392**
Individual/Group bit (I/G), 98
inet_addr, 531
infrastructure mode, wireless networks,
    352–353, *353*
inherent attenuation, 102
injectors, PoE, 326, *326*
inside global address, NAT, 243
inside local address, NAT, 243
Institute of Electrical and Electronics Engineers
    (IEEE), 42–43, 98, 338
    802, 43–44
    802.1D, 309
    802.1Q, 321
    802.1w, 311–312
    802.3, 99, 100, 101
    802.3ab, 103
    802.3af, 325
    802.3an, 104
    802.3at, 325
    802.3u, 103
    802.11, 338, **340–347**, *347*
    802.11a, 343–344
    802.11b, 341–342, *342*
    802.11g, 342–343
    802.11h, 344–345
    802.11n, 345–346
    803.3z, 103

insulation displacement connector (IDC),
  585–586
.int, 131
Integrated Services Digital Networks (ISDN),
  487, **504–505**
interior gateway protocols (IGPs), 264–266,
  265, 274
  BGP, 285
  IS-IS, 289
Interior Gateway Routing Protocol (IGRP),
  266, 275
intermediate distribution frame (IDF), **79**
Intermediate System-to-Intermediate System
  (IS-IS), 266, *289*, **289–290**, 621
internal routing protocols, 286
International Computer Security Association
  (ICSA), 431
International Electrotechnical Commission
  (IEC), 649
International Organization for Standardization
  (ISO), 28, 649
Internet, 8–9, *122*, *380*
Internet Control Message Protocol (ICMP),
  175, **175–176**, **415**, 621
  ACLs, 454
  IP routing, 257, 260, 262
  ping, 236
  traceroute, 520
Internet Engineering Task Force (IETF), 157
Internet Explorer (IE), 31
Internet Group Management Protocol
  (IGMP), **165**
Internet layer, DoD model, 159, **173–178**
Internet Message Access Protocol
  (IMAP), **162**
Internet Options, Security tab, 466, *466*
Internet Protocol (IP), 40, **155–187**. *See also*
  specific IP topics and processes
  ACLs, 378
  CLNS, 290
  encapsulation, **178–182**, *179*
  OSPF, 287
  SOHO, 140
Internet Protocol version 4 (IPv4),
  198–199, 291
Internet Protocol version 6 (IPv6), 40,
  200–205, *202*
  CLNS, 290
  IP routing, 254
  ipconfig, 522
  OSPF, 287

routing protocols, **290–291**
SOHO, 140
Internet Security Association and Key
  Management Protocol (ISAKMP),
  385–386
Internet service providers (ISPs)
  BGP, 265, 285
  cable modem, 502
  CIDR, 215
internetwork, 8, *8*
  devices, 39, *141*
  DV, 278, *278*
  routers, *41*, 121, *139*, *143*
  routing tables, 278
  SOHO, 140
  switches, *142*, *145*
Internetwork Package Exchange (IPX), 100,
  383, 458
Inter-Switch Link (ISL), 320–321
intranet, 8, 382
intrusion detection system (IDS), 433,
  468–472, **572–573**
  packet sniffers, *570–571*
intrusion prevention system (IPS), 423, 470,
  572–573
  packet sniffers, *570–571*
inverse multiplexing, 505
IP. *See* Internet Protocol
IP address, 7, 89–90, **189–210**
  ACLs, 379
  arp -a, 236
  BGP, 285
  DHCP, 127, 166
  DNS, 131–132, 165–166, 236
  DOS commands, 236–237
  evil twin, 424
  hierarchical addressing, **191–198**
  incorrect, 615
  network configuration, 122–123
  NICs, 235
  port security, 456
  private, **196–198**
  problem determination, *237*, **237–241**, *238*
  Smurf attacks, 415
  static, 168
  subnets, **212–234**
  switches, 121
  troubleshooting, *234*, **234–241**
  v4, **198–199**
  VLSM, 282
  WAP, 348, 359

IP header, 174, *174*
IP proxy, 460–461
IP routing, **253–272**, *256, 258, 263, 264. See
　　also specific routing types*
　ARP, 258
　CRC, 258, 259, 261
　default gateway, 261
　Destination Unreachable, 259, 261
　dynamic, **264–266**, *265*
　FCS, 259, 260
　frames, 259
　hardware address, 258, 260, 262
　HTTP, 263
　HTTPS, 263
　hybrid, 266, *266*
　ICMP, 257, 260, 262
　MAC address, 258
　OSI
　　Data Link layer, 258, 260, 261, 262
　　Network layer, 260, 261
　　Physical layer, 259, 262
　packets, 261
　packet switching, 260
　process, **257–262**
　Registry, 261
　static, **264–266**, *265*
IP Security (IPSec), **384**, *385*, 473
IP spoofing attack, 378–379, *424*, **424**, 454
IP stack, 235, 537
ipconfig, 502, 521–524
ipconfig/all, 236, 522–524
ipconfig/release, 517, 524
ipconfig/renew, 517, 524
IPS. *See* intrusion prevention system
IPSec. *See* IP Security
IPv4. *See* Internet Protocol version 4
IPv6. *See* Internet Protocol version 6
IPX. *See* Internetwork Package Exchange
ISAKMP. *See* Internet Security Association and
　　Key Management Protocol
ISDN. *See* Integrated Services Digital
　　Networks
IS-IS. *See* Intermediate System-to-Intermediate
　　System
ISL. *See* Inter-Switch Link
ISO. *See* International Organization for
　　Standardization
isotropic antennas, 350
ISPs. *See* Internet service providers

J

-j *host-list*, 527
jitter, 655

K

-k *host-list*, 527
Kerberos, **402**, *403*, 473
Kevlar, 62

L

-l *size*, 527
L2F. *See* Layer 2 Forwarding
L2TP. *See* Layer 2 Tunneling Protocol
LAN. *See* local area network
LAN Manager, 299
latching, 63
latency, 144, 302, 609
latency sensitivity, **653**
Layer 2
　bridges, **144–145**
　broadcasts, IPv4, 198
　port security, 456
　Spanning Tree Protocol, 309
　switches, **144–145**, 298, **302–309**
Layer 2 Forwarding (L2F), 383
Layer 2 Tunneling Protocol (L2TP), **383**
Layer 3
　broadcasts, IPv4, 198–199
　port security, 456
　switches, routers, 41, 122
layered architecture, OSI, **28–29**, **30–44**,
　　31, 32
LC. *See* Local Connector
Lcd, 558
LDAP. *See* Lightweight Directory
　　Access Protocol
learning state, 310
leased lines, 491
least significant bit (LSB), 99
LEDs. *See* light-emitting diodes
Length, IEEE 802.3, 100
light-emitting diodes (LEDs), 63, 119,
　　600–601

Lightweight Directory Access Protocol
     (LDAP), **165**
Link Aggregation, 101
link light, **600–601**
link state (LS), 266, *266*, 277, 283, **286–290**
link state advertisements (LSAs), 286
link state packets (LSPs), 286
link-local address, 204, 291
listening state, 310
LLC. *See* Logical Link Control
load balancing, **130**, 275, 278, **657**
load testing, 651
local address, 243, 262
local area network (LAN), *3*, **3–5**. *See also*
     Small Office, Home Office; virtual local
     area network; wireless local area network
     IP routing, 254
     packet switching, 492
     RJ-11, 61
     routers, *4*, *315*, 451
     switches, *301*
          bridges, 303
     VLSM, 281
     VPN, 380–382
Local Connector (LC), 64, *65*, 66
local loop, 489
logging, NIDS, 470
logical address, 41, 254
Logical Link Control (LLC), 43
logical network diagrams, **645**, *646*
LogMein, *519*, **519**
Long Term Evolution (LTE), 503, **504**
loop avoidance, 307–309, *308*
loopback plug, *578*, **578**
LS. *See* link state
Ls, 558
LSAs. *See* link state advertisements
LSB. *See* least significant bit
LSPs. *See* link state packets
LTE. *See* Long Term Evolution

M

MAC. *See* Media Access Control
macro viruses, **420**
magnetic flux, 71–72
mail exchanger (MX), 133
mail relay, 434

mail server, 6, 433, 456
main distribution frame (MDF), **79**
mainframes, **7**
man-in-the-middle attacks, *427*, **427**
mask netmask, 539
maximum burst rate (MBR), 507
maximum transmission unit (MTU), 103,
     615, 621
MB. *See* megabyte
MBR. *See* maximum burst rate
MD5. *See* Message-Digest algorithm 5
MDF. *See* main distribution frame
MD-IDS. *See* misuse-detection IDS
MDI/MDI-X. *See* medium dependent
     interface/medium dependent
     interface-crossover
mechanical transfer registered jack (MTRJ),
     64–65, *65*
Media Access Control (MAC), 43, 236,
     345, 379
     address, 88–90, 94, 98
          ARP, 529
          arp -a, 236
          bridges, 303
          DHCP, 127
          IP routing, 258
          ipconfig, 524
          IPv6, 202
          port security, 456
          PPPoE, 392
          switches, 120, 303
          TKIP, 366
          VLAN, 318
     authentication, 364
     forward/filter table, 304, *304*, *306*
media converters, **66–67**
medium dependent interface/medium
     dependent interface-crossover
     (MDI/MDI-X), 605
meet-in-the-middle attack, 387
megabyte (MB), 492
mesh topology, *15*, **15–16**
Message-Digest algorithm 5 (MD5), 405
metric, 40
metric metric, 539
mget, 559
Microsoft Challenge Handshake
     Authentication Protocol (MS-CHAP),
     391, **405–406**
microwave radio relay, 497

.mil, 131
Mills, David, 164
MILNET, 158
MIMO. *See* multiple-input multiple-output
misuse-detection IDS (MD-IDS),
    468–469, *469*
MLS. *See* multilayer switch
MMF. *See* multimode fiber
mobility, 201
modems, 434, 492. *See also* cable modem
modulation technique, 343
monitor viewing, 433
MPLS. *See* MultiProtocol Label Switching
MS-CHAP. *See* Microsoft Challenge
    Handshake Authentication Protocol
Mtr, **536–537**
MTRJ. *See* mechanical transfer registered jack
MTU. *See* maximum transmission unit
multicast packets
    bridges, 142
    EIGRPv6, 291
    IPv4, 199
    IPv6, 204
    RIPng, 290–291
    routers, 41
    switches, 142
multifactor authentication, 400
multilayer switch (MLS), 122, **130**
multimedia, **33**
multimeter, **582**, *583*
multimode fiber (MMF), 62, 63, 66,
    66–67, 103
multipartite viruses, *420*, **420–421**
multiple barrier system, 475, *476*
multiple-input multiple-output (MIMO),
    345–346
MultiProtocol Label Switching (MPLS), 9,
    9, 16
MX. *See* mail exchanger

N

-N, 531
-n, 537, 553–554
-n *count*, 527
NaaS. *See* network as a service
NAC. *See* Network Access Control
name resolution, 131

NAT. *See* Network Address Translation
National Fire Protection Association
    (NFPA), 56
National Institute of Standards and Technology
    (NIST), 388
National Security Agency (NSA), 386
nbtstat, **540–546**
NCP. *See* Network Control Protocol
near-end crosstalk (NEXT), 60, 606
neighbor table, 284, *284*
neighbor-discovery process, 291
NESSUS, 472
.net, 131
NetBIOS. *See* Network Basic Input/Output
    System
netstat, **546–554**
NetWare, 299–300
networks, 2, **21–26**, 89. *See also specific*
    network types and devices
    backbone, *20*, **20–21**
    bus topology, **12**, *13*
    client-server, **11**, *11*
    configuration, **122–125**
    devices, **115–153**
    documentation, **638–649**
    environment, **146–147**
    firewalls, **125–126**
    hosts, **7**, 39
    hybrid topology, **18**, *18*
    LAN, **3–5**
    mesh topology, *15*, **15–16**
    monitoring performance, **649–661**
    MPLS, 9
    operating system, 5
    peer-to-peer, *10*, **10–11**
    physical media, **55–70**
    physical topology, **12–18**
        selection, **18–21**
    point-to-multipoint topology, *17*, **17**, *18*
    point-to-point topology, **16–17**, *17*
    policies, **647**
    procedures, 648
    ring topology, **14–15**, *15*
    security threat mitigation, **428–430**
    security threats, **413–447**
    segments, *20*, 21
        SOHO, **137–147**
        troubleshooting, **604**
    servers, **5–6**, 7
    star topology, **13–14**, *14*

troubleshooting, **595–633**
WAN, **7–9**
workstations, **5**, 7
Network Access Control (NAC), **405**
Network Access layer, DoD model, 159
network address, 40, 190, *192*, **192–196**
    Class A, **193–194**, 215, 217
    Class B, **194–195**, 215, 216, **226–234**
    Class C, **195–196**, 215, **217–226**, *219*,
        220–221, *221*
    Class D, **196**
    Class E, **196**
Network Address Translation (NAT), 196,
    241–245, *245*, 621
    configuration, *242*
    IPv6, 200
    WAP, 348
network analyzer, 570
network as a service (NaaS), 661
Network Basic Input/Output System
    (NetBIOS), 540–546
Network Control Protocol (NCP), 157
Network Interface Cards (NICs), 39,
    118–119, *119*
    crossover cable, 75–76
    duplex, 93–94
    firewalls, 452
    half duplex, 123
    IP address, 235
    packet sniffers, 570–571
    ping, 236
    wireless, 348, *349*, 355–359, *357*
    xDSL, 500
network interface device (NID), 80
Network layer, OSI, **39–41**
    encapsulation, 179, 181
    firewalls, **461–463**
    IP routing, 260, 261
    SOHO, 139–140
network management stations (NMSs), 39
Network Mapper (NMAP), **472–473**, *575*, 674
Network Monitor, 517
network reconnaissance, **426**
network scanners, **570–576**
Network Time Protocol (NTP), **164**
network-based firewalls, **453**
network-based IDS (NIDS), **468–471**, *469*
NEXT. *See* near-end crosstalk
next-hop address, 291, 539
next-hop router, 41

NFPA. *See* National Fire Protection Association
nibble, 94, *95*
NICs. *See* Network Interface Cards
NID. *See* network interface device
NIDS. *See* network-based IDS
NIST. *See* National Institute of Standards
    and Technology
NMAP. *See* Network Mapper
NMSs. *See* network management stations
noise immunity, 71–72
nonces, 366–367
notification, 432, 470
Novell, 299–300
NSA. *See* National Security Agency
nslookup, **533–534**
NTP. *See* Network Time Protocol

O

OC. *See* optical carrier
octet, 190
OE. *See* operator error
OFDM. *See* Orthogonal Frequency Division
    Multiplexing
OLT. *See* optical line termination
omni directional antennas, 349–351
on-access virus scan, 440–441
on-demand virus scan, 440
one-to-many address, 204
ONUs. *See* optical network units
open access mode, WLAN, 363
open impedance mismatch, 606
open relay, 434
Open Shortest Path First (OSPF), 40, **287–289**,
    288, 621
    IP routing, 254
    IS-IS, 290
    LS, 266
    RIPv2, 280
    v3, **291**
    VLSM, 282
Open Systems Interconnection (OSI), **27–51**
    Application layer, **31–32**
        firewalls, **463–464**
    connection-oriented communication,
        34–35, *35*
    Data Link layer, *42*, **42–44**
        encapsulation, 179
        Ethernet, **94–101**

frames, 181
IP routing, 258, 260, 261, 262
routers, 41
DoD model, 158–159, *159*
encapsulation, *45*, **45**
flow control, **35–36**, *36*
layered architecture, **28–29**, **30–44**, *31*, *32*
MLS, 130
Network layer, **39–41**
encapsulation, 179, 181
firewalls, **461–463**
IP routing, 260, 261
SOHO, 139–140
PDU, 178
Physical layer, **44**
encapsulation, 179
Ethernet, **101–106**, *102*
frames, 182
hubs, **145–146**
IP routing, 259, 262
Presentation layer, 33
reference model, **30–44**
Session layer, **33**
TCP/IP, 157
Transport layer, **33–34**
ACK, **38–39**
encapsulation, 179
port numbers, 181, *181*, 245
reliable networking, *38*, **38–39**
windows, *37*, **37–38**
operating system, 5
operator error (OE), **602**
optical carrier (OC), 495, *496*
optical line termination (OLT), 497
optical network units (ONUs), 497
optical time-domain reflectometer (OTDR),
581–582, *582*
.org, 131
organizationally unique identifier (OUI), 98
Orthogonal Frequency Division Multiplexing
(OFDM), 343
OS/2, 299
OSI. *See* Open Systems Interconnection
OSPF. *See* Open Shortest Path First
OTDR. *See* optical time-domain reflectometer
OUI. *See* organizationally unique identifier
outbound ACLs, 456
out-of-order delivery, 655
outside global address, NAT, 243
outside local address, NAT, 243

overhead, 34
overloading, 243, 244, *245*

P

-p
netstat, 551–553
route, 538–539
-p *period*, 537
packets, 179. *See also specific packet types*
dynamic filtering, **459**
IP routing, 254, 257, 261
NAT, 244
OSI Network layer, 39–40
PDUs, 181
TKIP, 366
VLAN, 319
Packet InterNet Groper. *See* ping
packet shaping, 656
packet sniffers, **426**, **570–572**, *571*, 650–651
packet switching
Frame Relay, 506
IP routing, 260
LAN, 492
SOHO, 140
packet-filter firewalls, 462
PANs. *See* personal area networks
PAP. *See* Password Authentication Protocol
partial mesh topology, 16
passive detection, **429**
Passive Optical Network (PON), **496–497**
passphrase, 367
passwords, **396–400**
automatic account lockouts, 398–399
encryption, 386–387
security policy, 433
WAP, 359
password attacks, **426**
Password Authentication Protocol (PAP), 405
PAT. *See* Port Address Translation
patch cable, 74, 640
patches, **437–439**
security policy, 434
pathping, 536–537
payload protocol, 380
PDUs. *See* Protocol Data Units
PEBCAK. *See* problem exists between chair
and keyboard

peer-to-peer networks, *10*, **10–11**
penetration, 422
personal area networks (PANs), 497
PGP. *See* Pretty Good Privacy
phishing, 426, **427–428**
physical barriers, 475
Physical layer, OSI, **44**
   encapsulation, 179
   Ethernet, **101–106**, *102*
   frames, 182
   hubs, **145–146**
   IP routing, *259*, 262
physical network diagrams, **642–644**,
   643, *644*
physical security, **474–478**
physical topology, networks, **12–18**
   selection, **18–21**
ping, 176, 235–236, **526–529**
Ping of Death, **415**
PKI. *See* Public Key Infrastructure
plain old telephone service (POTS), 59, 487
   ADSL, 501
   ISDN, 504
   PSTN, 489
plennum-rated coating, 56, 62
PoE. *See* Power over Ethernet
point of presence (POP), 489
pointer record (PTR), 133
point-to-multipoint topology, *17*, **17**, *18*,
   349–351
point-to-point connection, 92
point-to-point link, 14
Point-to-Point Protocol (PPP), **391–392**, 491
Point-to-Point Protocol over Ethernet
   (PPPoE), **392**
   DSL, 499
point-to-point topology, **16–17**, *17*, 103,
   349–351
Point-to-Point Tunneling Protocol (PPTP),
   383–384
policies
   networks, **647**
   security, **430–436**, 647
polyvinyl chloride (PVC), 55, 62
PON. *See* Passive Optical Network
POP. *See* point of presence; Post Office
   Protocol
ports
   access ports, 319
   IDS, 470, *470*

   routers, 124
   security, **456**
   speed, 124, 614
   switches, 123, 310
   trunk ports, **319–320**, *320*
   USB, *70*
   WAN, 8
Port Address Translation (PAT), 243, 244, 245,
   245, 621
port duplex mismatch, 614
port mirroring, **326–328**, *328*
port numbers, **171–173**, *172*, 263
   ACLs, 379
   OSI Transport layer, 181, *181*, 245
port scanners, 426, **574–576**, *575*
port sweeping, 574
port-redirection attacks, **427**
Post Office Protocol (POP), **162**
POTS. *See* plain old telephone service
Power over Ethernet (PoE), 324–326, *325*
power switch, **601–602**
powers of 2, 214
PPP. *See* Point-to-Point Protocol
PPPoE. *See* Point-to-Point Protocol
   over Ethernet
PPTP. *See* Point-to-Point Tunneling Protocol
preamble, 99
prefix routing, 279
Presentation layer, OSI, **33**
Pre-Shared Key (PSK), 367–368
Pretty Good Privacy (PGP), 386–387,
   389, *390*
Primary Rate Interface (PRI), 504
print, 539
print server, 6
private cloud, 659
private IP address, **196–198**
private network, 451
private side firewalls, 125
proactive defense, **429–430**
problem exists between chair and keyboard
   (PEBCAK), 602
procedures
   networks, 648
   security, **436–441**
Process/Application layer, DoD model,
   158–168
protocol analyzers, **517–518**, **579–580**, 651
Protocol Data Units (PDUs), 45, 178, 181
protocol switching, **457–458**, *458*

Proxy ARP, 622
proxy server, 6, **135**, *136*, *460*, **460–461**
PSK. *See* Pre-Shared Key
PSTN. *See* Public Switched Telephone Network
PTR. *See* pointer record
public cloud, 659
public key encryption, 388, *389*
Public Key Infrastructure (PKI), **401**, *402*
public side firewalls, 125
Public Switched Telephone Network (PSTN),
     59, 487, **489–490**
punch-down tool, *585*, **585–586**, *586*
PVC. *See* polyvinyl chloride
Pwd, 558

Q

-q *num-queries*, 537
quality of service (QoS), 41, 144, **316–317**,
     655–656

R

-R, 527
-r, 544–545, 551
-r *count*, 527
rack-mounted switches, 641, *642*
radio frequency interference (RFI), 606
RADIUS. *See* Remote Authentication Dial In
     User Service
Rapid Spanning Tree Protocol (RSTP), **311–312**
RARP. *See* Reverse Address Resolution
     Protocol
RAS. *See* Remote Access Services
rate limiting, 656
RDC. *See* Remote Desktop Connection
RDP. *See* Remote Desktop Protocol
Real-time Transport Protocol (RTP), **163**
Recommended Standard 232 (RS-232), 69, *69*
recording equipment, **432**
reference model, OSI, **30–44**
registered jack (RJ), 640
     RJ-11, 60–61, *61*
     RJ-45, 60–61, *61*, 102, 500, *640*
Registry, 257, 261
regulations, **648–649**
reliable networking, 33, *38*, **38–39**

remote access, **390–392**
remote access server, 6, 236
Remote Access Services (RAS), **390–391**, *391*
Remote Authentication Dial In User Service
     (RADIUS), *365*, **365**, 403, 621
     PPPoE, 392
     VPN concentrator, 473
Remote Desktop Connection (RDC), 162, 391
Remote Desktop Protocol (RDP), **162**, **391**
Remote Desktop Services, 162
remote-access VPN, 382
repeaters, 39, 146
replay attacks, 366
Requests for Comments (RFCs), 164
resistance-to-change syndrome, 201
Reverse Address Resolution Protocol (RARP),
     177, *178*
reverse lookup zone, 134
RFCs. *See* Requests for Comments
RFI. *See* radio frequency interference
RG-6, *57*, 58
RG-58 A/U, 57
RG-58 U, 57
RG-59, 57
RG-62, 58
ring topology, **14–15**, *15*
RIP. *See* Routing Information Protocol
RIPng. *See* Routing Information Protocol
     next generation
RIPv2. *See* Routing Information Protocol
     version 2
Rivest, Shamir, and Adleman (RSA), 382, 388,
     391, 473
RJ. *See* registered jack
RJ-11, 60–61, *61*
RJ-45, 60–61, *61*, 102, 500, *640*
rogue access points, 423
rootkit, 425
round-robin load balancing, 278
route, **537–540**
routers, 4, **121–122**. *See also* IP routing
     ABRs, 288
     ACLs, *378*
     ASBR, 289
     broadcasts, 651
     collision domains, 143
     CPU, 274
     Internet, *122*
     internetwork, *41*, *139*, *143*
     IP routing, 255

LAN, *4*, *315*, 451

missing routes, 621

next-hop, 41

OSI

    Data Link layer, 42

    Network layer, 39–41

point-to-point topology, 16

ports, 124

QoS, 144

security zones, *478*

SOHO, 138

subnets, 220

traceroute, 236

WAN, 8

route-update packets, 40

routing by rumor, 278

routing flow tree, *275*

Routing Information Protocol (RIP), 40, 266, **279**, 283, 621

    AD, 275

    convergence, 278

    IP routing, 254

    OSPF, 287–288

Routing Information Protocol next generation (RIPng), **290–291**

Routing Information Protocol version 2 (RIPv2), **280**, 282, 283, 621

routing loops, 621

routing protocols, 254, **273–296**. *See also specific protocols*

    AD, **275–277**

    classes, **277**

    DV, 277, **278–286**

    hybrid IP routing, 277

    IPv6, **290–291**

    LS, 277, **286–290**

routing tables, 255, 257

    convergence, 278, *279*

    EIGRP, 283, 284

    internetwork, 278

    SOHO, 140

RS-232. *See* Recommended Standard 232

RSA. *See* Rivest, Shamir, and Adleman

RST (reset packet), 574

RSTP. *See* Rapid Spanning Tree Protocol

RTP. *See* Real-time Transport Protocol

S

-S, 545–546

-s, 531, 546, 551

-s *count*, 527

-S *srcaddr*, 527

SA. *See* Source Address

SaaS. *See* software as a service

Sarbanes-Oxley Act of 2002 (Sar-Ox), 648

SAs. *See* security associations

SATAN. *See* Security Administrator Tool for Analyzing Networks

SC. *See* subscriber connector

scanning services, **464–468**

schematics, 639–642

Scope Options, 127, *127*

SCP. *See* Secure Copy Protocol

SDH. *See* Synchronous Digital Hierarchy

SDSL. *See* symmetric digital subscriber line

Secure Copy Protocol (SCP), **165**

Secure File Transfer Protocol (SFTP), **161**

Secure Shell (SSH), **164**, **392**

    SFTP, 161

    Telnet, 561

Secure Sockets Layer (SSL), *383*

    tunneling, **382–383**

    VPN concentrator, 473

Secure Sockets Layer Virtual Private Network (SSL VPN), **382–383**

security

    antivirus programs, **439–441**

    DSL, 499

    hardware/software, **450–452**

    patches and upgrades, **437–439**

    physical, **474–478**

    policies, **430–436**, 647

    procedures, **436–441**

    server logs, 651

    threats, **413–447**

        mitigation, **428–430**

        wireless networks, **421–424**

    training, **436–437**

    wireless networks, **362–368**

Security Administrator Tool for Analyzing Networks (SATAN), 429

security associations (SAs), **385–386**

security audits, 397, **431**

security filtering, **377–392**
    ACLs, *378*, **378–379**
    encryption, **386–389**
    remote access, **390–392**
    tunneling, **379–380**, *380*
Security Services Module (SSM), 464
Security Set Identifier (SSID), 353, 357, 364
    evil twin, 423
    WAP, 359
    war driving, 422
Security tab, Internet Options, 466, *466*
security zones, **476**, *477*, *478*
segments
    networks, *20*, **21**
        SOHO, **137–147**
        troubleshooting, **604**
    OSI
        connection-oriented communication, 34
        flow control, 35
        PDU, 178
        TCP, 169, *169*
        UDP, *170*
sendmail, 425
serial cables, **68–70**
servers, **5–6**, *7. See also specific*
    server types
server logs, **651–652**
server mode, VTP, 322, *323*
service level agreement (SLA), 656
service packs, 438
Service Set Identifiers (SSIDs), **608**
Session Initiation Protocol (SIP), **163**
Session layer, OSI, **33**
session secret, 367
SetRequest, 638
SFD. *See* start frame delimiter
SFF. *See* small form factor
SFTP. *See* Secure File Transfer Protocol
shared keys, 360
shielded twisted-pair (STP), 58, 72
short circuits, 606
Shortest Path First (SPF), 286. *See also* Open
    Shortest Path First
show ip route, 255
show mac address-table, 307
shunning, 470
side channel attack, 388
signal degradation, 354–355
signature identification, 466

Simple Mail Transfer Protocol (SMTP),
    162, 560
    proxy, 461
Simple Network Management Protocol
    (SNMP), 121, **163**, 463, **638–639**
simplex, 33
single sign-on, 400
single-mode fiber (SMF), 62, 63, 66, **66–67**
    10GBase-LW, 104
    1000BaseLX, 103
SIP. *See* Session Initiation Protocol
site-to-site VPN, 382
SLA. *See* service level agreement
small form factor (SFF), 63–65
Small Office, Home Office (SOHO), 121,
    137–147, 501, 580
smart antennas, 345
smart jack, **80**
SmartDraw, 639, 644, *644*, *645*
SMF. *See* single-mode fiber
SMTP. *See* Simple Mail Transfer Protocol
Smurf attacks, **415–416**, *416*, 454
SNAT. *See* static NAT
SNMP. *See* Simple Network Management
    Protocol
Snort, 574
social engineering, **427–428**
software address, 174
software as a service (SaaS), 661
SOHO. *See* Small Office, Home Office
SONET. *See* Synchronous Optical Network
Source Address (SA), 100
SPAN. *See* Switch Port Analyzer
spanning trees, 303
Spanning Tree Protocol (STP), *309*, **309–312**,
    311, 620–621
spanning-tree algorithm (STA), 309
spatial multiplexing, 346
SPF. *See* Shortest Path First
split pairs, 579, 606
splitters, 501
SQL injection attacks, 574
SSH. *See* Secure Shell
SSID. *See* Security Set Identifier
SSIDs. *See* Service Set Identifiers
SSL. *See* Secure Sockets Layer
SSL VPN. *See* Secure Sockets Layer Virtual
    Private Network
SSM. *See* Security Services Module

ST. *See* straight tip
STA. *See* spanning-tree algorithm
Stacheldraht, **417**
standard ACLs, 455
star topology, **13–14**, *14*
start frame delimiter (SFD), 99
state table, 459, 462
state transitions, 44
stateful firewalls, **462–463**
stateful packet inspection, 462–463
stateless firewall, **462–463**
static ARP table entries, 530
static IP addressing, 168
static IP routing, 255, **264–266**, *265*, 275
static NAT (SNAT), 243, 245
static VLAN, 317–318
steady state, 257
STP. *See* shielded twisted-pair
straight tip (ST), 63, *64*
straight-through cable, **75**
strong passwords, 398
subnets
    autonomous systems, 265
    Class B network address, **226–234**
    Class C network address,
        217–226, *219*
    IP address, **212–234**
    VLSM, 281
subnet masks, **214–215**
    CIDR, 216–217, 225
    Class C network address,
        220–221, *221*
    DHCP, 166
    EIGRP, 283
    route, 539
    VLSM, 281
subscriber connector (SC), 63, *64*
supplicant, 405
surge protectors, 587
swipe mechanisms, 433
switches, **120–121**, **297–334**. *See also specific*
    switch and switching types
    address learning, 304–306
    broadcast domain, 140
    collision domains, *138*, 140,
        143, 302
    Ethernet, *121*
    forward/filter decisions, 306–307
    half duplex, 302
    hubs, 143

    internetwork, *142, 145*
    LAN, 4, *301*
        bridges, 303
    Layer 2, **144–145**, 298, **302–309**
    Layer 3, routers, 41
    loop avoidance, 307–309, *308*
    MAC address, 303
    multicast packets, 142
    nbtstat, 541–546
    netstat, 548–554
    networks before, **298–301**, *299*
    PoE, 324–326
    ports, 123, 310
    port mirroring, **326–328**, *328*
    PSTN, 490
    rack-mounted, 641, *642*
    services, **302–309**
    SPAN, **326–328**
    Spanning Tree Protocol, **309–312**
    VLAN, **313–321**, *316*, 451
    VTP, 322
    wireless networks, troubleshooting, 609
Switch Port Analyzer (SPAN), **326–328**
symmetric digital subscriber line (SDSL), 501
symmetrical key encryption, 387
SYN (synchronize), 34, 462, 674
SYN flood, 416, *417*, 463
    DoS/SYN flood attack, 416, *417*, 454
SYN/ACK (synchronize- acknowledgment), 34,
    416, 674
Synchronous Digital Hierarchy (SDH), 495
Synchronous Optical Network (SONET), *15*,
    104, 495
Syslog, **650**

T

-t, 527
T1
    crossover cable, **76**, *77*
    WAN connection, **494**
T3, **494–495**
TA. *See* terminal adapter
TACACS+. *See* Terminal Access Control
    Access-Control System Plus
tapping, 72
TCP. *See* Transmission Control Protocol

TCP/IP. *See* Transmission Control Protocol/
    Internet Protocol
TDM. *See* time-division multiplexing
TDR. *See* time-domain reflectometer
Teflon. *See* fluoroethylenepropylene
telephony server, 6
Telnet, **160**, 386, *560*, **560–561**
telnet, 561
temperature, 146, 588–589
Temporal Key Integrity Protocol (TKIP),
    366–367
Terminal Access Control Access-Control
    System Plus (TACACS+), **403–405**, *404*
terminal adapter (TA), 504–505
Terminal Services Client (TSC), 162, 391
TFN. *See* Tribe Flood Network
TFN2K. *See* Tribe Flood Network 2000
TFTP. *See* Trivial File Transfer Protocol
thicknet, 57, 102, 104
thin client, 661
thin computing, 661
thin protocol. *See* User Datagram Protocol
thinnet, 56, *56*, 102, 105
Third Generation Partnership Project 2
    (3GPP2), 503
thrashing, 308
3DES. *See* Triple Data Encryption Standard
3GPP2. *See* Third Generation Partnership
    Project 2
three-way handshake, 34, 36, 168
throughput, 495, *518*
    testing, **518–519**, 651
Time to Live (TTL), 236, 520
time-division multiplexing (TDM),
    493, 505
time-domain reflectometer (TDR), **581**
TLS. *See* Transport Layer Security
Token Ring, 299
toll network, 489
toner probe, **582–584**, *584*
topology table, 283–284, *284*
TPC. *See* Transmit Power Control
Traceroute, 176, 454
traceroute, 236, **520–521**
tracert, 236, 520
tracking, 433
traffic contract, 656
traffic shaping, **656**
transceivers, 39

Transmission Control Protocol (TCP), 33,
    168–169
    connection-oriented communication, 34
    DNS, 134
    full duplex, 168
    OSI Transport layer, 39
    port numbers, **171–173**, *172*
    port scanners, 574
    segments, 169, *169*
    stateful firewalls, 462
    throughput testers, 518
    UDP, 169–170
Transmission Control Protocol/Internet
    Protocol (TCP/IP), **7**, **157–177**
    ACLs, 379
    ARP, 529
    DoD model, **158–159**, *160*
    FTP, 554
    history, 157–158
    IGMP, 165
    IPSec, *385*
    L2TP, 383
    nbtstat, 540–546
    netstat, 546–554
    network segments, 604
    OSI
        Application layer, 31
        windows, 37
    ping, 526
    protocol switching, 457–458
    subnets, 213
    SYN flood, 416
    Telnet, 560
    traceroute, 520–521
transmission speeds
    cables, 71
    DSL, 499
    WAN, 492
Transmit Power Control (TPC), 344–345
transparent bridging, 145
transparent mode, VTP, 322–323, *323*
Transport layer, OSI, **33–34**
    ACK, **38–39**
    encapsulation, 179
    port numbers, 181, *181*, 245
    reliable networking, 38, *38*–39
Transport Layer Security (TLS), **163**, 382
traps, 163, 638
Tribe Flood Network (TFN), **417**

Tribe Flood Network 2000 (TFN2K), **417**

Triple Data Encryption Standard (3DES), 387–388

Trivial File Transfer Protocol (TFTP), 32, 161

Trojan horse, 421

troubleshooting
    ARP, **529–533**
    cables, **604–609**
    connectivity software, **519**
    FTP, **554–559**
    Hosts table, **535–536**
    ifconfig, **525–526**
    IP address, *234*, **234–241**
    ipconfig, *521–524*
    Mtr, **536–537**
    nbtstat, **540–546**
    networks, **595–633**
       segments, **604**
    nslookup, **533–534**
    ping, **526–529**
    protocol analyzers, **517–518**
    route, **537–540**
    steps, **609–623**
    Telnet, **560–561**
    throughput testers, **518–519**
    tips, **623–626**
    tools, **515–568**
    traceroute, **520–521**
    wireless networks, **607–609**
    workstations, **604**

trunk ports, **319–320**, *320*

trusted network, 451

Trusted Sites, 467, *467*

trust-exploitation attacks, **427**

TSC. *See* Terminal Services Client

T-series WAN connections, **492–495**

TTL. *See* Time to Live

tunneling
    IPSec, **384**
    L2TP, **383**
    PPTP, **383–384**
    security filtering, **379–380**, *380*
    SSL, **382–383**
    SSL VPN, **382–383**
    VPN, **380–382**

twisted-pair cable, **58–61**

Type, Ethernet, 100, **259–262**

U

UDP. *See* User Datagram Protocol

unicast, 199, 204, *550*

UNII. *See* Unlicensed National Information Infrastructure

uninterruptible power supply (UPS), 587

unique local address, 204

Universal Serial Bus (USB), 69–70, *70*

Unlicensed National Information Infrastructure (UNII), 339, *339*, 343–344, *344*

unreliable protocol, 170

unshielded twisted-pair (UTP), 58–59
    connecting, **60–61**
    Ethernet, 102
       crossover cable, 75
    ISDN, 504
    PSTN, 490
    wiring schematics, 639–640
    xDSL, 500

untrusted network, 451

upgrades, **437–439**

UPS. *See* uninterruptible power supply

uptime, **654**

USB. *See* Universal Serial Bus

user accounts, **393–396**

User Datagram Protocol (UDP), 33, **169–170**
    DHCP, 166–167
    DNS, 134
    netstat, *547*
    OSI Transport layer, 39
    packet sniffers, *572*
    port numbers, **171–173**, *172*
    port scanners, *574*
    RIPng, 290
    segments, *170*
    throughput testers, 518

UTP. *See* unshielded twisted-pair

V

-v, 531

-v *TOS*, 527

Variable Length Subnet Mask (VLSM), **280–282**, *282*, 287

VDSL. *See* very high bit-range digital
    subscriber line
very high bit-range digital subscriber line
    (VDSL), 501
video, 654
virtual circuits, 34, 36, **508**
virtual desktops, 660–661
virtual local area network (VLAN), 41, *313*
    broadcast domains, 143
    dynamic, 318
    identifying, 318–321
    incorrect, 615
    ipconfig, 524
    membership, 317
    QoS, **316–317**
    static, 317–318
    switches, 121, **313–321**, *316*, 451
    trunk ports, **319–320**, *320*
    voice, 319
virtual machines (VMs), 659
virtual networks, 658–661, *660*
Virtual Private Network (VPN), *381*. *See also*
    VPN concentrator
    packet sniffers, 571
    tunneling, **380–382**
virtual servers, 659
virtual switches, 660
viruses, **417–421**
virus definition files, **440**
VLAN. *See* virtual local area network
VLAN Management Policy Server
    (VMPS), 318
VLAN Trunking Protocol (VTP),
    321–324, *323*
VLSM. *See* Variable Length Subnet Mask
VMPS. *See* VLAN Management Policy Server
VMs. *See* virtual machines
Voice over IP (VoIP), 74, 163, 464, 501
    bandwidth, 654
    network configuration, 122
    PoE, 324
    switches, 121
voice VLAN, 319
VoIP. *See* Voice over IP
voltage event recorder, **587–588**
volt/ohm meter (VOM), 582
VPN. *See* Virtual Private Network
VPN concentrator, *137*, **137**, *473*, **473**
VTP. *See* VLAN Trunking Protocol
vulnerability scanners, **472–473**

W

-w *timeout*, 527, 537
WAN. *See* wide area network
WAP. *See* wireless access points
war chalking, **422**
war driving, 363, **422**
Wavelength Division Multiplexing
    (WDM), **496**
Web proxy server, 135, 461
web server, 6, 39, 456, 580
well-known port numbers, 172
WEP. *See* Wired Equivalent Privacy
wide area network (WAN), **7–9**, **485–514**, *489*
    broadband services, **498–503**, *499*
    cellular, **503**
    connection types, **490–495**, *491*
    demarc, 79
    IP routing, 254
    network segments, 604
    protocols, **504–509**
    subnets, 213
    VLSM, 281, 282
    VPN, 380–382
    wireless, **503–504**
    wiring, **495–496**
Wi-Fi, 345
Wi-Fi Alliance, 338, 339–340
Wi-Fi Protected Access (WPA), 366, **367–368**,
    423, 607
    cracking, **423**
    WAP, 360
WiMAX. *See* World Wide Interoperability for
    Microwave Access
windows, OSI, *37*, **37–38**
Windows Internet Naming Service (WINS),
    131, 166
Windows Update, **437–438**, *438*
WINS. *See* Windows Internet Naming Service
wire crimper, 586
Wired Equivalent Privacy (WEP), 357,
    364–365, 607
    cracking, **422**
    WAP, 360
wireless access points (WAP), **347–348**, *348*
    configuration, 359–362
    DHCP, 365
    installing, 355
wireless antennas, 349–351

wireless local area network (WLAN), **337–373**
  history, *339*
  IEEE 802.11, **340–347**
  ipconfig, 522
wireless networks, **335–373**
  ad hoc mode, 351–352, *352*
  authentication, 357
  components, **347–351**
  infrastructure mode, 352–353, *353*
  installing, **351–362**
  security, **362–368**
  security threats, **421–424**
  signal degradation, 354–355
  switches, troubleshooting, 609
  transmission media, **497–498**
  troubleshooting, **607–609**
wireless NICs, 348, *349*, 355–359, *357*
wireless WAN, **503–504**
wire-map testers, 578–579
Wireshark, 570–571
wiring. *See also* cables
  EIA/TIA, 640
  schematics, 639–642
  security policy, 432–433

standards, 72–78
WAN, **495–496**
WLAN. *See* wireless local area network
WLAN Association (WLANA), 338
workgroups, 3
workstations, 5, 7, **604**
World Wide Interoperability for Microwave
  Access (WiMAX), 503, **504**
worms, **421**
WPA. *See* Wi-Fi Protected Access

X

xDSL, 500–501

Z

Zimmerman, Phil, 389
zones
  firewalls, **466–467**
  security, 476, 477, 478

Free Online Study Tools

Register on Sybex.com to gain access to a complete set of study tools to help you prepare for your CompTIA Network+ Certification Exam

Comprehensive Study Tool Package Includes:

- **Assessment Test** to help you focus your study to specific objectives

- **Chapter Review Questions** for each chapter of the book

- **Two Full-Length Practice Exams** to test your knowledge of the material

- **Electronic Flashcards** to reinforce your learning and give you that last-minute test prep before the exam

- **Searchable Glossary** gives you instant access to the key terms you'll need to know for the exam

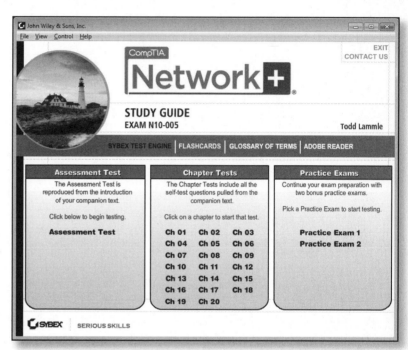

Go to www.sybex.com/go/netplus2e to register and gain access to this comprehensive study tool package.